Contributions to Political Science

The series Contributions to Political Science contains publications in all areas of political science, such as public policy and administration, political economy, comparative politics, European politics and European integration, electoral systems and voting behavior, international relations and others. Publications are primarily monographs and multiple author works containing new research results, but conference and congress reports are also considered. The series covers both theoretical and empirical aspects and is addressed to researchers and policy makers.

More information about this series at http://www.springer.com/series/11829

Michał Gierycz

European Dispute over the Concept of Man

A Study in Political Anthropology

 Springer

Michał Gierycz
Institute of Political Science and Administration
Cardinal Stefan Wyszyński University in Warsaw
Warszawa, Poland

ISSN 2198-7289   ISSN 2198-7297   (electronic)
Contributions to Political Science
ISBN 978-3-030-61519-2   ISBN 978-3-030-61520-8   (eBook)
https://doi.org/10.1007/978-3-030-61520-8

Original title: Europejski spór o człowieka. Studium z antropologii politycznej.
First edition in Poland by Wydawnictwo Naukowe UKSW, Warszawa 2017.
Research founded by National Centre for Science, Decision no. DEC-2011/01/D/HS5/05850
English translation by: Małgorzata Wójcik
Proofreading: Steve Jones
Reviewers: Prof. Tomasz G. Grosse, Ph.D. (University of Warsaw) and Prof. Marek Rembierz, Ph.D.
(University of Silesia in Katowice)

Contents

List of Abbreviations

7FP	Seventh Framework Programme of the European Community for research, technological development and demonstration activities
ALDE	Alliance of Liberals and Democrats for Europe (2004–2019 EP terms political group)
FRA	Agency for Fundamental Rights
DRC	Democratic Republic of the Congo
ECR	European Conservatives and Reformists (EP political group)
EFD	Europe of Freedom and Democracy (2009–2014 EP term political group)
ECHR	European Convention on Human Rights (Convention for the Protection of Human Rights and Fundamental Freedoms)
EPP/PPE- DE	European People's Party (Christian Democrats) (EP political group)
ECtHR	European Court of Human Rights
CJEU	Court of Justice of the European Union
EEC	European Economic Community
ECSC	European Coal and Steel Community
FEMM	European Parliament Committee on Women's Rights and Gender Equality
G7/G8	Group of Seven/Group of Eight: intergovernmental political forum of the USA, Japan, France, Germany, Canada, the United Kingdom, Italy (G7) and—until 2014—Russia (G8)
GJC	Global Justice Center
Greens/EFA	Greens/European Free Alliance (EP political group)
GUE-NGL	European United Left/Nordic Green Left (EP political group)
ICD-11	11th Revision of the International Classification of Diseases and Related Health Problems
ILGA	International Lesbian and Gay Association
IND/DEM	Independence/Democracy (2004–2009 EP term political group)

ISIS	Islamic State of Iraq and Syria
EC	European Commission
CFR	Charter of Fundamental Rights
LGB LGBT/ LGBTI/LGBTIQ	Lesbian, gay, bisexual, transgender, intersex, queer
NI	Non-Inscrits, non-attached Members of the European Parliament
UN	United Nations
UDHR	Universal Declaration of Human Rights
EP	European Parliament
PEP	Post-exposure prophylaxis of HIV
PSVI	Preventing Sexual Violence in Conflict Initiative
PES	Party of European Socialists
EC	European Council
CEU	Council of the European Union
S&D	Progressive Alliance of Socialists and Democrats (EP political group of PES)
TL	Treaty of Lisbon
TEU	Treaty on European Union
TFEU	Treaty on the Functioning of the European Union
ECC Treaty	Treaty Establishing the European Economic Community
UNFPA	United Nations Population Fund
UE	European Union
UEN	Union for Europe of the Nations (2004–2009 EP term political group)
WTO	World Trade Organization

List of Figures

List of Tables

List of Diagrams

Chapter 1
Introduction

If one were to make a list of issues which are nowadays the subject of heated public disputes, ethical questions related to fundamental human rights would certainly occupy a prominent place. From disputes concerning abortion, *in vitro*, euthanasia, the financing of stem-cell research, "same-sex marriage" and the right to conscientious objection, all the way to discussions about separate toilets for transsexuals—the public debate sweeping across Europe has been growing in intensity over the past decades. It is usually stormy, with mass protests and advocacies, online petitions, and even civic initiatives witnessed on a daily basis.

Institutions of the European Union have actively participated in the debate. Particularly after the Lisbon Treaty which consolidated the Union's axiological dimension,[1] they have made their presence felt in morality policy by "postulating," "expecting," "pointing out," "supporting," "demanding," financing, and sometimes even regulating. On the other hand, they are regularly deluged with thousands of letters (both of support and objection), and sometimes even taken to the Court of Justice about their decisions in this area. For even though EU institutions usually purport to be "neutral actors," not encroaching upon the Member States' jurisdiction in the field of ethics, their involvement often makes them perceived, both by the left and the right, as agents of cultural change. Consequently, even though this change is evaluated differently on each side of the political scene—considered by some to be a feat of Europe's (new) cultural identity, while others see it as its caricature—neither side questions the cultural impact of EU policy.[2] This fact alone seems to deserve the attention of political science, particularly if we bear in mind that the Union

---

[1]Cf. e.g. Jan Barcz, *Unia Europejska na rozstajach. Traktat z Lizbony. Dynamika i główne kierunki reformy ustrojowej*, 2nd edition, EuroPrawo, Warszawa 2010, pp.112–116 and 117–122.

[2]Cf. e.g. Mirosław Janicki, Wiesław Władyka, "Gabinet grozy," *Polityka* No. 20 (2858) of 16.05.2012, who, while deprecating the fears of the right, at the same time concur with their premises: "The right is afraid of Europe (. . .), because it is being invaded by moral norms and standards which are undesirable and scary, such as civil partnerships, *in vitro* insemination, euthanasia and apostasy, ideas of secular state and civic society, modern human rights (. . .) while

© Springer Nature Switzerland AG 2021
M. Gierycz, *European Dispute over the Concept of Man*, Contributions to Political Science, https://doi.org/10.1007/978-3-030-61520-8_1

represents a political form of the Old Continent which is not called a continent of culture by accident.[3]

Social sciences seem to have trouble understanding and explaining the relevance of these disputes for contemporary politics. The reasons are manifold. On the one hand, papers concerned with these issues are often ideologically biased, and written not so much (or at least not only) with cognitive objectives but rather with a political agenda in mind.[4] On the other hand, in view of the persistent ignorance of morality issues by European political science,[5] studies in this area, particularly as regards activities of the European Union, are contributory in nature. Finally, a large portion of the existing analyses consist in isolated studies concerning the LGB/LGBT/LGBTI discourse, the feminist discourse, the abortion discourse, etc., without even attempting to make any reference to the theses proposed by humanities concerning the crisis of Europe which is now facing a cultural "stress test."[6] No wonder, then, that political science is accused of lacking analytical depth.[7] As pointed out by one leading European intellectual, however, taking into account "the radical nature of the tensions that our continent has to face ... what is at stake in the debate about the definition of Europe, about its new political form, is not some nostalgic battle at the "rear-guard" of history, but rather a great responsibility for the humanity of today."[8] If he is right, then the issues outlined above, often portrayed in the media as "substitute topics," are of fundamental importance for the future of Europe, including the European Union.

There is much to support this claim. If the political and legal outcome of the culture of the Old Continent, or—more broadly—of the West, is a democracy based

---

refusing to acknowledge the fact that new norms are being formed right now, and that the ones they are defending were once just as new."

[3]Cf. Piotr Mazurkiewicz, *Europeizacja Europy. Tożsamość kulturowa Europy w kontekście procesów integracji*, IP UKSW, Warszawa 2001.

[4]For example, already in the introduction of a publication on transsexualism, printed by a renowned publishing house, we find a call to "file complaints against the actions of (or failure to take action by) the Polish government, so that in a few years the Polish transsexual community may celebrate a judgment on its behalf" issued by the European Court of Human Rights (Adam Bodnar, "Wprowadzenie," in: Anna Śledzińska-Simon [ed.], *Prawa osób transseksualnych. Rozwiązania modelowe a sytuacja w Polsce*, Wolters Kluwer Business, Warszawa 2010, p. 18).

[5]This issue had been rarely present in European political science until an opening of sorts provided by a series of articles published in the *Journal of European Public Policy* in the spring of 2013. Cf. Christoph Knill, "The study of morality policy: analytical implications from a public policy perspective," *Journal of European Public Policy*, 20:3, 2013; or Donley T. Studlar, Alessandro Cagossi, Robert D. Duval, "Is morality policy different? Institutional explanations for postwar Western Europe," *Journal of European Public Policy*, 20:3. For more on this issue, see Chap. 9.

[6]Joseph Cardinal Ratzinger, "Europe in the Crisis of Cultures," *Communio: International Catholic Review* 32 (2005), p. 348; cf. Joseph H.H. Weiler, *Un' Europa Cristiana: Un saggioesplorativo*, BUR Saggi, Milan, 2003.

[7]Cf. Roberto Esposito, *Terms of the Political: Community, Immunity, Biopolitics*, Fordham University Press 2013.

[8]Joseph Cardinal Ratzinger, op. cit., p. 348.

on respect for human rights, which by their very nature do not depend on a democratic majority, then the fact that in our times—within the framework of these very rights—fundamental values have become a matter of public controversy, and are at times stripped of any real protection, cannot be treated as politically inconsequential. This situation shows a progressive broadening of the area of politics, which refuses to accept any kind of order not dependent on a majority vote. It is thus encroaching upon a territory which has so far lain outside of its borders; these borders, until not long ago defined, *inter alia*, by public morals, are now being actually removed together with morality policy. The spreading of politicism in the name of freedom, or rather emancipation, seems to be turning politics into an area of omnipotence, at the same time potentially posing a threat to freedom itself. Consequently, particularly in political science, it is essential that we understand the meaning and consequences of European debates concerning the first principles, and the role of the European Union in this process. It is this very issue that this study examines.

When looking for a prism through which to look at the Union when discussing the problem outlined about, I have decided to adopt an anthropological perspective. There are two reasons for this. The first is a negative: a review of the literature on the subject shows that an analysis of cultural tensions in the ethical perspective has limited explicatory value—looking from the perspective of political science. This is not only because, due to an inflation of ethical theories,[9] merely making a diagnosis and naming diverse axiological positions, while cognitively valuable, often does not provide any data—particularly information that would be interesting to a political scientist—that would contribute to understanding the direction of social and political changes they entail. The problem consists, first of all, in that answers offered at the level of the theory of value (axiology) about the essence of the cultural debate do not provide any real explanation. For example, when discussing the nature of today's disputes about values, it is argued that the disputing parties, while essentially agreeing about the meaning of values, arrange them into different hierarchies. This is, naturally, quite true. One can hardly disagree, for example, with Marek Safjan, one of judges of Court of Justice of European Union, who claims that there is "consent as to the catalogue of principles and the locus of conflict, [while] there is no consensus as to the method of choosing the principle to be preferred in particular circumstances."[10] The problem is that such a reply leaves us, in essence, without an answer to the question we began with. It does not provide any explanation as to why such a serious conflict exists (particularly if the values are shared!) and what premises its parties rest their claims upon.

There is much to suggest, on the other hand, that the problem at hand is not only concerned with the hierarchical ordering of values. If, for instance, we were to analyze the dispute about the legalization of euthanasia, we would soon discover

---

[9]Cf. e.g. Peter Singer [ed.], *Ethics*, Oxford University Press 1994.

[10]Marek Safjan, "Prawo, wartości i demokracja," in: Michał Gierycz, Jan Grosfeld [ed.], *Zmagania początku tysiąclecia*, Łośgraf, Warszawa 2012, p.173.

that none of the parties challenge the supreme value of man's dignity.[11] At most, such a charge may be brought by one party against another. The dispute is not about identifying the value that is at the top of the hierarchy; it is about how the value should be understood, and what practical implication this may have. This may suggest that the contemporary dispute is concerned first and foremost with the way the content of certain categories (such as dignity, freedom, equality, etc.) is understood, and only secondarily, so to say, with the hierarchy of values. This situation brings to mind the eighteenth century dispute over ideas. At that time, concurrently with the emergence of a liberal type of democracy, a trend emerged from the same premises which Jacob Talmon calls totalitarian (messianic) democracy. While the former recognized the significance of endeavors "which are altogether outside the sphere of politics," understanding politics as "a matter of trial and error,"[12] the latter widened "the scope of politics to embrace the whole of human existence", postulating "a preordained, harmonious and perfect scheme of things, to which men are irresistibly driven, and at which they are bound to arrive."[13] Given the nature of contemporary disputes, some serious thought should be given to looking into those visions of man and politics for the source of today's cultural situation in which general consent about fundamental values is coupled with a major dispute over their content, and ultimately also a dispute about the competences of politics.

The other reason is a positive one. Since at the very heart of the world of values is man,[14] there can be no doubt that at the source of axiological tensions must be the dispute over the concept of man. It is therefore reasonable to assume that any differences in understanding values and their hierarchy must entail different anthropological standpoints. Ultimately, in order to say what rights are vested in man, i.e. what it justly due to man, we must consider some answers concerning the nature of man, or at least about man's condition,[15] to be adequate, and others to be inadequate.[16]

---

[11]Cf. e.g. Włodzimierz Galewicz, "Decyzje o zakończeniu życia," in: id. [ed.], *Wokół śmierci i umierania*, Universitas, Kraków 2009.

[12]Jacob L. Talmon, *The Origins of Totalitarian Democracy*, Butler & Tanner Ltd, London 1919, pp. 1–2.

[13]Ibid.

[14]Józef Tischner, "Etyka wartości i nadziei," in: Ks. Józef Tischner, Jan A. Kłoczowski OP, *Wobec wartości*, W drodze, Poznań 2001, p. 29.

[15]For example, in her reflections Hannah Arendt consistently tries to move away from the category of human nature. And yet, when stressing that "the sum total of human activities and capabilities which correspond to the human condition does not constitute anything like human nature" or "essential characteristics of human existence in the sense that without them this existence would no longer be human," she ultimately tries to find an answer to what is possibly the first philosophical question: "what is?". Consequently, she considers being "conditioned" an intrinsic element of being human, and thus as something proper to "human nature." Hannah Arendt, *The Human Condition*, University of Chicago Press 2018, p. 10.

[16]For example, to protect the freedom of thought and the right to education, we must share the assumption that man is a rational being who is capable of intellectual development.

In recognition of the fact that the concept of man is at the root of "every theory of state, law, justice,"[17] this study focuses on revealing the anthropological dimension of European politics. On the one hand, this should help establish a link with the European tradition of political ideas, where the anthropological question has often been explicitly afforded a central place. On the other hand, it should contribute to a better understanding of the meaning and potential consequences of the legal norms developed today in the European political process, which may at the same time be "an instrument ordering the public sphere at a given moment, and a tool used to implement social change."[18]

Consequently, it should be concluded that this book is a study in political anthropology. This is much easier said than done, however. For while it is beyond doubt that the anthropological process is, by the very nature of things, central to social reflection and analysis, an understanding of political anthropology in political science is yet to be fully achieved. The exuberant development of political anthropology in ethnology[19] as well as in philosophy,[20] is not coupled with an analogous process in political science.[21]

---

[17]Zbigniew Stawrowski, *Wokół idei wspólnoty*, OMP, Kraków 2012, p. 37.

[18]Piotr Mazurkiewicz, "Wokół Karty Praw Podstawowych UE," in: Michał Gierycz, Jan Grosfeld [ed.], *Zmagania początku tysiąclecia...*, p. 207.

[19]Cf. e.g. Cris Shore and Susan Wright, *Anthropology of Policy. Critical perspectives on governance and power*, Routledge, London and New York 2005; Irene Bellier and Thomas Wilson, *An Anthropology of European Union. Building, Imagining and Experiencing the New Europe*, Berg, Oxford, New York 2000, Joanna Tokarska-Bakir, *Cóż po antropologii?*, Collegium Civitas, Warszawa 2006; Mirosława Drozd-Piasecka, Aleksander Posern-Zieliński, *Antropologia polityki i polityka w antropologii*, KNE PAN, Warszawa 2010; Wojciech Dohnal, Aleksander Posern-Zieliński, *Antropologia i polityka. Szkice z badań nad kulturowymi wymiarami władzy*, KNE PAN, Warszawa 2011.

[20]Cf. e.g. Marian Grabowski [ed.], *O antropologii Jana Pawła II*, WUMK, Toruń 2004; ks. Stanisław Kowalczyk, *Zarys filozofii człowieka*, Wydawnictwo Diecezjalne, Sandomierz 2002; Henryk Piluś, *Antropologia filozoficzna neotomizmu*, Vizja, Warszawa 2010; Piotr Duchliński, Grzegorz Hołub [ed.], *Oblicza natury ludzkiej. Studia i rozprawy*, Ignatianum, WAM, Kraków 2010; Piotr Stanisław Mazur, *Spór o osobę w świetle klasycznej koncepcji człowieka*, Ignatianum, WAM, Kraków 2012.

[21]In Polish literature, for example, there are few contributing studies: Elżbieta Muciek, "Antropologia polityczna – między etnologią a politologią," *Roczniki Nauk Społecznych* 6 (42) 2014, pp. 195–213; Anna Popławska, "Podejście antropologiczne a metody historyczne i socjologiczne na terenie nauk politycznych," in: Bohdan Szklarski [ed.], *Mity, symbole i rytuały we współczesnej polityce*, Scholar, Warszawa 2008, pp. 29–36; Piotr Załęski, "Subdyscypliny empiryczne nauk o polityce," in: Wojciech Jakubowski, Piotr Załęski, Łukasz Zamęcki, *Nauki o polityce. Zarys koncepcji dyscypliny*, Wyd. Typografia Pułtusk, Pułtusk 2013, pp. 222–225; Michał Gierycz, "O pojmowaniu antropologii politycznej na gruncie politologii," *Roczniki Nauk Społecznych* 6 (42) 2014, pp. 171–193; Michał Gierycz, Piotr Mazurkiewicz, "Europejska antropologia i europejska polityka – obserwacja współczesności," in: Christoph Bohr, Christian Schmitz, *Europa i jej antropologia polityczna. Człowiek jako droga historii – o filozofii Karola Wojtyły*, KAS, Warszawa 2016, pp. 107–141.

It is characteristic in this context that in the *Lexicon of Political Science,* no entry on "political anthropology" is to be found at all,[22] just like in the *Encyclopaedia of Political Science.*[23] Considering the absence of an explicit theoretical and methodological standpoint of political science, the approach to political anthropology developed within cultural anthropology is now being transferred over to the domain of political science. Suffice to say that the *Concise Oxford Dictionary of Politics* includes only a single short entry under anthropology, identifying it with the study of primitive societies.[24] It is then not surprising, that the *Encyclopaedia of Political Science* presents political anthropology as an ethnological science which "by reconstructing the way of life in pre-human populations, argues that they were politically-oriented, as is demonstrated by the organizational forms of these communities.".[25] While this approach cannot be charged with being seriously wrong, it is not only narrow,[26] but also fails to achieve the goal which a political scientist considers to be essential, that is—according to the very same *Encyclopaedia,* incidentally—to study "the essence of politics, its governing rules and the functions of its components (. . .) with a view to constructing an overall theory of politics and understanding man's role in it;"[27] that is, a type of study which is far beyond the scope of archaeology or ethnology. It appears, therefore, that political science, while needing anthropology, is somewhat ill at ease with it. At the outset of our endeavor here, it is therefore necessary to take a seriously approach to the challenge of theoretically and methodologically placing political anthropology within the framework of political science. The first part of this study will be devoted to this very issue and outlines the approach to anthropological studies relevant to political science.

Chapter 2, which begins with a more precise elaboration on the essence of the anthropological problem, presents the existing approaches in other disciplines of science (physical anthropology, ethnology, philosophy, and theology), as well as their possible interrelations. I will demonstrate that the anthropological problem as such escapes the reach of individual sciences, and requires an interdisciplinary approach which may or may not be methodologically accurate. In the conclusion to Chap. 2, the basic criteria for a methodologically correct integration of anthropological perspectives will be defined; they will prove useful later on, in the course of further theoretical analyses. Chapter 3 analyzes the ways in which political anthropology is understood, and its significance for political science studies. Even though these analyses demonstrate the applicability of findings supplied by political and

---

[22]Cf. Andrzej Antoszewski, Ryszard Herbut [ed.], *Leksykon politologii,* atla2, Wrocław 2003.

[23]Marek Chmaj, Joanna Marszałek-Kawa, Wojciech Sokół [ed.], *Encyklopedia Wiedzy Politycznej,* wyd. Adam Marszałek, Toruń 2006, even though it includes such entries as anthropology, cultural anthropology, and social anthropology. Ibid., pp. 19–21.

[24]Cf. Alistair McMillan, *Concise Oxford Dictionary of Politics,* Oxford University Press 2003.

[25]Andrzej Chodubski, "Antropologia polityczna," in: Marek Żmigrodzki, Wojciech Sokół [ed.], *Encyklopedia politologii, tom 1: Teoria polityki,* Zakamycze, Kraków 1999, p. 30.

[26]It does not, for example, include a definition of the anthropology of politics developed on the grounds of cultural anthropology – see more in Chap. 3.

[27]A. Chodubski, "Antropologia polityczna," p. 29.

anthropological studies carried out in other disciplines (such as ethnology, philosophy, or theology), they also prove that none of them provides a complete answer to questions relevant to political science.

Consequently, in Chap. 4 a framework is constructed for a theory of political anthropology in political science, including its proper research objective, and the ways of integrating the achievements and study methods of anthropological studies relevant for analyses performed in political science, developed within the framework of other disciplines. To put it in more general terms, a case is made that just as cultural anthropology is founded on an analysis of the products of culture, and philosophical anthropology on intellectual reflection, so political anthropology should be grounded in an analysis—taking into account the ideological and cultural context—of legal regulations and political documents in order to reveal the underlying concepts of man. To this end, it may integrate and elaborate, in furtherance of its own goals and from the system paradigm perspective, on study techniques developed in cultural (social) and philosophical (theological) anthropology.

Based on the understanding of political anthropology outlined in the Part 1, I will then move on to the concept of man underlying the politics of the European Union. My main research objective is to reconstruct the sources and the specific nature of the EU's concept of man, as revealed both by primary legislation and the activities of EU institutions. The above goal is linked to two basic research questions. One is concerned with the relevance of the concept of man for the concept of politics. To be more precise, I am interested in what main currents of thought about man can be identified in European political thought, being the cultural context of European integration. Taking into accounts the findings of Jacob Talmon, Thomas Sowell, and others, who prove the existence of two contrary currents of thought in modern politics, this research examines the anthropological standpoints in which they are grounded.

The other question is concerned with the anthropological solutions adopted in the European Union. Since it groups together countries which endorse different hierarchies of fundamental values, while at the same time—owing to the dynamics of creation of primary legislation—avoids making any explicit statements in its treatises to settle axiological disputes between the Member States, the thesis to be verified in this part of the study is the claim that contradictory anthropological concepts co-exist in EU legislation. This implies a departure for EU axiology from the metaphysics of values characteristic of the constitutional tradition of Europe. This research aims to verify this claim, and try to reveal the political consequences of an inconsistent anthropological stance. An important auxiliary question which will be taken up in the course of functional analyses is whether particular institutions of the European Union (the Commission, the Council, the Parliament) represent the same or a different concept of man.

The intended goal of my studies, the questions asked, and the theses I propose require a two-stage research. The first, implemented in the second part of this book and engaged—in reference to Ferdinand Breudel's terminology—with the "long time span," is aimed at examining the cultural background of the political system and discovering the anthropological models characteristic of the European tradition of ideas, as well as outlining the core anthropological problems related to the political order. In reference to findings made by researchers who point to two, radically different, modern ways of understanding politics which developed from the same values in the Enlightenment,[28] an attempt will be made at offering a model presentation of two anthropological traditions within whose framework the cultural tensions specific to modern and late-modern politics may be considered. The starting point will be Thomas Sowell's theory presented in Chap. 5. With certain adjustments, it helps to describe two ideal anthropological types: a constrained and an unconstrained anthropology, representing two opposing sources of the vision of man specific to modern politics. These categories, encompassing major ideological traditions of politics, refer to the recognition (or non-recognition) of the objective boundaries of human nature whose transgression entails some form of dehumanization.

A constrained anthropology and its political and ideological interpretations has been described in Chap. 6, where I contend that a belief in the existence of objective boundaries of "the human" was a key element of political philosophy even in Antiquity. It was expressed clearly not only in the awareness of man's imperfection, but foremost in the idea of natural law which reveals an anthropological intuition about "the moral character of existence itself, and the indispensable harmony of human beings with the message of nature,"[29] and thus, ultimately being "none other than a question about the rational nature of reality".[30] Through Christianity, the anthropological concept which emerged in Antiquity is not only developed and theologically grounded, but also grafted onto the main trunk of European political thought, providing the foundations for understanding politics as a prudent, and therefore conscious of its own limitations, way of acting for the common good. Consequently, it should come as no surprise[31] that this anthropological perspective was also present in currents of thought which at times appeared to be distant from Christianity.[32]

---

[28]Cf. Jacob L. Talmon, *The Origins of Totalitarian Democracy,* Butler & Tanner Ltd, London 1919; or Thomas Sowell, *A Conflict of Visions. Ideological Origins of Political Struggles,* revised edition, Basic Books, New York 2007.

[29]Joseph Cardinal Ratzinger, *Czas przemian w Europie. Miejsce Kościoła i świata,* translated by Magdalena Mijalska, M, Kraków 2001, p. 25. [German original: *Wendezet für Europa? Diagnosen und Prognosen zur Lage von Kirche und Welt.*Einsiedeln: Johannes Verlag, 1991.].

[30]Zbigniew Stawrowski, *Prawo naturalne a ład polityczny,* Instytut Myśli Józefa Tischnera, ISP PAN, Kraków-Warszawa 2006, p. 9.

[31]Even if, as has been pointed out by Leo Strauss, "[t]he issue of natural right presents itself today as a matter of party allegiance." Id., *Natural Right and History,* University of Chicago Press 1965, p. 7.

[32]As noted by Zbigniew Stawrowski in the conclusion of his analyses of the understanding of natural law in Plato, Thomas Aquinas, Thomas Hobbes, Immanuel Kant, and Georg Hegel, it is for "all of them equally self-evident that man, by being part of the world, participates in its order and is subject to its laws. It is in this sense that we can talk of man's permanent nature." In addition, the author points out that even though the question of what elements are essential to this nature would certainly be a point of dispute between these philosophers, "an analysis of their concepts nevertheless seems to suggest that if they had a chance to actually continue this debate, four of them—all but

A different anthropological approach, although present in embryonic form already in some sophist writings,[33] appears in Europe with the political thought heralding the breakthrough brought by the Enlightenment, leaving a significant imprint on modern political thought. A feature characteristic of unconstrained thought, in all of its many guises, is the presumption of man's (at least potential) perfection. This presumption, as noted by Marcin Król, is thoroughly novel in that "even the—apparently—least religious thinkers, such as Machiavelli or Shakespeare, were very well aware of our imperfection, of the presence of evil."[34] The idea of perfection also entails the obliteration, *inter alia* by negating man's moral nature, of the hitherto clear boundaries of humanity. The borderline no longer necessarily runs between man and animal, but depends on various criteria: historical, ideological, or scientific.[35] These anthropological concepts are discussed in Chap. 7.

In view of the fact that the European Union is a community created in the late modernity, Chap. 8 discusses the cultural status of modernity. Referring to Gianni Vattimo and Chantal Delsol, I will demonstrate why post-modernism should be perceived not as a new cultural era, but rather as an age of "fulfilling" the promises of modernity. Consequently, this chapter will show the particular relationship between unconstrained anthropology and the late-modern cultural context. Recognizing the legitimacy of the claim, emphasized today in the humanities, that even the most secularized way of thinking is grounded in an implied choice which is theological in nature,[36] the conclusion of this section presents the implicit relationships between anthropological and theological standpoints which refer—in the case of constrained anthropology—to the logic of *veluti si Deus daretur* (vertical anthropology), or—in the case of unconstrained anthropology—to that of *etsi Deus non daretur* (horizontal anthropology).

The third part of this study is concerned with the second research question and is devoted to an analysis of the morality policy of the European Union. In Chap. 9 I will

---

Hobbes—would probably have reached an agreement as to the key points under dispute." Z. Stawrowski, *Prawo naturalne. . .*, pp. 433–434.

[33] Suffice it to cite the *homo-mensura* principle proposed by Protagoras: "Protagoras undoubtedly intended, by using the principle of *man-measure*, to deny than an absolute criterion exists by which do discriminate between being and not being, truth and falsity, and in general every value. The criterion is only relative, it is the man, the individual man." Giovanni Reale, *A History of Ancient Philosophy I: From the Origins to Socrates*, translated by John R. Catan, State University of New York Press, Albany, p. 157.

[34] Marcin Król, *Europa w obliczu końca*, wydawnictwo czerwone i czarne, Warszawa 2012, p. 12.

[35] Chantal Millon-Delsol, *Esej o człowiekupóźnejnowoczesności*, translated by MałgorzataKowalska, Znak, Kraków 2003, p. 18 [French original: *Éloge de la singularité, essai sur la modernité tardive*, La Table Ronde, 2000].

[36] Agata Bielik-Robson, *Kryptoteologie późnej nowoczesności*, Universitas, Kraków 2008, p. 8. This approach is frequently found in today's literature. Cf. eg. Creston Davis, John Milbank, Slavoj Ziżek, *Theology and the political. The new debate*, Duke University Press, Durham and London 2005; or Leszek Kołakowski, "Kapłan i błazen. Rozważania o teologicznym dziedzictwie współczesnego myślenia," in: Id., *Nasza wesoła apokalipsa. Wybór najważniejszych esejów*, Znak, Kraków 2010.

demonstrate the legitimacy of the claim that it is within the framework of this policy
that the anthropological tensions characteristic of late modernity are most emphatically present today. Some more background will be provided on the category of
morality policy itself, and its research tradition. I will also show the relevance of
anthropological models discovered in the course of studies on political ideas for
disputes raging around morality policy, and their impact on the language used by the
disputing parties. The chapter ends with a paragraph presenting the competences of
the EU in the area of morality policy. Chapter 10 moves on to an analysis of the
anthropological framework of the political discussion witnessed in the European
Union. Therefore, the main focus is on the key anthropological settlements of
primary legislation, first of all the Treaty on European Union and the Charter of
Fundamental Rights. By presenting the solutions they adopt against the background
of the document which is fundamental for the international system of human
rights—the Universal Declaration of Human Rights—I will demonstrate the legitimacy of the thesis concerning the coexistence of two contradictory anthropological
models, characteristic of the post-Enlightenment tradition in Europe, in the primary
legislation of the European Union. Chapters 11 and 12 are devoted to an inductive
study of the political consequences of this "coexistence." In Chap. 11, I will analyze
the language and contents of documents compiled by EU institutional actors,
documenting the prevalence, particularly in supra-national institutions (the Parliament, the Commission), of unconstrained anthropological thinking. In Chap. 12,
based on the premises of grounded theory, I will perform some functional analyses to
saturate the claims made in Chap. 11 by elaborating on the anthropological standpoints of the main institutional actors of the European Union (the Parliament, the
Commission, the Council, the Court) and the dynamics of their mutual influences in
the political process, which will allow me to answer the question about the specificity of the Union's way of thinking about man, and to verify the hypothesis about
institutional divergences as regards the vision of man.

I wish to make it clear that it is not my intention to explain all of the reasons for
which European institutions engage in the cultural debates discussed here; there are
certainly many different degrees of their involvement. Apart from the ideological
commitments of politicians and political groups, there are also the attempts made by
EU institutions to elicit social legitimization for their activities, to enhance their
terms of reference (or fear of losing them), to construct a European identity, etc.[37]
While this work does signal these issues in its analyses, they do not constitute the
main objective, which is to reconstruct the sources and specific way of thinking
about man in the EU. At the same time, the two-stage research strategy adopted here
helps to demonstrate that the EU's anthropological stance is not only an effect of the
evolution taking place among the community's elites (institutions), but also a

---

[37]Cf. e.g. Tomasz G. Grosse, *Europa na rozdrożu*, ISP, Warszawa 2008; or Michał Gierycz,
"Axiology of the European Union and Challenges of the Integration Process," in: Wojciech Gizicki
[ed.], *European Union. Present and Future*, KUL, Lublin 2009, pp. 9–26.

reflection (even if at times it resembles a hall of mirrors) of the broader changes in Western European culture in the age of late modernity.

The methodology of this study, stemming from the view of political anthropology proposed in Part 1, is discussed in detail in the last paragraphs of Chap. 4. At this point I would only like to mention that it is founded on a modified system approach referred to as in-depth system analysis. As will be demonstrated in Chap. 4, by focusing on micro-system and mezzo-system analyses, political science has essentially ceased, contrary to what had been expected by David Easton, to take the cultural background into account when examining the political process. In-depth system analysis restores this perspectives by having regard for the fact that "the conscious policies of men and governments are (...) deductions from our most basic ideas of human destiny."[38] Consequently, when seeking to capture the ways of thinking about man that are characteristic of a political system, its contents, outputs, and inputs, political activity must be seen as inherently linked to civilizational, cultural and religious ideas. In-depth system analysis thus strives to reveal the relationship between two levels: political developments examined over a short time span, and transformations in ideas and ways of thinking which define the standards of evaluation and norms structuring institutional activities. This seems particularly reasonable in the context of the research objective of reconstructing the sources and trajectories of thinking about man characteristic of European integration. Ultimately, the EU is to a large extent a political embodiment of the European cultural formation. One can hardly imagine understanding the anthropological debates present within it in isolation from the ideological disputes held at least since the Enlightenment. If the thesis to be verified states that there are mutually contradictory anthropological concepts coexisting in the legislation and politics of the European Union, then their proper identification (and thus their understanding) requires an analysis that reaches below the surface of political events.

The study is based on a variety of sources, largely due to the different character of each part. In somewhat simplified terms, the first part of the book is based on sources and scientific works in ethnology, political science, sociology, philosophy and theology, including methodological studies; the second—on classic and contemporary works in the philosophy of politics and researchers studying political thought; the third—on political and legal documents of the European Union, documents of institutions cooperating with the EU, press releases and information from the Internet, as well as political studies in morality policy. As an additional source, I have also used in-depth interviews [IDI] with actors of the European discussion on morality policy. Even though they have played a role in my search for clues to be followed, I only refer to them in the text when they contribute data which cannot be found elsewhere.

The findings should not be revealed in the introduction; nevertheless, being aware of the voluminosity of this study, despite the logical sequence of its parts, I do not expect all readers to quickly read the entire book. I am aware that the theoretical and

---

[38]Richard M. Weaver, *Ideas Have Consequences*, University of Chicago Press, 2013, p. 3.

methodological part, interesting—not only in my opinion, I trust—to those who have a predilection towards the theory and study of politics, does not necessarily evoke passionate interest among the less specialized of my readers. I do hope, however, that the second part, devoted to political ideas, and particularly the third part which analyses the legislation and politics of the European Union, may not only provide those interested in political matters with facts they have not been familiar with so far, but may also shed some light on the essence of the cultural debate in Europe, and the way the European Union has become involved in it; while at the same time also revealing the ambitions of contemporary Western politics.

Part I
Political Anthropology and Studies in Political Science

When looking for an approach to political anthropology that can satisfy the requirements of this study, one should first define the area and the research problem of anthropology. The term "anthropology", derived from ἀνθρωπος [*anthropos*: man] and Λόγος [*logos*: reason, study, science], refers to the study of man and knowledge of that which is properly human. Consequently, the issue of human nature and the forms in which it is actualized, that is—ultimately—of the unity and diversity of humankind, was the initial problem undertaken by the new discipline of anthropology as it developed in the nineteenth century. As pointed out by Ewa Nowicka, "the proper subject matter of this discipline is man in all of his aspects: social, cultural, psychological and physical."[1]

The belief in the holistic goals of anthropology as the science of man is deeply rooted in the anthropological tradition. Already in a 1901 essay entitled *Explanations of Cause and Origin*, Alfred L. Kroeber claimed that human life as a whole is the proper object of anthropology, whose task, consequently, is to present a coordinated concept of man.[2] In the early 1930s, Franz Boas stressed that its goal is to understand "the steps by which man has come to be what he is, biologically, psychologically and culturally," concluding that anthropological studies "must include the history of the development of the bodily form of man, his physiological functions, mind and culture."[3] In a much later work *The Church and Cultures*, Louis Luzbetak, one of the classics of cultural anthropology, emphasized that "whereas other sciences may study human beings from a *particular* perspective (for instance, from the physical, biological, psychological, social or historical perspective), anthropology focuses on something more than an understanding limited to any single point of view."[4] Aiming at a holistic description of man, it brings together "various

---

[1]Ewa Nowicka, *Świat człowieka – świat kultury*, PWN, Warszawa 2006, p. 34.

[2]Alfred L. Kroeber, *The Nature of Culture*, University of Chicago Press, Chicago 1952, pp. 12–19.

[3]Franz Boas, "The Aims of Anthropological Research," in: *Race, Language and Culture*, University of Chicago Press 1982, p. 244.

[4]L. J. Luzbetak, *The Church and Cultures*, Orbis Books 1989, p. 24.

perspectives or models of humanness and superimpose[s] them like transparencies, one on top of the other."[5] It is therefore interested both in describing man "in the externally-quantitative: somatic, biological, ecological, morphological, etc. dimension,"[6] and in characterizing man and society in their relation to culture. We may thus say that a holistic view of man which does not lose sight of his being "a bio-socio-cultural whole" may be treated as a characteristic feature of the anthropological approach.[7] This would mean that even if anthropology focuses on examining otherness, its goal is not merely to show the diversity of cultural perspectives. As pointed out by Louis Dumont, "ethnology, or more precisely social anthropology, would have only specialist interest if the subject of its study—'primitive' or 'archaic' societies and the great civilizations of other countries—revealed a human kind quite different from ourselves. Anthropology, by the understanding it gradually affords of the most widely differing societies and cultures, gives proof of the unity of mankind."[8] It tries to resolve the paradox of that "there is indeed a person, and individual and unique experience, but it is in large part made up of common elements."[9]

One can hardly fail to see, however, that this desire, deeply seated in the anthropological tradition, to explain "why people are so similar and yet so different,"[10] ultimately appears to be an area where cultural anthropology has fallen short. As pointed out by Louis Luzbetak, "no anthropologist could possibly master the entire field of anthropology."[11] This impossibility, let us add, results not only from the immensity of the material one would have to master. It is related, first of all, to the nature of the question, which goes beyond issues typically studied by social sciences, and refers to fundamental philosophical problems. Already in Plato's *States-man*, the Eleatic Stranger points out[12] that people have a predilection to two polar opposites in what they do. On the one hand, "since people aren't accustomed to look into things by dividing them according to forms, they right away throw these things that are so different together in the same group, deeming them similar," while on the other hand "they do the opposite of this with other things, failing to divide them according to parts." A wise man, however, once he "perceives the community of many things," should not "desist before he sees the differences within it, all those that lie within forms, and then again, in the case of all sorts of dissimilarities, whenever they're seen in multitudes," and keep on reflecting until "he encompasses

---

[5]Ibid.

[6]Stanisław Kowalczyk, *Zarys filozofii człowieka*, Wydawnictwo Diecezjalne, Sandomierz 2002, p. 7.

[7]E. Nowicka, *Świat człowieka. . .*, p. 35.

[8]Louis Dumont, *Homo hierarchicus. The Caste System and Its Implications*, University of Chicago Press 1981, p. 2.

[9]Ibid., p. 6.

[10]Ewa Nowicka, *Świat człowieka – świat kultury*, Wydanie nowe, PWN, Warszawa 2006, p. 21.

[11]L. J. Luzbetak, *The Church and Cultures*, p. 27.

[12]I owe this observation to Ottavio De Bertolis, *Elementy antropologii prawa*, Rhetos, Warszawa 2013 [Italian original:*Elementi di antropologia giuridica*, Edizioni Scientifiche Italiane 2010.].

and encloses with the being of some kind all the things that belong within the confines of one similarity."[13] Consequently, if it may be said that "to move from the multifariousness of a phenomenon to the unity of the concept, without ever claiming to have captured the whole of reality in its attempts at providing answers— is the task of a holistic and critical [...reflection on] man,"[14] then this anthropological task *par excellence* is ultimately a philosophical one. In fact, anthropologists are fully aware of the fact that the essence of man is beyond their reach. On the one hand, they admit, therefore, that attempts, based on social studies, "at creating a universal theory explaining the most important principles in the functioning of the world of the human spirit are doomed to failure, or boil down to platitudes."[15] On the other hand, however, they emphasize the immanent interdisciplinarity of the study of man, since "the search for properties specifically human is a thread linking sciences as far apart as the science of religion and the science of the development of man's physical structure."[16]

Therefore, as we stand at the threshold of a search for the proper meaning of political anthropology, we must first describe, at least briefly, the ways of understanding anthropology and their possible relationships (Chap. 2). This will pave the way for understanding the multiple meanings attributed to political anthropology today (Chap. 3), to then develop a theory of political anthropology adequate for political studies, and to identify its methodological consequences (Chap. 4).

---

[13]Plato, *The Statesman*, translated by E. Brann, P. Kalkavage, E. Salem, Focus 2012, p. 62.

[14]Ottavio De Bertolis, *Elementy antropologii prawa...*, p. 16 [Italian original: *Elementi di antropologia giuridica*, Edizioni Scientifiche Italiane, 2010.].

[15]Ewa Kopczyńska, *Metoda i pasja. Antropologia kulturowa Franza Boasa z wyborem pism*, Nomos, Kraków 2012, p. 66.

[16]E. Nowicka, *Świat człowieka...*, p. 41.

Chapter 2
Anthropologies and Their Relationships

An attempt at founding the science of man immediately leads to a paradox. In the light of the above observations, the principal aim of anthropology developing as a domain of social sciences would be related to philosophical reflection, and the empirical starting point for its research would be related to biological sciences. This set of disciplines should, in fact, be supplemented to include theological sciences. It is clear that, to use the terminology of Ferdinand Breudel, the deep structures of every civilization are related to convictions, entailed by religion, about who God is and who man is. In the European context, from the very beginning, religion has involved in-depth intellectual and scientific reflection—theology. Even though it is often institutionally relegated to the margins of modern science,[1] it remains relevant not only for an understanding of our pre-judgements about who we are, but also for philosophy[2] and social sciences. The classic works of Max Weber, Erich Voegelin, Carl Schmitt, or Raymond Aaron demonstrate the relevance of the often immanentized religious experiences and ideas for secularized societies.

---

[1] In Poland, the most apparent symptom of this process is e.g. the sustained exclusion of theological faculties from most universities.

[2] For example, N. Lobkowicz argues that—in philosophical terms—the doctrine of inviolable dignity of the human person "can hardly be upheld, much less substantiated, without the belief that the human person has been created by a personal God." Nikolaus Lobkowicz, *O pojęciu osoby*, in: Id. [ed.] Czas *kryzysu, czas przełomu*, translated by Grzegorz Sowiński, WAM, Znak, Kraków 1994, p. 105 [German original: *Das Erbe Europas*, Frankfurt a.M. 1989].

© Springer Nature Switzerland AG 2021

M. Gierycz, *European Dispute over the Concept of Man*, Contributions to Political Science, https://doi.org/10.1007/978-3-030-61520-8_2

2.1 Four Anthropologies

Even though anthropology emerges as a science of man *par excellence*, it has never been concerned with all aspects of human life.[3] Given the differences in methodology and problems outlined above, from the very beginning parallel studies have been involved, different in their goals and techniques, carried out under the name of anthropology. From the point of view of the functioning of science, it would therefore be legitimate to say that instead of an anthropology in the singular, since the turn of twentieth century multiple anthropologies have developed: physical, cultural (social), philosophical, and—much later—theological. Over time, each of them has defined its proper area of study and methodology, making its own, unique contribution to the study of man. Paraphrasing the famous concept of anthropology proposed by Franz Boas,[4] we may thus speak of a four-aspect concept of anthropology, taking up four types of issues, with the proviso that—already in their assumptions—they do not constitute a single discipline of science.

2.1.1 Physical Anthropology

The first application of the category of anthropology was its reference to what is nowadays called physical, natural or biological anthropology, studying people as biological organisms. An examination of the term "anthropology" as used in the first half of the nineteenth century clearly shows that anthropology meant "the theory of the human that can be derived from the research of anatomists, palaeologists, and biologists of race and heredity,"[5] which made some researchers conclude that "a broad view of anthropology has been narrowed down to the biological science of man."[6]

Anthropology in the naturalist approach thus means a science dealing with "the physical and biological properties of man";[7] it analyses properties of the human body and its functions. According to Andrzej Malinowski, such an anthropology has three main research areas: in the phylogenetic branch, "it studies the direction and pace of the evolution of humanoids based on analyses of human fossil remains." In the population branch (population anthropology) it examines "the variability of

---

[3]E. Nowicka, *Świat człowieka. . .*, p. 34.

[4]Cf. E. Kopczyńska, *Metoda i pasja. . .*, p. 76. It is worth noting that the concept of four domains of anthropological knowledge is still in use today in the USA. Cf. Alan Barnard, *History and Theory in Anthropology*, Cambridge University Press 2000.

[5]Helmuth Plessner, *Political Anthropology*, translated by Nils F. Schott, Northwestern University Press, Evanston, Illinois 2018.

[6]Andrzej Malinowski, *Wstęp*, in: Id. [ed.], *Antropologia fizyczna*, PWN, Warszawa—Poznań 1980, p. 9.

[7]Tadeusz Kuder, *Antropologia w zarysie*, WUJK, Kielce 2011, p. 11.

morphological and physiological features in human populations across geographical regions," while the ontogenetic branch is concerned with "the ontogenetic development of man, and the genetic and environmental factors affecting this process."[8] Some authors also refer to applied anthropology, e.g. criminal, forensic, or sports anthropology.[9] Irrespective of the differences in detailed approaches within physical anthropology, it may be said to focus on "studying those properties of man which are his biological equipment, while at the same time diversifying the human species from within."[10] Consequently, it is essentially a comparative biology of man, examining "the developmental processes of particular physical types, studying their susceptibility or resistance to change, tracking contacts between populations which have become reflected in changes in body structure and functions of human organisms."[11] It is, therefore, "an empirical, comparative study of the supposed beginnings of the human kind and its diverse manifestations in the races."[12] The emphasis on the issues of race is related to the fact that a characteristic feature of physical anthropology is its focus on population. Unlike genetics, for instance, which studies the concrete human genome, anthropology tries to identify features characteristic of entire groups of people. It is interested in man as a member of a community identified based on biological data. Consequently, one of the central categories of physical anthropology is the category of race as the biological type of differentiation within the *homo sapiens* species.

Physical anthropology uses research methods characteristic of natural sciences. Since its study is focused on population, it relies on "methods of measurement (rather than description) and compilation of statistical data based on the results of these measurements."[13] The most generally conceived research technique of physical anthropology is anthropometry "which is a collection of descriptive and measuring techniques and methods. It includes craniometry which deals with measurements of the skull, cranioscopy which is concerned with description of the skull (. . .). Similarly, as regards the rest of the skeleton, there is osteometry and osteoscopy, and as regards the living man—somatometry and somatoscopy."[14] Anthropologists also analyze other anatomical details, such as "the skin, hair, eyes, internal organs, blood, and the various bodily secretions."[15] In the search for explanations concerning the evolution and diversification of the human body, an important role is also played by archaeological research which allows to reconstruct the history of particular human groups: "by taking very minute and detailed measurements and making comparisons of fossilized and unfossilised bone structures

---

[8]A. Malinowski, *Wstęp. . .*, pp. 9–10.

[9]T. Kuder, *Antropologia. . .*, p. 12.

[10]E. Kopczyńska, *Misja i pasja. . .*, p. 71.

[11]E. Kopczyńska, *Misja i pasja. . .*, pp. 71–72.

[12]H. Plessner, *Political Anthropology*, p. 11.

[13]E. Kopczyńska, *Metoda i pasja. . .*, p. 71.

[14]A. Milanowski, *Wstęp. . .*, p. 10.

[15]L. Luzbetak, *The Church and Cultures*, p. 29.

from human and prehuman forms, the paleoanthropologist tries to discover the origins of the human body, its genetic relationships to lower forms, and its evolution through the thousands of years since the first appearance of humankind on earth."[16] All of this research is aimed at contributing to an understanding of the unity and biological diversity of the human as a natural species.

It should be stressed that the comparative and anatomical approach to natural anthropology was gradually superseded by "a new approach, centering anthropology on the study of man as the locus of social phenomena. This way, a shift occurred from considering man in the perspective of biological time to a study of man in the perspective of sociological time."[17] This outlined "a new understanding of anthropology as a science whose research area is on the borderline of biological and social forms of the movement of matter, while taking into account also its other, abiotic forms," introducing "anthropology into a system of particularly numerous and complex relationships with other disciplines of science."[18] This topic shall be revisited further on.

2.1.2 Cultural Anthropology

While physical anthropology is focused, so to say, on the animal (specific) features of man, studying their diversification over time and space, cultural anthropology is concerned with "the distinctly human aspect of peoples"[19]—their culture. As pointed out by Ewa Nowicka, culture "may be treated as the proper subject matter of anthropology" precisely because "it is a feature that is specifically human."[20] Even though some definitions of anthropology claim that it is a science "which consists in adequately describing and explaining the evolutionary processes of man as a bio-cultural species,"[21] and thus includes man's biological and cultural characteristics, combining the study areas of physical and cultural anthropology, it appears that this kind of holistic approach is methodologically untenable. By placing in the

---

[16]Ibid.

[17]Zbigniew Drozdowski, "Antropologia a nauki stosowane. Antropologia polska nadchodzących lat," *Przegląd Antropologiczny*," 1986, vol. 52, book 1–2, pp. 55–56.

[18]Ibid., p. 56. These relationships are considered important by anthropologists themselves. For example, in a study by Jan Strzałko, Maciej Hennenberg and Janusz Piontek, *Populacje ludzkie jako systemy biologiczne*, PWN, Warszawa 1980, already in the introduction the authors note that "when studying the contemporary problems of ecology and the evolution of man, we have strongly felt the absence of a theoretical link between the sciences of man," emphasizing the indispensability of contributions from philosophers, ethnographers, or archeologists to their research (pp. 7–8).

[19]L. Luzbetak, *The Church and Cultures*, p. 29.

[20]E. Nowicka, *Świat człowieka...*, p. 34.

[21]Andrzej Szyjewski, "Miara, liczba i waga – Andrzeja Wiercińskiego droga do poznania," in: Andrzej Wierciński, *Magia i religia. Szkice z antropologii religii*, Nomos, Kraków 2010, p. XIII.

centre of its attention "the cultures of relatively autonomous social wholes,"[22] cultural anthropology clearly separates itself in terms of the problems it studies from physical anthropology. Already Franz Boas, one of the founders of modern anthropology,[23] emphasized in his works that linguistic phenomena, somatic (physical) differences, and typically cultural processes (customs, rituals, attitudes) should be seen "as separate realities. Even though they come together in the life of a particular people (...) they should be studied as relatively independent, since differences and similarities in customs do not necessarily correspond to differences in language or physical features."[24] Seeing that "the results of classifications according to cultural groups disagreed with both the linguistic and the somatic classifications,"[25] cultural anthropology rejects "the concept of a biological origin of cultural differences, and consequently, any references to biological factors in explaining cultural differences."[26] In fact, looking from the historical perspective, cultural anthropology "developed largely from an opposition to biological determinism in the science of man—a somatic conditioning of cultural development and the psychical features of individuals and groups of people."[27] Almost from the very beginning it claimed,[28] therefore, that "every culture is learned and is not inherited through the genetic structure."[29]

A classic definition of culture, which may be said to have founded cultural anthropology as a discipline of science, was provided by Edward B. Taylor. In 1871, he defined culture as a "complex whole which includes knowledge, belief, art, morals, law, custom, and any other capabilities and habits acquired by man as a

---

[22]E. Nowicka, *Świat człowieka – świat kultury. . .*, p. 21. Understood this way, anthropology remains a science following specific paradigms or cognitive pre-assumptions. They include, first of all, a conviction about the equal ranking of cultures, and the right to cultivate one's own cultural identity.

[23]His division of anthropology into four disciplines represents one of the fundamental elements of its contemporary identity. Cf. E. Kopczyńska, *Metoda i pasja. . .*, pp. 70–78.

[24]E. Kopczyńska, *Metoda i pasja. . .*, p. 70.

[25]George W. Stocking, *The Shaping of American Anthropology, 1883–1911: A Franz Boas Reader*, Basic Books, New York, p. 29.

[26]E. Nowicka, *Świat człowieka – świat kultury. . .*, p. 20.

[27]Janusz Ziółkowski, "Antropologia kulturowa i społeczna," *Przegląd Antropologiczny* 1986, vol. 52, books 1–2, p. 36.

[28]This is a generalization, considering the significance of evolutionism at the early stage in the development of anthropologies which claimed that all cultural development may be explained by the operation of fixed laws which "required the simpler to precede the more complex, the less perfect to precede the more perfect. Their assumptions about progress were held as true whether they considered bodily forms, marriage, religious beliefs, or any other socially shared behaviour." L. Lutzbetak, *Church and Cultures. . .*, p. 37. Nevertheless, this generalization appears legitimate in that evolutionism soon paled into insignificance compared to other paradigms (particularly diffusionism and functionalism).

[29]Hanna Kostyło, "Rekonstrukcjonizm społeczny: wzajemność oddziaływań kultury i edukacji," *Forum Oświatowe* 2012 No.2 (47), p. 16.

member of society."[30] What is striking in this view of culture is its consistent descriptivism. By moving away from an evaluative approach to civilization, characteristic of the scientific theory and social awareness of the nineteenth century,[31] Taylor explicitly emphasized that "the condition of culture among the various societies of mankind (. . .) is a subject apt for (. . .) study."[32] Culture appears here in the plural, and its meaning in the singular moves entirely to the background.[33] By losing its evaluative character, culture simply becomes an attribute of social coexistence.[34] As noted by Janusz Ziółkowski, "Taylor provides the grounds for what has become the canon of modern cultural anthropology—cultural pluralism and relativism, the conviction that culture, a human phenomenon, is in fact a multitude of cultures, that every cultural behaviour may only be evaluated in the context of the system of values embraced in a particular culture. This entails a directive of respect and tolerance for every culture. There is no room here for cultural ethnocentrism, for judging other cultures according to the values and norms of our own culture. A division into higher and lower cultures, or primitive and developed ones, is pointless. These postulates were developed and realized later on, but formulated already at the birth of this new discipline; it became its *raison d'etre*."[35]

It is worth noting the radicalism of the anthropological stance presented by Ziółkowski, also on the lexical level (*vide* "pointless division"). It results from a specific anthropological trait of a worldview in which the normative idea of the equal ranking of cultures and the related relativist paradigm is of central importance.[36] Its source may be linked to the sociological theory of Emil Durkheim who "greatly influenced the direction of social anthropology," founding claims about social systems existing as independent organisms "sustained through the interdependence of their constituent parts."[37] This gave rise to the idea—so important in anthropology today—of explaining the studied systems solely in the categories of these very systems. As a further consequence, this led to the idea of respect for cultural diversity

---

[30]Edward B. Taylor, *Primitive culture: researches into the development of mythology, philosophy, religion, language, art and custom*, John Murray, London 1920, p. 1.

[31]It understood civilization to mean European civilization, providing the proper model and ultimate destination of other societies. Cf. Fernand Breudel, *Gramatyka cywilizacji*, translated by Hanna Igalson-Tygielska, Oficyna naukowa, Warszawa 2006, pp. 37–42 [French original: *Grammaire des civilisations*, Flammarion 1993].

[32]E. B. Taylor, *Primitive Culture*, p. 1.

[33]More on this topic, see: Piotr Mazurkiewicz, *Europeizacja Europy*, InstytutPolitologii, Warszawa 2001.

[34]The various definitions of culture in social sciences have been discussed by RadosławZenderowski, "Czym jest kultura? Kultura a cywilizacja. Spór o definicje podstawowych pojęć," in: Radosław Zenderowski, Krzysztof Cebul, Mateusz Krycki, *Międzynarodowe stosunki kulturalne*, PWN, Warszawa 2010, pp. 66–77.

[35]J. Ziółkowski, *Antropologia. . .*, p. 38.

[36]Cf. Jack David Eller, *Cultural Anthropology: Global Forces, Local Lives*, Routlege, 2016, p. 12ff; the author includes it among the three main characteristic features of the anthropological perspective (together with comparative studies and holism).

[37]L. Lutzbetak, *The Church and Cultures . . .*, p. 33.

and equality of cultures, whose essence "is understanding both the culture of a small isolated group, a nation organized into a state, and that of an entire cultural area as manifestations of cultural diversity, and therefore equally deserving study and examination. At the same time, it places the culture of the researcher and all other cultures on an equal footing in moral or any other terms."[38] This commitment to understanding the studied cultures—initially avoiding judgment, and ultimately prohibiting it altogether—makes cultural anthropology on the one hand a science that is considerably ideologically laden, "developed by constructing a concept of cultural relativism;"[39] and on the other hand, and to a large extent in contradiction to the postulated equality of cultures, an applied science,[40] which "conducts studies aimed at introducing particular solutions to improve the social, economic, or political situation of individual groups."[41] Consequently, anthropologists have begun to place themselves in the position of moderators in the dialogue of cultures.

Cultural anthropology, both in the academic and the applied variant, considers its main terms of reference to encompass "everything we think and do and have as members of society."[42] It is interested in cultural differences: human customs, beliefs and rituals, as well as the history of cultures, their mutual contacts and borrowings. An anthropologist tries to isolate the elementary particles of a culture (features, themes, cultural patterns, institutions, social roles) to discover the relations between them, and consequently the organization of the entire culture and forms of its configuration. It is interested in intra- and inter-cultural relations, the concepts of evolution, diffusion, acculturation, enculturation, or syncretism.[43] Thus, anthropology always studies "individual actions as manifestations of relatively permanent arrangements, characteristic of a given community, of behaviours, experiences and images which make up the basic 'cultural backbone'."[44] Even though interviews with individual persons are one of its primary research tools, it is ultimately interested not so much in man, but rather in the collective experience, in human cultures.

Distinctly different from physical anthropology in terms of sphere of interest, anthropology has had to develop its own, specific methodology. The task was not an easy one since social studies had already been conducted in sociology, developing in the nineteenth century, which was also interested in collective entities. The specific theoretical disposition and research instruments of cultural anthropology developed

---

[38]E. Nowicka, *Świat człowieka...*, p. 20.

[39]E. Nowicka, *Świat człowieka...*, p. 151. The author points out that even witnessing rituals which result in a "permanent mutilation of female or male sexual organs (...)" an anthropologist does not find in his discipline of science any moral directive other than the one which says: do not intervene, do not destroy cultural diversity." Ibid.

[40]This does not apply to the first generation of anthropologists, but becomes relevant already in the 1920s.

[41]E. Nowicka, *Świat człowieka...*, p. 41.

[42]R. Bierstedt, *The Social Order*, McGraw Hill, New York 1957, p. 135.

[43]Cf. E. Nowicka, *Świat człowieka – świat kultury...*, p. 23 and pp. 81–88.

[44]Ibid., p. 62.

directly in relation to the subject matter of anthropological studies. Ultimately, this led to the development of a characteristic methodological trait of anthropology—characteristic to such an extent that some authors claim today that the difference between anthropology and other social studies resides in how it conducts its research rather than in its subject matter.[45]

Cultural anthropology was born out of a fascination with otherness, with unknown societies and their cultures. Consequently, in the beginning it studied an area that lay beyond the field of interest of philosophy or the newly developing sociology.[46] While these sciences studied the developed societies of the West, researchers such as Richard Radcliffe-Brown or Bronisław Malinowski, who referred to the claims of Durkheim, endeavored to explain primitive social systems. Years later, Ruth Benedict called them "a laboratory in which we may study the diversity of human institutions,"[47] adding that it is "the only laboratory of social forms that we have or shall have."[48] This reference to the subject matter of research led to "a peculiar anthropological approach. It became a science studying phenomena which in structurally and economically more complex societies are investigated by entirely separate disciplines: economics, sociology, linguistics, art history, musicology, literary studies, etc."[49]

Due to the extensive subject matter to study, from the very beginning anthropologists narrowed down their research to small groups. At first, anthropology studied primitive (traditional) societies, as isolated from other as possible. As pointed out by Ruth Benedict, as well as others, they were simple enough for their tradition to be "contained within the knowledge of individual adults, and the manners and morals of the group [to be] molded to one well-defined general pattern."[50] Anthropological methodology therefore stemmed from the belief that it was possible to encompass all aspects of a culture by studying social consciousness, using quite simple tools. Contemporary anthropology essentially continues this tradition. Even though, due to limited possibilities of studying isolated societies, research is now conducted largely within the Western civilization, in essence its character has not changed. It is still carried out in small groups selected according to purpose-based criteria.[51] The goal is to investigate "a small number of cases, perhaps just one case, in detail."[52]

---

[45]Cf. e.g. Paweł Chlipała, "Podejście etnograficzne w gromadzeniu wiedzy o konsumentach," *Zeszyty naukowe Uniwersytetu Szczecińskiego* No. 660, p. 27.

[46]As noted by Jack Eller, it "did occupy the 'savage slot' (...) for tactical reasons (...) and for the simple reason that no other science did." J. D. Eller, *Cultural Anthropology...*, p. 8.

[47]Ruth Benedict, *Patterns of Culture*, Houghton Mifflin Company, New York 2005, p. 17.

[48]Ibid., p. 96. The categorical tone of this assertion is not readily concurred with by contemporary anthropologists, however. Cf. E. Nowicka, *Świat...*, p. 25.

[49]E. Nowicka, *Świat człowieka...*, p. 37.

[50]R. Benedict, *Patterns of Culture*, p. 18.

[51]P. Chlipała, *Podejście etnograficzne...*, p. 30.

[52]David Silverman, *Interpreting Qualitative Data*, SAGE Publications, 2019, p. 262.

The commitment to an in-depth analysis of the observed phenomena entails the primacy of qualitative research techniques in cultural anthropology. The basic study method is broadly-conceived fieldwork. It essentially consists—as described by James Clifford—in "physically going out into a cleared place of work," which allows for a direct, usually long-term, contact of the researcher with the object of his research, and involves "the specific practices of (...) focused, disciplined attention."[53] The fieldwork method is, by definition, related to external or participant (*incognito* or overt) observation, and often other qualitative techniques also: in-depth interview (controlled, structured, or free-flowing), thick description,[54] etc. A characteristic feature of the ethnological method is its bottom-up research perspective which is aimed at helping the researcher discover the hidden hierarchies of values specific to a particular group, its retained traditions etc. which are normally concealed from "strangers."

Finally, it should be stressed that anthropology tries to cultivate its (primary) idea of a holistic perspective. It remains in a relationship with physical anthropology (which belongs to the curriculum of a cultural anthropologist);[55] it includes in its terms of reference studies of language (linguistics),[56] and with regard to historic (extinct) societies, the field of cultural anthropology is considered to be archaeology.[57] Since the history of anthropological reflection has witnessed "a total terminological confusion, with the meaning of particular terms entirely lacking in clarity,"[58] we will not pursue the discussions held among anthropologists about the relationship between archaeology, ethnology, linguistics, cultural anthropology, and social anthropology. Let us assume, as suggested by the literature on the subject, that cultural anthropology is a category essentially identical with ethnology and social anthropology,[59] and different from physical anthropology, linguistics, and archaeology.[60] Given its cultural orientation and commitment to the study of groups, it is also clear that ethnology represents the very core of cultural (social)

---

[53]James Clifford, *Routes: Travel and Translation in the Late Twentieth Century*, Harvard University Press, Cambridge, MA 1997, p. 53.

[54]Cf. Clifford Geertz, "Thick Description: Toward an Interpretive Theory of Culture," *The Interpretation of Cultures: Selected Essays*, Basic Books, New York 1973, pp. 3–30.

[55]Cf. E. Kopczyńska, *Misja i pasja...*, pp. 76–78.

[56]L. Luzbetak, *The Church and Cultures...*, p. 29.

[57]Ibid. Even here there is no consensus concerning taxonomy. EwaKopczyńska, for instance, emphasizes that archeology is not a subdiscipline, but a "research tool," "one of the most important methods allowing for the reconstruction of historical change" (*Misjaimetoda...*, p. 75).

[58]Ewa Nowicka, *Świat człowieka...*, p. 39.

[59]Some interesting an most accurate comments on the relationship between cultural and social anthropology can be found in the work of C. Levi-Strauss, who showed the unity of the subject matter and research program of these two approaches, as well as the "subtle differences" between them. Cf. C. Levi-Strauss, *Structural Anthropology*, Basic Books 1974, p. 299f. Nevertheless, his distinction between ethnology and anthropology is not generally endorsed.

[60]Cf. E. Nowicka, *Świat człowieka – świat kultury...*, pp. 39–43.

anthropology understood in such terms.[61] This reveals—even in etymological terms—the essential research perspective of this science. At its core, it is a science not so much about the human and its essence, but rather a science of peoples (*ethnos*—people), human societies and their cultures.

2.1.3 Philosophical Anthropology

The above discussion clearly shows that the proper anthropological question "Who is man?" is to a large extent beyond the terms of reference of cultural anthropology. By studying cultures we may, indeed, discover that common, human content is not limited to that which stems from the common biological nature of man.[62] Nevertheless, we are still at the level of description, or typologisation. This way, we cannot arrive at the essence of man. As long as we believe it is possible, anyway,[63] we must move our search to the grounds of philosophy, one of whose questions is precisely the question about man.[64] This problem is central to philosophical anthropology, which aims at developing a theory of man to understand not only what man is on average, but also what man can and should be.[65] It is therefore focused on studying the very essence of man—of what man is not accidentally, at a time, or collaterally, but in his essence intrinsically linked to his existence;[66] it seeks to discover a *constans homo*, so to say, a common core of humanity.[67]

As noted by Elżbieta Paczkowska-Łagowska, "that which seems to have made a decisive contribution to moving the reflection concerning man onto the tracks of philosophical anthropology is the discovery of the 'problematics' of man."[68] At the end of the nineteenth century, known as the age of science, doubts about man reached unprecedented dimensions. There were considerable reasons for this: "the

---

[61]E. Kopczyńska, *Misja i pasja…*, p. 77.

[62]Cf. G. Haeffner, *The Human Situation: A Philosophical Anthropology*, University of Notre Dame Press, 1989. See for example the list of "human monopolies" by Martha Nussbaum (ibid.).

[63]Which is not an entirely obvious assumption. As Hannah Arendt, referring to Saint Augustine, points out, "if we have a nature or essence, then surely only a god could know and define it, and the first prerequisite would be that he be able to speak about a 'who' as though it were a 'what'." Hannah Arendt, *The Human Condition…*, p. 10.

[64]As noted by Tadeusz Szkołut, "it is quite possible that the most important philosophical problem is the issue sometimes called 'the problem of man'." Tadeusz Szkołut, "Słowo wstępne: Spór o naturę ludzką i jego konsekwencje aksjologiczne," in: Id. [ed.], *Antropologia filozoficzna i aksjologiczne problemy współczesności*, UMCS, Lublin 1997, p. 9.

[65]Cf. G. Haeffner, *The Human Situation …*, p. 9.

[66]Ibid., p. 4.

[67]O. De Bertolis, *Elementy antropologii…*, p. 15.

[68]Elżbieta Paczkowska-Łagowska, *Wstęp. Natura ludzka, historia, polityka w antropologii HelmuthaPlessnera*, in: H. Plessner, *Władza a natura ludzka. Esej o antropologii światopoglądu historycznego*, translated by Elżbieta Paczkowska-Łagowska, PWN, Warszawa 1994, p. IX.

Copernican Revolution relativized man's place in the world; the introduction of Europeans to foreign cultures relativized their own culture; Darwin's theory radically changed the traditional relationship between man and nature; the theory of alienation and psychoanalysis disillusioned man about the intrinsic value of higher culture."[69] Consequently, as noted by Max Scheler, "in no other period has man ever become more problematic to himself than in our own days".[70]

The age of reason has not only failed to provide answers to all of man's questions, but left him with new ones. Thus, even though a philosophy of man has always existed,[71] philosophical anthropology as a systematic subdiscipline of philosophy was born at the threshold of the twentieth century as an attempt to overcome this disillusionment.[72] It tries to understand the essence of man in order to create an actual definition that would tell us how to understand the contents of this particular form of being.[73] The anthropological-philosophical approach is then aimed at "constructing an idea of man—a human being, as a theoretical model of man, as an integral whole with particular emphasis on his intrinsic characteristics,"[74] looking for "features which are not merely an expression of the particular time and place in which man finds himself."[75] It is worth noting that this is true even of those philosophers who—like Helmuth Plessner—distanced themselves from substantializing human nature. Even adopting a historical perspective of looking at man and recognizing the impossibility of defining him in terms of "man is nothing but. . .", Plessner understands him as a "creative place," believing man to be "power . . . and authority over himself, a being who is capable of realizing himself,"[76] and

---

[69]E. Paczkowska-Łagowska, *Wstęp. Natura. . .*, p. IX.

[70]Max Scheler, *The Human Place in the Cosmos*, Northwestern University Press 2009, p. 35.

[71]In this sense, Helmuth Plessner noted that "philosophical anthropology is not (. . .) a discovery of our times. A philosophy of man has always existed, if 'man' is understood not only as a particular product of nature (. . .) but a horizon of tasks pointed out to us which—in various cultures and irrespective of all historical differences—have always been considered proper to man." Helmuth Plessner, *Zadanie antropologii filozoficznej*, translated by Elżbieta Paczkowska-Łagowska, in: Stanisław Czerniak, Jarosław Rolewski [ed.], *Studia z filozofii niemieckiej, v.4, Antropologia filozoficzna*, UMK, Toruń 2004, p. 23.

[72]We owe the belief that philosophical reflection on man should have a systematic form and become a philosophical anthropology to Max Scheler who considered it to be a discipline concerned with nine issues: a typology of consciousness, essential ontology of man, the differences between man and animals, old age and dying, the origins of man, social and historic transformations of man, humankind as a whole, comparative anthropology, and the principle of all things. Adam Węgrzecki, "Od filozofii człowieka do antropologii filozoficznej. MaxaSchelera koncepcja człowieka," in: Leszek Kusak [ed.], *Filozofia człowieka. Wybrane koncepcje epoki nowożytnej*, Wyd. Uniwersytetu Ekonomicznego w Krakowie, Kraków 2015, p. 50.

[73]Cf. G. Haeffner, *The Human Situation. . .*, pp. 1–3.

[74]J. Szczeniowski, *Metaantropologia filozoficzna. Zarys antropologii krytycznej*, Oficyna Wydawnicza
PolitechnikiWarszawskiej, Warszawa 1997, p. 38.

[75]J. Szczeniowski, *Metaantropologia. . .*, p. 38.

[76]E. Paczkowska-Łagowska, *Wstęp. Natura. . .*, p. XV.

thus, ultimately, defines him.[77] In post-Cartesian philosophy, the anthropological question is considered to be the central concern of philosophy as such. Immanuel Kant argued that "the field of philosophy (. . .) can be brought down to the following questions: (1) What can I know? (2) What ought I to do? (3) What may I hope? (4) What is man? Metaphysics answers the first question, morals the second, religion the third, and anthropology the fourth."[78] He pointed out, however, that "fundamentally (. . .) we could reckon all of this as under anthropology, because the first three questions relate to the last one."[79] Consequently, he considered the ultimate question of philosophy to be the question about man.[80] Even if we do not follow Kant in his reduction of philosophy to anthropology,[81] we should note that none of the questions he asks can be answered within the framework of natural or social sciences.

How, then, are we to discover what man is, understood "as such and as a whole"? How should we understand the essence of "an entirely different being from things"[82]? Gerd Haeffner notes that the process of defining consists in looking for features which are proper to all (and only to) representatives of a species, i.e. for so-called essential features.[83] This cannot be—as has already been pointed out—an empirical search. Naturally, a large group of philosophers—though not all of them[84]—are of the opinion that philosophical anthropology should rely on a variety of data: psychological, historical, social, ethical, religious, cultural, and consequently that "it must not ignore humanities, limiting itself to a pre-scientific experience", and neither can it ignore major achievements of empirical sciences which have now become "a permanent element of pre-scientific knowledge."[85] Nevertheless, even if we recognize the significance of broadly-understood empiricism for

---

[77]Even if we conclude—as proposed by Elżbieta Paczkowska-Lagowska—that this is a definition "at a deeper level" than that on which such definitions are usually developed (ibid., p. XV).

[78]Immanuel Kant, *Lectures on Logic*, Cambridge University Press 2004, p. 25.

[79]Ibid., p. 25.

[80]Aleksander Bobko, "Wstęp: Człowiek w filozofiiImmanuelaKanta," in: Immanuel Kant, *Antropologia w ujęciu pragmatycznym [Anthropology from a Pragmatic Point of View]*, translated by EwaDrzazgowska, Paulina Sosnowska, IFiS PAN, Warszawa 2005, p. XI.

[81]At first sight, this may appear unclear in the perspective of classical philosophy where "anthropology is not the main domain of knowledge" (P. Duchliński, *Uwagi o stylu klasycznej. . .*, p. 215), and to be open to theoretical criticism. Nevertheless, this position seems to be supported by some substantial reasons, even if probably quite distant from the views held by Kant himself. As pointed out by Dariusz Karłowicz in his analyses concerning antique philosophy, it may be "defined as a method of a full conversion of being and knowledge, a method of spiritual progress expressed in a complete transformation of life." Consequently, "the goal of philosophy is the complete perfection of human nature," and any attempts at detaching philosophy "from its strictly existential dimension only petrify anachronistic divisions into independent fields of philosophy." Dariusz Karłowicz, *Arcyparadoks śmierci*, Znak, Kraków 2000, pp. 63, 72, 73.

[82]Immanuel Kant, *Anthropology from a Pragmatic Point of View*, translated and edited by Robert B. Louden, Cambridge University Press 2006, p. 15.

[83]Cf. G. Haeffner, *The Human Sitaution. . .*, pp. 2–5.

[84]Note the fundamentally different standpoint of existential Thomism discussed in paragraph 1.1.2.

[85]S. Kowalczyk, *Filozofia człowieka. . .*, p. 31.

philosophical investigations, it is only a starting point for philosophical anthropology which—in addition—also depends on other philosophical disciplines (e.g. ontology, ethics, philosophy of nature, theory of knowledge, and aesthetics).[86] Ultimately, anthropology refers to a practical "knowledge of depths" (*Tiefenwissen*) which man as such has about himself.[87] In the language of modern philosophy, we might say this is about a transcendental consciousness.

Even though in the search for the essence of man in the field of philosophy, a variety of methods are used, Rev. Stanisław Kowalczyk says that "two varieties should be emphasized: the phenomenological (sometimes linked to hermeneutics), and the metaphysical one."[88] According to the father of philosophical anthropology, Max Scheler, phenomenology in particular corresponds to the desire to find the "essential notion" of man. By focusing on the diverse, indeed human, phenomena (manifestations) of man's life and activity, unburdened by any prior assumptions or convictions, in the course of subsequent reductions which consist in putting any non-essential elements in parentheses, the phenomenological method should achieve an "intuitive knowledge, or insight, into the essence" of man.[89] It has an "a priori validity holding in all instances to which the discovered essence applies."[90] In the case of hermeneutics, on the other hand, this would consist in the process of understanding man by "elucidating the meaning of spoken and written word" which is understood "as a 'coded meaning' whose logic reveals the meaning of human existence."[91]

Both of these methods, as pointed out by Rev. Kowalczyk, should be linked to the metaphysical method—not only due to its use of the language of ontology, but also because it offers insight into "explanations of the human person in the context of general metaphysics and the philosophy of nature. This way, human being would simply be a particularization of being in general," making it possible to construct "philosophical anthropology as a system correlating with the philosophical view of the universe as a whole."[92] At the same time, the phenomenological method contributes to the language of ontology which "does not have a description of man as a subject and a person, and neither does it have an axiological description."[93]

Naturally, even though the phenomenological and metaphysical standpoints may be perceived as methods of particular significance, nowadays they are but an example of the many different approaches in philosophical anthropology. There is no consensus as to how philosophizing about man should be conducted. Quite on the contrary, "the diverse anthropological styles of our times deny one another the right

---

[86]Ibid., p. 34.

[87]Cf. G. Haeffner, *The Human Sitaution* . . ., p. 25.

[88]S. Kowalczyk, *Filozofia człowieka*. . ., p. 34.

[89]A. Węgrzecki, *Od filozofii człowieka*. . ., p. 52.

[90]Ibid.

[91]S. Kowalczyk, *Filozofia człowieka*. . ., pp. 35–36.

[92]S. Kowalczyk, *Filozofia człowieka*. . ., p. 37.

[93]Ibid., p. 38.

to be the only and ultimate view explaining the condition of the *homo sapiens.*"[94]
There is no single answer to the key anthropological question. This situation is not
new, in fact. Historically speaking, the anthropological current in philosophy has
always presented "a diversity of ways in which man is described, a wealth of
concepts, and a multitude of alternatives in depicting the human phenomenon."[95]
In more general terms, "anthropology as a department of philosophy shares its
nature. Just like there is no single philosophy, so there is no single anthropology;
and just like there is no consent as to which philosophy is the right and true one, so
there is no consent on the grounds of philosophical anthropology, or, as some call it,
the philosophy of man. There is no anthropology shared by everyone."[96] This does
not deny the meaning of philosophical anthropology. Rather, it shows that man—the
subject matter of anthropology—probably cannot be explained on the grounds of a
single theory.

The significance of philosophical anthropology for the anthropological cognitive
process should be emphasized. While cultural anthropology demonstrates the diversity of the human species, philosophical anthropology—on each of its cognitive
paths—"assumes that the human species is one, and that the deep cultural differences
do not outbalance this unity,"[97] and consequently that "diverse cultural beliefs do not
prevent anthropological reflection concerning humanity as a whole (. . .), that there is
an individual called man who has similar features and an analogous condition
everywhere."[98] This is, let us stress, historically speaking a most obscure paradigm,
which makes it exceedingly important in cognitive terms. As pointed out by Alain
Finkielkraut, "what distinguished people for quite a long time from other species of
animals was precisely this—that they did not recognize one another (. . .). Initially,
the characteristic feature of man was that he reserved the title of humanity to
members of his own community."[99] Asking "Who is man?", philosophical anthropology *ex definition* defends humanity, showing the fundamental features which
demonstrate, to use Chantal Delsol's expression, man's constancy, or, in the language of classical philosophy, the existence of a human nature.

---

[94]P. Duchliński, *Uwagi o stylu klasycznej. . .*, p. 208.

[95]Ireneusz Bittner, *Filozofia człowieka. Zarys dziejów i przegląd stanowisk*, third ed., WUŁ, Łódź
2000, p. 29.

[96]P. Duchliński, *Uwagi o stylu klasycznej. . .*, p. 208.

[97]Chantal Delsol, *Czym jest człowiek? Kurs antropologii dla niewtajemniczonych*, translated by
Małgorzata Kowalska, Znak, Kraków 2011, p. 12 [French original: *Qu'est-ce que l'homme? Cours
familier d'anthropologie*, CERF edition 2008].

[98]Ch. Delsol, *Czym jest człowiek. . .*, p. 13.

[99]Alain Finkielkraut, *Zagubione człowieczeństwo*, translated by Mateusz Fabjanowski, PIW, Warszawa 1999, p. 9 [*L'Humanité perdue*, Seuil, 1996].

2.1.4 Theological Anthropology

Alongside and, to a significant extent, together with philosophy,[100] the question about man has been asked by theological anthropology. The central question which it wants to answer by studying Christian revelation is the issue of "who man is in relation to the One and Triune God revealed in Christ."[101] It is thus aimed at obtaining at a complete vision of man from the viewpoint of the Christian faith. Even though it avoids the pluralism of philosophical anthropology, thanks to a clearly defined point of view, they both ask the same fundamental question. Consequently, theological anthropology remains in a strict relationship with major currents of philosophical anthropology. Suffice to say that in the comments made by Thomas Aquinas about man in his Summa Theologica, philosophical questions already dominate theological issues sometimes. In fact, Aquinas should actually be credited for developing a philosophy of man which, in line with the approach characteristic of the Middle Ages, is worked into his great synthesis of theology. This is not about a particular, specific, historical experience, however. Since theology also takes into account the so-called "natural revelation"—that is, it refers in theological knowledge to intuition and theoretical reflection which guides us towards the truth about God's existence—[102] a correlation between these two disciplines is inevitable.[103] In essence, the very fact that—as has been stressed in the Catechism of the Catholic Church—"with his openness to truth and beauty, his sense of moral goodness, his freedom and the voice of his conscience, with his longings for the infinite and for happiness, man questions himself about God's existence,"[104] shows the great significance of the philosophical dimension of the anthropological question for theological reflection. Due to the close relationship between theological and philosophical reflection, Christian anthropology is sometimes described as a "philosophical-theological subdiscipline that examines what it means to be truly

---

[100] As noted by Tadeusz Gadacz, when philosophical and theological anthropology was developing in the twentieth century, a strong relationship existed between philosophy and theology. Theologians such as Paul Tillich or Rudolf Bultmann, considered to be one of the founders of modern hermeneutics, have left their mark on philosophical reflection. Also "theology drew for its inspirations on philosophy, including the philosophy of Nietzsche (Gogarten, Tilllich, J.B. Lotz, . . .), the philosophy of dialogue, or Heidegger's fundamental ontology." Cf. Tadeusz Gadacz, *Historia filozofii XX wieku. Nurty*, vol. 1, Znak, Kraków 2009, pp. 47–49.

[101] Luis F. Ladaria, *Wprowadzenie do antropologii teologicznej*, translated by Arkadiusz Baron, WAM, Kraków 1997, p. 11 [Spanish: *Introducción a la antropología teológica*. Editorial Verbo Divino 2010].

[102] Cf. Mieczysław Maliński, *Katechizm dla niewierzących*, WAM, Kraków, http://www.opoka.org.pl/biblioteka/K/kat_dla_nie3.html

[103] As pointed out by Stefan Świeżawski, "every complete philosophy is essentially religious," and "a true metaphysician is in a sense a theologian, because when analysing each thing in terms of its being, its existence, he must necessarily refer to the ultimate reason for its existence, that is to God." Id., *Święty Tomasz na nowo odczytany*, W drodze, Poznań 2002, pp. 24 and 36.

[104] *Catechism of the Catholic Church*, 33.

human."[105] Such a combination is possible as long as it takes into account the fact that theology should stress that which "does not come to be expressed in philosophical anthropology, at least not in the form and sense which we owe to faith in Jesus Christ. In Biblical language, this could be expressed in terms of sin and eternal life."[106] Consequently, it may be noted that theological anthropology has its own research program, so to say, one that goes beyond the philosophical perspective. As stressed by Gerhard Ebeling, "to develop a reliable anthropology which is based on the fall into sin and the call to eternal life so that it includes the entire experience of reality—this is the endless task facing theology."[107]

Even though anthropological problems have been present in theology from the very beginning,[108] the discipline as such only developed at the time of the Second Vatican Council. Already in 1957 Karl Rahner wrote that "anthropology as we understand it represents a task which is yet to be completed in theology; not in the sense, of course, that any particular claims or contents of this discipline should be rediscovered as new—it is more about extracting the claims about man present in the revelation—but in the sense that Catholic theology has not yet developed a complete anthropology starting from its initial assumptions."[109] A special impulse to the development of theological anthropology was the Constitution *Gaudium et Spes*, whose Chap. 2 "briefly explains and updates basic truths about man: his being created in the image of God; the sin through which man abused his freedom (. . .) and forfeited harmony in his relationship with God, with himself, other people, and the whole of creation; man's constitution based on the unity of body and soul; the dignity of human reason and conscience; the greatness of human freedom; the mystery of death (. . .)."[110]

Fundamentally important for the development of theological anthropology is *Gaudium et Spes* section 2 which says that "[t]he truth is that only in the mystery of the incarnate Word does the mystery of man take on light. For Adam, the first man, was a figure of Him Who was to come, namely Christ the Lord. Christ, the final Adam, by the revelation of the mystery of the Father and His love, fully reveals man to man himself and makes his supreme calling clear. (. . .) He Who is 'the image of the invisible God' is Himself the perfect man. To the sons of Adam He restores the divine likeness which had been disfigured from the first sin onward."[111] Commenting on this passage, Cardinal Luis Ladaria states that "this is not about

[105]L. Lutzbetak, *Kościół i kultury. . .*, p. 62.

[106]Gerhard Ebeling, "Przyczynek do definicji człowieka," in: *Człowiek w nauce współczesnej. Rozmowy w Castel Gandolfo*, Znak, Kraków 2006, p. 78.

[107]Ibid.

[108]Note e.g. Origenes's*De Principis* or Gregory of Nyssa's *De hominis opificio*.

[109]Karl Rahner, *Anthropologie, Theologiesche Anthropologie*, in: Michael Buchberger [hg.], *Lexiconfuer Theologie und Kirche*, Freiburg 1957, pp. 618–627, as quoted in: L. F. Ladaria, *Wprowadzenie. . .*, p. 23.

[110]L. Ladaria, *Wprowadzenie. . .*, p. 26.

[111]Vatican II, *Pastoral Constitution on the Church in the Modern World* Gaudium et Spes (hereinafter *Gaudium et spes*), 22.

the development of theological contents concerning man, but first of all about the principle which should be the foundation of theological anthropology. (. . .) Jesus reveals to man his own role (. . .). In Him, the fullness of humanity is revealed."[112]

It appears that, particularly in the European context, the theological dimension of reflections on man should be treated as an essential source of knowledge. Robert Schuman, a father of the integration process, argued that on the Old Continent there was no way one could ignore the "immense moral authority of the Church which is spontaneously accepted by a large number of citizens and the high value of its teaching that no other philosophical system has been able to attain up to the present."[113] More or less consciously, the view of man developed within the framework of theology has influenced both our philosophical thinking (for example, the idea of man's dignity) explored in philosophical anthropology, and the social practices studied by anthropologists of culture. Having realized this fact, we should now examine the relationships between each of these anthropological currents.

2.2 Relationships Between Anthropologies

In view of the fact that, as noted above, each anthropological approach represents a different scientific tradition, and thus to a certain extent—to use the language of cultural anthropology—a different cultural tradition, when analyzing their relationships we may try to adapt the theory of intercultural relations. Even though a number of different terminological approaches are used in the analyses of relationships between cultures, Rev. Piotr Mazurkiewicz points out that "theoreticians are quite in agreement as to the essence of the phenomenon (. . .). If we were to present it on an axis, at one extreme we would place various forms of conflict, or isolation, which are aimed at keeping one's own identity 'uncontaminated,' and at the other extreme there would be assimilation, meaning the actual absorption of a group by the dominant culture. (. . .) There can also be some intermediate states (. . .) in which cultures exist on the same territory and engage in interactions."[114]

Per analogiam, we can thus construct a hypothetical axis of all possible relationships between individual anthropological traditions in the world of science. At one extreme, we would place the equivalent of the model of assimilation, which in this context would mean ignoring the differences in methodological and problematic frameworks in an attempt to create an amalgam in which—with one tradition taking the dominant position—various (two or three) anthropological traditions become fused. At the opposite extreme, we could place the approach we may call isolation or separation, assuming a fundamental lack of correspondence between the results obtained within the frameworks of each separate anthropological reflection. This

---

[112]L. Ladaria, *Wprowadzenie. . .*, p. 27.

[113]R. Schuman, *For Europe*, Les Éditions Nagel, Geneva 2010, p. 51.

[114]P. Mazurkiewicz, *Europeizacja Europy. . .*, p. 53.

approach may involve the idea of domination by one of the perspectives, and—possibly—depreciation of the other standpoints, which would be an equivalent of the category of conflict described by Rev. Mazurkiewicz. Finally, a third approach is possible, one of integration, entailing interactions between various anthropological standpoints.

2.2.1 Extreme Models

It is worth noting that a consistent reliance on the initial, holistic aspirations of cultural anthropology to being the science of man *par excellence* is largely related to the logic of amalgamation. In this situation, with some simplification it may be claimed that philosophical conclusions about human nature are to be derived from fieldwork. Such a danger can be seen, for example, in the structuralism of Claude Levi-Strauss. In his works, he arranges anthropology in order by "distinguishing sub-disciplines based on the generality of the assertions they make. Thus, strictly descriptive and monographic studies are said to be the domain of ethnography; a more general level of comparative, intercultural assertions—of ethnology; and the highest level of general statements—of anthropology. These are three phases of the cognitive process (...). The highest and ultimate goal of anthropological knowledge is a synthesis which encompasses all human societies."[115] As pointed out by Levi-Strauss, such an anthropology "aims at a global knowledge of man—embracing the subject in its full historical and geographical extension",[116] leading to "conclusions (...) which are valid for all human societies."[117] The problem is that—as noted by Kowalczyk—a consequence of such an approach in structuralism seems to be a deprecation of historical thinking and absolutization of the synchronic-structural method, which reduces "human culture to physicochemical nature." In the end, the existential "peculiarity" of man becomes questioned: the personal self, society, history, spiritual culture. Kowalczyk points out that Levi-Strauss "reduced man's psyche to physiology, and that in turn to physics and chemistry. This way, anthropology boils down to entropy guided by blind chance and inevitably gravitating towards a disintegration of the human being."[118] Despite the initial data of ethnology and history, structuralism thus reveals clear philosophical, or—to be more specific—materialistic, inclinations. It appears to be a necessary consequence seeing that, as pointed out by Louis Luzbetak, "no anthropologist could possibly master the entire field of anthropology;"[119] consequently, all philosophical universalizing statements derived from empirical studies are burdened by the risk of, *nomen omen*, structural

---

[115]E. Nowicka, *Świat człowieka...*, p. 91.

[116]Claude Levi-Strauss, *Structural Anthropology*, Basic Books, 1974, p. 355.

[117]Ibid., p. 356.

[118]S. Kowalczyk, *Zarys teorii człowieka...*, p. 13.

[119]L. J. Luzbetak, *The Church and Cultures...*, p. 39.

imperfection and selectiveness. They are then often characterized by an "epistemo-logical monism, narrowing down the domain of scientific knowledge to limits which can be captured in the sensory knowledge of matter."[120]

It is not a coincidence that "the father of modern anthropology," Franz Boas, finally gave up on his attempts at identifying general laws governing human culture based on empirical material. Initially, he referred to two stages of anthropological knowledge, with the first "consisting in detailed studies of particular cultures, taking into account their particular context (...)", and the second being "aimed at formu-lating general laws of cultural development."[121] Still, not only did he never engage in studies characteristic of the second stage, but even wrote "at the end of his scientific career (...) that the material of anthropology determines its nature as necessarily historical; it is one of those sciences which focus more on understanding individual phenomena than establishing general laws."[122] A similar logic was adopted by Bronisław Malinowski or Alfred Kroeber, as well as the mainstream of modern anthropology.

The problem of amalgamating knowledge may also apply to the relationship between physical and philosophical/theological anthropology. This occurs when we try to fathom the essence of man by using the tools of biological anthropology. Biological anthropology, as mentioned above, demonstrates the differences between man and the entire world of animals. Even though this provokes us to take a stance on the essential difference between man and the animal world, by adopting it we are nudged toward the plane of philosophy. Some biologists refuse to acknowledge this boundary and try to define man within the framework of their science. Gerd Haeffner says that such attempts may consist, for example, in seeing the specifically human element of man—the "spirit"—only in the special means he employs to satisfy his basic needs and preserve himself and his species. Man is then perceived through the prism of an old theory, formulated already by J. G. Herder, which, as Haeffner explains, "views the human being, along with A. Gehlen, for example, as a 'faulty being' that attempts to compensate as well as possible for a lack of hair through clothing (...) and a lack of instinctual provisions through social institutions."[123] As he rightly points out, however, "the human being appears faulty only when one takes the animal's attainment of survival and reproduction of its species as the standard. Whether this standard is the correct standard for human beings, that is, is of its essence, is really the question."[124] If his philosophical significance is negated, we suddenly discover that, for example, the self-preservation instinct functions "as an

---

[120]S. Kowalczyk, *Zarys teorii człowieka. . .*, p. 12.

[121]E. Nowicka, *Świat człowieka. . .*, p. 96.

[122]Ibid.

[123]G. Haeffner, *The Human Situation. . .*, p. 16.

[124]Ibid.

abstract principle from which and toward which interpretation unfolds,"[125] which in fact results in biological metaphysics.

The phenomenon of amalgamation can also be observed in the relationship between physical and cultural anthropology. This is worth noting because the problem, though today already a historical one, was concerned with a key—even today—category of physical anthropology, namely that of race. As pointed out by Erazm Majewski already in 1905, "we keep hearing about 'pure and mixed races,' about the 'spirit of a race,' the 'brain of a race,' as well as the *racial* qualities or faults of this or that *people*. We hear of a German race when there is talk of longheads, and of a 'German race' when someone is simply talking about a group of Germanic peoples. Both individuals and peoples often boast their alleged 'purity' of race, without even being aware what this word is supposed to mean."[126] As stressed by the Polish scholar, this applies not to colloquial speech, but to scientific claims: "even in a journal recently founded for the purpose of studying races (*Archiv für Rassen- und Gesellschafts- Biologie*) there is absolutely no consistency in the way the term is understood: while some authors use it in its ethnic meaning, others in its morphological meaning, while Ammon, for instance, probably to honor long-headed Germans, identifies the term 'long-headed' with a spiritually gifted man, and the term 'short-headed' with the concept of a wimp, if not a moron! (see this year's first issue of the journal). This error has resulted in such widespread consequences like thoroughly false descriptions such as the "Slavic race," the "Roman race," the "Aryan race" used to talk about ethnic wholes such as Slavic "peoples," Romance "peoples," Aryan "peoples."[127] As a result, zoological terms are blended—in a methodologically illegitimate way—with cultural concepts (language, tradition, culture), and even with statements concerning the essence of humanity.

This amalgamation of knowledge, and the resulting inability to make a methodologically adequate distinction, lay at the root of racism, which was still perceived in the interwar period as a scientific theory. It was most enthusiastically developed in anthropological circles beginning from the nineteenth century. In France, a key role was played by "An Essay on the Inequality of the Human Races" by Joseph de Gobineau, scientifically substantiating the inequality of races. The subsequent development of racist theories was particularly intense among German scholars.[128] Its advocates derived cultural conclusions from biological factors, and even made determinist prognoses about the future of populations. As noted by Marcin Kula, "in Darwin's times, it was often believed that white people were descended from the

---

[125]Walter Schulz, *Philosophie in der veraenderten Welt*, Pfullingen 1972, p. 443, as quoted in: G. Haeffner, *The Human Situation. . .*, p. 31.

[126]Erazm Majewski, *Rasa a naród*, "Światowid" 1905 No 6, p. 163, available at BazHum: http://www.archeo.uw.edu.pl/swarch/Swiatowit-r1905-t6-s162-168.pdf [4.11.2015].

[127]E. Majewski, *Rasa a naród. . .*, p. 164.

[128]For example, already in 1905 Erazm Majewski blames Germans for disseminating an ill-founded concept of race. Cf. *Rasa a naród. . .*, p. 164.

orangutan, and black people from the gorilla."[129] The white race was considered superior, and consequently it was believed that a natural process would lead other races to extinction.[130] The influence of this intellectual climate across the entire Europe was most explicitly illustrated by the fact that "as late as in 1931 at a colonial exhibition in Paris, a group of women from an African tribe were exhibited. (...) These women were then exhibited at other cities, and finally, after 4 years, they were sent back home."[131]

It is worth emphasizing that racist doctrines encountered opposition in some scholars from the very beginning. Along with Erazm Majewski, quoted above, Franz Boas also pointed out that racism was based on two misconceptions: "the one, the confusion of heredity in a family and heredity in a population; the other, the unproved assumption that the differences in culture which we observe among peoples of different type are primarily due to biological causes."[132] Due to its amalgamated nature—Boas argued—racism is not a scientific theory, but echoes the logic of hostility "against the outside group" typical of all societies. With the important difference that "racism as a basis of social solidarity as against the cultural interest of mankind is more dangerous than any of the other groupings because according to its claims the hostile groups are biologically determined and therefore permanent."[133] We might thus say that a thorough look at racism from the anthropological perspective showed that it was merely a new form of the "old distinction of the in-group and the out-group."[134] It had no scientific foundations.

A radical reaction to the amalgamation of knowledge is the isolationist stance. On the grounds of philosophical anthropology, it is found in existential Thomism, for instance. Assuming that empirical sciences are not able to provide—due to their aspectuality—a methodological basis for anthropology, it considers philosophical anthropology to be a discipline which has nothing in common with scientific knowledge, and whose data cannot even "be a starting point in doing philosophy."[135] Understood in such terms, anthropology becomes a form of metaphysics, i.e. a theory of the ontic principles of man's existence and actions. Consequently, the achievements of modern science seem to be superfluous for a properly anthropological analysis, since "truth in the proper sense can only be grasped in the field of philosophy, which refers to so-called existential judgments directly capturing the act of existence, and thus providing a cognitive interface with actual being."[136] In

---

[129]M. Kula, *Najpierw trzeba się narodzić*, WUW, Warszawa 2011, p. 28.

[130]Ibid., p. 29. Marcin Kula points out further on that even "in an ethnologist such as Bronisław Malinowski one can find a note from his trip to Ceylon: 'When I look at the black monkeys playing Europeans on a tram, I have a sense of the superiority of the white race'".

[131]M. Kula, *Najpierw trzeba się narodzić...*, p. 30.

[132]F. Boas, *Race and Democratic Society*, Biblo and Tannen Publishers, 1969, p. 30.

[133]F. Boas, *Race...*, p. 29.

[134]R. Benedict, *Patterns of Culture*, p. 11.

[135]P. Duchliński, *Uwagi o stylu klasycznej...*, p. 210.

[136]S. Kowalczyk, *Zarys filozofii człowieka...*, p. 13.

empirical sciences, on the other hand, "truth can only be captured indirectly, as long as concepts and models correspond to reality. Essentially, however, scientific theories and models are not related to truth statements, since their role is generally instrumental."[137] In this approach, the epistemological role of science is questioned; it is assigned the phenomenal aspect, while philosophy is supposed to be concerned with the aspect of general existence or relevance. This represents the "ideal" of separation: "philosophy has one research aspect, empirical sciences another. These aspects do not intersect, which warrants their cognitive autonomy and peaceful coexistence."[138]

A similar approach can also be found in certain currents of cultural anthropology. In the second edition of Ewa Nowicka's well-known textbook we still find a note saying that the speculative nature of philosophical anthropology "distinguishes it from the research approach of anthropology; consequently, their historical relationships were largely irrelevant, and the two currents of thought followed divergent paths."[139] In short, this essentially represents the belief, analogous to the one we discovered earlier in philosophical anthropology, that these two views of anthropology generally have nothing in common.[140] Ultimately, it justifies the absence of references to philosophical anthropology in the discussion presented in the textbook. Characteristically, in the most recent edition, the category of philosophical anthropology is omitted altogether, even though the index lists more than 20 different types of anthropologies, including academic anthropology, anthropology of law, or anthropology of food.[141]

The problem, however, resides in the fact that the separatist paradigm ultimately seems impracticable, even in the case of physical anthropology. Though it might seem that a consistent separation of the evolutionary science of man beginning from animal forms appears much simpler than the recognition of the absence of any areas shared by physical and cultural anthropology, even this task faces major challenges. Claude Levi-Strauss is right to say that "to define it thus would be to forget that the last phases, at least, of human evolution—those which have differentiated the race *Homo sapiens*, and even perhaps the stages which led to him—occurred under conditions very different from those governing the development of other living species (...). Each human society conditions its own physical perpetuation by a complex body of rules, such as the prohibition of incest, endogamy, exogamy, preferential marriage (...), polygamy, or monogamy—or simply by the more or

---

[137]Ibid.

[138]P. Duchliński, *Uwagi o stylu klasycznej...*, p. 211.

[139]E. Nowicka, *Świat człowieka – świat kultury*, 2nd edition, PWN, Warszawa 1991, p. 51.

[140]Consequently, the comment made by EwaNowicka in her opening remarks on relationships between these two sciences that "another discipline of science linked to cultural anthropology is philosophical anthropology" (E. Nowicka, *Świat człowieka – świat kultury*, 2nd edition, PWN, Warszawa 1991, p. 50) should be seen more as a salvatorius rather than the author's actual belief in the existence of any essential relationships.

[141]Cf. E. Nowicka, *Świat człowieka – świat kultury*, PWN, New Edition, Warszawa 2006, pp. 458–459.

less systematic application of moral, social, economic, and aesthetic standards."[142] Even if Levi-Strauss seems to have made an exaggeration when he said that "form the time man acquired the power of speech (...) he himself determined (...) the process of his biological evolution,"[143] he is certainly right that it did influence the conditions in which evolution occurred.

2.2.2 Integrating Models

A review of literature of the subject clearly shows that even for the sake of rejecting the scientifically flawed logic of amalgamation, we are not doomed to a separation of anthropological approaches. Both in the case of scientific knowledge (in the sense of natural and social sciences), and in the case of philosophical or theological knowledge, the goal is ultimately to arrive at knowledge aimed, generally speaking, at developing a concept of man. Consequently, they may only be separated to a limited extent; both of these methods make up a single cognitive program which will never be fully realized. Referring to Kant's pair of concepts, we might say: in view of this goal, without the explanatory and synthesizing efforts of philosophy, empirical research projects relevant from the anthropological point of view would remain "blind," while philosophical reflection would be largely "void" if it tried to limit itself to its own field.[144] Let us take a closer look at this problem, referring to some examples.

The meaning of the mutual relationships between physical and cultural anthropology has been illustrated well by Ewa Nowicka. She says that natural anthropology "must take into account the cultural factor, studying the process of historical and spatial variability of the physical build of man who follows in his daily struggle for survival considerations which are largely cultural, such as the norms of aesthetics, eating habits, or lifestyle. At the same time, cultural anthropology desperately needs the findings of physical anthropology, since man's culture (...) is strictly related to the biological features of the *Homo sapiens* species."[145] Moreover, culture may to a certain extent be seen, especially in its beginnings, as a form of a non-biological adaptation mechanism, and—as long as this perspective is not absolutized[146]—the reasonability of such an approach is most apparent: "cultural patterns have developed not only in accordance with a certain biophysical structure, but also in line with this structure's relation to the surroundings. They were thus both a kind of

---

[142]C. Levi-Strauss, *Structural Anthropology...*, p. 353.

[143]Ibid., p. 353.

[144]G. Haeffner, *The Human Situation...*, p. 11.

[145]E. Nowicka, *Świat człowieka – świat kultury...*, p. 40.

[146]Its absolutization would amount to the amalgamation described above, As pointed out by Gerd Haeffner, for instance, no natural biological explanation can be offered of moral misgivings about killing, or gratitude for a good hunt or harvest. Cf. id., *The Human Situation*, p. 30.

superstructure and a substitute of biological structure in contact with the natural environment."[147]

Luis Luzbetak SVD points out that cultural and philosophical anthropology need to be integrated. He argues that "if a culture were its own ultimate measure of rightness or wrongness, headhunting, racism, and perhaps most social evils, inasmuch as they are integral parts of that 'sacred' and 'untouchable' whole, would be right and proper."[148] Such a perspective is too restrictive, at least in the sense that "they are all limited to localized microvalues of a particular social group and have little or no relation to the rest of humanity. Such criteria downplay or overlook the macrovalues and universal relations with and responsibility toward the rest of humanity."[149] He therefore postulates that broader philosophical concepts should be adopted, such as, for example, man's dignity. For even if such considerations are beyond the domain of cultural anthropology, by being philosophical or theological in nature "they can and indeed should be part and parcel of what one understands by 'being human' and 'human self-realisation'".[150] Consequently, they must be taken into account in anthropology, especially in applied anthropology.

Finally, in philosophy, the dominant view is criticism of the isolationist stance. As pointed out by Rev. Stanisław Kowalczyk, who cites the views of many contemporary philosophers (J. Ladiere, C. Peursena, L. Mascalla, and others), "while implying a diversity of subject matters and methods employed by empirical sciences and metaphysics, philosophical anthropology does not rule out their mutual complementarity (. . .), and points instead to their need of cooperation. It is particularly indispensable in the case of liminal problems, such as the origins of man, determinism and freedom, suffering and death, work, culture, man's place in society. Man is immanent with respect to the cosmos, and therefore natural sciences are indispensable in the description of his existential status. An analogous role is played by social sciences as regards the relationship between an individual and the society. In both cases, the philosopher must know at least the rudiments. Isolationism with regard to empirical sciences exposes philosophy to abstractionism and verbalism; one can then hardly speak of an existential description of the human person. There are, of course, limits to the empirical-sociological knowledge, as the world of person—its value and category—is essentially beyond its reach. This is already a domain of philosophical reflection, which uses its own proper methods. (. . .) Natural knowledge and philosophical knowledge differ in terms of methodology and scope of

---

[147]E. Nowicka, *Świat człowieka – świat kultury*. . ., p. 40.

[148]L. Luzbetak, *The Church and Cultures*. . ., p. 41.

[149]Ibid., p. 41.

[150]Ibid. The author qualifies this statement: "if one is to be both an applied anthropologist and a believing Christian". It does not appear to be an exclusively Christian issue, however. In essence, this is about taking heed of moral responsibility. Otherwise, an anthropologist becomes "a man without a face": a consultant advising his employer about "what must be done to assure the employer's stated goals." (Ibid., p. 40).

investigation, and therefore must not be mixed, much less identified. They are complementary, however, in the ultimate explication of human existence."[151]

The above standpoints—and many more could easily be listed—show how integration of anthropological perspectives may be perceived while respecting their diversity. Let us now try to discover their structural logic to identify possible models of integration as it should be understood. What is meant by model here is a tool which explains a large amount of data, useful in organizing the whole of knowledge in a logical and simple way, while recognizing its own limitations.[152]

The comments Ewa Nowicka makes about the relationship between natural and cultural anthropology reveal that the starting point for integration is consistent self-limitation, as it were—defining the subject matter and research goals while keeping to the terms of reference (as regards their subject matter and methodology) of each respective discipline, recognizing and respecting their autonomy. In the case of physical anthropology, such a research problem may be, for example, the spatial variability of physical build. And once this specific subject matter is defined as belonging to the sphere of physical anthropology, it becomes obvious that it must open up to interdisciplinarity: certain data which are required for the achievement of the specific research goal of physical anthropology must come from cultural anthropology. In this case, aside from atmospheric, geographic, or other similar factors, the anthropologist must also take into account the ethical or aesthetic norms prevailing among the peoples he studies. And to take them into account, he or she must rely on the findings of cultural anthropology. These findings—and this is where the need for an integrating perspective becomes apparent—are not facultative; they are indispensable for properly answering the research question asked within the framework of this particular discipline.

This issue may be further elaborated upon. In fact, integration does not always need to mean relying on the studies of cultural anthropologists, but may mean reference to data obtained by way of a methodology that differs from the one typically used in one's own field of study. For example, in the case of statements about the origin of man, both disciplines (physical and cultural) draw on archaeological knowledge. Only with this knowledge may anthropologists find answers to the questions they consider to be of essence.

It appears that the above mechanics of integration is also discovered in the relationship between cultural and philosophical anthropology. In this approach—as stressed by Kowalczyk—the point is not to turn philosophy into a "meta-science", a kind of "synthesis crowning the whole of empirical sciences."[153] On the contrary, integration begins by acknowledging the actual autonomy of philosophy, with recognizing its specific subject matter and methods, noting, for example, that "only philosophy is able to capture and explain the intellectual and spiritual values

---

[151] S. Kowalczyk, *Filozofia człowieka...*, pp. 14–15.

[152] Cf. L. Luzbetak, *The Church and Cultures...* pp. 135–136.

[153] S. Kowalczyk, *Filozofia człowieka...*, p. 13.

of man: truth, good, beauty, love, religion."[154] At the same time, however, aware-ness of the goal of philosophical anthropology which strives to answer the question about man prevents us from ignoring the knowledge about man collected by empirical sciences. Gerd Haeffner stresses that each philosophical anthropology must be open to empirical studies of man and his world. Openness means, on the one hand, interest in cross-curricular empirical studies of the human phenomenon, and on the other hand attempts to integrate the most reliable results of these studies relevant for its systematization.[155]

When discovering an analogous starting point in the integrating logic (recogniz-ing the autonomy of a scientific discipline), it should be noted, however, that some legitimate questions may be asked about the understanding of the process of integration itself. When discussing the relationship between natural and cultural anthropology on the one hand, and philosophical anthropology on the other, Stanisław Kowalczyk describes the former as "purely descriptive," and the latter as "evaluative-normative."[156] According to this logic, integration would consist in a philosophical analysis of data provided by natural sciences, and thus—neverthe-less—an attempt at a synthesis within the framework of philosophy understood as a meta-science. Paradoxically, this approach approximates the viewpoint of existential Thomism which questions the theoretical nature of science. At the same time, however, Kowalczyk criticizes such a standpoint, rightly pointing out that "truth is neither the exclusive privilege of the former nor of the latter."[157]

Even though the descriptive dimension remains a characteristic feature of cultural anthropology, it cannot be denied to have epistemological value. It appears, there-fore, that it is not a radical separation of description and theory that is the proper—also according to Kowalczyk—way of characterizing the mechanics of integration. The terms description and theory, perhaps applied somewhat inadequately, seem to suggest that the theory of philosophical anthropology is of a different kind than the theories of cultural anthropology;[158] it is an objection against the "philosophically universalizing" claims of empirical sciences.[159] Therefore, openness and integration in philosophical anthropology mean it must have its own foundations.[160] Conse-quently, all findings of scientific disciplines, even those of a theoretical, probabilis-tic, or generalizing nature, contribute to philosophical anthropology as input data necessary to avoid "abstractionism and verbalism" in the search for answers to the typical questions of philosophical anthropology. This corresponds to the model discovered in the course of analyses concerning the relationship between cultural and natural anthropology. On the other hand, in the case of descriptive data, they

---

[154]Ibid., p. 13.

[155]Cf. G. Haeffner, *The Human Situation. . .*, p. 25.

[156]S. Kowalczyk, *Filozofia człowieka. . .*, pp. 7–8.

[157]Ibid., p. 13–14.

[158]As noted by Kowalczyk, "philosophy and science emphasize" different aspects of truth" (p. 14).

[159]S. Kowalczyk, *Filozofia człowieka. . .*, p. 8.

[160]Cf. G. Haeffner, *The Human Situation . . .*, p. 26.

may serve as a confirmation or exemplification of theoretically conceptualized notions.

Once the significance of integration for a proper understanding or confirmation of study findings is acknowledged, the relevance of a comment made by Luis Luzbetak on the relationship between cultural and philosophical anthropology becomes apparent. While what we have established so far has led us mainly towards identifying the relationships between anthropologies in the course of asking research questions, selecting methods and sources—in other words, "on the input side," so to speak, Luzbetak insists that it is also necessary to integrate perspectives "on the output side." He emphasizes the significance of integrating the results of investigations performed in philosophical and theological anthropology with those carried out in cultural anthropology. This postulate—as proposed by Luzbetak—is a requirement of the ethics of science. He points out that if this reference is missing, it must be concluded that culture represents its own ultimate measure of rightness, which results in a relativist stance in ethics. In other words, it would amount to concluding that one cannot say what it essentially "means to be a human being."[161] And yet, as Luzbetak points out, it is owing to philosophy and theology that we can actually do it. Gerhard Ebeling identifies the relationship between these two theoretical perspectives. He argues that theology "should offer more than just knowledge about the anthropological structures and mechanisms or ethical norms. Its proper contribution consists in saying that once we leave God out of consideration, we also leave out man—as a sinful, created being in need of forgiveness."[162] Consequently, both philosophical and theological reflection about man makes it possible—in a cascade, so to say, level by level—to refer the discovered microvalues to macrovalues, and accurately direct our actions and thoughts with regard to the discovered cultural facts. It does not change the scientific findings, but informs our attitude towards them and deepens our understanding. In reference to the phenomenological tradition, we could speak of a philosophical reduction, revealing the essential content of an observed cultural phenomenon and the concept of man entailed by this phenomenon, or a theological reduction revealing its eschatological (the sinful nature of man, mercy, etc.) dimension.

When trying, in relation to the above conclusions concerning the possible models of integration, to determine the conditions of a model integration within the framework of anthropology, it should therefore be noted that the starting point in the process of integrating knowledge is the research problem to be investigated, which determines the methodological framework and the subject matter to be analyzed. The first step—however paradoxical this may appear—is to respect the boundaries, to separate and locate the problem within the relevant discipline. Only this procedure, by eliminating the temptation of amalgamation, opens the way to an integrating approach. It may be realized in three areas. One area of integration may be the subject matter of analyses—where the input data may include the findings of a

[161]L. Luzbetak, *The Church and Cultures. . .*, p. 27.

[162]G. Ebeling, *Przyczynek do. . .*, p. 78.

different current of studies on man. For example, an analysis of the anatomy of aboriginal peoples may require taking into account their aesthetic or ethical norms or eating habits described by anthropologists of culture. Another area of integration may be that of methodology. This applies to situations when for the purpose of collecting data for the primary research objective it is necessary to perform studies typical of a different research area. For example, studies in cultural anthropology also include archaeological analyses which belong to an independent discipline of science. Finally, a third area of integration may be that performed "on the output side," or, better perhaps, "at the foundations." This consists in taking into account the findings of another current of anthropology when drawing conclusions or developing research paradigms in a particular discipline. For example, this may mean referring to philosophical or theological reflection on what it means to be human when taking a stance on the phenomenon of "headhunters," or evaluating individualist philosophical standpoints in anthropology in the light of findings contributed by cultural anthropology about the "primeval" social life of human beings. This last example additionally shows the significance of a hierarchy of findings. Even though essentially the framework of reflections is related to more theoretical (philosophical, theological) approaches, in which empirically observed phenomena are evaluated, this is not a "unidirectional" movement. Also analyses which are less theoretical may affect philosophical reflection, and to a certain extent theological theories as well.[163]

---

[163]It is worth noting that in its documents Vatican II begins precisely with empirical experience, which leads it to re-reading, so to say, the meaning of revealed truths.

Chapter 3
Political Anthropologies

On the grounds of each of the disciplines of science described in Chap. 2, a reflection on politics has developed, sometimes in more theoretical, at other times in more applied, terms. It should be stressed, however, that today we would prefer not to embrace all of the traditions of broadly-conceived political anthropology. Some of them, to a large extent due to the amalgamation of knowledge discussed above, are not considered scientific today. A particularly infamous page in the history of science was written by the political application of physical and cultural anthropology in Nazi Germany. As pointed out by Andre Gingrich, representatives of both anthropological currents whose differentiation from *Voelkerkunde*, even though already beginning, was not yet complete in the Germany of the 1930s,[1] largely sympathized with Nazi politics and supported it on the scientific side (both in theoretical and applied terms).[2]

It should be stressed that the support provided to Hitler's regime by German anthropology did not only arise from pragmatic reasons, or the dismissals from work—if not persecutions—by the Nazis for scholars who thought differently.[3] To a large extent, it was related to the dominant scientific theories developing from the turn of the twentieth century. The racist ideas which then became characteristic of the Third Reich were provided with solid theoretical foundations by the strain of anthropology that had developed since the end of the nineteenth century. A good exemplification of this phenomenon is the case of Eugen Fischer, a professor of anthropology at the University in Freiburg, who presided over the Anthropological Association in the interwar period and headed major scientific institutions (e.g. the Kaiser Wilhelm Institut für Antropologie)—a renowned scientist, whose approach

---

[1]Cf. Andrew Gingrich, "Alliances and Avoidance: British interactions with German-speaking anthropologists 1933–1953," in: Deborah James, Evie Plaice, Christina Toren [ed.], *Culture Wars. Context, Models and Anthropologists' Account*, Berghahn Books, New York-Oxford 2012, pp. 20–21.

[2]Ibid., p. 21–22.

[3]Which did actually take place, of course. Cf. A. Gingtich, "Alliances...," p. 21.

© Springer Nature Switzerland AG 2021
M. Gierycz, *European Dispute over the Concept of Man*, Contributions to Political Science, https://doi.org/10.1007/978-3-030-61520-8_3

may be legitimately considered representative of the intellectual climate in German anthropological circles. Let us add that in 1951 he was awarded the title of Honorary Member of the German Anthropological Association. Together with other luminaries of contemporary science, Erwin Baur and Frid Lenz, in the early 1920s Professor Fischer wrote a two-volume work entitled *Menschliche Erblichkeitslehre und Rassenhygiene (Eugenik)*,[4] where he not only demonstrated the intellectual superiority of the Nordic race, but also emphasized "how science could explain the rise and fall of civilization, cure the diseases of the 'body politic,' and provide a scientific basis for population and racial politics."[5] From this point of view, broadly shared in the German anthropological community,[6] anthropology was intrinsically political. As stressed by another German anthropologist, the significance of "studies into peoples and races (...) must not be underestimated, as they are related to the most important political problems of peoples and races."[7] Indeed, Adolf Hitler was very much aware of the political nature of anthropology; when writing his *Mein Kampf*, he supported his theses with arguments taken from Professor Fischer's work mentioned above.[8]

Consequently, after Hitler came to power in Germany, anthropology fully blossomed precisely as a scientific substantiation of racial politics. Already in 1933, Eugen Fischer was made Vice-Chancellor of today's Humboldt University in Berlin. In his lectures, he stressed that "what Darwin was not able to do, genetics has achieved, it has destroyed the theory of equality of man,"[9] and elaborated on his earlier claims about the political role of anthropology. He understood it as an applied science, explaining that "so must each political regulation regarding the population be so scientifically supported that it will be untouchable and will work far into the future."[10] The same logic was also embraced by other scientific institutions, including those established by the Germans in occupied territories (like the Institute of German Work in the East—Institut für Deutsche Ostarbeit, IDO). Their goal was to "carry out anthropological studies aimed at implementing the Nazi concept of racial segregation and extermination in occupied countries. (...) Anthropological studies were supposed to help isolate basic ethic groups (...) and each of them would have its specific destiny assigned by the Nazi regime."[11] German anthropologists claimed

---

[4]First issued by Lehmann in Münich in 1921.

[5]Robert Wald Sussman, *The Myth of Race: The Troubling Persistence of an Unscientific Idea*, Harvard University Press, Cambridge, Massachusetts, London 2014, p. 116.

[6]Cf. A. Gingtich, "Alliances...," p. 21–22.

[7]As quoted in: Gretchen Engle Schafft, G. Zeidler, "Antropologia" Trzeciej Rzeszy, *"Alma Mater. Miesięcznik Uniwersytetu Jagiellońskiego"* 47/2003, http://www3.uj.edu.pl/alma/alma/47/01/05.html [13.09.2011].

[8]R. W. Sussman, *The Myth of Race...*, p. 116.

[9]As quoted in:R. W. Sussman, *The Myth of Race...*, p. 117.

[10]Gretchen Engle Schafft, *From Racism to Genocide: Anthropology in the Third Reich*, University of Illinois, Illinois 2004, p. 121.

[11]G. E. Schafft, G. Zeidler, *"Antropologia" Trzeciej Rzeszy....*

that "Middle and Eastern Europe were comprised of various 'racial strains.' Under the prevailing philosophy, each group should be assessed according to how the capabilities of its people could best assist in the development of the 'New Order' of Nazi Germany."[12] They believed one race to be useless for this purpose by definition—the Jews, whom Hitler compared to bacteria. These beliefs were supported by anthropological studies. For example, Julian Estreicher claimed that "the protein contained in the sperm of Jews is of a specific nature, so that it (...) permanently infects the woman to whom it is passed—which led to the conclusion that it must never be transferred to German women."[13]

The booming period of political anthropology understood in such terms in the Third German Reich was its final chord. After the scale of extermination on racial grounds was exposed, the current died out. From the perspective of today's science, the methodological inadequacy of deriving political or social abilities, much less the ontological value of a person, from the circumference of his or her skull or length of nose, is self-evident. In a most appalling way, it shows the potential consequences of amalgamating knowledge, in particular of attempting to provide a scientific explanation of the phenomenon of human existence.

The fall of anthropology in the Third Reich was not a decline of political anthropology as such, however. As pointed out by Ted. C. Lewellen, it was after World War II that "political anthropology [developed] within social anthropology."[14] Before that, from the beginning of the twentieth century, political anthropology had been developing within the field of philosophy. And it is to these approaches to political anthropology, today considered to be scientifically substantiated, that the main reflections in this chapter will be devoted. To make sure the significance of theological anthropology is not underestimated, in the last part of this chapter the place of political anthropology within it is discussed. It appears that, albeit in a slightly different sense than in the case of philosophy and cultural anthropology, within theology there is also room for reflection on political anthropology.

---

[12]Gretchen Engle Schafft, *From Racism to Genocide..*, p. 101. By way of illustration, let us take a look at Plügel's duties: "racial investigations of certain individual groups of population in the GG, racial-biological investigation of Polish resistance members; racial-biological investigation of groups whose value cannot immediately be determined, such as the Gorale, Ukrainian groups, etc.; identifying groups or clans that are suitable for Germanization [*Eindeutschung*]; providing information about German blood that is dissipating in the east; racial-biological investigations of family members of people of the east to determine to what extent their work in the Reich would create a biological contact with our Volk; putting our Volk in contact with those in the east and seeing what the results are." (p. 100).

[13]M. Kula, *Najpierw...*, p. 32.

[14]Ted C. Lewellen, *Political Anthropology: An Introduction*, Praeger 2003, p. 1.

3.1   Political Anthropology as a Subdiscipline of Cultural Anthropology

As we set out to discuss political anthropology developing within the framework of cultural anthropology, it must be made clear that the general recognition of the scientific nature of this discipline does not mean its studies are not politically implicated. Wojciech Dohnal says that "the birth of political anthropology was assisted by politics."[15] Nowadays this leads some researchers to conclude that "since the beginning of its existence, anthropology has been part and parcel of the European political project aimed at taking over control of the world," legitimizing "Europe's [*and then USA's—MG*] colonial policy and domination in the world."[16] Acknowledgment of this fact is significant, while it shows some crucial sources of the crisis of political anthropology in the 1980s and its contemporary rebirth with a considerably modified research agenda. Consequently, this section follows the historically-problematic perspective in the presentation of political anthropology. The research attention is focused first on the classical problems of political anthropology and its methodology, and then on its contemporary appearance. It seems reasonable to discuss both of these topics given that—despite the transformations continuing since the 1980s—the classical issues of political anthropology are still part of its investigations. At the same time, the contemporary form—so attractive to political science[17]—of political anthropology cannot be understood either in terms of the problems it undertakes or the methods it employs without referring to the earlier stages in its development.

3.1.1   Classical Political Anthropology

No definitive answer can be provided to the question about the beginning of political anthropology. Some authors consider the establishment of the Bureau of American Ethnology in 1879 by the US Congress to be a symbolic date, marking the start of "first professional studies on the political and legal organization of Indian peoples."[18] This experience was political in two ways: not only were its investigations concerned with primitive political institutions, but the institution was a political one itself. A considerable number of scholars do not consider the establishment of the

---

[15]Wojciech Dohnal, „Antropologia polityczna," in: Mirosława Drozd-Piasecka, Aleksander Posern-Zieliński, *Antropologia polityki i polityka w antropologii*, Komitet Nauk Etnologicznych PAN, Warszawa 2010, p. 9.

[16]Ibid., p. 19.

[17]This has been realized by anthropologists themselves; they seem to take pride in it, actually. Cf. Wojciech Dohnal, Aleksander Posern-Zieliński, "Wstęp," in: Ids. [ed.], *Antropologia i polityka. Szkice z badań nad kulturowymi wymiarami władzy*, KNE PAN, Warszawa 2011, p. 8.

[18]W. Dohnal, *Antropologia...*, p. 9.

Bureau, created at a very early stage in the development of cultural anthropology, to be the birth of the subdiscipline we are interested in, however. Not only may the results of works performed by the Bureau seem irrelevant today, but the then prevailing holistic model of anthropology does not really provide grounds for talking about a subdiscipline. For example, from the perspective of political studies, much more important than the Bureau's expert opinions were the works of "classical" anthropologists of culture, such as Henry S. Maine or Lewis H. Morgan. They demonstrated the thesis, for example, that "the primitive society was organized along the lines of kinship," which "may have been the basic socio-political structure."[19] So while political topics were certainly among the important issues studied by the then contemporary anthropology of culture, there may be doubts as to whether the birth of a political subdiscipline may be announced at a time when the discipline is only being formed itself.

Other authors[20] date the beginning of political anthropology to the 1920s. The study constitutive for political anthropology in this case is considered to be Robert Lowie's *Origin of the State* (1927). It certainly included "certain lasting ideas: that all societies recognize territory, that increases in population and in conflict lead to states, that class stratification is a key element in movement up the evolutionary ladder toward the state, and that the central element of the state is a monopoly of coercive power".[21] At the same time, however, even though "Lowie clarified a number of issues, asked some crucial questions, and presented anthropology with a fascinating challenge (. . .) unfortunately, the challenge was not taken up (. . .). [T]he begging of political anthropology was also its end—until 1940."[22]

Consequently, political anthropology as a specialization within social anthropology did not develop until the 1940s. Ted C. Lewellen, who locates its beginning as late as in the year 1940, says that it only began to function after the end of World War II, when the growing amount of data and number of professional anthropologists made specialization necessary, which resulted in an erosion of the ideal of a holistic anthropology. Whether we consider the year 1940 to be the beginning of political anthropology or not, it was certainly a breakthrough for the new discipline. A study published in that year, entitled *African Political Systems*, edited by Meyer Fortes and Evans-Pritchard, outlined "the problems, the theoretical foundation, the methodology, and the controversy for more than a decade of research into the politics of preindustrial societies."[23] While the years up until 1939 are sometimes called the formative period of political anthropology,[24] after *African Political Systems* it definitely entered its classical period.

---

[19]T. Lewellen, *Political Anthropology. . .*, p. 3.

[20]Cf. Georges Balandier, *Political Anthropology*, Random House, New York 1970.

[21]T. Lewellen, *Political Anthropology. . .*, p. 6.

[22]Ibid.

[23]Ibid., p. 7.

[24]W. Dohnal, *Antropologia. . .*, p. 9.

In the classical period, the problems studied by political anthropology differed from those investigated by political science not so much in terms of the subject matter, but the type of problems and the methods they employed. It was essentially interested in pre-industrial political systems, which were not of particular interest to political scientists at the time. Consequently, "a system of classification emerged between 1940 and 1980 that gained a general terminological acceptance, providing a common vocabulary of political difference."[25] It listed egalitarian systems (bands, tribes), and centralized ones (chiefdoms, states), arranged along the lines of evolution.[26] Political anthropology in its classical period was thus concerned with studies of "strangers." Its focus was then typical of cultural anthropology, but narrowed down to the problems of power. One could add also, that its researchers were to a large extent in the pay of the government. Wojciech Dohnal points out that "the theory of evolution (. . .) essentially affirmed the colonial policy. (. . .) [The peoples that were studied] were not so much interesting in themselves as in that they provided knowledge about the past forms of culture and law. It was also in this context that the genesis and development of political systems and legislation were investigated."[27]

The doubly political character of anthropology, related not only to the subject matter, but also to the political applicability of its studies, despite clearly having some negative aspects, such as, for example, the assumption of a cognitive neutrality of imperialism,[28] did support the development of studies into primitive societies, in the expectation that "anthropology would provide knowledge about the indigenous systems of law and government. Their accurate recognition warranted the success of current politics."[29] Consequently, studies on the peoples of Africa and Asia, discovery of the principles of their internal integration in the absence of state structures, including the particular significance of segmentary lineage structures, was to a large extent the result of colonial administration and its political agenda, as it made anthropologists study politologically relevant topics otherwise entirely neglected in political science.

Fieldwork was related to the theoretical aspirations and achievements of anthropology. In this area, the findings made by anthropologists clearly and directly interacted with political science almost from the very beginning. For example, studies on the origin of the state led anthropologists to falsify, and sometimes also

---

[25]T. Lewellen, *Political Anthropology. . .*, p. 17.

[26]It is this evolutionary argumentation that prompts Ted Lewellen to uphold the category of "tribe," nowadays largely contested. He argues that "the term is a recognition that in sociopolitical complexity and evolutionary development, there must be a form that bridges the gap between hunting-gathering bands and centralized systems". Ibid., p. 26.

[27]W. Dohnal, *Antropologia. . .*, p. 10.

[28]Wojciech Dohnal says that even such outstanding researchers as Evans-Pritchard "did not concern themselves with the influence which British colonial presence exerted on the life of the communities [they studied]. They did not realize the changes it made, or try to understand how this affected local politics," *Antropologia. . .* p. 15.

[29]W. Dohnal, *Antropologia. . .*, p. 13.

to develop, theories of the sources of government. As regards falsification, they played a corrective role—content-wise, as mentioned above—in the process of integrating knowledge. For example, referring to anthropological fieldwork, Elman Service criticized the Marxist theory of the class conflict as a source of the evolution of state, demonstrating that "there is absolutely no evidence in the early archaic civilizations themselves, nor in archeologically—or historically-known chiefdoms and primitive states, of any important private dealings—e.g., evidence of capitalism".[30] On the other hand, studies on the distribution of primitive societies contributed to the development of the theory of environmental circumscription (Robert Carniero) or the hydraulic theory (Karl Wittgfogel), thus helping understand the evolution of state. The former theory, by realizing that the common denominator in the development of primary states was that they were located in circumscribed rural areas,[31] demonstrated the significance of the geographic context for the form of state, including its centralization. The latter showed the significance of irrigation systems as a source of developing power elites. The case of Carniero's theory, who concluded—based on the observation of primary states—that the entire planet would become politically united by the year 2300, illustrated the risk of exaggerated extrapolation of the findings of political anthropologists. As their research developed, anthropologists gradually ceased to emphasize a single cause leading to the formation of state, and shifted towards theories accentuating interactions of multiple causes. In *The Early State*, written in the late 1970s, Henri Claessen and Peter Skalnik singled out four factors "as directly causal: (1) population growth and/or population pressure, (2) war or the threat of war, (3) conquest, (4) the influence of previously existing states."[32] This way, political anthropology in its classical period made a major contribution to the reflection on state in political science.

It is worth adding that anthropologists paid attention to topics which were generally absent in the reflection of political science. For example, one of the essential achievements of studies on primitive societies was to identify the significance of religion. As noted by Georges Balandier, "the sacred is always present in politics".[33] Fieldwork provided evidence that religion is manifested in various ways: "the government may be directly based on religion, as in theocracy; religion may be used to legitimize the ruling elite; religion may provide the underlying structures, beliefs, and traditions (. . .) religion can also be a powerful force of opposition."[34] For anthropologists, it was clear that religious rituals play important political functions, uniting "the entire community in a sacred bond."[35] These observations were generally ignored by political scientists who embraced the modern understanding of politics which was "inherently linked to a profound division between politics and

---

[30]T. Lewellen, *Political Anthropology*. . ., p. 65.

[31]I.e. surrounded by the mountains, sea, or desert.

[32]T. Lewellen, *Political Anthropology*. . ., p. 60.

[33]Ibid., p. 65.

[34]Ibid., p. 66.

[35]Ibid., p. 67.

morality"[36] and treated religion as a factor of negligible importance in scientific analyses of political processes.[37] Still, anthropology implicitly suggested that the prevailing secular paradigm in political science should be adjusted, which finally happened at the beginning of the twenty-first century.

The fact that classical political anthropology focused its research on primitive societies was related to its employment of a specific methodology. Seeing that "these societies are illiterate (...), the basic methods employed by anthropologists who study them include (...) direct interviews with informants combined with observation."[38]

In the context of interviews, the key problem is the selection of interlocutors and the form of interview. Anthropologists prefer free-form or unstructured interviews, which are very much like ordinary conversations, but help gather information which the anthropologist is interested in.[39] The more natural the interview, the more likely it is that the interviewer will be able to discover the meaning of patterns, norms, institutions in the lives of respondents. Consequently, in preparation for such a conversation, the researcher is not supposed to come up with a list of fixed questions, but an array of open-ended suggestions or topics, preferably carefully memorized by the researcher instead of being written down on a piece of paper.[40]

There are two main principles in the selection of interlocutors in classical political anthropology. Seeing that "in a primitive society (...) older people know more about tradition than the young," and women "usually know less about most aspects of social life,"[41] when studying primitive societies particular attention was paid to interviews with adult men. In classical political anthropology it was clear that aside from "female gestation, male impregnation and avoidance of incest," male domination was one of the four basic principles of kinship reflected in public and political life.[42] So even though anthropologists generally assume that "the greater the diversification of society, the greater the social distances in the community, the less representatives of various groups know about one another," in an effort to obtain

---

[36]Cf. P. Burgoński, M. Gierycz, "Politologia i religia," in: P. Burgoński, M. Gierycz, *Polityka i religia. Zarys problematyki*, Elipsa, Warszawa 2014. Consequently, in the beginning of the twentieth century they joined Vilfrido Pareto in his belief that metaphysical theories were "derivations," claiming that belief in "natural laws," "justice," or "law," is a kind of superstition or prejudice.

[37]Cf. Ernst-Wolfgang Boeckenfoerde, "Teoria polityki a teologia polityczna. Uwagi na temat ich wzajemnego stosunku," in: *Teologia polityczna* 3/2005–2006, p. 303. The author contends that by pushing away the question about God, political science "became an atheist science in the proper sense."

[38]Anna Popławska, "Podejście antropologiczne a metody historyczne i socjologiczne na terenie nauk politycznych," in: B. Szklarski [ed.], *Mity, symbole i rytuały we współczesnej polityce*, Collegium Civitas, Warszawa 2008, p. 31.

[39]E. Nowicka, *Świat człowieka...*, p. 114.

[40]Cf. Tim Rapley, *Doing Conversation, Discourse and Document Analysis*, SAGE 2008.

[41]E. Nowicka, *Świat człowieka...*, p. 113.

[42]T. Lewellen, *Political Anthropology...*, p. 132.

"multiple images of the same reality from persons holding different social posi-tions,"[43] these pictures most often came from men.

It should also be added that since "in primitive societies cultural participation is much greater than in societies which are more developed structurally and in terms of the size of population (...) it is more legitimate to employ techniques based on the experiences, emotions and motives of individuals as a source of knowledge,"[44] in the beginnings of classical cultural anthropology, including political anthropology, the autobiographic method was considered most significant. This is well illustrated by the fact that research into the political customs of Native American societies involved studies portraying Indian chiefs.[45]

Both the methods of interview and biography entail the need for in-depth knowledge of the studied culture. This is why the basic method, related to the two just mentioned, employed by political anthropologists, was that of participant (covert or overt) or external observation. Irrespective of the form, "anthropological obser-vation is direct, meaning that the researcher participates, even if just as an observer, in various moments or periods of life of the group he or she studies, such as religious rituals, social meetings, military ventures, travels, even family life. Participation consists at least in watching, taking notes, while at the same time interpreting the observed phenomena."[46] If done well, observation helps capture the customs and political institutions characteristic of a particular society. As an example, let us refer to an observation made by Claude Levi-Strauss on "the people of dust," illustrating the interdependence of long-term observation and interviews and discovery of the proper character of political institutions in primitive societies. Levi-Strauss notes: "political power among the Nambikwara is not hereditary. When a chief grows old (...), he himself chooses his successor: 'That one shall be chief...'. But this autocracy is more apparent than real (...) the final decision would seem to be preceded by an appeal to public opinion, so that the heir finally appointed is the man most acceptable to the majority. But (...) the leader-designate must be willing to take on the job and, not uncommonly, he answers with a violent 'No, I don't want to be chief!' (...) There does not, in fact, seem to be any great competition for power, and the chiefs whom I knew where more likely to complain of their heavy burdens and manifold responsibilities than to talk with pride of the chief's lofty position."[47]

This account clearly shows that discovering the system of power did not so much require conducting the interviews as setting them against the background of a longer observation so that they could be properly interpreted in the light of notes made by the researcher. Should any of these elements be missing, a mistaken view might be

---

[43]E. Nowicka, *Świat człowieka...*, p. 113.

[44]E. Nowicka, *Świat człowieka...*, p. 115.

[45]Cf. e.g. Paul Radin's book on the Indian Winnebago (1926), or Leo Smimson's book on the Indian Hopi (1964).

[46]E. Nowicka, *Świat człowieka...*, p. 112.

[47]C. Levi-Strauss, *A World on the Wane*, Criteron Books New York, 1961, p. 302.

taken on the chief's autocratic power which—as contended by Levi-Strauss—was to a large extent merely apparent.

Summing up, the first period in the development of political anthropology was related to "studying down" primitive political communities using qualitative research tools typical of anthropology (participant observation, thick description, in-depth interview, etc.). They reflected the typical orientation of cultural anthropology "towards strangers." Just like cultural anthropology engaged in research in an area which sociology was not interested in, so political anthropology studied communities which were of no interest to political science. These studies, in terms of their subject matter, were focused not only on the political problems specific to the communities concerned (as for example the issue of segmentary lineage structures), but also contributed to more general research problems of political science (the origin of state, the structures of power, etc.), sometimes emphasizing the significance of issues ignored by political science (e.g. the role of religion). Consequently, in addition to knowledge about primitive societies, anthropological studies brought their contribution to the theoretical findings of political science. A particular characteristic of these studies was their role in colonial politics, which they were to a large extent supposed to serve (so-called applied anthropology).

3.1.2   Contemporary Political Anthropology

In the 1980s, it seemed that the process of decolonization and the resulting self-criticism within anthropology related to its imperial implication,[48] as well as the disappearance of primitive societies in the age of globalization heralded the impending end of political anthropology as a subdiscipline of cultural anthropology. Not only, it seemed, were anthropologists finally losing grip on the subject matter of their studies, but also appeared to be losing confidence in their own independence and methodology. If from today's perspective one could hardly imagine a more mistaken diagnosis, this is because the 1980s also witnessed the beginning of a new type of studies, opening up entirely new perspectives hitherto unknown in political anthropology. A major contribution was made here by the process of European integration. Consequently, mostly (though not exclusively) works which discuss these problems in relation to the issues analyzed in this study have been used as exemplification of the new anthropological approach.[49]

---

[48]As a side remark, it is worth noting that an interesting research project—though one which is beyond the scope of this book—would be to examine the consequences of this rendering of accounts for the establishment of an explicitly relativist cognitive paradigm in cultural anthropology. Considering that in the 1950s imperialism was still considered not only natural, but even "cognitively neutral" (Dohnal, *Antropologia...*, p. 11), it might be hypothesized that the unchallenged domination of relativism today may be a form of "psychological repression."

[49]Which, obviously, does not mean that works concerning anthropological studies on the state which were published in the early 1990s should be disregarded. In this context, see for example

3.1.2.1   Continental Anthropology: "Studying Up"

As noted by Marc Abeles, one of the pioneers of the "new opening" in political anthropology, "for an anthropologist, Europe-building within the European Union (EU) presents at least two original features. First of all, the recent history of post-war European institutions shows an alternating acceleration and regression. One cannot describe it as a linear process, nor as something which might be considered a priority by the majority of Europeans. Secondly, the process of building Europe is never complete. (...) The most salient characteristic of EU officials' discourses and practices is the link between the immediate present and an indeterminate future. In some circles it does not seem possible to be European without projecting oneself into a world which does not yet exist, and which cannot be adequately understood using the classical notions of political science".[50] And yet it is precisely the tools and concepts of cultural anthropology that support—according to Irene Bellier and Thomas M. Wilson—such an understanding, by emphasizing not so much the description of institutions and their functions, but rather the problems, long marginalized, of culture (the role of local traditions, customs, etc.) and identity (both national and local, as well as tensions between different levels of loyalty, or ideological standpoints)[51] in the process of European integration.

Having spotted these opportunities, Marc Abeles used the instruments of ethnology to study the identity of European elites, and consequently of the Community itself. Implementing a research program already articulated in the 1970s,[52] he employed the classical tools of cultural anthropology (such as participant observation, in-depth interviews, thick description, etc.), which had so far been used to study primitive societies (that is, "downwards", in the direction of small groups), in order to study "upwards," i.e. the class of European politicians and officials. In the course of his observations and interviews, Abeles noted a specific tension between the thoroughly planned present of European institutions, rationally arranged and driven towards further integration, and a complete lack of clarity about its purpose and future which is nevertheless supposed to justify and drive its efforts, showing the impact of the process in which the present and the future overlap on the institutional

---

Anthropologie de l'Etat by Marc Abeles (Armand Colin, Paris 1990); *The social production of indifference: exploring the symbolic roots of Western Democracy* by M. Herzfeld (Berg, Oxford 1992); or the many case studies such as *Nationalism and the Politics of Culture in Quebec* by R. Handler (University of Winconsin Press, Madison 1988).

[50]Marc Abeles, "Virtual Europe," in: Irene Bellier, Thomas M. Wilson [ed.], *The Anthropology of European Union. Building, Imagining and Experiencing the New Europe*, Berg, Oxford, New York 2000, p. 31.

[51]Irene Bellier, Thomas M. Wilson, "Building, Imagining and Experiencing Europe: Institutions and Identities in the European Union," in: id. [ed.], *The Anthropology of European Union. Building, Imagining and Experiencing the new Europe*, Berg, Oxford, New York 2000, p. 1.

[52]A classic text here is Laura Nader's "Up the anthropologist – perspectives gained from studying up," in: Dell Hymnes [ed.], *Reinventing Anthropology*, Random House, New York 1972.

logic and developmental dynamic of the European project.[53] Abeles's study of the culture of the European "tribe of bureaucrats" proved to be a game-changer and gained wide recognition in the scholarly community. Abeles demonstrated that we can actually talk of a specific identity of European elites, which may be a harbinger or an avant-garde of the future European identity.

His findings, which were then confirmed by other researchers, showed that the widespread perception of members of the European Commission, the Council, or the European Parliament as so-called "true Europeans" entails much more than the somewhat disdainful term "Eurocrat."[54] The prospects, related to employment in European institutions, of becoming engaged in the service of "Europe," as well as daily work with "strangers" who become colleagues, turns European institutions into a laboratory in which perception of one's own national identity becomes transformed.[55] Abeles demonstrated that it is, on the one hand, characterized by a "political schizophrenia" which is "visible in the split (. . .) between national and European affiliation;"[56] on the other hand, it is historical amnesia: an identity without a past.

Secondly, Abeles's studies have shown that the "tribal identity" of European elites is in fact an incarnation of the identity of the European project itself. When analyzing empirical data, he notes that in the European Union "[e]verything happens as if Europe will be inventing itself every day (. . .) Reference to the past is usually limited to a brief remembrance of the founding fathers;" indeed, "any reference to tradition seems to be completely incongruous in the context of the European institutions."[57] This way, the Community becomes a space with no tradition of its own, driven towards a goal which is underspecified by definition,[58] reflecting the identity of European elites themselves.

Studies performed by Marc Abeles as well as other anthropologists (such as Irene Bellier, for example) have laid foundations for a European theory of cultural compromise, expressed in institutional practice in "laying aside" in the course of European integration, in the name of building a "new Europe," all that which divides, particularly national awareness. On the one hand, it establishes "the basis for a political culture of the compromise,"[59] while on the other practically prevents the achievement of any real common good by promoting a relativist paradigm within

---

[53]M. Abeles, *Virtual Europe*. . ., p. 31.

[54]Irene Bellier, Thomas M. Wilson, "Building, Imagining and Experiencing Europe. . .," p. 17.

[55]Ibid., pp. 17–18.

[56]K. Kowalski, *Europa: mity, modele, symbole*, Międzynarodowe Centrum Kultury, Kraków 2002, p. 12.

[57]M. Abeles, "Virtual Europe," in: Irene Bellier, Thomas M. Wilson [ed.], *The Anthropology of European Union. Building, Imagining and Experiencing the new Europe*, Berg, Oxford, New York 2000, p. 33.

[58]M. Abeles shows that all attempts at a more specific definition (such as the idea of federalism) have been rejected. He argues that it is precisely the fact that this is a project which must remain underspecified that is most interesting for anthropologists (cf. ibid., p 35).

[59]I. Bellier, T. M. Wilson, "Building, Imagining and Experiencing Europe. . .," p. 18.

EU institutions. Anthropological studies have also revealed the inviolable limits and challenges of a cultural compromise. An analysis of the process in which positions of the European Union have developed shows that "the process of deterritorialization does not necessarily facilitate the creation of a public space of debate in the EU. As in the Commission, intercultural contact may actually reinforce national barriers instead of generating a common identity."[60] Different traditions of thought, culturally "natural" ideological standpoints ultimately come to be expressed even within ideologically coherent parliamentary fractions,[61] despite efforts at downplaying or ignoring them.

An "insider" analysis of European institutions and the awareness of EU decision-makers performed using the classical instruments of ethnology, depicting the inner logic of these institutions and their cultural specificity, sheds much light on the sources of their political decisions and mode of operation, driven towards instant results, the creation of symbols, a constant search for ways to "approach the citizen" whom they have no points of contact with, in fact, as well as institutional tensions, etc. Consequently, the findings of political anthropology have turned out to be politically relevant, providing a deeper insight into the sources and conditions determining the political processes occurring in the EU.

Studies performed by Marc Abeles in the 1980s and his publications in the early 1990s shed a new light on the anthropology of politics which—to a large extent—was simultaneously being discovered by a new generation of anthropologists interested in politics. Their studies were enthusiastically received as they responded to the growing demand for discussions concerning issues other than the economic, political and legal problems involved in the process of unification. Ultimately, as Bellier and Wilson rightly pointed out, the processes of Europeanization concern the legitimation of EU institutions and their agendas just as much as the issue of creating, endorsing and accepting new forms of European identity. This is due to the fact that the processes of building and imagining Europe "are inextricably linked, dialectically related components of the EU's project."[62] Ultimately, the creation of Europe requires legitimization in which the "structures and aims of the EU must find approval (. . .) among its people."[63]

3.1.2.2 Anglo-Saxon Anthropology: Studying Through

Almost in parallel to the above anthropological current, which may be called continental, a different current of the "new opening" in anthropology developed,

---

[60]M. Abeles, "Virtual Europe. . .," p. 42.

[61]He notes that the dispute within the socialist fraction about the US intervention in the Persian Gulf shows "how difficult it is to harmonize political strategies in spite of belonging to the same parliamentary group and speaking a common political language." Ibid., p. 42.

[62]I. Bellier, T. Wilson, "Building, Imagining and Experiencing. . .," pp. 8–9.

[63]Ibid., p. 15. Consequently, they point out, the postulate of building entails various meanings.

which we may call Anglo-Saxon.[64] As discussed above, continental anthropology
was generally interested in "old" anthropological problems: group identity, the
meaning of symbols used and their narration, and ultimately "cultures owned by
relatively autonomous social wholes," the only difference being that they were now
referred to a new being created by the political process. In other words, it was
interested in "what" changes the political process and "why" (here: the process of
European integration) as regards culture and identity. British anthropologists, on the
other hand, were mostly interested in the "how." They saw it as being of key
importance to understand how "policies 'work' as instruments of governance, and
why (. . .) they sometimes fail to function as intended? What are the mobilizing
metaphors and linguistic devices that cloak policy with the symbols and trappings of
political legitimacy? How do policies construct their subjects as objects of powers,
and what new kinds of subjectivity or identity we are being created in the modern
world? How are major shifts in discourse made authoritative? How are normative
claims used to present a particular way of defining a problem and its solution, as if
these were the only ones possible, while enforcing closure or silence on other ways
of thinking or talking?"[65]

The emphasis on "how," a practical question, shows, firstly, that political anthropology is in its core related to a logic of unmasking. For anthropologists, politics is
seen not only and not so much as an instrument of government, but first of all as an
instrument of studying the system of government as such.[66] Studies on politicians
are supposed to reveal the "social totality" of politics, and consequently the fact that
"it influences the way individuals constitute themselves in terms of the norms
through which they are governed so that although 'imposed' on individuals (. . .)
[they] influence them to think, feel and act in certain ways."[67] In the context of the
European Union, for example, anthropologists have developed the notion of "imagined communities" in order to "look more closely at the way Europe is being
constructed as a symbolic and political entity—and therefore as a more knowable
and governable space."[68] Emphasis on the question "why" also reveals, in a way, the
applied character of anthropology. Its task is not so much and not only to explain but
rather "to unsettle and dislodge the certainties and orthodoxies that govern the
present."[69]

---

[64]To some degree, territorial names are a matter of general consent. Note e.g. that a close
collaborator of Irene Bellier was Thomas Wilson of Queens University in Belfast, and Cris Shore's
book includes a publication by Laurent Vidal of ORSTOM in Paris.

[65]Cris Shore, Susan Wright, "Policy. A new field of anthropology," in: id. [ed.], *Anthropology of
Policy. Critical perspectives on governance and power*, Routledge, London & New York
2005, p. 3.

[66]Ibid., p. 11.

[67]Ibid., p. 7.

[68]Cris Shore, *Building Europe. The Cultural Politics of European Integration*, Routledge,
New York 2005, p. 4.

[69]Cris Shore, Susan Wright, "Policy. A new field of anthropology," p. 17.

The nature of the research questions and the related goals reveals, first of all, a paradigm of political anthropology characteristic of contemporary anthropology as a whole, even though not so explicit in the anthropology of "studying up." For if researchers aim at unmasking and unsettling, as ideologies, all that we consider to be self-evident and just (moral), then the hidden assumption of this approach is a conviction about the non-existence of any real or proper order of human affairs, i.e. a profoundly relativist cognitive stance. Unmasking is possible once everything is considered a form—a mask hiding nothing but other masks. If the anthropological approach differs from post-modernist narratives of poetics or polyphony, this is only because it is aware that an equality of voices is impossible. Ultimately, it asks "Which voices will survive?" and "How have their discourses been made authoritative?", without determining in any way their objective or, to use Habermas's language, truth-based legitimation. This also shows the "totality of politics" whose actors strive in various ways (different in democracy and in totalitarianism) to "manufacture consent" by "naturalizing a particular ideology as common sense,"[70] without—apparently—ever objectively deserving it.[71] They cannot, since everything, even language, is considered to be socially established.

In substantiating the thesis about the totality of current politics, anthropologists have made many important discoveries. First of all, they have demonstrated that politics may not only reflect but also furnish symbols and moral principles for the entire cultural system. For example, the American policy of containment, articulated by Truman's doctrine in 1947, represents a model illustration of the core symbol and moral principles in action. "A metaphor more commonly when associated with contagious disease, containment became the idiom for rethinking not only US defense and foreign policy, but also internal political control (. . .) It was subsequently instrumental in redefining what it meant to be American. Thus, acting as a core symbol, the idea of containment spilled over into, and restructured, many different domains."[72]

Secondly, it was noticed that modern politics likes to wear the mask of neutrality by using "expert" knowledge developing institutions and procedures, and by employing the language of science. In fact, "the primary aim of policy language is to persuade rather than inform."[73] Consequently, anthropologists reveal "linguistic procedures which enable endowing words with such meanings as can be used either as handy operating tools, or as instruments of influencing people in order to obtain

---

[70]Ibid., p. 18.

[71]For example, the claim that the fundamental goal of the state is rooted in natural law would simply be one of the internalized ideological formulas.

[72]C. Shore, S. Wright, "Policy. A new field. . .," p. 8.

[73]Raymond Apthorpe, "Writing development policy and policy analysis plain or clear. On language, genre and power," in: C. Shore, S. Wright [ed.], *Anthropology of Policy. Critical perspectives on governance and power*, Routledge, London & New York 2005, p. 43.

particular results."[74] In the belief that the political nature of the policies they implement is hidden behind the language they employ—the legal and rational idioms which make politics appear merely as instruments of promoting effectiveness and efficiency—they analyze them using tools developed in the study of myths.[75] The fact that myths are no longer "a product of the social unconscious," but are the work of "dexterous craftsmen" does not modify their basic function.[76]

Thirdly, it has been noticed that even though politics contains the entire history and culture of the society which has generated it, their essential strength consists in "reconfiguring basic categories of political thought to create new kinds of political subjects [, seeing that] profoundly reshaping the citizen's constructions of the 'self'" is "one of the most effective strategies governments can employ to achieve this hegemonic power."[77] Consequently, anthropology as a concept of man appears here to be a key area of political engineering and involvement.

Research problems different from those studied by continental anthropology required a different research field and study tools. Indeed, "the sheer complexity of the various meanings and sites of policy suggests they cannot be studied by participant observation in one face-to-face locality. The key is to grasp the interactions (and disjunctions) between different sites or levels in policy processes."[78] Consequently, in the Anglo-Saxon approach it is not enough to use the standard anthropological tools and simply modify their direction (to study "up" instead of "down"). British researchers refer to "studying through," which they understand as "tracing ways in which power creates webs and relations between actors, institutions and discourses across time and space."[79] Their research tool consists in many-sided ethnographies which trace political links between various "organizational and everyday" worlds.

In the course of research, a standard anthropological practice is to focus on a concept which appears to be unproblematic in order to discover its various meanings and role in the organization of the society. Anthropologists thus look for myths in such "non-suspicious" notions as a free society or free market, which they treat as concepts constructed in order to veil the political reality and "transform people into consumers, who can chose between products."[80] Therefore, anthropological research is mostly a study of language or, to be more precise, of discourse. This term is understood as a configuration of ideas which make up an ideology, or, in

---

[74]Krzysztof Gładkowski, "Idealizacja, ideologizacja, indoktrynacja: mit „ludu" w naukach o polityce, w etnologii oraz masowych ruchach XIX i XX wieku," in: W. Dohnal, A. Posern-Zieliński [ed.], *Antropologia i polityka. . .*, p. 241.

[75]Ibid.

[76]Krzysztof Kowalski, *Europa: mity, symbole. . .*, p. 27.

[77]C. Shore, S. Wright, "Policy . . .," p. 24.

[78]Ibid., p. 14.

[79]Ibid., p. 14.

[80]Ibid., p. 8.

other words, "a particular way of thinking and arguing which involves the political activity of naming and classifying, and which excludes other ways of thinking."[81]

An analysis of discourse leads, on the one hand, to discovering who has the "power to define," that is, real power; who establishes reference categories and does not allow for or marginalizes alternatives. On the other hand, it helps track the process of developing a "keyword" and its capacity for attracting mass endorsement, and thus for becoming a "mobilizing metaphor." This last term refers to words which become "the center of a cluster of keywords whose meanings extend and shift while previous associations with other words are dropped. Their mobilizing effect lies in their capacity to connect with, and appropriate, the positive meanings and legitimacy derived from other key symbols of government such as 'nation', 'country', 'democracy', 'public interest and the rule of law'."[82] Finally, it helps identify changes in the strength of discourses, including "the different resources (linguistic and non-discursive) political actors bring to bear on policy processes to make their discourse prevail." For "although some discourses are deeply embedded in institutional policy and practice (. . .) they are constantly contested and sometimes fractured."[83]

The focus on discourse also results in a change in the way anthropologists approach their sources. Interviews or observations give way to analyses of various documents, both stenographic records of debates and official legislative proposals. This also helps capture the multiple layers of interactions and analogies in the way phenomena or problems the researcher is interested in are understood and approached. For example, by analyzing political documents and activities, Cris Shore demonstrated similarities between UE activities related to the construction of identity and those activities which had been successfully employed in the formation of national states. As he points out in his monograph, all three types of "inventing traditions," namely: symbols of social cohesion, traditions legitimizing institutions, and those related to socialization, are concepts "equally integral to understanding the cultural politics of European integration."[84]

---

[81]Gill Seidel, Laurent Vidal, "The implications of 'medical', 'gender in development' and 'culturalist' discourses for HIV/AIDS policy in Africa," in: C. Shore, S. Wright, *Anthropology of Policy. . .*, p. 16.

[82]C. Shore, S. Wright, "Policy. . .," p. 15: "Thus 'individual' became part of a cluster including 'freedom', 'market', 'enterprise' and 'family', and previous associations with 'society', 'public' and 'collective' were diminished."

[83]Ibid., p. 20.

[84]C. Shore, "Building Europe. . .," p. 41. In Polish literature, this issue has been discussed in theoretical terms by RadosławZenderowski. His interesting analyses show that if the contents corresponding to the notion of "national identity" can be "arranged into five most important components or 'pillars' (. . .):epos, genos, logos, etos, and topos," then "by undergoing a widening interpretation, they become universal." This way, they may very well also refer to European identity. Cf. Radosław Zenderowski, *Religia a tożsamość narodowa i nacjonalizm w Europie Środkowo-Wschodniej. Między etnicyzacją religii a sakralizacją etnosu*, FNP, Wrocław 2011, pp. 28–32.

Shore's studies, even though stemming from a slightly different methodological perspective, have led to conclusions consistent with the analyses performed by Abeles. It is characteristic that as regards "invented traditions," Shore mentions not only to the explosion of community symbols dating back to the middle of the 1980s, when the EEC adapted the flag of the Council of Europe for its purposes, turned the "Ode to Joy" into the Community anthem, or introduced the European passport. He believes other factors to be more important, such as creation of the category of "Community history" celebrated on the occasion of Treaty anniversaries or accession of new Member States. It has also been reflected in changes introduced into the classical calendar which now includes new holidays (such as May 9). Shore points out that the creation of European awards, weeks or years (such as the European Year of Cultural Dialogue), as well as the founding of university departments of European integration in fact leads to a reconfiguration of the symbolic order of time, space, information, education and media in order to give visibility to the "European dimension" and the presence of Community institutions. Shore makes it clear that these activities are aimed at creating a new political affiliation: a collective European identity.[85] His analyses of EU practices in this respect show that they are not merely aimed at emphasizing unity, but at constituting it. He concludes that historical reality gives way to constructivism. Abeles would add that this is an identity without a past.

* * *

The above ways of studying politics in contemporary political anthropology, anchored in culture, which represent its two main methodological schools ("studying up" vs "studying through"), clearly show the essential contribution of anthropological and social reflection to political analyses. While the "classical" political (institutional) understanding of the government process is related to analyzing the management of public affairs "from the outside" through norms, institutions and sanctions aimed at achieving desired results, the value added by the anthropological perspective consists in the inner dimension of the political process. Discovery of the cultural dimension of the observed processes—showing the internal cultural logic of institutions and political activities, officially presented as "neutral" or legitimized by a technocratic logic—leads to the discovery of cultural dynamics in political phenomena, adding much to their understanding and perception, often reduced in political science to the normative and institutional perspective. In this sense, political anthropology as cultural anthropology brings in tools (e.g. analysis of discourse) which may help unmask an apparently neutral political process, revealing its ideological implications.[86] On the other hand, it provides tools (e.g. participant observation, interviews) of insight into the "soft" tissue of the political process, related to identity, values, beliefs, worldview. At the same time, such an anthropology—in this respect remaining faithful to the traditions of cultural anthropology—leaves out the

---

[85]C. Shore, "Building Europe...," p. 51–52.

[86]Cf. Tomasz P. Grosse, "Trzy oblicza konstruktywizmu w Europie. Rozważania o kryzysie metody integracyjnej," *Chrześcijaństwo-Świat-Polityka* No. 17/18, 2014/2015, pp. 35–50.

fundamental anthropological problem (who is man?) as such entirely, and perhaps excludes the possibility of taking it up at all. The reduction of any cognitive standpoint to a single narration and the relativist paradigm, emphasized particularly in the "studying through" approach, ultimately seems to undermine the legitimacy of answering the question about the essence of humanity. We will come back to this issue later on.

3.2 Political Anthropology as a Form of Philosophical Anthropology

Considering the fact that in Plato's writings we already encounter the problem of the relationship between the structure of man's soul and organization of the state,[87] we might say that political anthropology has always been one of the key problems of philosophy. This is certainly true. Nevertheless, not every anthropological thesis found in the writings of philosophers or thinkers may be called philosophical anthropology *sensu stricto*. To cite Grzegorz Przebinda, if philosophy is understood as an accurate examination of reality using certain intellectual tools, then political thought does not have to satisfy the postulative accuracy of philosophy, being an "area between literature and philosophy."[88] It is worth noting, therefore, that even though reflection on man in the context of politics may, and does, appear in many philosophers and thinkers, this will not always be—from the philosophical point of view—a form of political anthropology understood as a philosophical subdiscipline.

---

[87] In the *Republic*, Socrates distinguishes between three parts of the soul: the sensual (appetite), the impulsive (spirit) and the rational one (reason), showing that the ideal state satisfies them all. Cf. Plato, *Republic*, Wordsworth Editions Ltd, 1999, p. 140 (book IV). "Here then, I proceeded, after a hard struggle, we have, though with difficulty, reached the land, and we are pretty well satisfied that there are corresponding divisions, equal in number, in a state and in the soul of every individual (...). And that as and whereby the individual is brave, so and thereby is the state brave (...). Is it not then essentially the province of the rational principle to command, inasmuch as it is wise, and has to exercise forethought in behalf of the entire soul, and the province of the spirited to be its subject and ally? (...) [A]nd so these two, having been thus trained, and having truly learnt their parts and received a real education, will exercise control over the concupiscent principle, which in every man forms the largest portion of the soul and is by nature the most insatiably covetous." It might be added that together with the segmentation of science, such issues have now become more a domain of social psychology and the psychology of politics than philosophy.

[88] Grzegorz Przebinda, *Od Czaadajewa do Bierdiajewa. Spór o Boga i człowieka w myśli rosyjskiej (1832–1922)*, Znak, Kraków 1998 p. 7.

3.2.1   The Genesis and Goal of Political Anthropology

Political anthropology in the strict sense, that is, as a philosophical discipline aware of its method, was born in the beginning of the twentieth century, along with philosophical anthropology. In the philosophical reflection on man a question appeared then—most significant in the context of the turbulent political events of the interwar period—about the status of politics: is it proper to the essence of man, or is it merely an "expression of the human's imperfection whose overcoming (...) is what the ideals of true humanity, what a moral education that liberates humans toward their authentic essence demand."[89] The question which had—though in a slightly different form—been asked for ages was now to be systematically analyzed, starting from an in-depth reflection on man as such. In other words, by "stemming from the spirit of politics," political anthropology wanted to understand politics in its human necessity. As explained by Helmuth Plessner, "just as art, science and religion became media for knowing the world because philosophy was able to turn each other of them into one of its tools, so politics will attain the same dignity only if philosophy, by turning politics into one of its tools, liberates it from its position as an area in which the human, which is tied to nature, acts merely contingently."[90]

Political anthropology is thus constituted as an effect of systematic, philosophical reflection on the essence of man. Its relations with philosophical anthropology remain complicated, not fitting—as will be discussed further on—within the simple scheme as one of the stories, or perhaps even the peak point, of the edifice of philosophical anthropology. The ways of philosophizing about man, in view of the intellectual climate of the historical moment, were related mostly to two perspectives of thought. One referred to Dilthey's historicism and the phenomenological standpoints, in many ways combined by contemporary thinkers like Arnold Gehlen, Georg Misch, Helmuth Plessner, Hans Freyer, or Max Scheler. On the other hand, it was linked to the broadly conceived existentialist current, with philosophers as diverse as Martin Heidegger, Karl Jaspers, and Nikolai Berdyaev. There is not enough room in this book to discuss all philosophical standpoints, of course. Consequently, the idea of a systematic anthropological philosophy of man and politics will be presented in reference to the political anthropology of Helmuth Plessner, not only because he is one of the first and leading authors of works in a philosophically-founded political anthropology, but also because almost all of the above-mentioned authors referred to Dilthey's philosophy of life,[91] representing the

---

[89]H. Plessner, *Political Anthropology (Studies in Phenomenology and Existential Philosophy)*, Northwestern University Press, 2018, p. 96.

[90]Ibid., p. 5.

[91]Even though the hermeneutics of *Dasein* may be said to have ultimately distanced Dilthey's hermeneutic of life, the genetic relationship of the philosophy of existence, hermeneutics with the philosophy of life are unquestionable. Cf. T. Gadacz, *Filozofia XX wieku. Nurty*, vol. 2, Znak, Kraków 2009, pp. 367–368.

philosophical fulcrum of Plessner's analyses which—also for this reason—seem to be representative of a certain type of anthropological-political reflection.

The essence of a philosophically-founded political anthropology is for Plessner "the genealogy of political life as it derives from the basic constitution of the human as an originary unity of mind, soul and body [*Geist, Seele und Leib*]. This genealogy is to be articulated according to the theory of drives and passions. It is, at the same time, a political theory of affects and a characterology, from which political practice could benefit. Second, a historically oriented reflection on the mutual dependence of a conception of human nature (...) and a conception of the state or the community."[92] This clearly illustrates the two political problems always present in reflection on politics: the relationship between the vision of man and the understanding of community, and the relationship between the ontological structure of man and the structure of political life. Plessner explains that this is about developing "the idea of the human as a microcosm, an elaboration guided by the political macrocosm," and discovering "the political a priori that turns out to be in effect in all notions of the human being its comprehensive intertwining with the world."[93]

The research problem is not particularly new. It generally refers to the classical problems of the philosophy of politics. In fact, already in the political tradition of Antiquity "philosophers discovered a certain concurrency between the spiritual 'self' and the ideal *polis*. Micropolis found its completion in the Macropolis."[94] It is the approach to its solution, however, that was new. Plessner, as well as other philosophers of the early twentieth century, believed that such a task of political anthropology lacks foundations today; that such a foundation is not furnished by "philosophy in its current state."[95]

The problem did not consist, however, in the absence of an anthropological theory. On the contrary, such theories were ten a penny. What many diverse and unremarkable standpoints concerning the nature of man had in common, according to Max Scheler, was their focus on a certain detailed aspect of human nature which then became generalized into a formula: "man is nothing but... (a social animal, a link in the evolutionary chain of nature, a bundle of passions, etc.)."[96] Elżbieta Paczkowska-Łagowska notes that "whatever the concept is content-wise, it will act as a sedative, if not an extinguisher, on our attention, making us reduce that which is human to a certain familiar horizon of phenomena. (...) The extent of the horizon in looking at man is always delimited by characteristics which belong to the past. (...) For it is man's history which tells man who he is, and history has not said its last

---

[92]H. Plessner, *Political Anthropology...*, p. 4.

[93]Ibid.

[94]P. Śpiewak, "Voegelina poszukiwanie Boga," in: E. Voegelin, *Od Oświecenia do Rewolucji*, translated by ŁukaszPawłowski, WUW, Warszawa 2011, p. X.

[95]H. Plessner, *Political Anthropology...*, p. 4.

[96]E. Paczkowska-Łagowska, "Wstęp. Natura ludzka, historia, polityka w antropologii HelmuthaPlessnera," in: H. Plessner, *Władza a natura ludzka...*, p. XI.

word yet."[97] The newly emerging political anthropology objects to such an approach. Also Plessner does not expect an anthropology of politics to furnish yet another description of man adding to the existing collection. Neither does he abandon the universalizing aspirations of anthropology, although his desire is to describe man not so much in the categories of "terms and definitions," but those of "openings and expositions." The basic problem, therefore, was the method.

3.2.2   The Methodology and Theory of Man

Given that the fundamental problem of political anthropology coincides with the traditional approach to the key questions of the philosophy of politics, and dissatisfaction is related to the "current state of philosophy," it may be assumed that political anthropology as a domain of philosophy will be characterized first of all by specific methods of analysis, or—more broadly—a specific research paradigm. It refers to Dilthey's philosophy of life, substantiating the cognitive relevance of historical experience, which helps—as noted by Plessner—expose "the idea of the human (. . .) attached to the historical perspective" in keeping with the meaning of politics.[98] It is only after Dilthey that the era of a new, proper, political anthropology begins, whose cognitive standpoint influenced the thought of authors as distant from one another as Max Scheler, Martin Heidegger, or Georg Misch, even if not all of them—according to Plessner—successfully followed the path discovered by Dilthey.[99]

What did the Diltheyan breakthrough consist in? According to Plessner, it could be compared to Kant's "Copernican revolution." While "[i]n Kant, we find the ethos of lawfulness, of the form of natural law in general (to be respected absolutely), of necessity and general validity. In Dilthey, we find the ethos of unforeseeability as the principle of viewing past life and one's own life, in its creative power and at the same time in its fragility, from out of the dark horizon from which and into which it proceeds. Just as the Kantian ethos of the categorical imperative lays the legal foundation for the legal categoricalness of critical philosophizing and its being guided by mathematical natural science, the Diltheyan ethos of that which is powerful beyond all possibilities lays the historical foundation for philosophy's being guided by history as its model, its object, its frame, and its form."[100] This does not simply mean adopting the perspective of historicism, yet it does consist in linking the study of man to history.[101] Philosophy does not turn away from standing

---

[97]Ibid., p. XII.

[98]H. Plessner, *Political Anthropology. . .*, p. 29.

[99]Cf. e.g. comments on Heidegger. Ibid., p. 22.

[100]Ibid., p. 45.

[101]E. Paczkowska-Łagowska, *O historyczności człowieka*, słowo/obraz terytoria, Gdańsk 2008, p. 85.

"face to face" with things themselves, but neither does it give up on the a priori perspective. Nevertheless, he stresses the fact that there are two ways of approaching the a priori procedure: "the possibility of defining human essence in terms of content, and the possibility of doing so formally; or, put differently: the possibilities of positing this essence in terms of a What and of positing this essence in terms of a How."[102]

While a priori thinking in terms of a What makes it necessary to specify the essence of man and is related to religious or dogmatic thinking, philosophical thought should remain rationally open to the "possibility a different humanity." Consequently, the paradigm of political anthropology is a formal one: "there is no compulsion concretely to specify the essence. There is only the compulsion to cover what is authentically human with a structure. This structure must be formal and dynamic enough to make the multiplicity spreading across the entire scope of ethnological and historical experience."[103]

In other words, by emphasizing the category of "how", political anthropology tries to combine a priori and empirical studies. On the one hand, it is thus aware that "a priori anthropology one way or the other produces an absolutization of particular human possibilities,"[104] and on the other that an empirical theory of essence is absurd. Plessner notes, however, that "[i]f we conceived of essence differently, not in conformity with notions of conceptual generality and ideational unity of form, but, for example, as a supporting substance or force, as what is really significant about a function that cannot be read off what is at issue, its secret, its hidden quality, then a doctrine of the essence of the human would have to be eminently empirical,"[105] or at least would not be purely a priori. From the methodological point of view, as noted by Elżbieta Paczkowska-Łagowska, this ultimately means acknowledging that "it is pointless to look in man for a substance that could be defined, since as a historical being man not so much develops his potential over time, but is formed over time."[106]

Political anthropology thus adopts a historical perspective "that goes to extremes" and is supposed to be an introduction to "a universal anthropology in conceiving of the human (also including its extra-empirical, purely intellectual dimensions) as the subject accountable for his world, as the 'point' where all supra-temporal systems, which accord meaning to its existence, emerge from."[107] Plessner points out that if we approach man in this way, "if we (...) conceive of humans also as creators who are of course bound to their own creatures and become subject to them, then we can, with regard to this possible conception of the human, which aligns with a historical conception of the world, clear the path to a universal doctrine of the essence of the

---

[102]H. Plessner, *Political Anthropology...*, p. 21.

[103]Ibid.

[104]Ibid., p. 24.

[105]Ibid., p. 17.

[106]Elżbieta Paczkowska-Łagowska, *Logos życia. Filozofia hermeneutyczna w kręgu Wilhelma Diltheya*, słowo/obraz terytoria, Gdańsk 2000, p. 294.

[107]H. Plessner, *Political Anthropology...*, p. 14.

human, to philosophical anthropology."[108] In this approach, man is the ultimate point of reference for all reality, and any supra-temporal spheres of meaning become relativized to a particular culture of man as their source in history.

In light of the above methodological paradigm, the destination point of Plessner's anthropology is explained, as it proposes that man should be understood as the creative birthplace of a spiritual world of values and categories which provide grounds for his self-conception and reference to himself and the world around him. Man is "not merely a process, a flow of time, but extracts from within himself and leaves behind 'supra-temporal units of meaning,' creates his own world on which then to rely as on something permanent, and which, in turn, has the power to define him."[109] Consequently, a key category becomes that of "unfathomability,"[110] and the corresponding "root of humaneness." Plessner says that acknowledgement of the binding character of unfathomability opens up the possibility of "gaining sight of something like an intellectual world and of history (. . .) [discovering] the temporal emergence of the non- and supratemporal (. . .) It is thus that the human reappropriates, by 'understanding' them, God and nature, law and morality, art and science as systems of reality, value, and categories," to ultimately "recognize oneself and one's world as having become out of the power of past generations."[111] For Plessner, history is a place of "creating and annihilating values, and not—as claimed by neo-Kantians—merely an arena on which timeless values become realized. Man is realized as long as he is creative, and what he creates is left behind as history."[112] Consequently, the idea of man's unfathomability or "open question" leads to viewing man as power.[113]

Such a view of man corresponds to Plessner's earlier conclusions presented in his *Levels of Organic Life and the Human*, in which the author—being a biologist[114]— adopts a biological standpoint. In this book, Plessner tried to overcome the dualism characteristic of the post-Cartesian understanding of man, without absolutizing either the internal point of consciousness, or the external perspective of the human body.[115] A key category here is that of "boundary" which helps distinguish the "inner" from the "outer": "inanimate bodies do not have one, they simply begin and end, and what might imprecisely be called their boundary is merely their outline. Having boundaries is the property of that which is alive." Indeed, one might say that

---

[108]Ibid., p. 16.

[109]Elżbieta Paczkowska-Łagowska, *O historyczności. . .*, p. 85.

[110]This idea has been borrowed from Dilthey's theory, for whom it was a "call sign" which helped "understand the historically developing human life, reaching a self-awareness whose supreme expression is philosophy." E. Paczkowska-Łagowska, *O historyczności. . .*, p. 76.

[111]H. Plessner, *Political Anthropology*, pp. 43–44.

[112]E. Paczkowska-Łagowska, *O historyczności. . .*, p. 85.

[113]H. Plessner, *Political Anthropology*, p. 50: "in conceiving of itself as power, the human conceives of itself as conditioning history and not only as conditioned by history."

[114]Elżbieta Paczkowska-Łagowska, *O historyczności. . .*, p. 86.

[115]E. Paczkowska-Łagowska, *Wstęp. . .*, pp. XVII–XVIII.

"the phenomenon of life consists in the relationship of the body and its boundary,"[116] which Plessner describes as positionality.[117]

Even though man, as an animal, is separated from his surroundings as a self-contained structure, he also has a distance from his own body, and furthermore—as the only being—a distance to his own self. Consequently, "if the life of the animal is centric, the life of the human, although unable to break out of centrality, is at the same time out of it and thus excentric. Excentricity is the form of frontal positioning against the surrounding field that is characteristic of the human."[118] This excentricity makes him predestined, so to say, to creating culture: "living—man always 'leads' his life. He does not fulfill it as a part of nature, but directs it from a distance provided by his excentric positioning."[119] And it is precisely in relation to the norms and values man establishes, providing support in the world he has created himself, that Plessner talks about man as a "creative breakthrough point." Consequently, in his studies on the anthropology of politics, the findings of his earlier studies in philosophical anthropology are extended to the spiritual world of culture and politics. In this context, we can see more fully Plessner's declaration made in the beginning of his treatise, that the genealogy of political life should be derived "from the basic constitution of the human," which is where he begins his study.

Plessner's methodology, related to the Diltheyan tradition and a holistic cognitive perspective, would not be fully characterized, however, if we failed to notice the influence of the hermeneutic current related to George Misch. Plessner interprets Dilthey in the spirit of the son-in-law of the author of the philosophy of life. Consequently, he declares "hermeneutics to be the method of his anthropology, in an attempt to understand man as a whole in the unity of his natural and spiritual aspect."[120]

Dilthey called the then newly emerging hermeneutics a theory of understanding externalizations of life recorded in writing. This understanding was thought of as a process in which the internal is discovered based on external manifestations, providing access to an extensive world of life possibilities. The process of understanding thus requires penetrating someone else's externalizations of life thanks to a transposition based on the fullness of our own experiences. Understanding consists in re-experiencing: "It is not a purely passive, receptive knowledge of someone else's experiences (. . .) but a kind of spiritual activity of the one who understands. Thus, one cannot understand others unless he understands himself."[121] Tadeusz

---

[116]Ibid., p. XVIII.

[117]Ibid.: "a plant represents an open form, an animal—a closed one. Open form makes the organism a dependent piece of the corresponding scope of life, its positional field; closed form, on the other hand, represents an independent fragment."

[118]Helmuth Plessner, *Levels of Organic Life and the Human: An Introduction to Philosophical Anthropology (Forms of Living)*, Fordham University Press, 2019, p. 271.

[119]E. Paczkowska-Łagowska, *Wstęp. . .*, p. XXI.

[120]E. Paczkowska-Łagowska, *O historyczności. . .*, p. 77.

[121]T. Gadacz, *Filozofia. . .*, p. 129.

Gadacz explains that understanding has its elementary and higher forms: "Elementary understanding is about the relationship between an expression and that which is being expressed. (...) Higher understanding is about a broader relationship. A fundamental principle of higher understanding is the relationship between parts and the whole, while elementary understanding is only about the relationship between that which is internal (impression) and that which is external (expression). Understanding spiritual products is focused exclusively on the arrangement which makes individual parts, taken one by one, form a whole."[122] Failure to understand individual parts in light of the whole makes it necessary to renew attempts at understanding and restating the meaning of the whole: "These attempts are made as long as the entire meaning of externalizations of life is exhausted. Individual parts are thus understood through the whole, and the whole through individual parts. This is what the hermeneutic circle consists in."[123]

The capacity for a hermeneutically conceived understanding, next to the idea—stemming from a holistic perspective—of an open question, and the idea—derived from Dilthey's philosophy of life—of unfathomability, was the third methodological foundation of Plessner's studies. He noted: "This is the only thing the human who has assumed the European principle of open immanence and of understanding the human from out of life and oriented toward life can do: despite and in its particularity, assert the universally binding position of the being human that is truly and authentically so only in this position; despite the monadic individualization and closedness of ethnic, philosophical, political positions against one another, creatively assert the continuous medium that connects them all, the medium that had come into view as a possibility in the Greek discovery of mathematical general validity, the medium they in fact now run the danger of losing in the de-deification of the world."[124] The ability to understand life opens up the possibility of a philosophical anthropology.

3.2.3 The Politics of Anthropology

Given the above conclusions, we might ask about the place of politics in Plessner's anthropology: why should there be a political anthropology at all? Plessner's conception of man as an open question leads him to grounding and providing a profoundly anthropological and philosophical substantiation of Schmitt's concept of the political as the distinction between enemy and friend:[125] "Plessner seems to

---

[122]Ibid., p. 131.

[123]Ibid., p. 132.

[124]H. Plessner, *Political Anthropology*, p. 76.

[125]As pointed out by Elżbieta Paczkowska-Łagowska, the Schmittan thread may be considered the other ideological current of Plessner's treatise, next to the hermeneutically-oriented philosophy of life. Cf. id. *O historyczności...*, p. 77.

attest, in his own way, to the legitimacy, phenomenological naturalness and existential accuracy of Schmitt's analyses."[126] How does this happen?

Firstly, we may notice that in Dilthey the elementary human situation already includes the fact that we experience some people as familiar and friendly, and others as strange and hostile. Consequently, an anthropologically essential distinction appears as the familiar vs strange dichotomy. Even more significant for the political nature of anthropology seems to be the very idea of man as an open question, or power. For "if man has no permanent nature, no essence, if his nature is history, then he determines who he is himself through his history."[127] Such a way of viewing man radically leads to emphasizing the political nature of man's fate.

On the one hand, it is the political in the most general sense, in relation to the weight of man's choices in life. For "[w]hat it thus wins in terms of a fullness of possibilities at the same time allows for a resolute limitation over against infinitely other possibilities of self-conception and world conception, which the human thereby already no longer has available."[128] Consequently, "[i]n its indeterminateness toward itself, that peculiar horizon takes shape inside of which everything appears to the human as known, familiar, and natural, appropriate to its essence and necessary, [and] outside of which everything appears as unknown, foreign, and unnatural, against its essence and incomprehensible."[129]

The political for Plessner has a much broader meaning than reference to the state. It is a quality present in all human relations: "[t]here is politics between man and woman, master and servant, teacher and student, (. . .), and whatever other private relationship you like, just as in the public sphere, there are, beside the politics proper of the state and of parties, politics and policies concerning the law, the economy, culture, and religion, as well as social policy."[130] It also encompasses the space of ethics. It is worth emphasizing: "man as the author of values" remains beyond a certain ethical horizon. This has been pointed out by Schmitt himself, who stressed that "for Plessner, man is initially a 'distancing' being whose nature is unspecified, unfathomable, an open question. Translated into the elementary language of this naïve political anthropology which relies on the distinction between good and evil, the open and dynamic disposition in Plessner, close to reality in an attitude of readiness for anything, would certainly be closer to evil than good in view of its share in risk and danger."[131]

On the other hand, politics in the narrow sense is also an important category for Plessner. Since man as an open question represents power, it is precisely by establishing and enforcing law that he sanctions the power to decide about himself. Politics appears here as a quintessence of anthropology, as it is "only politics that

---

[126]Ibid., p. 78.

[127]Ibid., p. 84.

[128]H. Plessner, *Political Anthropology*, p. 49.

[129]Ibid., p. 53.

[130]Ibid., p. 55.

[131]As quoted in E. Paczkowska-Łagowska, *O historyczności. . .*, p. 78.

tells man who he is, and it never says the last word—like Dilthey's history—since being an endangered being, man is at the same time a dangerous being; who he is also represents a dangerous surprise to himself."[132]

Generally speaking, "[i]t thus seems that to declare the unfathomable to be binding for knowledge of the human (...) is to declare the primacy of the political for insight into the essence of the human, for political anthropology."[133] Dilthey's elementary situation and the decisionist consequences of conceiving the human as power introduce into the heart of Plessner's anthropology the political question, showing—in reference to Schmitt—the enemy-friend relationship as part of the essential constitution of man, determining every way of associating and forming communities, which cannot be released even by the concept of humanity. For although "it does make the formation of the general concept *human* possible, which comprises, as subforms and cases, the differences of nations, races, states, cultures, and individuals, this pacifying discovery of a natural commonality cannot be secured in any absolute criteria that would not once more be tied to a one- sided reduction of what is human and the monopolization of a specific, historically become human- kind."[134]

In Plessner's view, political anthropology is not a branch of philosophical anthropology: "Philosophy, anthropology, politics instead belong together in another, central sense. They draw their possibilities from the same source of the principle of the unfathomability of life and the world."[135] The need to discover the political nature of anthropology results not only from conceiving man as an open question, but also from the political nature of anthropology; consequently, the fact that the opposition between friendship and hostility as a necessity of human fate cannot be overcome determines viewing man as a possibility and prevents the essence of the human from being ontologically established. Plessner contends: "Ability, the powerful are only expressions for the indeterminacy in which the subject of attribution of history—in the sense of a thinking that accords with life and remains within the open immanence of the interlocking perspectives of past and future—wins its determinacy in each case differently and always anew."[136]

* * *

---

[132]E. Paczkowska-Łagowska, *O historyczności...*, p. 91.

[133]H. Plessner, *Political Anthropology*, p. 60.

[134]Ibid., p. 54.

[135]H. Plessner, *Political Anthropology*, p. 62: "[E]ach independently seeks to take from the open ground of powerfulness, by which it knows itself to be empowered, that share of possibility that is traced out for each by the tradition it joins with this principle and which it acknowledges itself to be ready to accept." Plessner points out, therefore, that "[t]here is no general philosophical anthropology with various fields of application (the political, the religious, etc.); nor is there philosophy above anthropology, a philosophy that would as it were fan out according to particular fields of application to which belong, for example, the human and history."

[136]Ibid., p. 56.

Political anthropology as a philosophical anthropology appears to be relevant for political studies for a number of reasons. Firstly, it systemically demonstrates that "the intersecting of anthropology and politics [is] (. . .) a philosophically significant problem."[137] The relationship between Plessner's anthropology and Schmitt's political theory shows that at the foundations of political theory ultimately lies a— discoverable—deep vision of man, even if it is not explicitly or fully adequately articulated by the author of that theory. Secondly, political anthropology brings a whole range of tools which help analyze manifestations of human thought, of which the hermeneutic approach is of particular importance. Whether or not we treat hermeneutics broadly, as "a paradigm emphasizing the primacy of the linguistic (hermeneutic) nature of experience, which claims it is impossible to directly know oneself, others or the world other than in interpretations of language" or, traditionally, as "a theory of understanding aimed at capturing universal meanings,"[138] it is one of the key approaches to the analysis of cultural texts. Thirdly, political anthropology on the grounds of philosophy contributes important analytical categories, potentially relevant in the context of political analyses. In Plessner's case, these are, for example, the categories of "boundary" and "creative breakthrough point." Finally, it should be emphasized that political anthropology on the grounds of philosophy addresses the fundamental anthropological problem in the context of the conception of politics, society and the state. Thus, it remains an anthropology *sensu stricto*.

At the same time, however, it must be emphasized that political anthropology understood in such terms shares all the problems of the philosophical anthropology analyzed above. Each of its theories (including the one developed by Plessner) may be countered by a different theory and there is no way the dispute may be settled. In other words, every logical system works properly as long as we adopt its premises. At the same time, everyone claims the right to exclusivity. Plessner's theory, deriving a Schmittan vision of politics from the theory of organic layers, is a particularly explicit exemplification. But can it really be said that Plessner's theory ends the discussion, and Schmitt's theory is an anthropologically accurate view of politics? It is certainly debatable, especially since a meeting between Plessner's and Schmitt's theories is not as necessary as it might seem. As pointed out by commentators, Plessner accepts conclusions close to those made by Schmitt, which could, however, also lead in a slightly different direction.[139] In other words, such a form of political anthropology does not provide answers about the anthropological sources of various political traditions, but represents an independent reflection, sometimes intersecting with some currents of politics, on the political nature of man, following its own proper rules of reflection. So even though it does take up the problem of man's relation to politics, it does so in an abstract perspective, not referred in a

---

[137]E. Paczkowska-Łagowska, *O historyczności. . .*, p. 79.

[138]T. Gadacz, *Historia filozofii. . .*, vol. 1, p. 63.

[139]As stressed in this context by Helmut Fahrenbach, Plessner's treatise is not unproblematic in this respect. Cf. E. Paczkowska-Łagowska, *O historyczności. . .*, p. 80.

necessary way to the politics realized in a given place and time, or even the traditions of thought in which it is grounded.

3.3 Political Anthropology and Theological Anthropology

On the grounds of theology, no independent anthropological subdiscipline has developed dedicated to politics, even though there are a number of different interpretations of the political role of theology.[140] At the same time, however, theological reflection on politics attributes an important—if not crucial—place to the anthropological question. Already Leon XIII wrote in *Rerum Novarum* about the need for a healthy theory of state, reflecting—as noted by John Paul II—"a realistic vision of man's social nature, which calls for legislation capable of protecting the freedom of all."[141] In *Centesimus Annus* he explicitly emphasizes that "authentic democracy is possible only in a State ruled by law, and on the basis of a correct conception of the human person."[142] He also points out that the contribution made by the Church to the political order is anthropological, and consists in "a vision of the dignity of the person revealed in all its fullness in the mystery of the Incarnate Word."[143] In this sense, theological anthropology is also political, in the broad sense of the word,[144] as it defines the proper tasks of the state, resulting from the true identity of man revealed by God. The Church, "by its concern for man and by its interest in him and in the way he conducts himself in the world" believes that "the theological dimension is needed both for interpreting and solving present-day problems in human society."[145]

If in the sense outlined above, one can reasonably talk of a political anthropology also within theological reflection, it is necessary to further specify its character. To this end, it may be helpful to refer to the processes through which political anthropology emerged as a subdiscipline of philosophy or cultural anthropology. While in these cases it was an internal process within the respective discipline of science, consisting in an autonomization of the research problems of political anthropology through their emancipation from a broader anthropological context,[146] in the case of theological anthropology no such process has taken place. The separation of political anthropology from within its framework is more of an external research procedure,

---

[140]More on this subject, see: M. Gierycz, *Chrześcijaństwo i Unia Europejska*, WAM, IP UKSW, Kraków-Warszawa 2008, Chap. 2.

[141]John Paul II, *On the Hundredth Anniversary of Rerum Novarum: Encyclical Letter CentesimusAnnus of the Supreme Pontiff*, no. 44, St. Paul Books & Media, 1991–93.

[142]Ibid, no. 46.

[143]Ibid, no. 47.

[144]Cf. P. Mazurkiewicz, "Niepolityczna polityczność Kościoła," *Chrześcijaństwo-Świat-Polityka* No 13 (1) 2012, pp. 5–17.

[145]John Paul II, *On the Hundredth Anniversary...*, no. 55.

[146]More on the roads of autonomization, see: Janusz Ruszkowski, *Wstęp do studiów europejskich*, PWN, Warszawa 2007, pp. 17–18.

not related to the inner developmental dynamics of theological anthropology; it consists in extracting, or isolating from the overall reflection on man those issues which are linked particularly to political problems.[147]

3.3.1 The Anthropological Turn of Christianity

As noted by Benedict XVI, while "in history, systems of law have almost always been based on religion: decisions regarding what was to be lawful among men were taken with reference to the divinity,"[148] Christianity does not require religious legitimization to recognize the lawfulness of a legal regulation, or to acknowledge the divine provenience of particular authority. The roots of this unusual—from the perspective of comparative religious studies—approach to politics can be traced back to the well-known Gospel story of Jesus' conversation with Jewish teachers of the Law concerning the legitimacy of paying taxes to Caesar (Mk 12:13–17).[149] Asking to be shown a denarius with the image of Caesar, Jesus challenges his interlocutors: "Whose image is this? And whose inscription?". Only after they reply ("Caesar's") does he answer their question: "Give back to Caesar what is Caesar's and to God what is God's."

Jesus's listeners were amazed at the concept of His reply. It suggested that the order (fiscal, in this case) established by a pagan ruler was also morally binding for faithful Jews. It recognized the legitimacy of regulations imposed by pagan authorities, contrary to the Old Testament tradition which presented kings as chosen by God. Even though Caesar did not meet this criterion, he was to be obeyed as long as he did not require violation of God's law. It is worth noting that this new logic of legitimizing power is even more explicit in the apostolic letters. Note for example the well-known maxim from the Letter to Romans which says that "the authorities that exist have been established by God" (Rom 13:1). Making this statement in the context of pagan rule, St. Paul expressed a new understanding of legitimate authorities, claiming that "in the measure that they safeguard peace and uphold the law,

---

[147]Further on in this paragraph I refer to my findings presented in the article "Kościół, teoriaikryzyspolityki," in: J. Grosfeld [ed.], *50 lat później. Posoborowe dylematy współczesnego Kościoła*, IP UKSW, Centrum Myśli Jana Pawła II, Warszawa 2014, pp. 113–130.

[148]Benedict XVI, *The Listening Heart. Reflections on the Foundations of Law*, Reichstag Building, Berlin 2011 (http://www.vatican.va/content/benedict-xvi/en/speeches/2011/september/documents/hf_ben-xvi_spe_20110922_reichstag-berlin.html).

[149]Those asking the question try to set up the alternative: are we supposed to pay or not? It is a loaded question which makes any answer risky. Consent to pay would mean opposition to some zealous Jews who believe that "for religious reasons, taxes should not be paid." If Jesus objected to paying taxes, this would entail objecting to the law and risking charges from the Romans. It should also be noted that in asking this question, Jews refer to a specific version of the logic of division: either you are faithful to God (and His law), or you obey the state (which does not acknowledge the True God). Jesus cancels this logic in an exceptional way.

they correspond to a divine decree."[150] However paradoxical it may seem, St. Paul's maxim quoted above, harmoniously coinciding with the answer given by Jesus, made room in Christian tradition for secular power; secular in the sense of being independent from the religious community and religious legitimization. Its legitimacy was not based on divine anointing, but on warranting the true good of man and his overall development.

The discussion concerning taxes reveals the significance of the anthropological premise in the Christian theology of politics. It says that the political community and authority as such come from God and are necessary to man, representing the order resulting from creation, stemming from human nature. Already Thomas Aquinas stressed in his treatise *De Regno* referring to Aristotelian thought that while "for all other animals, nature has prepared food, hair as a covering, teeth, horns, claws, (..) man was endowed with reason," and "it is natural for man to be a social and political animal (. . .) It is, therefore, natural that man should live in the society of many."[151] The persistence of this belief is documented by *Gaudium et Spes* which says that "the political community and public authority are founded on human nature and hence belong to the order designed by God, even though the choice of a political regime and the appointment of rulers are left to the free will of citizens."[152]

The freedom of choice as regards the regime emphasized in the teaching of *Vaticanum II* shows the consequences of abandoning a religious legitimization of power. First, it eliminates the possibility of any "Christian" political order, reflecting the Divine order.[153] Catholic reflection tends to claim that such a reflection is not possible in a world tainted by original sin. The meaning of original sin in terms of

---

[150]J. Ratzinger, *Europe Today and Tomorrow: Addressing the Fundamental Issues*, Ignatius Press, 2007, p. 56.

[151]Thomas Aquinas, *De Regno: On Kingship*, Divine Providence Press, 2014, p. 1.

[152]Second Vatican Council, *Pastoral Constitution on the Church in the Modern World Gaudium et Spes*, Pauline Books & Media, 1966, no. 74.

[153]John Paul II, *Centesimus Annus*, no. 25: "no political society (. . .) can ever be confused with the Kingdom of God". The separation of that which is Caesar's and that which is God's ultimately concerns the scope of legitimate ambitions of power. By locating their hope in the true Messiah, Christians do not expect politics to create paradise in this world. Political attempts at responding to the yearning for a perfect world, even though historically present also in *Christianitas*, are treated with suspicion on the grounds of the Catholic theory of politics as efforts akin to idolatry. The teaching of the Church after Vatican II is very explicit on this point. *Centesimus Annus* explains that "when people think they possess the secret of a perfect social organization which makes evil impossible, they also think that they can use any means, including violence and deceit, in order to bring that organization into being. Politics then becomes a 'secular religion' which operates under the illusion of creating paradise in this world. But no political society—which possesses its own autonomy and laws—can ever be confused with the Kingdom of God". Contrary to the latter, the life of temporal communities "implies of imperfection and impermanence." This is yet another theoretical characteristic of the Christian approach to politics: the faith proclaimed by the New Testament points to the inherent limitations of power. Christians, as pointed out by Cardinal Joseph Ratzinger, "precisely, because they see the limits of the State, which is not God and cannot be presented as God, (. . .) recognize the purpose of its ordinances and its moral value" (J. Ratzinger, *Europe Today and Tomorrow*, Chap. 2). Referring in this aspect to the good traditions of the Roman

political anthropology, which will be discussed further on,[154] is a very important current in Catholic reflection, seeing in it a "great hermeneutical value" which helps understand the human reality[155] and emphasizes its significance for the stability of the social order.[156] Consequently, even if some historically developed preferences concerning the best social and political order do appear in Christian reflection,[157] they always have the form of conditional suggestions which point—based on certain premises—to those systems which best serve the overall development of man in a particular social and historical context.[158]

Orientation on the overall development of man results in a moral understanding and legitimization of politics. Above all, it means a negative specification of the purpose of government. Even though government means rule over people and is, as such, consistent with God's ordinance, the ruler may not use his authority to obliterate the divine image in man. Consequently, when the government promotes injustice, tries to strip man of his transcendental dignity, orders the subjects to do evil—it contradicts itself. And it is worth noting that this applies to every human being, and not a citizen or member of a nation—this is an important novelty compared to the social and political communities surrounding Christians.

Apostolic letters clearly already show that the negative program (prohibition of injustice) in the Christian understanding of politics is explicitly linked to the positive one. The goal of government is to safeguard justice—to give man what is due to him in view of his exceptional dignity. Consequently, belief in the moral character and goal of government is clearly visible in the letters of St. Paul and St. Peter.[159] Conviction about the ethical character of politics, developed and expressed in contemporary terms, is the central message of the Council's thought about the state. "The political community," we read in the Constitution *Gaudium et Spes*, "exists (. . .) for the sake of the common good, in which it finds its full justification

---

Empire, the state is seen as a space embodying peace and law (*Conservator*). Messianic hopes, on the other hand, are located solely in Jesus Christ (*Salvator*).

[154]See Part 2.

[155]John Paul II, *CentesimusAnnus*, no. 25.

[156]Ibid.

[157]Thomas Aquinas clearly pointed to monarchy. Cf. Thomas Aquinas, *De Regno. . .*, p. 20.

[158]For example, the acceptance of democracy in *CentesimusAnnus* is conditional on the reservation that it should be understood as a regime founded on values and the proper concept of the human person.

[159]The Letter to Romans says: "for rulers hold no terror for those who do right, but for those who do wrong" (Rom 13:3), and "the one in authority is God's servant for your good" (Rom 13:4). The First Letter to Timothy adds that it enables living a godly and holy life (1 Tim 2:2). Similarly, St. Peter in his letters explains that the role of authorities is to "punish those who do wrong and to commend those who do right" (1 Pet 2:14). It seems that these descriptions can reasonably be considered as depicting an ideal model of power as intended by God, committed to internal and external peace. Even if, as noted by Joseph Ratzinger, "this may sound rather commonplace, (. . .) in reality it expresses an essentially moral standard: internal and external peace are possible only when the essential rights of man and of the community are respected and guaranteed." (J. Ratzinger, *Europe Today and Tomorrow: Addressing the Fundamental Issues.*).

and significance, and the source of its inherent legitimacy. Indeed, the common good embraces the sum of those conditions of the social life whereby men, families and associations more adequately and readily may attain their own perfection."[160]

Finally, it is worth noting that even though in its reflection on politics Christian theology focuses on anthropology, it is an anthropology that is doubly theological, so to speak. The expression "Give back to Caesar what is Caesar's and to God what is God's" in fact ultimately teaches about who man is and what his relationship is with God. We can clearly see this is we note the image analogy implied in the passage from St. Mark. The denarius bears the image of Caesar, which tells us the coin belongs to him. And what belongs to God? The answer is provided in the Book of Genesis which says that man as the only being was "created in the image and likeness of God" (Gen 1:26–27), and therefore he himself—man—is the bearer of *imago Dei*. The anthropological anchoring of the Christian theory of politics is possible because in it "God is part of the definition of man."[161] John Paul II writes in *Veritatis Splendor* that "only God can answer the question about the good, because he is the Good. But God has already given an answer to this question: he did so by creating man and ordering him with wisdom and love to his final end, through the law which is inscribed in his heart (cf. Rom 2:15), the 'natural law'" which allows him to distinguish between good and evil.

3.3.2   Capacity for Moral Knowledge and Law as the Foundation of State

As noted above, the Christian approach to politics is anchored in an anthropological premise: the belief that in his being created in the image and likeness of God, by his very nature, through his reason, man has a share in God's wisdom. With this share, he is capable of knowing objective good and of growing in his humanity by striving towards it. Thomas Aquinas noted: "the rational creature is subject to divine providence in the most excellent way, insofar as it partakes of a share of providence, being provident both for itself and for others. Thus it has a share of the Eternal Reason, whereby it has a natural inclination to its proper act and end. This participation of the eternal law in the rational creature is called natural law."[162]

It should be stressed that this participation does not necessary require faith in God. It results from the specific nature of the human being: it is within himself that man discovers "a natural inclination to just acts and goals," discovers attitudes and actions which correspond to his ontological condition or which are contrary to

---

[160]Second Vatican Council, *Pastoral Constitution on the Church in the Modern World, Gaudium et spes*, no. 74.

[161]O. Piotr Roztworowski OSB, *W szkole modlitwy*, 5th ed., Wydawnictwo Benedyktynów, Tyniec 2011, p. 15.

[162]Thomas Acquinas, *Summa Theologiae*, I-II, q. 91, a. 2.

it. Thus, he discovers within himself an inner law which is "natural" to him, inherent to the human condition and—as emphasized by St. Paul—characteristic also of pagans (cf. Rom 2:14–15). In slightly different terms, John Paul II says that natural law expresses "the dignity of the human person and lays the foundation for his fundamental rights and duties."[163]

Based on the above anthropological premise, the Church proclaims as the fundamental norm for the state the requirements of natural law which says that "good is to be done and pursued, and evil is to be avoided."[164] This precept is "the foundation on which all other principles of natural law are based, namely all commandments and prohibitions which practical reason naturally considers to be good for man."[165]

When trying to define the main principles of natural law, Thomas Aquinas points first to the desire, common to all living creatures, to preserve life and health, so that "whatever is a means of preserving human life, and of warding off its obstacles, belongs to the natural law." Secondly, Aquinas notes that "those things are said to belong to the natural law which nature has taught to all animals (. . .), such as sexual intercourse, education of offspring and so forth." Finally, "there is in man an inclination to good, according to the nature of his reason, which nature is proper to him: thus man has a natural inclination to know the truth about God, and to live in society: and in this respect, whatever pertains to this inclination belongs to the natural law; for instance, to shun ignorance, to avoid offending those among whom one has to live, and other such things regarding the above inclination."[166]

It is thus clear that natural law is not a closed collection of detailed norms, but expresses the moral sense inherent to human nature, which allows man to recognize the proper good in a specific situation: "there is in every man a natural inclination to act according to reason (. . .) [and thus] all acts of virtue are prescribed by the natural law."[167] Consequently, natural law does not determine man's actions. For even though it does provide the essential direction to his development, it "does not expressly define those actions which lead to man's development, or the contents of the state of being towards which he is supposed to strive."[168] Thus, there is much room for the exercise of man's free will in choosing a particular good.

Revisiting reflections on the political role of natural law, it should be noted that natural law is the proper point of reference for the law established in a political community. Since natural law is not definitive, it should not be expected in this context that any rules of positive law should be derived from it directly.[169] Just like in the case of man's decisions, many roads may lead to the fulfillment of natural law.

---

[163]John Paul II, *Veritatis splendor*, no. 51.

[164]Thomas Aquinas, *Summa Theologiae*, q. 94, a. 2.

[165]P. Mazurkiewicz, *Europeizacja. . .*, p. 237.

[166]Thomas Aquinas, *Summa Theologiae*, q. 94, a. 2.

[167]Ibid, q. 94. a. 3.

[168]M. Piechowiak, *Klasyczna koncepcja. . .*, p. 11.

[169]As pointed out by Mieczysław Krąpiec OP, natural law is formulated in analogous rules, which do not yield to a syllogistic deduction *sensu stricto*.

The point is more to verify positive norms in the light of principles resulting from natural law: to see whether particular regulations developed by human reason are based on the precepts of natural law, and do not contradict the judgment: "good ought to be done and evil is to be avoided" in any detailed aspect.[170] In other words, due to its positive dynamics (towards the good of man and his development) natural law does not definitively set the upper limit of man's actions, but clearly sets the lower limit which, when trespassed, results in man doing evil and contravening his very nature.

The discovery of the specificity of natural law, binding closely together the human and the divine dimensions, provides foundations for a secular politics which satisfies the requirement of giving back to God what is His in the deepest sense. In the political context, natural law understood in such terms makes it possible to establish ethical principles of the state, defining the framework of justice and rule of law. On the other hand, it plays a critical role by helping verify the non-contradictoriness of positive law and the judgment: "evil is to be avoided." Such a verification helps determine whether a particular norm is lawful, or whether it is a kind of decreed lawlessness.

3.3.3   Original Sin and the Place of Religion in a Political Community

It might seem that, in a sense, the reference to natural law makes religion superfluous in political space. Since reason recognizes the principles stemming from eternal law and adapts them to particular situations, religion as such may appear politically irrelevant. Christian anthropology has not lost sight of the original sin, however. Even though, as noted by Aquinas, "the natural law, in the abstract, can nowise be blotted out from men's hearts," it is nevertheless "blotted out in the case of a particular action, in so far as reason is hindered from applying the general principle to a particular point of practice, on account of concupiscence or some other passion, as stated above (...) by evil persuasions, just as in speculative matters errors occur in respect of necessary conclusions; or by vicious customs and corrupt habits, as among some men, theft, and even unnatural vices, as the Apostle states, were not esteemed sinful."[171] In other words, the original sin calls for a special place of religion in the Christian theory of politics.

Even though Christianity does not aspire to impose laws on the political community or create political agendas, it recognizes its essential significance for the space of politics. Characteristically, from the Christian perspective on politics, it is mainly the state that should be committed to providing space for the influence of religion. Since politics is based on the foundations of natural law, and "the

---

[170]Cf. P. Mazurkiewicz, *Europeizacja...*, p. 242.

[171]Thomas Aquinas, *Summa Theologiae*, q. 94, a. 6.

knowledge of this law inscribed on the heart of man increases with the progress of the moral conscience," then "the first duty for all, and particularly for those with public responsibility, must therefore be to promote the maturation of the moral conscience."[172] The Church is the only institution which is by its very nature in the service of human conscience. As noted by John Paul II, "the Church puts herself always and only at the service of conscience, helping it (..) not to swerve from the truth about the good of man, but rather, especially in more difficult questions, to attain the truth with certainty and to abide in it."[173] Consequently, the fact that moral truth available to every human being through conscience and expressed in natural law[174] is also contained in the Revelation received from God primarily provides a safeguard for the political community.

In light of the above, it becomes apparent why Christians, even though interested in the independence of the secular and the religious orders, are at the same time conscious that the teaching of the Holy Scripture "throws light on the order of human society," ensures that "the requirements of a society worthy of man are better perceived, deviations are corrected, the courage to work for what is good is reinforced,"[175] and utopian political projects are disabled.[176] This way, religion enters into a relationship with politics not so much on the level of political parties (which is treated as an autonomous sphere of "the secular"), but indirectly, by safeguarding the deposit of transcendental truth "in obedience to which man achieves his full identity."[177] This means, let us add, a critical role of religion on the one hand, and its formative role, on the other.

On the one hand, religion is seen as a factor which plays a purifying role with regard to political reason in its moral search, clarifying whenever necessary the leading moral principles of the political order. By proclaiming the truth about the transcendental dignity of the human person, it relativizes the political claims to undivided competence,[178] directly influencing the political life only on the level of fundamental ethical principles. This can be clearly seen in the contemporary social teaching of the Magisterium, focused on the basic principles of the social and political order.[179]

---

[172]Benedict XVI, *To the participants in the International Congress on natural moral law*, Clementine Hall, 12 February 2007.

[173]John Paul II, *Veritatis Splendor*, no. 64.

[174]As a side remark, the same perspective is adopted in the Universal Declaration of Human Rights. Cf. M. Piechowiak, *Filozofia praw człowieka*, KUL, Lublin 1999, pp. 96–100.

[175]John Paul II, *Centesimus Annus*, no. 25.

[176]Benedict XVI discusses this issue at length in the Encyclical *Spe Salvi*.

[177]John Paul II, *Centesimus Annus*, no. 44.

[178]George Weigel, *The Final Revolution: The Resistance Church and the Collapse of Communism*, Oxford University Press, 2003, p. 196.

[179]In this context, see for example the Encyclicals *Evangelium Vitae* and *CentesimusAnnus*. It should be emphasized, however, that often the statements essentially made by the Church on principles are construed as political statements, due to the expansion of the sphere influenced by politics into the area which theologians of politics consider to be metapolitical.

On the other hand, it is the primary task of the Church, as emphasized by Benedict XVI during his visit to the Lebanon, "to illumine and purify consciences and to make it clear that every person is an image of God (...) and we must treat the other as an image of God."[180] This entails laying ground for the development of a political system that is worthy of man, oriented towards the search for common good. In simple terms, the Church does this by forming people to choose good, to live the fullness of their humanity. In view of the "double citizenship" of every Christian, by educating righteous people, religion educates righteous citizens of the state. As noted by George Weigel in his comments on democracy, "Democratic politics is impossible, over the long haul, without democratic civility. And democratic civility is impossible without a virtuous people, confident of their own ability to choose wisely, and committed to protecting individual liberty amidst genuine pluralism while concurrently promoting the common good.".[181] Consequently, while existing "beside" the political community, the Church justly understands herself as "as a leaven and as a kind of soul for human society."[182]

* * *

The above analyses show that the anthropological premise represents a key aspect of the theology of politics, revealing a clearly outlined political anthropology also on the grounds of theology. This discovery appears to have two important dimensions. Firstly, in the methodological dimension, it shows that political anthropology may be discovered through a process of extraction, and therefore is not necessarily related to self-knowledge and identity within a subdiscipline. Secondly, in terms of content, it implicitly reveals a relationship between religious and secular thought. From the perspective of political thought, it is clear that the understanding of politics outlined above, as a prudent commitment to the common good founded on the belief in the existence of an objective and knowable good, the dignity of every human being, and the independence of the state and the Church, being in harmony with and developing essential aspects of the classical understanding of politics, is at the source of the best traditions of specifically European politics. Indeed, we may say, as noted by Piotr Mazurkiewicz, that "democracy understood as a regime which recognizes the equal dignity of every human being is genetically Christian. It has only appeared where there had already been a widespread belief that man is a being created 'in the image and likeness' of God."[183] This shows the meaning of political anthropology developed within theology for the "secular" thought of politics.

---

[180]*Interview of Benedict XVI with journalists during his flight to Lebanon*, September 14, 2012.

[181]George Weigel, *The Final Revolution: The Resistance Church and the Collapse of Communism*, Oxford University Press, 2003, p. 196.

[182]Second Vatican Council, *Pastoral Constitution on the Church in the Modern World, Gaudium et Spes*, no. 40.

[183]P. Mazurkiewicz, "Religia i aksjologiczne podstawy polityki", w: P. Burgoński, M. Gierycz, *Religia i polityka. Zarys problematyki*, Elipsa, Warszawa 2014, p. 212–213.

Chapter 4
Towards a Politological Approach to Political Anthropology

The analyses performed so far show, on the one hand, the relevance of the results of studies carried out in various approaches to political anthropology for political science. At the same time, they also prove that none of the approaches presented above fully answers the questions specific to political science. One could hardly expect—from the perspective of the research field of political science—that political anthropology be reduced to philosophical or even cultural anthropology. In fact, it should be noted that a significant portion of sources and data relevant in political analyses, both concerned with political thought and the political process, are not taken into account in the above-mentioned studies.

On the other hand, a review of political anthropologies which have developed in various disciplines shows that—even in the absence of an inner process of autonomization of its research problems—it is possible to separate by extraction an area of problems studied by political anthropology within a broader discipline of science. This seems noteworthy particularly in a situation when the anthropological question is an essential aspect of research conducted within its framework.

If analyses performed in Chap. 3 suggest it is reasonable to look for a politological approach to political anthropology, the analyses presented in Chap. 2 provide tools which help build a framework for a theory of political anthropology in the framework of political science. Since a politological approach must provide for an integration of the achievements of various political anthropologies relevant for political analyses, and take into account the importance of their tools in political studies, we should refer to the integrating model discussed above as a point of reference for the model of political anthropology we want to build here.

In the light of conclusions made in Chap. 2, the starting point for a political anthropology on the grounds of political science would be to define its specific approach to the anthropological problem which determines—by informing the research question—the way political anthropology is understood within its framework. It will then be necessary to elaborate on the approach, specific to political science, to scientific analysis (research perspective) in the context of its being used in anthropological studies. The last stage would be to identify areas and principles of

© Springer Nature Switzerland AG 2021
M. Gierycz, *European Dispute over the Concept of Man*, Contributions to Political Science, https://doi.org/10.1007/978-3-030-61520-8_4

integrating the subject matter and methodologies of political anthropologies existing within other disciplines in a political anthropology grounded in political science, that is, to create instrumentation for studies to be undertaken further on.

4.1   Studies in Political Science and the Anthropological Question

The scientific character of political studies does not raise any reasonable doubts today. As noted by Janusz Ruszkowski, in order for a separate discipline of knowledge to exist, three elements must appear: researchers and institutions, research methods and techniques, and a proper conceptual framework.[1] This list should perhaps be supplemented to include a separate subject matter of research, unless it is implicitly included in the conceptual framework. In any case, political science satisfies these criteria. Nevertheless, even though it has its specific methodological trait,[2] well-developed institutions and scientific community, as well as its own analytical categories, political sciences pose certain problems compared to other scientific disciplines both methodologically and in terms of their subject matter.[3]

4.1.1   The Subject Matter of Studies in Political Science

Problems related to identification of the subject matter of political science can be easily seen in its dictionary definitions. For example, the *Lexicon of Political Science* defines it as follows: "political science analyses political phenomena and processes, their interdependencies and consequences."[4] Similarly, the *Encyclopedia of Political Science* says that political science is "an empirical and nomological social science studying political phenomena and processes."[5] While there is no logical error in saying that political science is a science of political processes, it does seem to border on a tautology.[6] Ultimately, the question is: what phenomena and processes

---

[1]Janusz Ruszkowski, *Wstęp do studiów europejskich*, PWN, Warszawa 2007, p. 9.

[2]Cf. e.g. Franciszek Ryszka, *Nauka o polityce. Rozważania metodologiczne*, PWN, Warszawa 1984.

[3]In fact, some researchers claim that it is still looking for its identity—see e.g. Hanna Dubrzyńska, *Elementy teorii polityki*, Uniwersytet Gdański, Gdańsk 1998, p. 20.

[4]A. Antoszewski, *Politologia...*, p. 326.

[5]Z. Kantyka, *Politologia...*, p. 229.

[6]Imagine defining history as a science studying historical processes, or biology as a science studying biological phenomena.

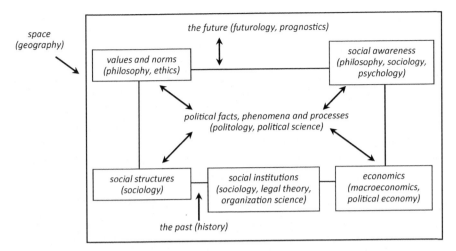

Fig. 4.1 Henryk Przybylski's Field of Politics Model. Source: Henryk Przybylski, *Politologia.* *Zarys problematyki*, 2nd extended edition, Wydawnictwo Naukowe Śląsk, Katowice-Warszawa 2004, p. 31

specifically are studied by political science; how is political reality distinct from social reality?[7] In other words: what is the field of study specific to political science?

The answer to this question has been sought in the theory of politics, by referring to the so-called "field of politics". Henryk Przybylski describes it as "the sphere of facts, phenomena and processes which are the product of existing social structures and economic relationships, whose development is influenced by social norms and values, the institutional and organizational structures of the society, as well as particular forms of social awareness which result in cooperation or power struggle over goods and values shared or rationed by public authorities."[8] This is schematically presented in Fig. 4.1.

Clearly, the idea of the field of politics as the area of studies in political science makes it much easier to understand its subject matter by presenting its relation to other areas of knowledge,[9] and the two-directional dynamics between the politic on the one hand, and the social, cultural, and economic on the other. In the context of the goals of the present study, it also reveals the natural relationship and relevance of philosophical, social and cultural reflection for political analyses. In terms of the theory of politics, it explains the relevance, noted in the previous chapters, of studies

---

[7]Cf. Dirk Berg-Schlosser, Theo Stammen, *Einführung in die Politikwissenschaft (Introduction to political science)*, 7.te Auflage, Verlag C.H. Beck, München 2003, p. 39.

[8]Henryk Przybylski, *Politologia. Zarys problematyki*, 2nd extendededition, Wydawnictwo Naukowe Śląsk, Katowice-Warszawa 2004, p. 30. Naturally, such a field of politics "feeds back to the condition of economics, social structures, social awareness, norms and values," etc. (ibid.).

[9]Even though the above diagram does not include the perspective of social anthropology, for example.

on politics performed within philosophy and cultural or theological anthropology for politological reflection.

Even though, as previously mentioned, the category of the field of political science helps understand its subject matter by revealing its relation to other areas of knowledge, it does not reduce the tautological potential of the definition of political sciences. According to the above diagram, political science studies the field of politics which is made up of political facts, phenomena and processes.[10] In fact, therefore, the existing definition is supplemented with one more category, just as underspecified as the previous ones.

This lack of definitive clarity reveals the problematic nature of the subject matter of political sciences.[11] This results from the ambiguity of the term "politics." This category appeared in Europe together with the first complete Latin translation of Aristotle's *Politics* by William of Moerbeke in the thirteenth century A.D.[12] It was subsequently included in reflections and theories of the system, to which Thomas Aquinas contributed his comments to Aristotle's *Politics*. In view of its genesis, in its primary definition referring to the classical tradition politics is understood as a normative and ontological concept. Consequently, as explained by Berg-Schlosser and Stammen, political analysis is not based solely on the examination of an empirically understood political reality, but on metaphysical studies: showing ways to the essential fulfillment of human existence. The concept of a "good life" is the central point of reference for political sciences, understood as one of the dimensions of practical philosophy.[13]

In this sense, Christian Schwaabe calls Aristotle "the creator of political sciences as an independent discipline."[14] The Stagirite's characteristic depiction of polis as the social order proper to man (*zoon politikon*) reveals the study of politics as a science most closely related to ethics—"the science of good and just actions of man" who can only "live a truly human and happy life"[15] in the polis. Ethics and politics come together here as the "science of man," making politics part of anthropology. As pointed out by Aristotle, "the student who is going to make a suitable investigation of the best form of constitution must necessarily decide first of all what is the most desirable mode of life. For while this is uncertain it is also bound to be uncertain what is the best constitution."[16] Politics is focused here on goods and values which the political order is supposed to serve as a condition of the "good life" of the people

---

[10]H. Przybylski, *Politologia. Zarys problematyki...*, p. 31.

[11]Cf. D. Berg-Schlosser, T. Stammen, *Einfuehrung...*, p. 23.

[12]Richard J. Regan, "Preface," in: Aquinas, *Commentary on Aristotle's Politics*, Hackett Publishing Company, Indianapolis, Cambridge 2007, p. vii.

[13]D. Berg-Schlosser, T. Stammen, *Einfuehrung...*, pp. 24–25.

[14]Christian Schwaabe, *Politische Theorie 1. Von Platon bis Locke*, 2., durchgesehene Auflage, Wilhelm Fink, Paderborn 2010, p. 50.

[15]Ibid., p. 51.

[16]Aristotole, *Politics*, Penguin Classics, 1981, 1323, p. 469.

who live in it.[17] In this sense, "political" means related to the circumstances of "good life," the "right order," or—in contemporary categories—the common good.[18] Authority is understood here as moral strength. Therefore, it "not only has the duty to establish laws, but also to establish just laws, i.e. such as correspond to man's dignity and the dictates of righteous reason."[19] In other words, anthropology is the key to political science. The anthropological problem: the question of who man is stands, in the classical approach to politics and political science, at the very heart of political studies. Politics in this sense has its own content, its substance— warranting a "good life," creating conditions for common good—which is what distinguishes it from other areas of social life.

While the political and the anthropological are closely related in the normative and ontological—or, better perhaps—substantial approach to politics, the situation becomes more complicated as newer definitions of the term are provided. To cite Berg-Scholosser and Stammen, three more key approaches to politics may be identified: the realistic one, the one based on the friend-enemy criterion, and the Marxist one. It appears they all ultimately refer, though in different ways, to a formal and functional concept of the politic.

Sources of the realistic approach may be sought in Antiquity in the thought of sophists, and in modern times in the writings of Hobbes, and particularly in Machiavelli, in whom—as pointed out by Pierre Manent—"modernity found an interpretation of itself that determined the orientation of the European mind, and hence of European political history."[20] By breaking with the belief that the essence of politics is to ensure order which is aimed at living "a good life," or, more broadly, with the focus on the ethical goals of politics, Machiavelli focuses his attention on political actions and their means—that is, on the formal dimension of the politic. Consequently, rather than ethos or participation, for both it is ultimately "power" that becomes the key category of politics.

This approach becomes endowed with particular meaning in modern times, with the development of thought in the categories of natural sciences. As has been rightly pointed out by Cardinal Joseph Ratzinger, in the course of the development since Francis Bacon's *Novum Organum* of so-called scientific rationalism, a reduction has occurred of "the rational" to "the experimentally demonstrable," relegating "moral-ity, just like religion (. . .) to the realm of the subjective."[21] Consequently, the fundamental political problem of classical philosophy is suspended in mid-air: no truly "good life" exists any more, there are only its subjective visions devised by

---

[17]D. Berg-Schlosser, T. Stammen, *Einführung. . .*, p. 25.

[18]Cf. Piotr Mazurkiewicz, "Polityka jako roztropna troska o dobro wspólne: koncepcja polityki w katolickiej nauce społecznej," in: Włodzimierz Wesołowski [ed.], *Koncepcje polityki*, Scholar, Warszawa 2009, pp. 98–126.

[19]Ibid., p. 109.

[20]Pierre Manent, *An intellectual history of liberalism,* Princeton University Press, Princeton 1994, p. 12.

[21]Joseph cld. Ratzinger, *A Turning Point for Europe?: The Church in the Modern World: Assessment and Forecast, Ignatius,* 2010, p. 37.

man. Concurring with this belief, the leading sociologist of politics of the early twentieth century, Vilfrido Pareto, considered metaphysical theories to be a "derivation," claiming that "a belief in 'natural rights,' in 'justice' or in 'law' is a kind of superstition or prejudice. None of them is a scientific concept, and hence none of them is rationally derived, rationally defensible, true or false."[22]

Since the politic no longer has any content, only its pure form remains, ultimately linking the concept of politics to the concept of violence. As pointed out by Max Weber, quoting Leo Trotsky for support, "in the final analysis the modern state can be defined only sociologically by the specific means that are peculiar to it, as to every political organization: namely, physical violence."[23] Consequently, in the realistic sense "politics" means the strife "for a share of power, or to influence the distribution of power, whether between states or between the groups of people contained within a state."[24] In other words, "power is made the central, if not the only, determinant of the politic."[25]

The relevance of this approach for contemporary political science is self-evident. It is not by coincidence that the *Lexicon of Political Science* says that "the essence of politics is power, particularly state power, a constitutive element of which is monopoly in the exercise of lawful—potential and real—coercion against individuals who do not respect authoritative decisions about the distribution of tangible and intangible goods."[26] In the same vein it is claimed that politics is "techniques, mechanisms, and not goals, values, ideals," stressing that "no politics can be done without the use of power."[27] Finally, David Easton notes that "the study of politics is concerned with understanding how authoritative decisions are made and executed for a society."[28] There are plenty of examples. They all clearly illustrate the formalism resulting from the new understanding of politics: the decisive factor is the possibility (tools, mechanics) to take decisions, in which a crucial role is played by power (coercion). The end to which this power is employed, i.e. the goal of political action, is not usually mentioned today as a defining element of politics. In fact, it is even suspicious, in a way. Some scholars see the specter of ideology in the very existence of a substance of politics.[29] Looking at the politic from the perspective of goals, according to Kenneth Minogue, "suffer[s] from the crucial difficulty of

---

[22]John H. Hallowell, *The Moral Foundation of Democracy*, Liberty Fund Inc., 2007, p. 9.

[23]According to Weber, in an address at Brest, Trotsky was supposed to say: "Every state is based on force." Max Weber, *The Vocation Lectures,* Hackett Publishing, 2004, p. 33.

[24]Ibid, p. 33.

[25]D. Berg-Schlosser, T. Satmmen, *Einführung...*, p. 27. Naturally, as the authors rightly point out, this assumption does not in fact make it possible to distinguish politics from other areas of social life, since power is understood here as a feature affecting all social relationships (ibid.).

[26]Leszek Sobkowiak, "Polityka," in: A. Antoszewski, R. Herbut, *Leksykon...*, p. 329.

[27]Marcin Król, *Słownik demokracji,* Res Publica, Warszawa 1991, p. 89.

[28]D. Easton, "An Approach to the Analysis of Political Systems," in: *World Politics*, 1957, vol. 9, No. 3, p. 383.

[29]Kenneth Minogue, *The Liberal Mind*, Liberty Fund, Indianapolis 2003, p. 80.

describing one brand of politics far better than other kinds of which we have some knowledge."[30]

The way of thinking characteristic of the realistic, or formal, in fact, concept of politics seems to have been carried to its ultimate conclusion in the famous saying of General Clausewitz[31] who saw in war the continuum of politics.[32] It also shows that a formal concept of politics *nolens volens* focuses on the issue of conflict. Such an approach is premised on the assumption that "politics occurs where people disagree about the distribution of goods, benefits or statuses, and have at least some procedures for the resolution of such disagreements."[33] It is not—unlike in the classics—a natural context and fulfillment of human life, warranting a "good life," but rather the effect of a particular antagonism.[34]

In this context, the theory of Carl Schmitt may be seen as a complement to the realistic, or formal, logic in viewing the politic.[35] It identifies the politic with an irremovable conflict between "us" and "them"—the politic becomes constituted a soon as we start looking at one another in the categories of friends and enemies.[36] "The political relationship—Schmitt says—expresses the utmost degree of opposition (to enemies) and union, agreement (with friends), the utmost degree of

---

[30]Ibid.

[31]Even though, as rightly pointed out by John Hoffman, politics is often portrayed as the opposite of military solutions. Cf. John Hoffman, *A Glossary of Political Theory,* Edinburgh University Press, Edinburgh 2008.

[32]As a side remark, it is worth noting that in the times of Clausewitz and after World War II, war was understood differently. As noted by Bertrand de Jouvenel, "[w]ar is not necessarily, has not always been, what we see it today. In the time of Napoleon only the men of military age were taken—and not all of them, for as a general rule the Emperor would call up only half a class. All the rest of the population were left, apart from having to pay war taxes of moderate size, to lead their normal lives." During the monarchy of Middle Ages, wars were necessarily limited in time, since the king could not count on his vassals for more than 40 days, and would not be able to pay an army over the long haul from his domain. Consequently, the Hundred Years War, for example, was a series of short campaigns, each paid for separately. Nevertheless, this does not mean that total war is not the logical consequence of the dynamics of approach to war in Europe. As noted by de Jouvenel, "if we arrange in chronological order the various wars which have for nearly a thousand years ravaged our Western World, one thing must strike us forcibly: that with each one there has been a steady rise in the coefficient of society's participation in it, and that the total war of today is only the logical end of an uninterrupted advance towards it." Bertrand de Jouvenel, *On Power. The Natural History of Its Growth,* Liberty Fund, Indianapolis 1993, p. 5.

[33]Lincoln Allison, "Politics," in: Iain McLean, Alistair Mcmillan [ed.], *The Concise Oxford Dictionary of Politics,* Oxford University Press, Oxford 2003, p. 423.

[34]Cf. Carl Schmitt, *The Concept of the Political,* translated by George Schwabb (expanded edition), The University of Chicago Press 2007.

[35]Essentially, this has also been noted by Berg-Schlosser and Stammen; they have not drawn any structural conclusions from this observation, however.

[36]As a side remark, it may be noted that Schmitt's theory is related to the concurrently developing sociological theories, including the fundamental theory of Ferdinand Tönnies who shows as the basic social fact the relationship of the familiar and the strange, and the related likes and dislikes, trust and mistrust. See Ferdinand Tönnies, *Community and Civil Society,* Cambridge University Press 2001.

dissociation and association. The division into us and them does not result directly from substantial disagreements over particular issues or differences between people (...), but when it appears, it is the decisive factor in defining the situation."[37] Politics has no substance of its own, then; it is a specific type of relationship which may develop on various subjective foundations: "the morally evil, aesthetically ugly, or economically damaging need not necessarily be the enemy; the morally good, aesthetically beautiful, and economically profitable need not necessarily become the friend in the specifically political sense of the word."[38] On the contrary, "the inherently objective nature and autonomy of the political becomes evident by virtue of its being able to treat, distinguish and comprehend the friend-enemy antithesis independently of other antitheses."[39]

It appears that Schmitt's theory reveals how the formal approach smoothly turns into a functional one. The definition of politics as the relationship between us and the enemy ultimately means that "the politicity of politics boils down to (...) the issue of safeguarding the social order and identifying anyone who might take action posing a threat to the state. (...) Without an enemy, there is no threat to order; and if the enemy poses a threat so great, then he must be existentially alien, and the conflict should be solved by way of direct confrontation rather than compromise."[40] In the context of our reflections here, this shows that in practice it is not possible to consistently understand the politic in formal terms.[41] Politics is always a politics "of something." Even if we focus our attention on the means employed, there is no avoiding the question about the ends they serve.

In this perspective, a "realistically" conceived politics seems to fulfill Thrasymachus' maxim: "The interest of the ruler and stronger, and the loss of the subject and servant."[42] For, ultimately—in the absence of other goals—the use of power serves the interest of those who use it. From the functional perspective, Lenin's claim, rooted in Marxism, that politics is the "class conflict" over power in the state is ultimately a functional variation of the friend-enemy model. Naturally, this is not the only possible "content filling" of the formal approach. As pointed out by John Hallowell, "if we are under the influence of Freudian psychology, we will be inclined to view political conflict as pathological in character and requiring the services of psychiatry to resolve it."[43] Finally, for a liberal, politics will be a

---

[37]Paweł Kaczorowski, *My i oni. Państwo jako jedność polityczna*, SGH, Warszawa 1998, p. 51.

[38]Carl Schmitt, *The Concept...*, p. 27.

[39]Ibid.

[40]Ryszard Skarżyński, *Od chaosu do ładu. Carl Schmitt i problem tego, co polityczne*, ISP PAN, Warszawa 1992, p. 121.

[41]Cf. Kenneth Minogue, *The liberal mind*, Liberty Fund, Indianapolis 2003, pp. 82–83.

[42]Plato, *The Republic*, translated by Benjamin Jowett, Neeland Media 2016, book I, p. 35.

[43]John Hallowell, *The Moral Foundation of Democracy*, Liberty Fund Inc., 2007, p. 90. In the same spirit, Harold D. Lasswell developed his vision of politics, claiming that "the preventive politics of the future will be intimately allied to general medicine, psychopathology, psychological psychology and related disciplines," H. D. Lasswell, *Psychopatology and Politics*, University of Chicago Press 1986, p. 203.

"peaceful resolution of conflict; a road leading to compromise, negotiation (. . .) the political relationship is a relationship between parties with a conflict of interest, but not to the extent that they would be forced to actually fight."[44] Without looking into other possible options, we may note, therefore, that the formal approach to politics, where the politic is understood as power, the realization of one's will, may evolve into various functional variants.

From the perspective of foundations that are being laid here for political anthropology, it seems important to ask whether the formal and functional approaches to the politic reduce the relevance of the anthropological question for political sciences. Clearly, the starting point in these theories is to negate the "true concept of man" and "the right social order"—always in quotation marks. As contended by Pareto, in the light of the "logical and experimental" method, all political and metaphysical theories, systems of ethics and philosophies prove to be mere verbal expressions of the dominant residual—[45] that is, manifestations of human irrationality and emotionality, forms of "wishful thinking" dominated by deception, lies and violence.[46]

Does the above worldview, clearly referring to the Machiavellian tradition,[47] make anthropology irrelevant for political sciences? Certainly, "Machiavelli's breakup with traditional political thinking is related to a deep-seated division between politics and morality."[48] The *novum* introduced by Machiavelli's works into the modern understanding of politics is therefore a turn in thinking about the politic: "if political action is not organized in view of a good (. . .) then all the goodness of the world belongs to the innocent passivity of those who ordinarily do not act in political terms."[49] Consequently, the division between morality and politics leads Machiavelli to concluding that in politics evil matters more than good.

The question whether the above standpoint may be considered anthropologically neutral appears to be a rhetorical one. As Irena and Julian Pańkow point out referring to Nederman, "at the basis of Machiavelli's political thought is his peculiar way of understanding man."[50] The famous, pessimistic diagnosis of the human condition found in Chap. XVII of *The Prince*[51] actually leads commentators to conclude that

---

[44]R. Skarżyński, *Od chaosu. . .*, p. 120.

[45]John Hallowell, *The Moral Foundation of Democracy*, Liberty Fund Inc., 2007, p. 2.

[46]Ibid., p. 13.

[47]Even if this is a simplification and a superficial reading of his work, we must agree with Pierre Manent when he says that in the case of an author of such a standing as Machiavelli, it is worth taking a closer look at this superficiality "because it is this surface that influenced men's minds (. . .) that contains, so to speak, the depth" P. Manent, *An Intellectual History of Liberalism*, p. 13.

[48]Ch. Schwaabe, *Politische Theorie 1. . .*, p. 107.

[49]P. Manent, *An Intellectual History of Liberalism*, p. 16.

[50]Irena Pańkow, Julian Pańkow, "Polityka jako sztuka skutecznego rządzenia: Niccolo Machiavelli," in: W. Wesołowski [ed.], *Koncepcje polityki. . .*, p. 131.

[51]As noted by Machiavelli: "because this is to be asserted in general of men, that they are ungrateful, fickle, false, cowardly, covetous, and as long as you succeed they are yours entirely; they will offer you their blood, property, life and children, as is said above, when the need is far

Machiavelli "persuades us to fix our attention exclusively, or almost exclusively, on pathologies."[52] For Machiavelli, Christian Schwaabe points out, man is no longer a *zoon politikon*, whose nature and essence fit into to the best *polis*, but first of all an "uncertainty factor,"[53] difficult to calculate, with respect to whom the ruler must employ various disciplining measures.

Machiavelli's anthropological standpoint is, naturally, much more complex than its popular reception,[54] but we are not interested in the details of his concept here, after all. From the perspective of this study, it is first of all important to see that "underlying every system of government there is some predominant conception of the nature of man and the meaning of human existence."[55] Suffice it to note that Schmitt's distinction between friend and enemy is a direct reference to Hobbes's anthropology presented in *Leviathan*. He says: "and therefore if any two men desire the same thing, which nevertheless they cannot both enjoy, they become enemies; and in the way to their End, (which is principally their own conservation, and sometimes their delectation only,) endeavour to destroy, or subdue one another."[56] Modern politics develops on the basis of a new anthropology. As David Lockwood rightly noted, "the step from Hobbes to Marx in this matter is a short one. The introduction of the division of labour transforms the war of all against all into the war of one class against another."[57] We will come back to this issue more extensively in the second part of this study.

At this point, it should be noted that due to the way politics is viewed in modernity, the anthropological premises of political concepts "more often than not (. . .) [*are*] implicit rather than explicit. But if not always explicit, [*they are*] always fundamental."[58] Consequently, the anthropological problem is by its very nature an essential element of analyses in political science, representing a more or less express background to political concepts, actions, and phenomena. It is not a coincidence that a one of recently published textbooks on political science emphasizes that "the point of reference in analyses performed in political science is the human person and his nature."[59] This shows a growing awareness that within the framework of political sciences there is not only room but also a need for a political anthropology which

---

distant; but when it approaches they turn against you." Machiavelli, *The Prince*, translated by W. K. Marriott, Dutton & Company 1908, chap. XVII.

[52]P. Manent, *An Intellectual History of Liberalism*, p. 13.

[53]Ch. Schwaabe, *Politische Theorie. . .*, p. 108.

[54]Cf. I. Pańkow, J. Pańkow, *Polityka jako sztuka skutecznego rządzenia. . .*

[55]John Hallowell, *The Moral Foundation of Democracy*, p. 89.

[56]Thomas Hobbes, *Leviathan, or The Matter, Form and Power of a Commonwealth Ecclesiastical and Civil*, Hackett Publishing Company, 1994, p. 75.

[57]David Lockwood, "Some Remarks on 'The Social System'". *The British Journal of Sociology*, 1956, 7(2), pp. 134–146.

[58]J. Hallowell, *The Moral Foundation of Democracy*, p. 89.

[59]Wojciech Jakubowski, Piotr Załęski, Łukasz Zamęcki, "Aspekty współczesnych badań politologicznych," in: Ids., *Nauka o polityce. Zarys koncepcji dyscypliny*, Akademia Humanistyczna im. A. Gieysztora w Pułtusku, Pułtusk 2013, p. 135.

reveals the views of human nature that, as has already been noted, often remain hidden behind political standpoints and actions. This need is particularly urgent seeing that, as has been pointed out, politics is moving away today from any explicitly embraced anthropology and the related normativity defining the goal of political action the way it once used to be defined—for example, by the category of common good. Even human rights, analyzed in the third part of this study, are sometimes deprived of their ontological foundations today.

Once the significance of the vision of man for the understanding of politics is recognized, the "anthropological problem" as examined by political anthropology on the grounds of political sciences may be distinguished from the way it is approached in the other disciplines of science discussed above. In contrast to the anthropology of politics developed within cultural anthropology, political science is interested in the central anthropological question of who man is, generally given little weight to in the ethnological tradition focused on communal issues. Unlike philosophical anthropology, however, which does consider the above question, the anthropological problem is of interest to political science not so much, or not mostly, as a metaphysical or existential problem, but one considered in the context of a particular political community. To be more precise, political science is interested in how man is understood in the context of ideological standpoints present in political life, in political actions, legal acts, as well as the "extra-source" knowledge, so important for the functioning and analysis of political processes.[60] Consequently, even if politics, "as understood in political science, is seen as the total of relationships and processes related to the problems of broadly conceived power and its functioning in political life,"[61] the anthropological problem remains a central one, determining the goals of actions pursued by those in power, the vision of social relationships, and thus the foundations of political action and the political community as such.

Political anthropology on the grounds of political science seems—primarily—to be not so much a normative or a descriptive discipline, but mostly a theoretical one. It helps discover, reconstruct, and name the vision of man shared by a particular community or inherent to a particular political standpoint,[62] to better understand and explain political processes and the direction of postulated social changes.[63] Its goal may be also, for example, to discover the relationship between the traditions of anthropological thought characteristic of a political community and its political activity. The source base of such an anthropology may, in the light of what has been established so far, be both ideological standpoints and specific political decisions or legal documents, and even observation of political life. Ultimately, each of

---

[60]H. Przybylski, *Politologia...*, pp. 19–20.

[61]Marek Jeziński, "Polityka," in: Marek Chmaj, Joanna Marszałek-Kawa, Wojciech Sokół [ed.], *Encyklopedia Wiedzy Politycznej*, Adam Marszałek (publ.), Toruń 2006, p. 255.

[62]As noted by Franciszek Ryszka, "theory is a thinking that leads from the knowledge to the concept of an object." Id., *Nauka o polityce. Rozważania metodologiczne*, PWN, Warszawa 1984, p. 357.

[63]Cf. Piotr Mazurkiewicz, "Wokół Karty Praw Podstawowych," *Chrześcijaństwo-Świat-Polityka* Nr 7, 2010, p. 29.

these sources may lead to discovering the anthropology embraced by a particular group or political community. If the goal and subject matter of studies in political anthropology within political science seems precise enough now to engage in research, the issue that needs to be considered is the question of methodology.

4.1.2   Methodological Currents in Political Studies

Andrzej Antoszewski says that political science "has not developed its own proper research method."[64] On the contrary, it embraces a "pluralism of subject matter, methodology and research techniques."[65] This does not mean a methodological confusion, however. The methods form distinctly distinguishable groups, established over subsequent periods in the development of political science. For the sake of order in our narration, let us take a look at the main methodological currents from the theoretical and historical perspective.[66]

Political sciences, developing in the context of sciences of the state, were initially influenced by the normative and institutional approach, as well as the historical perspective. "The historical emphasis produced detailed descriptions of the developments leading to political events and practices. Legalism, on the other hand, involved the study of constitutions and legal codes, while the concentration on institutions included studies of the powers and functions of political institutions such as legislatures, bureaucracies, and courts."[67] Consequently, "traditional political science focused on formal governments and their legally defined powers"[68] and has been criticized for not only failing to take into account informal political processes, but also for being essentially descriptive, without performing an explicatory function.[69] Its main sources were considered to be legal and historical documents (philosophical writings, chronicles, literature, etc.). In addition to the above,

---

[64]Andrzej Antoszewski, "Politologia," in: Andrzej Antoszewski, Ryszard Herbut [ed.], *Leksykon politologii*, atla 2, Wrocław 2004, p. 328.

[65]Jan Woleński, "Spór o status metodologiczny nauk o polityce," in: Kazimierz Opałek [ed.], *Metodologiczne i teoretyczne problemy nauk politycznych*, PWN, Warszawa 1975, p. 34.

[66]Naturally, the approach employed here is not the only possible one. Zbigniew Kantyka suggests that we distinguish "four orientations in approaching the problems of political science: (a) the social-behavioural one (empirical study of actual political behaviour of groups and individuals); (b) the philosophical-normative one (philosophy of politics, construction of political theories defining the criteria of political action and norms of relationships); (c) the historical one (political phenomena as seen over time); (d) the legal-institutional one (analysis of institutions and legal norms regulating the functioning of the state)." Z. Kantyka, *Politologia...*, p. 230.

[67]Janet Buttolph Johnson, Henry T, Reynolds and Jason D. Mycoff, *Political Science Research Methods*, CQ Press; 2015, p. 36.

[68]Ibid, p. 37. The authors say that "in the heyday of the traditional approach (...) when separate departments did appear, they were frequently called departments of government."

[69]Ibid, p. 37. This charge seems rather short of the mark, considering for example the theoretical achievements of Carl Schmitt or Max Weber.

primary, characteristics of political sciences, it should be noted that it was a normatively-oriented science. If, as proposed by Christian Schwaabe, Aristotle is considered to be the father of political science, it becomes obvious that it initially developed normative theories concerning the essence of politics, the goals of government and its best form.

Has political science understood in such terms had at its disposal any specific research instruments? As euphemistically stated by Marek Sobolewski, as regards the relationship between political science and history, attempts made by political scientists at describing history using a different instrumentation have brought "very mixed" results.[70] If we are looking for a contribution of political science to the study of recent history and the history of ideas, we will not find it in the area of developing their own instruments, but rather in paying attention to issues marginalized in traditional historiography. They may include, for example, "the study of the social makeup of representative bodies, particularly the parliament; study of the contents of journals and the political role of newspapers; study of the development of an organization of 'interests'; and study of the genesis of political parties."[71] Political science, when engaging in studies of the genesis of political institutions or ideologies, or looking for an empirical basis for generalization and verification of scientific laws, is "doomed" to methods and techniques characteristic of historical sciences. An analogous situation occurs as regards the relationship between political science and legal sciences and philosophy. Normative, exegetic analyses or hermeneutical tools are nowadays adapted to the studies of political science with the instruments of the sciences mentioned above.

The traditional approach to the study of politics was increasingly contested from the 1950s onwards. The main charge against such political studies was the fact that "verbal theories"[72] were not subjected to empirical verification, which—particularly in view of the development of sociology and cultural anthropology—made it appear as though political sciences were "methodologically backward." In the United States in the early 1960s a so-called "behavioral revolution" began which consisted, very briefly, in "shifting the emphasis from what political phenomena, processes or activities should look like to the actual political phenomena and processes themselves, and the actual behaviour of individuals in political situations."[73] In terms of the methodological paradigm, this was an empirical or positivist revolution in political sciences.

The beginning of behaviorism in political science was marked by the well-known study by Paul F. Lazarsfeld, Bernard Berelson and Hazel Gaudet on the electoral behavior of a selected group of the inhabitants of Erie County in Ontario State during

---

[70]Marek Sobolewski, "Historyczne ujęcie zjawisk politycznych," in: K. Opałek [ed.], *Metodologiczne...*, p. 242.

[71]M. Sobolewski, *Historyczne...*, p. 243.

[72]J. Buttolph, H. Reynolds, J. Mycloff, *Political Science Research Methods*, p. 67.

[73]Piotr Sztompka, "Analiza systemowa w naukach politycznych. Próba rekonstrukcji," in: Kazimierz Opałek [ed.], *Metodologiczne...*, pp. 80–81

the presidential elections of 1940.[74] Its goal was to examine the relationship between voting decisions and the education, social and economic status, age and sex of the voters. Even though reception of this approach was not immediate, over the following decades the role of political studies focused on political behavior radically increased. They relied mostly on statistics and methods of social studies characteristic of sociology, and partially also for cultural anthropology. Consequently, today the empirical method seems to define the main research current in political science,[75] with its multiple applications: starting from statistical analyses of "political activity, aimed at detecting patterns in voting behaviour or relationships between such behaviour and social background," through survey studies and opinion polls aimed at "identifying political views and standpoints," to laboratory experiments "which consist in simulating certain types of political relations, with the widest range of applications in the study of international relations."[76]

Almost from the very beginning, the empirical movement has been criticized as well, however. The triteness of its "allegedly scientific" conclusions was emphasized,[77] as well as ignorance of vital social problems and the fact that "in the effort to be scientific and precise (. . .) political science overlooks the moral and policy issues that make the discipline relevant to the real world;"[78] finally, the fact that "many predictions in political science and the explanations that underline them turn out to be weak or even false."[79] In opposition to the empirical standpoint, a constructivist paradigm has emerged and grown in significance since the end of the 1970s. Its advocates claim that "humans do not simply discover knowledge of the real world through neutral processes, such as experimentation or unbiased observation; rather, they *create* the reality they analyse. In other words (. . .) what people often assume to be pure facts are conditioned by the observers' perceptions, experiences, opinions, and similar mental states."[80] Consequently, scientific research (if this concept is still adequate, anyway[81]) carried out within this current is focused around the problem of interpretation, restoring normative reflection as an essential element in the study of politics. Methods derived from linguistic studies, such as critical analysis of

---

[74]The study was entitled *The People Choice*.

[75]J. Buttolph, H. Reynolds, J. Mycloff, *Political Science Research Methods*, p. 67.

[76]Hanna Dubrzyńska, *Elementy teorii polityki*, Uniwersytet Gdański, Gdańsk 1998, p. 19.

[77]See for example the spatial theory of voting by James Enelow and Melvin Hinch (*The Spatial Theory of Voting: An Introduction*, Cambridge University Press, New York 1984), claiming that people support those parties and candidates who are closest to them; or the—otherwise valuable— work by Jurg Steiner proving that sometimes politicians follow their conscience in making political decisions (cf. Juerg Steiner, *Conscience in Politics: An Empirical Investigation of Swiss Decision Cases*, Routledge, 1996). It appears that empirical studies often lead to a scientific "discovery" of obviousness.

[78]J. Buttolph, H. Reynolds, J. Mycloff, *Political Science Research Methods*, p. 38.

[79]Ibid., p. 29.

[80]Ibid., p. 40.

[81]Ultimately, constructionism seems to challenge the idea of an objective epistemology or theory of knowledge.

discourse or interpretative analysis, have also been adapted, therefore, for use in political studies.[82]

Considering the fact that none of the traditions of viewing political studies briefly discussed above has been ultimately refuted by any other,[83] it is important that we realize the accumulation of research methods employed in political science. And it should be stressed that these methods are derived from essentially disparate ways of understanding the goal of science itself. While the normative approach refers to classical reflection on politics related to philosophy, the empirical approach strives at providing political science with a scientific model characteristic of exact sciences. Allan Cribb describes this dispute as one between the positivist and the hermeneutic paradigm within the framework of political sciences. While the former aims at eliminating interpretations and value judgements from observation and description by radically separating the subject and object of research; the hermeneutic current underscores the distinction between the respective objects of exact and social sciences, emphasizing the multifaceted nature of human behavior.[84]

This methodological heterogeneity of political science reveals a heterogeneity of all political knowledge. Henryk Przybylski suggests that in this context we should talk of source based and non-source based political knowledge. While the former "comes from a source, a reliable document, direct observation of a phenomenon, material trace of an activity, etc. which can be described as concrete and verifiable," the latter represents "an interiorized knowledge which (...) by merging into all layers of our personality, speaks in us as 'the voice of conscience' when we evaluate a particular fact."[85]

In other words, the empiricism and nomology of political science are not necessarily directly related. The identification of patterns and formulation of general laws about the political reality is not related in political science only to empirically investigated processes (even though—naturally—empirical observation always plays an essential role), but also to the operation of ideas, values, worldviews, and the entire "soft" sphere of our reflection on social life. This means that in his studies, a political scientist may—depending on the range of problems—resort both to the instrumentation of social sciences and that of humanities.[86] From the point of view of this research into anthropology, this is both an advantage and a challenge.

---

[82]Cf. e.g. Dvora Yanow, *Conducting Interpretive Policy Analysis*, Sage Publications, Thousand Oaks, London, New Dehli 1999.

[83]Some researchers claim that what we are witnessing today is their "peaceful coexistence." Cf. J. Buttolph, H. Reynolds, J. Mycloff, *Political Science Research Methods*. . . .

[84]Alan Cribb, *Values and Comparative Politics. An introduction to the philosophy of political science*, Avebury, Adershot 1991, p. 18.

[85]H. Przybylski, *Politologia. Zarys problematyki*. . ., pp. 19–20.

[86]As a side remark, this issue seems to deserve broader reflection in the context of the classification of political sciences used in Poland. Considering the field of research proper to political science, the classification of political science as a social science appears to ignore its proper identity, almost as though a portion of its research field were amputated. It would be much more legitimate to consider political science as being on the border of social sciences and humanities.

On the one hand, the fact that "political science has few research methods of its own [and] usually adapts for its purposes those methods which are proper to other social sciences"[87] seems advantageous in that it offers a perspective of founding political anthropology on the grounds of political sciences. In relation to the integrating models described in Chap. 2, it opens opportunities for integrating within political sciences the research instrumentation which belongs to research traditions other than political sciences, such as cultural or philosophical anthropology. In the context of the research and theoretical reflections proposed in this study, the methodological heteronomy of political sciences seems to be an advantage.

On the other hand, however, the radically different problematization of research goals and methods in the hermeneutic and positivist current, to use Cribb's terminology, presents a considerable problem to anthropological studies. For if we recognize that political anthropology is interested not only in "hard facts" (concrete decisions, support structure, etc.), but first of all in the context of ideas related to political thought, values, etc., we stand before a serious methodological challenge: the need to integrate two research programs within political science. From the point of view of anthropological studies on the grounds of political sciences, the question is, therefore, what perspective can help combine these two approaches into a single model of political analysis.

4.2   System Perspective

Considering the multiplicity of methods, corresponding to the multiplicity of issues related to the problems of government, political science runs the immanent risk of disciplinary decompression, so to say, or of remaining a collection of various scientific sub-disciplines "dealing with the investigation of political phenomena and processes by employing their own peculiar views and methods."[88] This threat is not purely theoretical. As David Easton has pointed out, in the 1950s in the United States it was difficult to justify the existence of a theory of politics as part of political science at all.[89] He indicated that the fact "we can try to understand political life by viewing each of its aspects piecemeal"[90] is methodologically problematic. Naturally, "we can examine the operation of such institutions as political parties, interest groups, government, and voting; we can study the nature and consequences of such political practices as manipulation, propaganda, and violence; we can seek to reveal the structure within which these practices occur. By combining the results we

---

[87]Zbigniew Kantyka, "Politologia," in: *Encyklopedia politologii*, vol. 1, p. 230.

[88]Zbigniew Kantyka, "Nauki polityczne," in: Wojciech Sokół, Marek Żmigrodzki, *Encyklopedia politologii*, vol. 1: *Teorie polityki*, Zakamycze, Kraków 1999, p. 199.

[89]David Easton, *The Political System. An Inquiry Into the State of Political Science*, H. Wolff, New York 1959, p. IX.

[90]D. Easton, "An Approach . . .," p. 383.

can obtain a rough picture of what happens in any self-contained political unit."[91] Nevertheless, this way we cannot capture the whole, and "in combining these results (...) there is already implicit the notion that each part of the larger political canvas does not stand alone but is related to each other part."[92]

If Easton actually wanted to help "in some small way to win back for theory its proper and necessary place,"[93] he achieved much more. By suggesting that political life should be viewed as a system of interrelated activities, thus opening political analysis to the systemic paradigm (pluralist orientation), he in fact paved the way for an operationalization of the field of research in political sciences (pluralistic orientation), and ultimately its conversion into politology/political science (monistic orientation). Consequently, system analysis still remains "one of the most influential theoretical and methodological orientations in political analysis,"[94] making it possible to interpret not only various spheres of political life as "internally integrated wholes which are distinct from their environment and follow their proper rules,"[95] but also the relationship between political processes and other (cultural, economic, or social) phenomena.

When looking for a methodological approach, therefore, which would afford us a holistic perspective when studying political phenomena, it seems necessary to begin by referring to this paradigm. For if we want to understand the anthropological meaning of political decisions, we need to take into account both their sources or promotors, and the framework conditions which influenced them; and thus—at least to a certain extent—we need to look at European integration as a process taking place within a system.

4.2.1 The Essence of the System Approach

The essential step we need to take now is to establish what a system approach is. In political studies, it is sometimes treated as a theory, and at other times as a research technique. It does not appear to be either of the two, however.

As pointed out by Franciszek Ryszka, system analysis is more of a "methodological proposal rather than a complete theory."[96] The system here is a model or scheme which provides "a conceptual frame of reference within which the theory itself is to be built."[97] Therefore, "conceptual models represent a useful tool of research created at an initial stage in developing a theory, but may not be identified

---

[91] Ibid.

[92] Ibid.

[93] D. Easton, *The Political System...*, p. IX.

[94] Andrzej Chodubski, "Analiza polityczna," in: W. Sokół, M. Żmigrodzki, *Encyklopedia...*, p. 28.

[95] A. Chodubski, "Analiza polityczna," p. 28.

[96] F. Ryszka, *Nauka o polityce...*, p. 360.

[97] Barbara Krauz-Mozer, *Teorie polityki*, PWN, Warszawa 2005, p. 58.

with it."[98] The employment of a system perspective does not determine the form of the theory, therefore, but enables—by taking into account all essential elements and their interrelations—its construction. It delineates the area of legitimate searches and hypotheses.

The system approach is not a research method in the narrow sense of the word either. It should be considered as a methodological proposal in a broad sense: as a perspective highlighting elements of a system and the existence of relationships between them, which helps us observe a certain phenomenon. It does not, in itself, offer tools for investigating it, however. From this perspective, the methodological eclecticism of political science proves to be an advantage. From its diversified arsenal of research instruments, mostly borrowed from other humanistic and social studies, it may choose those techniques which are most useful in the investigation of an element or relationship perceived thanks to the system perspective.

The essence of the system approach is looking at political life as a system of interrelated activities,[99] which determines the way they can be analyzed. Firstly, "the very idea of a system suggests that we can separate political life from the rest of social activity, at least for analytical purposes, and examine it as though for the moment it were a self-contained entity surrounded by, but clearly distinguishable from, the environment or setting in which it operates."[100] The boundaries of this system are those activities which are directly related to the making of authoritative decisions, and the way in which it works is in part "a function of its response to the total social, biological, and physical environment."[101]

Secondly, "if we hold the system of political actions as a unit before our mind's eye, as it were, we can see that what keeps the system going are inputs of various kinds. These inputs are converted by the processes of the system into outputs and these, in turn, have consequences both for the system and for the environment in which the system exists."[102] The outputs of the system are decisions made by the government, and the inputs are demands which require an organized effort on the part of the society, and support.

Both forms of inputs (demands and support) are of two different kinds. Demands may be external or internal. They may come from the environment (i.e. other systems: the economic, cultural, social, or demographic one), or from the inside. Internally inspired inputs, according to Easton, have more direct consequences than

---

[98]Ibid.

[99]This is reasonable in view of the fact that, as explained by Easton, "these activities derive their relatedness or systemic ties from the fact that they all more or less influence the way in which authoritative decisions are formulated and executed for a society." D. Easton, "An Approach . . .," p. 384.

[100]Ibid.

[101]Ibid., p. 385.

[102]Ibid., p. 384.

Fig. 4.2 David Easton's Model of a Political System. Source: Easton D., "An Approach to the Analysis of Political Systems," in: World Politics, 1957, vol. 9, No.3, p. 384

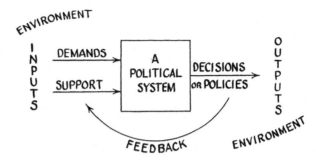

those coming from the outside.[103] Support, on the other hand, may consist either in actions "promoting the goals, interests, and actions of another person", or it may "involve not external observable acts, but those internal forms of behaviour we call orientations or states of mind."[104] It each case, support refers to one of three objects: the political community, the regime, or the government.

Support is generated by inputs of the system (political decisions) which he believes to constitute "a body of specific inducements for the members of a system to support that system,"[105] which are also of two kinds: positive and negative inducements, or rewards (satisfying some demands of its members), and sanctions.[106] In this sense, there is feedback between the inputs and the outputs of a system which ensures its balance, thus being a "vital mechanism in the life of a political system."[107] Easton's formula is expressed in the model shown in the diagram (Fig. 4.2).

This diagram, even though created by David Easton himself, is imperfect as it does not take into account all internal demands (all seem to be inspired by the environment), and in fact underestimates the process of politicization as a source of the system's stability, being an equivalent to the process of socialization in sociological analysis.[108] Moreover, it appears as though all support and demands were empirically measurable, while even the dual nature of the former makes it clear that they are not simply "observable". In this sense, the superficially model nature of the above diagram, suggestive of a positivist paradigm of scientificity, is somewhat misleading. To paraphrase Pierre Manent's opinion about Machiavelli, one might

---

[103]As an example of such demands, Easton mentions "changes in the process of recruitment of formal political leaders, or modifications of the way in which constitutions are amended." Ibid., pp. 388–389.

[104]Ibid., p. 390. Easton emphasizes here that "supportive states of mind are vital inputs for the operation and maintenance of a political system." (Ibid., p. 391).

[105]Ibid., p. 395.

[106]Easton also mentions a reserve of support, which is the support resulting from the conviction (mental state) that the government is generally favorable to the interests of its supporters, which allows it not to meet all of their demands.

[107]Ibid., p. 391.

[108]Cf. D. Easton, "An Approach ...," pp. 383–400.

say, however, that in the case of an author of Easton's standing, it may be worthwhile taking a look at this superficiality, as it has influenced and is still influencing human minds.

4.2.2 Applications of the System Approach in Political Science

It will not be an exaggeration to say that the understanding of system analysis which results from the above diagram corresponds to the typical way in which it is viewed in political studies. It is assumed that "system inputs are supports originating in the environment (e.g. payment of taxes, compliance) and demands (e.g. reduction of unemployment),"[109] and thus internal and external elements are integrated as system inputs. For example, in one study on the European Parliament system, inputs include "measures available to Polish Members of the Parliament", while bodies of the Parliament, the procedures and mechanism they employ are treated as the inside of the system.[110] In this way, Members of the Parliament—who are undoubtedly part of the system of the European Parliament—were placed outside of it, as carriers of "inputs" into the system.

The above approach is justified to the extent that, as pointed out by Anatol Rapoport, the system approach "places no restrictions on the sort of entities which can be taken as the 'elements' of the system. (. . .) Nor is any restriction placed on the sort of relations which can obtain among the elements. The only restrictions implied by the requirement of rigor is that both the elements and the relations are unambiguously specifiable."[111] Consequently, meso- and micro-level system analyses prevailing in political studies view the political system as the environment of the sub-system under investigation. This way, however, the research field of political science becomes narrowed down to its core. All that which is its actual environment, and which is therefore qualitatively different from the system itself, is no longer included in the researcher's perspective. This politological reduction results in an explicitly behavioral orientation of system analysis. In contemporary political science, it is viewed as an approach which may be adequately "applied to the knowledge of so-called hard problems: institutions, social organization or structure, but is

---

[109]Waldemar Żebrowski, *Badanie polityki. Ogniwa procesu badawczego na studiach politologicznych*, INP UWM, Olsztyn 2012, p. 30.

[110]Adam Szymański, "Systemowe podejście w badaniach europejskich," in: Wojciech Jakubowski, Konstanty Adam Wojtaszczyk, *Studia europejskie. Zagadnienia metodologiczne*, WAiP, Warszawa 2010, p. 176.

[111]Anatol Rapoport, "Some System Approaches to Political Theory," in: David Easton [ed.], *Varieties of Political Theory*, Prentice-Hall, Englewood Cliffs 1966, p. 130.

not convincing when applied to the study of 'soft' problems: systems of beliefs, meanings, norms and rules, forms of discourse, collective mind, etc."[112]

Indeed, a narrowly understood system analysis, even if it provides for subsequent stages of the political process—and in this sense corresponds to this research project—seems to have nothing in common with anthropological research. If, as we have concluded above, anthropological standpoints are implicitly contained in political standpoints, related to the cultural context in which a particular political discourse is present, and define the frameworks of the decision-making process, they can hardly be simply "observed." It is even more difficult to understand why they are what they are, or why some standpoints dominate over others. We may thus say that system analysis does not provide sufficient tools to—to use the language of hermeneutics—understand the observed phenomena.

Finally, it should be noted that the European Union is, on the whole, a difficult area for a classic system analysis. While inputs in a typical political system are largely related to social activity (including a society's economic and cultural system, etc.), the influence of particular societies on the EU political system is generally negligible. If in elections to the only institution elected by European societies, the European Parliament, in only 8 out of the 28 member states voter turnout exceeded 50%,[113] and in half of them did not even reach 40%,[114] then—even setting aside the fundamental issue of the absence of a European *demos*—the society can hardly be considered a real source of inputs into the system. A formal approach could be adopted, and initiatives of the Commission or of parliamentary groups (in the case of the political standpoints of the EP) could be considered as such a source. The problem with this approach, however, is that only 6%, approximately, of all legislative proposals have its source in an initiative of the Commission as such. A radical "majority of the submitted projects were a response to various demands and appeals from the outside, including lobbying groups and organizations."[115] An informal approach would be even more problematic, however, as the search for sources of proposals would begin to look very much like detective work.[116] We will come back to this issue further on in this chapter.

---

[112]A. Chodubski, *Analiza...*, p. 28.

[113]Moreover, the three member states where voter turnout was the highest (above 75%) are small: Belgium, Luxembourg and Malta https://www.europarl.europa.eu/elections2014-results/en/turnout.html [15.03.2020].

[114]"Record-holders" did not even achieve a turnout of 20%: in Slovakia it was 13%, and in the Czech Republic 18%; in Poland it was just below 24%. https://www.europarl.europa.eu/elections2014-results/en/turnout.html [15.03.2020].

[115]*Lobbing a instytucje UE*, http://www.europedirect-bydgoszcz.byd.pl/index.php?id=244 [30.03.2016].

[116]The interest groups standing behind a particular legislative proposal need to be identified, which is not always possible. Taking into account the fact that "Commission officials rely heavily on (...) expert support, since they do not have sufficient knowledge (...), [and] lobbyists form part of expert groups or supply the required expert opinions, analyses," proposals developed by the Committee are not simply the effect of "the efforts of an interest group or an individual lobbyist, but the

If the empirical and functional approach to the system method prevailing in political science, while being legitimate, does not capture the complexity of political processes, this is due to the fact that it always remains, so to say, on their "surface". It prevents their complete understanding, particularly as regards the anthropological problem we are interested in. In this context, Robert Esposito points to the deficit of depth and substance in the language of political science.[117] Just like Simone Weil, who actually claimed that "on inspection, almost all the words and phrases from our political vocabulary turn out to be hollow."[118] Let us take for example the contents of such terms as non-discrimination, sovereignty, democracy, tolerance, etc. and ask the following questions: what anthropological content is expressed today by anti-discrimination directives? What vision of man and political community do they imply? Who pushes them through, and why? Who objects to them, and why? And, finally: why does the political system function according to a particular set of rules?

A political system is more than just the issue of an *ad hoc* majority and its demands or expressions of support. Both the form of the system and its inputs and outputs are much more deeply rooted in the ways of thinking and understanding the world prevailing in a given culture, including the key aspect of "pre-judgments" concerning man. A system analysis on the grounds of political science, if it is to be of any use in analyses of anthropological standpoints, needs not only analytic breadth, but analytic depth as well. It must take into account the specific nature of the research field of political science.

4.3 Towards In-Depth System Analysis

It might appear that the empirical and functional understanding of the system method is fully compatible with the methodological orientation of David Easton himself, who may be considered a representative of the empirical revolution in political science. Nevertheless, the situation is not as obvious as it might appear. It is true that—from the vantage point of Eastonian studies—a broadly understood behavioral perspective is fully substantiated. Still, Easton's theory also has the great potential—

---

outcome of a number of analyses and standpoints." http://www.europedirect-bydgoszcz.byd.pl/index.php?id=244 [30.03.2016].

[117]Roberto Esposito, *Terms of the Political: Community, Immunity, Biopolitics*, translated by R. N. Welch, Fordham University Press 2013, p. 47.Further on he points out that even though "[e]very political concept has an illuminated part that is immediately visible, [it also has] a dark zone, a cone of shade from which, only through contrast, such light bursts forth," which cannot be discovered by typical analytical reflection: "This is the case because, while the manifest meaning of political concepts is always univocal, monolinear, and self-enclosed, their underlying sense is more complex, often contradictory, and capable of containing reciprocally opposing elements." (Ibid., p. 48).

[118]Simone Weil, "The Power of Words," in: id., *An Anthology*, edited and introduced by Siân Miles, Weidenfeld & Nicolson, New York 1986, p. 230.

which seems not to have been fully taken advantage of—of carrying out an in-depth analysis of politics.

4.3.1   Culture in System Analysis

In the above context, we may wish to consider the approach to culture and its role in the area of politics presented by David Easton. He pointed out that "the members of every society act within the framework of an ongoing culture that shapes their general goals, specific objectives, and the procedures that the members feel ought to be used."[119] He emphasized that "the typical demands that will find their way into the political process will concern the matters in conflict that are labeled important by the culture. For this reason we cannot hope to understand the nature of the demands presenting themselves for political settlement unless we are ready to explore systematically and intensively their connection with the culture."[120] This reflection points not only to the possibility, but in fact to the indispensability of an in-depth analysis if the system model is to be applied properly. Furthermore, analyzing the process of politicization—not represented in the above diagram—as an important factor consolidating the political system, the author of *The Political System* underlined the fact that "the various political myths, doctrines, and philosophies transmit to each generation a particular interpretation of the goals and norms,"[121] providing the foundations which determine the appropriate or expected behavior in specific political situations.

   The above observation—let us make it clear—is not some kind of a research directive detached from the system approach, and added for no apparent reason to reflections on the political system. On the contrary, it is consistent with the entire logic of systemic thinking in social science, which assumes that "the regularity, or patterning, of interaction becomes possible through the existence of norms which control the behaviour of the actors. (...) Indeed, a stabilized social system is one in which behaviour is regulated in this way and, as such, is a major point of reference for the sociological analysis of the dynamics of social systems."[122] Social order is possible thanks to a normative order, which—even recognizing the legitimacy of Lockwood's criticism of Parsons[123]—unless it is the only variable, represents,

---

[119]D. Easton, "An Approach...," p. 388.

[120]Ibid.

[121]Ibid., p. 399.

[122]D. Lockwood, "Some Remarks on The Social System", *The British Journal of Sociology,* 1956:7 (2), p. 135.

[123]Talcott Parsons distinguished between three subsystems of the environment, resulting from the functionalist approach: economy and technology (the function of adaptation); family (the function of pattern maintenance); culture, religion, art (the function of integration) As quoted in: P. Sztompka, "Analiza systemowa w naukach politycznych...", p. 96.

together with the social stratum, one of the two key ones.[124] Easton was fully aware of this. He emphasized that "it is essential for the viability of an orderly political system that the members of the system have some common basic expectations with regard to the standards that are to be used in making political evaluations, to the way people will feel about various political matters, and to the way members of the system will perceive and interpret political phenomena."[125]

Once we realize the meaning of normative standards, we are able to ask the anthropological questions we are interested in. One might say that the accepted norms, including "the most important are moral standards,"[126] ultimately represent the social, or political answers to anthropological questions.[127] In this sense, system analysis requires depth—to uncover the sources and possible trajectories of political thought and action, thus outlining the field of political anthropology. At the same time, one must admit that in Easton's model the issue of accounting for normative standards has not been operationalized, and remains more a theoretical directive than an instrument of research praxis.[128] In other words, the point is to take the theoretically recognized role of the surroundings of the political system seriously as an environment exerting fundamental influence on its functioning. Theoretically, the system model is premised on this assumption. In the practice of political studies—as has been demonstrated above—the environment and its role are considerably restricted by a "politological reduction" that focuses on intra-systemic inputs, or applies the system model to micro-level and meso-level system analyses, where the problem under investigation is merely a section of the broader political system, which thus becomes the environment for the political sub-system concerned.

This practical reduction of the role of the environment comes as no surprise. The above-mentioned problem with the operationalization of in-depth system analysis seems to arise from the temporal incompatibility of the cultural and political context. Referring to the theoretical work of Fernand Breudel, we may note that there are "at least three planes. One, which we may call A, is that of traditional history, habitual narrative, hurrying from one event to the next like a chronicler of old or a reporter of today (...). A second plane—B—is that of episodes, each taken as a whole: Romanticism, the French Revolution, the Industrial Revolution (...). They can be regarded as events of long duration, stripped of superfluous detail. A third plane—C—transcends these events: it considers only phenomena that can be measured over a century or more. (...) On this last level (...) civilizations (...) reveal their longevity, their permanent features, their structures—their almost abstract but yet

---

[124]Cf. D. Lockwood, "Some Remarks...".

[125]D. Easton, "An Approach...", p. 398.

[126]D. Lockwood, "Some Remarks..." ..., p. 135.

[127]As noted by Rev. Józef Tischner, ethics is "a science of the 'human score' (...), a theory of man." *Etyka wartości i nadziei...*, pp. 13–15.

[128]Piotr Sztompka points out that Easton's classification of the environment "lacks any explicit theoretical basis; it does not result from any general assumptions, but is developed on an *ad hoc* basis." Id., "Analiza systemowa w naukach politycznych"..., p. 95.

essential diagrammatic form."[129] The model of system analysis prevailing in political science is concerned with short duration: that of political processes happening "right now", the so-called events history. The cultural context of key importance—according to Easton himself—for understanding these processes is the dimension of long-term duration, revealing fundamental structures and thinking patterns delineating its trajectories in the short term.

Consequently, in-depth political analysis should strive towards uncovering the relationship between two levels of time: political events studied in the short-term perspective, and transformations in ideas and ways of thinking which determine the standards of value-judgments and norms defining the structures of institutional operation. In this perspective, analysis of political processes should take into account the fact that "the conscious policies of men and governments are (...) deductions from our most basic ideas of human destiny, and they have a great, though not unobstructed, power to determine our course."[130] This is fully consistent with the system approach, where "the environment is everything that remains in relevant causal relations with the system."[131] Consequently, when looking for ways to capture the view of man characteristic of a particular political system, its inside, its outputs, and its inputs, political behaviors must be seen as deeply related to civilizational, cultural, mental and religious transformations.

4.3.2 The Methodological Perspective and Time Frame

The above general comments on the methodological perspective need to be further elaborated in the context of our studies concerning the European dispute over the vision of man. In the context of the research goal which is to reconstruct the sources and ways of thinking about man characteristic of European integration, reflected both in primary legislation and in the activity of EU institutions, it seems particularly reasonable to depict the relationship between the above-mentioned levels of duration (long and short). All in all, the EU is to a large degree a political embodiment of European cultural formation. The anthropological disputes present in it today can hardly be understood without referring to the ideological disputes which have been around at least since the Enlightenment. If the thesis to be verified is the claim that the Union encompasses several co-existing anthropological concepts—some based on an anthropology which embraces a holistic definition of the concept of man and claims exclusivity, and some which do not refer to a holistic concept of man—then their accurate identification (and thus, understanding) requires a deeper analysis, one that reaches below the surface of historical events.

---

[129]Fernand Breudel, *A History of Civilizations*, Penguin Books, 1995, p. 34.

[130]Richard M. Weaver, *Ideas Have Consequences*, University of Chicago Press, Chicago and London 1984, p. 3.

[131]P. Sztompka, "Analiza systemowa w naukach politycznych...", p. 94.

The main purpose of referring to long duration is to identify structuralizing norms, in this case models of or approaches to man characteristic of the Western political tradition, defining the possible trajectories of political standpoints in anthropology within the EU, including its constitutive identity. Identification of these models will help understand the anthropological standpoints which are usually only implied, and thus not necessarily consistently or completely presented in political discourse. Indeed, this may turn out to be a condition for perceiving and identifying those standpoints which—as demonstrated by the culturally-oriented anthropology of politics—may be obscured in the political discourse, just like other ideologically relevant categories, by a technocratic and efficiency-based jargon.[132]

Generally, taking into account the long time span in system analysis means focusing not only and not exclusively on the ongoing political process, but also on its cultural and ideological context, which helps understand it while at the same time restoring depth to political analysis. The point would therefore be to reinstate the real role of the environment in system analysis—in this case, the cultural and ideological context in whose light the inside of the system along with its inputs and outputs should be analyzed. Consequently, research questions should not only be concerned with what anthropological concepts are reflected in EU legislation and politics, but also how they are embedded in the European tradition of thinking about man. This latter question, let us stress once again, not only provides depth to the answer given to the former, but seems to make it possible at all in the first place.

The thesis, goal, research question and methodological perspective outlined above suggest two main stages of this research project. The first stage involves examination of the cultural environment of the system. The second stage—relying on the findings made in the first stage—is focused on the anthropological solutions adopted in the EU political process.

The first stage of research will thus consist in a study of ideas and be concerned with the anthropological models in European thought which can be observed from the perspective of long duration. The primary goal of this part of the study will be to identify the sources of the dispute over the vision of man, to reveal the key issues of this dispute, and to operationalize the categories which may be used to describe it. It will therefore consist in singling out and operationalizing the approaches to the concept of man characteristic of European political reflection. This will require constructing a typology of anthropological models present in European traditions of ideas, and outlining the core anthropological problems related to the political order. In the course of studies, the theoretical claim will be verified about the existence in the ideological tradition of Europe of an anthropology which offers a holistic concept of man and which claims exclusivity, and of anthropologies which approach the problem of man differently. In this study, they will be referred to as constrained and unconstrained anthropologies.

---

[132]Cf. Chap. 3. In the EU context, this issue seems to be of particular significance.

The second stage of the study will be concerned with the anthropological solutions adopted within the EU political system. The starting point here will be defining the area of politics in which the anthropological tensions characteristic of late modernity, observed in the analysis of ideas, are present most emphatically. As will be demonstrated, they are especially discernible in the area of morality policy, which will be discussed in the chapter opening the third part of this book. Consequently, further analyses of the anthropological dispute will focus on this problem area.

The analyses performed in the second stage, in line with the logic of system analysis, will be focused—on the one hand—on an anthropological analysis of system frameworks, i.e. the legal circumstances of the intra-systemic conversion of anthropologically relevant system inputs into political decisions; and on the other hand—on an anthropological analysis of system inputs and outputs, as well as the process of conversion itself. Since the goal of the study is to answer the question about the Union's anthropological orientation, particularly important from the perspective of this research project are the "outputs," i.e. the decisions made by its key institutions: the European Commission, European Parliament, Council of the European Union, the Court of Justice of the European Union, and possibly also other EU agendas, particularly relevant for the EU approach to the core problems of morality policy. They will also be the main focus in analyzing the language and objectives of political documents. In relation to the above-mentioned distancing of EU institutions from the citizens who—other than the European civic initiative—have no direct say about the direction EU politics, and the exclusive initiative of the European Commission which often makes it difficult to prove the "primary" initiators of a particular legal or political solution coming from lobbying communities, proposals for actions to be taken by the Commission, in particular legislative proposals, will be treated in this study as system inputs, so as to enable tracking the process of intra-systemic conversion. Nevertheless, in the course of case studies, the role of inter-institutional and external lobbying will be presented as well, together will the approach to civic initiative in the area of morality policy.

Studies performed in the second part could be based either on the black-box or the transparent-box model.[133] Since in-depth system analysis helps to reveal the relationships between the system and the environment, the black box perspective seems to be most natural. Nevertheless, taking into account the anthropological dimension of the inside of the system and its impact on the conversion process, an analysis of inputs and outputs must show the practical meaning of anthropological solutions adopted in primary legislation for the decisions being made. In this sense, the "box" may not be fully obscured, even if—due to the massive volume of documentation—it cannot be made fully transparent. We should, perhaps, talk of a "diaphanous box"

---

[133]The first consists in "focusing on the relationships between the system and the environment, on the system's behaviour as a whole in the environment, without analysing the intra-systemic mechanisms which this behaviour stems from;" the other enables looking into "the inside of the political system in the course of its operation, as inputs are being transformed (converted) into outputs." P. Sztompka, "Analiza systemowa w naukach politycznych"..., p. 100.

which allows us to capture some elements of system conversion. To ensure reliability of conclusions, analyses in the second stage will be performed in line with the grounded theory, gradually saturating the theoretical claims in the course of subsequent reveals of the "box."

In order to engage in-depth system analysis which requires integration of the long and short duration perspectives, it is necessary to define the timeframe in which analyses are to be performed. As regards short duration, the period of interest is the time after the European Union was formed as a political organism. There are three possible caesuras to consider. The year 1992, when the Union was formed; the year 2000, when its constitutional framework (Charter of Fundamental Rights) was established; and the year 2007, when the EU was constituted as a legally and internationally independent being in a form which—as of today—may be considered final. It seems reasonable to set the short duration timeframe for the period after 2000, i.e. when the terms of the system's functioning were conclusively established. The end of the studied period has been set as December 31, 2016. This date is not content-based, but functional, connected with moment of performing the study and time-frame of the grant provided by National Center of Science. Nonetheless, it also provides insight into nearly two last decades of European integration, what seems to be long enough to note the anthropological dynamic of the EU's policy. Naturally, the adopted caesura does not mean that the studies may not, in justified cases, take into account the genesis of the anthropological solutions reflected in the legislation and practice of the EU.

English edition appears 3 years after Polish one. It is, on the one hand, too short timescale to make a full update of the book; on the other, some not resolved in 2016 issues, got in the meantime solution as well as some described processes developed. Consequently, apart from obvious time adjustment, I decided to develop third part of the book in two ways: quantitative data presented in Chap. 11 cover last full two decades (so the period till December 31, 2019), and, where it was needed, I signalize development of presented cases after December 31, 2016.

It seems more problematic to define the time span of long duration. Breudel's paradigm in the part encompassing the long time span perspective refers to ages-long processes and, in terms of plane B, to decades. It appears that in the context of research into the European anthropological discourse, it would be necessary to mediate, so to say, between these two perspectives. In the context of this research project, it seems reasonable to adapt the long time span to encompass the period from the beginning of modernity (seventeenth/eighteenth century) until the present, since it is this period that has been marked by an unprecedented acceleration of civilizational changes. It will allow us to identify the main currents of anthropological thought relevant for modernity. Nonetheless, as Enlightenment started a dispute with classical and Christian philosophical thought, rooted in antiquity, to understand the novelty of modern currents of anthropological thought, one must refer to ideas removed further in time, yet relevant to today's anthropological discourse.

Summing up, we may say that in-depth system analysis is an attempt to take into account, within the now prevailing research current of political science, its initial epistemological orientation,[134] while having regard—as will be discussed further on—to certain research techniques developed on the grounds of constructivism.[135] It thus complements the empirically oriented system approach with the ideological and cultural dimension, which—on the one hand—is fully substantiated in the context of Easton's theory of political system, while on the other helps restore a desirable depth to political analyses. Finally, in the context of this research project, it founds its methodological framework.

4.3.3   Research Methodology

Once the approach of political science to the anthropological problem has been identified, and a methodological perspective rooted in political science, which we have called in-depth system analysis, has been developed, we are now able—in terms of research methodology—to creatively integrate the instrumentation of the cultural and philosophical/theological anthropology in order to decipher the visions of man reflected in the politics of a particular community or group, and their social consequences.

First, it should be noted that in relation to the goal and the two stages of our studies, they need to be based on two, essentially different, types of sources. While in the first stage, research must be based on the works of classic political thinkers and studies on political thought and political philosophy, in the second stage the sources will mostly consist of documents—an array of legal and political acts, expert opinions, reports and stenographic records of institutional activities, etc., their scientific analyses and discussions, as well as interviews with actors of public life as an auxiliary source.

4.3.3.1   Research Techniques of the Anthropological Dimension of Political Ideas

In relation to the sources and research goal of the first stage, of particular importance will be the hermeneutic research method, discussed at length in Chap. 3, often used together with the phenomenological method within the framework of philosophical anthropology. The way it is employed in this study requires one comment, however.

In Chap. 3 it was mentioned that just as political thought does not satisfy the strict criteria of a philosophy of politics, so political anthropology in the politological approach is not the same as philosophical anthropology even with regard to research into the works of philosophers of politics. The latter—as previously explained—

---

[134]Whether we derive it—like Schwaabe—from Aristotle, or from the works of twentieth century theoreticians like Carl Schmitt.

[135]Without endorsing the philosophy of science entailed in this approach, however.

involves taking a holistic look at man within the framework of a systematic intellectual reflection, while the former is concerned with discovering the visions of man inherent to works, each displaying a different level of systematization, of philosophers, thinkers, or political actors of key importance to a particular culture.[136] In the case of philosophical anthropology, the research work is creative in the strict sense of the word; it is aimed—by employing the phenomenological method and the related reduction—at "reaching to the core," and offering "not only a view, but an insight." In the case of political anthropology, the situation is different. Its role is theoretical, and therefore to some degree reconstructive and systematic, looking to understand the observed phenomena. Naturally, also here the basic interpretive aim is to "capture the idea of the text... through in-depth study and repeated analyses in order to extract from the text its riches and its multiple meanings;"[137] nevertheless, one could hardly agree that "understanding a text in this research perspective does not consist so much in revealing multiple layers of meaning, but rather in capturing the sense of the whole through intuitive insight."[138] In other words, while in philosophical anthropology the very experience of man is the starting point of the process of understanding,[139] in anthropology developed on the grounds of political science the starting point is some record of this understanding, its interpretation, sometimes implicitly present in the concept of politics embraced by the author. Consequently, a particular role seems to be played by the hermeneutic method, taking precedence over the phenomenological method.

Hermeneutics, as has been pointed out by Wilhelm Dilthey, is a theory of the art of interpretation of written artifacts. This knowledge is obtained through construction, i.e. interpretation. This is clearly the aftermath of the exegetic tradition. Referring to one of the most outstanding Polish philosophers whose reflection focused on the anthropological research program, the understanding of hermeneutics adopted here would thus consist in explaining the studied texts, conceived integrally, "focusing our attention particularly on those points that directly present (...) its anthropological stratum."[140] The point is not so much to simply read "the text from the viewpoint of its anthropological content," but—which is particularly important when studying political thought—to "penetrate into the profound significance of this content, searching for the coherence among the formulations that seem to be 'dispersed' throughout the document, (...) and, in a certain way, in the different

---

[136]These two roles sometimes overlapped in a single person; note Tocqueville, for example.

[137]Rev. Mariusz Sztaba, *Przykładowe metody użyteczne w pisaniu pracy teoretycznej*, http://pracownik.kul.pl/files/12843/public/Metody_uzyteczne_w_pisaniu_prac_teoretycznych_z_pedagogiki.doc. [31.03.2016].

[138]M. Sztaba, *Przykładowe...*, p. 2.

[139]Karol Wojtyła, "Osobowa struktura samostanowienia," in: id., *Osoba i czyn oraz inne studia antropologiczne*, TN KUL, Kraków 2000, p. 425 [See: Karol Wojtyła, *The Acting Person*, Springer 1979.].

[140]Wojtyła, Karol, "The Anthropological Vision of *Humanae Vitae*," trans. William May, *Nova et Vetera*(English edition) 7, no. 3 (2009).

circumstances created by the guiding thread"[141] of the text. This way, textual analysis also becomes a synthesis of a particular way of thinking about man, revealing the anthropological contours of a particular tradition of thought. Once it is discovered, it is possible—in line with Dilthey's comment about the "unwitting author"—to enrich "it with a content that will be simultaneously more detailed and more systematic. A penetrating reflection on individual formulations of the text allows us to ascertain how (. . .) from this emerges that coherent image that we can rightly call the 'anthropological vision'."[142]

The ultimate goal is to uncover the visions of man, as well as—through idealization—to systematize them into model standpoints. Consequently, we may agree with Wilhelm Dilthey when he says that "the ultimate goal of the hermeneutic process is to understand an author better than he understood himself,"[143] which in our context means locating the anthropological vision within the broader framework of anthropological models present in the European tradition of ideas. It should be added that, since the study of ideas in Europe has a long tradition, in our search for an adequate typology of anthropologies we will start with works already present in literature, mainly by Jacob L. Talmon and Thomas Sowell, whose theoretical conclusions will be corrected and supplemented along the way.

4.3.3.2 Research Techniques of the Anthropological Dimension of EU Politics

With regard to studies concerned with the anthropological dimension of EU politics, it is crucial to "transcend the EU institution as an object,"[144] which is the only way to understand "the roles which culture and identity play in the institution, as well as the roles the institution plays as an agent of political and cultural change."[145] In order to accomplish this "transcending," we may use various techniques, depending on the type of documents to be analyzed.

In the normative analysis of constitutional texts—that is, documents which refer to fundamental rights and which explicitly have considerable anthropological content—the analytical-synthetic method described above will be used in line with the hermeneutic approach, together with the comparative method. This will facilitate a comparison of how man is seen in the context of human rights as interpreted in the EU and as they are commonly understood, which in turn will let us capture the

---

[141]Ibid.

[142]Ibid.

[143]Wilhelm Dilthey, *Hermeneutics and the Study of History*, Princeton University Press, 2018, p. 250.

[144]I. Bellier, T. Wilson, *An Anthropology of the European Union:Building, Imagining and Experiencing...*, p. 11.

[145]Ibid.

specificity of the anthropological contours endorsed in the primary legislation of the European Union.

In view of the flexibility of axiology present in the treatises documented in literature of the subject,[146] as well as the politological goal of this study aimed at revealing the actual anthropological model they reflect, analyses of primary legislation may not be considered as the answer to the research question. In line with the methodological and theoretical assumptions presented above, it will be treated as a reconstruction of the anthropological framework within which EU institutional actors operate, shaping the Union's actual anthropological profile.

The preliminary technique which will help "uncover" the anthropological dimension of decisions made by EU institutional actors will consist in analyses of the language and contents of EU political documents. Clearly, "language is the mirror of the society (. . .) it is the manifestation *par excellence* of transformations occurring in the society and its culture."[147] Linguists argue that "we see and hear and otherwise experience very largely as we do because the language habits of our community predispose certain choices of interpretation."[148] Consequently, our study will begin with identification—in reference to works concerning morality policy and observation of the related discourse—of the characteristic concepts and categories they employ, and with revealing their relation to the anthropological models identified in the first stage of research. Once these concepts and categories have been singled out, they may then serve to create conceptual matrices to be used in analyzing documents issued by EU institutions. The concept of discourse is understood here in the broad sense, echoing Foucault's belief that it represents an "epistemological category," which ultimately serves to examine "not so much the language, but rather systems of knowledge," encompassing "both a certain way of seeing the world, and the corresponding practice."[149] Consequently, this way of understanding discourse is premised on the assumption that "in the social reality, there are many independent discourses functioning side by side. Each of them is a comprehensive take on or a fragment of a certain system of knowledge."[150]

Of particular significance for the analysis of language are the central concepts of a discourse, or so-called mobilizing metaphors. As has been discussed at length in Chap. 3, they are words which become "the center of a cluster of keywords whose

---

[146]Cf. Michał Gierycz, "The European Union's axiological credo and morality policy tensions", *Studia Philosophiae Christianae*, No. 3, 2015, p. 159–192

[147]Anna Siewierska-Chmaj, *Język polskiej polityki. Politologiczno-semantyczna analiza expose premierów Polski w latach 1919-2004*, Wyższa Szkoła Informatyki i Zarządzania, Rzeszów 2005, p. 14.

[148]E. Sapir, "The Status of Linguistics as a Science," [in:] *Selected Writings of Edward Sapir*, ed. D.G. Mandelbaum, University of California Press 1949, p. 162.

[149]Jerzy Szacki, *Historia myśli socjologicznej. Wydanie nowe*, PWN, Warszawa 2002, p. 905

[150]Aleksandra Synowiec, "W stronę analizy tekstu – wprowadzenie do teorii dyskursu," *Zeszyty Naukowe Politechniki Śląskiej*, no. 65, 2013, p. 188.

meanings extend and shift while previous associations with other words are dropped. Their mobilizing effect lies in their capacity to connect with, and appropriate, the positive meanings and legitimacy derived from other key symbols of government such as 'nation', 'country', 'democracy', 'public interest and the rule of law'."[151] In this sense, as noted by Lakoff and Johnson, "metaphor plays a role in the creation of reality."[152] Consequently, an analysis of mobilizing metaphors provides an insight into what anthropological standpoint has the "power to define"; it specifies the framework of ideas, or context, for the entire discourse. As pointed out in Chap. 3, politics, in appropriate circumstances, may not only reflect cultural norms, but establish them, modifying the cultural system. Thus, they are a particularly important aspect of the analysis of both the inputs and outputs of the system.

As regards works in linguistically-oriented political science, the starting point of linguistic analyses are statistical findings, which show the lexis prevailing in European documents; by identifying the dominant mobilizing metaphors, they point to the anthropological model prevailing in the European Union, as well as its possible changes. With objective statistical indicators, it is possible to "identify preferences in the choice of words, both as regards individual authors and particular historical moments."[153]

Concurring with the assumption, however, that "statistical analysis alone may only contribute to finding the right lead in research, it must be concluded that it is also necessary to analyse the uses and contexts in which certain words are employed."[154] The first stage in saturating theoretical claims concerning the dominating anthropological models will therefore consist in an analysis of the content of political documents. In line with its assumptions, after constructing and performing a preliminary statistical falsification of the conceptual (categorizing) framework, relevant documents will be reviewed in terms of their content in order to identify connotations related to the choice of terminology, and verify their relation to the anthropological models discussed in the second part of this study.[155] In the case of analyses concerning programming or decisional documents, this will help discover, either ultimately or—as will be discussed below—to be further investigated, the anthropological orientation of particular institutional actors. Consequently, by analyzing content related to the employed linguistic categories, it will be possible to reveal, based on analyses of metaphors, concepts, categories, or narrative models, as

---

[151]C. Shore, S. Wright, "Policy. . .," p. 15: "Thus 'individual' became part of a cluster including 'freedom', 'market', 'enterprise' and ' family', and previous associations with 'society', 'public' and' collective' were diminished."

[152]G. Lakoff, M. Johnson, "The Metaphorical Logic of Rape," *Metaphor and Symbolic Activity* 2(1) 1987, p. 79, as quoted in: D. Yanow, *Conducting. . .*, p. 43.

[153]A. Siewierska-Chmaj, *Język polskiej polityki. . .*, p. 15.

[154]Ibid., pp. 15–16.

[155]Cf. Satu Elo and Helvi Kyngas, "The qualitative content analysis process," *Journal of Advanced Nursing* 62(1) 2007, pp. 111–112.

well as the existing interpretive communities,[156] the implicit ways of thinking about man in specific decisional or programming acts of European institutions. This way, we will be able to track down the anthropological orientation of the European Union as such.

From what has been established so far it may be concluded that the search for anthropological visions characteristic of EU institutional actors, beginning with the concepts specific to a particular discourse, is inductive in nature. The methodology employed in the second stage of research, i.e. the third part of this work, will rely to a considerable degree on the logic of the grounded theory, with the proviso, however, that while the categories we are looking for are identified based on elements of the observed reality, they are related to models developed when analyzing political thought.[157] Consequently, while conclusions concerning anthropological models developed in the first stage of research are theoretical, model and ideal in nature, theoretical claims made in the second stage concerning the anthropological orienta- tion of European politics are based, from the very beginning, on systematically collected empirical data. Theoretical proposals are not built, therefore, only by employing "a logically deductive method based on pre-defined axioms," but "refer to the observed fragment of [political] reality."[158] The construction of theories in the second stage of this study is strictly related to the research process itself.[159]

Given that the standpoint of European institutions, other than those which, like the Court of Justice of the European Union, settle cases by rulings, may be expressed not only in the documents they adopt, but also in concrete political actions (e.g. refusing to adopt a document, or acting contrary to declarations), the second stage of saturating the theory developed based on linguistic analyses will be an examination of decision-making processes. Since—for obvious reasons—it is not possible to review all decision-making processes over the past 20 years, I have opted for the case study method, focused on detailed analysis of particular decision- making processes.

Due to the rather widespread view that case study is of little use in the verification of hypotheses, this approach calls for a brief substantiation. It should be stressed that limiting the scientific role of case study to the construction of hypotheses has no

---

[156]The concept of interpretive communities refers here to—analytically identified, but also naturally existing—groups of political actors who "engage in the same or similar acts, and use the same or similar language to talk about thought and action." Even though the category of "community" may suggest geographical location, it is "borrowed into a policy context with broader reference points (. . .): 'location' within an organizational structure, professional training and membership, sex and gender, and a myriad of other possible dimensions lead to a set of values, beliefs, and feelings that can bind people together in communities of meaning." It refers to groups of people who share the same understanding of political ideas and language, and in the case of proposed action—the same (or similar) anthropological views, resulting in an essential community of political action (political initiatives, voting, implementation, etc.). Cf. D. Yanow, *Conducting. . .*, p. 10ff.

[157]Cf. Krzysztof Konecki, *Studia z metodologii badań jakościowych. Teoria ugruntowana*, PWN, Warszawa 2000, r.2.

[158]K. Konecki, *Studia z metodologii badań. . .*, p. 26.

[159]Ibid.

substantive justification. In the mid-1970s, Harry Eckstein already argued that case studies "are valuable at all stages of the theory-building process, but most valuable at that stage of theory building where least value is generally attached to them: the stage at which candidate theories are tested."[160] Ultimately, as Bent Flyvbjerg rightly points out, when looking at the development of science we can see that "[c]arefully chosen experiments, cases, and experience were also critical to the development of the physics of Newton, Einstein, and Bohr, just as the case study occupied a central place in the works of Darwin, Marx, and Freud. In social science, too, the strategic choice of case may greatly add to the generalizability of a case study."[161] A contrario, William Ian B. Beveridge notes that "more discoveries have arisen from intense observation than from statistics applied to large groups."[162] Consequently, there are no substantive grounds for questioning the relevance of case studies for the saturation or testing of theoretical claims. The key condition for successfully saturating a theory is to make the correct choice of cases.

The selection of cases made for the purposes of this study was oriented at obtaining information from small samples and individual cases, that is, on maximizing the usefulness of information. Consequently, the cases presented here generally represent two types: critical and paradigmatic. Critical cases are ideal for "generalizing using the type of test that Karl Popper called 'falsification,' which in social science forms part of critical reflexivity. (. . .) [I]f just one observation does not fit with the proposition it is considered not valid generally and must therefore be either revised or rejected."[163] They are those cases which serve to "achieve information which permits logical deductions of the type, 'if this is (not) valid for this case, then it applies to all (no) cases."[164] Paradigmatic cases emphasize more general characteristics of the studied objects, establishing "a school for the domain which the case concerns."[165] In order to fully saturate the constructed theory with reference to a single case, the process-tracing method has been employed, with its own, specific rigors; it "helps analyse the way in which a hypothetical cause affects the observed result."[166]

While comparative analysis, the qualitative and quantitative analysis of language, and case study are the main research techniques employed in the second stage, they are further supplemented with auxiliary techniques. In relation to certain data which cannot be found in, or are difficult to be extracted from, the documents themselves

---

[160]Harry Eckstein, "Case Study and Theory in Political Science," in: *Regarding Politics. Essays on Political Theory, Stability, and Change*, University of California Press, 1991, p. 80.

[161]Bent Flyvbjerg, "Five Misunderstandings About Case-Study Research," *Qualitative Inquiry*, vol. 12, no. 2, April 2006, p. 229.

[162]Ibid., p. 230.

[163]Ibid., p. 230.

[164]Ibid., p. 233.

[165]Ibid.

[166]Cf. Kamil Ławniczak, "Process tracing. Śledzenie mechanizmów przyczynowych," in: id. [ed.], *Metody jakościowe i ilościowe w badaniu organizacji i działania Unii Europejskiej*, WDiNP, Warszawa 2013, p. 69.

(such as the context in which the document was drafted, non-public negotiations, the meaning of terms, etc.), in-depth interviews have been used with political actors representing various standpoints in the anthropological discussion. The interviews—representing qualitative data—were based on a broad approach to values, leading the interviewees to express their own evaluative declarations, freely formulated, giving insight into their hierarchy and evaluation of goals within the framework of an axiological discussion (desirable/undesirable goals, realized/unrealized goals, identified/unidentified goals, etc.).[167] When analyzing documents, the analytic-synthetic method was used, and the case studies employed, as applicable, the techniques of quantitative studies, including basic statistical methods.

The diversity of research methods employed shows that owing to the distinctly separate research goal,[168] different from that of other approaches to political anthropology, on the grounds of political science political anthropology may integrate within the paradigm of deep system analysis the research techniques characteristic of philosophical and theological anthropology, particularly the hermeneutic method, as well as techniques developed by cultural anthropology.[169] Even though the research is focused on the text, or, more precisely, on the language (the concepts, categorizations, metaphors used) as an externalization of anthropological assumptions, it does not abstract from empirical data. Nevertheless, it is oriented qualitatively, as results directly from the research goal of understanding and reconstructing the anthropological models hidden behind the narrative structures used by participants in social life, expressed through their adopted system of signs and preferences.[170] The point, therefore, is not only to understand a broadly-understood "text" (e.g. a legal act, a legislative proposal, a postulate of a lobbying group, a parliamentary debate, etc.), but to analyze "the text in its context", to reveal the anthropological logic behind particular solutions, and the related direction of potential social change.

Consequently, even if historically and, indeed, in the first place, political anthropology was a subdiscipline of other domains of science: cultural (social) anthropology, philosophy and theology, within whose framework attempts were made at capturing—from various vantage points—the specificity of the political nature of human beings, it seems nevertheless possible and reasonable to approach political anthropology as a subdiscipline of political science. As noted above, on politological grounds, its specific goal and character, as well as its proper methodology may be identified. From this point of view, just like cultural anthropology is based on analyzing the products of culture, and philosophical anthropology—on intellectual reflection, so political anthropology is grounded on the analysis of political thought, legislation and documents with a view to revealing the concepts of man which stand

---

[167]Cf. Jacek K. Kołodziej, *Wartości polityczne. Rozpoznanie, rozumienie, komunikowanie*, Księgarnia Akademicka, Kraków 2011, pp. 252-271.

[168]The significance of this issue for the possibility of integrating research approaches without the risk of amalgamation is discussed in greater detail in Chap. 2.

[169]See more on this topic in Chap. 3.

[170]Cf. David Silverman, *Qualitative Research*, Sage Publications Ltd, 2016.

behind them, dominate, or compete with one another within the particular political system.

* * *

Even though—as has already been mentioned—such a form of political anthropology is neither descriptive, nor normative, but primarily theoretical, we may still ask about its descriptive and normative role. Naturally, it plays the former role only incidentally, so to say, while performing the theoretical function. The question regarding its normativity remains open, however. On the one hand, in the normative aspect, in relation to the theoretical findings made in Chap. 2 concerning "integration on the input side", the approach of political science could become integrated with that of philosophy or theology. A philosophically and theologically grounded political anthropology could provide a context for evaluating the findings of political anthropology in the politological approach. Such a standpoint would mean recognizing that political anthropology on the grounds of political science is not able to develop autonomous normative directives. Such a solution does not appear to be the only possible one, however. Naturally, a political anthropology within the framework of political science does not have any tools to metaphysically or existentially "weigh up" the politically dominant anthropological attitudes, i.e. to provide an absolute normative criterion. By employing its model approach it may, however, show the ideological links between one anthropological standpoint and another standpoint whose social value is now available for historical evaluation. Therefore, by revealing the ideological "interpretative communities" which transcend the perspective of just one or two generations, a political anthropology on the grounds of political science may also be an indirectly normative discipline. As long as we agree, of course, that history may indeed be a *vitae magistra*.

Part II
The Anthropological Dispute in European Political Thought

As we set out to study the anthropology of the European Union, we must begin with the specific view of man in its cultural context, referred to as late modernity or postmodernism. Since our époque, as will be demonstrated more extensively further on, does not so much overcome the logic of modernity, as continue and fulfill it in its own way by processing certain modern categories,[1] the starting point of our analyses must be the anthropological problem of modern politics that has developed since the Enlightenment.

Obviously, studies into the ideological and political consequences of the Enlightenment are hardly *terra incognita*. From the perspective of the problem addressed here, of particular relevance seems the fundamental political tension, discussed in literature, which emerged in European tradition at that time, linked to the coexistence of two radically opposite currents of political thought which referred—and this is especially interesting in the context of reflections on contemporary axiological disputes—to the very same values. Jacob Talmon notes that together "with the liberal type of democracy there emerged from the same premises in the eighteenth century a trend towards what we propose to call the totalitarian type of democracy. These two currents have existed side by side ever since the eighteenth century. The tension between them has constituted an important chapter in modern history, and has now become the most vital issue of our time."[2] A slightly different approach to the same problem is found in Thomas Sowell. He points to the dispute, characteristic of the beginnings of modernity, which he believes to be exemplified by two revolutions: the American and the French. He argues that it was not a coincidence that the efforts made—on both sides of the Atlantic—in the name of freedom, equality, and human rights led to a lasting political regime in the USA founded on the idea of a constrained government, respecting the religious social context, while in France they resulted in unsteady dictatorships which proclaimed terror in the name

---

[1] Michał Wróblewski, "Zatarg Jeana – Francoisa Lyotarda czyli o postmodernizmie raz jeszcze," *Diametros* 24/2010, pp. 132–134

[2] Jacob L. Talmon, *The Origins of Totalitarian Democracy*, Secker & Warburg, 1952, p. 1.

of democracy and entailed radical secularization.[3] The difference—according to Sowell—resulted from the vision of politics.[4]

Thus, modernity begins with an enormous paradox: the modern political spirit, apparently based on the same ideals or values, results in radically different concepts of social and political order. The political tension specific to modernity is not necessarily related to spatial and political distance, however. It may also appear within a single political community. As regards the American society, such a situation is picturesquely described by Gertrude Himmelfarb,[5] arguing that "the most significant battle raging on in America is the fight for values (...) between two (...) worldviews".[6] The existence of this dispute means that the modern tension around the concept of the politic may be "intra-systemic," touching upon the very core of the existing political regime. In his broadly discussed encyclical *Centesimus Annus*, John Paul II reveals the theoretical dimension of this problem in modern politics. When analysing democracy, i.e. the system which is considered to be a self-evident value and a cream of the crop, so to say, of the political achievements of the West, distinguishes between its two models. He writes about "authentic democracy" and "disguised totalitarianism," a fake democracy. The Pope argues that the former requires a recognition that "obedience to the truth about God and man is the first condition of freedom;"[7] it is "possible only in a State ruled by law, and on the basis of a correct conception of the human person."[8] Failure to meet these conditions results in an axiological decomposition of the system, as "democracy without values easily turns into open or thinly disguised totalitarianism."[9] In the latter case, it still

---

[3]Thomas Sowell, *A Conflict of Visions. Ideological Origins of Political Struggles*, Basic Books, New York 2007, p. 25ff. Suffice it to cite Robespierre's speech to the National Convention on 5 February 1794: "La terreur n'est autre chose que la justice prompte, sévère, inflexible; elle est donc une émanation de la vertu; elle est moins un principe particulier, qu'une conséquence du principe général de la démocratie, appliqué aux plus pressants besoins de la patrie." ("Terror is nothing more than speedy, severe and inflexible justice; it is thus an emanation of virtue; it is less a principle in itself, than a consequence of the general principle of democracy, applied to the most pressing needs of the *patrie*".) M. Robespierre, "On the Principles of Political Morality," February 1794, Fordham University Internet Modern History Sourcebook, https://sourcebooks.fordham.edu/mod/1794robespierre.asp (taken from M. Robespierre, *Report upon the Principles of Political Morality Which Are to Form the Basis of the Administration of the Interior Concerns of the Republic* [Philadelphia, 1794].).

[4]Ibid.

[5]Cf. Gertrude Himmelfarb, *One Nation, Two Cultures: A Searching Examination of American Society in the Aftermath of Our Cultural Revolution*, Vintage, 2001.

[6]Piotr Skurowski, *Wprowadzenie*, in: G. Himmelfarb, *Jeden naród...*, p. 9.

[7]John Paul II, *Centesimus Annus, Encyclical Letter to His Venerable Brother Bishops in the Episcopate, the Priests and Deacons, Families of Men and Women Religious, All the Christian Faithful and to All Men and Women of Good Will on the Hundredth Anniversary of Rerum Novarum* (hereinafter *Centesimus annus*), no. 41.

[8]John Paul II, *Centesimus Annus...*, no. 46. More about the reasons and conditions for the Church's acceptance of democracy, see: Aniela Dylus, *Polityka w perspektywieetycznejireligijnej*, UKSW, Warszawa 2016, pp. 434–444.

[9]John Paul II, *Centesimus Annus...*, No. 46.

keeps up the appearances of democracy. What John Paul II has in mind is a situation where in a formally democratic reality, such ideological and political standpoints begin to dominate as eliminate the core contents of "authentic democracy" from the "inside." Not necessarily all of them at the same time, and not evidently; the essence of this change consists in that it is difficult to spot right away, precisely because it is "disguised." Modern democracy itself, or, more broadly, modern politics appear here, just like in Talmon's theory, to be a regime that is subject to constant inner tension. *Per analogiam* to the "creeping revolution of fundamentalism" diagnosed by Piotr Kłodkowski,"[10] it is threatened by a "creeping revolution of totalitarianism" which step by step, from the inside, makes democracy "inauthentic" while formally respecting the democratic mechanisms. A key aspect of this transformation would—in light of the comments made by John Paul II—be an anthropological change, i.e. negation of the truth about man.

When looking for a key to the anthropological study of contemporary political disputes, it is worth considering the work of Thomas Sowell. He is one of the few authors to have paid special attention to the anthropological problem, demonstrating its presence at the very foundations on which social theories are built. His reflections (Chap. 5), critically discussed in the context of findings made by other authors, have therefore been designated as the starting point for theoretical conclusions which end up revealing the two opposing anthropological models characteristic of modernity (Chaps. 6 and 7), and then their postmodern form (Chap. 8) which is a key factor in contemporary European politics.

---

[10]Cf. Piotr Kłodkowski, *O pęknięciu wewnątrz cywilizacji. Ideologiczny spór między modernistami a fundamentalistami w islamie i hinduizmie w XX i na początku XXI wieku*, Dialog, Warszawa 2005.

Chapter 5
Two Visions of Politics and Two Visions of Man

When looking for the sources of modern political disputes, Thomas Sowell suggests that we focus on "social visions," which he refers to as "the foundations on which theories are built."[1] They represent a pre-analytical cognitive act which is the foundation of political action. His goal is therefore to discover what we believe or feel[2] even before we engage in systematic inference, and what reflects our most deeply held convictions about how the world works.[3] Social visions are important because, as he emphasizes, they fill in the unavoidable gaps in individual knowledge, setting out the trajectories for thought and action.[4] Moreover, they spread easily across societies and their impact extends over generations. By unearthing the visions which are at the very core of metapolitics, we may find the key to understanding the dynamics of modernity, which Sowell believes to have been forged—as mentioned above—in the fire of two political revolutions, reflecting two different social visions: the "constrained" (the case of America) and the "unconstrained" (the case of France).

---

[1]"Visions are very subjective, but well-constructed theories have clear implications, and facts can test and measure their objective validity. The world learned from Hiroshima that Einstein's vision of physics was not just Einstein's vision." T. Sowell, *A Conflict...*, p. 4.

[2]Meaning not so much the state of an emotional impression, but rather an intellectual sense of something.

[3]Ibid., p. 105.

[4]He argues that "for example, an individual may act in one way in some area in which he has great knowledge, but in just the opposite way elsewhere, where he is relying on a vision he has never tested empirically". T. Sowell, *A Conflict...*, p. 7.

© Springer Nature Switzerland AG 2021
M. Gierycz, *European Dispute over the Concept of Man*, Contributions to Political Science, https://doi.org/10.1007/978-3-030-61520-8_5

5.1   The Constrained and Unconstrained Vision of Politics

One fundamental difference between Sowell's unconstrained and constrained visions of politics is apparently the fact that the former strives towards implementing a knowable and identifiable social good, or, better perhaps, a supreme value (e.g. the Marxist ideal of a classless society), while the latter is an attempt at accommodating conflicting interests and beliefs about what this "social good" may be.[5] Sowell's dichotomy is thus a variation of political intentionalism and contingentism.[6] In functional terms, and using Sowell's terminology, it is based on different ways of understanding two key criteria: the source of decisions, or, in other words, the location of discretionary powers (*locus of discretion*), and the way they are implemented (*mode of discretion*).[7]

Advocates of the unconstrained vision of social processes locate the power to rule in representatives of the social elite, or avant-garde—those who are most competent in identifying the knowable good. The avant-garde operates on expressly rational premises, and their actions are teleological. Decision-makers lead their societies towards "ever-higher levels of understanding and practice (. . .) pending the eventual progress of mankind to the point where all can make social decisions,"[8] at times even allowing for the temporary need to use violence. Consequently, the government acts as a surrogate: it operates "in the stead" of the society, so to say, and the dynamics of authority leaves no room "for the idea of subjecting the political process to general rules and institutional constraints. On the contrary, such constraints are only perceived as hindering or obstructing an effective implementation of the 'known good'."[9]

The advocates of constrained vision locate the power to decide in (every) citizen; they believe not so much in the citizens' ability to properly understand and regulate social matters, but in the inner logic of social processes which ultimately lead to an appropriate form of social relationships. The constrained vision is therefore based on historically evolving processes which are verified not so much by the intentions behind them, but rather by their efficiency in guaranteeing the common good

---

[5]Cf. Victor Vanberg, *Conflict of Visions. Thomas Sowell*, "Cato Journal," Vol.7, No.2 (Fall 1987), p. 548.

[6]Bogdan Szlachta notes that the former substantiates the establishment of social order by individuals who are deliberately striving towards particular goals, while the latter denies the thesis that man can intentionally create any institutions, norms, etc. Cf. Bogdan Szlachta, "Indywidualizm," in: id. [ed.], *Słownik społeczny*, WAM, Kraków 2006, p. 412.

[7]T. Sowell, *A Conflict. . .*, p. 106.

[8]Ibid., p. 110. Naturally, this may come in many different varieties. For example, "a special variant in Godwin is that each individual acts essentially as a social surrogate, making decisions individually but with social responsibility rather than personal benefits uppermost in his thinking. This tradition of 'social responsibility' by businessmen, universities and others implies a capacity to discern the actual social ramifications of one's acts—an assumption implicitly made in the unconstrained vision and explicitly rejected by those with the constrained vision" (ibid.).

[9]V. Vanberg, *Conflict. . .*, p. 548.

through socially developed incentives and modes of social interactions.[10] The way to realize competences is, therefore, the gradual, systemic evolution of the social institutions they entail.

The different ways of perceiving and moderating the dynamics of social processes result from a different concept of political reason in the advocates of the two visions. The advocates of the unconstrained vision believe that it is possible to find a rational answer to all problems and challenges, if only "the forces of intelligence and of virtue could be made to prevail over ignorance and wickedness."[11] Consequently, the unconstrained vision relies on intellectual reflection to find a solution to the political problem and establish some form of ideal order. Every social change which brings us closer to achieving this desired ideal should be preferred, no matter the cost.[12] At the same time, advocates of the unconstrained vision believe it to be self-evident that since knowledge is an element of diversification between people, citizens of narrow horizons should submit to the leadership of the elites who cultivate reason: philosophers or qualified experts.[13] The special role of the "thinking people" or "the brightest and the best" was, according to Sowell, a central theme of the unconstrained vision for centuries.[14]

In the constrained vision, reason is treated with much more scepticism. Knowledge is understood first of all as social experience, passed on in non-articulated forms of traditions, customs, habits, sentiments, feelings and modes of behavior; it is the everyday experience of people, succeeding in the Darwinian competition between what works and what does not.[15] Consequently, knowledge is universally accessible, but always shared and dispersed, so that ultimately even the most outstanding individuals are unable to distinguish between what they invented themselves, and what they learned from others. The advocates of constrained vision strongly believe that individual reason is much too insufficient to capture the diversity and take the right decisions, both in private and social matters, and consequently politics must be limited to looking for solutions which are satisfactory, and introduce reforms only if absolutely necessary and always with great caution. Since systemic rationality is more reliable than individual reality, a cautious reformer respect people's well-established customs and pre-judgments, "not disdain[ing] to ameliorate he wrong."[16] A key category in the constrained vision is that of a trade-off developed within the framework of systemic processes.[17] We might say that

---

[10]Cf. T. Sowell, *A Conflict. . .*, p. 70.

[11]I. Berlin, "Political Ideas in the Twentieth Century," in: id., *Liberty*, ed. H. Hardy, Oxford University Press, 2002, p. 59.

[12]T. Sowell, *A Conflict...*, p. 29.

[13]See, for example, the well-known claim by Voltaire who said that philosophers have no particular interest to defend and only speak up in favor of reason.

[14]T. Sowell, *A Conflict. . .*, p. 43.

[15]Ibid., p. 36, 64, 71.

[16]Ibid., p. 33.

[17]Ibid., p. 26–37.

imperfection is understood as a socially perfect solution. As Edmund Burke said: "(...) I must bear with infirmities until they fester into crimes."[18]

As a result of the above approach, the constrained model of politics respects the existing social institutions, particularly religion, which it perceives as a special repository of social traditions and an instrument in mitigating the human tendency to egotism. Advocates of the unconstrained logic assume, on the other hand, that "the circumstances of the world are continually changing, and the opinions of men change also; and as government is for the living, and not for the dead, it is the living only that has any right in it."[19] This impacts the process of designing political solutions (there is no need to take into account pre-existing institutions), as well as the understanding of political commitments in everyday practice (the principle *pacta sunt servanda* seems an anachronism here: submitting to past decisions means losing opportunities which may arise with more knowledge).[20] Since all is about progress, whether moral, social, or political, such actions may be justified whereas in the light of traditional ethics they would be considered immoral. However, in the light of unconstrained anthropology, they are essentially immoral only at a given stage in development. By helping overcome it, they obtain legitimization.

The revolutionary potential of unconstrained politics is most clearly revealed with regard to religion, a basic structure of long duration. It was not by coincidence that, in his reflections on the Enlightenment, Kant said that one must reject "dogmas and formulas" which are "the ball and chain of (...) permanent immaturity." Longstanding traditions, in particular religion, its institutions and beliefs are seen by the advocates of unconstraint as a source of contamination. Jacob Talmon points out that "no eighteenth-century thinker recognized any distinction between membership of a kingdom of God and citizenship of an earthly state, in the Christian sense."[21] Consequently, "[t]he philosophical line of attack on the Church was that apart from the historic untruth of the revealed religion, it also stood condemned as a sociological force. It introduced 'imaginary' and heterogeneous criteria into the life of man and society." The proper goal was a political and religious monism instead. It was not only Helvetius who believed that "[i]t is from the legislative body only (...) that we can expect a beneficent religion," and the idea of public cult was not incidentally a lasting element of the French Revolution.[22]

Owing to the different solutions as regards the concept of political reason and the dynamics of social processes, the two visions of politics differ radically in the way

---

[18]Ibid., p. 42.

[19]Cf. Thomas Paine, *Rights of Man*, http://www.let.rug.nl/usa/documents/1786-1800/thomas-paine-the-rights-of-man/text.php [15.09.2016].

[20]Sowell notes: "Being bound by past decisions whether in constitutional law casus or in marriage for life is seen costly and irrational," T. Sowell, *A Conflict...*, Ibid., p. 79.

[21]Jacob L. Talmon, *The Origins of Totalitarian Democracy*, Secker & Warburg, 1952, p. 23.

[22]Ibid. More on this topic, see: Michał Gierycz, Piotr Mazurkiewicz, *Europäische Anthropologie und europäische Politik. Beobachtungen in der Gegenwart*, in: Christoph Bohr, Christian Schmitz [ed.], *Europa und die Anthropologie seiner Politik. Der Mensch als Weg der Geschichte—Zur Philosophie Karol Wojtyłas*, Berliner Wissenschafts-Verlag, Berlin 2016, pp. 133–176.

they conceive of fundamental values. Since the advocates of unconstrained vision believe it is possible to find a rational answer to all problems and challenges, then also freedom, justice, and equality in the unconstrained approach are verified by the goal—fulfilled equality, justice as social justice, equality as making everyone equal (social cohesion). As noted by Robert Dahl, freedom "finally depends on attaining important prime goals such as dignity, respect, love, affection, solidarity, friendship. To the extent that individuals lack these, they cannot be free."[23] Consequently, equality is seen as the equality of outcome: "to apply the same criteria to those with radically different wealth, education, or past opportunities and cultural orientations is to negate the meaning of equality (. . .). [E]quality of opportunity means equalized probabilities of achieving given results, whether in education, employment or the courtroom,"[24] which requires "compensatory advantages" for the weaker. In the constrained vision, on the other hand, freedom, justice, equality are characterized in terms of a process. Thus, freedom is an absence of any externally imposed obstacles, freedom from the arbitrariness of another; justice is the application of the same rules, and equality is ensured when social processes guarantee equal treatment, irrespective of whether the results are identical or not.[25]

Consequences of the above assumptions for law as a key institution of the state are quite self-evident. For the advocates of a constrained vision, such as Holmes or Hayek, law is in the first place a record of experience which sums up, so to say, not only our own lives, but also the lives of all those who have ever been.[26] So even though it is created, it remains a function of longstanding customs and beliefs without which the entire system of law would be inoperative. Even though the law, as well as the entire social system, may be changed, it should only be done so when necessary, with much caution and prudence. For advocates of the unconstrained vision, like Ronald Dworkin, law is a plastic, man-made creation; it requires "an activist court" which should read its own meanings into the words of the Constitution.[27] Ultimately, it is not so much about the letter of the law, but about its spirit, interpreted by a competent judge in order to achieve socially desirable outcomes.[28] Just like social change, the "right" interpretation of law should be preferred as long as it helps achieve the desired ideal. The apogee of this logic is found in the Marxist theory of law which says that "legislation [is] intended to benefit only a section of the people, or the ruling interest."[29]

---

[23]Robert A. Dahl, Charles E. Linborn, *Politics, Economics and Welfare*, University of Chicago Press, Chicago 1967, p. 518, as quoted in: T. Sowell, *A Conflict. . .*, p. 95.

[24]T. Sowell, *A Conflict. . .*, p. 123.

[25]Ibid., pp. 121, 200.

[26]Ibid., p. 52. In this context, he cites Hayek: "all the famous early law-givers did not intend to create new law but merely to state what law was and had always been."

[27]Ibid., p. 53.

[28]Ibid., p. 179.

[29]J. M. Kelly, *A Short History of Western Legal Theory*, Clarendon Press, 1992, p. 22. Naturally, in a communist state the law (just like other bourgeois elements of the superstructure) were to disappear. Its presence after the revolution of 1917 was explained as a transitory phenomenon.

5.2 Anthropological Sources of Political Visions

Sowell is aware that the functional criteria he refers to (*locus* and *mode of discretion*), while explaining why the way social life is understood in both visions leads to different outcomes, call for an explanation themselves. In looking for such an explanation, he refers to the anthropological question. Anthropology is not only the starting point for his work, but in fact its undercurrent which continues to add precision to the assumptions about human nature which are the basis for two different visions of social and political order.[30] He notes that "despite necessary caveats, it remains an important and remarkable phenomenon that how human nature is conceived at the outset is highly correlated with the whole conception of knowledge, morality, power, time, rationality, war, freedom, and law which defines a social vision."[31]

Sowell's key thesis is that the visions of social order, political reason, understanding of values, and the resulting concepts of power and law are based on a certain understanding of human nature. As paraphrased by one commentator, "those who see the potentialities of human nature as extending far beyond what is currently manifested have a social vision quite different from those who see human beings as tragically limited creatures whose selfish and dangerous impulses can be contained only by social contrivances which themselves produce unhappy side effects."[32] Even if Sowell's theses are somewhat overplayed here, he does believe that a different view of the moral and intellectual potentialities of man is at the basis of the different concepts of knowledge and social processes.[33] Consequently, the constrained vision of social processes stems from the appreciation of the fundamental significance of imperfection, or, in other words, of man's brokenness or corruption. The unconstrained anthropological vision appears to be the negative of the anthropology of brokenness. Advocates of the unconstrained vision—according to Sowell—consider human beings as morally perfect and altruistic, and their reason as being capable of obtaining accurate knowledge.

According to PēterisStučka, the first People's Commissar for Justice, "Soviet law is 'bourgeois' law, but without the bourgeoisie," and serves the new ruling class—the proletariat.

[30]T. Sowell, *A Conflict...*, p. 30. As a side remark, even the very structure of his book emphasizes the thesis that social visions ultimately rest on the view of human nature: its inherent potentialities and limitations.

[31]Ibid., p. 38. Sowell has also been accused of "cherry picking, hedging and mitigating" to find examples that fit his theory, for example, by considering Jefferson an advocate of the constrained vision, while in fact he was most explicitly an advocate of the unconstrained one. Cf. D. S. Wright, "Book Review: *A Conflict Of Visions*," Progressive Friends of the Library Newsletter, http://www. dailykos.com/story/2012/02/21/1052864/-Book-Review-A-Conflict-Of-Visions-Part-1 [12.09.2013].

[32]Ibid., p. 35.

[33]T. Sowell, *A Conflict...*, p. 93.

5.2.1 Constrained Anthropology

The essence of constraint is vividly painted by F. von Hayek, who points out that "in the view of those British philosophers, man was by nature lazy and indolent, improvident and wasteful and that it was only by the force of circumstances that he could be made to behave economically or would learn carefully to adjust his means to an end."[34] The anthropology of constraint assumes that the human person is "never wholly free and to some degree, but never entirely, good."[35] It is not, as held in the classical realism of Machiavelli, that people are bad by nature[36] (if this was the case, there would probably be no point in a theory of justice as we usually understand it). We are following more in the footsteps of one of the forefathers of modernity, Thomas Hobbes, who saw man as an egotist, "completely uninterested in the value (...) of other lives (...) [but] capable of co-operating for mutual advantage."[37] It is not by coincidence that right at the very beginning of his reflections on man, Sowell cites the story by Adam Smith who stresses in his *Theory of Moral Sentiments* that an earthquake in China will not impress us as much as the prospect of losing a finger. When all is said and done, man is, as emphasized by advocates of the constrained vision, centered on himself.

The moral limitations of man in general, and his egocentrism in particular, are not a problem, however. On the contrary, they are accepted as a fact one must live with, somehow.[38] This is a characteristic trait of this vision of man: limitations are something natural which cannot and should not be changed. The logic of trade-off mentioned above[39] helps mitigate egotism, which does not have to determine people's behavior. The existence of incentives such as honor, morality, religion, in practice inclines people to sacrifice their interest for the sake of higher goods. Ultimately, as pointed out by János Kis, "if we want them [egoists] to co-operate in accordance with the basic requirements of morality—'laws of nature'—they must be given incentives in terms of their selfish interests."[40]

The advocates of the constrained vision, according to Sowell, would not readily agree with the above claim. Instead, they would say that such incentives develop in the course of social processes,[41] instead of being (intentionally and rationally)

---

[34]Friedrich von Hayek, *The Constitution of Liberty*, University of Chicago Press, 2011, p. 120.

[35]I. Berlin, "Political Ideas...," p. 60.

[36]Cf. Machiavelli, *The Prince*, Translated by W. K. Marriott, Dutton & Company, 1908.

[37]János Kis, *Politics as a Moral Problem*, Central European University Press, 2008, p.13.

[38]T. Sowell, *A conflict...*, p. 16.

[39]Some in this context refer to combinations of preferences—cf. Will Kymlicka, *Contemporary Political Philosophy*, Oxford University Press, 2001.

[40]János Kis, *Politics as a Moral Problem*, p. 13.

[41]Sowell points out further on that man's internal and external resources are insufficient to satisfy his needs, while at the same time individuals refuse to accept limits on the satisfaction their own desires, unless inherent social constraints are imposed through social mechanisms (such as prices, etc.). T. Sowell, *A Conflict of...*, p. 100.

constructed. At this point we touch upon the other essential limitation of human nature. It is epistemic in nature, referring to the possibilities of human reason. Even though the advocates of a constrained anthropology are not always as pessimistic as Blackstone, for whom reason is corrupted and man's understanding full of ignorance and error,[42] they are convinced that individual reason is way too insufficient to capture diversity and take the right social decisions.[43] The knowledge of every individual is perceived here as radically inadequate considering the inner social complexity and the requirements of decisions that affect it. Consequently, confidence should not be placed so much in reason understood as the effect of reflection by outstanding individuals, but as the entire human experience, the "systemic rationality" mentioned above. Even though it takes away some of man's intellectual satisfaction, suggesting the primacy of non-reflexive knowledge,[44] it makes all people to some degree successors to knowledge through social experience. At the same time, no one has enough knowledge to design a model of politics that would make it possible to overcome the imperfections of nature.

The above anthropology explicitly suggests that due to his moral and intellectual faults, man is not able to build an ideal world. Therefore, as argued by one of the contemporary philosophers, "a theory of justice that accounts for the anthropological circumstances of justice in a realistic manner must be a partial (rather than strict) compliance theory."[45] A constrained anthropology grounds a constrained model of politics, suggesting a reconciliation with the world's imperfection, including morally negative phenomena and some degree of social injustice; aware that it is "the limitations and passions of man himself [that] are at the heart of these painful phenomena;"[46] it substantiates the "minimalist" claims to equality and the limits of power. The advocates of this anthropology ultimately acknowledge the frailty of institutions as entailed by the general infirmity of human nature, recognizing—to cite Edmund Burke—that "true political sagacity manifests itself in distinguishing that complaint which only characterizes the general infirmity of human nature from those which are symptoms of the particular distemperature of our own air and season." What needs to be explained, they believe, is not so much the afflictions that beset mankind (as they are a natural consequence of human nature), but the ways which have made it possible to avoid or mitigate them. At the same time, they are of the opinion that social life may also bring unexpected benefits resulting from activities oriented on the achievement of individual goals. The invisible hand of the market doctrine, even if somewhat mythologized by Sowell, would probably be a flagship example.

---

[42]T. Sowell, *A Conflict of. . .*, p. 178.

[43]As noted by Edmund Burke: "we are afraid to put men to live and trade on his own private stock of reason, because we suspect that this stock in each man is too small". Edmund Burke, *Reflections on the Revolution in France*, Seeley, Jackson and Halliday, 1872, p. 84.

[44]Cf. T. Sowell, *Conflict. . .*, p. 82, 100.

[45]János Kis, *Politics as a Moral Problem*, p. 31.

[46]T. Sowell, *A Conflict. . .*, p. 31.

5.2.2 Unconstrained Anthropology

Sowell believes that a view characteristic of the advocates of the other anthropological model was expressed by Godwin when he said that "man [is] capable of directly feeling other people's needs as more important than his own, and therefore consistently acting impartially, even when his own interests or those of his family were involved,"[47] presenting man as a being who is both morally and epistemically perfect. Such claims may be found at the sources of thought by many other thinkers. Voltaire, for example, radically opposed Pascal's arguments about the corruption of human nature, saying that "he is determined to depict us all as evil and unhappy. (...) He attributes to the essence of our nature what applies only to certain men."[48] In fact, as noted by Condorcet, human nature promises progress, since "no bounds have been fixed to the improvement of the human faculties,"[49] and "the perfectibility of man is absolutely indefinite."[50] Radical anthropological optimism is an essential feature of the Enlightenment thought from which—according to Sowell—stems the unconstrained vision of politics.

The fathers of unconstrained anthropology, even if their theses might suggest otherwise, are not pure apriorists. As emphasized by Voltaire, "we know nothing in this world but by experience."[51] Thus, they cannot entirely ignore expressions of man's limitations and errors. It is not a coincidence that Voltaire refers to "certain" evil men. Their existence introduces a problematic cognitive dissonance, however. For how can the theory of a perfect man be reconciled with empirical contacts with our next door neighbor? A solution for this dissonance according to the *philosophes*, to the extent they considered the "canaille" (or mob) as belonging to the category of Man in the first place,[52] was to find external sources of man's infirmity, not related to human nature. At this point, "eighteenth-century philosophy was immensely helped by associationist psychology of Condillac" which claimed that "the mind is at birth a tabula rasa, with no innate ideas, characteristics or vices. All are formed by education, environment and associations of ideas and impressions."[53] Man is a product of education—one needs only to know how to educate him. It is not a coincidence that in *Code de la Nature* Morelly places "on the one side the science of natural morality

---

[47]Ibid., p. 24. It seems, however, that there is a work even earlier than Godwin's study cited by Sowell, namely Morelly's *Code de la Nature* of 1735, which expresses the premises of eighteenth century thought.

[48]Francois Marie Arouet Voltaire, *Letters on England*, trans. Leonard Tancock, Penguin, London 2005, p. 120.

[49]Antonie Nicolas Condorcet, *Sketch for a Historical Picture of the Progress of the Human Mind*, J. Johnson,1795, p. 366.

[50]Ibid.

[51]Francois Marie Arouet Voltaire, *The Ignorant Philosopher*, Haldeman-Julius Co., 1922, p. 9.

[52]As noted by Talmon, some thinkers "rejected the idea. Only the bourgeoise is Man. Those beneath him were too ignorant, too brutalized, had too little share in maintaining the society, to be counted at all." Jacob L. Talmon, *The Origins Of Totalitarian Democracy*, Secker & Warburg, 1952, p. 50.

[53]Ibid., p. 34–35.

(...) and on the other side the chaos of errors (...) presented by the whole human history. Morelly's aim was to find a situation where it would be almost impossible for man to be depraved and vicious."[54] Mably's belief that "politics could develop from the most conjectural into a most exact science, once the recesses of the human heart and passions had been explored, and a scientific system of ethics defined" was shared by many others. As noted by Jacob Talmon, "Helvetius, Holbach, Mably, the Physiocrats and others, in the same way as Rousseau himself, believed that ultimately man was nothing but the product of laws of the State, and there was nothing that a government was incapable of doing in the art of forming man."[55]

If the main point of political measures is to locate evil and find ways to eliminate it,[56] then the human mind, on which the success of these measures depends, becomes a central anthropological category. Its advocates essentially believe that "[m]an is in principle at least, everywhere and in every condition, able, if he wills it, to discover and apply rational solutions to his problems. And these solutions, because they are rational, cannot clash with one another, and will ultimately form a harmonious system in which the truth will prevail, and freedom, happiness, and unlimited opportunity for untrammelled self-development will be open to all."[57] For "if we employ our rational faculties, we cannot fail."[58] Consequently, it is believed that "the patterned behaviour of society is successful, just, and progressive insofar as it reflects the articulated rationality of man in general and of the most intellectually and morally advanced people in particular".[59] Such an anthropological perspective justifies the search for a solution as the essence of politics. Premised on unlimited possibilities of reason, "the unconstrained vision promotes pursuit of the highest ideals and the best solutions."[60] Their rational discovery calls for effective implementation, without regard to what it might cost.

The idea of man as the effect of state education, and the comment on there being people who are "the most morally advanced", reveals the hierarchical or elitist dimension of the anthropology of unconstraint, concealed beneath the cloak of enthusiasm about man's perfection. It implies the existence of a group of "educators" and those who are "educated."[61] The advocates of this way of thinking—once again, aware of the empirical dimension of this perspective—agree that a majority of the

---

[54]Ibid., p. 26.

[55]Ibid., p. 35.

[56]Separating ourselves from old mistakes – to quote Condorcet – with an "everlasting barrier (...) that will forever preserve us from a relapse into former ignorance". Cf. T. Sowell, *A Conflict . . .*, pp. 18–19.

[57]I. Berlin, "Political Ideas. . .," p. 62.

[58]William Godwin, *Enquiry Concerning Political* Justice, University of Toronto Press, Vol. I, Toronto 1969, p. 80, as quoted in: T. Sowell, *A Conflict. . .*, p. 46.

[59]T. Sowell, *A Conflict. . .*, p. 90.

[60]Ibid., p. 26.

[61]Note that this way of looking at man is found already in the thought of Machiavelli who "seems to share the view that man has a free will but (...) only to an extent. (...) Only "few outstanding individuals' are endowed with it to a higher degree." Romuald Piekarski, *Makiawelizm, patologia*

population represent narrow horizons, and the group cultivating reason forms a narrow circle.[62] They treat this as a call to action: those "most intellectually advanced" should wield power, since "well-being of the masses is achievable only through the leadership and commitment of the elite."[63] Consequently, Helvetius and Holbach believe that "legislators, moralists and natural scientists should combine to form man on the basis of their teachings. (. . .) Governments have it in their power to rear genius, to raise or to lower the standard of ability in a nation."[64] Intellectuals, according to Godwin, are precursors of their contemporaries in the discovery of truth.[65] This needs to be emphasized, as it shows that the unconstrained anthropology is not so much an anthropology of perfection as rather an apology of the perfection of the (future, constructed) man, or, better, mankind, being essentially a synthesis of claims about the ethical and cognitive perfection of man (*per se*) and the actual imperfection of the real one.

Such a way of looking at human affairs explains the political views held by advocates of the unconstrained vision, where every step bringing us closer to the ideal should be preferred at all cost. This is well illustrated in Jefferson's comment on the French Revolution: "My own affections have been deeply wounded by some of the martyrs to this cause, but rather than it should have failed, I would have seen half the earth desolated."[66] What Jefferson is saying here is that he could not condemn the methods of the French Revolution which his conscience objected to and which were emotionally loathsome to him. They were a necessary, if painful, means to achieving a perfect end. Their immorality was relative: justified on the one hand by the good cause,[67] and on the other by the progress in whose light moral categories may change as well. Essentially, for Jefferson and other advocates of an unconstrained anthropology, the French Revolution represented the unconstrained sovereignty of man in a purer form than the American Revolution.

---

ducha, sacrum i polityka. Eseje z filozofii politycznej, Spódzielczy Instytut Naukowy, Sopot 2016, p. 21.

[62]T. Sowell, *A Conflict. . .*, p. 106.

[63]Ibid., p. 137.

[64]J. Talmon, *The Origins. . .*, p. 34.

[65]Ibid.

[66]T. Sowell, *A Confllict. . .*, p. 29.

[67]The equality of people is an end so important that achievement of the final solution to the problem of inequality justifies the interim solutions, treated as temporary, which would otherwise be considered unacceptable.

5.3 The Strengths and Weaknesses of Thomas Sowell's Theory

As regards his basic thesis about the conflict of two visions of politics, Thomas Sowell is convincing. He argues fervently[68] that the two perspectives of approaching social processes he has sketched out are an important key to understanding the inner tension of modernity, showing that "there are not merely differences of visions but conflicts of visions."[69] His conclusions are confirmed by some works of other authors, more thoroughly immersed in the study of political thought. Jacob Talmon refers to the same reality when he writes about liberal and totalitarian democracy. He confirms that "the tension between them has constituted an important chapter in modern history, and has now become the most vital issue of our time."[70] Sowell has a point in illustrating the two visions of politics with two revolutions. The extensive competences, including power over life and death, awarded in the course of the French Revolution to those who spoke "in the name of 'the people', expressing the Rousseauean 'general will'"[71] are an accurate exemplification of the unconstrained logic. Likewise, a good example of constrained logic is the check and balance system developed in the course of the American Revolution and characteristic of the constitutional tradition of the United States. The French Revolution, in line with the spirit of unconstraint, was a "total revolution," leaving "no sphere and no aspect of human existence untouched, whereas the American Revolution had been a purely political change-over (...) content to achieve a balance of social powers based on inequality and compromise."[72]

Another valuable solution is the categorization Sowell employs in the way of ideal types. The concepts of constraint and unconstraint, being "an abstract construct made up of the essential features"[73] of a particular political standpoint, elude typical

---

[68]And in a most straightforward and engaging style, let us add. As noted by one of his critical commentators: "The first thing that strikes you when reading Thomas Sowell is what a fine writer he is. The initial reaction from a man of the Left at this realization is chagrin. Reactionaries often, and with no awareness of irony, justify their belligerence by appealing to tradition while simultaneously murdering the English language. It would seem any persuasive argument on the glory and necessity of preserving established culture should, in the first instance, pay homage to the rules of the language the culture being venerated writes and speaks. This is rarely the case with conservative books, especially ones by those who fashion themselves the equivalent of public intellectuals, though no right thinking dittohead would dare use the hated and maligned word *intellectual* (*public* seems to also be on the ropes)". D.S. Wright, "Book Review: A Conflict of Visions," Progressive Friends of the Library Newsletter,http://www.dailykos.com/story/2012/02/21/1052864/-Book-Review-A-Conflict-Of-Visions-Part-1 [12.09.2013].

[69]T. Sowell, *A Conflict of...*, p. 39.

[70]J. Talmon, *The Origins...*, p. 1.

[71]T. Sowell, *A Conflict...*, p. 32.

[72]J. Talmon, *The Origins...*, p. 27.

[73]Roman Bäcker, *Czym jest teoria w politologii? O znaczeniukategoriitypuidealnego*, a paper presented at the conference "Czym jest teoria w politologii?", Poznań 12 May 2010, p. 2, wnpid. amu.edu.pl/attachments/787_Prof.%20Backer%20-%20referat.pdf [10.09.2013].

patterns of studies in political thought. They are not burdened like Talmon's typology, for example. And the burden concerns not only the content load of the concept of totalitarianism. It is worth noting that in Talmon, who uses the classical terminology, despite the depth of his analyses which Sowell's work stands no comparison to, we are witnessing a confusion of concepts. Ultimately, in the light of his theses and contrary to the popular understanding of the liberal-totalitarian dichotomy, it is in fact liberal democracy that may have a totalitarian character. He understands "liberal" in the etymological sense of the word, related to freedom, without referring to the long tradition of liberal thought at all. This shows that the application of classical categories used in the study of ideologies to describe contemporary political and ideological tensions may be misleading.

The categories used by Sowell ward off this risk, implicitly pointing to the key aspect of the two views: a different approach to the limits of the politic. This helps show not only the obvious contradictions between different families of ideas, but also identify major cracks and differences within these families, as well as relationships between ideological currents which are usually analyzed separately. Even if Sowell exploits this potential only to a limited degree, by employing a Weberian approach to the problem he reveals lines of thinkers distant from one another in their theoretical concepts, beginning with precursors of liberalism, through luminaries of the Enlightenment, to twentieth century economists. This way, he potentially also opens the door to revealing a relationship between the primary ideas of modernity and contemporary politics.

Finally, the greatest advantage—from the point of view of this study—of Sowell's theory is the link between the political and the anthropological problem. The two visions of politics that he presents correspond to two anthropological visions, showing the anthropological dispute as a foundation of the political dispute. Sowell arranges this into a neat dichotomy: a constrained anthropology, which is essentially an anthropology of (moral, cognitive) corruption, is paired with an unconstrained one, being an anthropology, if not apology, of man's perfection. These two stances lie—in his opinion—at the source of the different social visions and divergent visions of politics.

However paradoxical it may sound, the "greatest advantage" of Sowell's theory is also the most problematic. Of course, as regards anthropological sources of the unconstrained vision of politics, Sowell's claims appear to be most reasonable and find confirmation in other authors. Belief in the "essential goodness and perfectibility of human nature"[74] has always been held by the broadly-understood Left which, as noted by Talmon, even "resorting to force, does so in the conviction that force is used only in order to quicken the pace of man's progress to perfection and social harmony."[75] Eric Voegelin proves that this idea is rooted in the spirit of the *Encyclopaedia*, expressed in the conviction that "we are on the path of truth. We are not in the future to which this path will lead, but we are right on the path and we

---

[74]J. Talmon, *The Origins...*, p. 7.

[75]Ibid., p. 7.

will definitely know the direction."[76] It may thus be demonstrated that it was precisely due to the "vague, Messianic expectations"[77] concerning politics, characteristic of the logic of unconstraint, that "when the Revolution came to test the eighteenth-century teachings, the sense of an imminent and total renovation was almost universal."[78]

If we conclude, however, like the above-mentioned scholars, that the logic of unconstraint has its sources in the Enlightenment which "aimed at liberating men from fear and establishing their Sovereignty;"[79] and that by being related to broadly-understood leftism, it has an immanent revolutionary potential resulting, as Leszek Kołakowski argued in his treatises, from the "Promethean faith in the self-liberation of mankind,"[80] it seems unclear why Sowell should have excluded Marxist thought from the tradition of anthropological and political unconstraint. After all, it was precisely Morelly's mid-eighteenth century *Code de la Nature*, standing on the grounds of the logic of unconstraint, that was the first book "in modern times to put fully-fledged communism on the agenda as a practical programme, and not merely as a Utopia."[81]

According to Sowell, however, "the Marxian theory of history is essentially a constrained vision, with the constrains lessening over the centuries, ending in the unconstrained world of communism."[82] Sowell makes a fundamental distinction between the Marxist approach to the past and to the future, considering it a hybrid theory. He points out that unlike other socialists, for whom capitalism was simply immoral, Marx appreciated its "greatness and temporary necessity for the bourgeois regime."[83]

This reveals the first problems with Sowell's anthropology. It is true that Marx did not consider capitalism to be immoral. But not because he considered it moral and right, but because—as will be demonstrated further on—he abolished moral categories, understood in their proper sense, altogether, subordinating them to class interests. One can also hardly agree with Sowell that Marx believed in any "inherent constraints,"[84] considering that he refused to acknowledge the existence of a "human nature." Constraints resulting from historical, economic and social circumstances obviously have a place in Marxist theory. Nevertheless, like constraints, they may be

---

[76]E. Voegelin, *From Enlightenment to Revolution*, Duke University Press Books, 1982, p. 86.

[77]J. Talmon, *The Origins . . .*, p. 19.

[78]Ibid., p. 20.

[79]Max Horkheimer, Theodor W. Adorno, *Dialectic of Enlightenment*, Verso, 1997, p. 3.

[80]Leszek Kołakowski, *O duchu rewolucyjnym*, in: Id., *Czy diabeł może być zbawiony i 27 innych kazań*, Znak, Kraków 2006, p. 311.

[81]J. Talmon, *The Origins. . .*, p. 17.

[82]T. Sowell, *A Confllict of Vision. . .*, p. 105.

[83]T. Sowell. *A Conflict of Vision. . .*, p. 105. The Marxist attempts at abolishing it were based on "on the premise that new options now made capitalism both unnecessary and counterproductive." Ibid., p. 106.

[84]Ibid., p. 105.

seen as subsequent stages of man's self-emancipation. In fact, Sowell points this out himself. He says that for Marx capitalism was "a great step forward," and communism will be "the final form of human emancipation."[85] Since also for Rousseau, Condorcet and other *philosophes* man is in the process of liberation from bonds, and so his unlimited potential is yet to be fully realized, one can hardly argue that the Marxist logic is essentially different. Rather, it may be a sign that the theory of anthropological unconstraint needs to be given more thought. It seems to be an oversimplification to say that its essential feature is the Godwinian moral and epistemic perfection.

Even more serious questions arise from Sowell's understanding of constrained anthropology. It clearly refers to the reflections of Friedrich von Hayek, and particularly his criticism of constructivist rationalism.[86] Consequently, as has been rightly pointed out by Victor Vanberg, Sowell's vision of constraint does not sufficiently appreciate the human mind. It underplays the difference between the logic of social planning on the one hand, and rational judgment and establishment of institutional frameworks within which social relations have their place on the other.[87] The problem—simply put—lies in the fact that the view that "man is wicked and corrupt" supports not so much the check and balance system, but rather—as noted by Jacob Talmon—rightist totalitarianism.[88] It is not a coincidence that the *homo homini lupus* premise leads Hobbes to a vision of the state as Leviathan, rather than a constrained government. Constraint which places the main emphasis on moral and intellectual infirmities is, by its very nature, oriented more on emphasizing inequality and the role of power than on grounding the republic. Isaiah Berlin notes that as long as appropriate safeguards are in place to prevent treading on the "sacred past", already in the nineteenth century conservatives "no less than liberals were prepared to look upon the conscious direction of human affairs by qualified experts."[89]

Once Sowell's anthropological claims are accepted, several other, minor concerns arise. For example, it is not clear from what level of injustice the advocates of constraint should begin to strive towards changing the political *status quo*. Sowell stresses that Burke—whom he believes to be a classical representative of constrained anthropology—opposed slavery. On the grounds of a consistent logic of constraint, it is not clear why. After all, it was on the grounds of the belief in the epistemic and moral limitations of human nature that Aristotle argued that "a great number of men were slaves by nature (. . .) [and] did not possess the moral and intellectual resources with which to face the prospect of responsibility, of too wide a choice between alternatives."[90] It seems that some other anthropological premises are necessary here

---

[85]Ibid., p. 107.

[86]Cf. Victor Vanberg, *Conflict of Visions. Thomas Sowell*, "Cato Journal,"Vol.7, No.2 (Fall 1987), p. 547.

[87]V. Vanberg, *Conflict. . .*, p. 548–550.

[88]J. Talmon, *The Origins. . .*, p. 13.

[89]I. Berlin, "Political Ideas. . .," p. 63.

[90]Ibid., p. 73.

as well. Similarly, we will not learn from Sowell's text anything about the sources of the claim about the permanent, unchanging nature of man, and very little about the role of community in such a view of human nature. Belief in the innate infirmities of man seems to be necessarily related to the belief in the essential role of community in man's life.[91] Sowell makes only marginal comments regarding this issue. On the one hand, he emphasizes the conservative idea of an (intergenerational) community, while on the other, his standpoint, at least implicitly, is that of individualism (primary egotism). It thus appears that his view of constraint as corruption is rather limited and requires correction.

Moreover, referring to Berlin's thought, it may be argued that a constrained anthropology, as an anthropology of corruption, and an unconstrained anthropology, as an apology of man's perfection, are in fact two sides of the same political logic coin. Ultimately, Lenin also "started with the egalitarian belief that with education, and a rational economic organization, almost anyone could be brought in the end to perform almost any task efficiently. But his practice was strangely like that of those irrationalist reactionaries who believed that man was everywhere wild, bad, stupid, and unruly, and must be held in check and provided with objects of uncritical worship. This must be done by a clear-sighted band of organizers, whose tactics— if not ideals—rested on the truths perceived by elitists—men like Nietzsche, Pareto, or the French absolutist thinkers from De Maistre to Maurras, and indeed Marx himself (. . .). Only thus (in this view) can the founder of the new free society control whatever threatens to dissipate human energy or to slow down the relentless treadmill which alone prevents men from stopping to commit acts of suicidal folly, which alone protects them from too much freedom, from too little restraint, from the vacuum which mankind, no less than nature, abhors."[92] This way, as a result of a painful confrontation of the a priori ideal of the individual and the actual condition of the masses, the apology of man's perfection implicitly leads to the recognition of the profound corruption of human nature. Corruption which—and here it differs from the anthropology of corruption—can nevertheless be removed.[93]

The "convergence" of Sowell's constrained and unconstrained anthropology demonstrated by Berlin is a special proof of the legitimacy of concerns raised above. For while the characteristic features of these two visions of politics do seem to have been aptly illustrated by Sowell, their anthropological foundations appear to be oversimplified. And yet it is precisely their accurate definition that is of key importance in the context of contemporary disputes over the first principles. We

---

[91]As noted by Berlin, in the constrained vision typical of conservatism, man is "unable to save himself by his own wholly unaided efforts; and therefore rightly seek[s] salvation within the great frameworks – states, churches, unions. For only these great edifices promote solidarity, security and sufficient strength to resist the shallow joys and dangerous, ultimately self-destructive, liberties peddled by those conscienceless or self-deceived individuals who (. . .) ignore or destroy the rich texture of social life heavy with the treasures of the past". Ibid, p. 60.

[92]I. Berlin, "Political Ideas. . .," p. 74.

[93]The difference exists, but is not absolute. Ultimately, Leviathan also removed the corruption, at least in the social dimension. In this sense, the ideal of the state as an instrument of change is similar.

do not usually observe systemic symptoms of either of these two visions of politics, after all. On the contrary, we witness intra-systemic tensions about the essence of the politic. In other words, we are not fighting about democracy, but, if at all, about its "authenticity" or "disguise."[94] The ability to identify the vision of man behind postulates made in the political battle may help reveal the vision of politics they imply.

There are two questions, then. The first concerns the understanding of constrained anthropology. The issue of infirmity, well-defined by Sowell, needs to be complemented. Constrained politics, as demonstrated above, seems to require an understanding of the anthropological constraint that is broader than just the claim about infirmity. The second question concerns the very essence of unconstraint. Although the idea of human perfection is undoubtedly attractive to the advocates of unconstrained politics, they do not, in fact, believe in man's perfection—as Sowell has demonstrated himself. The core of the anthropological unconstraint must be hidden in another idea, then.

---

[94]Cf. Introduction to this Part of the book.

Chapter 6
Constrained Anthropology

In his analyses of Marxist thought, Leszek Kołakowski points out that the Promethean revolutionary project rejects "the idea of original sin understood so that it requires a redemptive intervention from the outside,"[1] suggesting the hermeneutic usefulness of theology in understanding political ideas. This seems to be entirely reasonable, particularly since—as argued by Agata Bielik-Robson—even the most secularized thinking is founded on an underlying theological choice.[2] Looking at Sowell's understanding of constraint from this perspective, we may find in it an approach to original sin that is the opposite of that of Marxism. When describing constrained anthropology, Sowell implicitly emphasizes the significance of sin which made "Adam, the first man, transgress God's commandment and lose the holiness and justice in which he was made, holiness and justice which were received not only for himself but for all of humanity."[3] Consequently, his brokenness affects not only himself—the corruption of his nature is inherited by all humanity: "it is a sin which will be transmitted by propagation to all mankind, that is, by the transmission of a human nature deprived of original holiness and justice."[4]

Clearly, as stressed by John Paul II, as well as others, the doctrine of the original sin is not only "an integral part of Christian revelation; it also has great hermeneutical value insofar as it helps one to understand human reality".[5] He agreed, we might say, with Sowell that "the social order will be all the more stable, the more it takes this fact into account."[6] It is not a coincidence that the recognition of some form of

---

[1] L. Kołakowski, *O duchu rewolucyjnym...*, p. 311.

[2] Agata Bielik-Robson, *Kryptoteologie późnej nowoczesności,* Universitas, Kraków 2008, p. 8.

[3] Pontifical Council for Justice and Peace, *Compendium of the Social Doctrine of the Church,* no. 115.

[4] Ibid., no. 115.

[5] Jan Paweł II, *Centesimus Annus...,* no. 25. Note that this sentence seems to positively verify the stability of the order which is the effect of the American Revolution, and the instability of the order which resulted from the French Revolution.

[6] Ibid.

© Springer Nature Switzerland AG 2021

M. Gierycz, *European Dispute over the Concept of Man*, Contributions to Political Science, https://doi.org/10.1007/978-3-030-61520-8_6

corruption in human nature is a recurring undertone of contemporary political theories.[7] Failure to bear in mind the imperfection of human nature makes "people think they possess the secret of a perfect social organization which makes evil impossible," and "that they can use any means, including violence and deceit, in order to bring that organization into being;" consequently, "politics (. . .) becomes a 'secular religion' which operates under the illusion of creating paradise in this world."[8]

Nevertheless, in keeping with the theological inspiration, it should be stressed that the constraint which affects man due to original sin is secondary. However paradoxical this may seem, in the theological perspective the fact that "man, against God's prohibition, allows himself to be seduced by the serpent and stretches out his hand to the tree of life," thus "challenging God, his sole Lord and the source of his life," in fact describes man's strife to "break through his limits as a creature."[9] Thus, the sin that is the source of the corruption of human nature is motivated by the desire to overcome the much more primary constraint that is proper to man.

6.1 Towards an Adequate Theory of Constraint

What does this basic constraint consist in? The simplest, theological lead is probably found in the prohibition God imposes on man after creating him in His own image and likeness: "you must not eat from the tree of the knowledge of good and evil, for when you eat from it you will certainly die" (Gen 2:17). This prohibition, seen in the context of God's blessing and the perspective of man's freedom (cf. Gen 1:28; 2:16), is not arbitrary. In its very essence, it expresses God's concern for man. Nevertheless, it does limit the field of man's activity. It is a reminder that "throughout his existence man is bound by the need to submit to the will of the Creator (. . .;) by the fact he is not God, but depends on Him. Through this prohibition, he is bound to ask about the will of the Creator, and by the limitation of his freedom, he is called to make decisions."[10] In this sense, man's limitedness is first of all related to the fact that his condition is that of a created being. It thus expresses the historically verifiable experience of man who has always been aware of the presence of The Other. The Other who is not only incomparably greater, but who is the guarantor of

---

[7]See for example the "envy test" in Dworkin's theory, or the key category of Rawls's "veil of ignorance." Ultimately, the point of drawing the veil is to lead to a situation where egotism "achieves the same purpose as benevolence." J. Rawl, *A Theory of Justice*, Belknap Press, Harvard University Press 2005, p. 148.

[8]John Paul II, *Centesimu Annus. . .*, no. 25.

[9]Pontifical Council for Justice and Peace, *Compendium of the Social Doctrine of the Church*, no. 115.

[10]Rev. Piotr Mazurkiewicz, *Grzech*, in: B. Szlachta [ed.], *Słownik społeczny*, WAM, Kraków 2006, p. 388.

human life. This dependence thus means that "if man forgot the word 'God' so that he also forgot that he had forgotten, he would cease to be a man."[11]

The discovery that God is part of the definition of man[12] refers us to the deepest relationship between the Creator and his creation recorded in the Book of Genesis: the fact that man is created in the image and likeness of God (Gen 1:27). Even though we are still moving within the limits of constraint, it is clearly not a negative one. By analogy to the typology of freedom proposed by Berlin, we could talk not so much of "constraint from," but of "constraint to." Constraint is not related primarily to any human flaw; on the contrary, it emphasizes the fact that (1) man has a nature, an identity—that he is "someone;" (2) his being "someone" is related not only to the nature of other created beings (corporeality), but primarily to the nature of God, in whom he finds his fulfillment. In the theological perspective, man's nature is related first of all to an exceptional and extraordinary dignity, resulting not only from the fact that man is created in the image and likeness of God, but also from the incarnation of God and redemption of man. The human person is at his source depicted "in relation to God and the whole of creation, as well as to other people, referring to the long philosophical tradition concerned not so much with an individual as the center of instinct, feelings, or random impressions, but rather with an intransient, self-conscious substance endowed with reason (spiritual nature), who is free, able to intellectually know reality independent from him, and to choose particular moral values."[13] It is the greatness, and not the smallness of man that is the first sign of constraint from the viewpoint of the hermeneutics of creation.[14]

If right at the heart of concept of human nature we touch upon the limits of man and of politics, the issue of the fall and sin only results in constraint being endowed with a dimension that was not intended by God. In this sense, the anthropology of creation also takes into account the anthropology of corruption, albeit without focusing on it.[15] We might say that just like in the case of other human characteristics, so too is constraint corrupted by sin. First of all because man wants to deny objectively existing constraint. Sin makes it more difficult for him to recognize the good that is inherent in his nature and to follow it—not only his mind, but also his

---

[11]Ibid. This would be a situation where man "understood himself as an entirely immanent being, (...) having nearly complete certainty that decomposition of matter marks the absolute end of his existence (...). Plunging into compete immanence would not only eliminate the problem of God, but also remove the drama of being a man."

[12]Fr. Piotr Roztworowski, *W szkole modlitwy*, 5th edition, Wydawnictwo Benedyktynów, Tyniec 2011, p. 15.

[13]Bogdan Szlachta, *Indywidualizm*, in: id. [ed.], *Słownik społeczny...*, p. 417.

[14]"The name for that deep amazement at man's worth and dignity—John Paul II boldly writes in *Redemptor Hominis*—is the Gospel, that is to say: the Good News." John Paul II, *The Encyclical Letter Redemptor Hominis to His Venerable Brothers in the Episcopate, the Priests, the Religious Families, the Sons and Daughters of the Church and to All Men and Women of Good Will at the Beginning of His Papal Ministry*, no. 10.

[15]This is also the point where the Protestant and the Catholic anthropologies diverge. Cf. Aniela Dylus, "Chrześcijaństwo," in: P. Burgoński, M. Gierycz, *Religia i polityka. Zarys problematyki*, Elipsa, Warszawa 2014.

will is wounded. Consequently, original sin reveals a new kind of tension in man: it is now up to a tainted man to decide whether to "exist in the image of God." The decision in which man "takes into his hands his own fate, and often the fate of other people,"[16] is placed in the hands of a being who can only see "dimly," "in part" (see 1 Cor 13:12). Nevertheless, it is still a being who can see clearly enough to be able to make the right choice, even if the choice has become much more difficult. As a consequence of sin, the difference between the nature of man and its laws, and the nature of the rest of the created world is seen in a new light. For while "[t]he laws of nature, as applied to stones or trees, may only mean 'what Nature, in fact, does'," when applied to man the law of nature no longer describes "what human beings, in fact, do," and often starts to mean "what human beings ought to do and do not."[17]

The limitation of reason—this should be most emphatically pointed out—as regards the search for moral good and common good is not primarily related to man's inherent infirmity; that is secondary, while the limitation is primary. It results from the fact that it is God (*Logos*) himself who represents proper reason. Consequently, man's rationality will always only be a reflection. "No one has ever seen God," St. John expressly writes (John 1:18). We are taught about wisdom; it is not man-made. Frederic Nietzsche wrote about this with respect to morality, saying that justifications supersede the rules.[18] Constraint from the perspective of the hermeneutics of creation does not weaken, but sharpens intelligence and cognition, leading towards the depth of knowledge which is contained in God, inaccessible to "purely human" rationality.[19] It reveals, in a way, the meaning of the spiritual and corporeal unity of the person who—despite his biological and intellectual limitations—can access truth, even if after the fall this requires more effort, since cooperation with God's grace no longer comes naturally to man.

The concept of person will be broached again soon. At this point, let us note that from the perspective of the hermeneutics of creation constrained anthropology proves to be simultaneously an anthropology of infinity and an anthropology of limits: infinity, because owing to the relationship of his nature with the Absolute, man as "a being who is rational and autonomous in his actions, different from what surrounds and singularizes him; while maintaining the nature of his species, endowed with freedom, responsibility, and grace; and when called upon by God, deciding about his own salvation and eternity;"[20] and limits, because he nevertheless has the "nature of his species," which is not only biological, but moral and spiritual as well. This nature allows us to talk of a "freedom characteristic of man which

---

[16]Mieczysław Albert Krąpiec OP, *Człowiek i polityka*, Towarzystwo św. Tomasza z Akwinu, Lublin 2007, p. 33.

[17]Clive Staples Lewis, *Mere Christianity*, HarperOne, 2015, pp. 27–28.

[18]Robert Spaemann, *Granice*, translated by Jarosław Merecki, Oficyna naukowa, Warszawa 2006, p. 83. [*German original: Grenzen. Zurethischen Dimension des Handelns*].

[19]In this context, John Paul II wrote that "faith and reason are like two wings on which the human spirit rises to the contemplation of truth." See: id., *Encyclical Letter Fides et Ratio of John Paul II to the Bishops of the Catholic Church on the Relationship Between Faith and Reason*, par. 1.

[20]B. Szlachta, *Indywidualizm...*, p. 417.

brings human cognition and love (desire) together in a single act of decision-making."[21] It is precisely this tension between the infinity of a person and his limitations, resulting both from his nature and from its corruption, that delineates Spaemann's normality of man in the light of the anthropology of creation: the specificity of being "someone."

To summarize, once constrained anthropology is complemented with the perspective of creation, we discover that "constraint" in the first place refers here not so much to any intellectual or moral "limitation," but to the existence of a human nature which has its "limits" and remains in a relationship with "that which is Higher," here: with its Creator. It thus refers to (1) the existence of twofold limits to humanity (related to its nature and to its corruption); (2) the constitutive tension between these limitations and the transcendental character of the person. This approach may be called holistic in the sense that it attempts to depict the comprehensive, both in the horizontal and the vertical dimension, specifically human identity.[22] It results directly from the logic of creation that being human is related to the awareness of limits which may be trespassed, but whose trespassing entails some form of dehumanization. To use philosophical categories, we might say that it is a realistic rather than a constructivist approach: man is a creation, and therefore a being who is formed in his very foundations, instead of being a plastic being that could be imagined any way we wanted. What man is, even taking into account the phenomenon of original sin, is not contained here in his weakness, but in his essence.

6.2 The Experience of Antiquity

We should now ask whether the essential elements of the understanding of constraint described above are specific only to Christianity, or whether they can also be found in other, pre-Christian ways of thinking significant for European culture. No doubt awareness of the "secondary" constraint was very widespread in Antiquity. The political system of Athens was full of "hedges" against human infirmity and the temptations of power—from rotating offices to the principle *Graphe Paranomon*. Similarly, republican Rome not only had the system of plebeian assemblies, but also the shared supreme power of two consuls. Was there an awareness, however, of the primary constraint described above?

It is worth noting that it is in Antiquity that we see a deeply-seated belief that it is the existence of a higher constraint, not dependent on the will of man, that founds

---

[21]Mieczysław Albert Krąpiec OP, *Człowiek i polityka*, Towarzystwo św. Tomasza z Akwinu, Lublin 2007, p. 31.

[22]A perceptive reader will notice that I have borrowed this concept from Charles Taylor, who in turn borrowed if from Mimi Bick. In Taylor's approach, holistic anthropology is contrasted with atomistic anthropology which assumes that social goods may and should be interpreted in terms of a collection of individual goods. Nevertheless, as will transpire in due course, I fill this concept with somewhat different content.

political order. In this context, Robert Spaemann refers to *The Eumenides* by Aeschylus, noting that right at the very beginning of the establishment of political community, the Erinyes, who represent the non-rational, archaic taboo of the matrilineal tribal ethics, are not banished from the polis. On the contrary, Athena, the goddess of reason, attributes the success of the polis to the worship of the old goddesses who existed before it was founded. "While traditional ethics is rejected, its place is not taken by any other. (...) The principle of rationality attributed to the polis reveals its power to humanize and bring peace in that it is open—so to say— 'downwards' and 'backwards,' i.e. open to what has not been established by itself."[23] On the grounds of philosophy, this is expressed by Aristotle in *Magna Moralia*, when he says that "it is not the case, as the others think, that reason is the originating principle and guide of virtue: rather, the emotions are. For there must first be produced in us (as indeed is the case) an irrational impulse to the noble, and then later on the reason must put the question to the vote and decide it."[24] The directness of valuation which is not mediated by any arguments precedes the final settlement made by reason which "judges them critically from the point of view of the goal which is good life as a whole."[25] In fact, we might say that the greatness of classical philosophy is due to the fact that it actualized rationality which did not transform into irrationality because it remembered its "pre-rational premises."[26]

Starting with the Aristotelian conviction that reflections on morality are "a starting-point of statecraft,"[27] the classical expression of this approach to man is represented by the natural law current. It is not, as should be stressed from today's perspective, just one more current of the ancient political philosophy. Quite the opposite, "the birth of natural law is also the beginning of ancient philosophy of law stretching across about 11 ages (sixth century BC—fifth century AD)."[28] In fact, therefore, the discovery of "nature" is the beginning of philosophy per se. As noted by Robert Reilly, mythical logic made no distinction between custom and nature: "a dog wagged its tail because that was the way of a dog. Egyptians minted their funeral caskets in bright colors because that was the way of the Egyptians. There was no way to differentiate between the two—the one being according to Nature and the other according to custom—because the word Nature was not available in the vocabulary of the prephilosophical world."[29]

Obviously, one might easily make the charge that—particularly in the sophist thought—nature "like the mythological Proteus, began to take on any such content

---

[23]R. Spaeamann, *Granice*, p. 93.

[24]Aristotle, *Magna Moralia*, Book II, 1206b in: *Aristotle's Ethics: Writings from the Complete Works*, Princeton University Press, 2014, p. 453.

[25]R. Spaemann, *Granice*, p. 92.

[26]Ibid., p. 96.

[27]Aristotle, *Magna Moralia*, Book I, 1181a.

[28]Roman Tokarczyk, *Filozofia prawa*, UMCS, Lublin 2005, p. 76.

[29]Robert R. Reilly, *Making Gay Okay. How Rationalizing Homosexual Behaviour is Changing Everything*, Ignatius Press, San Francisco 2014, p. 17.

and form as a particular thinker might imagine."[30] Nevertheless, even the sophist reflection was characterized by an attempt to emphasize the existence of some permanent rules, irrespective of the positive order, which must always be respected; in other words: limits which must not be trespassed by the lawgiver. Their universal incumbency was inherently linked to the issue of man's fundamental interests, i.e. that which people strive for by nature.[31] Plato and Aristotle "take up the distinction made by the Sophists between the laws that have their origin in a convention, that is, in a purely positive decision (*thesis*), and those that have force 'by nature'. The first are neither eternal nor are they in force everywhere and they do not oblige everyone. The second oblige everyone, always and everywhere,"[32] outlining the space of properly human action. What belongs to a convention must not contravene nature.

An important novelty introduced by Plato and Aristotle is the concept of that which is right by nature. Contrary to the hedonist current, it is based "on two premises. One says that in nature subjective pleasure always has a function, i.e. it is rooted in the objective teleological constitution of individual *physis*. (. . .) Pleasure is a subjective way of experiencing the realization of objective *telos*. The other premise is as follows: man—unlike other living creatures—may realize this function, which otherwise remains hidden."[33] This also means that man may try to circumvent *telos* in seeking pleasure.[34] Here, man's freedom is made manifest—he may walk towards a false happiness which leads to a sickness of the soul.[35]

For Plato, the incomparable depth of happiness resulting from realization of the *telos*, i.e. a man's objective good, is obvious: "a rational being realizes his essence through express thematisation of that which is objectively good, finding in it a happiness compared to which the happiness of a hedonist counts nothing at all."[36] If someone strives towards it, it is only because he is blind to the consequences, treating "the threat to the wellbeing of his soul as fictitious, non-urgent, and one which may be removed into the future,"[37] too distant to overcome the temptation of what is instantly available. Consequently, however, even for a man who makes a false turn, only the objective good represents a goal. This insight allowed the great minds of antiquity to stand on the threshold of natural law.

---

[30]R. Tokarczyk, *Filozofia prawa*, p. 83.

[31]R. Spaemann, *Granice*, pp. 191–192.

[32]International Theological Commission, *In Search of a Universal Ethic: A New Look at the Natural Law*, no. 19.

[33]R. Spaemann, *Granice*, pp. 191–192.

[34]Ibid., p. 193. Such conduct is destructive, however, "and Plato believes it to be the reason for all cultural decline."

[35]Ryszard Legutko, *Sokrates*, Zysk i ska, Poznań 2013, p. 255. He notes there that—according to Socrates—this process is not entirely conscious: "No one says to himself—unless we are dealing with pathology—that he cares nothing about the perspective of an illness of his soul, and that he prefers wickedness."

[36]R. Spaemann, *Granice. . .*, p. 193.

[37]R. Legutko, *Sokrates. . .*, p. 255.

A "textbook" antique formulation of natural law is found in Cicero who says that "true law is right reason in agreement with nature, it is of universal application, unchanging and everlasting; it summons to duty by its commands, and averts from wrongdoing by its prohibitions. And it does not lay its commands or prohibitions upon good men in vain, though neither have any effect on the wicked. It is a sin to try to alter this law, nor is it allowable to attempt to repeal any part of it, and it is impossible to abolish it entirely (. . .) for all nations and all times, and there will be one master and ruler, that is, God, over us all, for he is the author of this law, its promulgator, and its enforcing judge. Whoever is disobedient is fleeing from himself and denying his human nature, and by reason of this very fact he will suffer the worst penalties, even if he escapes what is commonly considered punishment."[38]

The above passage clearly shows both the power and the weakness of natural law. The power is related to its invariability, its divine provenience, its permanence, finally its fundamental significance for developing in humanity, related to its orientation towards good. Weakness—due to the absence of coercion on the part of the conscience, and the fact it may be violated by men with apparent impunity. Apparent, because in its essence such a transgression is an abuse; indeed, a self-abuse. This blunt allegory seems justified. Natural law, from the perspective of constrained anthropology, defines the criteria of normality; it establishes them. Robert Spaemann emphasizes that nature is that which "is in principle beyond discursive problematisation;" it is an "anthropological minimum of that which is normal."[39] Consequently, by transgressing it, we enter the sphere of degeneration, denying the ability to perceive the proper measures of existence itself, which Plato called "nous."[40]

6.3   The Christian Tradition

Although conviction about the existence of a primary limitation of human nature was already found in antiquity, the blooming period of the theory of normality, understood in Spaemann's terms, in European tradition is related to Christianity. The

---

[38]Cicero, *On the Republic*, translated by C.W.Keyes, Harvard University Press, 1928, book III, no. 22, p. 211.

[39]R. Spaemann, *Granice*, pp. 197–198. Robert Spaemann notes that the concept of normality flows out of the concept of human nature in two ways. Firstly, because the existential significance of normality is entailed by man's nature as a living creature. And secondly because this nature itself also establishes a basic normality. To exemplify this nondiscursive naturalness, Spaemann refers e.g. to the fact that since it is women who get pregnant, they are the ones who bear the first responsibility for the child's life. This initially unequal distribution of duties, resulting from nature, does not require a justification, even though it entails legal obligations. Similarly, the fact that children need the presence of their parents establishes the anthropological criteria for justifying the divestment of parental rights, etc.

[40]Cf. Joseph Cardinal Ratzinger, *Turning Point for Europe?: The Church in the Modern World: Assessment and Forecast*, Ignatius, 2010, p. 136.

easily noticeable difference introduced by Christianity concerned the applicability of anthropological postulates previously discovered by "the greatest minds of the ancient world: Plato, Aristotle, Cicero, Sophocles, Euripides."[41] While for the Greeks, as taught by Aristotle, "barbarian and slave are by nature one and the same,"[42] once man redeemed by Christ was recognized as an *imago Dei*, this logic was ultimately rejected. For St. Paul, "there is neither Jew nor Gentile," for they are all "one in Christ Jesus" (Ga 3:28).

In this perspective, the classical political theory which says that the role of government is to ensure that norms which are self-evident to a righteous mind (as they result from natural law) are enforced by positive law, has been developed and deepened. In Aquinas's interpretation, the law—as the road that leads to happiness[43]—is a "an ordinance of reason for the common good, made by him who has care of the community, and promulgated."[44] Characteristically, the way to happiness is directly related to constraint: to norms (nor arbitrary, but reasonable) oriented towards the actualization of man's inherent potentialities. This gives rise to the question about how reason has access to discernment between right and wrong. Already in ancient philosophers, as can be seen, for instance, in the passage from Cicero quoted above, reference was made in this context to the idea of a god who is "'the measurement of measurements,' that is, the standard according to which cities may be founded and rules of behaviour laid down."[45]

It is worth noting that the "automatic" Christianization of the ancient idea of natural law could have led to forsaking the secular character of politics and claiming, as one of the currents in Judaism, that natural law is the same as revealed law.[46] Even though for Aquinas it was clear that "the world is ruled by Divine Providence (. . .) [and] that the whole community of the universe is governed by Divine Reason,"[47] the theory he developed did not follow this "simplified" path. Concluding that eternal law, which is nothing other than God himself,[48] "directing all actions and

---

[41]Rev. Piotr Mazurkiewicz, "Chrześcijańskie korzenie Europy," in: Maciej Koźmiński [ed.], *Cywilizacja europejska. Wykłady i eseje*, Scholar, Collegium Civitas Press, Warszawa 2004, p. 48.

[42]Aristotle, *Politics*, Oxford University Press 1946, Book 1, p. 3.

[43]To quote Aristotle who said that "all the various pronouncements of the law aim (. . .) at the common interest of all (. . .) so that in one of its senses the term 'just' is applied to anything that produces and preserves the happiness, or the component parts of the happiness, of the political community." Aristotle, The Nicomachean Ethics, Harvard University Press 1934, p. 76 [1129b17].

[44]Thomas Aquinas, *SummaTheologiae*, XIII q. 90 a. 4. This definition clearly refers to the ancient philosophy of politics mentioned above, from which Aquinas took not only the concept of the state as an ideal community, but also of politics as the space of realizing a good life.

[45]Hannah Arendt, *Between Past and Future: Eight Exercises in Political Thought*, The Viking Press 1968, p. 131.

[46]Cf. R. Tokarczyk, *Filozofia. . .*, pp. 152–153, or Piotr Burgoński, "Judaizm," in: P. Burgoński, M. Gierycz [ed.], *Polityka i religia. Perspektywa politologiczna*, Elipsa, Warszawa 2014.

[47]Thomas Aquinas, *SummaTheologiae*, XIII q. 91 a. 1.

[48]Cf. Ibid q. 91 a.1 ad. 3, where Aquinas says: "but the end of the Divine government is God Himself, and His law is not distinct from Himself."

movements," Aquinas also notes that no one—apart from the saints in heaven—is able to know eternal law the way it is in and of itself.[49] This means that the necessary participation of man in eternal law must happen otherwise. Recapitulating Aquinas's thought, we might say that people "are subordinated to eternal law in two ways: by the features they share with all created beings, and in a way that is specifically human—by reason."[50] And it is precisely due to the light of reason, which allows us to discern between right and wrong, that it is "evident that the natural law is nothing else than the rational creature's participation of the eternal law."[51]

Analogously to the thought of Plato and Aristotle, the fundamental principle of natural law is based on the concept of good. The commandment: "good is to be done and pursued, and evil is to be avoided"[52] "is the foundation on which all other precepts of natural law are based, i.e. all those imperatives and prohibitions which practical reason naturally considers to be good for man."[53] Thus, in Aquinas, it first of all represents this anthropological normality—that which is good and therefore right for man. It should be emphasized already here, even though this thought will be elaborated further on in the summary, that this solution "works" only on the assumption that there is a God who does not enter into man's life only "from 'the outside,' but from 'the inside,' as the voice of conscience."[54] Natural law represents the order resulting from creation which bears the imprint of God and his law. It is not merely man's cognitive abilities, but their participation in higher wisdom that provides man with certainty about the uniqueness and universality of the principles of natural law. It helps man recognize in the diversity of cultural customs one recurring motif in understanding what is good. With regard to the ancient version, we may thus speak of a secularization of the law of nature, but not in the sense of forsaking its relationship to the Absolute, but of an indirectness of reference to God in the process of defining what is natural.

6.3.1 The Value of Life and the Equality of Personal Dignity

Despite his awareness that it is impossible to encompass the full expanse of natural law, Aquinas considers it legitimate to define its basic requirements, understood as fundamental anthropological borders. Beginning with the nature of man as a living being, he constructs an area of an anthropological minimum safeguarded by natural law.

---

[49]Ibid q. 93 a.2.

[50]P. Mazurkiewicz, *Europeizacja Europy...*, p. 237.

[51]Thomas Aquinas, *SummaTheologiae*, XIII q. 91 a. 2.

[52]Ibid q. 94 a. 2.

[53]P. Mazurkiewicz, *Europeizacja...*, p. 237.

[54]P. Mazurkiewicz, *Europeizacja...*, p. 349.

In the first place, he points to the desire, shared by all living beings, to preserve their life and health, with the following result: "whatever is a means of preserving human life, and of warding off its obstacles, belongs to the natural law."[55] This, essentially rather commonplace, statement entails significant anthropological content. All human relations are ultimately based on the idea that "man is first respected in the integrity of his bodily *physis*,"[56] which is the basic limitation to human freedom. From the outside, "we cannot separate the subject of freedom from his physical existence as the first sphere of this freedom—as though to respect freedom by destroying physical existence. A person as the subject of freedom may only be respected if we recognize as a taboo the sphere in which the person appears: his existence as a natural living being."[57]

Special respect for human life is thus the first measure of humanity resulting from natural law. The germ of this thought can already be found in the ancient Hippocratic Oath. With the emergence of Christianity, this logic reaches its apex.[58] In its light, the core meaning is revealed of the conviction about the difference between man and animal, or—more broadly—the human world and the animate/inanimate world. The idea of human unity implicitly present in the approach to human life is premised on "the great, common and primitive world—the world of mankind. 'Humans' are treated here as a group that is one of a kind, within which all individuals have the same substantial value and which differs from all other groups."[59] To quote Leszek Kołakowski, we might say that humankind is a "moral concept" here.[60] This is due to the abyss which "the Biblical story has dug between man and animal."[61] Rooted in the redemption of man created in the image and likeness of God, the idea of human dignity,[62] premised on "the essential, radical separation between the world of man and the rest of nature, and at the same time the essential bond between all men,"[63] is the deepest foundation for the belief that "man may not be treated like an object."[64]

---

[55]Thomas Aquinas, *Summa Theologiae*, XIII q. 94 a. 2.

[56]R. Spaemann, *Granice...*, p. 199.

[57]Ibid.

[58]Though from today's perspective, antiquity would appear "inhuman" to us. As noted by Remi Brague, not only abortion and slavery were quite widespread. Also abandoning unwanted babies was not "a crime which should be prevented at all cost." Id., *Europe, Christianity and the Modern Age*, a lecture delivered at the International Conference "John Paul II and the Spiritual Foundations of European Unity" on June 11–12, 2014.

[59]Chantal Delsol, *Esej o człowieku późnej nowoczesności*, translated by Małgorzata Kowalska, Znak, Kraków 2003, p. 16 [*Éloge de la singularité, essai sur la modernité tardive*, La Table Ronde 2007].

[60]Leszek Kołakowski, "Kant i zagrożenie cywilizacji," in: id., *Czy diabeł może być zbawiony i 27 innych kazań*, Znak, Kraków 2006, p. 197.

[61]Ch. Delsol, *Esej o człowieku...*, p. 16.

[62]L. Kołakowski, "Kant i zagrożenie cywilizacji," p. 197.

[63]Ch. Delsol, *Esej o człowieku...*, p.16.

[64]Ibid.

As noted by Robert Spaemann, "the content of the word dignity is difficult to conceptualize because it expresses a non-definable, simple quality."[65] It refers to the special value of man, who is not only "for himself an end in itself," but simply "and end in and of himself." He notes that "if value exists only in view of the valuating subjects, then the destruction of all valuating subjects cannot be called a crime. Existence is not a property whose absence makes man poorer, because one cannot be poorer if one does not exist."[66] Only once the value of man "in and of himself," i.e. not only for man himself, is recognized can the source of the irreplaceable value of every human being be discovered, revealing the ontological dimension of human dignity which turns out to be an essentially religious and metaphysical concept. As emphasized by Spaemann, for dignity to exist, either man must "live after his physical death, so that the subject who has been wronged continues to exist," or there must be a God "about whom Psalm 116 says: 'Precious in the sight of the Lord is the death of his faithful servants'."[67]

If constrained anthropology, by emphasizing the dignity of man, understands him not only as an individual, but also as a being who transcends "the dimension of goals and desires proper to the organization of social life, and strives towards the supernatural order,"[68] these "manifestations of transcendence by the human spirit of man's determined biological nature and the society have taken on [in the history of philosophy] the form of the so-called theory of personal existence."[69] Without recapitulating here the studies on the category of person,[70] extensively discussed in literature, it should be stressed that the concept of personal dignity, which penetrated anthropology from Trinitarian theological reflection, is associated in the Christian tradition first of all with qualities such as reason, capacity for moral knowledge, free will, dominion over the created world, immortality, or the calling to social life. Consequently, all human actions are forms in which personhood is made manifest, expressed in "three characteristic ways of acting (...) specifically, the ways of personal knowledge, personal acts of love, and the freedom characteristic of man which brings human knowledge and love (desire) together in a single act of decision-making."[71]

One more thing that needs to be stressed is the equality potential of the theory of personhood. The significance of Christianity for the concept of man's dignity, one that is of key importance for contemporary Europe, is also of fundamental significance for the idea of equality. "In dismantling barriers of race, social status and gender, Christianity proclaimed from the first the equality of all men and women

---

[65]R. Spaemann, *Granice...*, p.150.

[66]Ibid., p.155.

[67]Ibid., p.155.

[68]MichałBardel, Tadeusz Gadacz, "Osoba," in: B. Szlachta [ed.], *Słownikspołeczny...*, p. 786.

[69]Mieczysław Albert Krąpiec OP, *Człowiek i polityka...*, p. 31.

[70]Cf. e.g. Nicolas Lobkowicz, *Czas kryzysu, czas przełomu...* [German original: *Erbe Europas*], or P. Mazurkiewicz, *Europeizacja Europy...*.

[71]M. A. Krąpiec OP, *Człowiek i polityka...*, p. 31.

before God."[72] It was never about equality understood as identicalness, however. As will be demonstrated in the next section, awareness of the fundamental significance of difference is inherent to the Christian concept of man in view of its recognition of the anthropological significance of sex. Consequently, also the "dismantling of barriers" mentioned by John Paul II should be seen in terms of long duration, since Christianity was never about a social revolution.[73] It was a transformative force, however. Taking the stance that "the basis of an organic social order is fraternity uniting parts that are distinct,"[74] in long duration it revealed the social consequences of Paul's thesis that "[t]here is neither Jew nor Gentile, neither slave nor free, nor is there male and female," for all are "one in Christ Jesus."[75]

Summing up, it should be emphasized that the concept of equality in personal dignity is strictly linked to the approach to human life, which Aquinas presents as the first principle of natural law. We might say that a test of respect for this dignity is the attitude to human life. Once it is separated from life, dignity—as Eduard Picker points out—loses "its substratum, and thus its significance" as the highest good that must be protected.[76]

6.3.2   Sexuality and Marriage

When discussing *inclinationes naturales*, Aquinas lists the uniting of man and woman and the education of their offspring as the second natural inclination.[77] By making the sexual drive the starting point which is the basis for the fact that "our whole body is saturated with our relationship to the opposite sex,"[78] Aquinas shows monogamy and indissolubility of marriage as an expression of anthropological normality, being a good in itself and a social good.

Even though "the central feature of the vision of man as originating from the God of Abraham, Isaak and Jacob is the mutual complementariness of man and woman,"[79] this standpoint does not, of course, represent a *differentia specifica* of the Christian tradition. So too in ancient Rome was marriage "monogamous. As noted by Modestinus, it was a union of man and woman for life, a community of

---

[72]John Paul II, *Fides et Ratio...*, 38.

[73]Cf. Jacek Salij OP, *Eseje tomistyczne*, W Drodze, Poznań 1995, pp. 180–182.

[74]Richard M. Weaver, *Ideas Have Consequences*, University of Chicago Press, 2013, p. 40.

[75]St. Paul, *Letter to Galatians* 3:28.

[76]E. Picker, *Godność człowieka a życie. Rozbrat dwóch fundamentalnych wartości jako wyraz narastającej relatywizacji człowieka*, Oficyna Naukowa, Warszawa 2007, p.35 [German original: *Menschen würde und Menschenleben*].

[77]Thomas Aquinas, *Summa Theologiae*, XIII q. 94 a. 2.

[78]M.A. Krąpiec, *Człowiek...*, p.57.

[79]Jan Grosfeld, "Mężczyzna i kobieta," in: M. Gierycz, Jan Grosfeld, *Zmagania początku tysiąclecia*, Łośgraf, Warszawa 2012, p. 49.

divine and human law."[80] Even earlier, Plato exhorted his fellow citizens that they "should not fall below the other animals, who live all together in flocks, and yet remain pure and chaste until the time of procreation comes, when they pair, and are ever after faithful to their compact."[81] Nevertheless, it is "Judaism [that] is credited for having accomplished a sexual revolution which considered as good only the relationship between a man and a woman."[82] Consequently, development of the recognition of the exceptionality of monogamous union is related strictly to the Christian tradition,[83] which developed and deepened the ancient intuitions about the meaning of the relationship between a man and a woman.

The Book of Genesis portrays the original loneliness of the first man—Adam who falls to sleep "with the desire of finding a being like himself." His circle of loneliness is filled once "the first 'man' awakens from his sleep as 'male and female'," discovering "homogeneity of the whole being of both."[84] The fact that—as specified in the Jahwist description of creation—God created "man and woman" in his image leads to the conclusion that "man became the 'image and likeness' of God not only through his own humanity, but also through the communion of persons which man and woman form right from the beginning."[85] Consequently, "from the beginning" man reflects the "inscrutable divine communion of persons." John Paul II says that this may well be "the deepest theological aspect of all that can be said about man. In the mystery of creation—on the basis of the original and constituent 'solitude' of his being—man was endowed with a deep unity between what is, humanly and through the body, male in him and what is, equally humanly and through the body, female in him. On all this, right from the beginning, the blessing of fertility descended, linked with human procreation."[86]

From this perspective, the natural desire to be united with the opposite sex has a profoundly personal meaning. Manhood and womanhood express not only "the dual aspect of man's somatic constitution, (. . .) [but also] a new consciousness of the sense of one's own body. It can be said that this sense consists in a mutual enrichment (. . .): femininity finds itself, in a sense, in the presence of masculinity, while masculinity is confirmed through femininity."[87] The experience of sexuality is here "something more than the mysterious power of human corporality, which acts

---

[80]Rafał Kamprowski, *Miejsce i rola kobiety w rodzinie na przestrzeni wieków. Od Antyku po I wojnę światową Zarys problematyki*, https://repozytorium.amu.edu.pl/bitstream/10593/3835/1/kamprowski.pdf [07.09.2016], p. 35.

[81]Plato, *The Laws*, translated by Benjamin Jowett, Pantianos Classics 2016, p. 44.

[82]Jan Grosfeld, "Żydowski wymiar chrześcijaństwa," in: M. Gierycz, J. Grosfeld [ed.], *Zmagania. . .*, p. 19.

[83]Note that in ancient Rome, the sacral form of marriage, *confarreatio*, celebrated only once in a lifetime, was reserved "only for the higher social strata." Ibid.

[84]John Paul II, *The Redemption of the Body and Sacramentality of Marriage*, Libreria Editrice Vaticana 2005, p. 23.

[85]Ibid., p. 25.

[86]Ibid.

[87]Ibid., pp. 26–27.

almost by virtue of instinct. At the level of man and in the mutual relationship of persons, sex expresses an ever new surpassing of the limit of man's solitude that is inherent in the constitution of his body, and determines its original meaning."[88] Consequently, a sexual act is not an act driven by instinct, but one of the many dimensions of a personal union "intended to go along with it and make up the total union."[89] For "right from the beginning, that unity which is realized through the body indicates not only the 'body,' but also the 'incarnate' communion of persons— *communio personarum*—and calls for this communion."[90] Therefore, it must be related to the choice of another person as a party to the "covenant of persons,"[91] i.e. the contract of marriage.

Since sex and sexuality belong to the essence of personhood, abstraction of the experience of sexuality from the marital relationship between a man and a woman would be an exemplification of the circumvention of *telos* in the search for pleasure described by Plato. It may be achieved, but doing so manifestly contravenes the good that is inherent to marital union; just like it would be a contravention to derive pleasure from eating without swallowing and digesting the food, "by chewing things and spitting them out again."[92] In the perspective of constrained anthropology, monogamous marriage thus appears to be a phenomenon of key importance for man's integral development. Sex is "a constituent part of the person," showing "how deeply man, with all his spiritual solitude, with the never to be repeated uniqueness of his person, is constituted by the body as 'he' or 'she'."[93] We thus discover here, similarly to when we were first looking for an adequate view of constraint,[94] a "constraint to"; not so much a lack of something, but an element that is constitutive of man.

Marriage, however, as noted by Aquinas, is a good not only for the persons who engage in it. Considered "objectively, the martial relationship", as Karol Wojtyła wrote, "is therefore not just a union of persons, a reciprocal relationship between a man and a woman, but is essentially a union of persons affected by the possibility of procreation. This term is more appropriate here than 'reproduction', which tends to have a purely biological meaning. We are speaking of course, not merely of the beginning of life in a purely biological sense but of the beginning of a person's existence."[95] Consequently, the order of nature (geared toward procreation) and the personal order (expressed in the love between persons) are strictly related: "each depends upon the other. In particular, the correct attitude to procreation is a condition

[88]Ibid., pp. 27–28.

[89]C.S. Lewis, *Mere Christianity,* HarperOne 2015, p. 105.

[90]John Paul II, *The Redemption of the Body and Sacramentality of Marriage*, p. 26.

[91]Ibid., p. 109.

[92]C.S. Lewis, *Mere Christianity*, p. 105.

[93]John Paul II, *The Redemption. . .*, p. 27.

[94]Cf. Sect. 6.1.

[95]Karol Wojtyla, *Love and Responsibility*, Ignatius Press 1993, p. 226.

of the realization of love."[96] In the light of constrained anthropology, the offspring which is "the fruit and the sign of conjugal love"[97] makes marriage and family inseparably related.

Marriage is not only a condition for the birth of children, but also for their personal development. As noted by Chantal Delsol, the question of education in a family based on marriage is ultimately the question of human subjectivity—which may exist or not: "the ability to take initiative and assume responsibility depends entirely on educational communities, beginning with family which is a spacer between the individual and the institutional."[98] So much so that "the survival of an autonomous subject is strictly related to education in the family."[99] Considering that only a monogamous marriage promotes the "normal, mental development of a human being (from birth up to the independent, mature period of human life)" who can be raised to be responsible for the life of another,[100] constrained anthropology understands marriage and family as the second measure of Spaemann's normality. Let us add—in the light of Delsol's reflections—that it conditions, to a degree, the first measure: for "if an individual subject disappears, it will not be possible for the dignity of an individual being to survive either."[101]

6.3.3   Man's Rational and Social Nature

"Thirdly,"—as pointed out by Thomas Aquinas—"there is in man an inclination to good, according to the nature of his reason, which nature is proper to him: thus man has a natural inclination to know the truth about God, and to live in society: and in this respect, whatever pertains to this inclination belongs to the natural law; for instance, to shun ignorance, to avoid offending those among whom one has to live, and other such things regarding the above inclination."[102]

The other *inclinationes* Aquinas lists are not related to the personal experience of aspects of existence common to all animate nature, but the specific (in the sense of exclusivity) experience of man. Interestingly, the Angelic Doctor includes in this

---

[96]Ibid, p. 226.

[97]John Paul II, *Apostolic Exhortation (FamiliarisConsortio) of His Holiness Pope John Paul II to the Episcopate to the Clergy and to the Faithful of the Whole Catholic Church Regarding the Role of the Christian Family in the Modern World*, No. 28.

[98]Ch. Delsol, *Esej o człowieku. . .*, p. 86.

[99]Ibid. She notes that "in this respect, our democracy is now at the ultimate crossroads, as it must decide whether to develop welfare state and matriarchies, affording the individual privileged treatment, or to develop a more liberal economy and uphold family institutions which forge the individual's responsibility." (*Esej*, p. 84).

[100]M.A. Krąpiec, *Człowiek. . .*, p. 61. He stresses that these goals of marriage "cannot be realized in other types of marriage (and the related family life)."

[101]Ch. Delsol, *Esej o człowieku. . .*, p. 92.

[102]Thomas Aquinas, *Summa Theologiae*, q. 94 a. 2.

group the concept of man as a social being, which seems to be an extension of the phenomenon of man's sexuality. It reveals man as a being saturated with "relations to others, enabling him to actualize his humanity."[103] This should be understood so that while "a community is more of a work of nature and more nearly related to the biological; a society is more of a work of reason, and more nearly related to the intellectual and spiritual properties of man."[104] In this sense, for Aquinas social life is primarily a dictate of reason, an element which no longer belongs to the aspects of human nature shared with all animate beings. It is a "necessary complement—a complementary formation—ensuring the possibility of personal development which in the chief sense is common good."[105] It is worth noting that constrained anthropology in the Christian approach upholds the conviction, in a somewhat different form already expressed by Aristotle, that an "asocial" man is unthinkable, being a "poor sort of being, or a being higher than man."[106] The emphasis on man's social nature implicitly curbs the ambitions of the state which—as already illustrated in Aristotle's *Politics*—may only intervene where smaller communities are no longer self-sufficient. This idea, fully developed in the context of the Christian principle of subsidiarity,[107] shows the secondary role of the state not only with regard to the family as the first natural community, but also with regard to other communities closer to man, thus helping subordinate politics to the objective good of a person and respect for his or her subjectivity.

If community is a dictate of reason, then in the light of constrained anthropology rationality itself, related to the Absolute, represents a key attribute of person. It is not incidentally that Boetius defines person as "naturae rationabilis individua substantia."[108] For the people of Middle Ages, it was quite obvious that "a person is something independent (. . .), endowed with reason (. . .), and something that has a

---

[103]Ch. Millon-Delsol, *Esej o człowieku. . .*, p. 92.

[104]Jacques Maritain, *Man and the State*, CUA Press 1998, p. 2.

[105]M. A. Krąpiec, *Człowiek. . .*, pp. 57–58.

[106]Aristotole, *Politics*, Book I §9, p. 5.

[107]This term was first used by Bishop Wilhelm von Ketteler in the second half of the nineteenth century. The political influence of the idea of subsidiarity in modern politics is strictly related to the social teaching of the Church. Cf. Anton Losinger, "Einfluss auf das Menschen- und Gesellschaftsbild der Katholischen Soziallehre," in: Wolfgang J. Mückl [Hg.], *Subsidiarität. Gestaltungsprinzip fuer eine freiheitliche Ordnung in Staat, Wirtschaft und Gesellschaft*, Verlag Ferninand Schöningh, Paderborn-München-Wien-Zürich 1999; or Otfried Höffe, "Subsidiaritaet als europapolitisches Prinzip," in: Rudolf Hrbek [Hg.], *Die Anwendung des Subsidiaritätsprinzips in der Europäischen Union—Erfahrungen und Perspektiven*, Nomos Verlagsgesselschaft, Baden-Baden 1995. In literature, it is sometimes even considered impossible to detach the principle of subsidiarity from the context of the social teaching of the Church without blurring its semantic contours. Cf. Winfrid Böttcher, Johanna Krawczynski, *Europas Zukunft: Subsidiaritaet*, Shaker Verlag, Aachen 2000, p. 22.

[108]Boetius, *De duabis naturis Christi*, V, 4, 20–22, as quoted in: Berthold Wald, "Bycie człowiekiem jest byciem osobą. Kontekst chrześcijański i podstawy filozoficzne," in: Piotr Stanisław Mazur [ed.], *Spór o osobę w świetle klasycznej definicji człowieka. Studia i rozprawy*, Ignatianum, WAM, Kraków 2012, p. 20.

dignity."[109] Unlike the idea of dignity, since Greek times the "love of wisdom" has been a characteristic trait of pre-European intellectual culture. Nevertheless, the novelty brought by Christianity was "the affirmation of the right of everyone to have access to the truth."[110] While in antiquity, philosophy was an elitist occupation, in the Christian world this could no longer be the case—since "access to the truth enables access to God, it must be denied to none."[111] Having noted that along with the thesis concerning dignity, rationality is another premise of the egalitarian trait of the Christian tradition, let us also note that the concept of rationality deepens the concept of rationalism seen in antiquity. So, rationalism—as mentioned above in reference to Spaemann—was already potentially "open to what had not been established by itself."[112] In the Christian tradition, rationality refers both to the mind's faculties to know the sensuous world, to moral knowledge described as conscience and sinderesis,[113] and finally—to spiritual knowledge, an encounter with God who himself manifests rationality (logos).

The breadth of the understanding of rationality in constrained anthropology corresponds to the breadth of human freedom. After all, only "the freedom to take a stance on the most essential issues concerning the meaning of life, man's place in the universe, and the existence of God enables [man's] comprehensive personal and social development."[114] Looking from another side, the rational, spiritual and moral dimension of human existence protects the space of man's freedom in a particular way. The Absolute which operates in man as the voice of conscience allows him to rise above the purely human opinions or social circumstances, and to refer his actions to objective good. This upper limitation is of key importance for the subjectivity of the human person. Consequently, Aquinas supplements the Boetian definition of person, emphasizing that he is also "the master of his cognitive and volitional acts, and is therefore not the object of action, but its subject."[115]

The sovereignty of the person this entails is the basis of "the sovereignty of all institutions we encounter in this world. After all, it is in the act of man's personal decision that we first encounter the existential sovereignty of the human person, and it is modeling on this sovereignty that we develop the idea of the sovereignty of a family, a nation, or a state."[116] The idea of dignity and the elements of anthropological normality outlined above in the light of the philosophy of natural law clearly

---

[109]N. Lobkowicz, *Czas kryzysu. . .*, p. 96.

[110]John Paul II, *Fides et Ratio. . .*, 38.

[111]Ibid.

[112]N. Lobkowicz, *Czas kryzysu. . .*, p. 93.

[113]Aquinas distinguished it from conscience, understanding it as "the capacity of reason to know the first principles of moral behaviour; conscience is only revealed on the grounds of sinderesis, as an act of practical reason which adjudicates about the moral rightness of particular actions." Rev. Henryk Skorowski SDB, "Sumienie," in: B. Szlachta [ed.], *Słownik społeczny. . .*, p. 1384.

[114]Wojciech Janyga, "Wolność sumienia," in: P. Burgoński, M. Gierycz [ed.], *Polityka i religia. . .*, p. 471.

[115]N. Lobkowicz, *Czas kryzysu. . .*, p. 96.

[116]P. Mazurkiewicz, *Europeizacja. . .*p. 349.

delineate the framework of political action. Man—this dimension is explicitly underscored by the anthropology of constraint—may "transfer to the society, and then to the state only as much authority as he has over himself (. . .) the limits inherent to individual freedom must also be transferred to the society and the state."[117] In this sense, as rightly noted by Jacques Maritain, the sovereignty of the state, in the sense of absolute autonomy and power, "which in their proper sphere are supreme absolutely or transcendently, not comparatively or as a topmost part in the whole"[118] in fact does not exist.[119] Only God is fully sovereign. Man is—also in his sovereignty—limited by his very nature. The measures of the freedom to act, which make this freedom possible in the first place, are the convictions about human dignity which prohibits the instrumentalization of man-person, human sexuality, rationality, sociality and equality, as well as everything that righteous reason (*recta ratio*) recognizes as good, and therefore necessary for his development.[120] The fact that man is considered here to be a rational (in the sense of moral and not only instrumental reason) social being for whom the basic social unit is marriage and family, defines the framework of man's choices, at the same time defining the areas of potential dehumanization. Constraint is not a limitation here, but a constitutive element of identity.

It should also be stressed that since natural law is not a closed collection of detailed norms, but expresses the capacity which enables man to recognize his proper good in a concrete situation,[121] constrained anthropology is not—as it might seem—a rigid, deterministic anthropology. Natural law, precisely because it expresses the rational component, does not determine man's actions. On the contrary, it creates a space of freedom to moral action. Even though it defines the essential direction for the development of those who follow it, its framework "does not expressly define those actions which lead to man's development, or the contents of the state of being towards which he is supposed to strive."[122] Even though the anthropology of limits is based on teleological metaphysics premised on the assumption that a thing inherently contains its own purpose, it leaves a broad space of man's

---

[117]Ibid.

[118]Jacques Maritain, *Man and the State*, p. 38.

[119]He stresses that "the question is not a question of words only. Of course we are free to say 'Sovereignty' while we are thinking full autonomy or right to decide without appeal—as we are free to say 'omnipotence' while we are thinking limited power, or 'drum' while we are thinking flute." Ibid, p. 49.

[120]Acts which violate these boundaries, and which are therefore contrary to what is recognized by a *recta ratio*, may be said to be abnormal in that they trespass beyond the area of lawful, in the deepest sense, acts of the state. In other words, the freedom of human actions—as long as they are to remain human—is realized within the field delimited by these categories.

[121]Thomas Aquinas, *Summa Theologiae*, q. 94, a. 3: "each one's reason naturally dictates him to act virtuously (. . .) there is in every man a natural inclination to act according to reason."

[122]Marek Piechowiak, "Klasyczna koncepcja osoby jako podstawa pojmowania praw człowieka. Wokół św. Tomasza z Akwinu i Immanuela Kanta propozycji ugruntowania godności osoby," in: Piotr Dardziński, Franciszek Longchamp de Berier, Kazimierz Szczucki [ed.], *Prawo naturalne – natura prawa*, C. H. Beck, Warszawa 2011, p. 11.

free will as regards the choice of a concrete good. As noted by Marek Piechowiak, we might even say that it is the free choices man makes that help better define the contents of eternal law and natural law as they apply to a particular person.[123] It is a diversity which keeps within the limits of that which is proper to the dignity and ontology of man.

6.4   Liberal Interpretation

An important question from the point of view of modern politics appears to be whether the logic of constrained anthropology is only a philosophical foundation of various currents in political thought inspired directly by Christianity, for instance personalism, or whether it is also found in other, more secular, ideological traditions. A key issue in the context of Europe is, of course, the status of liberal thought. It may be noted that some liberal postulates are quite in harmony with the anthropology outlined above. In the context of the social dimension of man, let us note for example the communitarianist standpoint which says that it is part of anthropological normality that every man is a member of various communities: "families, neighborhoods, innumerable social, religious, ethnic, workplace and professional associations. Neither human existence nor individual liberty can be sustained for long outside the interdependent and overlapping communities to which all of us belong."[124] Finally, at the heart of liberalism we may find the idea of truth. As pointed out by Will Kymlicka, "what we want in life is something more than, or other than, the acquisition (. . .) of any kind of 'inner glow,' enjoyable or otherwise. We do not just want the experience of writing poetry, we want to write poetry."[125] In line with this theses, liberalism looks for the real good, not its substitutes, which evokes the idea of rationality discussed above.

In this context, it is worth noting that the writings of John Locke, a precursor of liberalism, expressly reflect a belief in the existence of a reasonable law of nature. He says that it teaches "all mankind, who will but consult it, that being all equal and independent, no one ought to harm another in his life, health, liberty or possessions: for men being all the workmanship of one omnipotent, and infinitely wise maker; all the servants of one sovereign master (. . .) are his property, [his] workmanship (. . .) Every one, as he is bound to preserve himself, and not to quit his station willfully, so by the like reason, when his own preservation comes not in competition, ought he, as much as he can, to preserve the rest of mankind."[126]

---

[123]Marek Piechowiak, *Klasycznakoncepcja. . .*, p. 12. This means that in the temporal perspective "man actively fills in the contents of eternal law and natural law."

[124]Amitai Etzioni [ed.], *The Essential Communitarian Reader*, Rowman & Littlfield Publishers 1998, p. xxv.

[125]Will Kymlicka, *Contemporary Political Philosophy*, Oxford University Press 2002, p. 14.

[126]John Locke, *Two Treatises of Government*, Whitmore and Fenn 1821, p. 191.

This passage clearly echoes the classical thought of natural law,[127] emphasizing not only the vertical dimension of the law of nature and its universal validity, but also its weakness, so to say, in that it is a point of reference for those only who "will but consult it." Nevertheless, this law of nature which dictates "peace and preservation of the whole of mankind" shows that in the liberal tradition there is a deeply rooted belief in the existence of measures, inherent to human nature and related to moral discernment, justifying "the normative boundaries of choices made by individuals; measures common to the minds of all individuals which may serve to evaluate ideological projects and to find them dangerous, because irrational."[128] It is not a coincidence that Friedrich von Hayek considered Cicero "the main authority for modern liberalism,"[129] and Leo Strauss believed that Aristotle's philosophy contained some early forms of liberal categories.[130] The widespread belief that a liberal society should not be based on any specific concept of good life cannot be unequivocally upheld.[131] The diversity present in the bosom of the liberal tradition emphasized in literature[132] is also manifested in this issue. Not surprisingly, as pointed out by Bogdan Szlachta, human rights are a point in ethics that are accepted by both contemporary liberals and Catholics,[133] "outlining the boundaries which must not be trespassed either by individuals, or by the democratic majority."[134]

The freedom beloved by liberals remains, for some of them, the opposite of absolute freedom. There is a dispute in this area clearly visible in the liberal tradition. While for the most outstanding liberal-utilitarianist, J. S. Mill, freedom means "the liberty to pursue one's own good in one's own way," for Locke it is activity ordered by the light of reason and conscience.[135] It is this light, delimiting the boundaries of human action, that ultimately delimits the space of personal sovereignty. By acknowledging this constraint, coming from "the inside" of man, so to say, from

---

[127]Cf. John Gray, *Liberalism*, University of Minnesota Press 1995, or Zbigniew Rau, "Wstęp," [in:] J. Locke, *Dwa traktaty o rządzie*, translated by Zbigniew Rau, PWN, Warszawa 1992.

[128]B. Szlachta, *Indywidualizm. . .*, p. 424.

[129]John Gray, *Liberalism*, University of Minnesota Press 1995, p. 6.

[130]Anna Krawczyk, *Hobbes i Locke. Dwoiste oblicze liberalizmu*, WDiNP UW, Warszawa 2011, p. 18. Though in view of the different vision of liberty so skillfully demonstrated by Benjamin Constant, it should be remembered that these leads operate by analogy.

[131]Charles Taylor, "Cross-purposes: The Liberal-Communitarian Debate," in: *Philosophical Arguments*, Harvard University Press 1995 p. 194. As he points out further on, the misunderstanding arises, on the one hand, from confusing the ontological level with the level of preference; and on the other hand from confusing the two senses of the word "good." "In the broad sense, it means anything valuable we seek; in the narrower sense, it refers to life plans or ways of living so valued." Even in procedural liberalism, good is understood in this broader sense.

[132]Cf. Sławomir Sowiński, "Religia i polityka w tradycji liberalnej," *Studia Bobolanum* 1/2013.

[133]Even if interpreted differently—which is where the discrepancy of liberal currents comes in.

[134]Bogdan Szlachta, "Katolicyzm—liberalizm: obszary konfliktu i dialogu," in: *Liberalizm i katolicyzm dzisiaj*, Wydawnictwo DiG, Warszawa 1994, p. 27.

[135]Cf. John Locke, *Two Treatises of Government*, p. 234, where he notes in his comments on punishments that they may only be imposed as dictated by the light of reason and conscience. As he expressly states in par. 57, there is no liberty without law.

his conscience, Locke situates himself on the other side of the anthropological thought, across from both Mill and Hobbes. The existence of conscience not only sets the limits to the liberty of pursuing one's own good, but also prevents an annihilation of man's sovereignty within the political community.[136] As noted by Locke in his polemic with Hobbes, "a man, not having the power of his own life, cannot, by compact, or his own consent enslave himself to any one, nor put himself under the absolute, arbitrary power of another," for "nobody can give more power than he has himself."[137] The constrained sovereignty of a person, characteristically of the current of constrained anthropology, translates into a constrained sovereignty of the state, whose laws "are only so far right, as they are founded on the law of nature, by which they are to be regulated and interpreted."[138] It is no coincidence that Benjamin Constant wrote that "there are deeds which can never be sanctioned by anything,"[139] linking "the problem of the borders of the freedom-independence of an individual with the existence of inherent rights, not only warning against the threat posed by the majority, but also finding it problematic to accept the proposal of conservatives who—invoking tradition or God's decisions as the basis of a normative order binding for all—lose sight of the individual and his inherent rights."[140]

While noting those aspects of understanding human constraints in the current of liberal tradition which are clearly convergent with the tradition of natural law outlined above, we should refer to one fundamental difference, often emphasized in literature. In liberal thought concerning social and political life, including the current which highlights the limitation of human nature, the emphasis is placed on individualism. It is argued that "since Hobbes and Locke, both political communities (state, nation, society) and religious communities (churches, religious associations, religious majorities and minorities, families) have been treated in liberalism (...) first of all as groups made up of actual beings, i.e. individual people."[141] This issue is discussed at length by Charles Taylor who points out that it is an atomistic anthropological perspective in which communities are seen as beings which are inherently instrumental: "established by collections of individuals to obtain benefits through common action (...) the action is collective, but the point of it remains individual. The common good is constituted out of individual goods, without remainder."[142]

---

[136]Locke notes that "he who attempts to get another man into his absolute power, does thereby put himself into the state of war with him." Ibid, pp. 200–201.

[137]Ibid., p. 206.

[138]John Locke, Two Treatises of Government, Whitmore and Fenn 1821, p. 197.

[139]Benjamin Constant, *O monarchii konstytucyjnej*, Warszawa 1831, Vol. I, p. 37, as quoted in: B. Szlachta, *Indywidualizm...*, p. 433 [French original: *Réflexions sur les constitutions, la distribution des pouvoirs et les garanties dans une monarchie constitutionnelle* (1814)].

[140]Ibid., p. 433.

[141]S. Sowiński, *Religia i ....* He notes, in unison with Jadwiga Staniszkis, that sources of such a way of viewing social life may be sought in the European tradition in the Reformation and the so-called nominalist breakthrough. Cf. Jadwiga Staniszkis, *O władzyibezsilności*, WydawnictwoLiterackie, Kraków 2006, p. 51 ff.

[142]Cf. Charles Taylor, "Cross-purposes...," p. 188.

This approach—as pointed out by Taylor—is neither obvious nor necessary, however.

It is not obvious because already the first liberal's standpoint on this issue was not as unequivocal as is commonly believed. Locke clearly distanced himself from the atomistic anthropological vision.[143] It can be validly claimed that in terms of people having a natural tendency to "seek community with others", he understood human nature as social.[144] Referring to the classical interpretation of Aristotle and Thomas Aquinas, he wrote that "God having made man such a creature, that, in his own judgement, it was not good for him to be alone, put him under strong obligations of necessity, convenience and inclination to drive him into society, as well as fitted him with understanding and language to continue and enjoy it."[145] Consequently, as noted by Taylor, even in atomistic liberalism there is room for family[146] and friendship.

And it is not necessary since—as argued by Taylor—procedural liberalism too may, or perhaps must if it is to survive, be based on an anthropology which takes into account relations between the members of a society that are deeper than merely instrumental. He is not alone in this view: the standpoint of the communitarian movement which aims at emphasizing the social dimension of human existence within the framework of liberalism[147] is the best example of the obscurity of the atomistic ontology of liberalism. In this context, it is worth noting the phenomenon of patriotism, one of key importance to the continuing existence of the state, which "is somewhere between friendship, or family feeling, on one side, and altruistic dedication on the other."[148] Taylor also argues that one can validly claim that a "purely" liberal, procedural standpoint is in fact a cultural option characteristic at the most of the USA and England.[149]

---

[143]I am aware that this thesis does not appear to be self-evident. StanisławFilipowicz stresses, for example, that already in Locke we can see "the triumph of an emancipated *ego*, an isolated man" (*Historia myślipolityczno-prawnej*, Arche, Gdańsk 2001, p. 215). The problem is, however, that the thesis is not obvious either, even to the author himself. He also admits that for Locke society "is not an (...) artificial formation" (p. 216), and therefore—*tertio non datur*—it is a natural one. Consequently, he softens the strong initial thesis about the triumph of "an isolated man" with the reservation that Locke's man "is not autistic, however" (p. 2150).

[144]Cf. A. Krawczyk, *Hobbes...*, pp. 67–71.

[145]John Locke, *The Second Treatise of Government and A Letter Concerning Toleration*, Courier Corporation, Mineola, New York 2012, p. 35.

[146]Citing Witold Wundl, Anna Krawczyk notes that even in Hobbes family is portrayed as an element of the state of nature. Cf. A. Krawczyk, *Hobbes...*, p. 47.

[147]"Komunitariańska Platforma Programowa. Społeczeństwo Responsywne: Prawa i Obowiązki," in: P. Śpiewak [red.], *Komunitarianie. Wybór tekstów*, Aletheia, Warszawa 2004, p. 17.

[148]Ch. Taylor, "Cross-purposes...," p. 166. He stresses that apart from convergent common goods (or collective instrumental action), there are also goods which are indirectly and directly common that give meaning and character to social life.

[149]Charles Taylor, "Cross-purposes...". He notes that the procedural model would not fit Quebec's distinct society which "cannot make cultural-linguistic orientation a matter of indifference". Ibid, p. 140.

Nevertheless, even assuming that Taylor's interpretation at this point is disputable, we must note that liberalism modifies the interpretation of ontological constraint, but does not reject it entirely. It thus reduces, albeit inconsistently and non-necessarily, the classic moral discernment about the social nature of man, yet upholds it—even if sometimes interpreting it differently—in practically all other areas.[150] It refers to the moral and rational condition of man, acknowledging the inalienability and naturalness at least of the basic social structures within which man can realize his freedom.

Anthropological modifications within liberalism which refers to the idea of the law of nature are also expressed in the emphasis placed on the meaning of the right of ownership. Even though the attitude to property was markedly different in antiquity and, particularly in early, Christianity, in neither of these traditions did it belong to the law of nature. Although according to Aquinas, private property "corresponds better to human nature than shared property,"[151] it is treated as a purely human right. Aquinas explicitly writes: "the division of possessions is not according to the natural law, but rather arose from human agreement which belongs to positive law."[152] It is therefore a relative value: "whether it is good or bad depends on how it is used."[153] In liberalism, property becomes endowed with a metaphysical meaning. Polemicizing with utilitarianism, Richard M. Weaver points this out when he stresses that the essence of property is that "it does not depend on any test of social usefulness. Property rests upon the idea of the hisness of his: *proprietas, Eigentum,* the very words assert an identification of owner and owned (. . .) in the hisness of property we have dogma; there discussion ends."[154]

Considering that the context in which liberalism emerged was a confrontation with absolutism and Filmer's idea of patriarchal society, in the above-mentioned "uncertainty" as regards the social dimension of human condition, and the emphasis placed on the natural right of ownership we may see a defensive reaction against absolutist claims placing the rights of a community above the rights of an individual. However, this leads to the assertion that in liberalism "the concept of man was added as an afterthought, after the desire for and sense of freedom had been articulated."[155] Consequently, as noted by Wojciech Chudy, unlike in classical philosophy where

---

[150]Cf. J. Turek, *Dobro wspólne.* . . .

[151]Kazimierz Zając, "Św. Tomasz z Akwinu – Jego zapatrywania socjalne i ekonomiczne," *Annales. Etyka w życiu gospodarczym* No 1 (8) 2005, p. 114. The author notes that Aquinas provides three arguments for private property: "(1) people care and are concerned more about their own than about shared property, so it is the most important incentive to work; (2) it is a better safeguard of order in the society; and, finally, (3) it ensures peace in the society, as most disputes arise over shared property." (Ibid.).

[152]Thomas Aquinas, *Summa Theologiae,* 2–2, q. 66, a. 2.

[153]K. Zając, *Św. Tomasz z Akwinu.* . ., p. 114.

[154]Richard M. Weaver, *Ideas Have Consequences,* p. 132.

[155]Wojciech Chudy, "Miejsce prawdy w systemie wartości. Postawa klasyczna a postawa liberalistyczna i ich konsekwencje aksjologiczne," in: *Liberalizm i katolicyzm dzisiaj,* Wydawnictwo DiG, Warszawa 1994, p. 67.

"the concept of freedom is aligned with anthropology and metaphysics, and man's freedom is placed against the complete background of definitions explaining who he is, what he may, and what he ought to do," in liberalism "there is no metaphysics of man."[156] It is not possible to discuss this claim at length here, even though it could explain how Locke's anthropology might—based on other works—be interpreted in the spirit of unconstrained anthropology.[157] The self-evident nature of the above observation is revealed in later liberal thought (e.g. Mill's utilitarianism). In its beginnings based on metaphysical substantiations and in the interpretations which refer to them it appears less obvious.

Even if we do not finally resolve the above dilemma, the fact that "the Lockean political society is a community whose essence lies in the fact that the reason for its formation and the goal of its actions is the exercise of rights indicated by the law of nature"[158] suggests the existence of significant interpretations of liberalism which link it to the logic of constraint. In this perspective some scholars argue that it may protect "individual liberty not because it does not care about what people do with their lives, but because it believes that freedom is of fundamental importance for people to be able to live well,"[159] even if the task of developing such models of a good life falls to communities other than the state.[160] Thus, there can be a liberal state which, by following the logic of natural rights, protects conditions which make it possible to achieve a good life.

Such an approach to liberalism, referring to the logic of constrained anthropology, seems to be akin to some contemporary thinkers who emphasize the falsity of the liberal concepts of abstract individualism.[161] It acknowledges, as noted by Sławomir Sowiński, "its inherent limitations" and therefore "humbly looks for various (social, cultural and religious) allies to ensure that the difficult and demanding truth about human freedom is neither banal nor cruel."[162] Aware that "unlimited

---

[156]Ibid.

[157]Cf. Piotr Stanisław Mazur, "Spór o substancjalną koncepcję osoby," in: Tenże [ed.], *Spór o osobę w świetle klasycznej koncepcji człowieka. Studia i rozprawy*, Ignatianum, WAM, Kraków 2012.

[158]J. Turek, *Dobro. . .*, p. 139.

[159]Ibid., p. 141.

[160]The author stresses (ibid., p. 143) that "Locke believed the task of moral upbringing and education belonged not to politics, but to social institutions, families, churches and schools (Thoughts on Education). He stressed that individuals developed in such institutions. He believed that the society was the source of common "spiritual" goods: models of virtue, moral rules, or customs against which everyone measures their own actions."

[161]As noted by John Gray: "we can begin to perceive the spuriousness of liberal notions of universal humanity and abstract personhood—notions whose only value is to summarize or abbreviate (very imperfectly) certain passages in the historic experience of specific liberal societies." J. Gray, *Liberalisms: Essays in Political Philosophy*, Rutledge 2009, p. 240.

[162]S. Sowiński, "Liberalizm. Przed kryzysem, po kryzysie," in: K. Wielecki, p. Sowiński, *Co po postindustralizmie?*, Centrum Europejskie UW, Warszawa 2013, p. 152.

freedom for all means unlimited rule of the stronger,"[163] it sees—like Christian tradition, and the ancient tradition before it—in the reference to conscience a key dimension of personal sovereignty, remaining within the circle of constrained anthropology. As argued by Lord Acton, liberalism is in fact founded on the idea of conscience, outlining for the government "bounds it had never acknowledged; and they were the repudiation of absolutism and the inauguration of freedom."[164] Respect for the primacy of conscience in politics, and thus the idea of constrained authority, is, according to Acton, strictly related to the Christian context.[165]

* * *

The above analyses show that it is reasonable to adopt a broader view of constraints on man than what is proposed by Sowell. In their light it should be concluded that in principle, constrained anthropology should take into account man's twofold limitation.

One, which Sowell focuses on in his analyses, is a consequence of the original sin. Whatever man endeavors is corrupted by imperfection. Sin, which has "impaired" man's intellect and will, results in the effects of his work always being at odds, to some extent, with his original intentions. Instead of "plants of the field" which were "good for food," the earth produces "thorns and thistles" (Genesis 3:17–18). Awareness of the consequences of original sin present in social life leads to the establishment of mechanisms which control the government to prevent abuse (through a check and balance system). The need for such mechanisms of control is clearly reflected in the words of James Madison: "If men were angels, no government would be necessary. If angels were to govern men, neither external nor internal controls on government would be necessary."[166]

The other limitation, the one our reflection in that chapter has been focused on, is much more fundamental. It does not result from the "corruption" of human nature, but from the fact that man is a created being. Man is constrained in his nature because he is not almighty God. For as long as he exists, he is bound by the need to refer to "that which is Higher" and to make his own decisions in this context. Taking this into account in the area of politics means recognizing that there are inviolable anthropological limits to the exercise of political power and law making. There are political acts which are inherently wrong (*intrinsece malum*), which "poison human

---

[163]L. Kołakowski, "Samozatrucie otwartego społeczeństwa," in: id., *Cywilizacja na ławie oskarżonych*, Res Publica, Warszawa 1990, p. 173.; he adds: "hence, to quote Dostoyevsky, absolute freedom equals absolute slavery."

[164]John Emerich Edward Dalberg Acton, "The History of Freedom in Antiquity," in: *The History of Freedom, and Other Essays*, Freeport 1967, p. 29.

[165]Ibid. He notes that this is possible because "our Lord not only delivered the precept, but created the force to execute it."

[166]J. Madison, "The Federalist Papers" No. 51, *Independent Journal*, Wednesday, February 6, 1788 (https://www.constitution.org/fed/federa51.htm).

society" while doing "more harm to those who practice them than those who suffer from the injury,"[167] and which must never be done by any government.

In relation to the above analyses, such acts should be understood as including all those which contradict the personal dignity of man, organizing the world "as if God did not exist" (*esti Deus non daretur*), thus questioning the existence of objective measures of humanity, independent of man's will—boundaries beyond which stretch the fields of dehumanization. In this context, a characteristic comment has been made by the philosopher Marcelo Pera in response to a proposal made by Cardinal Ratzinger that the above postulate be reversed and that the political sphere be organized "as if God existed" (*velutisi Deus daretur*). Marcelo Pera, an agnostic, replies as follows: "This proposal should be accepted, this challenge welcomed, for one basic reason: because the one outside the Church who acts *veluti si Deus daretur* becomes more responsible in moral terms. He will no longer say that an embryo is a 'thing' or a 'lump of cells' or 'genetic material.' He will no longer say that the elimination of an embryo or a fetus does not infringe any rights. He will no longer say that a desire that can be satisfied by some technical means is automatically a right that should be claimed and granted. He will no longer say that all scientific and technological progress is per se a liberation or a moral advance. He will no longer say that the only rationality and the only form of life outside the Church are scientific rationality and an existence bereft of values. (...) he will no longer think that a democracy consisting of the mere counting of numbers is an adequate substitute for wisdom. (...) We act in liberty and equality as if we were all sons of God."[168] This also shows that constrained anthropology is naturally open to theologization, while remaining a secular concept. We shall return to this issue later on.[169]

---

[167]Vatican II, *Gaudium et Spes*, 27; Cf. John Paul II, *Veritatis Splendor*, 79–81.

[168]M. Pera, "Introduction: A proposal That Should Be Accepted," in: J. Ratzinger, *Europe in the Crisis of Cultures*, Ignatius Press, San Francisco 2006.

[169]Cf. Sect. 7.5.

Chapter 7
Unconstrained Anthropology

As noted above, one of the sources of the vision of unconstrained politics is the concept of man. In view of the doubts concerning the way it is approached by Sowell, which—or so it seems—has resulted, among other things, in cutting Marxism from the main current of unconstrained politics, we should ask about the core vision of man characteristic of unconstrained politics. When seeking an answer to this question, we must begin with the works of eighteenth century thinkers in whom—as demonstrated in literature—the new vision of politics was first expressed. A special place among them belongs to Jean-Jacques Rousseau, who made anthropology *expressis verbis* the foundation of his reflections.[1] His position among thinkers of the Enlightenment is special in view of—as Robert Spaemann describes it—"the model character of Rousseau's existence."[2] It was in his works that the "paradoxes of the modern, non-teleological concept of nature"[3] were expressed for the first time. His vision of the beginnings of man, meticulously reproduced in the *Discourse on Inequality*, is therefore the starting point for our analyses here, revealing the anthropological leads whose ideological consequences will be described in the paragraphs below.

Why start with a vision of the beginnings? Precursors of unconstrained thought loved to invoke the concept of "the state of nature"; it was a fashion of sorts, even, of the Age of Lights. Looking for a "new unitary principle of social existence," they claimed that "events and facts have no claim to be taken for granted, and to be considered natural, if they do not conform to one universally valid pattern, no matter

---

[1] Stressing that "knowledge of the natural man (*l'homme naturel*) is a preliminary condition for determining the laws which should guide culture." Andrzej Gielarowski, "Natura, jako to, co upragnione. Analiza koncepcji natury ludzkiej u J. J. Rousseau," in: *Oblicza natury ludzkiej*, WAM, Kraków 2010, p. 57.

[2] Robert Spaemann, *Rousseau – człowiek czy obywatel. Dylemat nowożytności*, Oficyna Naukowa, Warszawa 2011, p. 11.

[3] Ibid.

© Springer Nature Switzerland AG 2021
M. Gierycz, *European Dispute over the Concept of Man*, Contributions to Political Science, https://doi.org/10.1007/978-3-030-61520-8_7

whether such a pattern has ever existed."[4] Rousseau argued that "as long as we are ignorant of the natural man, it is in vain for us to attempt to determine either the law originally prescribed to him (...), to be natural, it must come directly from the voice of nature."[5] By applying the method, proposed by Bielik-Robson, of looking for theological sources of secular categories we can easily see in this a secularized vision of paradise. Referring to Schmitt's thought, we may thus speak of a structural analogy between these two concepts.[6] The state of nature, like the Biblical Eden, is supposed to communicate—in philosophical language—key truths about man and his Creator.[7]

7.1 Atomistic Anthropology of the "State of Nature"

In analyses of Rousseau's thought, the idyllic motif of a good savage is often emphasized, presented in his *Discours sur les sciences et les arts (Discourse on the Sciences and Arts, 1750)* where he indicated civilization—that is, the product of human reason—as the source of man's decline. It might appear, therefore, that his concept of nature is the antipode to another key thinker of modernity—Thomas Hobbes. Rousseau polemicized with Hobbes in his writings, arguing that the state of nature is "the best calculated to promote peace, and the most suitable for mankind."[8] Nevertheless, it should be noted that he agreed with Hobbes, that other father of modernity, on a much more fundamental issue. As is well known, the author of *Leviathan* believed that in a state of nature "an individual has not only an actual, but also a legitimate possibility (...) to do all things necessary to satisfy the requirements of the instinct of self-preservation, and may act only in accordance with the rules he defines himself, using his mind only when called to do so by the instinct or the emotions it stirs up, and not in order to recognize universal norms, for instance."[9] This fundamental assumption made by Hobbes, which lies at the bottom of his depiction of the state of nature as a state of war, is in fact fully shared by Rousseau. The only objection he makes is against Hobbes's inconsistency. He argues that since in the state of nature people had "no moral relations or determinate obligations one

---

[4]Jacob L. Talmon, *The Origins Of Totalitarian Democracy*, Secker & Warburg, 1952, pp. 18–19.

[5]Jean-Jacques Rousseau, *Discourse on Inequality*, Penguin Classics 1985, p. 70.

[6]Cf. Carl Schmitt, *Political Theology,* University of Chicago Press 2006. As regards Schmitt's concept of political theology against the background of other approaches to the relationship between theology and politics, I have discussed this issue at length in Chap. 1 of *Chrześcijaństwo i Unia Europejska. Rola religii w procesie integracji europejskiej*, WAM, Kraków-Warszawa 2008.

[7]Cf. Rev. Michał Kaszewski, *Raj upragnionym przez Boga losem człowieka*, http://www.teologia.pl/m_k/zag03-09.htm#5, 25.03.2014.

[8]Jean-Jacques Rousseau, *Discourse on Inequality*, p. 44.

[9]Bogdan Szlachta, "Indywidualizm," in: id. [ed.], *Słownik społeczny*, WAM, Kraków 2006, p. 413.

with another," they "could not be either good or bad, virtuous or vicious."[10] Consequently, contrary to the popular image of a "good savage," Rousseau believes that man in the state of nature is not good. Nor is he bad. In moral terms, his status is similar to that of an amoeba: morality is simply irrelevant.

The attitude to morality outlined above is one of the key assertions of unconstrained anthropology which is shared with Rousseau not only by Hobbes, but by practically all luminaries of the Age of Lights and their heirs, revealing the relativity and historicity of moral convictions. Suffice it to cite d'Alembert's introduction to the *Encyclopaedia* in which he derives the idea of good and evil from a revolt against oppression,[11] or the arguments of Newton and Voltaire[12] who derive it from biological instincts. Its persistence in the logic of unconstraint is documented by claims made by J. S. Mill who argued that moral dispositions are not innate[13] but "susceptible, by a sufficient use of the external sanctions and of the force of early impressions, of being cultivated in almost any direction: so that there is hardly anything so absurd or so mischievous that it may not, by means of these influences, be made to act on the human mind."[14] Naturally, like most other advocates of unconstraint, J. S. Mill would not have wished for man's moral degradation. On the contrary, at the very beginning of his ethical treatise, he complains about "the little progress which has been made in the decision of the controversy respecting the criterion of right and wrong,"[15] which he wanted to remedy with utilitarian ethics.[16] Of key importance here, however, is the assumption that there is no morality intrinsically linked to being human; that the categories of good and bad are relative, and consequently that morality may "be flexibly adjusted."[17]

Negation of the moral nature of man is a key element of the vision of the state of nature. It is not, by any means, a state of moral values. Even though it is presented as a state of peace, war is not raging only because people are too weak to wage it. "It is impossible—Rousseau writes—to make any man a slave, unless he be first reduced to a situation in which he cannot do without the help of others: and, since such a situation does not exist in a state of nature, everyone is there his own master, and the law of the strongest is of no effect".[18] The state of nature is not so much a state of

---

[10]J.-J. Rousseau, *Discourse on Inequality*, p. 35. Rousseau claims that "savages are not bad merely because they do not know what it is to be good: for it is neither the development of the understanding nor the restraint of law that hinders them from doing ill; but the peacefulness of their passions, and their ignorance of vice" (p. 35).

[11]E. Voegelin, *From Enlightenment to Oppression*, Duke University Press, Durham, 1975, p. 77.

[12]Ibid., pp. 24–25.

[13]Cf. John Stuart Mill, *Utilitarianism*, Batoche Books, Kitchener 2001, p. 31.

[14]Ibid. As a side remark, this was one of Mill's arguments for the possibility of impressing on man the principle of utility.

[15]Ibid., p. 5.

[16]Cf. par. 6.3.

[17]Monika Małek, *Liberalizm etyczny Johna Stuarta Milla. Współczesne ujęcia u Johna Graya i Petera Singera*, FNP, Wrocław 2010, p. 170.

[18]J.-J. Rousseau, *Discourse ...*, p. 183.

peace, but a permanent armistice, interrupted sporadically and for a short while by stronger individuals. This also means that the state of nature is not a state of equality: some people are stronger than others, which forces some to submit to the will of others. A sense of relative equality results from the fact that "it is impossible to make any man a slave," and therefore inequality "is hardly felt."[19] This clearly shows that as a consequence of considering the state of nature a "pre-moral" state, categories of valuation do not properly apply here: in fact, we are dealing neither with peace nor equality.

Consequently, neither is the state of nature—contrary to what is claimed by some commentators—a state of personal freedom.[20] In light of the above findings, it should at most be considered a state of relative individual independence. This "individualist moment," to use Bogdan Szlachta's expression, realigns the analyses of Rousseau and Hobbes. As pointed out by Zbigniew Stawrowski, also for the author of *Leviathan* freedom has no trace of affinity to will, meaning "solely the absence of external obstacles,"[21] which in fact means "a set of external circumstances which (. . .) enable a greater or lesser degree of mobility."[22] Consequently, according to Rousseau, in a state of nature no natural communities or bonds exist: the life natural to man is individual and self-sufficient. For the author of *The Social Contract*, even family, which the treatise presents as a natural community (in terms of physical necessity) is not entirely natural (in terms of its essence). It was only occasionally, and driven merely by natural instincts, that the opposite sexes turned to each other "as accident, opportunity or inclination brought them together," and parted "with the same indifference."[23] In the primitive state, family was reduced to the satisfaction of the sexual need, following which "the two sexes knew each other no more"[24] and did not even feel the need to communicate verbally,[25] while "the offspring was nothing to its mother, as soon as it could do without her."[26] The state of nature is here a kingdom of an atomized individual. The need to relate with other people is treated by Rousseau as an experience of dependence. His anthropology is consistently atomistic, negating the social nature of man, who is presented as self-sufficient.

It would seem paradoxical that, despite all the rapture with *homme naturel*, Rousseau does not consider the state of nature as the ideal state. Although in his

---

[19]Ibid.

[20]Tokarczyk argues that in Rousseau "nature gave man freedom," *Filozofia prawa. . .*, p. 129. In view of the above findings, one can also hardly agree with the author's claim that in Rousseau "the state of nature is 'an oasis of goodness'" in which people enjoyed freedom, happiness and equality.

[21]He points out that "this way it turns out that water flowing along the riverbed is free." Zbigniew Stawrowski, *Wokół idei wspólnoty*, OMP, Kraków 2012, p. 69.

[22]Ibid.

[23]J.-J. Rousseau, *Discourse. . .*, p.165.

[24]J.-J. Rousseau, *Discourse. . .*, p. 113.

[25]Rousseau writes: "the sexes united without design, . . . nor had they any great need of words to communicate their designs to each other." Ibid., p. 165.

[26]Ibid., p. 185.

famous statement about fencing in land and establishing property Rousseau appears here—like elsewhere—to be an admirer of the state of nature,[27] he will eventually write that the state of primitive societies was better—a state which was the effect of progress, the development of man and of human affairs. It was not by wandering alone in the forests, but living together in their mud huts that people "lived free, healthy, honest and happy lives, so long as their nature allowed."[28] They were free because "they undertook only what a single person could accomplish," and so their independence was only marginally limited: they remained essentially autarchic, while already enjoying some benefits of communal life. This weighing of benefits is an important current in Rousseau's analysis. The value of change, including that which brought about the emergence of property and which—as a source of destruction of the state of nature—should be seen as unequivocally negative, is determined by utility. The move from complete independence and absence of property to primary societies with a "fenced-in field" was useful, and therefore good. Moreover, according to reasonable judgement based on the observation of savage peoples, Rousseau considered it self-evident that it was this very state of primitive societies that should be the final stage of development. He notes that "for the public good [. . .] men were meant to remain in it."[29] It was precisely the state of independence enjoyed in a small group, with some degree of ownership, that was "the real youth of the world." All the progress that followed—by some random accident—even though it lead "towards the perfection of the individual," in reality led "towards the decrepitude of the species"[30] and submission to all kinds of fetters. It is worth taking a closer look at these theses: the ambivalent attitude to the state of nature, the role of utility as a criterion in evaluating reality, and finally, the randomness of changes in man's condition. They entail important anthropological contents which seem to ground the unconstrained vision of politics.

7.2 Fluid Humanity

The visible contradiction between admiration of the state of nature and the distancing from it, followed by a yearning for the world as it was at the initial stages of its development seems to be necessarily entailed by the unconstrained vision of man. Thus, it is not a lack of consistency in the view of man, but its very manifestation. The turn towards individual autarchy, as noted by Bogdan Szlachta, began the

---

[27]"The first man who, having fenced in a piece of land, said 'This is mine,' and found people naïve enough to believe him, that man was the true founder of civil society. From how many crimes, wars, and murders, from how many horrors and misfortunes might not any one have saved mankind, by pulling up the stakes, or filling up the ditch (. . .)." J. J. Rousseau, *Discourse. . .*, p.185.

[28]Ibid., p. 165.

[29]Ibid., p. 114.

[30]Ibid., p. 115.

"process of 'depersonalization of the subject,' who gradually lost his personal identity and was overtaken by the newly emerging individual."[31] Certainly, the individual depicted by Rousseau, standing outside the sphere of good and evil, not related necessarily to any other being, can hardly be called a person. He does not—in a stark contrast to the Biblical image—resemble a social being endowed with special dignity, ontologically superior to all other creatures, integrating in himself the spiritual and the corporeal element. This observation, by the way, was made by the author of the *Discourse* himself when he stressed that human life in a state of nature is "the life of an animal limited at first to mere sensations, and hardly profiting by the gifts nature bestowed on him, much less capable of entertaining a thought of forcing anything from her."[32]

7.2.1 The Lost Boundary

Clearly, Rousseau effaces, in the spirit of unconstraint, the hitherto clear boundaries of humanity separating man from the rest of the natural world. The anthropology of unconstraint changes this fundamental boundary into a borderland, "a blurry and neutral space in which distinctions are disputable."[33] He anticipates, in a way, the theory of evolution which makes "man so close to monkeys that the boundary becomes liquid."[34] This has far-reaching anthropological and political consequences. Ultimately, as pointed out by Delsol, "the boundary line of respect, subjective, and therefore changeable, will henceforth depend on historical, ideological, or scientific criteria. It no longer necessarily runs between man and animal; it may run between various groups of human beings, so that some are treated as subhumans, or even as animals."[35]

One more comment should be added to Delsol's apt observation, namely that the "liquid boundary of humankind" may also operate in the opposite direction, expanding the category of "person" to include animals. This issue is being explicitly articulated now. Singer explains that the awkwardness of calling an animal a person

---

[31]B. Szlachta, "Indywidualizm," p. 420. He points out that this is "a process, visible particularly in the nineteenth century, of liberating the individual of Leibnitz's 'pre-established harmony' or Smith's 'invisible hand,' of 'leading' it beyond the 'background of rationality' which had so far bound independent beings together, progressing since G. W. Hegel who no longer treated man as the subject of history but as its object, and thus linking the value of individuality to the values of rationality, to Friedrich Nietzsche who crowned this trend with his thesis about the "revaluation of all values."

[32]J.J. Rousseau, *Discourse...* p. 24.

[33]Ch. Millon-Delsol, *Esej o człowieku poźniej...*, p. 19.

[34]Ibid., p. 17.

[35]Ibid., p. 18. Delsol stresses further on that it is "the terrible consequences of this obliteration of boundaries that make us consider them sacred, inviolable: in answer to the question: 'Who is man,' not everything is possible" (p. 19).

is only apparent and "may be no more than a symptom of our habit of keeping our own species sharply separated from others."[36] What we should be asking is whether "animals are rational and self-conscious beings, aware of themselves as distinct entities with a past and a future."[37] Thus, the belief, characteristic of constrained anthropology, in the existence of a special dignity as an intrinsic attribute of every human being may be seen by the heirs of atomist thinking as a symptom of the chauvinism of our species.

Even though Gielarowski is right to point out that Rousseau's concept of man's freedom "is defined so ambiguously that (. . .) it is possible to dispute what differs man from animals,"[38] one could hardly defend the thesis that in Rousseau's logic man is simply an animal. This is most clearly visible in the role he plays in creating the ideal state. As mentioned above, according to the author of *The Social Contract,* the equivalent of biblical Eden, the world of primitive communities, is created by men (even if it is also corrupted by them; this is a critical element). Man in fact also acts as the Creator: he leads himself, on his own, out of animal into human life, in its ethical and social dimension. He creates himself as a person. This approach to man echoes Descartes's description of the "self" which he presents "as though it was God."[39] Consequently, we can see in Rousseau's view of man a harbinger of "exclusive humanism," in its peak form developed by Comte, where man as such is the highest being who will not suffer anyone above himself. Clearly, man appears here as an entirely sovereign being whose power soars above truth and the laws of nature.[40]

Depending on the perspective we adopt, the life of the *homme naturel*, being an archetype of the modern man, may have more affinity either to animal or to divine life,[41] which explains the contradiction in the approach to the state of nature noted at the beginning of this section. The concept of absolute individual independence combines the ideas of Descartes's anthropology[42] and Leibniz's monadology.[43]

---

[36]Peter Singer, *Practical Ethics*, Cambridge University Press, New York, 2011, p. 94.

[37]Ibid. Singer believes the answer is already known, and that in some animals we have a "strong evidence of a sense of self."

[38]A. Gielarowski, *Natura, jako to, co upragnione. . .*, p. 62.

[39]More on this topic, see: Piotr Mazurkiewicz, *EuropeizacjaEuropy. . .*, p. 322.

[40]Cf. R. Brague, *The Legitimacy of the Human,* translated by Paul Seaton, St. Augustine's Press, Chicago, 2017.

[41]And therefore—even though for reasons somewhat different than in Hobbes—deplorable rather than desirable. As Rousseau says in *Emile*, "[b]orn in the depths of a forest he would have lived in greater happiness and freedom; but being able to follow his inclinations without a struggle, there would have been no merit." Rousseau, *Emile: or On Education*, NuVision Publications, 2007, p. 453.

[42]Which, as pointed out by Bogdan Szlachta, was premised not only on the assumption that "the self is given to an individual consciousness, but also that the consciousness of an individual should be considered the basis of the existence of societies and social order." Id., "Indywidualizm. . .," p. 416.

[43]Cf. Janusz Sytnik-Czetwertyński, "Pojęcie monady w koncepcjach Gottfrieda Wilhelma Leibnitza i Immanuela Kanta," *Diametros* No. 15 (March 2008), pp. 38–56.

The latter replaced the "rationalist *cogito*" with a "monadological *cogito*", and consequently "every individual became a separate world, self-sufficient, perfectly independent from the influence of other creatures, encompassing infinity and expressing the universe."[44]

This reduction of man to animal and his absolutization show that unconstrained anthropology can no longer describe that which is specifically human, and drifts into opposite extremes. The problem of man's depersonalization, already visible in Rousseau, takes on two main forms in the tradition of philosophic thought. On the one hand, there is the idea, descended directly from Descartes, of identifying a person with a thinking substance, which "no longer applies to man as a whole, but only to his soul."[45] In this context, consciousness, or, better, self-consciousness constituted over time is a criterion which serves to distinguish people from animals. This has important social and political implications. For while "in the classical tradition, man became a person from the moment he began to be a human being," in the light of post-Cartesian theories "developed by David Hume or Christin Wolff, abortion would be taking the life of a human being, but not of a person. A similar thinking process could be applied to persons who have lost their consciousness."[46] This thread will be taken up again with redoubled strength in the age of late modernity.

On the other hand, there is the view, which seems to be more akin to Rousseau's thought, that it is the human environment that "constitutes a person, since a condition for being a person—as demonstrated by G. W. Hegel and his example of the relationship between a master and a servant—is recognition by others."[47] One of the most outstanding heirs of this tradition today is Jürgen Habermas who—while fending off liberal eugenics—nevertheless adopts the concept of "gradual protection of pre-personal human life," using the category of "potential person" to refer to human beings who have not yet entered the process of socialization and social relations.[48] A special version of this interpretation is Marxism, analyzed below.

Irrespective of the above discrepancies, the anthropological belief which links these concepts is that man not so much is, intrinsically, a person, but becomes a person in view of some functional reasons. It is of secondary importance whether they are bodily functions which he cannot control (consciousness), passions which he is able to rein in (feelings, defiance, work, emancipation, etc.), or social relationships. The important thing is the belief that personal dignity is not an immanent, inherent property of human beings, but that it is linked to some disposition, mode of acting, or behavior.[49] Even though as far as the assumptions are concerned, this

---

[44]B. Szlachta, "Indywidualizm. . .," p. 419.

[45]P. Mazurkiewicz, *Europeizacja. . .*, p. 322.

[46]Ibid., p. 323.

[47]Ibid., p. 324.

[48]Cf. Jurgen Habermas, *The Future of Human Nature*, Polity 2003.

[49]Cf. Barbara A. Markiewicz, "Nowożytne prawa obywatela – albo co można było kupić za 50 franków złotem, czyli 'markę srebra' (marcd'argent)," *Civitas* No. 6 (2002), p. 85.

approach is supposed to emphasize the exceptionality of human beings, its results are quite paradoxical. For regardless of the intentions, the very possibility of separating the concept of person from the concept of man opens the door to challenging the thesis about man's dignity. If man is merely a specimen of a certain, somewhat more intellectually developed, species of animals which may for some reasons become endowed with personal features, man's uniqueness recognized solely based on his species becomes legitimately open to challenge.

7.2.2 The Ideal of Authenticity

The reverse of the "liquid humanity" outlined above is another, practically axiomatic,[50] claim of atomistic anthropology. Since man is not distinguished from animals by reason,[51] and even "free agency" may be "the subject of some discourse,"[52] the question is: what is the *differentia specifica* of man? As rightly noted by Gilarowski, for Rousseau the only faculty which differentiates man from animals is the potential for self-improvement.[53] He says in the *Discourse* that it is "the faculty of self-improvement, which, by the help of circumstances, gradually develops all the rest of our faculties, and is inherent in the species as in the individual."[54] Rousseau substantiates this belief in various ways, arguing that people "learnt to surmount the obstacles of nature," and "grew enlightened," which increased their inventiveness, opening the road to "a first revolution, which established and distinguished families, and introduced a kind of property."[55] While Rousseau's opinion about this process was negative, this conviction, combined with the understanding of freedom as self-determination,[56] clearly reveals the sources of the key belief—particularly for modern liberalism—that man is by nature predisposed to achieve autonomy.[57] "Human nature," wrote John Stuart Mill, "is not a machine to be built after a model (. . .) but a tree, which requires to grow and develop itself on all sides, according to the tendency of the inward forces which make it a living thing."[58] This logic flows directly from the spirit of the Age of Lights, proclaiming—in the words of Condorcet—that "no limit to the development of human talents has been

---

[50]Even though it seems that this belief can be related to the idea of self-awareness as a key attribute of personhood.

[51]Rousseau sees this as a "qualitative" difference only. Cf. J.J. Rousseau, *Discourse. . .*, p. 153.

[52]Cf. ibid., p. 157.

[53]A. Gielarowski, *Natura. . .*, p. 62.

[54]Jean-Jacques Rousseau, *Discourse...*, p. 151.

[55]Ibid., p. 181.

[56]Cf. Charles Taylor, *The Ethics of Authenticity*, Harvard University Press 1992, p. 27.

[57]Cf. Zbigniew Rau, *Liberalizm. Zarys myśli politycznej XIX i XX wieku*, Aletheia, Warszawa 2000, p. 75.

[58]John Stuart Mill, *On Liberty*, Fields, Osgood & Company 1869, p. 107.

set." Indeed, an autonomous individual "never represents a completely formed personhood. He is always involved in the search for new forms of life, new experiences."[59] This way, we stand at the threshold of the ideal of authenticity whose early exponent was Herder who claimed that everyone has his own measure: "each of us has an original way of being human."[60]

As emphasized by Taylor, authenticity as a moral ideal is thoroughly modern; it is therefore a legacy actively influencing the understanding of man in Western civilization. "It accords crucial moral importance to a kind of contact with myself (. . .) Being true to myself means being true to my own originality, and that is something only I can articulate and discover. In articulating it, I am also defining myself. I am realizing a potentiality that is properly my own."[61] In the idea of authenticity expressing the idea of autonomy we can therefore see a reflection of the claim about the independence of an individual, inherent to the concept of a state of nature. This is, in fact, another way of defending the same anthropological assumption: a belief in the atomistic nature of man, understood as an individual, being at the same time his own creator and the supreme being.[62]

The above ideal, let us add, has its own social and political implications. Zbigniew Rau notes that since "it is not possible to predict the direction of an individual's development, autonomy is premised on pluralism as a form of social and political life."[63] One clarification needs to be made here, however: constrained anthropology also, claiming that the contents of the state of being human are not fully specified (though at the same time clearly defining the boundaries of human nature), founds pluralism. Nevertheless, it fits within clearly defined ontological and moral boundaries. The difference lies elsewhere—in the understanding of pluralism. It is linked here to the fact that man himself becomes the object of self-creation, and moral categories are relative. Any solution potentially has the right to be present in public life as being equally good or bad for man, since there is no objective, substantive norm which it could be referred to or evaluated against. Only a surrogate of such a norm can exist, as we will see below.

Once this new approach to pluralism is identified, it becomes apparent that by breaking away from the first, fundamental constrain of the human condition, the anthropology discovered in Rousseau also rejects the other constraint. "For Rousseau, original sin is a deception. The primitive man had been innocent and pure until he became depraved by culture and society."[64] The essence of this logic was clearly

---

[59]Z. Rau, *Liberalizm. . .*, p. 76.

[60]Charles Taylor, *The Ethics of Authenticity,* p. 28.

[61]Ibid, p. 29.

[62]It is worth emphasizing that in Taylor's approach, authenticity, which he interprets as an actual moral idea, contradicts the idea of self-determination or anthropocentrism. He contends that "[a] uthenticity can't, shouldn't, go all the way with self-determining freedom. It undercuts itself." Ibid, p. 68.

[63]Ibid.

[64]Ch. Delsol, *Esej o człowieku. . .*, p. 188.

articulated by Fichte: "It is an absurd slander on human nature to say that man is born a sinner (. . .) His life makes him a sinner."[65] This has important implications. People—some, at least, for example those educated like Rousseau's Emile, and thus not submitted to the negative influence of culture—may be innocent. Founding the logic of initial sinlessness, Rousseau provides strong foundations for a Manichean view of the world and an elitist logic. Considering himself to be the only primitive and pure man to have survived depravation, he establishes a group of the innocent who will eventually be able to restore the lost society.[66] Delsol points out that "rejection of the idea of original sin, understood as the evil rooted in our condition, leads to two consequences: there is hope for the evil to be removed, and there is the need to locate its causes. The professed certainty that evil may become eradicated from the earth leads to a question about the means by which such an earthly redemption could be accomplished. The only possible solution is to locate evil in some groups, identifiable and recognizable, which then simply need to be eliminated."[67] It is not so much "the perfection of man," but rather liquid humanity, with all of its inherent contradictions, that lays the foundations for the unconstrained vision of politics, accurately diagnosed by Sowell and Talmon, among others. As noted by Delsol, "the madness revealed in the 20th century [is] still concealed in Rousseau's and Fichte's philosophical innocence."[68]

7.3 Rationalism Instead of Rationality

The logic of unconstraint thus rejects the belief that obligation is inherent to being human, that moral obligations result from the essence of being. Nevertheless, in its beginnings it is far from nihilism: it believes in the power of reason and looks for permanent moral criteria. At this point, it is worth taking a look at the model of morality and rationalism it proposes.

7.3.1 Utilitarianism as the Abolition of Morality

Even if in the light of atomistic anthropology moral categories are relative, this does not mean an absence of rules. Though Rousseau, who proclaimed *le sentiment de l'existence*, can hardly be classified as a pure utilitarian, it is precisely this criterion of the moral evaluation of man's progress that we find—as has been mentioned

---

[65]Johann Gottlieb Fichte, *Addresses to the German Nation*, Cambridge University Press 2009, p. 135.
[66]Ch. Delsol, *Esej o człowieku. . .*, p. 189.
[67]Ibid.
[68]Ibid.

above—in the *Discourse*.[69] The desire to explicitly define clear moral criteria will never leave modernity. After all, it was the insecurity and indistinctness of the "moral instinct" which some who had "pretensions to philosophy"[70] believed in, the inability to define "one first principle (. . .), the common ground of obligation,"[71] that would become the incentive for creating a precise, rational moral doctrine, referring to the utilitarian logic of the *Discourse*.

The modern sources of the utilitarian logic, as pointed out by Eric Voegelin, are already to be found in Locke and Helvetius. It was the latter who, founding anthropology on a genealogy of passions, claimed that sensuous sensitivity produces in man "a sentiment of love for pleasure, and of hatred for pain."[72] The utilitarian principle, later developed by Bentham and James Mill, among others, only reached its maturity in the middle of the nineteenth century, in the works of John Stuart Mill. In his well-known definition he argued that "[t]he creed which accepts as the foundation of morals, Utility, or the Greatest Happiness Principle, holds that actions are right in proportion as they tend to promote happiness, wrong as they tend to produce the reverse of happiness. (. . .) According to the Greatest Happiness Principle, as above explained, the ultimate end, with reference to and for the sake of which all other things are desirable (whether we are considering our own good or that of other people), is an existence exempt as far as possible from pain, and as rich as possible in enjoyments, both in point of quantity and quality."[73]

While hedonistic utilitarian interpretations fail to convince due to the oversimplification of human motivations and experiences, the mature criterion presented in J. S. Mill's work avoids the shallows, to use Voegelin's expression, of intellectual nonchalance. Mill's logic is far from simple hedonism, and takes into account social goods which bring happiness to the general population. He writes: "happiness which forms the utilitarian standard of what is right in conduct, is not the agent's own happiness, but that of all concerned."[74] Consequently, "the standard of morality, which may accordingly be defined, the rules and precepts for human conduct, by observance of which an existence such as has been described might be, to the greatest extent possible, secured to all mankind, and not to them only, but far as

---

[69]This seems to be documented by the Rousseau phenomenon, identified by Spaemann, being a synthesis of modernity in the sense of simultaneously evoking every modern thesis and its antithesis.

[70]J. S. Mill, *Utilitarianism*, Longmans, Green 1870, p. 3.

[71]Ibid., p. 4.

[72]Helvetius, *De l'Esprit: or: Essays on the Mindand its Several Faculties*, Dodfley& Co., London 1759, p. 121, as quoted in: E. Voegelin, *From Enlightenment. . .*, p. 39. As ironically pointed out by Voegelin, "it seems almost unbelievable that such cavalier pieces of verbiage should be the foundation of a system of morals in emulation of physics. But, as a matter of fact, that is all there is." Ibid.

[73]J. S. Mill, *Utilitarianism. . .*, pp. 9 and 17.

[74]Ibid., p. 24.

the nature of things admits, to the whole sentient creation."[75] A noble goal, without doubt. And yet, it gives rise to serious concerns.

Firstly, if utilitarianism depicts people as producers or consumers of a good, linking their duties "to that good, not to other people," then it "violates our core intuition that morality matters because human beings matter."[76] This shows that the egalitarian intuition, though sometimes tacitly identified with utilitarianism, is not inherent to it. On the contrary, Will Kymlicka argues that "utilitarianism has misinterpreted the ideal of equal consideration for each person's interests, and, as a result, it allows some people to be treated as less than equals, as means to other people's ends."[77] This way, while beginning with the ideal of a free, self-perfecting individual who is equal to others, atomistic anthropology ultimately leads in its moral doctrine to justifying inequality,[78] reinforcing from another angle the above-mentioned departure from the idea of the unity of mankind and a Manichean view of the world.

The problem lies deeper, however. As noted by Leszek Kołakowski, "if what is beneficial to one man or to one group is harmful to another man or other people; if, just as obviously, what is harmful to a man or a group may at some point be beneficial in the long run; if, in short, there is no concept of what is beneficial or harmful in general, it seems that to say that moral rules coincide with utilitarian criteria is to say that there are no moral rules at all."[79] Utilitarian ethics implicitly abolishes morality. Consequently, in a somewhat convoluted way, it remains faithful to its foundational anthropological conviction about the lack of any moral law inherent to man's condition.

Of course, the problem pointed out by Kołakowski was lost on Mill, who believed that he was actually creating a proper, coherent ethical system. He did see the problem of the conflict of goods, however. Looking for a solution, he proposed an elitist answer. The quality of pleasure "and the rule for measuring it against quantity [is] the preference felt by those who in their opportunities of experience, to which must be added their habits of self-consciousness and self-observation, are best furnished with the means of comparison."[80] The subjectivity of moral evaluations and their arbitrariness is upheld, but at the same time subjective boundaries are delineated: there is a higher, indisputable opinion of "competent judges,"[81] which cannot be objectively verified in any way, however. Even if, as emphasized by Mill,

---

[75]Ibid., p. 17.

[76]Will Kymlicka, *Contemporary. . .*, p. 34.

[77]Ibid., p. 36.

[78]This shows the deep sources of the contemporary discussion concerning the risk of liberal eugenics. Cf. Jurgen Habermas, *The Future of Human Nature*.

[79]Leszek Kołakowski, "Kant i zagrożenie cywilizacji," in: id., *Czy diabeł może być zbawiony i 27 innych kazań*, Znak, Kraków 2006, p.187.

[80]J.S. Mill, *Utilitarianism*, p. 17.

[81]As Mill authoritatively puts it: "From this verdict of the only competent judges, I apprehend there can be no appeal." Ibid, p. 15.

this does not necessarily contradict the traditional ethical norms, it relativizes their value and modifies their sense. From now on, they are binding only until philosophers have "succeeded in finding better ones."[82] Their value is no longer linked, to use categories proposed by Wojciech Chudy, to theoretical truth about the society, but to practical truth of the society.[83] Practical rationalism, oriented towards the utility of all, realized by the elites, now becomes the substantiation and the ultimate criterion of morality. In an almost perfect way this creates grounds for an unconstrained vision of politics.

It should be noted that the above logic ultimately shows the profoundly problematic nature of utilitarianism from the perspective of liberal ideals. At the level of social praxis, the above approach to morality in the name of autonomy and self-creation ultimately introduces, through "the back door," so to say, a conformist logic. It is the vote of the elites, and not the individual, developing "on all sides, according to the tendency of the inward forces," that sets the directions of development. It is a surrogate of "that which is Higher," a prelude to the liberal eugenics that is observed with apprehension today by Habermas, as well as others.[84]

7.3.2 Rationalism Outside of the Structure of Sense

Even though atomistic logic puts man on a pedestal, making him play the role of "that which is Higher" and absolutizing his decisions, it is entangled in an insolvable paradox. It is aware that being one's own creator does not mean that man can control the process of creation. A characteristic comment is made in this context in the *Discourse* when Rousseau says that "the youth of the world" was left "through some fatal accident, which, for the public good, should never have happened."[85] It reveals the belief that just like individual development is free and depends only on the individual concerned, without representing any higher teleology, so the development of mankind and—generally speaking—the development of the world does not, in the end, have any intrinsic sense. On the contrary, it is haphazard and random, and is just as likely to lead to perfection as to the demise of our species.[86] Utilitarianism may inform man's moral behavior, but does not guide the logic of the world's development.

The belief that the world in which individuals develop their rationalism is irrational as a whole, that history "has no recognizable structure,"[87] seems to be emblematic of the modern anthropological vision. Even though it is mentioned by

---

[82]Ibid., p. 35.

[83]W. Chudy, *Prawonaturalne...*, p. 35.

[84]Cf. J. Habermas, *The Future....*.

[85]J.-J. Rousseau, *Discourse on Inequality*, p. 194.

[86]Ibid., p. 195.

[87]Eric Voegelin, *From Enlightenment to Revolution,* Duke University Press Books, 1982, p. 9.

Rousseau as a side remark, as though not considered particularly important, it is of fundamental significance. In fact, it undermines all anthropological optimism, relativizing the belief in the meaningfulness of human life. In the long run, it logically leads to existentialist claim about the absurdity of human existence.[88] Since everything happens by chance, and man's existence, just as incidental, "leads to death, to nothingness,"[89] then man has the right—to use Sartre's terminology—to conclude that he is "left to himself;" that he has no raison d'être. This changes not only the mood of philosophy which slides into a gloomy pessimism, but also the approach to morality. As pointed out by Władysław Tatarkiewicz, "19th century radicals said that God was a superfluous hypothesis which should be rejected, yet this did not change anything in ethics (. . .) *a priori* was certain. (. . .) Existentialists looked at things differently: they believed that together with God, all *a priori* values had disappeared as well; if there was no God, then there were no imperatives,"[90] for man found within himself "nothing to lean against."[91] Clearly, Rousseau's optimism of the Age of Lights reveals a foretoken of a crisis of rationalism, fully uncovered in the post-modern logic.

The world's irrationality undermines not only individual rationalism, but collective rationalism as well. "As soon as the question is raised why one should know with any degree of completeness whatever has happened in the existence of mankind in time," Eric Voegelin notes, "the curiosity shop is revealed as senseless. Encyclopaedic knowledge, collected in handbooks, has to be moved into the functional position of a collection of materials which ultimately might become of importance for a relevant interpretation of history. And when historians do not entertain the idea of such ultimate use of their inquiries, historical research develops into a practice of vocational asceticism".[92] Nevertheless, as Voegelin goes on to stress, this approach is only "a transitory position in the movement of ideas". Man needs sense, and if he does not find it, he begins to create it himself. Like Voltaire, who saw the sense of history in revealing the process of extinction, revival and progress of the human spirit, the historian "selects a partial structure of meaning, declares it to be total, and arranges the rest of the historical materials more or less elegantly around the preferred centre of meaning."[93] These constructs, let us add, "are of decisive importance in the history of political ideas because they are genuine evocations of new communities which tend to replace the Christian *corpus misticum*."[94] This way, in trying to endow reality devoid of any objective sense with meaning, unconstrained anthropology proves to be an excellent breeding ground for utopia. The next section

---

[88]Sarte wrote: "It is absurd that we are born; it is absurd that we die." Id., *Being and Nothingness*, p. 567.

[89]WładysławTatarkiewicz, *Historia filozofii*. Vol. 3, PWN, Warszawa 1997, p. 351.

[90]W. Tatarkiewicz, *Historia. . .*, p. 351.

[91]Ibid..

[92]E. Voeglin, *From Enlightenment . . .*, p. 9.

[93]Ibid., p. 11.

[94]Ibid., p. 11.

will discuss one of the more important of such creations, one that is particularly relevant from the perspective of anthropological reflection, namely the concept of Marx.

7.4   Collectivist Anthropology

Even though in the end Rousseau "came to terms" with the fencing-in of the field and private property being a fact, not all visionaries of unconstrained anthropology were so submissive. In fact, this submissiveness was an inconsistency. As pointed out by Jacob Talmon, in the very idea of natural, rational order, "in the conception of the individual Man as the first and last element of social edifice, there was inherent the implication that all existing forms and interests may and should be upset and entirely reshaped, so as to give Man his due. On these principles property could not be regarded as a sacred natural right to be taken for granted."[95] It is not a coincidence that Rousseau presents the state in *The Social Contract* as "the master of all the goods of its members;" for Helvetius, Diderot, Mably and other contemporary thinkers the evil of the world was related to property. Nevertheless, in the eighteenth century the idea of abolishing property was "contradicted by the very same writers who put them forward. Rousseau, Helvetius and Mably concurred that private property had become the cement of the social order, and the foundation stone of the Social Contract."[96] With the exception of Morelly, this dimension of the dynamics of unconstraint was not to be realized until the nineteenth century.

By claiming that the source of human alienation was the division of labor which had led to the emergence of private property, communism could sum up its theory—in the words of Marx and Engels—"in the single sentence: abolition of private property."[97] Even though they did not, of course, wish to go back to any state of nature, ultimately their goal was essentially to realize Rousseau's desire and reconcile man and the world, to overcome alienation so that man may become "one with the world."[98] Their goal was to emancipate man,[99] to free him of the fetters—even though they understood them very differently than their eighteenth century predecessors.

[95]Talmon, *The Origins...*, pp. 50–51.
[96]Ibid., p. 52.
[97]Karol Marks, Friedrich Engels, *The Communist Manifesto,* Wiley-Blackwell 1995, p. 24.
[98]Erich Fromm, *Marx's Concept of Man*, Marino Publishing, Mansfield Centre 2011, pp. 58–59.
[99]E. Fromm, *Marx's Concept...*, p. 38.

As noted by Leszek Kołakowski[100] or John Paul II,[101] the entire structure of Marxism, including its attitude to property, is based on an anthropological standpoint. The key *novum* in Marx compared to the above-discussed thinkers representing unconstrained anthropology seems to be the fact that while sustaining the inner-worldly perspective of looking at man, it breaks up with the premise, fundamental to atomistic anthropology, about the existence of a *cogito*—a subject in himself, cleansed of his entanglement with historical circumstances. On the contrary, "the materialist interpretation of consciousness as it was understood by Marx is that human knowledge, as well as desires, ideals, sentiments, images, in short—all conscious content—is the product of man's social and historical existence."[102] Man is historical, and his features "depend on the circumstances, on his social position."[103] His essence, as he writes in *Theses on Feuerbach*, "in its reality (. . .) is the ensemble of the social relations."[104] And as regards social factors, "of primary importance are material factors, and among these—the economic ones."[105]

From the above perspective, the solution, typically of the logic of unconstraint, to the social problem, the road to man's liberation was not so much the discovery of human nature or enhancing the spirit of free emancipation,[106] but discovering the laws of social and historical development. Since man is "a configuration of data, a combination of objective tendencies,"[107] and—to quote Marx—"man's ideas, views, and conception, in one word, man's consciousness, changes with every change in the conditions of his material existence, in his social relations and in his social life,"[108] the oppression that afflicts man cannot be removed from within the very system in which this oppression is grounded. Therefore, the purpose of science is to discover the laws governing history to enable the inevitable, revolutionary

---

[100]Cf. Leszek Kołakowski, *Główne nurty marksizmu. Część I. Powstanie*, Zysk i ska, Poznań bdw, p. 16.

[101]Cf. John Paul II, *CentesimusAnnus*, No. 13: "the fundamental error of socialism is anthropological in nature. Socialism considers the individual person simply as an element, a molecule within the social organism, so that the good of the individual is completely subordinated to the functioning of the socio-economic mechanism. Socialism likewise maintains that the good of the individual can be realized without reference to his free choice, to the unique and exclusive responsibility which he exercises in the face of good or evil."

[102]L. Kołakowski, *Główne. . .*, p. 487.

[103]Jan Baszkiewicz, Franciszek Ryszka, *Historia doktryn politycznych i prawnych*, PWN, Warszawa 1973, p. 363.

[104]Karl Marx, *Theses on Feuerbach*, Thesis VI.

[105]J. Baszkiewicz, F. Ryszka, op.cit., p. 363.

[106]As pointed out by StanisławFilipowicz, in the light of Marxist thought "the entire concept of emancipation related to the bourgeois revolution was (. . .) misconceived. It should be treated as a symptom of false consciousness." *Historia. . .*, p. 318.

[107]S. Filipowicz, *Historia. . .*, p. 317.

[108]Karl Marks, Friedrich Engels, *The Communist Manifesto*, Wiley-Blackwell 1995, p. 27.

changes and thus to ultimately remove the fetters shackling mankind.[109] In the middle of the nineteenth century, such optics fit well with the then popular view that "human civilization develops according to strictly defined rules."[110] Consequently, Marxism claimed to "direct the process of history based on scientific theses."[111]

Before we refer to the necessary rules of history specified by Marx, we should note that the modified unconstrained concept of anthropology made one more premise next to its claim about the historical and social (economic, in fact) conditioning of a person, an essentially axiomatic one, though related to its assumed logic of history. Namely, it treated human labor as a key anthropological factor. To capture man in Marxism as a complete being, as noted by Leszek Kołakowski, is not only do depict him as a physical being (materialism), but also as one that "works, wrestles with nature."[112] Work was for Marx an essential factor in human existence, a particular form of affirming humanity.[113] This assumption was important for three reasons. Firstly, it showed the source of the dynamics of social transformations. Like for the luminaries of the Age of Lights or J. S. Mill the "tendency of inward forces" was an axiom which explained progress, so for Marx it was labor and its effects that became the driving force for economic change. Secondly, the special role of labor justified the need for a revolution in a situation where, in the circumstances of capitalism, labor became something alien to, even hostile to man: "when selling his labor, he only received a little portion of its value in the form of wages, whose amount was not determined by his effort or the value of the goods he produced, but by the level of costs he had to incur in order to survive."[114] And thirdly, it justified the possibility of reconciling existence in a communist society. Marx wrote: "in a higher phase of communist society, after enslaving subordination of the individual to the division of labour (. . .) has vanished; after labour has become not only a means of life but life's prime want; after the productive forces have also increased with the all-round development of the individual, and all the springs of co-operative wealth flow more abundantly—only then can the narrow horizon of bourgeois right be crossed in its entirety and society inscribe its banners: From each according to his ability, to each according to his needs!"[115] Liberation of man means liberation from the potential of labor on an unprecedented scale, and "a future society without scarcity, conflicting economic interests, ethnic or religious divisions, or imperfect

---

[109]As rightly pointed out by Leszek Kołakowski, this reveals the Hegelian optics of Marx (different from Engel's perspective), who also envisaged at the end the ultimate reconciliation of existence. Cf. L. Kołakowski, *Główne. . .*, pp. 489–491.

[110]Włodzimierz Bernacki, *Marksizm*, in: B. Szlachta [ed.], *Słownik społeczny*, WAM, Kraków 2004, p. 642.

[111]Jan Baszkiewicz, Franciszek Ryszka, *Historia doktryn politycznych i prawnych*, PWN, Warszawa 1973, p. 360.

[112]L. Kołakowski, *Główne. . .*, p. 490.

[113]W. Bernacki, *Marksizm. . .*, p. 643.

[114]Ibid.

[115]Will Kymlicka, *Contemporary. . .*, p. 166.

rationality."[116] The desire for work that is inherent in man is essential, therefore. Not only for practical reasons (if the communist society project is to succeed, there must be prosperity), but first of all because in the historical process man creates himself through work, which will reach its full potential after the alienation is overcome.[117] Consequently, as noted by Will Kymlicka, Marx's concept of alienation is an example of perfectionist argumentation which says that resources should be distributed so that they serve "the realization of distinctively human potentialities and excellences and to discourage ways of life which lack these excellences. Such theories (...) claim that certain ways of life constitute human 'perfection' (or 'excellence'), and that such ways of life should be promoted, while less worthy ways of life should be penalized."[118]

Once we note the anthropology of a materialist *homo laborens*, we can understand the "historical laws" discovered by Marx, presented in *The Communist Manifesto* as "the history of class struggles" which made "freeman and slave, patrician and plebeian, lord and serf, guild-master and journeyman, in a word, oppressor and oppressed, [stand] in constant opposition to one another, [carry] on an uninterrupted, now hidden, now open fight, a fight that each time ended either in a revolutionary reconstitution of society at large, or in the common ruin of the contending classes."[119] In this sense, capitalism is a harbinger of socialism. In *A Contribution to the Critique of Political Economy* Marx wrote: "in the social production of their existence, men inevitably enter into definite relations, which are independent of their will, namely relations of production appropriate to a given stage in the development of their material forces of production. The totality of these relations of production constitutes the economic structure of society, the real foundation, on which arises a legal and political superstructure and to which correspond definite forms of social consciousness."

The acceptance of class logic in which being/not being an owner determines a special kind of consciousness necessarily means the need for a "falsification of all earlier philosophical systems and political theories."[120] In Marx, truth becomes class-bound, which abolishes the possibility of a universal ethics. From now on, any ethics that is formulated only expresses class awareness. There is no personhood any more, or freedom, or independence; now, there is a "bourgeois" personhood, freedom, and independence, all of which should be abolished.[121] "Law, morality, religion, are (...) bourgeois prejudices, behind which lurk in ambush just as many bourgeois interests," as Marx and Engels wrote in the *Communist Manifesto*,

---

[116]Ibid., p. 173.

[117]Cf. S. Filipowicz, *Historia...*, p. 320.

[118]Will Kymlicka, *Contemporary...*, pp. 186–187: "In Marx's case, our distinctive excellence is said to be our capacity for freely creative co-operation production. To produce in a way that stunts this capacity is to be 'alienated' from our true 'species-nature'."

[119]K. Marks, F. Engels, *The Communist...*, p. 16.

[120]W. Bernacki, *Marksizm...*, p. 646.

[121]Cf. K. Marks, F. Engels, *The Communist Manifesto*.

debunking false consciousness. "Unethical" acts are only "unethical" in the bourgeois logic. In the revolutionary fight, violence is justified. Of course, it may be argued that "by claiming a dialectical changeability of the world, Marxism proclaims the view that moral and ethical truths are changeable as well."[122] In fact, however, it makes an even stronger claim: it negates the possibility of the existence of universal truths. Consequently, Marx's "political, social and economic doctrine was not supported by ethical findings, because ethics was class-bound. In view of Marx's goal of building a scientifically substantiated political theory, developed in the spirit of positivist philosophy, rejecting all great axiological systems allegedly to fend off the charges of subjectivism, also moral imperatives (...) were negated."[123] Commenting on Marx's contempt for theoreticians who tried to justify socialism in ethical terms, Will Kymlicka writes, somewhat ironically, that "when Marxists believed that socialism was inevitable, there was no need to explain why it was desirable."[124]

Since social rules are not based on a universal morality but are the product of social and economic conditions, it becomes understandable why "bourgeois private property," which in accordance with Marx's "scientific socialism" was "the final and most complete expression of the system of producing and appropriating products that is based on class antagonisms, on the exploitation of the many by the few,"[125] could never be accepted. It was the abolition of property that would lead to the expected total revolution: social, legal, political, spiritual. According to Marx, once man is liberated from property and the social relationships that are based on ownership, having overcome alienation, he will be able to "devote himself freely to self-fulfillment (...) creating his own world through the process of work."[126] Thus, unlike in Rousseau's vision, it is not by trying to go back to nature, but "through continued technical efforts and by forcing the existing society to reveal its utmost potential, through man's further expansion in ruling over the powers of nature"[127] that we will arrive at the gates of Paradise, where we will meet a "new man," however, as new economic conditions will engender new social relationships. This also means that our knowledge about the future, just like the mystics' knowledge about God,[128] can only be negative. We can predict what will not happen, but not what new is to come. Positive knowledge, as argued by Frederic Engels, will become available to us "when a new generation has grown up (...) when these people are in the world, they will care precious little what anybody today thinks they ought to do; they will make their own practice and their corresponding public

---

[122]J. Baszkiewicz, F. Ryszka, *Historia...*, p. 364.

[123]W. Bernacki, *Marksizm...*, p. 644.

[124]Will Kymlicka, *Contemporary...*, pp. 167–168: "the death of 'scientific' Marxism as a theory of historical inevitability has helped give birth to Marxism as a normative theory."

[125]K. Marks, F. Engels, *The Communist...*, p. 24.

[126]S. Filipowicz, *Historia...*, p. 320.

[127]L. Kołakowski, *Główne...*, pp. 499–500.

[128]Cf. Anonymous, *The Cloud of Unknowing,* translated by James Walsh, Paulist Press 1981.

opinion about the practice of each individual—and that will be the end of it."[129] This comment by Engels shows what revolutionary anthropological content is entailed by the postulate of abolishing property.

Of course, in the above theory, like in all unconstrained concepts, there is one irremovable problem. If "all conscious content is the product of man's social and historical existence,"[130] a question arises about the possibility of "anticipating" history and discovering its laws. Marx's writings give no explicit answer to this problem; one is provided by his heirs, however. Antonio Gramsci, attributing a subjective role to politics in Marxism, expressly declares that revolution is possible if the "masses [become] united behind the intellectuals."[131] The latter, possessed of deeper insight, will be able—"by virtue of their educative role"—to persuade the masses to accept their domination "which will therefore be entirely without a coercive basis."[132] Under its leadership, a synergy will be accomplished of two forces: "that exerted from above by the communist intellectuals, (...) and that exerted from below by the 'masses,' who bear within themselves the new social order that has grown from their labour."[133] As a result, the Enlightenment dream of the "city of man," free from superstition and any social and cultural structures which alienate him from his essence,[134] will be achieved thanks to the enlightened leadership of the far-sighted elites.

7.5 Initial Conclusions

Our reflections concerning unconstrained anthropology began by asking about its essence. From the perspective of philosophy, we may note that the difference in approaching the essence of humanity—compared to constrained anthropology—boils down to the ontological question. While the ontology of personhood delineates a space of plasticity within the logic of constrained anthropology, considering it possible to rationally capture the moral (and not only physical) boundaries of human nature, unconstrained anthropology does not have a metaphysics of man to rely on. In the end, it founds the idea of liquid humanity with blurred boundaries, whose definition—depending on the perspective—coincides either with the definition of animal, or that of the Absolute.

---

[129]Friedrich Engels, *The Origin of the Family, Private Property and the State*, Penguin Classics 2010, p. 73.

[130]L. Kołakowski, *Główne...*, p. 487.

[131]Roger Scruton, *Fools, Frauds and Firebrands: Thinkers of the New Left*, Longman Group 1985, p. 82.

[132]Ibid., p. 83.

[133]Ibid., p. 81.

[134]As noted by W. Bernacki, "for Marx, culture, as a tool of class rule, also lost the values it had theretofore been attributed. Works of material culture were but expressions of the ambitions and class aspirations of the wealthy." *Marksizm...*, p. 647.

The above difference may also be described otherwise. One might say that the dispute is about the concept of rationality and conscience. In the current of constraint, rationality is understood as a disposition with an inherent moral sense allowing man to refer to "that which is Higher," to a universal norm that is independent from man and related to his nature. In the unconstrained current, ethical rules are instrumental (e.g. in utilitarianism, the overriding value is utility, in Marxism—class interests), so the classical category of reason and conscience, as well as moral categories, become irrelevant in a sense. Eric Voegelin says that "the thinkers of the eighteenth century have mutilated the idea of man beyond recognition. In the case of D'Alambert (. . .) man was deprived of his *bios theoreticos* and reduced in essence to the utilitarian level of a *homo faber*. In Voltaire we have seen the fierce attack on the life of the spirit (. . .) Diderot has spoken of the 'useless contemplator'."[135] If, as put by J. S. Mill, moral dispositions do not form part of our nature,[136] then they do not belong to the area of rationality, at least if morality is to be understood as something more than consequentialism (i.e. the reduction of morality to the practical cause-and-effect rule evaluated according to the logic of economic benefits). Consequently, once we reject conscience as a tool which helps prevent rationality from turning into (ir)rationalism we downplay the understanding of human life in a dimension deeper than just the material and sensuous one; the recognition that it leads to an "understanding of man himself and of his place in the universe."[137]

Naturally, the two issues outlined above are intrinsically interlinked. It is the rejection of metaphysics that makes it possible in the unconstrained current to assign rationality to the domain of objective facts which stand in opposition to subjective experiences and feelings, which from now on will include morality and religion. This leads not only to undermining the deepest foundations of morality, but also the sense of rationality which in itself calls for the recognition that the world may have its origin in the rational.[138] Such a claim is challenged as unscientific or irrational. The logic of "pure facts" means that the only permissible (progressive, non-metaphysical, for metaphysics becomes here a synonym for backwardness) perspective is the rule of contingency. Thus, the thesis that is considered properly rational now is that about the meaninglessness of history, which is reduced to a combination of more or less surprising coincidences. The "accidental" evolution of man described by Rousseau finds its complement in nineteenth-century theories of evolution expanded into a universal worldview.[139]

---

[135]E. Voegelin, *From Enlightenment. . .*, p. 95.

[136]Cf. J.S. Mill, Utilitarianism, p. 30. Note that for Mill, nature only means the physical, experimentally verifiable.

[137]E. Voegelin, *From Enlightenment. . .*, p. 79.

[138]Cf. J. Ratzinger, *A Turning Point for Europe?: The Church in the Modern World: Assessment and Forecast*, Ignatius Press 1994.

[139]Cf. e.g. Richard Dawkins, *The God Delusion*, Mariner Books 2008.

Refusal to believe in the existence of substantiations of sense and morality that are deeper than can be discovered scientifically results in the experience of the directness of judgment being identified in the current of unconstrained anthropology with the education of feelings, which may be freely formed through the process of socialization. Consequently, as regards substantiations of morality, unlike in the classical tradition which sought to open "downwards", to pre-rational truth and its understanding, reason is now supposed to help unmask justifications which are in any way transcendental. This approach was characteristic not only of Enlightenment thinkers, but even more of their followers, including the utilitarian tradition analyzed above declaring that moral rules should be evaluated against the standard of utility, or leftist currents which referred to the Marxist legacy.[140] In this last approach, moral categories make no sense at all outside of the political process. Ultimately, it is political praxis, striving to further the inevitable victory of the proletariat and annihilation of the capitalist class, that makes particular actions right or wrong. Consequently, the categories of good or bad no longer have any raison d'être. For Vilfredo Pareto, who places the sociology of politics within the logic of Marx, they are derivations, a kind of superstition or prejudice: "none of them is a scientific concept and hence none of them is rationally derived, rationally defensible, true or false."[141] In this sense, we might say that collectivist anthropology goes a step further than atomistic anthropology. Unlike the latter, which still looks for objective moral criteria in the utilitarian current, the former rules out any possibility of objectivism. Nevertheless, this should be seen more as a subsequent stage in development than a breakup. Returning to the image of paradise, we might say that in its expository endeavors and attempts at revealing "the proper" sense of morality, the logic of collectivist and atomistic anthropology invokes a similar image: that of the Biblical snake—the tempter. It was the first exposer, suggesting that "God prohibits eating from the tree of life because he does not wish for people to become his equals. The unmasked basis of morality is design, purpose—and a hidden purpose at that, (. . .) contradicting the purposes which this morality advocates."[142] The true good was to be seen by man only after he had negated God's law, and thus—at least for a moment—by establishing himself as the highest being.

When looking at the specificity of unconstrained anthropology, there is no way we could ignore the significant discrepancy between atomistic and collectivist anthropology; namely, the collectivist thesis that man is wholly defined by his social existence. While this seems to be very far from liberal theses, in fact this premise appears to be an implication of atomistic logic. This can be seen very clearly in the works of a precursor of this logic—Turgot, the prior of the Sorbonne. He was one of the first thinkers to embrace the thoroughly modern view, resulting from the above-mentioned logic of "pure facts," that for an individual man, history has no meaning. Consequently, he performed a kind of replacement: "since concrete man cannot be

---

[140]Will Kymlicka, *Contemporary. . .*, p. 21.

[141]John Hallowell, *The Moral Foundation of Democracy*, Liberty Fund 2007, p. 2.

[142]R. Spaemann, *Granice. . .*, p. 85.

the subject for whom history has a meaning, the subject has to be changed—man is replaced by the *masse totale*."[143] In result, and this can be clearly seen in Marx, even though the view of man's anthropological "input" changes, the structure of anthropological thought characteristic of unconstraint remains intact: the universalism of the individual is recreated at the level of the collective. In Marx and his heirs, it is the proletariat—analogically to the individual in Rousseau—that has neither nation nor state.[144] In its own way, this is even more consistent with the idea of perfection referred to in the atomistic current, in which it ultimately applies more to the species than to an individual. It was Marx who claimed that "in the future world, all mediation between an individual and mankind will be abolished."[145] For the heirs of either current of unconstrained anthropology, this goal is worthy of the necessary sacrifices.

The dominant, despite all differences, core shared by collectivist and atomistic anthropology is uncovered, almost inadvertently, by Leszek Kołakowski in his analysis of Marxism. He contends that "in Marxism it is almost as though there are no such circumstances of life that people are born or die, that they are young or old, that they are men or women, that they are healthy or sick, that they are genetically unequal and that all such divisions may affect their social development irrespective of class divisions; that these circumstances place limits on man's projects to improve his world. Marx does not believe in the fundamental finiteness and limitedness of man, he does not believe in the essential limits to his creativity. Evil and suffering appear as the leverages of future liberation, they have no meaning of their own, they are not necessary components of life—they are entirely social facts."[146] If we substituted Marx's name with that of Rousseau, J. S. Mill, or Helvetius, the above description would essentially hold just as well.

The significance of this approach to rationality and conscience as categories differentiating two opposite anthropological standpoints, and thus the approach to the existence of a universal norm that is higher than man, reveals the significance of theological standpoints for the anthropologies outlined above. Just like for constrained anthropology the existence of the Absolute makes it possible to think about man as a being who has his own concrete, permanent (though not necessarily static) ontological structure (or, in other words: a nature which can be known and which is anchored in a rational reality), so the foundation of unconstrained thinking considers the "God hypothesis" to be irrelevant. Perceiving man as the highest being who leads himself from animal to human life implies an atheistic logic. In this view, atheism is the "ontological condition of man,"[147] if he has any ontology at all. This

---

[143]E. Voegelin, *From Enlightenment...*, p. 94.

[144]Cf. K. Marks, F. Engels, *The Communist Manifesto*, p. 23.

[145]L. Kołakowski, *Główne...*, p. 498.

[146]L. Kołakowski, *Główne...*, p. 502.

[147]Cf. Marek Rembierz, "Tropy transcendencji... Współczesne myślenie religijne wobec pluralizmu światopoglądowego i relacji międzykulturowych," *Świat i Słowo* No. 2(23)/2014, pp. 30–31.

cannot be without consequences for the reinterpretation of rationality and morality, or the meaning of basic values (freedom, equality, justice, etc.). In other words, opposite to the logic of transcendence characteristic of constrained anthropology stands the anthropology of immanence specific of unconstrained anthropology.

In contrast to unconstrained rationality, it is easier to see that openness, even if only potential, to the existence of the Absolute is a condition for rationality to be open—to use Spaemann's expression—"downwards," towards non-rational, though not necessarily irrational, sources. It is by referring to this openness that constrained anthropology avoids understanding nature as facts which can be seen through, and thus also mastered. Unlike unconstrained anthropology, it does not close itself to the moral message which reaches man from "beyond himself," so to speak. For while in the current of unconstrained thought about man morality undergoes a calculated transformation which makes the good (or wrong) of an act dependent on its foreseeable consequences,[148] the acknowledgement of limitations to human reason and the recognition that Revelation "throws light on the order of human society",[149] which ultimately expands the cognitive perspective rather than reducing the categories of good and bad to the calculus of benefits. It was no coincidence that John Locke believed it was necessary to discover God in order to "set the direction of life and formation of character," that "this way man recognizes himself as a moral being, who must live a life in accordance with the reason he has been given by God, a being who is trusted by his Creator and a being who is trustworthy."[150] In the constrained current, it is therefore assumed that without breathing "the air of faith" man also loses the ability to know the truth about himself,[151] that his reason—in the long run—is curtailed, and his conscience distorted.

The thesis that it is precisely the approach to the Absolute, the verticality of the anthropological perspective, that determines whether we may ground constrained anthropology is not an obvious one, however. Constrained thinking has often succumbed to the secularist logic. In a way, we might even say that the very category of natural law encourages such succumbing, making the "God issue" relevant only on the level of an inessential hypothesis. Since ultimately it is the human reason that discovers moral truth as permanent, eternal principles, and adapts them to concrete situations, the issue of the reality of Transcendence seems secondary, in a manner of speaking. This road, explicitly rejected by Aquinas[152] and his successors, was

---

[148]Cf. J. Ratzinger, *Christianity and the Crisis of Cultures*, Ignatius Press 2006. Elsewhere Cardinal Ratzinger points out that "the opposing worldviews of today have a common starting point in the rejection of the natural moral law and the reduction of the world to 'mere' facts. The measure with which they illogically hold on to the old values differs, but, at their core, they are threatened with the same peril." Id., "Consumer Materialism and Christian Hope," Fisher Lecture (1988), reprinted in *Teachers of the Faith*, London 2002, pp. 78–94.

[149]John Paul II, *CentesimusAnnus*. . . No. 25.

[150]J. Turek, *Dobro*. . ., p. 135.

[151]Cf. John Paul II, *Veritatis Splendor*. . .

[152]Aware that while "the natural law, in the abstract, can nowise be blotted out from men's hearts", it may nevertheless be "blotted out in the case of a particular action, in so far as reason is hindered

developed in the modern theory of natural law. Hugo Grotius, a precursor of this approach, believed that this law "results from man's inner principles and is a dictate of righteous reason which indicates the compliance or incompliance of human actions with man's rational nature,"[153] and exists "with full force, even if God did not exist."[154] For his successors, Samuel von Pufendorf, Christian Thomas (Thomasius) or Christian Wolff, the thesis *etsi Deus non daretur* was already natural. It was an attempt at keeping the constraint anthropology within the logic of immanence. Nevertheless, as pointed out by Javier Hervada, "keeping up the relationship between God and natural law while arguing for the latter's immanence is artificial"[155] and could not be upheld in the long run, proving to be merely a concession to the cultural context of the time. In its inner logic, the modern law of nature abandoned any reference to the creator of human nature, or to human sinfulness.[156] Consequently, as noted by Jacek Salij OP, it contributed to compromising the idea of natural law and "instead of building a comprehensive system of the law of nature as a complete code, binding all nations and for all times, the school of natural law finally led to doubts in the existence of any positive content in natural law. Indeed, the last and most important representative of this school, the great Kant, reduced natural law to an empty, purely formal principle"[157] of the categorical imperative. This way, the "diffusion of God" from the logic of constraint finally led to the diffusion of that logic itself.

The comment about Kant, considered to be one of the leading advocates of human dignity in the logic of immanentism, reveals that the "God issue" is relevant not only for the metaphysics of man, the understanding of his attributes (rationality, morality, freedom, etc.), but also for the possibility of substantiating human dignity. For Rousseau, man's nature was not human in a sense deeper than applicable to the species. This conviction—as has been demonstrated—is emblematic of the unconstrained paradigm. The above-discussed interpretations, particularly relevant in politics, do not provide satisfactory answers as to how, in this perspective, one should justify and warrant man's dignity, since they are premised on a functional understanding of dignity which may be easily undermined. The example of Kant shows, however, that there were also other attempts within this current of reflection which tried to break out of the functional logic. Apart from Kant, who built his ethics

---

from applying the general principle to a particular point of practice, on account of concupiscence or some other passion, as stated above (...) either by evil persuasions, just as in speculative matters errors occur in respect of necessary conclusions; or by vicious customs and corrupt habits, as among some men, theft, and even unnatural vices as the Apostle states, were not esteemed sinful." Thomas Aquinas, *Summa Theologiae*, q. 94 a. 6.

[153]Javier Hervada, *Historia prawa naturalnego*, Petrus, Kraków 2013, p. 173 [Spanish original: *Historia de la Ciencia del Derecho Natural*, EUNSA, Pamplona 1987.].

[154]Ibid.

[155]Ibid., p. 188.

[156]Jacek Salij OP, *Eseje tomistyczne*, W drodze, Poznań 1995, p. 186.

[157]Ibid., pp. 186–187.

referring solely to the inner logic of the ethical sphere, they included the phenomenological tradition.

Without going into a detailed discussion of these important attempts, it should be noted that they ultimately lead to doubtful results as far as the substantiation of human dignity is concerned. The self-evidences which phenomenologists refer to in fact depend on the culture, and are therefore relative; moreover, "many of the phenomena they talk about are in fact linguistic phenomena."[158] As regards the logic of the categorical imperative, it turns out that knowledge derived "from a formal 'inner logic' is, in the final analysis, too abstract to be the source of the substance of ethics." Lobkowicz points out that even though Kant claimed that his concept of ethics was based solely on formal reasons, he constantly played around with arguments, or, to be more precise: cited or invoked arguments which were not formal at all.[159] In the end, as pointed out by Giovanni Reale, even though "Kant's doctrine is believed to be based on pure reason, it could only have emerged in the Christian culture, and cannot be justified other than theologically."[160] The uniqueness and inviolability of every person "can only be substantiated in the last instance if we believe that the ruler of the universe cares about the person as a unique individual."[161] Consequently, the "God issue" proves to be of key importance for the doctrine of the inviolable dignity of the human person. This doctrine "cannot really be upheld, much less substantiated, without the belief that the human person (as well as the soul, since we come into this world through biological processes) has been created by a personal God."[162] Consequently, if unconstrained anthropology wants to avoid the shallows of challenging the idea of inviolable dignity, it may only accept it without substantiation: as an imperative of practical reason, or an axiom.[163] Most often, however, it undermines it—whether explicitly or otherwise.

---

[158] Nicolas Lobkowicz, *Czas kryzysu, czas przełomu*, WAM, Kraków 1995, p. 105. He continues: "we think that we 'see' something, because this is what our language suggests. But not all languages allow us to see 'the same thing;' to refer to a well-known example: in languages which do not use the auxiliary verb "to be," it would be unlikely for a "philosophy of being" to emerge."

[159] Cf. N. Lobkowicz, *Czas...*, p. 106.

[160] Giovanni Reale, *Karol Wojtyła. Pielgrzym Absolutu*, translated by Małgorzata Gajda, Centrum Myśli Jana Pawła II, Warszawa 2008, p.72 [Italian original: *Karol Wojtyla un pellegrino dell'assoluto*, Bompiani 2005].

[161] Ibid., p. 106.

[162] N. Lobkowicz, *Czas...*, p. 105.

[163] Leszek Kołakowski notes that "Kant believed, in fact, in an inalienable equality of people in their dignity of rational and freely acting subjects." Id., *Kant i zagrożenie cywilizacji*, p. 191.

Chapter 8
The Anthropology of Late Modernity

The radical dissimilarity between unconstrained and constrained anthropology, inherently linked to different approaches to Transcendence, may easily make us forget what these two perspectives have in common. To identify their shared area, let us refer to the understanding of the role of philosophers which the two adversaries subscribe to. In order to avoid shortcuts, let us refer to eighteenth-century claims made by Johann Gottlieb Fichte, who said that the philosopher's role is to make people aware of their true needs and to show them how they should be satisfied.[1] Whether or not Socrates would have accepted such a definition of the term philosopher, he would certainly have agreed with Fichte about one thing: that the truth about reality is key, and that philosophy is a privileged way of arriving at this truth intellectually. Here is where we discover a lead to discovering a profound affinity between the perspective of constraint and that of unconstraint, at least in the beginnings of the latter. A commitment to discovering the true needs, the real human condition, and the condition of the world was made, to the best of their belief, by Socrates as much as Descartes, Thomas Aquinas as much as Rousseau, Ockham as much as Feuerbach. Even though not all of them considered themselves to be, to use Thomas Carlyle's expression, "the light of the world (...) guiding it (...) in its dark pilgrimage through the waste of time,"[2] they all believed in the fundamental significance of the correspondence between the description and the thing being described, which gave "strength" to their claims. In this sense, Aquinas' involvement in disputes with Averroists resembled Voltaire's later disputes with the "Catholic superstition." In both cases, the goal was to set man free from the fetters of error. For "following the footsteps of Descartes, the *philosophes* believed in truth that is objective and stands on its own, and which can and would be recognized by

---

[1]Cf. Piotr Mazurkiewicz, "Odpowiedzialność uczonego w ponowoczesnym świecie," in: P. Mazurkiewicz, K. Wielecki [ed.], *Inny człowiek w innym społeczeństwie? Europejskie dyskursy*, Centrum Europejskie, Warszawa 2008, p. 79.

[2]Thomas Carlyle, *The Selected Works of Thomas Carlyle*, edited by F. Randolph Ludovico, The Bibliotheca Cakravarti Foundation, p. 199.

© Springer Nature Switzerland AG 2021
M. Gierycz, *European Dispute over the Concept of Man*, Contributions to Political Science, https://doi.org/10.1007/978-3-030-61520-8_8

man."[3] In somewhat simplified terms, the difference consisted in that Aquinas wanted to liberate the heretics from wandering away from the Church by referring to the authority of reason enlightened by faith, while the Enlightenment wanted to liberate believers (now treated as heretics, since "eighteenth-century *philosophes* were never in doubt that they were preaching a new religion"[4]) from religion by referring to reason enlightened by science. Richard Rorty expressed this aphoristically saying that "in secularized culture the scientist replaces the priest."[5]

The above examples of evident parallels visible in antithetic contexts show that under the surface of all the wrangling there was consent on a much deeper level. In this case, it was the essential (but, let us add for formality's sake, not complete—owing to the different concept of reason, as discussed above) consent about man's epistemic capacity. In the anthropological context, it was of fundamental importance. For in order to be able to reasonably argue about "who man is," or "what makes his flourishing,"[6] it was first necessary to agree that it is possible to arrive at any knowledge in this matter at all. This belief remained unshaken in the Enlightenment which cut itself off from the tradition of Revelation and postulated a new anthropological vision. It is true that, as discussed previously, the understanding of reason changed, and did so radically. Nevertheless, belief in the ability to discover the truth remained. In fact, much more remained as well. The genetically Christian conviction about the logocentric character of the world was still generally upheld.[7] As rightly noted by Lech Morawski, the modernist view of the world and all the theories built around it "were premised on the assumption that the world is a coherent, well-ordered and determined whole, governed by fixed rules which make processes occurring in the world predictable, calculable, and controlled."[8] The "great narrative" about the world was still based, as argued by Nietzsche, "on three basic elements: firstly, on belief in the meaningfulness of the world, the conviction that existence, the process of reality's becoming leads to some goal, e.g. realization of moral principles, salvation, or universal happiness. Secondly, on belief in the existence of a wholeness, an organic unity of the world which may be understood as a pantheist deity or a society which gives the individual a sense of participating in something higher than himself, and thus—a sense of greater value. And thirdly, on the belief that apart from the sensuous, temporal world, considered to be illusive, there is allegedly a true world, indestructible and permanent—like the

---

[3]Jacob L. Talmon, *The Origins Of Totalitarian Democracy*, pp. 28–29.

[4]Ibid., p. 21.

[5]Richard Rorty, *Objectivity, Relativism, and Truth*, Cambridge University Press 1991, p. 35.

[6]Cf. Robert R. Reilly, *Making Gay Okay. How Rationalizing Homosexual Behaviour is Changing Everything*, Ignatius Press, San Francisco 2014, p. 15.

[7]It is not a coincidence that the Enlightenment so readily embraced deism holding that the world was like a clock whose movements were well-ordered and predictable, and which was not in any particular need of God.

[8]Lech Morawski, *Co może dać nauce prawa...*, p. 26.

world of Plato's ideas."[9] This was the case because "Enlightenment thought, and Western culture in general, emerged from a religious context which emphasized theology and the achievement of God's grace. Divine providence had long been a guiding idea of Christian thought. Without these preceding orientations, the Enlightenment would scarcely have been possible in the first place. It is in no way surprising that the advocacy of unfettered reason only reshaped the ideas of the providential, rather than replacing it. One type of certainty (divine law) was replaced by another (the certainty of our senses, of empirical observation), and divine providence was replaced by providential progress."[10] It was this logocentric approach that made it possible to elevate the status of science, even though from now on it was to be "strictly empirical, hostile to all metaphysics," and was further to be "engaged in practical and technical applications,"[11] as a tool in transforming the world. The word "scientific" became synonymous to "true,"[12] which—this goal had remained unchanged ever since the Gospel was first preached by the Lord—was to set man free. Except that together with the immanentization of reason, liberation had become immanentized as well, usually turning into its very opposite.[13]

In the context of the great narrative it should be noted, however, that the situation before and after the Enlightenment differed not only in the standpoint concerning God. While until the Enlightenment there had essentially been only one great narrative in Christian Europe in which inhabitants of the Old Continent found the meaning of their lives, and the differentiation of Christian reflection, first of all into "Dominican" realism and "Franciscan" nominalism, did not lessen the uniqueness of the Christian thought horizon, after the Enlightenment the situation changed.[14] Not only was a new great narrative initiated under the banner of *etsi Deus non daretur*, still upholding the axiomatic convictions outlined above, but simultaneously, and as a consequence, a door was opened to various mutually contradictory narratives aspiring to become *the* "great narrative." Abandoning the vertical perspective and reducing knowledge to the activity of "pure reason," rationalism now stood before the daunting challenge of inconsistent interpretations. A challenge dramatic in that, as Michael Oakeshott tersely put it, a rationalist finds it "difficult to believe that

---

[9]Andrzej Zawadzki, "Pojęcie nihilizmu u Nietzschego, Heideggera i Vattimo," *Słupskie Prace Filologiczne*, Seria Filologia Polska 3/2004, pp. 211–212.

[10]Anthony Giddens, *The Consequences of Modernity,* John Wiley & Sons 2013, p. 48. He also notes that the parallel "growth of European power provided, as it were, the material support for the assumption that the new outlook on the world was founded on a firm base which both proved security and offered emancipation from the dogma of tradition." Ibid, p. 48.

[11]Andrzej Zawadzki, op. cit.

[12]It is no coincidence that Marx's socialism was supposedly scientific, and Comte called his third phase of development not only positive, but scientific as well.

[13]Simply put, such an approach opened the road to a politicization of Messianic hopes. Cf. Benedict XVI, *Encyclical Letter Spe Salvi to the Bishops, Priests and Deacons, Men and Women Religious, and All the Lay Faithful on Christian Hope.*

[14]Cf. M. Gierycz, P. Mazurkiewicz, *Europejska antropologia i europejska polityka…*, pp. 107–114.

anyone who can think honestly and clearly will think differently from himself."[15] Consequently, a number of narratives were produced, all sharing the above-mentioned expository zeal striving to reveal the "real" deep structure of social life, and consequently to endow human and social life with meaning. At the same time, however, the contents of theories built within their frameworks were growing further and further apart, with the distance between them gradually turning into chasms.[16]

It seems that it is this "war of rationalists" that may have been an important source of the contemporary cultural situation,[17] which, as suggested by Chantal Delsol or Gianni Vattimo,[18] may be called late modernity, and which is commonly associated with postmodernism.[19] If there is any element common to all of the diverse

[15]Michael Oaksechott, *Rationalism in Politics and Other Essays,* Basic Books 1962, p. 2.

[16]It may justifiably be argued it was not a coincidence that in this context of ideas, such great career was made by the idea of legal positivism, which was inherently aphilosophical and which could easily be combined with various philosophical doctrines and political programs (which became the obvious source of its demise in the age of Nazism). Cf. L. Morawski, *Co możedaćnauceprawa. . .,* pp. 19–25.

[17]Naturally, there have been other sources as well. The ones usually mentioned are the economic and cultural factors, such as globalization and the related eclecticism, which Lyotard calls "the degree zero of contemporary general culture" (Cf. Jean-Francois Lyotard, "Answering the Question: What Is Postmodernism?", translated by Regis Durand, [in:] The Postmodern Condition: A Report on Knowledge, Manchester University Press 1984, p. 76). I am aware of the radically different approaches to the problem. The growing interest in interpretations of the so-called late left makes it necessary to note that in the light of their analyses "the complete picture of the postmodern condition is, on the one hand, postmodernism, rampant fragmentation, games and para-logic, local identities, Babel, Babylon, pragmatism, relativism and mixed-up languages. On the other hand, the imperial supremacy of capital in the global reality." (Bartosz Kuźniarz, *Goodbye Mr. Postmodernizm. Teorie społeczne myślicieli późnej lewicy,* FNP, Toruń 2011, p. 19). From the correlation of these two phenomena, the late left draws a conclusion about the economic sources of today's alienation of man. This interpretation, though not entirely lacking in apt observations, tries—ineffectively, in my opinion—to resurrect the Marxist thesis about the primacy of economy over culture, now apparently combined into a single formation (cf. e.g. Fredric Jameson, Postmodernism, or, the Cultural Logic of Late Capitalism, Duke University Press 2013).

[18]Cf. Chantal Delsol, *Éloge de la singularité, essai sur la modernité tardive,* La Table Ronde 2007; Gianni Vattimo, The End of Modernity, The Johns Hopkins University Press, 1991. Of course, the interpretations proposed by these two authors differ as well. For Vattimo, it is about a form of abolishing the category of novelty, an experience of "the end of history", and not yet another, however advanced, phase of history. Delsol, on the contrary, points out that "the late time does not mean—or does not only mean—a decline of strength, withdrawal and weariness, but also the beginning of one culture being replaced with another. (. . .) Since cultures, unlike people, do not die, or at least never die for good." (*Esej o człowieku. . .,* p. 11).

[19]Opinions on the relationship between these concepts, as well as their accompanying notions: postmodernity (Zygmunt Bauman), second modernity (Urlich Beck), sur-modernity (George Baladier) are divided, both among researchers studying the phenomenon and among representatives of postmodern thought themselves (some of whom, let us add, like Richard Rorty or Jacques Derrida, refused to have these categories applied to their work at all.) Sometimes (Ryszard Nycz [ed.], *Postmodernizm. Antologia przekładów,* Wyd. Baran i Suszczyński, Kraków 1997) postmodernism is treated as a concept essentially identical to late modernity. It is considered to be both the name "of the period in the history of Western thought that followed modernity" and "a phase in the development of highly advanced societies of the West," as well as the name for (by reference to its

postmodern currents,[20] it could be "the considering of many truths which earlier generations had considered inviolable to be fragile and uncertain."[21] Post-industrial civilization, contributing to and generating processes of the autonomization of individuals,[22] left them with "questions where once there appeared to be answers."[23] Anthony Giddens says that not only philosophers are aware of this: "a general

---

beginnings in literary criticism) "a period of changes in literature and arts" (p. 9). Sometimes these two concepts, though still related, are filled with different content, so that "[p]ostmodernity is for postmodernism what modernity was for modernism" (Z. Bauman, *Ponowoczesność*, in: B. Szlachta [ed.], *Słownikspołeczny*, p. 903). Postmodernism is then seen as the driving force and the GPS of postmodernity. For just like modernism sharpened and promoted change, "postmodernism is a reflection which, as a rule, contains a programming, designing element [an element] which is either not present or avoided in postmodernity, being a sociological description of the realities of postmodern life" (p. 904). A different understanding of late modernity (the equivalent of postmodernity) is embraced by Vattimo, for whom there is no room in it for any designing element, due to its essentially anti-metaphysical, nihilistic character (cf. G. Vattimo, "Dialectics, Difference, Weak Thought," in: *Weak Thought*, Gianni Vattimo, Pier Aldo Rovatti (eds.), translated by Peter Carravetta, State University of New York Press 2012, pp. 39–52)]. In this approach—or so it appears, for Vattimo himself does not develop a semantic analysis—late modernity would simply be the cultural form of postmodernism. Finally, there are also those interpretations which separate postmodernism from postmodernity. Some, like Giddens, does this using the objective criterion, and says that postmodernism refers to the "aesthetic reflection upon the nature of modernity" (Anthony Giddens, *The Consequences of Modernity*, p. 45) and "is best kept to refer to styles or movements within literature, painting, the plastic arts, and architecture" (ibid). Postmodernity in this approach refers, on the other and, to the theory of social life, defining a different type of social order whose germ forms are already visible (p. 46). Others, like Życiński, while locating both categories within the area of social reflection, contrasted the proper spirit of postmodernity, following the classical models of rationalism and sense, with the "populist," relativistic and nihilistic version of postmodernism corresponding to the "mentality of customers in a supermarket" (Abp. Józef Życiński, *Bóg postmodernistów*, RW KUL, Lublin 2001, pp. 17–20). It seems, however, that this approach, being an attempt at entering into a dialogue with at least some part of postmodernity, ultimately leads to breaking up the relationship between the cultural and mental condition of modernity. The former is treated as inessential and populist, and the latter—radically different—is attributed the proper value. This model, though it may lead to entering into a dialogue, seems unconvincing in the context of the intellectual explications of contemporary cultural tensions.

[20]For example, Życiński points to reconstructive (eliminative) postmodernism, or to ultramodernism (trying to eliminate the concepts of God, soul, sense, truth, objective values from the philosophical picture of the world), and the antithetical constructive (revisionist) postmodernism which finds a hierarchy of values in the practice of our actions (*Bóg postmodernistów...*, p. 27); American postmodernism, heavily influenced by pragmatism, and French postmodernism, related to deconstructivism; finally, Christian postmodernism, combining a criticism of the Enlightenment "with a positive view of Christianity's relation to contemporary cultural challenges," and populist (ideological) postmodernism in which the entire Socratic and Enlightenment tradition is rejected (ibid., p. 24).

[21]J. Życiński, *Bóg postmodernistów...*, p. 29. The paradox of this situation is pointed out e.g. by Henryk Kiereś who stresses that "today's European—the creator of philosophy, which is the disinterested love of wisdom!—does not understand the world or himself." (Henryk Kiereś, "Kultura klasyczna wobec postmodernizmu," *Człowiek w kulturze*, 11/1998, p. 235).

[22]Wojciech Jakubowski, *Społeczna natura człowieka*, Elipsa, Warszawa 1999, p. 106.

[23]A. Giddens, *The Consequences of Modernity*, p. 49.

awareness of the phenomenon filters into anxieties which press in on everyone."[24] Consequently, the discovery which constitutes late modernity seems to be that "nothing can be known with any certainty, since all pre-existing 'foundations' of epistemology have been shown to be unreliable" and "'history' is devoid of teleology and consequently no version of 'progress' can plausibly be defended."[25] These diagnoses, in a more or less elaborated version, are subscribed to by most researchers,[26] who point to the anti-metaphysical character—consistent with Życiński's "populist postmodernism"—of late modernity, undermining not only the classical understanding of truth, but also the idea of progress—one of the key ideas of the Enlightenment.[27]

The comment on "violating the inviolable" is most significant in the context of reflections on politics and anthropology. It reveals an important, in view of our analyses here, problem related to the experience of the age of postmodernism: the question about its relationship to modernity. There can be no doubt that such a relationship exists—as has already been mentioned in the introduction to this chapter. Jean-Francois Lyotard argues, trying to turn the discourse "upside down" so to say, that in fact "a work can become modern only if it is first postmodern."[28] Though in the end he distances himself from such a "mechanical" view of the problem, it points to the inseparability of these two experiences. Nevertheless, answers to the question about its actual nature remain ambiguous. There seem to be two general standpoints.

The first is premised on the assumption that the meaning of socially and culturally significant changes in the age of postmodernism is properly described by the category of "postmodernity"; the other says that the proper term is "late modernity." These are not merely "linguistic games", so cherished in postmodernism. The talk of postmodernity suggests that contemporary civilization has moved beyond modernity (entering the end of history, or the beginning of a new era), resulting in a "rejection

---

[24]Ibid., p. 49.

[25]Ibid., p. 46.

[26]As noted by Andrzej Szahaj, who attempts to synthesize information about postmodernism, "in the postmodern logic, mistrust about the correspondent concept of truth, (. . .) a cognitive skepticism is usually accompanied by emphasis on the axiological and political danger of any thought claiming to know the entire Truth." As a consequence, it is characteristic of this current to "emphasize the partiality and relativity of all thought as being always ethically and politically involved." Andrzej Szahaj, "Postmodernizm," in: B. Szlachta [ed.], *Słownik społeczny*, WAM, Kraków 2006, p. 938.

[27]The modern idea of progress was premised on the assumption that the replacement of old "institutions with new ones, tailored to human capacities and needs, would be a one-time task, even if requiring the effort of many generations. The progress that mankind was now embarking on might be a long and exhausting venture, but the destination was already known (. . .). After a period of disturbances, an era of stability and universal peace would follow (this time eternal), safe from any surprises because built on unshakeable foundations of reason and in accordance with its infallible guidelines." (Z. Bauman, *Ponowoczesność*, p. 905).

[28]Jean-Francois Lyotard, "Answering the Question: What Is Postmodernism?", translated by Regis Durand' [in] *The Postmodern Condition: A Report on Knowledge*, Manchester University Press 1984, p. 44.

of the old word, and considering the changes that are underway as having already been completed."[29] The advocates of "late modernity" claim, on the other hand, that such assertions are ideological (designatory and, ultimately, normative), since in fact all we know is "that we are at the end of an epoch, but it is not known whether a return or a rebirth will be possible."[30] This approach does not proclaim an overcoming of the earlier epoch, but rather the fact that—as put by Giddens—it begins to "understand itself."[31] For the purposes of these reflections, a resolution of this dilemma with respect to anthropology, even if only a partial one, seems to be of key importance. As has been shown, modern political thought, standing in opposition to the classical tradition, represents an anthropology that supports the unconstrained vision of politics. If those who advocate calling it "late modernity" are right, postmodernism will refer to anthropologies grounding unconstraint as their new mutation. Still, since the mission statement of postmodernism includes a departure from the correspondence approach to truth, weakening, deconstruction, relativization, etc., the question is whether we should not be witnessing a weakening of the unconstrained tendencies instead. It would then make sense to talk about postmodernity as a standpoint founding new anthropological approaches, different from those we already know (both constrained and unconstrained).

8.1   The Anthropological Relevance of Nihilism

A consistent and philosophically well-developed description of the intellectual condition of our age has been presented by Gianni Vattimo, who describes it as *il pensiero debole*. Aware of the key role of departure from the correspondence approach to truth, he describes the contemporary intellectual condition using the category of "weak thought." Weak, because standing in opposition to the "strong thought" characteristic of both the classical tradition and modernism,"[32] "considering being, or beings, in the categories of presence, permanence, stability."[33] It is a special kind of opposition, we should add. The disputes held hitherto between the "classics" and "modernists" ultimately always touched upon the problem of beginnings, foundations, "whether in the traditional version of Aristotelian metaphysics, emphasizing the significance of the first principles, *archai*, or in the historicist,

---

[29]Ch. Delsol, *Esej o człowieku...*, p. 9.

[30]Ibid.

[31]A. Giddends, *The Consequences...*, p. 38.

[32]Andrzej Zawadzki notes that "the distinguished forms of strong thought include dialectic philosophy, transcendental philosophy, particularly phenomenology and its concept of *epoché*, suspension of references to concrete historical and cultural horizons, as well as various philosophies modelled on exact, deductive sciences premised on a referential concept of truth—though Vattimo pays the least attention to the latter." (*Literatura a myślstaba*, Universitas, Kraków 2009, pp. 61–62).

[33]Ibid.

Hegelian version, using the categories of fulfillment, culmination, finality," premised on "the possibility of direct access to being, with no cultural, historical, or linguistic mediation."[34] *Il pensiero debole* characteristic of late modernity wants to invalidate this dispute, in a way, claiming that such access is impossible. Vattimo is aware that this gives the impression—despite all disclaimers—of a dialectic logic where, in opposition to the strong claim about being, there is a strong claim about non-being. He notes, however, that even though the "overcoming of metaphysics seems to involve a dialectical overcoming," yet "it is different precisely insofar as it is a *Verwindung*. [...] This relation of overcoming and distortion is already exemplified in Nietzsche's announcement that God is dead, which is *not* a metaphysical utterance on the nonexistence of God." It is simply to be acknowledged as "an 'event' since the death of God means mainly the end of the stable structure of Being, hence also the end of the possibility of stating God's existence or nonexistence." It is "a historicist (as opposed to metaphysical) thesis which charges the death of God with value, cogency, 'logical necessity'."[35] Therefore, as noted by Andrzej Zawadzki, "weak ontology which is supposed to express the experience of being characteristic of the world of late, accomplished modernity, is premised on an understanding of being not in broadly-conceived "strong" categories, that is, as being, structure, reality that exists objectively, independently, fully, authentically, but quite on the contrary—in weak categories, as traces, remnants, that which is left of the full and intact presence, or self-presence, of being."[36]

   If we have no access to being and the logocentric interpretation of the world cannot be upheld, we are left with nihilism which—as noted by Lyotard—in general experience essentially boils down to an attitude of "anything goes."[37] Consequently, it is precisely nihilism, or "accomplished nihilism," to be more exact, that Vattimo considers to be the key experience of contemporary times.[38] He explains that "the accomplished nihilist has understood that nihilism is his or her sole opportunity. What is happening to us in regard to nihilism, today, is this: we begin to be, or to be able to be, accomplished nihilists."[39] And as such, we do not feel the depression

---

[34]He notes further on that this is "irrespective of whether the emphasis is placed on the directness of pure sensory data, as in the empiricist variant, or on the transcendental conditions of possible experience, as in the many rationalist variants." A. Zawadzki, *Literatura...*, p. 61.

[35]G. Vattimo, "Dialectics...," p. 46.

[36]A. Zawadzki, *Literatura...*, p. 70.

[37]J.-F. Lyotard, "Answering...," p. 76. He sees in this approach the triumph of capital (ibid.: "in the absence of aesthetic criteria, it remains possible and useful to assess the value of works of art according to the profits they yield." A question left unanswered is why the same should not be the case in the ethical sphere, considering the abolition of moral universals), and his thesis is developed by researchers of the "late left" current.

[38]As pointed out by Zawadzki, "according to Vattimo, nihilism is a central event and the destiny of late modernity, determining its characteristic way of experiencing the being of its existence" (A. Zawadzki, "Koniecnowoczesności: nihilizm, hermeneutyka, sztuka," in: G. Vattimo, Koniecnowoczesności, Universitas, Kraków 2006, p. X).

[39]G. Vattimo, *End of Modernity...*, p. 19.

resulting from the forsaking of values. Vattimo believes that metaphysical categories "such as the good, morality, truth, meaning and the wholeness or unity of being" were only "antidotes" against nihilism, doubt, the sense of pointlessness of human efforts. These antidotes are no longer required by contemporary Europeans, though, for their lives are much less marked by insecurity or fear which characterized human existence in traditional, pre-modern societies. This emancipation of the modern subject makes it possible to "loosen" the traditional, rigorous bonds of morality, to "weaken"—using the language of Vattimo who often refers to this particular fragment of Nietzsche's reflections—"strong" metaphysical categories.

The specificity of weakening "strong" categories is best illustrated by the approach to truth. In late modernist logic it becomes a synonym of violence which should not be succumbed to. For if everything is but a trace, then "all this talk about the world, in the sense of attributing to such talk any relation to objective truth about things, is constructed by man and imposed onto others by force in order to subordinate them."[40] Pierre Bourdieu's theory of habitus is a good exemplification of this logic. It justifies talking about (symbolic) violence "even when people unwittingly submit to imposed cultural patterns."[41] Consequently, as noted by Życiński, in late modernity "even the very concept of dialogue should be considered a great illusion, which prevailed during the moderne but has since been definitely abandoned."[42] The point is no longer to seek truth, but to fight "regimes of truth", to use Judith Butler's expression.[43] The emancipatory ambitions of modernity seem to have reached their fulfillment in late modernity.

We discover a paradox here. The proclaiming of inability, fragility, traces instead of possibility, certainty, being ultimately means, as regards its intellectual implications, not so much a weakening the earlier categories, but their (classically dialectic) negation. Not so much a nostalgic *pietas*, but a huge conflict. It is no coincidence that Lech Morawski, describing the dynamics of postmodernism, does not hesitate to use military categories. He stresses that postmodernism not so much weakens as "declares a war on logocentric (. . .) images and theories of the world and society," questioning "the idea of the world as a uniform, coherent whole, governed by universal laws."[44] This results from the fact that even if "eclecticism, collage, pastiche are [indeed] concepts which adequately describe the distinctive features of postmodernist culture,"[45] the intellectual mosaic of late modernity only admits

---

[40]Rev. Piotr Mazurkiewicz, *Ideologia gender jako wyzwanie dla chrześcijańskiej antropologii*, http://tydzienwychowania.pl/wp-content/uploads/2015/08/TW-ks-Mazurkiewicz-gender.pdf [27.06.2016].

[41]P. Mazurkiewicz, *Ideologia. . .* p. 67. Cf. S. Lee Bartky, "Foucault, Femininity and the Modernization of Patriarchal Power" [in:] K. Conboy, N. Medina, S. Stanbury (eds.), *Writing on the Body: Female Embodiment and Feminist Theory,* pp. 129–154, Columbia University Press, New York 1997.

[42]J. Życiński, *Bóg. . .*, p. 90.

[43]Judith Butler, *Gender Trouble. Feminism and the Subversion of Identity*, Routledge 1990, p. 10.

[44]L. Morawski, *Co może. . .*, p. 36.

[45]Ibid.

those voices which agree to be merely a "trace," and thus embrace the relativistic and nihilistic paradigm. Bauman describes this as a move away "from a hierarchy of goals, standpoints and actions, to a 'hetearchy' where differences exist side by side, but without having anything in common, without any order. Movement seems to be everything, and the goal is nothing. (...) [T]he movement is chaotic, leads nowhere and can never come to an end. Man immersed in the postmodern world is doomed to (...) 'self-creation,' or the freedom to become anyone."[46] This clearly shows the fulfillment or self-realization of the ideal of unconstrained anthropology birthed in the eighteenth century.

Striking at the idea of truth and man's rationality,[47] the logic of late modernity challenges especially the existence of moral truth. It comes as no surprise that Vattimo considers the "loosening of traditional moral bonds" to be the fundamental aspect of late modernity. As has been discussed more extensively in the description of unconstrained anthropology, the undermining of the idea of rational nature and the related logic of "pure facts," or—in the case of late modernity—traces of such facts, ultimately results in a situation where "no moral message outside ourselves can now come to us. Morality, just like religion, now belongs to the realm of the subjective; it has no place in the objective."[48] Modernity, while considering these claims to be true with respect to traditional morality, assumed that moral progress was possible and that new, scientific foundations of morality could be found. This logic, in a "weakened" form, comes back in late modernity. On the one hand, since nothing can be said about man, Vattimo holds that "there are hardly any philosophers today who claim that there is an absolute morality, objective truth, or natural laws."[49] At the same time, however, such claims—if they nevertheless appeared—must not be accepted. Ultimately, as Judith Butler rightly points out, this is about opposing "regimes of truth,"[50] which means "opening up possibilities"[51] and developing new normative standpoints, but now within a "positive normative vision."[52]

Despite all of Vattimo's disclaimers, weak thought turns out at its core to be a new mutation of the unconstrained logic; it means not so much opposition to as continuation and strengthening of the logic of modernity,[53] an invitation to freely mould the social reality. For if everything has been "constructed, it can also be

---

[46]Z. Bauman, *Ponowoczesność...*, p. 907.

[47]It should be stressed that late modernity does not consistently negate the idea of truth itself—for example, it considers the thesis that there is no objective truth to be objectively true.

[48]Ratzinger, *A Turning Point...*, p. 37.

[49]G. Vattimo, "Kościół popełnia samobójstwo," *Europa. Tygodnikidei*, 14–15.03.2009, p. 13.

[50]J. Butler, *Gender Trouble...*, p. viii.

[51]Ibid.

[52]Ibid., p. xxii. The author's explanation that she does not intend to create a single prescription which, if complied with, will ensure that "life will be good," does not really change much.

[53]The difference, if any, would consist only in that having accepted, for the first time in history in a consistent way, the relativist *dictum*, late modernity would not produce any new, positive modes of living, but effectively undermine the old ones. Also this claim, as will be demonstrated further on, is far from self-evident, however.

deconstructed. The only question is what tools to use."[54] Thus, constructivism turns out to be the reverse of nihilism, demonstrating the validity of Sowell's claims about the revolutionary potential of the logic of unconstraint.

The commitment to constructing new norms in late modernity appears to be natural. Even if we accept as true Bauman's claim that "the essential norms and values regulating human existence and the principles organizing human coexistence which we used to associate with the modern era have disappeared [or...] are experiencing a major crisis, waiting in vain for a new set of norms, values, and principles,"[55] the question is: what should we found social life on? After all, we must live somehow. In practice, therefore, also postmodernists usually refer to the supra-systemic character of certain values (e.g. liberation of minorities, social justice, etc.).[56] The link between this standpoint and the nihilist standpoint outlined above has been justified in theoretical terms by Jean-Francois Lyotard. He argues that "certain truths of fundamental significance may be entirely inaccessible to reason, and yet be knowable as truths by persons who have the ability to transcend the situational and cultural circumstances."[57] The freedom to become anyone thus leads—like in the entire tradition of unconstraint—to recognition of the leading role of the elites. As noted by Życiński, such an "epistemology introduces into our knowledge an element of arcane truth accessible to chosen individuals, but impossible to rationally justify."[58] The difference compared to the rational elites of modernity would only consist in that now it is not even necessary to rationally substantiate one's position. Like in the case of the approach to morality, this is a deepening rather than a negation of modernity, which justifies—at least in the area of anthropological reflection—rejecting the category of post-modernity, and referring to "late modernity" instead.

8.2 Man as an Exchangeable Value

In light of the above reflections, it may be noted that even though the anthropology of late modernity is largely negative, related to the logic of nihilism and deconstruction, it is the fulcrum of new social constructs. Deconstruction of man's epistemic faculties and the category of truth is related—as noted above—with deconstruction of the concept of subject which had become "tremendously exaggerated" in the past. In late modernity, as Vattimo points out, it becomes unmasked as fiction, in order to

---

[54]P. Mazurkiewicz, *Ideologia...*, p. 119.

[55]Z. Bauman, *Ponowoczesność...*, p. 902.

[56]J. Życiński, *Bóg...*, p. 90.

[57]Ibid., pp. 90–91.

[58]Ibid., p. 91.

"safely allow for a certain dose of randomness or even senselessness of existence."[59] Let us now take a closer look at this anthropological *dictum* and its consequences.

What does the weakening of the "tremendous exaggeration" of the concept of subject specifically mean? Vattimo is clear that the nihilist standpoint has fundamental consequences for thought about man. He claims that "metaphysical anthropology consists in the description of the universal structures of the occurrence of the human phenomenon. If we want to avoid this because we take seriously the historical (*geschicklich*) 'thrown-ness' of Dasein, then we must develop our thought in the direction of cultural anthropology."[60] This inevitably leads to the adoption of a relativist paradigm, premised on the assumption that it is impossible to develop a meta-cultural narrative by way of compromise.[61] In Vattimo's logic, this is self-evident since nothing can be said about man as such, "abstract" man, considering that nihilism is a process that concludes in "nothing left of Being as such."[62] What could remain is a "concrete man" at the most, understood as a monologous being, doomed to "becoming inevitably locked up in the cave of his own cultural tradition."[63] Consequently, Vattimo says, nihilism "concerns first of all Being itself (. . .) 'simply humanity',"[64] proving to be a "reduction of Being to exchange-value."[65]

The idea of being as an exchangeable value in the anthropological context is certainly a strong implication of "weak thought." Vattimo does not only say that he does not know what man's nature is; he says that there is no human nature, that nothing can be said about it, that we can only access traces of ideas of what it might consist of. This resembles an onirist nightmare of a pile of masks, with nothing underneath but more masks, each exchangeable for any other—at no loss, but no gain either. This way, weak thought undermines—most powerfully—the idea of a constitutive human condition, or, in other words, of human nature per se. If, however, "man is no longer distinguished by his condition, then he joins the animal species and is no longer distinguished by dignity."[66] The fundamental difference in the essence of being between animal and man seems to be implicitly ignored, even if this conclusion is not always clearly articulated. Consequently, the "weak thought" of late modernity supports, on the one hand, those proposals which postulate that the category of man's inherent dignity should be abandoned and replaced by the dignity of the person—a category which may include both people and animals, as long as they satisfy certain conditions (e.g. self-consciousness),[67] in other words—certain

---

[59] A. Zawadzki, "Pojęcie nihilizmu u Nietzschego, Heideggera i Vattimo," *Słupskie Prace Filologiczne*, Seria Filologia Polska 3/2004, p. 213.

[60] G. Vattimo, *End of Modernity. . .*, p. 146.

[61] Cf. J. Życiński, *Bóg postmodernistów. . .*, p. 90.

[62] G. Vattimo, *End of Modernity . . .*, p. 39.

[63] J. Życiński, *Bóg postmodernistów. . .*, p. 90.

[64] G. Vattimo, *End of Modernity. . .*, p. 20.

[65] Ibid., p. 21.

[66] Ch. Millon-Delsol, *Esej o człowieku. . .*, p. 26.

[67] Cf. Peter Singer, *Practical Ethics. . .*, p. 74.

functional criteria. On the other hand, it is the source of standpoints which consider the concept of "person" suspicious itself.[68] These standpoints claim that the "the subject, the self, the individual, are just so many false concepts, since they transform into substances fictitious unities having at the start only a linguistic reality."[69]

Irrespective of the adopted strategy of deconstructing the "tremendous exaggeration" of the subject, it leads to negating the special status of the human person and dignity. It is a standpoint that is revolutionary at its core, considering that in everyday life "everyone subscribes to the assertion about the inviolability of man's dignity (. . .) which is universally recognized as 'the highest value,' the fundamental constitutional principle, and perhaps even 'the highest leading idea.'"[70] Due to the absolutization of dignity in the public sphere, as demonstrated by Eduard Picker, a test which helps falsify this approach is the attitude to the absolute value of human life. The negation of man's uniqueness, which owing to the context of Western culture may be difficult to openly, theoretically defend, may proceed much more easily on the theoretical level: human life as an exchange value is not absolute *ex definitione*.

A particularly valuable exemplification of the consequences of the intellectual and spiritual climate of late modernity for the approach to human dignity seems to be the thought of Peter Singer. His work gathers the dispersed ethical intuitions of late modernity into a single, coherent system, without avoiding the theoretical arguments which are usually provided only reluctantly. Interested in practical questions, Singer draws practical conclusions from the deconstruction of the subject, explicitly claiming that "treating the lives of all members of our species as uniquely valuable (. . .) cannot be defended."[71] He asserts that "our present attitudes date from the coming of Christianity. There was a specific theological motivation for the Christian insistence on the importance of species membership: the belief that all born of human parents are immortal (. . .). During the centuries of Christian domination of European thought, the ethical attitudes based on these doctrines became part of the unquestioned moral orthodoxy of European civilization. Today, the religious doctrines are no longer universally accepted, but the ethical attitudes to which they gave rise fit in with the deep-seated Western belief in the uniqueness (. . .) of our species; these attitudes have survived. Now that we are reassessing our speciesist view of nature, however, it is also time to reassess our belief in the sanctity of the lives of members of our species."[72]

In the above argumentation, it is clearly visible that the late-modern "relaxation" of the rigorous constraints of morality is revealed in the first place as the challenging

---

[68]Cf. J. Butler, *Gender Trouble. . .*, p. 23.

[69]Michel Haar, "Nietzsche and Metaphysical Language," in: David Allison [ed.], *The New Nietzsche: Contemporary Styles of Interpretation*, Delta, New York 1997, pp. 17–18, as quoted in: J. Butler, *Gender Trouble. . .*, p. 29.

[70]Eduard Picker, *Godność człowieka. . .*, p. 5.

[71]Peter Singer, *Practical Ethics. . .*, pp. 75–76.

[72]Ibid.

of the special protection of man's fundamental good which is his life.[73] A fact which had so far been morally obvious and whose self-evidence is not questioned by Singer, who only blames the Christian tradition for its emergence, is now negated. The negation of man's dignity and the special value of his life is a specifically late modern phenomenon. On the one hand, it is done—in line with the classical canons of modernity—in the name of rationalism understood in utilitarian terms. Singer explains that the "preference utilitarianism," which is a mutation of the classical utilitarianism, evaluates the moral value of actions "by the extent to which they accord with the preferences of any beings affected by the action or its consequences."[74] The value of life, as well as the status of a person, are therefore relative and temporal, depending on his or her current functionalities. At the same time, however, this negation seems to satisfy Vattimo's criteria of overcoming and distortion. Singer does not claim to provide the ultimate answer about the right approach to be adopted. He does, of course, make his own proposal which he considers to be the best,[75] but he is aware of other proposals, also legitimate in a way.[76] Moreover, however paradoxical this may sound, Singer quotes R. M. Hare to emphasize that "it will be better if we adopt some broad ethical principles ["that experience has shown over the centuries"—MG] for our everyday ethical life and do not deviate from them."[77] Such an approach has a positive effect on our choices.[78] Thus, Singer does not negate the significance of a "trace" of strong metaphysics, even though he challenges its validity. He treats such a "trace" as an intuitive principle which—while not meeting the proper truth-value criteria—is a useful guideline in everyday life. Thus, classical moral claims may be accepted, as long as we agree that they do not declare what truly is—that they do not satisfy the criterion of truth, but that of an opinion (doxa). Let us emphasize this: the novelty of this approach to understanding man and the value of his life is not expressed—due to the contestation of epistemic capacities—in providing the final, new answer, but in an absolute negation of the one embraced so far and in defining the mandatory framework of "correct" answers, consistent—to put it somewhat contrarily—with nihilistic metaphysics.

Its specific expression today seems to be transhumanism. The common element in this diversified current of thought is rejection of the concept of human nature, premised on the assumption that all human features are merely the evolutionary product of adaptation to living conditions, and when such conditions change, they should change as well. Transhumanists consider even "the biological conditioning of

---

[73]Cf. Barbara Chyrowicz, "Eutanazja i spór na argumenty," in: id. [ed.], *Eutanazja. Prawo do życia. Prawo do wolności,* TN KUL, Lublin 2005, p. 150.

[74]P. Singer, *Practical...*, p. 94.

[75]He believes that the right to live should be determined by rationality and self-consciousness. Cf. ibid., p. 74.

[76]E.g. those of Joseph Fletcher or John Locke.

[77]P. Singer, *Practical...*, p. 79.

[78]Even if simply because of "what will pay off most of the time." Ibid., pp. 92–93.

man as an inner environment which may be objectified, reified and shaped just like the external circumstances of man's life."[79] Consequently, the basic postulate of transhumanism is "self-evolution, i.e. modernization of the human condition along guidelines which man has created himself, and its adjustment to the possibilities and requirements which arise from civilizational changes."[80] The goal of this controlled evolution is a "posthuman," symbolizing the abolition (in part or whole) of the limitations of "the human mode of being."[81] Transhumanists promise that the space of possible modes of being accessible by posthumans will be incomparably greater than that accessible by humans in terms of lifespan, intellectual capacity, sensory modalities, or bodily functionality.[82] Nevertheless, one can hardly fail to notice that as human possibilities expand, transhumanism foresees a replacement of humans with posthuman people, and thus aims at closing the history of mankind. In this case, not only individual human beings, but the entire human species has become an exchangeable value.

8.3   A New Concept of Sexuality

The new, expository approach to the subject in late modernity is not limited only to the general question of man's ontological status; it also undermines another attribute of the human person which had so far been treated as self-evident. It is not a coincidence that "over the past years *Gender Trouble*, written in 1990, has become a fundamental book not only for feminism, but for thinking about the foundations of culture as well."[83] It is the issue of gender, treated consistently in the spirit of postmodernism, that symbolically opened the gates to late modernity, striking at one of the axioms[84] which had never been questioned in any culture before.

As emphasized by Carole S. Vance, the social constructivism which has been developing since the 1970s "suggested that one of the last remaining outposts of the 'natural' in our thinking was fluid and changeable, the product of human action and history rather than the invariant result of the body, biology, or the innate sex

---

[79]Błażej Skrzypulec, Marta Soniewicka, *Transhumanizm to nowa forma wiary, gdzie nie ma miejsca na ludzką wolność*, https://klubjagiellonski.pl/2018/03/24/transhumanizm-nowa-forma-wiary-gdzie-nie-ma-miejsca-na-ludzka-wolnosc-rozmowa/#

[80]Anna Cieślak, "Golem czy postczłowiek? Transhumanizm z perspektywy nie-ludzkiej," *Acta Humana* No. 4 (1/2013), p. 96.

[81]Nick Bostrom, *Transhumanist Values*, https://www.nickbostrom.com/ethics/values.html

[82]Ibid.

[83]Olga Tokarczuk, "Kobieta nie istnieje", in: Judith Butler, *Uwikłani w płeć. Feminizm i polityka tożsamości*, translated by Karolina Krasucka, Wyd. Krytyki politycznej, Warszawa 2008, p. 5.

[84]Cf. J. Butler, *Gender Trouble. . .*, p. xxxiv.

drive."[85] Even though it embraces various views about "what might be constructed, ranging from sexual acts, sexual identities (...) to sexual impulse or sexuality itself,"[86] it ultimately always undermines—to a lesser or greater degree—the legitimacy of the category of "sex,"[87] arguing that it has been mediated by cultural and historical factors. Consequently, instead of speaking of sex as such, it prefers a narrative referring to gender, which is initially neutral and in which various forms of sexual orientation may become rooted; the primary asexuality thus becomes in a way the basic norm in defining human relationships.[88]

There are three direct contexts which contribute to the above overturn in the understanding of sex. The first one is the feminist theory in which the struggle against the idea of sex was initially related to objection against considering the male model as the general one, and that which is related to sex as the female one. As noted by Simone de Beauvoir "the identification of women with 'sex,' (...), is a conflation of the category of women with the ostensibly sexualized features of their bodies and, hence, a refusal to grant freedom and autonomy to women,"[89] characteristic of men. In this perspective, femininity appears to be an "internalization of patriarchal standards,"[90] and the deconstruction of sex becomes a way for women to achieve the status of a universal subject.[91]

On the other hand, we should note the deep-running relationship between constructivism and gay and lesbian activism.[92] The effort to find a substantiation for "non-normative" sexual practices and gay identity has led, as an initial reaction, to questioning the axiological framework "for examining the 'facts' about sex and gender"[93] and looking for hidden (concealed) manifestations of gay identity in history.[94] Then, when it turned out that sodomy had always been historically—as remarked by Foucault—"a temporary aberration," the fact that "the homosexual was

---

[85]Carole S. Vance, "Social Construction Theory: Problems in the History of Sexuality," in: Denis Altman (ed.), Homosexuality, which Homosexuality?: International Conference on Gay and Lesbian Studies, An Dekker/Schorer 1989, p. 13.

[86]Ibid., p. 18.

[87]Cf. Ibid., p. 21.

[88]Tony Anatrella, Definition of Terms in the Neo-Language of the Philosophy of Constructivism and Gender, Pontificum Consilium Pro Familia, Vatican City 2008, p. 4.

[89]J. Butler, Gender Trouble..., p. 27.

[90]Cf. S. L. Bertky, Foucault, Femininity and the Modernization of Patriarchal Power, Columbia University Press 1997.

[91]J. Butler, Gender Trouble..., p. 45. One can hardly fail to notice that from the perspective of the interests of women, this solution seems to be just about as effective as relieving a patient's suffering by means of euthanasia. The logic of both solutions is analogous: elimination of the subject is considered to be the solution to his problems.

[92]C. S. Vance, "Social ConstructionTheory...," p. 13.

[93]Ibid.

[94]Paul Berman, A Tale of Two Utopias: The Political Journey of the Generation of 1968, W. W. Norton & Company 1997, p. 189.

now a species" was an unprecedented move.[95] Homosexuality was no longer seen as "an unchanging essence which defied legal and religious prohibitions; homosexuality increasingly came to be seen as a variable experience whose boundaries and subjectivity were shaped through complex negotiations between state institutions, individuals, and subcultures."[96] Let us stress this: the lack of grounds for rooting gay identity in the history of humanity[97] did not lead to rejecting the treatment of homosexual predilection in the categories of identity, but to a paradigmatic change in social sciences. Turning "gay identity" into an axiom thus necessarily led to undermining the idea of identity as such, understood in terms of essence, and to considering it a social and cultural construct. Once that perspective was adopted, it was then only necessary to justify why gay identity was not able not evolve until the beginning of the twentieth century,[98] since the idea of identity itself was *a priori* assumed.

Finally, the broadest context for the new view of sexuality was provided by the revolution of 1968. Paul Berman writes in his monograph that "already in the hippie sensibility, bisexuality glowed with special prestige (...) [and] in the preguerilla revolutionary cells of SDS's Weatherman, bisexuality became, by the early months of 1969, positively mandatory (...). Every month that passed seemed to bring crashing to the ground some taboo or inhibition that used to be regarded as basic to civilization."[99] The obvious relationship between the new approach to human sexuality (or its negation, actually) and the cultural revolution of 1968 leads us to the deep-seated, Marxist ideological sources of this anthropological approach. It is not difficult to see that the writings of Engels already reflect the belief that "when monogamous marriage first makes its appearance in history, it is not as the reconciliation of man and woman, still less as the highest form of such a reconciliation. Quite the contrary. Monogamous marriage comes on the scene as the subjugation of the one sex by the other (...). The first class opposition that appears in history coincides with the development of the antagonism between man and woman in

---

[95]Ibid.

[96]C. Vance, "Social Construction Theory...," p. 27.

[97]Not only in social and historical, but in biological (genetic) and psychological terms as well. As late as in 1973, psychiatric organizations officially declared that homosexuality was a mental illness. Cf. P. Berman, *A Tale...*, p. 134.

[98]Nell Miller concluded from his observations that "modern-style homosexual identity (...) crops up only at a particular moment in the development of society. This moment (...) arrives when four minimum requirements have been fulfilled: a fair amount of personal freedom and tolerance; a degree of economic development that is strong enough to allow people to get away from home and move about at will; a relatively high status for women; and (...) a decline in the power of the family and religious institutions in defining and determining every aspect of an individual's life." Paul Berman, *A Tale...*, pp. 189–190.

[99]P. Berman, *A Tale...*, p. 138.

monogamous marriage, and the first class oppression coincides with that of the female sex by the male."[100]

Nevertheless, as pointed out by researchers, this is not so much a simple continuation, but adoption of an analogous structure of thought. Just like Marxism tried to eliminate the differences between social classes, so constructivists "aim to make differences between the sexes irrelevant. (. . .) Like in Marxism, their goal is to create a utopian society in which anatomy has no role to play. Once there are no men or women in it any more, once the institution of marriage and family disappears, the patriarchal epoch will come to a definite end. Like the goal of Marxism was to build a classless society, so (. . .) [here the goal] is to build a sexless, post-human society, made up of post-women and post-men."[101] As noted by Sandra Lee Bartky, while "liberals call for equal rights for women, traditional Marxists for the entry of women into production on an equal footing with men, the socialization of housework and proletarian revolution," the new ideology "calls for the deconstruction of the categories of masculinity and femininity. Femininity as a certain 'style of the flesh' will have to be surpassed in the direction of something quite different, not masculinity, which is in many ways only its mirror opposite, but a radical and as yet unimagined transformation of the female body."[102]

Due to the "gender trouble," we leave the land of realism and walk into the land of imagination as the foundation on which to construct a new world. Since nature is "seen as meaningless and arbitrarily imposed/imposing,"[103] no wonder that "[a]ll movements of sexual liberation, including lesbian and gay, are built on imagining: imagining that things could be different, other, better than they are."[104] This late modern premise, typical of the logic of unconstraint, about the plasticity of human beings and social life differs from the modern approach only in that it has not yet been finally decided what this new world is to look like. Vance continues: "[t]o the extent social construction theory strives for uncertainty through questioning assumptions rather than seeking closure, we need to tolerate ambiguity and fluidity."[105]

The above assertion seems to touch upon the very core of the constructivist approach, and in a broader view—the entire logic of late modernity. Indeed, "to some extent" late modernity embraces uncertainty, challenging unchallengeable premises. In this challenging, however, it is not and does not want to (and is probably also unable to[106]) be consistent to the last. Ultimately, therefore, it entails unchallengeable normative content which Vance has aptly defined in her appeal

---

[100]F. Engels, *The Origin of the Family, Private Property and the State,* https://www.marxists.org/archive/marx/works/1884/origin-family/ch02d.htm

[101]P. Mazurkiewicz, *Ideologia gender. . .*

[102]S. L. Bertky, *Foucault. . .*, p. 147.

[103]Aneta Gawkowska, *Skandal i ekstaza. Nowy Feminizm na tle koncepcji pojednania Jana Pawła II*, WUW, Warszawa 2015, p. 229.

[104]C. S. Vance, "Social Construction Theory. . .," p. 30.

[105]Ibid.

[106]Cf. Ibid., p. 21–23.

to: "tolerate ambiguity and fluidity." Indeed, like in the approach to truth, so in the concept of subject and human sexuality this norm defines the *credo* of late modernity, including the framework of what must be accepted, with no room for retreat. This *credo*, or, rather, *dictum* is relativist, expecting that every assertion agrees to remain a "trace"; it rejects thinking in the categories of truth value. Consequently, late modernity abandons the logic of nature for good, and thus the logic of boundaries even on the most fundamental level: "exposing" the truth, it undermines all moral and anthropological ideas which have so far been self-evident, beginning with the foundations: human dignity, and human sexuality. Not only does this enhance its unconstrained tendencies (individualism, self-creation, horizontality, collectivism, etc.), but also founds them on primary grounds which have been entirely unknown so far, engendering a culture "that constitutes the absolutely most radical contradiction not only of Christianity, but of the religious and moral traditions of humanity."[107] This way, "weak" thought becomes much stronger than the "strong" standpoints of modernity; indeed, it proves to be their, almost perfect, fulfillment. While Nietzsche could still complain that he was, however unwillingly, a metaphysician, taking his "fire from the conflagration kindled by a belief a millennium old, the Christian belief, which was also the belief of Plato, that God is truth, that the truth is divine,"[108] nihilists as well as constructivists near perfection in their invalidation of the issue of truth, considering science an ideology,[109] and moral issues a space of unrestrained creation. At the same time—in terms of theoretical reflection—they make all effort to purify their standpoint, as far as possible, of any remnants or influences of essentialism.[110]

We discover a paradox. The nihilist approach, which breaks up with the optimistic and logocentric approach of modernity, at its very core proves to be a continuation, even a reinforcement of the Enlightenment logic. The nihilistic "theory of relativity" may be inconsistent, but it is certainly not a "weak" approach. How should this be explained?

From the perspective of the history of ideas, an interesting answer has been suggested by Anthony Giddens. He points out that "the seeds of nihilism were

---

[107]J. Ratzinger, *Europe's Crisis of Culture,* p. 48.

[108]F. Nietzsche, *Joyful Wisdom,* Macmillan 1911, p. 279.

[109]Cf. C. Vance, "Social Construction Theory. . .," pp. 13 and 23, where the fact that mainstream works in medicine and sexology define sexuality through the prism of biology, the body and its needs is also considered an expression of scientific ideology and therefore *a priori* rejected.

[110]Ibid., p. 26. It may be noted that this approach is ultimately perceived as a threat also by the LGBT community and the feminist movement. Constructivists believe this to be an effect of failure to sufficiently distinguish between the political objectives of a movement and social theory: "Within the lesbian and gay community's internal discussions and self-education, the failure to make a distinction between politically expedient ways of framing an argument and more complex descriptions of social relations promoted an increasingly rigid adherence to essentialism as an effective weapon against persecution." (Vance, p. 28). It seems, therefore, that also the LGBT community proves to be backward-looking and will have to be converted to the right orthodoxy by the "knowing elite" whose theory "may be the new orthodoxy in feminist, progressive, and lesbian and gay history circles" (ibid., p. 368).

there in Enlightenment thought from the beginning. If the sphere of reason is wholly unfettered, no knowledge can rest upon an unquestioned foundation, because even the most firmly held notions can only be regarded as valid 'in principle' or 'until further notice.' Otherwise they would relapse into dogma and become separate from the very sphere of reason which determines what validity is in the first place. Although most regarded the evidence of our senses as the most dependable information we can obtain, even the early Enlightenment thinkers were well aware that (. . .) sense data could never provide a wholly secure base for knowledge claims. Given the greater awareness today that sensory observation is permeated by theoretical categories, philosophical thought has in the main veered quite sharply away from empiricism. Moreover, since Nietzsche we are much more clearly aware of the circularity of reason, as well as the problematic relations between knowledge and power."[111] As a consequence, he notes, "rather than these developments taking us 'beyond modernity'," they provide a better understanding of modernity itself. And as we begin to understand it, we start to see it as unsettling not only "because of the circularity of reason, but because the nature of that circularity is ultimately puzzling. How can we justify a commitment to reason in the name of reason? (. . .) Modernity turns out to be enigmatic at its core, and there seems no way in which this enigma can be 'overcome.'"[112] This enigma also results in the ontologically "weak" thought—despite all the disclaimers—to have strong normative consequences.

8.4   Summary

In light of the above reflections, we may attempt to provide an answer to the question about the status of late modernity, which turns out to be a continuation and development of the logic of unconstraint initiated in the Enlightenment. It may be considered its fulfillment in that it has also challenged those truths which, even a hundred years after the Enlightenment, still appeared to be unshakeable. Referring to the thought of Thomas Aquinas, we might say that the Enlightenment directly challenged the third type of *inclinationes*, adopting a new model of reasonability, deciding that the "God hypothesis" is no longer needed, and proposing an atomistic vision of man. In the long term, however, as demonstrated by the experience of late modernity, the logic of unconstraint also challenges the first two *inclinationes naturales*: the conviction about the dignity of human life and human sexuality, opening a specifically "late-modern" space in the dispute about man. Consequently, the dispute between constrained and unconstrained anthropology becomes particularly meaningful.

---

[111] A. Giddens, *The Consequences of Modernity,* p. 37.
[112] Ibid.

8.4.1 Constrained Anthropology

Adequate description of the contemporary cultural dispute in the categories of constraint and unconstraint depends first of all on the understanding of man's limitedness. As discussed above, constraint may be understood in two ways: either in view of the corruption of human nature (*vide* e.g. Hobbes), or the very existence of human nature (*vide* Aquinas).[113] As also mentioned above, the anthropology of corruption in fact gravitates towards unconstrained anthropology, proving to be a variation on the theme of the impossibility to control man from within. If man is seen as essentially unable to discover truth or pursue good, as a being who is merely a more intelligent animal, this ultimately leads in the political context to a vision of political community that is typical of Rousseau, where every individual is entirely independent from others, but totally dependent on the state. This idea is expressed in similar terms in the vision of general will presented in *The Social Contract*, or the state seen as the *Leviathan*. In this sense, the anthropology of corruption and the anthropology of perfection ultimately found a similar vision of politics: unconstrained politics where sovereignty of the state is real and complete. Therefore, the proper sense of constraint as the opposite of unconstraint cannot be the logic of corruption alone.

Constrained anthropology—as examined in Chap. 6—should in principle take into account the twofold limitation of man. Even though it does acknowledge the problem of man's corruption and agrees that whatever man attempts to do is corrupted by imperfection, it sees in it a "secondary" constraint, leading to the introduction of mechanisms to check the government and prevent abuse (check and balance systems). The foundation of constraint is a "primary" limitation, entailed by man being a creation. Consequently, the existence of ontological boundaries "enables one person to recognize another person as a human being." In this view, "all human beings have a human Nature, which means that all human beings are fundamentally the same—and different from all other things—in their very essence, which is immutable."[114] This does not mean an attempt at encapsulating human nature in a rigid formula. On the contrary, as demonstrated above, the classical interpretation of the logic of constraint allows for a broad spectrum of personal freedom, without reducing the diversity of paths to personal development and realization of common good. It means that the dignity of man outlines the objective, though violable, boundaries to choices which may be considered truly human.

A key component in the above approach to man is considering him a moral being, able to recognize and choose good, endowed with a reason that is theoretical, and not

---

[113]In fact, we may note that on the grounds of philosophy there is also a third approach. Next to the two mentioned above, there is also a Socratic ethical intellectualism which seems to identify rationality with will, throwing doubt on the thesis about the corruption of human nature in the pursuit of good.

[114]Robert R. Reilly, *Making Gay Okay...*, p. 19.

merely instrumental. In this perspective, man employs his reason to discover his own nature and the actions which are proper to it, contributing to the realization of man's *telos*, or—in other words—comprehensive development. It is not whether an action can be performed (Can I?) but whether an action is right (Should I?) that is the problem characteristic of human affairs. The boundaries defined by human nature are constitutive, delineating the proper space of human normality and freedom.[115] In this current of anthropology, the key significance of "human ecology" is emphasized, that is, the agathological (concerning good) limits of human actions. These limits can be trespassed, since they are primarily internal, and only secondarily social or legal. Once they are violated, however, some form of dehumanization ensues. It is in this sense that this is a constrained anthropology: humanity is related to the existence of a nature which is not only and not primarily physical, but moral. These boundaries also delimit the influence of politics and the state, whose aim is to enable and actualize a good life, but not to define its contents.[116]

Understood in such terms, constrained anthropology is a strong anthropology, related most explicitly, though not exclusively, to the tradition of natural law where "definition of the contents of natural law is premised on the knowledge of being."[117] It is epistemically strong in that it puts its trust in reason and its ability to discover the truth about being, including human nature. In this sense, it is a holistic anthropology: it tries to capture the essence of man without reducing the complexity of human existence. For even though it is aware that it is not possible to "define the concept of personhood fully and completely,"[118] it also recognizes the common "nature which makes man the person who he is and the subject whose depth goes beyond the world of objects."[119]

A strong metaphysical standpoint translates into a strong axiological standpoint, based on cognition and nonnegotiable claims about objectively existing anthropological "data" which must be protected by the political system. Their classical depiction is found in Thomas Aquinas's description of *inclinationes naturales*.[120] Natural inclinations represent here a record of constitutive elements of existence, and include "all that irrespective of the will or constitution determines the modes in which the subject is actualized."[121] At the same time, they are the basis for determining "what is destructive for man, what prevents or hinders the development of his being."[122] Aquinas—largely following the Stoic tradition –believes at the same time that "man is the most perfect spiritual and physical being in nature, distinguished

---

[115]Cf. Remi Brague, *The Legitimacy...* .

[116]Cf. R. Spaeamann, *Granice...* p. 95.

[117]M. Piechowiak, *Filozofia praw...*, p. 296.

[118]Henryk Piluś, *Antropologia filozoficzna neotomizmu*, Wizja, Warszawa 2010, p. 168.

[119]Ibid.

[120]Arguing that "according to the order of natural inclinations is the order of the precepts of the natural law." Thomas Aquinas, *Summa Theologiae* 1–2, q. 94, a. 2.

[121]M. Piechowiak, *Filozofia praw...*, p. 299.

[122]Ibid.

(...) by his cognitive capacity, the freedom of his will, personal love, and orientation towards God."[123] Consequently, all *inclinationes naturales*—even if two of them are common to all animal organisms—become endowed with special, personal content. In the logic of human nature, they translate into three basic claims defining the space—to use Spaemann's expression—of human normality. Firstly, the conviction that man as a being who exceeds the animate world, free and equal to other people in dignity, endowed with reason capable of discovering eternal moral principles, is a non-exchangeable being. Secondly, man is a non-homogenous being: he is determined by his sexuality which entails not only biological, but also anthropological content, and which results in the social mode of living proper to man being family formed by a man and a woman. Thirdly, and in a way as a consequence, man as a rational and sexual being is also a social being who is not reducible to a collectivity, as well as a spiritual being who is able to freely discover God—first the god of philosophers, and then the One God.

The issue of freedom in the religious search reveals a relationship, discussed in more detail in Chap. 6, between constrained anthropology with vertical anthropology. On the one hand, it is only in the light of Revelation that the source of the special dignity of man is ultimately explained: from the perspective of his being created in the image and likeness of God, man's dignity may be independent from individual attributes and be related to human nature itself.[124] On the other hand, only reference to Transcendence makes it possible to build a systemic barrier to absolutist claims made by the government. In this sense, as has been pointed out, constrained anthropology is *ex definitione* open to theologization which guarantees an eschatological distance of politics. Its paradigm is the *etsi Deus daretur* approach, which is—so to say—a "God fearing" agnosticism, in the biblical understanding of fear.

It is worth noting that constrained anthropology is strong in a twofold sense. First, in its theoretical dimension: it is based on lasting foundations on which a vision of man may be constructed. They include conviction about the epistemic capabilities of man which allow him to understand human existence, and reference to Transcendence. Second, in the normative dimension: it presents a holistic anthropology which, while creating a broad space of man's freedom, clearly defines the boundaries of agathological choices. Consequently, it makes claims to the universality of its moral precepts related to the good discovered by man.

8.4.2 Unconstrained Anthropology

An anthropological antithesis to the above model is the model of unconstrained anthropology which—following Rousseau—believes there are no limitations

---

[123]Henryk Piluś, *Antropologia...*, p. 167.

[124]In this approach, being human—to quote Robert Reilly—means that "every human soul is ordered to the same transcendent good, or end." R. R. Reilly, *Making Gay Okay...*, p. 19.

inherent to human nature. The essence of this approach is revealed in late modernity which questions all permanent aspects of human nature, including those rooted in biology and common to all other animate beings.[125] Consequently, all constraints are considered here to be a form of oppression imposed on man's freedom: "society in any form is fundamentally alien [in this approach], and alienating, to individuals. In his origins, man was isolated and essentially complete on his own and in himself."[126] The unconstrained anthropological perspective negates the entire tradition of seeing man as a being who has his proper *telos*, of understanding freedom as oriented towards perfection. In the perspective of unconstraint, "history moves on, and man and all his social arrangements change, or 'evolve', with it; or rather, man can change himself according to his desires, as long as he has the means to do so."[127] Nature (or should we say: "so-called nature") is a product of history, social relations, self-creation, etc.

As rightly pointed out by George Weigel, if there is no such thing as human nature, "then there are no universal moral principles (. . .). That means that morality is simply law and obligation, and law is always something outside me. Law, in other words, is always coercion."[128] This thesis had not been fully expressed until late modernity, which embraced accomplished nihilism as the adequate ethical standpoint. Even though already in both atomistic and collectivist anthropology the existence of objective, non-rational moral norms had been questioned, an effort was made to find their rational basis: in Rousseau they were emotions; in Mill—benefits; in Marx—class interest. Thus, while challenging the idea of conscience, they were still trying to save morality. The late-modern logic of "weak thought" finally suspended this search: unbelief in the possibility of discovering the supreme moral rule is the crowning point of the logic of unconstraint.

By reference to Giddens, we might say that unconstrained thought is, at its roots, a weak thought based on a profound conviction that it is impossible to know objective good, to get in touch with reality as it actually is. This is so as long as we refer only to the theoretical dimension of the perspective of unconstraint; the foundations on which this thought is based. For—as has been demonstrated above—in the normative dimension, it is a thought at least as strong as the logic of nature.[129] The perspective of unconstraint requires that its relativist claims be universally recognized, demanding that all accept the freedom to become "whoever you

---

[125]T. Sowell, *A Conflict of Visions. . .*, pp. 24–25.

[126]R. R. Reilly, *Making Gay Okay.*, p. 16. The ideological sources of this approach may essentially be found already in nominalism, the first standpoint to have claimed there is no such thing as "human nature," and that there are only individual beings.

[127]Ibid., p. 31.

[128]George Weigel, *The Cube and the Cathedral. Europe, America and Politics Without God,* Basic Books 2006, p. 83.

[129]Perhaps even stronger, actually, in that it does not allow for such space of freedom and diversity as the tradition of constraint, and at times borders on fundamentalism. Cf. P. Berman, *A Tale. . .*, Chapter V. For more about secular fundamentalism see: Michał Gierycz, "Religion: A Source of Fundamentalism or A Safeguard Against It?" *Religions* 2020, 11, 104.

want."[130] The weakness of the theoretical foundations of this perspective results only in a multitude of selective normative claims aspiring to a universal status. We might say that in this perspective it is known for certain what must not be, but the question of what should be still remains impossible to fully imagine.[131] Unconstrained thought thus also represents a strong anthropological standpoint, provided, however, that it is only strong in one dimension: in normative, but not in theoretical terms.

Owing to the affirmation of indifferential freedom, in each subsequent version of unconstraint more and more fundamental anthropological "data" have been negated, related to human nature (the social nature of man in the atomistic current, his rationality in the Enlightenment current,[132] freedom in the collectivist current, etc.). Initially—as can be seen in Rousseau or Mill, for instance—this was done in a way that was not fully consistent, with some premises of the constrained concept acknowledged as self-evident. In each new version, for example in the thought of Marx or Engels, new anthropological visions were more and more fully expressed, and their culmination came with the late modern undermining of the axioms of Western civilization which had so far been unquestioned: the conviction about the special dignity of man and the value of human life (which, in the case of transhumanism, leads to the idea of a replacement of humans with posthuman people), and the conviction about the fundamental significance of sexuality for the identity and development of people and the organization of social life.

Consequently, in the unconstrained vision—a kernel of which can be found in Rousseau, and a full-blown version in the postmodernist mantra about the death of God—man is the highest being, a self-creator. Unconstraint and fluid humanity are therefore immanently linked to the logic of *etsi Deus non daretur*, a horizontal logic of radical secularism which does not acknowledge any general norms not willed by man.[133] The thought rooted in modernity reveals its genetically nominalist turn towards willfulness which "severs human beings from each other in most dramatic way,"[134] reducing all relationships to the Schmittean distinction between enemy and friend.[135] Since in the beginning instead of the Word there was only a Big Bang, there is no truth and no science, but merely the cunning of smart animals which use

---

[130]Cf. S. L. Bartky, "Foucault...," pp. 140ff.

[131]Ibid.

[132]However paradoxical this may seem, it appears that reason was the first to be negated. In Rousseau it is already portrayed as an accidental product of irrationality. As pointed out by Joël-Benoit d'Onorio, the Enlightenment obscured the fundamental truth about man as created by a rational Being, and therefore rational himself. Cf. J.-B. d'Onorio, *Le Vatican et la politique européenne*, Paris 1994, p. 25.

[133]As noted by Maria Marczewska-Rytko, the void left by religion does not remain empty. Science and technology are treated by the advocates of scientist views as "new gods which must be worshipped." Maria Marczewska-Rytko, *Religia i polityka w globalizującym się świecie*, UMCS, Lublin 2010, p. 56.

[134]G. Weigel, *The Cube...*, p. 84.

[135]C. Schmitt, *The Concept...*, p. 11.

words to impose their will on others.[136] The path from god to animal turns out to be short indeed. . .

It should also be stressed that there is a diversity of unconstrained visions. The differences between the new ways of understanding sexuality in late modernity, emphasized by Vance, seem to be consistent with the entire history of this way of thinking. Let us note that in its beginnings, in Rousseau for example, unconstrained anthropology retained some essential elements of the logic of constraint (such as sexuality or property), to subsequently "deepen" the emancipation of man with each new reveal. In addition, the inconsistencies witnessed today in "projections" about man show that the anthropology of unconstraint is gradable *ex definitione*: it may be more or less shallow, "conservative" or radical. This has two theoretical implications. Firstly, it shows that anthropological unconstraint is not related to any single vision, but to many visions which all have in common a negation of any limits on political decisions independent from man's will. In other words: anthropological unconstraint means a lack of anthropological boundaries not so much in the practical or declarative terms, as in the ontological sense: it is premised on the assumption that they may be freely established and redefined. Secondly, historically speaking, the fluidity of boundaries is essentially unidirectional: over time, the rejection of objective boundaries seems to result in a deepening of unconstraint, effortlessly steamrollering the relics of constrained logic.

---

[136]"But what I have in view will now be understood," Nietzsche writes, "namely, that it is always a *metaphysical belief* on which our belief in science rests,—and that even we knowing ones of to-day, the godless and anti-metaphysical, still take *our* fire from the conflagration kindled by a belief a millennium old, the Christian belief, which was also the belief of Plato, that God is truth, that the truth is divine." F. Nietzsche, *Joyful Wisdom* (*The Complete Works of Friedrich Nietzsche, Volume Ten*), translated by T. Common, The Macmillan Company, New York, 1924, p. 278.

Part III
EU Political Disputes in the Anthropological Perspective

As explicitly stated in Article 2 of the TEU, the European Union is founded on values. Even though this declaration may be far less than obvious for those who are familiar with the history of European integration, it defines the core of the European project today. On the threshold of the twenty-first century, it was made to reflect the normative question characteristic of every culture and civilization: the question of what should be.[1] In other words, the problem of *ethos*, of defining the proper living environment for Europeans, is presented as the fundamental problem of the Union, which considers its goal not only to advance peace and prosperity, but also its own values.[2]

The significance of values explicitly stated in EU legal documents is most relevant for the goals of this study. The problem of ethos is inseparably related to the anthropological problem. In interpersonal relationships, values are the prism through which "man formulates his attitudes in life, his actions, according to which he judges the attitudes and actions of others."[3] To use Rev. Józef Tischner's expression, values are a specifically "human score."[4] The same applies to societies and their institutions. The values which these institutions are supposed to serve and which determine their scope of work, operations, as well as the evaluation of actions taken by others (states, social groups, individuals, etc.) express, at least implicitly, the theory of man. Therefore, the special role of values in the EU justifies the anthropological analysis of the integration process in a particular way. For it is clear that it is at present and is supposed to be, a cultural project oriented towards the good of EU citizens.

Naturally, the problem of the actual existence of an EU ethos and, even more so, the issue of its primary importance, remains a matter of controversy. The questions are many: from functional ones, related to the instrumental treatment of values by the

---

[1]Cf. Ch. Delsol, *Czym jest człowiek?...*, pp. 87–88.
[2]Cf. Article 3 TUE.
[3]Józef Tischner, op. cit., p. 13.
[4]Ibid.

EU,[5] to structural ones, related to the weakness of the public sphere or the non-existence of a European *demos*.[6] Nevertheless, Andrew Williams is right to say that even if due to the lack of clarity about the form of the EU project, one may hardly make any strong claims about the existence of a public European ethos, there clearly exists what might be called an institutional, or communal, ethos. Williams suggests that this term should be understood as "the collective disposition, character and fundamental values that capture the existent sense of the EU as an institution in terms of both its particular formally constructed arrangement and its general pattern of activity."[7] Thus, the search for an EU anthropology is justified.

William's definition implies that even though there is an important relationship between the formally defined values of the EU as well as its fundamental patterns and ways of acting, these categories are not identical. Referring to this view, we may distinguish between two key elements of the EU ethos. One is normative and relates to the character of fundamental EU values. Its pillars include the constitutive acts of primary law—first and foremost, the Treaty of the European Union, the Treaty on the Functioning of the European Union, and the Charter of Fundamental Rights—as well as the axiological standpoints of the major political forces influencing the EU decision-making process. The other is functional, so to speak, and relates to the character of the collective disposition of the EU as a community, a disposition ultimately specified, according to Williams's definition, not so much by normative declarations, but by political practice—by decisions taken by Community institutions which add precision to, if not actually define (for example when legal norms are constructed so that there is room for their interpretation) the character and meaning of EU values. When looking for an anthropology characteristic of the European integration, in addition to normative (legal and political) declarations, it is also necessary to look into the axiological standpoints reflected in the legislation and political decisions, to capture the real ethos, and thus the concept of man actually embraced in the EU.

The above comments on the specificity of the EU ethos reveal the relevancy of employing an in-depth system analysis. As the first step, it is therefore necessary to reveal the framework conditions of system conversion, i.e. the fundamental normative anthropological assumptions expressed in the legal system of the European Union (Chap. 10). This way, the key components of the inside of the system will be described, where system conversion takes place, as well as the hypothetical, probable course of this conversion. Then, as the second step, an anthropological analysis of European politics will be carried out, focused particularly on the language (Chap. 11) and decision-making processes of the EU (Chap. 12), to reveal the actual

---

[5]Note for example the well-known objection voiced by Havel who points out that the EU treats values "simply as pretty packaging for the things that really matter. But aren't these values what really matter, and are not they, on the contrary, what give direction to all the rest?" Cf. Vaclav Havel, *Speech*, European Parliament, Brussels, November 11, 2009.

[6]Cf. Jan Zielonka, *Europa jako imperium*, PISM, Warszawa 2010, p. 177.

[7]Andrew Williams, *The Ethos of Europe. Values, Law and Justice in the EU*, Cambridge University Press, Cambridge 2010, p. 10.

nature and meaning of the EU ethos, illustrating the vision of man prevailing in European politics. These analyses ought to be preceded, however, by a more thorough understanding of the very phenomenon of morality policy. Chapter 9 provides thus an introduction to this area of politics and answers why, and on what basis, such problems should be present in the EU.

Chapter 9
Around Morality Policy

According to American and European researchers, morality policy includes "the regulation of issues like abortion, euthanasia, gun control, same-sex unions, pornography, prostitution, drugs."[1] This list is not exhaustive, however. Other authors consider the "obvious" issues to include problems related to assisted reproduction, stem-cell research, capital punishment,[2] religion, assisted suicide,[3] publicly subsidized art, sexual education, prayer at school,[4] access to weapons,[5] alcohol,[6] and even cigarettes.[7] Some emphasize that in fact "no definite list of morality issues has been offered and there may be some variation across space and time."[8] Others, on the other hand, object to such a broad treatment (and not without substantial arguments—which will be discussed below), arguing that morality policy should be narrowed down to "fundamental decisions related to death, marriage and

---

[1]Christoph Knill, "The study of morality policy: analytical implications from a public policy perspective," *Journal of European Public Policy*, 20:3, 2013, p. 309.

[2]Isabelle Engeli, Christogger Greek-Pedersen, Lars Thorup Larsen, "Theoretical Perspectives on Morality Issues," in: ids. [ed.], *Morality Politics in Western Europe. Parties, Agendas and Policy Choices*, Palgrave Macmillan, New York 2012, p. 25.

[3]Christopher Z. Mooney, "The Public Clash of Private Values," in: id. [ed.] *The Public Clash of Private Values. The Politics of Morality Policy*, Chatman House Publishers, New York-London 2001, p. 3.

[4]Donald P. Haider-Markel, "Morality in Congress? Legislative Voting on Gay Issues," in: Ch. Z. Mooney [ed.], op. cit., p. 115.

[5]Christoph Knill, op. cit., p. 312.

[6]David L. Schecter, "Legislating morality outside of the legislature: Direct democracy, voter participation, and morality politics," *The Social Science Journal* 46 (2009), p. 90.

[7]Michael J. Liciari, *Smoke Gets in Your Eyes: The Politics of Tobacco Policy*, Ph.D. Dissertation, University of Wisconsin – Milwaukee, 1997, as quoted in: Kenneth J. Meier, "Drugs, Sex and Rock and Roll: A Theory of Morality Politics," in: Ch Z. Mooney (ed.), op. cit.

[8]Donley T. Studlar, Alessandro Cagossi, Robert D. Duval, "Is morality policy different? Institutional explanations for postwar Western Europe," *Journal of European Public Policy*, 20:3, 2013, p. 354.

© Springer Nature Switzerland AG 2021
M. Gierycz, *European Dispute over the Concept of Man*, Contributions to Political Science, https://doi.org/10.1007/978-3-030-61520-8_9

reproduction."[9] Tensions around the definition of morality policy are even more intensified by divided opinions about whether it should be defined substantively[10] or (and) functionally;[11] some (though this is a rather marginal opinion) believe the term morality policy should only be used to refer to a certain kind of a "moralizing" narrative framework.[12]

Even though these discrepancies should not be overestimated, they do reveal two main approaches to understanding and defining morality policy which should be taken into account in order to properly situate the anthropological problems in the context of morality policy. One lead to take is the well-known definition of morality policy formulated by Christopher Z. Mooney. He proposes that morality issues are those "involving clashes of first principles on technically simple and salient public policy with high citizen participation." As rightly noted by Engeli, Greek-Pedersen and Larsen, this definition combines two different aspects: the substantial (first principles, technical simplicity) and the functional one, related to the political process around morality policy (social salience, high participation).[13] These aspects, combined in Mooney's definition, reveal two currents of understanding and studying morality policy which should be considered at the outset.

9.1   The Processual Approach to Morality Policy

The first approach to morality policy is characteristic of research carried out in the United States, where studies on this policy were first undertaken.[14] In the 1970s it has already been noticed that some types of important political disputes were related to arguments which—due to their moral nature—could not be submitted to public, rational (in the instrumental sense) falsification, and which led to unresolvable disputes over values. They eluded the standard analyses of political science. Moreover, by moving researchers out of the area of hard data and instrumental rationality into the area of values, they left them essentially helpless in the face of their observed facts. The prevailing political theories at the time emphasized the meaning of class

---

[9]I. Engeli et al., op. cit., p. 26.

[10]Cf. e.g. I. Engeli, Ch. Greek-Pedersen, L.T. Larsen (ed.), *Morality Politics ...*; Ch. Knill, op. cit.

[11]Cf. e.g. Ch Z. Mooney, [ed.] op. cit.

[12]Cf. Gary Mucciarioni, "Are Debates about 'Morality Policy' Really about Morality? Framing Opposition to Gay and Lesbian Rights," *The Policy Studies Journal*, Vol. 39, No. 2, 2011, pp. 188–218.

[13]I. Engeli et al., op. cit., p. 23.

[14]In Europe, the problems of morality policy and politics was first studied on a systemic basis nearly three decades later. In the broader scientific discourse, these problems only came to view in recent years, when major scientific periodicals dedicated their issues to these problems (such as the *Journal of European Public Policy*), and first monographs were published devoted entirely to analyses of politics from the perspective of morality policy (e.g. *Morality Politics in Western Europe*, 2012 – issued in the USA, but written by European scientists).

conflicts and commitment to one's own economic interests. Even though standpoints on moral issues sometimes correlated with the economic and social status, such correlations were indirect and evidently weaker than in the case of politics concerning the economy.[15]

While observing moral disputes, researchers noticed that such issues generated civil behaviors that were different than in the case of other types of policies or political institutions, causing anomalies in the ordinary functioning of the democratic system. Consequently, in the American tradition a new approach developed for studying morality policy, emphasizing processual and functional factors. It was claimed that "the definition of morality policy lies not in any intrinsic, objective characteristic of a policy or the substantive topic,"[16] but in the nature of public debate and political decisions.[17] The most radical advocates of this perspective contend that "any policy can be 'radicalized' by injecting a moral dimension into the debate,"[18] sometimes even arguing that morality policy *per se* does not exist at all.

Even though the above approach, theoretically eliminating morality policy, has been aptly and justifiably criticized,[19] the idea of a strictly processual approach to morality policy requires some more consideration. It has born the fruit of important, and largely pioneering, research into contemporary political processes touching upon essential moral issues, showing that they differ from other types of political processes in aspects as fundamental as the political actors' mode of behavior, citizen participation, and the use of institutional structures and decision-making procedures.

9.1.1 Morality Policy and the Behavior of Political Actors

As regards political actors, the specificity of the political process surrounding decisions concerning moral issues can be already observed, according to American researchers, at the level of the functioning of political parties and coalition majorities. Empirical studies have shown that while in a normally functioning parliamentary system, legislative proposals submitted by the government are endorsed in the parliament by the supporting party, the presence of a moral factor in legislation proposed by the government results in "frequent splits in party voting."[20] Consequently, it is argued that even though "party positions and cleavages are classical,

---

[15]Ch. Z. Mooney, op. cit., p. 5.

[16]Ibid., p. 6.

[17]Ibid., p. 4.

[18]Theodore J. Lowi, "New Dimensions in Policy and Politics," in *Moral Controversies in American Politics Cases in Social Regulatory Policy*, ed. Raymond Tatalovich and Byron Daynes, Armonk, N.Y.: M.E. Sharpe 1998, p. xxiv.

[19]See more on this subject in the next Section. Cf. also e.g. Ch. Knill, op. cit., pp. 309–317.

[20]C. T. Studlar, et al., op. cit., p. 354.

explanatory factors in public policy[, . . .] it is questionable whether they are of equal relevance when it comes to morality issues."[21] In such matters "members of the legislature vote according to their personal convictions rather than party political positions,"[22] and parties (as will be discussed further on) avoid explicit declarations. Moreover, in the case of voting on ethically sensitive issues, parties often allow their members a free vote, slacking party discipline typically exercised in other matters.[23]

The broader context of this phenomenon, according to researchers who adopt the functional paradigm, is the claim that political parties do not essentially define their political identity in reference to moral problems, and in fact even avoid putting such issues on their agenda. Consequently, morality policy apparently suspends the division, essential for partisan systems, between the left and the right. As pointed out by Engeli et al., the left-right division is unlikely to serve as the basis for an intense political conflict or politicization of morality issues. In the light of their research they claim that it may only serve as a source of the politicization of moral issues when "conservative parties for historical reasons have a strong religious profile without being formally Christian Democratic."[24] Nevertheless, Christian democratic parties also avoid defining their identity through the prism of morality issues, trying to establish a non-secular, yet also a non-confessional, political agenda. From this perspective, "morality issues are becoming increasingly unpleasant because they tend to threaten the broad appeal of these parties by pushing them to reaffirm a set of potentially divisive Christian moral values."[25] As a consequence, formally confessional parties also demonstrate considerable ambivalence as regards morality issues.[26]

Studies carried out at the European Parliament make it necessary to reconsider (if not challenge) the claim that parties distance themselves from tackling "ethically sensitive" problems, and that the right-left division is inadequate. They clearly demonstrate that neither the significance of these issues in their agendas nor the divisions running "across" party affiliations are equally distributed among parties or fit precisely within the right-left division. While left-wing parliamentarians (socialists, greens, communists, liberals) have clear, essentially permissive political goals as regards morality issues and remain consistent in ethically sensitive votes, central and right-wing MPs represent diverse standpoints in disputes over values, sometimes even contrary to the central values of their political groupings.[27] So even though an

---

[21]Stephan Heichel, Christoph Knill, Sophie Schmitt, "Public policy meets morality: conceptual and theoretical challenges in the analysis of morality policy change," *Journal of European Public Policy*, 20:3, 2013, p. 327.

[22]Ibid.

[23]I. Engeli et al., op. cit., p. 20.

[24]Ibid., p. 15.

[25]Ibid.

[26]Cf. Arco Timmermans and Gerard Breeman, op. cit., in: I. Engeli et al. [ed.], op. cit., pp. 35–61.

[27]Cf. Michał Gierycz, "Chrześcijańscy politycy w ponadnarodowych sporach o wartości. Perspektywa europejska," in: Anna Solarz, Hanna Schreiber [ed.], *Religia w stosunkach międzynarodowych*, WUW, Warszawa 2012.

overcoming of party divisions does indeed occur, it happens mostly on one side of the political scene, leading—obviously—to a permissive direction of changes in this area. Changes which, as has been stressed by researchers, usually contradict the prevailing social opinions.[28]

Some explanation of discrepancies between the above theory and the practice which can be observed in the European Parliament as well as elsewhere may be found by examining them against their cultural background. Analyses of disputes over values and the role played by parties in these disputes demonstrate that the role and functioning of parties in debates on morality issues is strictly related to the cultural substratum of the political system. Isabelle Engeli and others say that there are "two worlds": the religious and the secular, with individual countries belonging to either of the two. The religious versus secular dichotomy does not refer to the degree of secularization in the society and the state, but the tradition of conflict between the Church and the state (the religious world) or its absence (the secular world),[29] and thus a historically grounded conflict between religious (confessional) and secular parties, reflecting *de facto* the division into Catholic and protestant countries.[30]

According to Engeli et al., arguments about a different functioning of political parties and coalitions in relation to a greater split of votes on morality issues are more characteristic of the secular than the religious world. In the religious world, "political parties are central actors around morality issues and their positions on these issues are defined by the conflict between religious and secular positions."[31] In this sense, perhaps, the processual observations made in the USA do not fully reflect the European specificity. This explanation could be considered satisfactory if it were not for the studies performed by Donald Haider-Markel which prove that also in the United States "morality politics often inflames partisan conflict."[32] It seems, therefore, that processual differences in the functioning of party politics as regards morality policy result globally in a greater diversification of votes; this occurs mostly in the right wing of the political scene, albeit without necessarily eliminating the left-right division over regulations applicable to morality policy.

---

[28] As noted by Donley T. Studlar, Alessandro Cagossi and Robert D. Duval, the direction of changes in morality policy "is likely to be along the lines preferred by a more post-material, permissive elite than generally more restrictive public opinion." D.T. Studlar et al., op. cit., p. 357.

[29] I. Engeli et al., op. cit., p. 18.

[30] Even though the authors expressly object to such a way of viewing the problem (p. 16), in the religious world they include: Italy, Spain, and Holland, and in the secular world: Scandinavian countries and Great Britain. Not a single exception to this rule has been identified.

[31] Ibid., p. 16.

[32] He argues that "[a]s morality issues, gay issues frequently divide Republicans and Democrats, with Republicans tending to view homosexuality as a threat to traditional moral values. Democrats, meanwhile, are more likely to define homosexuality in less negative terms and be more supportive of gay and lesbian civil rights." (Donald P. Haider-Markel, "Morality in Congress? Legislative Voting on Gay Issues," in: Ch. Z. Mooney, op. cit., p. 119).

As regards actors informing political agendas, researchers also point to a different functioning of interest groups. The classic Anglo-Saxon model of interest groups proposed by Anthony Birch[33] distinguishes between material interest groups, focused on their own benefits, and promotional interest groups, focused not so much on their own interests but on resolving matters in accordance with their understanding of common good.[34] An example of this second type of interest group are opponents of the death penalty, who usually do not belong to any environment at risk of this punishment. A functional specificity identified by researchers studying morality policy involves interest groups developing and acting in these disputes according to different rules than in the case of a typical conflict of interest. So-called promotional interest groups have been observed to dominate, engaged in the debate but not deriving any measurable benefits from the proposals they advocate. These actors have included churches, among them the Catholic Church which has become—also in the United States—one of the key actors influencing morality policy debates ever since morality policy has emerged as an important dimension of politics.[35]

Even the above observation requires comment, however. It is clear that promotional interest groups play a special role in morality disputes. Nevertheless, one can hardly fail to see that in most such disputes their domination only occurs on one side of the political and moral dispute, usually politically affiliated with "the right." While organizations representing the opponents of abortion, *in vitro*, homosexual unions, etc. are mostly promoting groups, on the other side of the dispute stand groups which usually combine promoting goals with their own interests, thus falling into the category of material interest groups. In the case of the supporters of gambling, legalization of drugs, as well as *in vitro* clinics advocating "the right to a child," organizations like Planned Parenthood or the Center for Reproductive Rights supporting those who fight for "the right to abortion," the issue of important economic interests—independent from the morality rhetoric—is obvious.[36] Even in the case of organizations representing the gay community, at least in the European Union, the role of direct benefits is not without significance.[37] It thus appears that—

---

[33] Anthony Birch, *The British System of Government*, Boston 1973.

[34] Donley T. Studlar, "What Constitutes Morality Policy? Cross-National Analysis," in: Ch. Z. Mooney [ed.], op. cit., p. 38.

[35] Cf. Paul J. Fabricio, "Evolving into Morality Politics: U.S. Catholic Bishops' Statements on U.S. Politics from 1792 to the Present," in: Ch. Z. Mooney [ed.], op. cit., pp. 73–88.

[36] This includes both revenues from *in vitro* or abortion clinics and funds received from governments and international organizations. For example, in the years 2005–2009 the European Commission provided nearly 16 million pounds to finance the operation of the abortion organization *Marie Stopes International* (MSI), a portion of which was then spent on so-called "menstrual regulation," which is a form of abortion. As quoted in: European Dignity Watch, *The Funding of Abortion Through EU Development Aid. An Analysis of EU's Sexual and Reproductive Health Policy*, EDW, Brussels 2012.

[37] It is worth noting that in the years 2007–2010, as part of supporting the EU dialogue with LGBT groups, the International Lesbian and Gay Association received grants worth the total of four million euros, which represents about 80% of its operating costs. Cf. http://ec.europa.eu/budget/fts/

like in the case of political actors—also lobbying looks different on the right side of the political divide. In circles cooperating with the left wing of the political scene and lobbying for permissive changes in legislation, interest groups seem to represent the same material type as in other lobbying areas, even if they espouse the grand rhetoric of human rights and values. In functional terms, therefore, a thesis that requires further studies is the proposition that for the right wing morality policy is mostly concerned with "morality": a particular area of meta-political decisions; while for the left wing it is mostly about "policy": a decision-making area which does not substantially differ from other political acts of government.

9.1.2 Morality Policy and Participation

Aside from the mode of acting employed by political actors and interest groups, another difference characterizing morality policy from the perspective of the political process is the level of social participation in debates and resolutions concerning these matters. According to Mooney, if citizen participation is predictable in any area of the political process, it is so precisely in the area of morality policy.[38] This is especially interesting considering that this area is characterized by low economic impact,[39] which means that it is not material interests—so frequently emphasized in political theories—that engage the citizens.

On the one hand, it should be noted that morality policy issues are a special area of civic initiative, both legislative and otherwise. In Poland this is documented for example by the citizens' legislative initiatives concerning the education of 6-year olds, prohibition of eugenic abortion, or the large number of petitions concerning the Istanbul Convention or *in vitro* legislation.[40] On the supranational level in Europe, a particular expression of this engagement is the One of Us initiative signed by nearly two million citizens from all EU Member States in order to oblige the EU to prohibit the financing of activities which involve the killing of human life in the prenatal stage (e.g. for the purposes of scientific research).[41] The public debate in this area also takes the form of large demonstrations, associations, conferences. Marches for the Family against the legal equalization of same-sex unions, which gathered hundreds of thousands of people in France,[42] are now organized in several

---

[1.12.2011]. None of the pro-family or pro-life organizations has received any comparable support (both in percentages and actual amounts), even though they represented incomparably broader social groups.

[38]Ch. Z. Money, op. cit., p. 8.

[39]Ibid., p. 5.

[40]http://fakty.interia.pl/tylko-u-nas/news-in-vitro-przeciwnicy-kontra-zwolennicy-trwa-zbieranie-podpis,nId,1853169 [24.07.2015].

[41]See the European initiatives One of Us or Free Sunday Alliance.

[42]http://www.lemonde.fr/societe/article/2013/04/21/pro-et-anti-mariage-homosexuel-manifestent-dimanche-a-paris_3163619_3224.html [26.07.2015].

European states.[43] On the opposite pole are the annual Gay Pride events organized by LGBT communities throughout Europe. This appears to be a characteristic trait of civic engagement in morality policy. It may be argued that while other, redistributive issues, can mobilize large crowds of citizens on the occasion of a specific crisis against which a demonstration is being organized, moral issues generate structural (cyclical) activity in public demonstrations. High civic participation in events such as the "Manif Pour Tous", "March for Life" or "Gay Pride" show that public manifestations become an ordinary element of civic participation in the area of morality policy.

Increased civic engagement is also observed when citizens are asked to decide about ethically sensitive matters in a referendum. By comparing twentieth century referenda in Oregon, California and Arizona, David Schecter demonstrated higher civic participation in votes on morality policy matters. Commenting on some of his data, he says that "voters were much more interested in having their say on cigarettes, abortion and monitoring sex offenders than they were on nearly every other issue."[44] Saying in more general terms that "morality policy questions have higher rates of voter participation than their non-morality counterparts,"[45] he stresses that his analyses "lend strong support to the notion that morality policy ballot questions produce high rates of voter participation."[46]

The issue of referendums refers us to the third dimension of the functional differences of morality policy—namely to a specific way in which institutional structures and decision-making procedures are used. Studies show that in some democratic countries there is a tendency to shift the burden of decisions on moral issues directly onto the citizens. Moral issues have been demonstrated to be some of the most important referendum questions,[47] and the tendency to settle them by public ballot has been on the rise.[48] This seems to lend support to the thesis that the area of moral issues enhances the elements of direct democracy in representative democracy.

The above conclusion would be an unwarranted extrapolation, however. In political processes involving morality policy there are also tendencies that are the exact opposite of those described above. Researchers note the phenomenon of the total exclusion of citizens from the decision-making process owing to morality policy issues being settled by the judiciary. Naturally, it may be argued that modern democracies generally experience a juridization of a whole range of issues.

---

[43]Including Poland, Italy, and Germany, as well as other countries.

[44]David L. Schecter, "Legislating morality outside of the legislature: Direct democracy, voter participation, and morality politics," *The Social Science Journal* 46 (2009), p. 103.

[45]Cf. ibid.

[46]Ibid., p. 102–103.

[47]Cf. David Butler and Austey Ranney [eds.], *Referendums around the world: the growing use of direct democracy,* American Enterprise Institute for Public Policy Research, Washington, DC, 1994.

[48]D. L. Schecter, op. cit., p. 90.0.

Nevertheless, one may hardly fail to notice that morality policy has been the subject matter of major judicial decisions "even in countries where this rarely occurs (Austria, Sweden)."[49] As regards the USA, researchers point out that morality issues are usually elicited by a "political shock" following court decisions,[50] often passed by a very slim margin. A good example is the famous 2015 decision of the US Constitutional Court granting gay couples the right to marry in the USA and removing restrictions imposed by individual states in this respect, passed by a majority of one vote (5:4).[51] It seems that a similar role in Europe is attempted— to the extent of its abilities—by the European Court of Human Rights, which has tried to reinterpret fundamental human rights over the past years, invoking the idea of consensus.[52] It should therefore be noted that the process of reducing the role of the legislature in deciding on moral issues may be related not only to empowering citizens in the process of political decision-making, but also to enhancing the role of the judiciary which acts, in a way, as a substitute for the legislature as regards constitutional issues.

It appears that the different way of taking the public opinion "into account" in regulating morally sensitive issues could be explained by the weight of the matter at stake. Referendums analyzed by Schecter usually concerned issues like gambling, taxes on cigarettes, the treatment of sexual offenders, etc.[53] They were mostly concerned with unmoral behavior which did not constitute a violation of human rights, or the technical details secondary to previously made decisions concerning the protection of human rights. Court decisions, on the other hand, in most cases concern the interpretation of basic human rights by upholding or changing the existing interpretation of a legally protected good.[54] Functional analyses thus seem

---

[49]D. T. Studlar et al., op. cit., p. 356.

[50]Cf. Ch. Z. Mooney [ed.], op. cit.

[51]Samuel G. Friedman, "Push Within Faith for Same-Sex Marriage Gets Little Attention," *The New York Times National*, July 25, 2015, p. A16. The author emphasizes not only the religious associations' objection to the new law, but also—with some exaggeration—the intra-religious differences of opinion concerning so-called "gay marriage."

[52]Gregor Puppnick, "Abortion and the European Convention on Human Rights," *Irish Journal of Legal Studies* Vol. 3 (2) 2012, pp. 142–194.

[53]Cf. David L. Schecter, op. cit., pp. 89–111.

[54]Such a role was also played by the Polish Constitutional Tribunal in the dispute around the act which depenalized abortion. The Tribunal derived constitutional protection of life from the principle of the democratic rule of law. In its ruling, it explicitly stressed that "if the substance of the rule of law is a set of fundamental directives derived from the essence of democratically established law and guaranteeing the minimum of justice, the first such directive must be respecting in the rule of law the value without which any legal subjectivity is nonexistent, i.e. human life from the moment it comes into existence. Democratic rule of law considers the supreme value to be man and the goods which are most valuable to him. One of such goods is life, which in a democratic rule of law must be constitutionally protected at each stage of its development." For the avoidance of doubt, the Tribunal also emphasized that "the value of the constitutionally protected good which is human life, including life developing in the prenatal phase, must not be differentiated. There are no sufficiently precise or substantiated criteria allowing for such a differentiation based on the developmental phase of human life. From the moment of conception, human life thus becomes a

to suggest that it is necessary to take into account certain distinctions as regards the substantive understanding of morality policy. We will come back to this issue later on.

Even though the question whether morality policy in the political process contributes to the empowerment of citizens, or whether in fact the opposite is the case, is a significant question which deserves more in-depth study. It should be noted that— irrespective of their possible outcome—it is clear that normal procedures of parliamentary governments as regards morality policy are an exception rather than the norm. As pointed out by Studlar et al., morality policies lead to a slackening of the typical context of institutional rules, including the effect of overflow to other institutions.[55] Indeed, the issue of referendums and court decisions suggests that their characteristic trait is the delegation of decisions outside of the legislative. Researchers point out that this is also manifested in the establishment of various committees, expert advisory bodies, which are supposed to arrive at an "ethically right" decision. For example, in Holland in 1970, in the very beginning of the discussion about abortion, the government already established "an expert committee, and left the issue to the medical community, organized in the Royal Dutch Society for the Advancement of Medicine."[56] Consequently, it may be argued that the specificity of morality policy consists also in procedural and institutional differences, expressed in "the involvement of multiple institutions in this policy, including legislative initiatives on policy by opposition, (. . .) party divisions on legislative votes, constitutional disputes, participation of the judiciary at various levels, and, where available, decentralized institutions and referendums."[57]

9.1.3 Ways of Explaining Functional Anomalies

The processual distinctness of morality policy, observable at the level of the functioning of political actors and interest groups, civic engagement, as well as decision-making structures and institutions, requires an explanation. Some researchers representing the functional approach treat substantive explanations with a hint of irony[58] and try to explain disparities by the different functional characteristics of morality policy. For example, high civic participation is explained in literature by the high political (structural) relevance of the issues at stake, and above all by the fact

---

value protected by the Constitution. This applies also to the prenatal phase." For more on strategies adopted in the face of cultural changes within the framework of the rule of law and the EU, see Michał Gierycz, "EU's Axiological Credo and Morality Policy Tensions," *Studia PhilosophiaeChristianae* No. 3/2015, pp. 159–193.

[55]D. T. Studlar et al., op. cit., p. 357.

[56]Article Timmaermans, G. Breeman, op. cit., pp. 48–49.

[57]D. T. Studlar et al., op. cit., p. 357.

[58]Cf. Ch. Z. Mooney, op. cit.

that "morality policies are assumed to be technically less complex."[59] This last factor is supposed to operate like a kind of *perpetuum mobile*, since "higher public participation and technical simplicity favour high political salience of morality policies,"[60] which translates into higher participation. Analogically, high diversification of votes on moral issues may be explained by the lack of party discipline,[61] and the fact the legislative shrinks from settling these issues—by a fear of political conflict.[62] While these functional explanations are not wrong, they are evidently superficial. Firstly, they seem—at best—a partial explanation. One can hardly fail to notice that not only moral issues are structural, or even technically simple. The decision on single-mandate electoral districts is no less structural than the legalization of drugs, and the principle of resolving matters by fiscal authorities to the benefit of the citizen is not technically simpler than an explanation of the *in vitro* procedure. Clearly, it is not the simplicity of the case and its structural relevance that is the decisive factor which determines the specific functioning of morality issues in politics. Secondly, functional explanations call for an explanation themselves. True, the lack of party discipline does result in a greater potential for diversified voting. The key question, however, is: why this lack of discipline? Why is discipline given up even at the risk of losing the vote on an important political decision when, after all, studies show that morality issues are considered publicly salient?

On the grounds of functional analyzes, an important lead is provided by an analysis of the processes of political change. In accordance with the classical model developed by Hall,[63] political change may concern (1) policy paradigms;[64] (2) policy instruments; and (3) the calibration of those instruments. Paradigmatic changes refer to fundamental changes, such as modifications of legal status (e.g. a total ban on some behaviors, or—on the contrary—their decriminalization). Instrumental changes concern the means employed to achieve the existing ends.[65] Finally, calibration refers to the least radical form of change in the functioning of an instrument. In light of this theory, as regards morality policy, an example of paradigmatic change would be decriminalization of abortion; instrumental change would include, for instance, increased access to pregnancy termination procedures available through a new medical program; and calibration would be exemplified by a change in the number of weeks from conception during which abortion is permissible. Even though this may be theoretically differentiated, in practice discussions

---

[59]Christoph Knill, op. cit., p. 310. Cf. also e.g. C.T. Studlar, op. cit., pp. 37–59.

[60]Ch. Knill, op. cit., p. 310.

[61]Cf. e.g. I. Engeli et al., op. cit., p. 20.

[62]Cf. A. Timmaermans, G. Breeman, op. cit.

[63]Cf. Peter A. Hall, "Policy paradigms, social learning, and the state: the case of economic policymaking in Britain," *Comparative Politics* 25(3) 1993, pp. 275–296.

[64]In his paper, Hall calls this a "third order change," emphasizing—by reference i.a. to Kuhn's theory—its distinctness in character from the two other types of change. Cf. "Policy paradigms. . .," pp. 285–291.

[65]Cf. S. Heichel et al., "Public policy meets morality. . .," pp. 318–334.

concerning all of these issues would be paradigmatic. Dominance of the conflict of values results in that "any morality policy change is *per se* paradigmatic. As long as decisions over societal values are at stake, policy change is always about paradigmatic core issues rather than instrumental aspects."[66] Consequently, a model of political change that can be accurately applied in other areas of politics is essentially useless in the area of morality policy. It should be added that it is useless not due to processual or functional, but substantial factors—the content of regulations which is inherently paradigmatic.

Thus, ultimately also functional analyses draw our attention to substantive issues as the theoretical foundations for distinguishing morality policy, which seem to make "morality policy different."[67] In the course of further reflections we should consider questions which arise from functional analyses. First, do the contents of morality issues justify the tendency to escape into anomalies in the political process, particularly the greater-than-average civil engagement and the tendency to settle issues outside of the ordinary legislative process? Secondly, what are the sources of disparity in actions and behavior on the right and left wing of the political scene in settling these issues (inconsistent vs consistent voting; promotional vs material interest groups)? Can the substantive perspective contribute to the thesis about the tendency to politicize morality on the left wing of the political scene? Thirdly, can the diversification of problems related to morality issues explain the different role of public vote in each case (the thesis about a relationship between certain moral issues and basic human rights)?

9.2   The Substantive Approach to Morality Policy

However paradoxical this may be, despite the enumeration of moral problems found in many works, a substantive definition of morality policy presents a problem. In fact, the multiplicity of issues related to morality, some of which have been discussed at the beginning of this chapter, leads some researchers to deny that there is any moral substance to political discourse. We should, therefore—even briefly—first take a look at this standpoint.

9.2.1   Morality Policy: Lacking Substance?

As mentioned above, it is sometimes claimed that morality policy *per se* does not exist. It is then assumed that morality only constitutes a strategic approach to framing

---

[66]Ibid., pp. 321–322. The authors argue that even the discussion about tax regulations applicable to legalized same-sex unions is not a discussion about instruments, but a paradigmatic one.

[67]D. T. Studlar et al., op. cit., pp. 353–371.

public policy issues, i.e. a way of presenting issues in a discourse.[68] The essence of this approach consists in the claim that it does not matter what problem a political dispute is concerned with; what is important is whether policies may be presented as morality issues. This approach to morality policy situates reference to moral principles as one (sometimes very valuable) of many instrumental substantiations which may be used by the advocates of a particular solution to frame a political problem.[69] While non-morality frameworks emphasize instrumental rationality and evaluate policies based on whether they help achieve particular goals, the essential feature of morality frameworks is that those who employ them refer to morality as a basic instrument of political argumentation. In this approach, morality policy (if such term may reasonably be used at all) is related to whether its advocates want to and are able to use morality issues to frame a particular political problem. Consequently, morality policy (or moral framing) would refer to all instances when any party to the conflict presents the issue at stake in moral categories.[70]

The above argumentation about morality policy is additionally based on the claim that all politics (from the abolition of taxes to phone tapping) contain some axiological component which may be used to turn the discourse about it into a morality issue.[71] Nevertheless, it may also become shorn of it. Many issues which used to be morally "hot," such as divorce, racially mixed marriage, etc., have now become lukewarm at most, or even lost their moral aspect altogether. This is supposed to be an additional argument in support of the key claim of the advocates of "morality framing" that there are no political problems whose core constitutes an objective moral problem.[72] This also means that the scope of morality policy could, by definition, include an unlimited number of issues, differing depending on space and time.[73] It is worth adding, even though this already introduces us into the area of the anthropological dispute we are analyzing, that a theoretical grounding of these claims is provided by the assumption that morality is a social or political construct.[74]

It is not a matter of profound insight that not each one political decision has similar potential to become a moral problem. Suffice to say that the number of ethically acceptable solutions concerning the organization of waste removal or even taxes is practically unlimited. This does not apply, however, to possible legal regulations concerning the permissibility of abortion or human trafficking. Everyday experience shows that people rarely propose to "morally frame" a discussion about the development of railway infrastructure, while discussion about euthanasia does not need "framing" to become a moral discussion. At the level of empirical experience, one can hardly agree that there are no political problems whose core constitutes

---

[68]Cf. G. Muccaroni, op. cit., pp. 188–218.

[69]Christoph Knill, op. cit., p. 311.

[70]Ch. Z. Money, op. cit., pp. 4–5.

[71]G. Mucciaroni, op. cit., p. 191.

[72]Cf. ibid., pp. 189–190.

[73]Ch. Knill, op. cit., p. 311.

[74]Ch. Z. Mooney, op. cit., p. 10.

an objective moral problem. Unless for the sake of theory we negate experience. Such a methodological approach is possible on the grounds of a new interpretation of so-called methodological realism, which should not be confused with philosophical realism.[75] The so-called methodological realism says that "there are deep structures that cannot be observed and what can be observed may offer a false picture of those phenomena/structures and their effects."[76] One example of such realism was Marxism.[77] Just like a Marxist would not ask workers about their proper interests, as they would not know the correct answer, so a researcher-realist mounts the "high horse" of smart-aleckism. In the case of morality policy, this means that even if all those involved in the dispute say they are concerned about moral norms, he will know best—that they are "in fact" after something entirely different. The methodological problems of this standpoint are related to the fact that it contradicts the basic principles of scientific explanation applied in social sciences, which say that "a scientific assertion must have both logical and empirical support: it must make sense and, it must not contradict actual observation,"[78] and further that it must be open to falsification. Consequently, the fact that moral issues are emphasized in a dispute should make one consider their significance instead of *a priori* relativizing them.

9.2.2   Two Approaches to the Essence of Morality Policy

Both the methodological wasteland of reducing morality policy to moral framing, and the imperfection of functional explanations direct our attention to a substantive description of morality policy.[79] The road to doing so is not as simple as it may seem. Literature includes several significant attempts at a substantive definition which—while not mutually contradictory—view its essence differently on major points.

The classical substantive approach, born on American ground, to morality policy views it in the context of the category of sin. In this approach, morality policy is defined as the regulation of issues related to the demand for or desire of "what some people think of as sin."[80] It is then assumed that morality policy is what we are dealing with if "at least one advocacy coalition involved has portrayed the issue as

---

[75]It refers not so much to the tradition of Thomas Aquinas, but that of Karl Marx.

[76]David Marsh, P. Furlong, "A Skin Not a Sweater: Ontology and Epistemology in Political Science," in: D. Marsh, G. Stoker, *Theory and Methods in Political Science*, Palgrave McMillan, 2002, p. 30.

[77]Ibid., p. 31.

[78]Earl Babbie, *The Practice of Social Research*, Cengage Learning, 2007, p. 4.

[79]This standpoint is taken by most European researchers: cf. I. Engeli, et al., "Theoretical Perspectives on Morality..." or Ch. Knill, "The Study of Morality Policy...".

[80]K. J. Meier, op. cit., p. 682.

one of morality or sin."[81] Since "preferences for sin (...) have some unique characteristics that make them different from preferences for potatoes, baloney, or Republicans,"[82] also a policy that deals with regulating these preferences should have a particular character, generating the functional differences described above.

Clearly, a large portion of issues in morality policy meet the above criterion. From gambling to prostitution to abortion or euthanasia, we are in the area of regulating "what some people think of as sin."[83] Nevertheless, such issues as religious education, freedom of conscience, ownership of weapons, etc., are beyond the logic of sin as an analytical category. As a considerable number of researchers have pointed out in the course of their analyses concerned with morality policy, reference to the category of sin alone is too narrow. It does encompass some issues in morality policy, but if we were to adopt this definition, we would lose sight of all those issues which refer to a different kind of moral argumentation. Focusing on morally regulated "access to sin," we would thus leave out public discussions which are positive, and concern the guaranteeing or protection of fundamental societal values. It is worth adding that one other objection raised against the category of sin is that it refers to just one (Christian) moral tradition as the point of reference, while in contemporary societies there are many coexisting moral standpoints.[84]

Taking all of the above arguments into account, researchers understand morality policy in broader terms now: as politics concerned with issues touching upon the "first principles,"[85] claims about right and wrong,[86] and thus the moral foundations of the political community. Most generally speaking, morality policy would thus be a policy which legally sanctions good and evil, legitimizing one set of fundamental values and delegitimizing another one.[87] Such an approach to the problem would also explain the structural character of moral disputes, observable in functional terms, and their high social salience. One could hardly imagine how the moral foundations of a political community, defining the essential goods it protects and the principles regulating its life, could not be an issue of essence to that community.

Even though the above approach to the problem seems to be right on the mark, solving problems with the reference to sin in the definition of morality policy, it opens up other problems related to the great variety of topics attributed to morality policy. For example, as regards the issue of granting or refusing gays the right to marry we are dealing with legitimization of some values and delegitimization of

---

[81]Donald S. Haider-Markel and Kenneth J. Meier. 1996. "The Politics of Gay and Lesbian Rights: Expanding the Scope of Conflict," *Journal of Politics* 58, p. 333, as quoted in: G. Mucciaroni, op. cit., p. 188.

[82]K. J. Meier, op. cit., p. 682.

[83]Ibid.

[84]Cf. e.g. G. Mucciaroni, op. cit., pp. 188–189.

[85]Ch. Z. Mooney, op. cit., p. 3.

[86]D.T. Studlar et al., op. cit., p. 354.

[87]Ch. Z. Money, op. cit., p. 3; I. Engeli, et al., op. cit., p. 24; K. J. Meier, op. cit., p. 21.

others, as well as with a clearly structural act and a socially engaging problem. Does the same happen also in the context of the legalization of casinos and gambling?

The above question makes it necessary to ask about the internal diversification of issues attributed to the area of morality policy and their significance. This problem has been discussed in recent theoretical works concerning morality policy. Christoph Knill shows that in terms of substance there are four subfields that may be identified in morality policy:

(a) Issues of life and death (including abortion, euthanasia, artificial insemination, stem cell research or capital punishment);
(b) Issues of sexual behavior (homosexuality, prostitution, pornography);
(c) Issues related to addictive behavior (gambling, drugs);
(d) Issued referring to basic decisions over the relationship between individual freedoms and collective values (e.g. religious education, gun control).[88]

In functional terms, Knill points out that the first two types of problems and religious education "refer to issues in which value conflicts constitute the standard mode of political decision-making (. . .) material gains and losses are of minor importance." Knill calls these issues manifest morality policies. In this area, he notes, "individual values and beliefs, by contrast, play a central role", both internally and externally. On the one hand, they constitute the basic criteria determining individual preferences. On the other hand they are an instrument of social and political power which various groups and actors—e.g. liberals, conservatives or churches—"may gain or lose if certain values prevail or change."[89] Consequently, even minor issues related to the choice of instruments or their application and calibration (e.g. shifts in the time frame after fertilization in which abortions may still be legally performed) may easily trigger a fundamental conflict over values.[90]

The other type of morality policy according to Knill is what he describes as latent morality policies. They are characterized—aside from being related to fundamental values—also by a combination of concentrated economic benefits and highly dispersed costs, resulting in considerable economic significance for certain groups. Knill points out that "this constellation favours that political debates are framed as instrumental, focusing on the design of effective solutions to existing problems. At the same time, however, the regulatory matter contains elements that can easily be 'morally exploited'. Competing advocacy coalitions might try to shift the political debate from an instrumental one towards a value conflict."[91]

It seems that Knill's categories point to an important distinction in morality policies, intuitively observed, and found also in works by other authors. At the same time, the criterion he uses is disputable. Even though the issue of abortion or *in vitro* should be considered an example of manifest morality policies, the

---

[88]Ch. Knill, op. cit., p. 311.

[89]Ibid., p. 312.

[90]Ibid.

[91]Ibid., p. 313.

assumption that the financial factor is irrelevant in political disputes around these issues is most debatable. As noted above, there are major interest groups behind those who advocate the liberalization of abortion regulations, related to the pharmaceutical and abortion industry, funding a major part of the activities of lobbying groups. Knill's assertion that "material gains and losses are secondary" is wrong. For some participants in this debate they are very important, perhaps even of paramount importance.

If the difference between manifest and latent policies cannot result only from different values (moral vs material-and-moral) or the character of groups involved in the dispute (promoting vs material), we must look for another explanation of the above divide. The inadequacy of Knill's proposal shows that it is pointless to relativize the moral character of some of these disputes, in fact undermining their affiliation with morality policy. It seems that a valuable substantive criterion is found in the discussion concerning the definition of morality policy which has continued over the years: whether it is about "sin" or about "values." It may be hypothesized that latent politics concern the issue of "redistribution of sin," while manifest morality policies concern the "legitimization of values." Let us briefly discuss this proposition.

9.2.3 A Synthesis of Two Substantive Approaches

As emphasized by Kenneth J. Meier, a characteristic feature in the case of legalizing various perversions (such as prostitution or gambling) is that "no one is willing to stand up for sin. Legislators do not rise and recite the joys of drunk driving, the pleasures of prostitution, or the thrill they get from serial killings."[92] In these cases, the legislator does not ask about the value of a particular activity (it being clear that it is—in the moral sense—an anti-value), but about whether it is possible to legalize something that people want to do, even though it results in their depravation. Thus, the question lies within the confines of discussion about the autonomy of law, and concerns the acceptable areas of disparity between legal and moral norms, without challenging the applicability of the latter, however.[93] The legitimization of prostitution, the sale of alcohol or cigarettes is not motivated by their merits, but by the legitimacy—essentially resulting from the awareness of man's weakness—of distinguishing between morality and law; between that which man should do and that which he is coerced to do by sanctions.

While in the case of latent policies the crux of the dispute concerns the scope of the autonomy of law within the framework of a universally accepted morality, in the

---

[92]K. J. Meier, op. cit., p. 683.

[93]Cf. Marek Safjan, "Recht, Werte, Demokratie," *Christentum-Welt-Politik*, No. 3, 2008, pp. 5–27, and Rev. Franciszek Longchamps de Berier, "Rechtsautonomie und Moral," *Christentum-Welt-Politik*, No. 3, 2008, pp. 29–37.

case of policies which Knill calls manifest something much more important is at stake. In this case, a new aspect appears, related to the fact that solutions which are to be legally sanctioned (such as legalization of abortion, same-sex marriage, *in vitro*, etc.) are no longer presented as moral "offenses," but are awarded the status of values which should be recognized and guaranteed by the state.[94] Thus, it is not about legally permitting—for certain reasons, to an extent—something that depraves man, but about saying that what "some people think of as sin" not only does not contradict human dignity, but is an element of its protection and development. It should be stressed that this change in the character and essence of moral dispute is not necessarily clear at first glance. Sometimes moral discourse may begin in a way similar to the dispute about latent policies. For example, in the case of the dispute over abortion in the 1970s and 1980s it was often argued that it was necessary to separate that which is legal from that which is moral. A careful observer of the discourse might notice, however, that in the depths of the pro-abortion argumentation an entirely different argument was found. As penetratingly observed by Kazimiera Szczuka, a Polish feminist and scholar of the feminist discourse, the most important argument for abortion, from the very beginning of the dispute, was "a reversal of values."[95] The discourse concerning gay rights was conducted in an analogous way. In the course of court cases at the end of the 1950s, Franklin Kameny, a pioneer of the modern gay movement, emphasized that "homosexuality is not only not immoral, but is affirmatively moral,"[96] to finally coin the phrase "gay is good" in 1968.[97] Contemporary discussions around *in vitro* or surrogate motherhood are proceeding in the same spirit.

Looking from the substantive perspective, the distinction between manifest and latent policies would therefore be related to a different approach to the system of values prevailing in a particular political community. Latent policies accept it, demanding only a "space" for human weakness. Manifest policies aim at a redefinition of values and public affirmation of actions which are considered contrary to human dignity. It appears that this substantive distinction better explains the observable difference in the social attitude to the problem of abortion compared, for example, to the problem of gambling. This difference, let us add, also seems to reflect the social awareness of a different moral responsibility of the political community in these two cases. While the issue of gambling or alcoholism is concerned with the way responsible people use their freedom, the issue of abortion, euthanasia, *in vitro*, as well as so-called "same-sex marriage" (in the context of raising children) concerns the community's responsibility for people who are not

---

[94]Cf. John Paul II, *Evangelium VitaeEncyclical to the Bishops, Priests and Deacons, Men and Women religious, lay Faithful, and all People of Good Will on the Value and Inviolability of Human Life* (hereinafter *Evangelium Vitae*), No. 11.

[95]Kazimiera Szczuka, *Milczenie owieczek*, WAB, Warszawa 2004, p. 145.

[96]David W. Dunlap, *Franklin Kameny, Gay Rights Pioneer, Dies at 86*, "New York Times" 12.10.2001, as quoted in: R. R. Reilly, op. cit., pp. 3–4.

[97]Ibid.

(yet or are no longer) able to provide for their own good. The way this good is defined is of key importance. Manifest policies are thus related to a dispute not only about the guarantees of dignity, but also about how dignity is understood.

The awareness of a substantive difference between manifest and latent policies has significant consequences for the understanding of morality policies. If we agree that morality policy is understood as a dispute concerning the first principles, then— paradoxically—the category of sin turns out to have a greater capacity content-wise. The dispute over the first principles only concerns manifest policies. In the case of latent policies, the argument is essentially not about principles, but about the necessary scope of their legal protection. This would mean that morality policy is in fact concerned with disputes around the issues of life, death, marriage, and reproduction, which is consistent with the general intuitive understanding of the substance of morality policy.[98] Consequently, it appears that it would make more sense to talk about primary and secondary morality policies. Primary, because they are related to disputes over the first principles; secondary, because they are linked to clashes about their political and legal implementation.

* * *

In the context of the above reflections, it is worth referring to the questions asked at the end of functional analyzes. It seems reasonable to conclude that substantive questions are what explain the particularly high social participation in disputes over and the settlement of moral issues, as well as the functional anomalies related to these politics. One could hardly imagine that—particularly the primary—morality policies, concerned with the foundations of the political system, the sense of communal life, could remain the subject of unnoticed discussion and legal decisions made by a "simple majority" without the requirement of a qualified quorum. What, if not discussions about the first principles, should generate high social engagement, reference to the guardians of the constitution (Constitutional Tribunal, Supreme Court) and, finally, reliance on direct settlements by the citizens? After all, what is at stake is the ethical orientation of the community as a whole, the way it understands common good, and even the question whether the category of common good can still be justifiably applied. The substance and the structural nature of decisions related to primary morality policies substantiate the assertion that these are metapolitical disputes in fact, establishing the framework conditions for the political process that follows. By defining the axiological orientation of the political community, primary morality policy specifies the ultimate goals, character and direction of, or limits to, political action. In this sense, it belongs to metapolitics.[99]

The metapolitical nature of primary disputes concerning morality confirms the thesis about the special relationship between anthropology and morality policy

---

[98] As noted by I. Engeli et al., the definitive aspect of these politics are the fundamental decisions concerning life, marriage, and reproduction. I. Engeli et al., op. cit., p. 24.

[99] Cf. Maciej Zięba OP, "Kościół wobec liberalnej demokracji," in: Michael Novak, Anton Rauscher SJ, Maciej Zięba OP, Chrześcijaństwo. Demokracja. Kapitalizm, Wydawnictwo Polskiej Prowincji Dominikanów W drodze, Poznań 1993.

decisions. For since—as has been discussed more extensively in Part I—these values are "a theory of the other as well as a theory of my own self,"[100] key ethical decisions implicitly reflect the anthropological identification of the community as a whole. They are concerned with the understanding of human dignity and the fundamental goods man is entitled to. As previously stated, the essence of primary morality policies is not a dispute over "permitting iniquity," but over the ethical legitimization of immorality. It is precisely this "reversal of values" that is at the very heart of the anthropological problem of late modernity. As noted in Part II, the reinterpretation of man in the spirit of unconstraint that has been gaining traction since the Enlightenment, results in viewing the person as a mere "trace," understood as an exchangeable value with no sexual identity. This approach—already previously discussed—is not only inconsistent with the vision, prevailing in Europe and built on the moral traditions of antiquity and Christianity, of man as a constrained being, but also incompatible with the constitutional traditions of European countries.

It does not seem an exaggeration to say, therefore, that in contemporary politics the dispute about man is nowhere more explicitly and fundamentally present than in the area of primary morality policies. Note that we land right in the heat of the dispute as soon as we say that the first principles involve the area of metapolitics. Such a statement implies that there are some non-political, objective limits to the politic. By saying this, we claim that there is a morality as a space of objectively existing properties recognized by the conscience; in other words, that human conscience is an element of the power of reason which is capable of knowing objective moral reality. If we do not recognize such a conscience, the term metapolitics only has a functional meaning (and should, in fact, be called by a different name): it refers to an area of politics which has particular relevance for other political decisions, but which is governed by the same (majority) rule.

The above anthropological perspective is essential for morality policy discussions and the understanding of politics in general. Flagship issues of morality policy centered around the protection of life, the status of marriage, and religious freedom, touch upon three fundamental dimensions of humanity, essential to constrained anthropology, which result in strong claims about the foundations of political order. In this view, irrespective of the form or type of the political regime, the state should be based on the recognition of the special dignity of man, be committed to the protection of human life, marriage, and family, and guarantee free social life and the freedom of confession.

In light of a constrained view of politics, these expectations are not political, but metapolitical: they are settled on a level that is entirely different from the political one. They are considered an element of moral order, guaranteeing respect for human dignity on which politics should be founded. A politic that is grounded on constrained anthropology does not consider itself competent to politically decide in these matters; it only declares that it recognizes these fundamental values and

---

[100]Rev. Józef Tischner, op. cit., p. 17.

guarantees their protection.[101] What may, if at all, be a matter of political dispute is only the scope of protection, as an element related to the scope of governmental powers, rather than matters of substance. Let us stress, therefore, that in the perspective of constrained anthropology there is essentially no room for morality policy *sensu stricto*, understood as discretionary acts depending on man's will. The very fact of its existence is understood as a usurpation of power: since the boundaries of human nature define the limits of man's freedom, then too fundamental moral goods delimit the freedom of political arrangements. There is no room here for political compromise—there is the duty, instead, to protect man's inherent, fundamental rights which guarantee his ability to live a life that is truly human.[102] Constrained anthropology takes a strong stance in disputes concerning the first principles, treating the postmodernist thesis about the end of great narratives as just such a narrative, which it is not willing to submit to.

The adoption of unconstrained logic has significant consequences for morality policy and the understanding of politics as such. They first include, obviously, issues of substance, and are related to the implementation of a new vision of humanity. There are also some other, less obvious, structural consequences. The late-modern disintegration of the boundaries of humanity also means eliminating limits to the operation of the state. As rightly pointed out by Robert R. Reilly, already Rousseau intended "to politicize society totally and his first target was society's foundation—the family—the primary means by which men are curbed of that total self-absorption to which Rousseau wished them to return. Rousseau proposed that its primary function of educating its children be taken from it and given to the state (. . .) the father is supposed to console himself with the thought that he still has some authority over his children as a 'citizen' of the state."[103] Rousseau's proposal is a logical solution if family is but a historical, artificial construct. If there is no nature, any change is merely a change of convention. The above anthropological perspective swings wide the door to morality policy understood *sensu stricto*. Morality indeed becomes here a space of political decisions through which man (also politicized, for having no natural communities, i.e. such as are not related to the state) is formed according to his own will.

It appears that this is where we can find the key to answering the second question that followed our analysis of the functional interpretations of morality policy. The source of differences in the left and right wing's approach to morality issues, expressed in a consistent vote on the left and a dispersed vote on the right, seems to be connected precisely to the fact that they embrace different anthropologies. As a consequence, the left may consider morality as an area subordinated to political

---

[101]Cf. e.g. *Universal Declaration of Human Rights.*

[102]In this context, researchers sometimes use the term non-negotiable values, which include the first principles (protection of human life, marriage, religious freedom), of the fundamentalism of human rights. Cf. J. Węgrzecki, *Wartości podstawowe w polityce. Debata w latach 2005–2008*, in: S. Burgoński, S. Sowiński [ed.], *Ile Kościoła w polityce, ile polityki w Kościele?*, Księgarnia św. Jacka, Katowice 2009.

[103]R. R. Reilly, op. cit., p. 31.

will—just like any other area; while for the right this still remains (irrespective of how the matter is approached) an area of individual moral decisions—subordinated to the judgement of objective conscience.

Excursus: Morality Policies and Religion

Although it might seem that everything has been explained, one more thing needs to be considered. When presenting his typology, Knill includes religious education in manifest policies. He does so even though it evidently complicates the simplicity of his typology. This issue should also be taken seriously. We need to see to what extent the inclusion of religion can be explained by the proposed substantiation of the internal division of morality policies into primary and secondary ones.

It should be noted that some researchers place morality policies almost by default in the context of the dispute between the religious and the secular. As emphasized by Izabelle Engeli et al., "precisely because morality issues involve fundamental values of right and wrong, they are intimately linked to religion and religious arguments, or values in particular."[104] Consequently, even conceding that relevant morality issues should be defined in reference to basic decisions about life and death, marriage, and reproduction,[105] the authors point out that this is "what connects them to the existing conflict between secular and religious political groups."[106]

One can hardly polemicize with the fact that nearly all axiological systems have developed under the influence of religions dominating in a given area. Classical studies on the origins of civilizations show the central significance of belief in the formation of fundamental values and their relationships.[107] In this sense, an attempt at "a reversal of values" in Europe must mean taking a stance in opposition to the canon of morality stemming from the Christian background. Nevertheless, the conclusion that due to this fact axiological opposition should be identified with religious opposition seems to be considerably premature. Moreover, opposition to the traditional understanding of values today does not need to mean standing in opposition to religion at all.

The system of values grounded in the context of Christianity never had a confessional character. In fact, we may talk of a genetically inherent independence of law from religion in Christianity. Even though "in history, systems of law have almost always been based on religion: decisions regarding what was to be lawful among men were taken with reference to the divinity,"[108] in the Church tradition it has never been held that religious legitimization was necessary to substantiate the lawfulness of a legal regulation. Fundamental moral rules entailed by a doctrine have always been considered universal—binding irrespective of whether one knows the

---

[104]I. Engeli et al., op. cit., p. 24.

[105]Ibid., p. 26.

[106]Ibid.

[107]Cf. Braudel, *A History of Civilizations*, Penguin Books, 1995.

[108]Benedict XVI, "The Listening Heart. Reflections on the Foundations of Law", Visit to the Bundestag, Reichstag Building, Berlin 2011, https://insidethevatican.com/news/the-listening-heart-reflections-on-the-foundations-of-law/ [28.05.2020].

doctrine or not. Christianity never established specifically religious laws characteristic of other monotheistic traditions. Already Thomas Aquinas emphasized in his treatise *De Regno* referring to Aristotelian thought that while "for all other animals, nature has prepared food, hair as a covering, teeth, horns, claws, (. . .) man was endowed with reason," and this reason, particularly moral reason, teaches him about right and wrong. The biblical expression of this assumption is found in St. Paul who writes in his Letter to Romans: "when Gentiles, who do not have the law, do by nature things required by the law, they are a law for themselves, even though they do not have the law. They show that the requirements of the law are written on their hearts, their consciences also bearing witness, and their thoughts sometimes accusing them and at other times even defending them."[109] For St. Paul and the Christian doctrine he was constructing, the matter was obvious: there is a moral sense inherent in the nature of every human being, which makes even Gentiles, who do not know God, bound through their conscience (internally) by the law which later on, in the Christian tradition—which adopted Cicero's term, in fact—came to be called natural law.[110]

To make a case for values recognized by the conscience it is not necessary to invoke the religious versus the secular opposition. Quite on the contrary, values—precisely as universal properties—have always been and still are an area where the secular and the religious worlds can meet. This is illustrated both by the constitutional traditions of European countries which subscribe to a neutral worldview and refer to the axiological community as the basis of political community,[111] and by the observation of political discourse in which the same values are defended by Christians and by non-believers, or non-practicing believers.[112] To quote C. S. Lewis, "the question has nothing to do with the difference between Christians and those who (unfortunately, since the word has long borne a useful, and wholly different meaning) have been called 'humanists'."[113] The difference is anthropological: it is about how the good that is proper and due to man is understood; about values which correspond to his dignity.

---

[109]Romans 2: 14–15.

[110]As noted by Roman Tokarczyk, "biblical scholars generally agree [. . .] that these words mark the beginning of the development of Christian law of nature." Id., *Filozofiaprawa* . . ., p. 91.

[111]Cf. Constitution of the Republic of Poland of April 2, 1997, which reads: "We, the Polish Nation—all citizens of the Republic, both those who believe in God as the source of truth, justice, good and beauty, as well as those not sharing such faith but respecting those universal values as arising from other sources."

[112]This was witnessed in France where objection to same-sex unions being granted the status of marriage was also voiced by homosexuals: see Jean-Pierre Delaume-Myard, spokesman of the homosexual organization HOMOVOX, who objected to adoption by same-sex couples and said that his desire to become a father cannot take away from the child the love of a mother: "Je me suisengagéparce que mon manque d'enfant ne doit pas avoir pour conséquence de priver un enfant de l'affectiond'unemère.", http://leplus.nouvelobs.com/contribution/845347-je-suis-homo-contre-le-mariage-gay-m-hollande-arretez-la-democratie-a-deja-perdu.html [20.08.2015].

[113]C.S. Lewis, *The World's Last Night and Other Essays*, Harcourt Brace Jovanovich 1973, p. 49
C.S. Lewis, *The World's Last Night and Other Essays*, Harcourt Brace Jovanovich 1973, p. 49.

Secondly, it should be noted that endorsement of so-called "traditional values" today does not necessarily mean agreement with religious doctrine. Quite the opposite, the sheer number (though not necessarily the membership) of Christian churches in which traditional values have been—at least partially—negated is probably greater than of those where they have not. In some cases, like in the case of the attitude to homosexuality in the Swedish church, this results in a direct contradiction between the moral doctrine of a church and the moral standpoint expressed in the New Testament, or, like in the case of the Anglican community, a risk of breakup within the church community itself.[114] However we look at this, the reality of diverse Christian communities and churches in Europe and around the world, including their diverse moral teachings, is very complex. Naturally, most researchers who refer to the Christian moral standpoint *implicitly* refer to the standpoint of the Catholic Church. This is quite reasonable given that the Catholic Church is not only the largest and the most doctrinally and organizationally coherent Church of the West,[115] but first of all a Church which cultivates the traditional moral teaching of Christianity. Nevertheless, in light of the diverse faces of Christianity in Europe, the dispute cannot simply be placed on the religious versus the secular axis.

If the above argumentation is correct, both the relationship between religion and values and that between religious and axiological communities requires a more nuanced standpoint than is usually presented in literature of the subject. An axiological standpoint is not "intimately linked to religion" or religious arguments. Nevertheless, since the doctrines of religious communities entail a moral message, religions are committed to influencing the formation of the citizens' conscience (the educational role of religion).[116] Moreover, as part of the process of forming the conscience, they participate in public discussion as advocates of one of the competing moral standpoints. Consequently, even though moral dispute is not religious dispute, since Church doctrine includes a moral component, disputes over religious

---

[114]Jacek Dziedzina, *Sól utracona*, http://gosc.pl/doc/1121852.Sol-utracona [20.08.2015].

[115]One might add that such an approach is quite widespread in the literature – Cf. J. Weiler, *Chrześcijańska Europa*, W drodze, Poznań 2003 [*Un'Europa Cristiana: Un saggio esplorativo*].

[116]The educational role, clearly linked to the cultural role, is well developed in Christianity. Even though, as pointed out by Aquinas, "the natural law, in the abstract, can nowise be blotted out from men's hearts, (. . .) it is blotted out in the case of a particular action, in so far as reason is hindered from applying the general principle to a particular point of practice, on account of concupiscence or some other passion (. . .), either by evil persuasions, just as in speculative matters errors occur in respect of necessary conclusions; or by vicious customs and corrupt habits, as among some men, theft, and even unnatural vices, as the Apostle states, were not esteemed sinful" (Summa Theologiae, q. 94, Article 6). Consequently, Churches understand their role in politics as the service of "enlightening" human conscience. As noted by John Paul II—and his words would be subscribed to by representatives of most Christian denominations—the Church wants to help it "not to swerve from the truth about the good of man, but rather, especially in more difficult questions, to attain the truth with certainty and to abide in it" (*Veritatis splendor*). Consequently, religion is an important educational element and provides support to the defenders of values in the political process: it strengthens their conviction about the recognized good, showing the limit to equitable negotiations. A similar role is played by public statements made by the Church on moral issues. Let us add that the significance of this role goes beyond the community of believers.

education can justifiably be included, for substantive reasons, in primary morality policies, i.e. disputes over the content of moral disputes. Moreover, it should be noted that changes in morality policy regulations may affect the scope of religious freedom and education protected by political authorities (since restrictions may be imposed e.g. when the moral teaching of the Church contradicts state legislation), as well as the Churches' moral standpoints (which may become more permissive in an attempt to keep up with the changing public moods).

9.3 Anthropological Models and the Language of Morality Policy

There can be no doubt that "through their rhetoric, political elites reinforce the connection between particular moral foundations and specific public policies."[117] Consequently, as George Lakoff argues in his well-known monograph, when conservatives suggest "that liberals don't understand what they say, that they just don't get it, they are right."[118] That being the case, it should be expected that different anthropological visions, in contemporary times related on the intellectual level—as has been pointed out in the chapter on late modernity—on the one hand with the dispute about understanding man as an exchangeable value, and on the other with the dispute about the understanding of human sexuality, and expressed on the political level in primary morality policies,[119] will employ different semantics. Evidence in support of this hypothesis has been provided by in-depth interviews. As in the scenarios categories characteristic of both anthropologies were mixed, the respondents—identifying concepts inconsistent with their perspective—sometimes displayed a strong reaction, either deprecating the justifiability of using such concepts in the questions asked,[120] or, on the contrary, wholeheartedly approving the

---

[117]Scott Clifford, Jennifer Jerrit, *How Words Do the Work of Politics: Moral Foundations Theory and the Debate over Stem Cell Research*, "The Journal of Politics", 75, 2013, p. 659.

[118]George Lakoff, *Moral Politics. How Liberals and Conservatives Think*, University of Chicago Press, Chicago 2001, p. 24.

[119]As regards the former—moral disputes over abortion, euthanasia, *in vitro*, research on embryos, i.e. the entire area of disputes concerning life; as regards the latter—disputes over the concept of marriage, "LGBT rights," or sexual orientation.

[120]For example, when asked about the justifiability of protecting unborn life, a respondent representing the so-called feminist community answered: "You know what? These questions must have been written by some hardcore conservative. Such an idea could only have come up in Poland . . . It is only in Poland that people talk of unborn life. This is simply sick. If you took this [elsewhere], if you translated this into French or English, they would simply tap their foreheads at you, thinking you must be from Opus Dei or something. I am sorry about this comment, but that's the way it is." *In-Depth Interview (IDI)—1*. UKSW Institute of Sociology, UKSW Institute of Political Science.

categories and emphasizing the importance of expressions used in the scenarios.[121] Clearly, the language used in debates concerning the areas we are interested in is worth paying attention to.

9.3.1 Bioethical Discourses

Let us first note that after World War II the protection of human life at all of its stages was generally not a matter of dispute. Due to the German practices of eugenics, the constitutional traditions of Western countries (most emphatically in Germany) were supplemented with clauses explicitly making the protection of human life mandatory. The same applied to the European Convention on Human Rights, which includes a statutory obligation to protect human life.[122] It only permits one exception for deliberately taking human life, namely in the case of a valid death sentence. It may thus be said that Western post-war politics in the area of bioethics stemmed from an unequivocal anthropological standpoint related to the logic of constraint. In view of the tragic consequences of its instrumentalization, it was considered justified to protect human life at all of its stages. The first deviation occurred at the end of the 1960s, when some states began to respond to demands made by a fraction of feminism which, like Shulamith Firestone, saw pregnancy as barbarianism, and its termination as "the most important point of feminist politics."[123] The feminists argued that "only women can get pregnant, yet men, almost exclusively interpret the morality of and make the laws about abortion."[124] Thus, the dispute over abortion became a key element in the process of woman's emancipation. An element of particular significance, because expressly coupled with the thesis, characteristic of the cultural revolution of the 1960s, about sexual freedom as "an expression of one's personal freedom."[125]

---

[121]For example, when asked about sexual minorities, a respondent representing the gay community asked the interviewer: "Do you have it written: sexual or LGBT minorities?" and after having been assured that the wording used in the scenario is LGBT, added "When you say 'sexual,' the connotation is always with sex … We try not to use [the term] 'sexual'." *In-Depth Interview (IDI)—2.* UKSW Institute of Sociology, UKSW Institute of Political Science.

[122]Cf. ECHR Article 2.

[123]Marielouise Janssen-Jurreit, *Die Zukunft der Reproduktion – Niederlage oder Befreiung der Frau?,* in: id. [ed.], *Frauen und Sexualmoral,* Fischer Taschenbuch Verlag, Frankfurt am Main 1986, p. 346.

[124]Beverly Wildung Harrison, *Our Right to Choose. Toward a New Ethic of Abortion,* Beacon Press, Boston 1983, p. 2.

[125]Kevin White, *Sexual Liberation or Sexual License? The American Revolt Against Victorianism,* Ivan R. Dee Publ., Chicago 2000, p. 134. The author points out that this way of thinking was inspired by many intellectuals, including Wilhelm Reich who "believed that the cause of neurosis was the patient's inability to enjoy sufficiently intense orgasms." Wherefore the historian of culture Susan Warren calls the 1960s "the decade of Wilhelm Reich." Ibid., p. 135.

Even though female participation in legislatures did not rapidly increase in the 1970s, both legislators and courts gradually became more favorably disposed to abortion. The breakthrough came in 1973 with the U.S. Supreme Court decision in *Roe vs. Wade*.[126] While the idea of human dignity was not officially negated then, it clearly began to become devoid of substance.[127] Another challenge which inflamed the dispute have been the achievements of biotechnology. Since the 1980s, the issues of *in vitro*, stem cell research, or transplantation have been major areas of confrontation over the protection of human life in morality policies. Finally, the end of the twentieth century brought the problem of euthanasia, presented as a humanitarian and humanistic response to the problem of human suffering in the terminal phase.[128]

9.3.1.1 Two Standpoints

In the dispute over human life in the prenatal phase, there are, generally speaking, two main standpoints in the public debate. One declares that "the fetus has the same right to live as the woman"[129] and as any other human being, since every human life is a fundamental value which is irreplaceable and which, due to its personal character (dignity and/or sanctity), requires absolute protection at all of its stages. The other claims that "it does not have equal rights,"[130] and consequently often distinguishes between a person and a human being, and argues that human life is a relative value[131] which depends on conflicting values, e.g. the quality of life or freedom. In the dispute over abortion, these two standpoints are usually described, respectively, as "pro-life" and "pro-choice."

It is worth noting that the popular names of these two standpoints also reveal the dispute between constrained and unconstrained anthropology. Pro-life advocates who demand that the state provide statutory protection of human life at all of its stages consider the obligation to protect human life as an inviolable boundary of humanity, an objective limit to man's decisions. Pro-choice advocates consider this an area of objectively unconstrained human decisions. In the context of the dispute

---

[126]Cf. Johanna Schoen, *Abortion after Roe: Abortion after Legalization*, University of North Carolina Press, North Carolina 2015.

[127]Cf. E. Picker, op. cit.

[128]Cf. Jacek Malczewski, *Eutanazja – z dziejów pojęcia*, "Diametros" 2004, No. 1; or Rafał Citowicz, *Prawnokarne aspekty ochrony życia człowieka a prawo do godnej śmierci*, Kodeks, Warszawa 2006.

[129]Ewelina Wejbert-Wąsewicz, *Aborcja w dyskursie publicznym. Monografia zjawiska*, Wydawnictwo Uniwersytetu Łódzkiego, Łódź 2012, p. 69.

[130]E. Wejbert-Wąsewicz, *Aborcja w dyskursie . . .*, p. 70.

[131]See also Hugo Engelhardt's claim that "[n]ot all humans are equal (. . .) not all humans are persons. Not all persons are self-conscious, rational, and able to conceive the possibility of blaming and praising. Fetuses, infants, the profoundly mentally retarded, and the hopelessly comatose provide examples of human nonpersons." Hugo T. Ingelhardt, *The Foundations of Bioethics*, Oxford University Press, New York 1996, p. 135.

concerning abortion, even though they explain that "pro-choice is not just inter-changeable with pro-abortion (. . .) or anti-child,"[132] they also say that "it is about giving women a choice between continuing a pregnancy than either raising the child or giving it up for adoption, or having an abortion."[133] The fact that the choice is about killing a human life does not represent a moral constraint.[134] In this sense, both emblems accurately reflect the anthropological foundations of the two opposite standpoints. What according to unconstrained anthropology is a choice, according to constrained anthropology is a violation of inviolable boundaries—not freedom, but self-will and, in fact, an attempt to evade the consequences of one's decisions. As argued by pro-life advocates, "abortion is not a just another 'choice.' Rather, it is a flight from responsibility. Abortion is a response to choice, that is, the decision to have sex. (. . .) Sometimes the result is an unwanted baby. (. . .) Abortion has become a leading means to avoid taking responsibility for the life created."[135]

It is worth emphasizing that the thesis about the relative value of human life in the pro-choice current is rarely presented—as in the case of Singer's works mentioned above—as a theoretical thesis. It usually appears as a practical thesis, without openly engaging in a dispute about the claim that a fetus is a human being.[136] It tries to reconcile these theses by emphasizing the legitimacy, if not obviousness, of weighing human life (of the child) against another well-being (of the mother),[137] or by differentiating the scope of protection afforded to human life at its various stages, depending on the degree of biological or social development.[138] The latter, much more widespread standpoint apparently helps support the theoretical thesis of constrained anthropology (about the exceptional value of human life), while at the same time removing its practical meaning.[139] As a consequence, the advocates of

---

[132]Bertha Alvarez Manninen, *Pro-Life, Pro-Choice. Shared Values in the Abortion Debate*, Vanderbilt University Press, Nashville 2014, p. 89.

[133]B. A. Manninen, *Pro-Life, Pro-Choice . . .*, p. 90.

[134]Cf. e.g. B. W. Harrison, op. cit., p.231, where the author stresses that "elective abortion is morally appropriate." As a side remark, it is worth noting that such a standpoint results in women who have decided to have an abortion distancing themselves from the pro-abortion movement. In this context, Bertha Manneinen quotes 42-year-old Heidi who had an abortion when she was 24, and who, according to Manneinen, does not regret it. Nevertheless, the author says: "Heidi admits having trouble relating to reproductive rights activists because she perceives them as treating abortions too causally: 'I find myself not being a great supporter of the pro-choice movement. When I ask myself why that is, since I believe in the right to choose, what comes back as my answer is that it is something you are killing. You are killing a child.' She says that many pro-choice advocates treat abortion as 'just a medical operation,' rather than 'the taking of, at least, a potential life.'" Ibid., p. 89.

[135]Doug Bandow, *Roe v. Wade: Four Decades of Tragedy*, in: Noel Merino [ed.], *Abortion*, Greenhaven Press, Farmongton Hills 2014, p. 21.

[136]Cf. Mary Elisabeth Williams, "The Choice to Abort Is Up to Women," in: Noel Merino [ed.], *Abortion,* Greenhaven Press, Farmington Hills 2014, pp. 26–31.

[137]M. E. Williams, *The Choice . . .*, pp. 30–31.

[138]Cf. e.g. Jurgen Habermas, *The Future of Human Nature,* Polity Press 2003, pp. 37–53.

[139]An extensive discussion of this issue is found in Eduard Picker, *Godnośćczłowieka . . .*

abortion, euthanasia, or embryonic stem cell research do not publicly refer to the theses made by Singer or Ingelhard. On the contrary, they try to argue instead why a particular phase of human life does not yet deserve the protection due to a human person. Sometimes, as a complementary strategy, ethical arguments are invoked for suspending the general principles of protecting life. For example, as noted by Scott Clifford and Jennifer Jerrit who study the bioethical discourse, the advocates of embryonic stem cell research argue that the society has the "ethical obligation to carry out life-saving bio-medical research."[140] Note, however, that the moral justification of the thesis about the instrumental use of the human embryo requires a major linguistic shift. It succeeds to the extent that the embryo becomes "dehumanized" in the discourse. Consequently, the dispute over language, i.e. over what the human life that the dispute is concerned with is to be called, is vital for controlling the bio-ethical discourse.[141]

For actors subscribing to the constrained anthropological perspective, the term human life in the prenatal phase refers first of all to the fact that it is human life. Hence the term "pro-life" which is the general name of the anti-abortion movement emphasizes its focus on the life of an unborn human being. In its rhetoric, the movement refers to concepts traditionally used in legislation, such as "human life," "child," "nasciturus," sometimes introducing their own new forms such as "unborn child," "conceived life," "life in the prenatal phase," "every life,"[142] and generating slogans like: "yes to life,"[143] "one of us,"[144] or "the sanctity of life."[145] Media campaigns cite the cases of famous people who—like Andrea Boccelli—were at the risk of being aborted (in accordance with medical recommendations received by their mothers) and who live because their parents chose otherwise.[146] Another tool illustrating the legitimacy of using the above terms is the presentation of a recorded procedure of abortion, starting with *The Silent Scream* which has been known since the 1980s, to the most recent productions visualizing the process of removing the fetus.[147] The image of an unborn baby is often used as an emblem identifying pro-life groups.[148] All of these activities are aimed at making the

---

[140]S. Clifford, J. Jerrit, op. cit., p. 659.

[141]In Polish literature this has been expressively described by Agnieszka Graff who called the dispute about abortion "a war about language," which she believes to have been lost by the feminist community as "phrases like 'free choice' or 'the woman's right to choose' used by liberal circles in the West have never felt right in Polish." Cf. Agnieszka Graff, *Świat bez kobiet. Płeć w polskim życiu publicznym*, W.A.B., Warszawa 2008, pp. 131–133.

[142]Cf. e.g. http://www.pro-life.pl/ [15.09.2016].

[143]Cf. e.g. https://prawy.pl/28420-tak-dla-zycia/ [15.09.2016].

[144]Cf. e.g. https://oneofus.eu/ [15.09.2016].

[145]Cf. e.g. http://www.oaza.pl/cdz/index.php/pl/2011/612-warszawa-marsz.html [15.09.2016].

[146]http://info.wiara.pl/doc/566000.Andrea-Bocelli-moja-matka-nie-dokonala-aborcji [15.09.2016].

[147]Cf. e.g. https://www.lifesitenews.com/pulse/abortionist-quits-when-he-holds-a-living-baby-in-his-hands-after-an-abortio [28.06.2016] https://www.youtube.com/watch?v=10nryBtML_Q [15.09.2016].

[148]Cf. e.g. http://www.pro-life.pl/ [15.09.2016].

addressees realize that the dispute about abortion or *in vitro* ultimately concerns everyone, since every person who is alive was once in the situation of an unborn child; that when talking about a human embryo, we are talking—as the European Citizens' Initiative puts it—about "one of us."

Advocates of the other anthropological logic try to frame the debate so as to avoid defining the status of human life in the prenatal phase. In this context, it is characteristic that the abortion movement defines itself as a pro-choice movement. Thus, the attention rests not so much on the *nascitirus*, but on the woman in whose womb it exists. It is her choice about its life that is to be protected. Consequently, the pro-choice movement centers the discussion about abortion on the issue of women's rights, talking about "the right to manage one's reproductive life,"[149] the right to birth control and family planning,[150] the right to privacy,[151] the right to decide about oneself and one's own body,[152] and even the right to abortion.[153] These communities also generate mobilizing metaphors, some of which are populist ("fight for your own belly"), while other are an element of the language of political and legal decisions ("reproductive and sexual rights"). Concurrently with its emphasis on the language of (women's) rights, this movement fights against "the phantasmatic image of a Child who is symbolically killed,"[154] proposing either medical terms used to describe the first stages of human life, such as embryo or fetus, or even the term "fetal tissue."[155] The significance of this reorientation of the language of public debate is illustrated by the fact that in 2016 the National Institute for Reproductive Health Action Fund launched a Google application which, when installed, automatically changed the expression "pro-life" into "anti-choice" in all searches in the Internet."[156]

---

[149]Magdalena Stoch, "Reprodukcja i reprezentacja – analiza związków w obrębie dyskursu feministycznego," *Annales Universitatis Paedagogicae Cracoviensis. Studia de Cultura* VII (2015), p. 88.

[150]Cf. e.g. http://www.federa.org.pl [15.09.2016].

[151]In this area, they may refer to ECHR case law. Cf. e.g. http://www.prawaczlowieka.edu.pl/index.php?orzeczenie=ef9cb1abfdb1d45bb08bd2742f179591c8266187-b0 [15.09.2016].

[152]Cf. Sławomir Sierakowski athttps://wydawnictwo.krytykapolityczna.pl/pro-odzyskajmy-prawo-aborcji-katha-pollitt-94#.V9rIgK1XrgY [15.09.2016].

[153]Cf. Katha Pollitt, *Pro: Reclaiming Abortion Rights*, Picador 2014.

[154]Magdalena Stoch, op. cit., p. 94.

[155]J. Schoen, op. cit., p. 69.

[156]Tara Culp-Ressler, *A New Google Extension Will Change Every Mention of 'Pro-Life' to 'Anti-Choice'*, http://thinkprogress.org/health/2016/02/20/3751397/extension-anti-choice/ [13.06.2016]. The author notes that NIRH President Andrea Miller said "it was a really interesting and creative idea [. . .] we agreed with her [lady who created that app] that the language in this discussion really matters." It is worth citing the argumentation of the advocates of abortion who subscribe to this standpoint. As noted by Katha Pollitt, even though "in general it makes sense to call people what they wish to be called (. . .), 'pro-life' encodes too much propaganda for me: that a fertilized egg is a life in the same sense that a woman is, that is has the right to life as she does." This shows that in those who do not share the view about equal right to life, this generates a linguistic objection. At the same time, the author calls those who support abortion "pro-choicers," that is, in the way they

9.3.1.2 Two Languages

From the point of view of further analyses, it would seem particularly relevant to explicate the specific concepts used in the bioethical discourse, in order to better understand the politics of the European Union. Given that a large number of concepts used in political decisions and legal documents concerning bioethics belong either to the traditional language of law and ethics (e.g. child, human life, pre-born life, *nasciturus*), their anthropological explication does not seem necessary. Being related to constrained anthropology, they explicitly state the thesis about the exceptional dignity of man, and protect it. Though they still may, of course—as is illustrated by the case of personism—become subject to reinterpretation. Nevertheless, we should focus our attention on those concepts which, by entering the bioethical discourse, not only play the role of political emblems, but also constitute the language of political and legal decisions.

In this context, it is especially important that we understand both the concepts borrowed by legal sciences from the language of medicine,[157] and the new terms found in political and legal decisions.

The use of medical terms may influence the framing of the bioethical discussion. For example, Encyclopedia Britannica defines the term "embryo" as "the early developmental stage of an animal while it is in the egg or within the uterus of the mother. In humans the term is applied to the unborn child until the end of the seventh week following conception." It is worth noting that while applying to man terminology which applies to all animals, this definition respects the special, personal nature of human beings by referring to the category of "unborn child" which implicitly shows that the human embryo belongs to the community of personal beings. This example is particularly illustrative in that the Polish translation of the same Encyclopedia defines the embryo differently, as "the early developmental stage of an animal, including man, while it is in the egg or within the uterus. In humans the term embryonic stage is applied until the end of the seventh week of pregnancy."[158] While both definitions are similar as regards the biology, it is worth noting that Polish translation by deletion of the specifically personal element makes the category of embryo merely a general animal category which is applied in this sense to the human kind as a biological species. The relationship of the embryo defined in such terms to the community of persons is much less clear than in the case of the former of

---

describe themselves, explaining that she does so "because it is an accurate term for those who support woman's right to decide for themselves whether to end a pregnancy or carry it to term." Katha Pollitt, *Pro: Reclaiming Abortion Rights*, pp. 13–14.

[157]Cf. Jelena Kondratiewa-Bryzik, *Początekprawnejochronyżycialudzkiego w świetlestandardówmiędzynarodowych*, Wolters Kluwer, Warszawa 2009; or Marek Safjan [ed.], *Prawowobecmedycynyibiotechnologii: Zbiórorzeczeń z komentarzami*, Wolters Kluwer Bussines, Warszawa 2011.

[158]"Embryo," in: *Encyclopaedia Britannica: Micropaedia*vol. 4, Encyclopaedia Britannica, Inc. 1993, p. 471; *Encyclopaedia Britannica. EdycjaPolska*, vol. 47, Wyd. Kurpisz, Poznań 2005, p. 465.

the two definitions. The issue of the embryo's personal status is particularly important in view of the fact that the category of embryo frequently appears in the context of embryonic stem cells. Stem cells are "cells that can divide and differentiate into the cells of various tissues (...). There are two main types: embryonic stem cells and adult stem cells."[159] Since only the former, coming from the early phases of embryonic development, are totipotent, which means they can potentially develop into any other cell, they are a particularly desirable material for biomedical experiments. Therefore, the bioethical debate in the EU regarding this issue concerns mostly the funding of scientific research.[160] It should be added that while embryo is the medical term applied "until the end of the seventh week following conception," from the on it is called a fetus.[161] This term is applied to the embryo "after it has attained the basic form and structure typical of its kind."[162]

While pro-choice groups take advantage of the zoological provenience of medical categories to emphasize the distance between man and an "embryo" or a "fetus," stressing the radical difference between personal life and embryonic life, pro-life groups highlight the ethical community of people in all stages of development. While the former consistently force categories which were also (originally) used to describe the life of animals, and sometimes even plants (as is reflected in European documents), the advocates of protecting human life take care to at least precede them with the adjective "human," and consequently in EU documents we also find such terms as "human egg cells."

As regards new terms coined, so to speak, within the framework of bioethical discourse, a particularly important role is played by four interconnected categories: reproductive health and sexual health, and reproductive rights and sexual rights. The category of "health" and "rights" endows these concepts with significant political and legal potential, incomparable with other, new categories, fitting them within the human rights discourse. This can be easily done because in their structure "reproductive rights" do not stand in obvious opposition to other rights (unlike "the right to abortion," for instance), and do not suffer from the demagoguery syndrome (unlike, for example, "the right to one's own belly"). Their meaning is particularly significant in view of the fact that nowadays not only "pro-choice," but also "pro-life" groups begin to refer to these categories.[163]

At the same time, the meaning of these categories is far from unequivocal. Magdalena Stoch says that "the problems of reproductive rights were explicitly defined in the program of the first openly feminist organization: the National

---

[159]http://portalwiedzy.onet.pl/122853,,,,komorki_macierzyste,haslo.html [14.06.2016].

[160]Cf. M. Gierycz, *Chrześcijańscy politycy...*

[161]Marian Machinek MSF, *Embrion ludzki*, in: *Wielka Encyklopedia Nauczania Jana Pawła II*, Polskie Wydawnictwo Encyklopedyczne, Radom 2014.

[162]"Fetus," in: *Encyclopaedia Britannica*: *Micropaedia* vol. 4, Encyclopaedia Britannica, Inc. 1993, p. 754.

[163]https://agendaeurope.wordpress.com/sexual-and-reproductive-health [14.06.2016].

Organization for Women, established in the United States in the 1960s."[164] In the 1967 *Bill of Rights for Women* it demanded that "the right of women to control their own reproductive lives [besecured] by removing from penal codes the laws limiting access to contraceptive information and devices and laws governing abortion."[165] The feminist postulate of reproduction control coincided in time and content to high level political enunciations which—like the Declaration on Population presented by 12 states to the United Nations Secretary-General U Thant in 1966—asserted that "the opportunity to decide the number and spacing of children is a basic human right."[166] The fear of overpopulation increasingly overwhelming the world's elites coincided in the late 1960s with expectations of the feminist movement, beginning a road which ultimately led to a situation where "'reproductive health' language has been adopted in many nations."[167]

As part of a legally binding instrument, the thesis about family planning as a human right was included in the Convention on the Elimination of All Forms of Discrimination Against Women of 1979, which says that "the States Parties shall take all appropriate measures to eliminate discrimination against women in all matters relating to marriage and family relations and in particular shall ensure, on a basis of equality of men (...) [t]he same rights to decide freely and responsibly on the number and spacing of their children and to have access to the information, education and means to enable them to exercise these rights."[168] As claimed by the feminist activists Hilkka Pietila and Jeanne Vickers, "the recognition of the right to family planning (...) is a historic step (...) they [women] may eventually have the right to control their own lives."[169] Moreover, "another basic human right becomes a reality: the right to be born a wanted child."[170] Consequently, in view of the obviousness of the new law, the only matter that remained to be regulated was access to tools which enabled its implementation.

As noted by Susan Yoshihara, while the idea of a human right to family planning was definitively introduced into UN language, "the reproductive health language

---

[164]M. Stoch, op. cit., p. 89.

[165]*Bill of Rights for Women*, National Organization for Women 1968, Article VIII.

[166]T. Ayala & Lord Caradon, "Declaration on Population: The World Leaders Statement," in: Susan Yoshihara, "Lost in translation: the failure of the international reproductive rights norm," *Ave Maria Law Review*, Vol. 11:2, 2013, p. 372. It is worth noting that nowadays the assertion that "the right to freely and responsibly decide whether, when, and how many children to have—is a fundamental human right which allows women to participate more fully in social life," is an element of the educational and informative strategy of the Polish government. Cf. Wanda Nowicka, Aleksandra Solik, *Międzynarodowestandardyzdrowiaiprawreprodukcyjnychorazseksualnych a ich realizacja w Polsce*, Secretariat of the Government Representative for the Equal Status of Men and Women, Warszawa 2003, p. 10.

[167]Susan Yoshihara, op. cit., p. 367.

[168]*Convention on the Elimination of All Forms of Discrimination Against Women*, The Office of the United Nations High Commissioner for Human Rights, New York 1979, Article XVI.

[169]HilkkaPietila, Jeanne Vickers, *Making women matter. The role of the United Nations*, Zed Books, London 1990, p. 125.

[170]Ibid., pp. 123–124.

seeped in through routine reports, advanced by advocates among the U.N. staff."[171] This happened with considerable contribution by the World Health Organization, including its directors José Barzelatto and Mahmoud Fathall. Without going into the details of this process,[172] it should be noted that "[f]rom the beginning, reproductive health was a concept aimed at limiting pregnancy and childbirth, and included 'fertility regulation,' which in turn included 'pregnancy interruption' or abortion."[173] It should be added that with the development of reproductive techniques, these rights also came to include artificial fertilization—*notabene* originally applied to breeding animals.[174]

As noted by Wanda Nowicka and Aleksandra Solik, "a real breakthrough in the approach to reproductive and sexual health came with the International Conference on Population and Development held in Cairo in 1994."[175] It defined reproductive health as "a state of complete physical, mental and social well-being and not merely the absence of disease or infirmity, in all matters relating to the reproductive system and to its functions and processes. Reproductive health therefore implies that people are able to have a satisfying and safe sex life and that they have the capability to reproduce and the freedom to decide if, when and how often to do so."[176] The non-legally binding Action Plan to the Conference specified that implicit in the above definition was "the right of men and women to be informed and to have access to safe, effective, affordable and acceptable methods of family planning of their choice, as well as other methods of their choice for regulation of fertility which are not against the law, and the right of access to appropriate health-care services that will enable women to go safely through pregnancy and childbirth and provide couples with the best chance of having a healthy infant."[177] The Conference on Women held a year later in Beijing not only upheld the Cairo definitions, but added an article on sexual health. According to the Beijing action platform, the rights of women "include their right to have control over and decide freely and responsibly on matters related to their sexuality, including sexual and reproductive health, free of coercion, discrimination and violence."[178]

It may be noted, quoting Jerzy Kropiwnicki who developed the Polish government's agenda at the two Conferences, that the "new terms they introduced in English, which have no equivalents in any other language, particularly with regard

---

[171]S. Yoshihara, op. cit., p. 377.

[172]Cf. Ibid., pp. 377–378.

[173]Ibid., p. 377.

[174]Cf. R. Amy Elman, *Sexual Politics and European Union: The New Feminist Challenge*, New York 1996, p. 105.

[175]W. Nowicka, A. Solik, op. cit., p. 12.

[176]*Report of the International Conference on Population and Development*, Cairo 1994, p. 40.

[177]Ibid.

[178]*Beijing Declaration and Platform for Action*, The Fourth World Conference on Women, Beijing 1995, p. 36.

Cf. also S. Yoshihara, op. cit., p.379.

to man, like for example 'reproductive health'," seem appropriate "more in the area of zoology and veterinary science than medicine."[179] This association is not groundless. According to the Merriam-Webster Dictionary the term "reproduction" means "the process by which plants and animals give rise to offspring and which fundamentally consists of the segregation of a portion of the parental body by a sexual or an asexual process and its subsequent growth and differentiation into a new individual".[180] Similarly it is defined in other languages.[181] Moreover, other appearing meanings of the term, such as "a copy of the original made to any scale using print or photography," "the action of recreating something,"[182] etc. point to the essential imitativeness or exchangeability of the obtained good, which, by the way, reflects the common approach to plants and animals. The use of this term in the context of human beings clearly refers to the anthropological tendencies of late modernity discussed in Part II, and in its essence ultimately to Rousseau's thought: the terms applied to man are devoid of any moral connotation, so the effects of reproductive activity may be objectified. Thus, the use of zoological terminology removes a potential ethical problem. It does have serious anthropological consequences, however. To see them more clearly, note that theoretically speaking the term "procreative rights" could be used instead. In such case, man would not be the author of a more or less successful copy of himself (reproduction), but would take part in an activity that exceeds his terms of reference; he would participate in creation (pro-creation), without claiming to play the role of the Creator, however. The juxtaposition of these two terms illustrates the impact of language on political decisions.

Despite the clear connection between the category of reproductive rights and unconstrained anthropology, and in spite of the evident genetic, terminological and political connection between these rights and abortion postulates, neither the Beijing nor the Cairo platform made any direct reference to abortion. On the contrary, neither in Cairo nor in Beijing was abortion "listed as a family planning measure."[183] Moreover, "both documents contained 'sovereignty' clauses allowing nations to apply the language according to national laws, both included language calling for the reduction of abortion, and both evoked strong opposition to abortion in country reservations that accompanied the final outcome document."[184] This "incomplete" definition of reproductive rights results in that despite the evident bias towards unconstrained anthropology, attempts are sometimes made at reinterpreting reproductive and sexual rights in the spirit of constrained anthropology. This is rare,

---

[179]Jerzy Kropiwnicki, "Rodzina i ochrona życia poczętego na sesjach nadzwyczajnych ONZ (Kair plus pięć, Pekin plus pięć, Stambuł plus pięć)," *Annales. Etyka w życiu gospodarczym* 2008, vol. 11, no. 2, p. 185.

[180]https://www.merriam-webster.com/dictionary/reproduction [28.08.2020].

[181]See f.e. *Dictionary of Polish Language*, http://sjp.pl/reprodukcja [22.06.2016], which states that reproduction means "thebreedingofanimals and propagationof plants forhusbandrypurposes".

[182]Ibid.

[183]J. Kropiwnicki, op. cit., p. 186.

[184]S. Yoshihara, op. cit., p. 379.

Table 9.1 Central and borderline concepts in bioethical discourses

Constrained anthropology (pro-life)		Unconstrained anthropology (pro-choice)	
Central	Borderline	Borderline	Central
Procreation *Nasciturus* (conceived child, unborn/preborn child)	Human (embryonic, fetal) life Person Human embryo Human fetus Pregnancy	Embryo Fetus Embryo cells Stem cells Menstrual regulation	Reproduction (reproductive rights, reproductive health) Sexuality (sexual life, sexual rights) Abortion

Source: own compilation

however. As interviews and participant observation have demonstrated, the advocates of constrained anthropology are very reluctant about this term.[185]

The above example shows that some terms are so explicitly related to a particular anthropology that they are almost never used by advocates of the opposite anthropological standpoint. This does not apply to all terms, however. For example, the category of "embryo"—although its biologistic provenience makes it considerably easier to adopt in the unconstrained anthropological perspective—is also used by the advocates of ethical boundaries, who, as mentioned, often add the adjective "human" to it. On the other hand, the term "person" which was originally explicitly related to the perspective of constraint has been subjected to a rather effective reinterpretation as a consequence of Singer's personism. Therefore, we may try to construct a scale of terms used in bioethical discourses and their relations to the two types of anthropology discussed above. For, as pointed out, each party to the dispute uses its own language.

Table 9.1 lists the terms which may be considered central for the advocates of both anthropological approaches and thus almost impossible to "take on" by the other interpretive community, as well as those which—while being more related to one than to the other standpoint—are less clearly unequivocal, positioned on the borderline of the two discourses and consequently used or reinterpreted by the other party. In the case of constrained anthropology, such central categories include the terms "procreation," "conception" and "*nasciturus*" (characteristic concepts: conceived child, unborn child). In the case of unconstrained anthropology, they include the categories of reproduction (the concepts of reproductive health, reproductive rights), sexuality (the concepts of sexual rights, sexual health), abortion, choice. The "in between" concepts which, depending on the context and modality of use, belong to both parties, consist in the medical lexis: embryo, fetus, stem cells, embryonic cells, menstrual regulation, as well as terms which have been more or less successfully reinterpreted by the other party to the anthropological dispute. Such a reinterpretation is illustrated, for example, by the differentiation between human life and personal life, or reinterpretation of the very concept of "person" in personism. The

---

[185] As a prominent pro-life activist said in reaction to an organization's use of the term, it was "regrettable" and "imprudent."

list of concepts presented below is not exclusive. For example, it deliberately excludes those "mobilizing metaphors" which are non-translatable or nonspecific to the language of law and political documents (e.g. "one of us," "right to free choice," "right to decide").

9.3.2 Discourses About Sexuality

Generally speaking, the issue of sexuality and the related social and legal regulations had not been a matter of political dispute in Western civilization until the nineteenth century. Consequently, the terms used were univocal. Marriage as a permanent union between a man and a woman, entered into by the couple to be wed of their own free will, had been treated as indissoluble since the thirteenth century, essentially reflecting the Christian ethics of marriage.[186] The anthropological meaning of the sexes was unquestioned, and behaviors contrary to the norms related to human sexuality were called a deviation which—aside from the pejorative connotation of the word—described the conviction that they were a departure from behaviors which became man and his dignity. As has been demonstrated by studies on the history of homosexuality in the USA, including in the beginning of colonization "sodomy—then understood as any unnatural, non-reproductive sexual act—was a temptation and sin to which anyone, male or female, could fall victim, as to envy or theft (. . .). [T]he colonial society did not seem to conceive of a unique type of person—a homosexual—who engaged in these acts, nor did it provide a homosexual identity on a cultural level or anything resembling a homosexual subculture on a social level."[187] Consequently, it should be said that traditional legal concepts (such as marriage, sex, engagement) referred to the logic of constraint: they were related to the conviction that there is an objectively knowable human nature, of which the sex is an essential determinant. Biological nature was a point of reference for understanding the essence of man. In this perspective, it was considered possible to specify which behaviors were proper to his nature, and which contradicted it. The choice of terms shows that the former were evaluated positively, and the latter negatively also on the linguistic level.

Even though the beginning of divergence between Christian ethics and civil law as regards the approach to marriage may be dated back to the end of the eighteenth century in Austria,[188] with a special role played in the process by the Napoleonic

---

[186]Cf. Andrzej Dziadzio, *Skąd się wzięły rozwody? Historia prawa małżeńskiego*, https://www. gloria.tv/article/Re9J8fh6WS1c2Q5uaHpKgALSo [23.06.2016].

[187]C. S. Vance, op. cit., pp. 13–34.

[188]As noted by Professor Andrzej Dziadzio, "the first state to have recognized in its legislation that marriage is exclusively a civil contract rather than a sacrament was the Catholic Austria. This was during the reign of Emperor Joseph II whose enthusiasm for the Enlightenment ideals led to an attempt, partially successful, to limit the heretofore unquestioned rights of the Church, including its say on the valid form of marriage. While introducing a lay concept of marriage, the 1783 patent of

Code implemented in Europe which introduced divorce and upheld "the fully secular system of personal marriage law adopted in the first phase of the Revolution,"[189] the category of the sexes and the sexual behaviors proper to them, as well as the understanding of the basis of the institution of marriage (consent by two persons of the opposite sexes) remained unaffected. Until 1973 homosexuality was treated by psychiatrists, and until 1991 by psychologists as a mental illness. It was not until May 17, 1990 that it was stricken off of the list of mental disorders by the World Health Organization.[190] This change of standpoint in the field of medicine whose mainstream representatives now say that "sexual orientation cannot be changed,"[191] paved the way for undermining "one of the last remaining outposts of the 'natural'."[192]

In theoretical terms, these efforts were supported by constructivism. As emphasized by Caroline Vance, "the links between social construction theory and gay activism run very deep. Efforts to transform society inevitably raised questions about the past and the future, as they also called into question prevailing ideological frameworks for examining the 'facts' about sex and gender."[193] While in the beginning it was assumed that once documents about homosexual acts from the past have been found and resurrected, it would be possible to write a history of gays and lesbians, as the studies went on it turned out that sexual acts described in American documents from the period of colonization could not be identified with contemporary homosexuality. Consequently, as stressed by the author, "all movements of sexual liberation, including lesbian and gay" have been built "on imagining: imagining that things could be different, other, better than they are."[194]

If imagination has become the basis of "a new sex history,"[195] the instrument of causation was language which defined the existing cultural patterns as "heteronormative," questioning their universality. Heteronormativity, according to Wiktor Dynarski of the Trans-fuzja association, means "a configuration of culture which reduces sexuality to heterosexuality," and thus excludes "non-heterosexual

---

Joseph II, the first state marriage act to have ever been enacted, did not introduce secular contracts. It did, however, take jurisdiction in matrimonial matters away from the Church entirely. It introduced a mixed system of personal marriage law in which the church form of marriage contract was retained and marriage remained subject to the religious regulations of the couple's confession, with divorce being granted by state courts only to those persons whose confession permitted it. Consequently, Catholics could not obtain a divorce." A. Dziadzio, op. cit.

[189]Ibid.

[190]http://dayagainsthomophobia.org/what-is-may-17th/ [23.06.2016].

[191]Wiesław Czernikiewicz, *Czy homoseksualizm można wyleczyć?*, http://www.medonet.pl/zdrowie/zdrowie-dla-kazdego,czy-homoseksualizm-mozna-wyleczyc-,artykul,1643684.html [23.06.2016].

[192]Cf. C. S. Vance, op. cit., p. 13.

[193]Ibid.

[194]Ibid., p. 30.

[195]Ibid., p. 13.

identities and defines them in terms of margins, degeneration, or deviation."[196] This statement clearly shows that the concept of heteronormativity, describing the mutual attraction of the opposite sexes in terms of a particular anthropological standpoint, and not statements on the objective condition of man, creates a space for the emergence of a homosexual identity and other sexual identities which had not been known in history so far. Consequently, the discussion about human sexuality has become the arena for a contest over language.

9.3.2.1 Stances on Homosexuality

A comparison of the definitions of homosexuality found on two twin websites modelled on Wikipedia: Homopedia and Conservapedia, shows the significance of the dispute over concepts. Homopedia says that homosexuality is "one of the psychosexual orientations, along with heterosexuality and bisexuality, in which the psycho-emotional involvement is directed towards persons of one's own sex."[197] It also claims that "scientists have established that man is born with a predefined, unchangeable orientation," and "statistical studies show that (depending on the definition) homosexual persons represent between several and a dozen or so percent of the population."[198] Conservapedia, on the other hand, says that even though "homosexuality is sometimes also defined in terms of (. . .) orientation," this term is "particularly favored by those who are promoting public acceptance of homosexuality," while the phenomenon itself refers to "sexual desire or behavior directed toward a person or persons of one's own sex,"[199] without being rooted in genes.[200] This shows that while Homopedia tries to show homosexuality as one of many equivalent forms of human sexuality, stemming from man's biological nature and having a significant representation in the population, Conservapedia considers this entire narration to be a tool of political campaigning, and views the phenomenon of homosexuality in the categories of an inclination to or the practice of sexual behaviors which are negligible in terms of the population. Consequently, for the former it is a "homosexual orientation," while the latter describes it as "homosexuality," meaning a particular form of sexual behavior.

In the above perspective, it comes as no surprise that Homopedia questions the term "homosexualism." It says that "the terms *homosexualism* and *bisexualism* (as well as the hardly ever used term *heterosexualism*) are taken from medical discourse and regrettably suggest pathology of the characteristics they describe. The terms *homosexuality* and *bisexuality*, while being equivalent in denotation,

---

[196]Wiktor Dynarski, "Glosariusz," in: Anna Śledzińska-Simon [ed.], *Prawa osób transseksualnych. Rozwiązania modelowe a sytuacja w Polsce*, Wolters Kluwer Business, Warszawa 2009, p. 282.

[197]http://www.homopedia.pl/wiki/Homoseksualizm [22.06.2016].

[198]http://www.homopedia.pl/wiki/Homoseksualizm [22.06.2016].

[199]http://www.conservapedia.com/Homosexuality [22.06.2016].

[200]Ibid.

have a neutral and positive tone to them."[201] Even this stance is sometimes contested, however. "Ponton," a group of progressive sexual educators, say on their website that also that vocabulary could have a negative connotation. As they explain: "In the English language, the word 'sex' means not only sexual intercourse, but also gender, and so the word 'homosexual' means someone who prefers persons of their own gender. In our [Polish] language the word sex has only one meaning, and consequently the word homosexual immediately brings to mind sexual intercourse, while sexual orientation is not only about a person's sexuality, but involves their emotionality as well (. . .). As a synonym, we may use the expression 'homosexual person,' which has a less negative overtone and which underlines the subjectivity of the person concerned. Likewise, we talk of bisexual persons and bisexual orientation."[202] Consequently, "the most neutral and appropriate nouns are 'gay' and 'lesbian'."[203] Indeed, as demonstrated by interviews, it is these concepts— as having a positive overtone—that are promoted by leading representatives of the gay community in the public dispute. In fact, it appears that compared to data found in Homopedia, current discourse has moved even further on, aiming at a complete elimination of references to sexuality. As pointed out by one interviewee related to the gay and lesbian community, the very concept of sexuality "is always associated with sex (. . .). [W]e try not to use the term 'sexual' [minorities]."[204] The desirable term, according to the interviewee, is the "LGBT" community.[205]

The LGBT category seems to be another, along with homosexuality, concept gathering steam in the public discussion about human sexuality, promoted by the advocates of social and legal change. The term is "the most commonly used acronym defining non-heteronormative persons, i.e. lesbians, gays, bisexuals and transsexual persons; other variants include LGBTQ (queer), LGBTQI (intersexual persons), LGBTQIA (asexual persons), LGBTQIAO (others), LGBTQIAO(H) (heterosexual persons with a friendly attitude to non-heteronormativity)."[206] It is worth noting that the category of "others" is all-important here, as even in its extended version the acronym still does not include important categories such as e.g. omnisexualism, or pansexualism, described in one of scientific studies as "an orientation of the sexual drive regardless of the gender identity or physical sex of the other person",[207] or "dual role transvestitism;"[208] finally, it does not include polyamory, etc.[209]

---

[201]http://www.homopedia.pl/wiki/Homoseksualizm [22.06.2016].

[202]http://ponton.org.pl/pl/strona/plec-i-mniejszosci-seksualne [22.06.2016].

[203]http://www.homopedia.pl/wiki/Homoseksualizm [22.06.2016].

[204]*In-Depth Interview (IDI) – 2.* UKSW Institute of Sociology, UKSW Institute of Political Science.

[205]Ibid.

[206]W. Dynarski, op. cit., p. 283.

[207]W. Dynarski, op. cit., p. 283.

[208]W. Dynarski, op. cit., p. 286.

[209]Note, for example, that the Australian Human Rights Commission lists 23 cultural genders which apart from those mentioned above include, without limitation, "crossdresser, drag king, drag queen,

The above concepts show that the logic behind sexual orientation and gender identity terms is essentially the logic of unconstraint. The perspective of sexual orientation which describes "orientation of the sexual drive"[210] even when—as in the case of pansexualism—it is *ex definitione* lacking in any specific orientation, and gender identity as "a sense of one's own gender, also preferred gender"[211] opens up unlimited possibilities of "imagining" man. It is not merely a theoretical assumption. The Australian Human Rights Commission which officially promotes 23 cultural genders has made it clear that the list is not exclusive.[212]*A contrario*, it may be pointed out that in constrained anthropology it is not entirely clear what sexual orientation is supposed to mean at all. If this term were to mean sexual attraction to a person of the opposite sex (man's attraction to woman, woman's attraction to man), it would not need to be distinguished from the category of sex. In fact, the meaning of this term only comes to view when we adopt a different anthropology at the outset, were woman's sexual attraction to man and a man's sexual attraction to woman is not natural either in the biological sense or in terms of essence. Reference to the concept of sexual orientation as a variable independent from the category of sex results in a new division of the human species. Being a man or a woman is no longer related to human sexuality. The latter is now defined by other criteria. Ultimately, the new division undermines the logic of sex which—looking from the theoretical perspective—should be replaced by the category of sexual orientation.[213]

9.3.2.2 Different Ways of Understanding Sex

In the above context, it comes as no surprise that in discourses concerning sexuality, the category of "sex" is no longer a term referred to by both anthropologies, but is now mostly used by those who refer to constrained anthropology. In the English language, this can be clearly seen in the categories of "sex" and "gender" having gone their separate ways. The latter term, in Poland sometimes translated as "the

---

genderfluid, genderqueer, intergender, neutrois." Cf. Babete Francis, "Gender bending: let me count the ways," http://www.mercatornet.com/articles/view/gender_bending_let_me_count_the_ways/ [24.10.2016].

[210]W. Dynarski, op. cit., p. 283.

[211]W. Dynarski, op. cit., p. 284.

[212]Cf.B. Francis, op. cit.

[213]This is so because if we consider e.g. transsexuality to be a sexual orientation, then the man/woman category no longer has any raison d'être. This is already now reflected by Australian law where citizens have "as many as three options available when stating their sex in passport applications." As reported—also in 2011—by the media, as a result of "the enactment of new antidiscrimination regulations, transsexuals and persons who are unable to unequivocally specify their sex will have the option to have it identified in the passport as 'unspecified'." In the document, this will be denoted by the character 'X'." http://www.tvn24.pl/wiadomosci-ze-swiata,2/trzy-plcie-w-paszporcie-w-australii,184317.html [25.04.2016]. This way, the construction of sexual orientation based on the category of non-discrimination makes the category of sex inadequate.

cultural aspects of sexual behaviors,"[214] is clearly preferred by the advocates of unconstrained anthropology. This was not the case right from the beginning, though. The concept of "gender" was built on the intellectually obvious premise of biological sex defined in the body being distinguished from its (psychical and social) experience.[215] Thus, it did not undermine the concept of sex. Corresponding to the two sexes were the two genders: male and female. This approach was reflected both in international documents and scientific studies.[216]

Nevertheless, the concept of "gender" entailed an essential ambiguity. Judith Bulter, one of the first theoreticians of gender, claimed that the goal was to oppose "regimes of truth that stipulated that certain kinds of gendered expressions were found to be false or derivative, and others, true and original."[217] Consequently, the category of gender, unlike the category of sex, has ultimately helped substantiate the claim that "that which is conditioned culturally develops entirely independently from that which is conditioned biologically,"[218] founding the thesis—commonly accepted in sexual minority groups, though far from obvious—about the severability of "the sex of external genital organs"[219] and gender identity. The latter, it has been claimed, "may also have an unspecified form,"[220] since it expresses the "individual experience of gender,"[221] which is not defined by the binary structure: male-female.[222]

The widespread discovery of the ideological nature of gender by the advocates of constrained anthropology came in the beginning of the twenty-first century.[223]

---

[214]W. Dynarski, op. cit., p. 282.

[215]As noted by Rev. Piotr Mazurkiewicz, "since man is not simply an animal, human sexuality cannot be reduced to something that is determined by nature in the biological sense. The ability to create culture is inherent to that which we call human nature (by contrast to animal nature). As regards the experience of sexuality, this cultural element also plays an important role." Rev. Piotr Mazurkiewicz, *Ideologia gender . . .*, p. 4.

[216]Which is why articles on gender have been published in periodicals concerned with the sex. Cf. e.g. Diane Felmlee, Elizabeth Sweet, H. Colleen Sinclair, "Gender Rules: Same- and Cross-Gender Friendships Norms," *Sex Roles* (2012) 66, pp. 518–529. As a side remark, based on their in-depth qualitative studies, the authors come to the rather obvious conclusions that men are generally more reluctant than women to being kissed in greeting by their colleagues, or that most respondents believed that women and men can be friends.

[217]J. Butler, op. cit., p. VIII.

[218]P. Mazurkiewicz, *Ideologia gender . . .*, p. 4.

[219]W. Dynarski, op. cit., p. 284, which, the author explains, is "determined by the presence of a vulva in women and of a scrotum and a penis in men."

[220]W. Dynarski, op. cit., p. 284.

[221]https://en.wikipedia.org/wiki/Gender_identity [27.06.2016].

[222]Cf. https://en.wikipedia.org/wiki/Gender_identity [27.06.2016].

[223]Ebert Foundation experts seem to be right in considering one of the breakthrough points to have been a text published by Volker Zastrow, "Gender – the political gender transformation" in *Frankfurter Allgemeine Zeitung* in 2006. Cf. EszterKováts, MaariPõim [ed.], *Gender as symbolic glue. The position and role of conservative and far right parties in the anti-gender mobilizations in Europe*, Foundation for European Progressive Studies, Friedrich Ebert Stiftung, Budapest 2015, p. 13.

Consequently, the concept was entirely rejected by the circles defending the family and traditional values. As noted by Marguerite A. Peeters, even though "not all that the gender ideology says is false," it would be naïve to try to "separate grain from straw. The term 'gender' is not clearly defined, and this lack of a clear definition is— in her opinion—deliberate and strategic. Once it is rationally used in one place, it can then be deliberately abused elsewhere. All attempts at recovering the term 'gender' and using it in accordance with its definition provided in one document are counter-productive, because others will use it in accordance with a definition provided in another text."[224]

What terms are used by the advocates of constrained anthropology, then, to refer to the phenomena of experiencing sexuality described above? On the one hand, as has already been mentioned, they refer to medical categories (homosexualism, bisexualism, transvestitism, transsexualism). On the other hand, they sometimes adopt a statistical perspective and refer to "sexual minorities." It seems, however, that there is yet another narrative strategy, most interesting from the anthropological point of view. It is illustrated well by the standpoint of the Catholic Church. Its Catechism says that "the number of men and women who have deep-seated homo-sexual tendencies is not negligible. This inclination, which is objectively disordered, constitutes for most of them a trial. They must be accepted with respect, compassion, and sensitivity. Every sign of unjust discrimination in their regard should be avoided. These persons are called to fulfill God's will in their lives and, if they are Christians, to unite to the sacrifice of the Lord's Cross the difficulties they may encounter from their condition."[225] This text talks not about homosexuals or homosexual persons, but about persons who have homosexual tendencies. Such a position emphasizes the possibility that there may be tendencies in man which are "objectively disordered," because contrary to his nature, understood here in the sense of essence, and not just biology. These tendencies do not determine man's sexual identity, which is objective and which is expressed by the category of "sex." In this perspective, the divergence between sexual tendencies and sexual identity is a problem which should be responded to by offering professional help and a specific lifestyle.[226]

Considering the radical divergence between the anthropology expressed in the Catechism and that expressed in gay constructivism, the question arises whether the very likely objection to this interpretation on the part of the advocates of unconstrained anthropology is also reflected in language. In this context, a good example is provided by the *Manifesto* of Rev. Krzysztof Charamsa, a former employee of the Congregation for the Doctrine of the Faith, who publicly revealed his homosexual relationship right before the Synod on the family. The main charge

---

[224]As quoted in: P. Mazurkiewicz, *Ideologia gender. . .*, pp. 4–5.

[225]*Catechism of the Catholic Church*, Libreria Editrice Vaticana 2012, Article 2358.

[226]The Church recommends sexual abstinence, which—let us add—is nothing new in the Catholic tradition where celibacy is related not only to monastic life, but also to priesthood.

Rev. Charamsa brought against the Church was homophobia.[227] He argued that it was expressed in the fact that "in sections 2357-2359 the *Catechism of the Catholic Church* teaches that not only homosexual acts, but homosexual orientation itself is 'objectively disordered.' It also stresses that there is naturally no emotional complementariness in homosexual persons with other human persons they love. And adds that for most of us orientation is a difficult experience which calls for the compassion of our neighbors, but not without avoiding just discrimination."[228] The *Manifesto* says that "[t]he teaching of the Catechism is offensive, not to mention the fact that the very definition of homosexuality is defective, if not altogether false. Also the analysis of the situation of homosexual persons is false,"[229] since their suffering and hardship consists "not in their sexual orientation, but the homophobia of the Church."[230]

The concept of "homophobia" and the way it is used in the *Manifesto* is not a *differentia specifica* of Rev. Charamsa. Quite the opposite, it has been very widespread for years and used analogously in the gay-lesbian discourse on sexuality.[231] It is also used by political institutions. Note, for example, that more than 130 countries celebrate the International Day Against Homophobia in some way.[232] The term "was first used by the journalists Jack Nichols and Lige Clarke in the pornographic magazine *Screw* in 1969. It was popularized by the American psychologist and gay activist George Weinberg, who was initially not sure, in fact, in what sense he wanted to use it."[233] Etymologically, the use of the term homophobia is flawed—it means fear of man, not fear of homosexuals or homosexuality. As pointed out by Marek Drzewiecki, those who coined the term were ignorant of the difference between "the Latin noun *homo*—man and the Greek adjective ὁμόιος—the same (in Geek, man is referred to by the term ανθρωπος). If they wanted to correctly name what they were trying to name, they should have coined the term: homoisophobia."[234]

In psychiatric terms, homophobia is nowadays understood as "uncontrolled fear" related to the thought of homosexuality, "the sense that one must do all they can to

---

[227]Rev. Krzysztof Charamsa, *Manifest księdza Charamsy do Kościoła katolickiego. Po l. "Wyzbycie się homofobii"* ..., http://wiadomosci.gazeta.pl/wiadomosci/1,114871,18960940, manifest-ksiedza-charamsy-do-kosciola-katolickiego-po-1-wyzbycie.html [23.06.2016].

[228]Ibid.

[229]Ibid.

[230]Ibid.

[231]It is even used in the names of organizations committed to striving for social and legal change, such as the Campaign Against Homophobia, which is engaged in "counteracting violence and discrimination on account of sexual orientation and gender identity." http://kph.org.pl/o-kph/misja-i-wizja-dokumenty/ [23.06.2016].

[232]http://dayagainsthomophobia.org/what-is-may-17th/ [23.06.2016].

[233]Andrzej Margasiński, "Homofobia. Co to znaczy?," *Uważam Rze*, http://www.uwazamrze.pl/artykul/935705/homofobia-co-to-znaczy [23.06.2016].

[234]Rev. Marek Dziewicki, *Homofobia istnieje naprawdę!*, http://www.opoka.org.pl/biblioteka/P/PS/md_homofofo.html [23.06.2016].

avoid a different orientation, inability to function normally due to this fear and the awareness that it is irrational coupled with the patient's inability to overcome it on their own."[235] Nevertheless, in public discourse homophobia is understood much more broadly. LGBT circles present it as "unreasonable fear of homosexual persons [. . . or] all non-heteronormative persons."[236] The fact that the Day Against Homophobia is celebrated on May 17 to commemorate the above-mentioned striking of homosexualism off the WHO list of mental disorders shows that homophobia is in fact identified with all, even those rationally formulated, assertions challenging the claims of LGBT communities. Ultimately, even the supporters of talking about homophobia believe that, just like the assertions of twentieth century medicine, arguments against LGBT theses are based on prejudice and fear, representing forms of heteronormative thinking. In this context, it comes as no surprise that the Polish Campaign Against Homophobia is committed not only to helping gays affected by violence, but works first of all "on behalf of lesbian, gay, bisexual and transgender persons (LGBT) and their relatives, through political, social and legal advocacy, as well as creating and implementing educational solutions for various professional groups and building a broad alliance movement."[237] It understands the fight against homophobia as leading to cultural, social and legal change: the removal of heteronormativity which is inherently homophobic. Even though in light of the above comments on the understanding of the "heteronormativity of culture," such a broad understanding of homophobia is not particularly surprising, showing that it is not so much a descriptive or medical term, but an ideological one, it has the characteristics of a mobilizing metaphor and is aimed at taking control of the discourse about human sexuality by excluding voices which represent a different anthropological standpoint.

Summing up the above comments on discourses about sexuality held within the frameworks of morality policy, a comparison may be proposed, analogous to that presented in the previous section, of terms used in morality policy discourses on human sexuality. The central concepts of unconstrained anthropology include the category of gender, which opens the discourse to a redefinition of human sexual identity manifested in concepts such as gays, lesbians, and, more broadly, LGBTIQ. . .; the category of sexual orientation which expresses this in legal terms, and the concept of homophobia as an answer to the claims of constrained anthropology. On the opposite anthropological pole stand the concepts of sex, man and woman, their union called marriage, and the concept of "homo- (bi-) sexual tendency" as an answer to the claims of unconstrained anthropology about homosexuality as a gender identity. The concepts situated on the borderline of the two anthropologies include homosexualism, homosexuality, sexual minority—once used by both sides of the anthropological dispute, but in recent years more and

---

[235]Karolina Skrzek, *Objawy homofobii*, http://www.psychiczne.objawy.net/Objawy+Homofobii [23.06.2016].

[236]Wiktor Dynarski, op. cit., p. 282.

[237]http://kph.org.pl/o-kph/misja-i-wizja-dokumenty/ [23.06.2016].

Table 9.2 Central and borderline concepts in discourses about human sexuality and sexual behaviors

Constrained anthropology		Unconstrained anthropology	
Central	Borderline	Borderline	Central
Sex	Homosexualism	Homosexual person	Gender/gender identity
Homosexual tendency	Sexual minority	Homosexuality	LGBT...
Marriage	Family	Bisexuality	Sexual orientation
		Heteronormativity	Homophobia

Source: own compilation

more clearly attributed to one of the parties. Finally, there are concepts like family and heteronormativity which are being "intercepted" by the two opposite anthropological camps (Table 9.2).

* * *

The above analyses not only show the fundamental significance of the two anthropological approaches analyzed in detail in Part II for primary morality policies, but also reveal that each of these perspectives creates its own conceptual structure within the discourses they propose. In the case of both anthropologies, their respective central concepts form a coherent structure in which one concept implies another. For example, if the point of departure is the existence of two sexes, this founds marriage and family based on marriage as a social institution,[238] and substantiates considering homosexualism (as well as bisexualism, transsexualism, etc.) a psychological tendency which does not determine the identity of the person who experiences it. In other words, sexual tendencies do not determine the sex, a concept which refers only to man and woman. *A contrario*, the unconstrained approach to sexuality expressed in the category of gender develops into the idea of sexual orientation understood essentially as an orientation—not related to a person's sex—of the sexual drive, generating innumerable gender identities. The attitude to "heteronormativity" is expressed in the concept of homophobia. Likewise, in the case of bioethical discourse, if the starting point is reproduction, this opens the way to the introduction of the categories of reproductive rights, sexual health, and abortion into the discourse. The concept of procreation, which by definition means "conceiving and giving birth to offspring,"[239] rules out any abortion postulates since it focuses the attention on the unborn child.

Despite the similarities of semantic structures related to the two anthropologies, there is a great qualitative difference between them. The general characteristic of the concepts of constrained anthropology is their clear-cut meaning—each term has its concrete referent. For example, sex means male or female; marriage: the union of a man and a woman; child: a human being from conception to the age of majority, etc. The general characteristic of concepts typical of unconstrained anthropology is their ambiguity. Reproductive and sexual rights, gender, or homophobia are categories

---

[238]In view of the growing number of "single-parent families" located among borderline concepts.

[239]http://sjp.pwn.pl/sjp/prokreacja;2572612.html [27.06.2016].

which are semantically "half-open." Reference to reproduction may mean access to abortion, or the exact opposite; gender may *de facto* mean the same as sex, but may also "have an unspecified form;"[240] homophobia may be a disease entity, but may also be a tool of political struggle against "heteronormativity," etc. Even medical terms, such as embryo or fetus, are anthropologically "blurred," as their personal status may be questioned. It may be observed that this ambiguousness reveals a deep-seated affiliation of this standpoint with the spirit of late modernity, corresponding to the ideological postulate of Judith Butler. It should be remembered, however, that also in her writings this ambiguousness has a political goal: it is—as has been rightly pointed out by Peeters—an instrument of social and cultural change.[241]

9.4 Primary Morality Policies and EU Competences

Rounding up the introductory comments on morality policy, one cannot ignore one question that is fundamental from the perspective of our further analyses: how do they relate to the jurisdiction of the European Union? There can be no doubt that "ethical and bioethical questions in general were not seen, for a long time, as an issue for the European Community" and "even today, the EU does not have any legislative competence for policy areas in which bioethical questions are central. Rather, the principle of subsidiarity applies; that means that it is the EU Member States that take the fundamental decisions in this area."[242] This premise is often invoked both by European institutions and some (mainly pro-life) groups lobbying at the EU, emphasizing—for example—the fact that "abortion is outside the competence of the EU."[243]

The matter is not as obvious as it might seem, however. Simple institutional observation clearly shows that the Union is aware of operating in an "ethically sensitive" area as regards its policies. In this context, consider for example bodies such as the *Inter Service Group on Ethics and EU Policies*, or the *European Group on Ethics in Science and New Technologies*. Their tasks include coordination of activities in the area of bioethics by services of the European Commission,[244] or

---

[240]W. Dynarski, op. cit., p. 284.

[241]Cf. M.A. Peeters, *The Globalization of the Western Cultural Revolution: Key Concepts, Operational Mechanisms*, Institute for Intercultural Dialogue Dynamics 2012.

[242]Secretariat of the Commission of Bishops' Conferences of the European Union (hereinafter: COMECE), *An Overview Report on Bioethics in the European Union*, COMECE, Brussels 2009, p. 9.

[243]Cf. European Dignity Watch, *The Funding of Abortion Through EU Development Aid. An Analysis of EU's Sexual And Reproductive Health Policy*, Brussels 2012, p. 9.

[244]http://ec.europa.eu/european_group_ethics/platform/index_en.htm [2.11.2010].

preparing ethical opinions for the European Commission concerning policies drafted or implemented by the Union.[245]

The presence of the above groups, and of ethical issues in general, in European policies seems to be a consequence of the expanding scope of EU policies which are now influencing almost all areas of politics, as well as—in the European context stimulated largely by the EU—expansion of the trans-border dimension of international cooperation. Consequently, one can hardly imagine that the EU might not take a stance, as part of its policy of financing scientific studies, on stem cell research accepted in some of its Member States. And when taking such a stance, it makes bioethical decisions, indirectly affecting the bioethical standpoints of all Member States.[246] Similarly, when taking up the issue of the workers' right to freedom of movement, fundamental from the perspective of the common market, it regulates the issue of who has the right to migrate together with them, thus entering the area of the theoretically exclusive competence of the Member States as regards family law, etc.

9.4.1   Bioethical Issues

As noted by Maja Grzymkowska, "paradoxically, the question concerning bioethical standards comes up in surprising areas of competence, related strictly to the market dimension of the Community."[247] Based on studies carried out in this area,[248] four areas of EU competence may be listed which are relevant for bioethical issues. The first one is related to the original purpose of the Communities which were formed to establish and ensure "the functioning of the internal market," i.e. "an area without internal frontiers in which the free movement of goods, persons, services and capital is ensured."[249]

The relevance of the above provision for morality policy became apparent already in the early 1990s in the context of case C-159/90 *The Society for the Protection of Unborn Children Irleand Ltd (SPUC) v. Grogan and others*, considered by the European Court of Justice. In 1989 SPUC called upon Stefan Grogan and others to desist from disseminating in Ireland information about English abortion clinics, and when they did not comply, petitioned "the District Court for an injunction

---

[245]http://ec.europa.eu/european_group_ethics/index_en.htm [2.11.2010].

[246]COMECE, *An Overview* ..., p. 9. For example by the fact that Member States are supposed to co-finance from the common budged (i.e. from their contributions) practices which are not permitted under their legal regulations.

[247]Maja Grzymkowska, *Standardy bioetyczne w prawie europejskim*, Wolter Kluwers, Warszawa 2009, p. 207.

[248]Cf. e.g. Michał Gierycz, *Chrześcijańscy politycy* ...; Id., *Rola polskich posłów do Parlamentu Europejskiego VI kadencji w kształtowaniu jego polityki w obszarze aksjologii praw człowieka*, WDiNP UW, Warszawa 2010; COMECE, *An Overview* ....

[249]*Treaty on the Functioning of the European Union* (hereinafter TFEU) [2008] OJ C115/13, Article 26 §1.

prohibiting assistance in abortion."[250] In compliance with the EEC Treaty, the Court referred to the Court of Justice the question whether "the organized activity or process of carrying out an abortion or the medical termination of pregnancy comes within the definition of 'services' provided for in Article 60 of the Treaty establishing the European Economic Community." In its reply the Court of Justice ruled that "[w]hatever the merits of those arguments on the moral plane, (...) the answer (...) must be that medical termination of pregnancy, performed in accordance with the law of the State in which it is carried out, constitutes a service within the meaning of Article 60 of the Treaty."[251]

As noted by Leszek Bosek, the consequences of this ruling for Community law and the law of the Members States can hardly be overestimated, not only in view of its relevance for the development of the common healthcare market, but also considering its bioethical consequences. He points out that "there can be no doubt that this interpretation stimulates liberalization of legal regulations in the area of biomedicine, facilitates so-called biomedical tourism, and indirectly stimulates the development of biotechnological enterprises."[252] Based on this ruling it may be concluded that services include also other modern medical procedures, such as methods of artificial procreation or genetic testing.[253] If an individual has the right to use and obtain information in his or her country about such services legally offered in another Member States despite the restrictions imposed on the provision of a particular type of services by national legislation, this means that in the area of bioethics "the rules of Community law may in certain circumstances weaken the provisions of the Member States' national law."[254]

The importance of this issue is reflected by the fact that—in accordance with the Treaty—in view of the weight of the four liberties for the integration project, the Union may harmonize national legislation to the extent necessary to achieve it. Article 114 of the Treaty on the Functioning of the European Union (ex Article 95 TEC) says that "[t]he European Parliament and the Council shall, acting in accordance with the ordinary legislative procedure and after consulting the Economic and Social Committee, adopt the measures for the approximation of the provisions laid down by law, regulation or administrative action in Member States which have as their object the establishment and functioning of the internal market."[255] Even though this "shall not apply to fiscal provisions, to those relating to the free movement of persons nor to those relating to the rights and interests of

---

[250]Leszek Bosek, "Aborcja a swoboda przepływu usług," in: M. Safjan [ed.], *Prawo wobec medycyny...*, p. 128.

[251]Ibid., p. 129.

[252]Ibid., p. 131.

[253]M. Grzymkowska, op. cit., p. 244.

[254]The author illustrates this with the example of the development of the artificial procreation market in Europe. Ibid., pp. 244–245.

[255]TFEU, art.114, §1.

employed persons," it may apply, among other matters, to issues "concerning health."[256]

Consequently, a number of legislative solutions relevant for bioethical issues are based on Article 114.[257] Note for example Directive 98/44/EC on the legal protection of biotechnological inventions (Biotech Directive)[258] adopted with a view to facing up to global competition in this area.[259] Aside from various technical matters, the Directive regulated major bioethical issues in a way that arose controversy. Even though it excluded elements of the human body, including tissues, from patentability, it permitted "the patenting of such elements as exist naturally in the human body, as long as they are artificially produced," as well as "the patenting of human genes and their sequences in the sense of the means by which they are produced and their possible industrial applications."[260]

The legally binding force of legislative acts adopted based on Article 114 TFEU should be emphasized. After they are adopted, an EU Member State may introduce other solutions only based on "new scientific evidence relating to the protection of the environment or the working environment on grounds of a problem specific to that Member State arising after the adoption of the harmonisation measure."[261] Considering that in its conclusions based on Article 114, the Commission takes "as a base a high level of protection, taking account in particular of any new development based on scientific facts,"[262] it can hardly be considered realistic that any Member State should introduce its own legislation after the EU has entered a particular area.

An even more explicit basis for the adoption of bioethical regulations, often used in conjunction with Article 114,[263] is Article 168 TFEU concerning the protection of health. Even though it provides that activities of the Union "which shall complement national policies, shall be directed towards improving public health, preventing physical and mental illness and diseases, and obviating sources of danger to physical and mental health,"[264] it also says that "Member States shall, in liaison with the Commission, coordinate among themselves their policies and programmes", and "[t]he Commission may, in close contact with the Member States, take any useful initiative to promote such coordination."[265] This solution provides a broad field

---

[256]Ibid., §3.

[257]COMECE, *An Overview* . . ., p. 11.

[258]Directive 98/44/EC of the European Parliament and of the Council of 6 July 1998 on the legal protection of biotechnological inventions, L 213/13.

[259]M. Grzymkowska, op. cit., p. 215. The author points out further on that "harmonized rules of patent protection were supposed to contribute to the development of European biotechnology. By providing patent protection to biotechnological inventions, they were to result in an inflow of capital to finance research and thus help develop the biotechnological industry." (p. 216).

[260]Ibid., p. 218.

[261]TFEU, Article 114, §5.

[262]TFEU, Article 114, §3.

[263]Cf. COMECE, *An Overview* . . ., p. 13.

[264]TFEU, Article 168, §1.

[265]TFEU, Article 168, §2.

for the Commission's political activity. Moreover, Article 168 says that "[t]he European Parliament and the Council, acting in accordance with the ordinary legislative procedure and after consulting the Economic and Social Committee and the Committee of the Regions," shall adopt, firstly, "incentive measures designed to protect and improve human health;"[266] and secondly, "in order to meet common safety concerns", "measures setting high standards of quality and safety of organs and substances of human origin, blood and blood derivatives; (. . .) measures setting high standards of quality and safety for medicinal products and devices for medical use."[267] While the first case deals with typical measures excluding harmonization of laws, in the second case Article 168 presumes harmonization activities. Moreover, it should be noted that Article 168 also provides for the EU Council's "recommendations for the purposes set out in this Article"[268] at the Commission's request. As pointed out by Katharina Schauer, "a number of legislative and other measures are based on this Article."[269] These include e.g. Regulation 1394/2007 on advanced therapy medicinal products,[270] or Directive 2004/23/EC on setting standards of quality and safety for the donation, procurement, testing, processing, preservation, storage and distribution of human tissues and cells.[271] To exemplify the bioethical relevance of this legislation, it may be noted that "by setting standards applicable to all processes involved in the taking of tissue to be transplanted or used in therapy,"[272] while regulating technical matters the Directive also contains "provisions which set bioethical standards,"[273] such as prohibition on the commercial use of human tissues or organs, or the absolute requirement of the donor's informed consent.[274]

Another area of EU competence in which the Union enters the area of bioethics is that of scientific research policy.[275] Article 179 TFEU says that "[t]he Union shall have the objective of strengthening its scientific and technological bases by achieving a European research area in which researchers, scientific knowledge and technology circulate freely, and encouraging it to become more competitive, including in its industry, while promoting all the research activities deemed necessary by virtue

---

[266]TFEU, Article 168, §5.

[267]TFEU, Article 168, §4.

[268]TFEU, Article 168, §6.

[269]COMECE, *An Overview* . . ., p. 13.

[270]Regulation of the European Parliament and of the Council on advanced therapy medicinal products and amending Directive 2001/83/EC and Regulation (EC) No 726/2004, OJ L 324, 10.12.2007, p. 121.

[271]Directive 2004/23/EC of the European Parliament and of the Council of 31 March 2004 on setting standards of quality and safety for the donation, procurement, testing, processing, preservation, storage and distribution of human tissues and cells, L 102/48, 7.4.2004, pp. 48–58.

[272]M. Grzymkowska, op. cit., p. 213.

[273]Ibid.

[274]Cf. Directive 2004/23/EC aa. 13 and 14.

[275]Cf. M. Gierycz, *Chrześcijańscy politycy w sporze* . . ..

of other chapters of the Treaties."[276] To this end, the Treaty (Articles 182–188) provides for the adoption of a multiannual framework programme to "establish the scientific and technological objectives to be achieved," and to "fix the maximum overall amount and the detailed rules for Union financial participation in the framework programme and the respective shares in each of the activities provided for."[277] As the development of biomedicine "is one of the strict priorities of the Community's policy of scientific research,"[278] the program's provisions were related to the establishment of EU bioethical standards which changed over time, with the Fifth Framework Programme beginning to display a slackening tendency.[279] It should be stressed that—even though it is not legislation which harmonizes national legislation—bioethical standards adopted as part of the scientific policy represent a powerful instrument of political and financial influence. Scientific policy takes up about 6% of the entire budget of the EU. Consequently, "it is not unreasonable to say that the Community may influence the standards adopted in its Member States (at least in some areas) by setting guidelines specifying which projects may rely on funding under Framework Programmes."[280] All of this is taking place, let us add, in a situation when—objectively speaking—there is no "common European standard."[281]

Finally, it should be noted that the Union also has jurisdiction that allows it to tackle issues related to its characteristic approach to human life outside of Europe. Article 208 TFEU provides for the Union's competence to conduct development cooperation policy, complementing and reinforcing the policies of the Member States in this regard. Although the Treaty says that the policy "shall have as its primary objective the reduction and, in the long term, the eradication of poverty,"[282] Article 209 specifies that agreements concluded with third countries based on development cooperation provisions may have priorities broader than merely economic ones—they are to help achieve the objectives referred to in Article 21 of the TEU. The said Article says that "[t]he Union's action on the international scene shall be guided by the principles which have inspired its own creation, development and enlargement, and which it seeks to advance in the wider world: democracy, the rule of law, the universality and indivisibility of human rights and fundamental freedoms, respect for human dignity, the principles of equality and solidarity, and respect for the principles of the United Nations Charter and international law,"[283] stressing that "[t]he Union shall define and pursue common policies and actions" in order to: "a) safeguard its values, fundamental interests, security, independence and integrity; b)

[276]TFEU, Article 179, §1.

[277]TFEU, Article 182.

[278]M. Grzymowska, op. cit., p. 225.

[279]Ibid., pp. 226–227.

[280]M. Grzymkowska, op. cit., p. 229.

[281]Ibid., p. 226.

[282]TFEU, Article 208, §1.

[283]TUE, Article 21, §1.

consolidate and support democracy, the rule of law, human rights and the principles of international law (. . .)."[284]

This way, as part of its development policy, the Union is granted the right to promote its values and its own view of human rights. This is important in view of the fact that—as pointed out by Katharina Schauer—"it is primarily by the notion of 'human rights' that the EU's policies can pose bioethical problems, in particular when it comes to the issue of so-called 'reproductive health and rights' and abortion."[285] The relevance of this is global because together with its Member States who conduct their own policies in this regard, the EU is the biggest provider of developmental aid in the world. It is worth adding that—as in the case of the above-discussed provisions—"[t]he Commission may take any useful initiative to promote the coordination"[286] of developmental cooperation between Member States. The role of EU competences is emphasized by the fact that Member States are bound by the Treaty to "contribute if necessary to the implementation of Union aid programmes."[287]

The case is similar with the Union's humanitarian policy. Even though Article 214 says that its "operations shall be intended to provide ad hoc assistance and relief and protection for people in third countries who are victims of natural or man-made disasters, in order to meet the humanitarian needs resulting from these different situations,"[288] it also provides that "the Union's operations in the field of humanitarian aid shall be conducted within the framework of the principles and objectives of the external action of the Union,"[289] specified in article 21 TEU. Considering the ambiguous wording of the Union's fundamental rights,[290] the question about how human rights are to be understood remains open. Likewise, considering the catalogue of the Union's protected characteristics, the Declaration found in the same Article that "humanitarian aid operations shall be conducted in compliance with the principles of international law and with the principles of impartiality, neutrality and non-discrimination"[291] provides plenty of room for axiological disputes around specific financial and political solutions.

The legally required application of developmental and humanitarian policy to the promotion of values and human rights embraced by the Union shows it is necessary to consider the political initiatives of EU institutions, which are largely not provided for in the Treaty but which—as will be discussed further on—influence the activities conducted within its terms of reference. The literature indicates that particularly the

---

[284]TUE, Article 21, §2.

[285]COMECE, *An Overview . . .*, p. 13.

[286]TFEU, Article 210, §2.

[287]TFEU, Article 210, §1.

[288]TFEU, Article 214, §1.

[289]Ibid.

[290]Cf. M. Gierycz, 'Anthropologicalshift? EU human rights' anthropology in view of life and family', Prudentia Iuris, s No. 89 (2020).

[291]TFEU, Article 214, §2.

European Parliament, in view of its political identity,[292] is a "privileged locus of the bioethical debate within the institutional frameworks of the European Union."[293] In fact, however, it is not only the Parliament. In its document *Human Rights and Democracy: EU Strategic Framework and EU Action Plan* the Council says that "the entry into legal force of the EU Charter of Fundamental Rights, and the prospect of the EU's acceptance of the jurisdiction of the European Court of Human Rights through its accession to the European Convention on Human Rights, underline the EU's commitment to human rights in all spheres. Within their own frontiers, the EU and its Member States are committed to be exemplary in ensuring respect for human rights. Outside their frontiers, promoting and speaking out on human rights and democracy is a joint responsibility of the EU and its Member States."[294] This position, expressing the consensus of the Member States, shows that the EU as a whole considers itself to be a guarantor and promoter of human rights, even though it is not a human rights organization and its jurisdiction "does not include the authority to establish legal standards in the area of human rights."[295] Consequently, political involvement in bioethical issues resulting from the Union's commitment to human rights should be expected either "alongside" its competences provided for in the Treaty, or even outside of its competences.[296]

9.4.2   The Issues of Sexuality and Marriage

It would seem that the issues of sexuality, relations between the sexes, or the valuation of sexual behaviors are way beyond the scope of EU competences, particularly seeing that politics concerning marriage and family are recognized as belonging to the sole jurisdiction of the Member States, and that the EU does not have any competence in the area of public morals. And yet, like in the case of bioethics, it may exert its influence in this area based on jurisdiction in entirely different areas. The basic competences which allow the Union to take up issues belonging to this area of morality policy are those related to counteracting discrimination and equality provisions.

---

[292]Cf. Michal Gierycz, "Unijne spory o wartości podstawowe. Źródła, kluczowe problemy i "polski głos" w Parlamencie Europejskim," in: Piotr Burgoński, Sławomir Sowiński [ed.], *Od akcesji do prezydencji. Kościół Katolicki w Polsce i Unia Europejska*, Adam Marszałek, Toruń 2011, pp. 134–139.

[293]M. Grzymkowska, op. cit., p. 59.

[294]Council of the European Union, *Human Rights and Democracy: EU Strategic Framework and EU Action Plan*, 11855/12 https://data.consilium.europa.eu/doc/document/ST-11855-2012-INIT/en/pdf [05.09.2020].

[295]Maja Grzymkowska, op. cit., p. 207.

[296]Suffice to say that the European Parliament already adopted its first resolution on *in vitro* and *in vivo* on March 16, 1989, when these competences remained entirely beyond the Communities' scope.

It is interesting to note that the antidiscrimination policy actually exceeded its boundaries outlined by the Treaty right from the very beginning. Initially, in accordance with the Treaty, it referred mainly to discrimination on grounds of nationality. Under the then Article 12 TEC, now existing almost in identical wording as Article 18 TFEU, "[w]ithin the scope of application of the Treaties, and without prejudice to any special provisions contained therein, any discrimination on grounds of nationality shall be prohibited. The European Parliament and the Council, acting in accordance with the ordinary legislative procedure, may adopt rules designed to prohibit such discrimination." Nevertheless, almost from the very beginning, the Court of Justice "has treated the prohibition of all discrimination on grounds of nationality as a general principle of non-discrimination."[297] Consequently, it has applied an "expanded interpretation,"[298] not only "by applying a broad interpretation of the premise concerning the 'scope of the application of the Treaty,' but also by applying the prohibition of any discrimination on grounds of nationality to ever broader groups of individuals."[299] For example, in the mid-1980s it ruled that "the right of a migrant worker to obtain permission for his unmarried companion to reside with him falls within the scope of Community law,"[300] thus strongly encroaching upon the competences of the States in the area we are interested in.

The other area which has "forever" been subject to the logic of non-discrimination is the area of men's and women's pay. Like in the case of discrimination on grounds of nationality, as a result of numerous acts of secondary legislation adopted on the basis of both Article 119 TEU and Article 235 TEU, as well as the activity of the Court of Justice, this prohibition has gradually been extended to include the entire sphere of employment, and even that of social security.[301] Consequently, in the course of the Amsterdam reform, Article 157 TFEU was already considerably expanded so that the Parliament and the Council were provided with the ability to take "measures to ensure the application of the principle of equal opportunities and equal treatment of men and women in matters of employment and occupation, including the principle of equal pay for equal work or work of equal value,"[302] and Article 8 TFEU in its present wording says that "[i]n all its activities, the Union shall aim to eliminate inequalities, and to promote equality, between men and women."

Based on the above regulations, the EU has adopted various regulations touching upon problems of morality policy, like the Directive of 24 July 1986 on the implementation of the principle of equal treatment for men and women in

---

[297]Justyna Maliszewska-Nienartowicz, "Geneza i rozwój prawa antydyskryminacyjnego Unii Europejskiej," in: Anna Zawidzka-Łojek, Aleksandra Szczerba-Zawada, *Prawo antydyskryminacyjne Unii Europejskiej*, Instytut Wydawniczy EuroPrawo, Warszawa 2015, p. 17.

[298]Ibid., p. 19.

[299]Ibid., p. 29.

[300]Ibid., p. 19.

[301]Ibid., p. 32.

[302]TFEU Article 157 §3.

occupational social security schemes, or of 15 December 1997 on the burden of proof in cases of discrimination based on sex, which were replaced in 2006 by Directive 2006/54/EC of 5 July 2006 on the implementation of the principle of equal opportunities and equal treatment of men and women in matters of employment and occupation. Their relevance for morality policy is illustrated for example by the fact that—as will be discussed in more detail further on—"CJEU ruled that a case of discrimination on grounds of sex includes discrimination on grounds of transsexuality."[303] Thus, the term "sex," as has been aptly put by one author, was used "in a more abstract meaning."[304] Moreover, the above-mentioned Articles of the TFEU serve as the basis for the Union's program documents. In this context, consider for example the "Gender Equality Strategy" which is a "comprehensive commitment of the Commission to act for gender equality in all areas of politics, including equal economic independence of men and women; gender roles; legislation and instruments of government, implementing the general idea of gender mainstreaming expressed in Article 8 TFEU."[305]

Together with the Amsterdam Treaty, "a special norm concerning the competences was established in Article 13 §1 TEC (currently Article 19 §1 TFEU) which expanded the scope of potential anti-discrimination regulations."[306] From then on it was possible, providing the Council expressed their unanimous consent, to "adopt antidiscrimination laws prohibiting discrimination not only on grounds of sex, but also race, ethnicity, religion, beliefs, disability, age, or sexual orientation. It may thus be said that the problem of equal treatment has become a matter of priority in the Community's employment regulations."[307] Currently, the EU's obligation to counteract discrimination also results from Article 10 TFEU which says that "[i]n defining and implementing its policies and activities, the Union shall aim to combat discrimination based on sex, racial or ethnic origin, religion or belief, disability, age or sexual orientation."

Based on the antidiscrimination norm expanded in Amsterdam, two Directives were already adopted in 2000: 2000/43/EC of 29 June 2000 implementing the principle of equal treatment between persons irrespective of racial or ethnic origin, and 2000/78/EC of 27 November 2000 establishing a general framework for equal treatment in employment and occupation, which "considerably expanded the subjective scope of discrimination criteria."[308] From the point of view of morality

---

[303]Krzysztof Ślebzak, "Antydyskryminacyjne prawo Unii Europejskiej w dziedzinie zatrudnienia w orzecznictwie TSUE – zakres i podstawowe pojęcia," *Praca i Zabezpieczenie Społeczne* No. 9/2013, p. 7.

[304]Anna Pudło, "Niedyskryminacja osób transseksualnych w świetle prawa europejskiego," *Roczniki Administracji i Prawa*, rok XIV, p. 81.

[305]http://ec.europa.eu/justice/gender-equality/index_pl.htm [04.08.2016].

[306]Krzysztof Ślebzak, op. cit., p. 3.

[307]Ibid.

[308]Ibid. The author also mentions Council Directive 2004/113/EC of 13 December 2004 implementing the principle of equal treatment between men and women in the access to and supply of goods and services.

policy, of particularly great importance was the adoption of the latter directive which listed sexual orientation as one of the protected characteristics; since Amsterdam, it has become a fully-fledged category in European jurisprudence.

Aside from the strictly legal impact, the introduction of new protected characteristics considerably expanded the political influence of the EU in the area of morality policy. In this context, note for example the information campaigns conducted by the EU (e.g. For Diversity—Against Discrimination; European Year of Equal Opportunities for All) aimed at "raising the awareness of antidiscrimination provisions and the scope of the Union's responsibility."[309] As pointed out by Piotr Burgoński, such campaigns and programs operate as "a mechanism called social learning, i.e. contribute to a greater acceptance of pro-equality and anti-discrimination norms in the society," which is ultimately aimed at preparing social ground for the introduction of further EU norms."[310] In this context, it is worth noting especially the Horizontal Antidiscrimination Directive proposed in 2008.[311]

The provisions of Article 10 TFEU combined, as will be discussed in more detail in the next chapter, with the proclamation of a broad catalogue of characteristics protected by the principle of nondiscrimination in the EU Charter of Fundamental Rights, result in the problem of morality policy as regards gender and sexual behavior playing an important role in foreign policy which—pursuant to Article 21 TEU—is oriented on the protection and promotion of EU values. In the case of the EU, this is not only a slogan. It is no coincidence that in the theory of international relations, the Union is referred to as a "civil," "soft power,"[312] or normative power.[313] These assertions show that despite its rather modest possibilities of exerting influence "in the 'hard' external policy areas [. . . the EU] exercises a significant influence on the world stage"[314] by playing various international roles, including in particular the economic and cultural-civilizational one.[315] They are related to each other: the cultural role is enabled by the fact that the Union is "an economic tycoon."[316] This is reflected in the area of morality policy. The Union's power of influence is demonstrated for example by the Declaration of the 21st

---

[309]Piotr Burgoński, "Europeizacja polskiej polityki równościowej i antydyskryminacyjnej," *Przegląd Europejski* Nr 2, 2012, p. 153.

[310]Ibid.

[311]See more in Chap. 11.

[312]Cf. e.g. Dariusz Milczarek, "Rola międzynarodowa Unii Europejskiej jako 'mocarstwa niewojskowego'," *Studia Europejskie* 2003, No. 1, pp. 33–54.

[313]Ian Manners, "Normative Power Europe: A Contradiction In Terms?," *Journal of Common Market Studies* 2002, No. 2 (40), pp. 235–258. Concerning the adequacy of this theoretical view of the EU, cf. Anna Skolimowska [ed.], *Normatywna potęga Unii Europejskiej w obliczu umiędzynarodowionych konfliktów wewnętrznych*, Elipsa, Warszawa 2015.

[314]Neill Nugent, *The Government and Politics of the European Union*, Palgrave, London 2017, p. 395.

[315]Cf. Ryszard Zięba, *UE jako aktor stosunków międzynarodowych*, Scholar, Warszawa 2003, p. 267

[316]Ibid., p. 267.

Session of the African, Caribbean and Pacific Group of States Parliamentary Assembly on the peaceful co-existence of religions and the importance given to the phenomenon of homosexuality in the ACP-EU Partnership of September 2010.[317] The ACP Assembly urgently appealed to the European Union to "refrain from any attempts to impose its values which are not freely shared in the framework of the ACP-EU Partnership."[318] The above unilateral declaration demonstrates the scale of the cultural pressure, not accepted in this case, exerted by the EU on the ACP.

Even though the equality and antidiscrimination policy is a particularly important tool of the influence exerted by the EU in the area of morality policy we are interested in, it is not the only instrument at its disposal. Other tools include provisions concerning the free movement of workers and persons, and the provisions on enhanced cooperation.

Article 21 TFEU states that "every citizen of the Union shall have the right to move and reside freely within the territory of the Member States, subject to the limitations and conditions laid down in the Treaties and by the measures adopted to give them effect. If action by the Union should prove necessary to attain this objective and the Treaties have not provided the necessary powers, the European Parliament and the Council, acting in accordance with the ordinary legislative procedure, may adopt provisions with a view to facilitating the exercise of the rights referred to in paragraph 1."[319] Based on this provision, on April 29, 2004 the European Parliament and the Council adopted Directive 2004/38/EC on the right of citizens of the Union and their family members to move and reside freely within the territory of the Member States. The Directive defines the term "family member" as including the spouse and "the partner with whom the Union citizen has contracted a registered partnership, on the basis of the legislation of a Member State, if the legislation of the host Member State treats registered partnerships as equivalent to marriage and in accordance with the conditions laid down in the relevant legislation of the host Member State,"[320] which in view of the various conceptions of marriage and partners in the Member States generates significant political and legally-axiomatic tensions in relation to the principle of mutual recognition.[321]

---

[317]*Declaration of the 21st Session of the ACP Parliamentary Assembly on the peaceful co-existence of religions and the importance given to the phenomenon of homosexuality in the ACP-EU Partnership*, Brussels, 28. September 2010, ref. 2/3/15 (Vol.1) 10.

[318]Ibid.

[319]TFEU, Article 21 §§1 and 2.

[320]Directive 2004/38/EC of the European Parliament and of the Council of 29 April 2004 on the right of citizens of the Union and their family members to move and reside freely within the territory of the Member States amending Regulation (EEC) No 1612/68 and repealing Directives 64/221/EEC, 68/360/EEC, 72/194/EEC, 73/148/EEC, 75/34/EEC, 75/35/EEC, 90/364/EEC, 90/365/EEC and 93/96/EEC, Article 2.

[321]For example, in 2009 the European Parliament called on "Member States to fully implement the rights granted under Article 2 and Article 3 of Directive 2004/38/EC not only to different sex spouses, but also to the registered partner, member of the household and the partner, including same-sex couples recognized by a Member State, irrespective of nationality and without prejudice to their non-recognition in civil law by another Member State, on the basis of the principles of

Article 20 TEU says that "Member States which wish to establish enhanced cooperation between themselves within the framework of the Union's non-exclusive competences may make use of its institutions and exercise those competences by applying the relevant provisions of the Treaties."[322] From the perspective of these reflections, it is worth noting that when the mechanism was first applied, it was to a matter of morality policy, namely regulations concerning the law applicable to divorce cases.[323] It enables "international couples (. . .) to know in advance which law will apply to their divorce or separation."[324]

* * *

The review of the competences of the European Union presented in the above section, while not exhausting the problem, negates the assumption that the issues of primary morality policies we are interested in are beyond the EU's reach and influence. On the contrary, in spite of its limitations, the Union may and does play an important role in a key area of the anthropological disputes of late modernity.

---

mutual recognition, equality, non-discrimination, dignity, and private and family life." European Parliament Resolution of April 2, 2009 on the application of Directive 2004/38/EC on the right of citizens of the Union and their family members to move and reside freely within the territory of the Member States (2008/2184(INI)), Article 2.

[322]TEU Article 20 §1. It ends as follows: "subject to the limits and in accordance with the detailed arrangements laid down in this Article and in Articles 326 to 334 of the Treaty on the Functioning of the European Union."

[323]Council Regulation (EU) No 1259/2010 of 20 December 2010 implementing enhanced cooperation in the area of separation the law applicable to divorce and legal, L 343/10.

[324]https://www.consilium.europa.eu/ueDocs/cms_Data/docs/pressData/en/jha/118100.pdf [21.05.2020].

Chapter 10
Anthropological Pillars of European Politics

When looking for the most axiologically relevant part of any constitution laying down *expressis verbis* the "ethical foundations" of the political community we should look at the issue of human rights.[1] In the European Union, they are called fundamental rights. This term, until recently still evoking major doctrinal disputes,[2] is considered in contemporary literature equivalent to human rights.[3] This assumption has been made here as the input premise.

The issue of fundamental rights which provide the basis of the EU's axiological system most explicitly reflects the anthropological anchoring of the ethos of the

---

[1]Cf. Zbigniew Stawrowski, *Wokół idei wspólnoty*, OMP, Kraków 2012, p. 179.

[2]There has been a major debate in the doctrine around the term referring to fundamental rights (Fr. *droit fundamentaux*, Germ. *Grundrechts*) and their substance. In Poland, researchers have interchangeably used the terms "basic rights" (cf. e.g. C. Mik, K. Gałka, *Prawa podstawowe w prawie i praktyce Unii Europejskiej*, Dom Organizatora, Toruń 2009), "fundamental rights" (cf. Maciej Dybowski, *Prawa fundamentalne w orzecznictwie ETS*, Beck, Warszawa 2007), and "essential rights." This last term has been advocated by Jarosław Sozański, pointing out that it reflected most fully the difference between the rights referred to by the EU and the concept of fundamental rights and human rights. Essential rights would in this approach be narrower in scope than human rights (not including e.g. the right to complain to the ECtHR), and at the same time broader in that they include "many economic and social categories" (J. Sozański, *Prawa człowieka*, p. 38). This approach is disputable, however. The right to complain is more an element of the law of human rights than the human rights themselves, while economic and social rights belong to subsequent generations of human rights. A possible distinction—supported by the interpretation of fundamental rights in the history of the Court's rulings—could be the fact that the respective subjects of fundamental rights and human rights are understood differently (fundamental rights are also vested in legal persons, while human rights only in natural persons).

[3]For example, as pointed out by Cezary Mik, "fundamental rights are essentially identical with human rights." Id., *Europejskie Prawo Wspólnotowe. Zagadnienia teorii i praktyki*, vol. 1., Warszawa 2000, p. 440. Agnieszka Florczak is of the same opinion, saying that „there is no substantive justification for a different understanding" of human rights and fundamental rights (Agnieszka Florczak, *Ewolucja ochrony praw człowieka w systemie prawa wspólnotowego*, in: id. [ed.]., *Ochrona Praw Podstawowych w Unii Europejskiej. Wybrane zagadnienia*, WAiP, Warszawa 2009, p. 14).

© Springer Nature Switzerland AG 2021
M. Gierycz, *European Dispute over the Concept of Man*, Contributions to Political Science, https://doi.org/10.1007/978-3-030-61520-8_10

European, or any other, political community. For if these rights are considered today to be "the universally adopted standards of liberty, limits to the power of the state and the performances (. . .) owed to every individual in his or her relations with the state or any other power which may use coercion,"[4] i.e. the basis of a just order, it is because "they have as their basis something that is independent from the will of individuals, societies, or international agreements":[5] the good of every and the whole of man (hence the various generations of rights, referring to various areas necessary to man's development), which are "an integral element of any law."[6] Thus, the ultimate reason for "the particular substance [of the rights] is man (. . .). Consequently, the ultimate point of reference for any positive legal order protecting or respecting human rights are not the rights themselves, but the human person."[7] This means that human rights by their very nature express and reveal the fundamental, pre-analytic or axiomatic, so to speak, anthropological premises which are the anchorage of the entire axiological and constitutive order of a state or—as in the case of the European Union—a supra-national structure. In other words, they are the anthropological pillars of the entire legal and political system of the EU, or—to use systems categories—the framework conditions of system conversion; the normative form of the inside of the system.

When verifying the thesis about the dispute between two anthropologies in the European Union, we should first see how the EU conceives of values, particularly of human rights. Theoretically speaking, the Union, declaring its commitment to the respect for fundamental rights, yet not being a human rights organization, "not so much defines but respects the already recognized standards of human rights."[8] Nevertheless, by adopting the Charter of Fundamental Right and its Explanatory Notes, the EU has explicitly stated how it understands these standards. Taking into account the debate, growing in intensity since the end of the twentieth century, around the interpretation of human rights in the Western hemisphere, it may be expected that in the EU catalogue, formulated in an entirely different social and political context than was the case with almost all major international constitutional acts and human rights declarations/conventions, there will be a tension between the traditional understanding of values and human rights and the new approach, reinterpreting the traditional categories, present both in the contemporary

---

[4]Wiktor Osiatyński, *Prawa człowieka i ich granice,* Znak, Kraków 2011, p. 23.
[5]Marek Piechowiak, *Filozofia praw człowieka*, KUL, Lublin 1999, p. 49.
[6]Ibid., p. 78.
[7]Ibid.
[8]M. Grzymkowska, op. cit., p. 208.

constitutional law, the case law of European courts, and some political documents concerning human rights.[9]

The relevance of changes, if any, in the understanding or founding of human rights consists in that a policy based on the unconstrained anthropology does not need to undermine the language of human rights; it is enough to change their meaning or the philosophy behind them. If this is the case, the theory of human rights is not so much a record of ethical boundaries related to human nature, but, "a theory of will, a will presupposed to nothing but itself. In its politicized formulation, it has been the most enduring and dangerous alternative to a natural law that is based in this ontological reality of what man is."[10]

In view of the above findings, the hypothesis to be verified in this chapter is the claim that there are two coexisting anthropological approaches present in EU legislation based on the language of human rights: that of a constrained and that of an unconstrained anthropology. Our analyses will be aimed both at verifying this thesis and at identifying the consequences of this coexistence discernible at the level of primary law.

In accordance with the theoretical assumptions described in Part I, analyses have been carried out using the comparative method. Our reflections will begin with a look at the approach to values and human rights that is typical in international and constitutional law, with particular emphasis on problems relevant to morality policy. The reason is that the foundations for this concept have been laid by Europeans drawing heavily on the cultural achievements of the Old Continent. To this end, we will reveal the anthropological layer of the Universal Declaration of Human Rights, and the European Convention on Human Rights which refers to it. The anthropological assumptions of the EU will then be examined, paying special attention to the analysis of solutions concerning fundamental rights. Once they are shown against the background of solutions adopted in international law, the differences, if any, in the Union's approach to human rights may be identified. Like in Part II, the analysis will be based on exegetic and hermeneutic methods and will thus focus on seeking cohesion between expressions used in legal documents, becoming a synthesis of how they think about man, and a comparative analysis of various anthropological perspectives present in legal regulations. Its application should help us identify the anthropological framework conditions of the EU's political system.

---

[9]Cf. e.g. K. Remin [ed.], *ZasadyYogakarty. Zasadystosowaniamiędzynarodowegoprawaprawczło wieka w stosunku do orientacjiseksualnejoraztożsamości płciowej*, KampaniaprzeciwHomofobii, Warszawa 2009.

[10]James V. Schall and Ken Masugi, "An Easter Conversation with James V. Schall, SJ," Claremont Institute, as quoted in: R. R. Reilly, op. cit., p.32.

10.1 The Anthropology of Human Rights

Even if some say that "human rights are the history of mankind,"[11] their history is much shorter.[12] Being ideologically related to the Christian idea of man as *imago Dei*, redeemed by God incarnate, having its antecedences in the school of natural law, the constitutions proclaimed by American states, the Declaration of the Rights of Man and of the Citizen,[13] finally in humanitarian and minority law, had not been articulated until the twentieth century in the context of communism and Nazism,[14] subsequently becoming the guiding idea of the United Nations.[15] The unprecedented crimes perpetrated by Germany and the Soviet Union contributed to the introduction of human rights, referring to natural law, into international law, and their dizzying career in international and constitutional law in the second half of the twentieth century.

In this section, the main point of reference for an anthropological analysis of human rights will be the Universal Declaration of Human Rights (UDHR) adopted in 1948 by the General Assembly of the United Nations, and the 1950 European Convention on Human Rights (ECHR)[16] which referred to it. Given that the goal is to show the anthropology of human rights characteristic of Europe, this solution does not seem to require any special substantiation. Let us only say that the Declaration is an unquestioned foundation for the entire system of human rights, exerting a major influence on both the European constitutional law and the formation

---

[11]Laura Koba, Robert Zydel, "Dzieje, charakter i treść praw człowieka," in: Laura Koba, Wiesław Wacławczyk, *Prawa człowieka. Wybrane zagadnienia i problemy*, Oficyna Wolters Kluwers, Warszawa 2009, p. 13.

[12]As noted by Alastair Davidson, even "declaring universal human rights did not lead to their automatic implementation. Indeed, the history of 1789-1815 was rather a history of their practical failure." A. Davidson, *The Immutable Laws of Mankind. The Struggle for Universal Human Rights*, Springer, Heidelberg, New York, London 2012, p. 234.

[13]This should not be taken literally, however. Note for example that "as they were understood in the Enlightenment, they were limited to a small group of owners and excluded women, children, non-owners and the entire non-white population of the world." (W. Osiatyński, op. cit., p. 31). For the publication in 1791 of *The Declaration of the Rights of Woman* which said, among other things, that "Women are born free and remain equal to man in rights," Olympe de Gouges was convicted for treason and executed during the Revolution. (cf. L. Koba et al., "Dzieje charakter i treść praw człowieka . . .," p. 23).

[14]Probably the first person to have proposed the idea of international human rights was André Mandelstam who published the *Declaration of the International Rights of Man* at the International Law Institute in November 1928.

[15]Cf. United Nations Declaration signed on August 1, 1942.

[16]A review of regulations concerning the scope of human rights law can be found in: Mariusz Jabłoński, Sylwia Jarosz-Żukowska, *Prawa człowieka i systemy ich ochrony. Zarys wykładu*, WUWr, Wrocław 2010. I am aware, of course, of the extended system of human right protection in Europe which could provide a point of reference.

of the international system of protecting human rights.[17] The European Convention on Human Rights, on the other hand, was intended as a special, European instrument established in order to ensure effective enforcement of the rights laid down in the Declaration.[18] The two documents remain in a special relationship: the goal of the Convention was practical, while the Declaration was intended as the "fundamental ideological document on human rights."[19] Rene Cassin said—not without some emphasis, but not without good reason either—that the Declaration was to become (and in fact has become to a large extent) a sort of Ten Commandments of the great human society "that must serve as a guide for the politics of the state."[20] It is in the latter that we find a much broader exposition of the philosophy,[21] and especially of the anthropology of the adopted rights which the European Convention no longer develops, but—in view of its practical goal—which it implements, elaborating on the rights it proclaims so as to ensure their effective legal protection.[22]

When presenting the anthropology of human rights inherent to the UDHR and the ECHR, references will be made to other documents, including the European constitutional traditions, to show the philosophical and legal convergence of the UDHR perspective and the approach to these problems that is characteristic of the constitutional tradition of Europe. It should be added that in view of the abundant literature on this subject, the goal of this section is not to perform a novel, source-based analysis, but rather to offer a synthetic presentation, based on available and reliable sources, of the anthropological logic characteristic of the law of human rights, which will contribute to achieving the proper research goal of this study.

Consequently, the analysis performed here of the international and the EU approach to values and human rights follows the methodology adopted by Marek Piechowiak, focusing on the axiological and anthropological foundations of law. By

---

[17]As noted by Mariusz Jabłoński and Sylwia Jarosz-Żukowska, "this document has become a particular kind of model to be followed—without having any legal force, it outlined the scope of constitutional regulations implemented by democratic states one by one. Subsequent acts of the UN in the form of international agreements (. . .) created a developed system providing protection for individual rights." Ibid., p. 173.

[18]*Preamble to the Convention for the Protection of Human Rights and Fundamental Freedoms*, Rome, 4 June 1950. European governments created the Convention in order to "take the first steps for the collective enforcement of certain of the Rights stated in the Universal Declaration."

[19]Sebastian Sykuna, "Powszechna Deklaracja Praw Człowieka," in: Michał Balcerzak, Sebastian Sykuna [ed.], *Leksykon ochrony praw człowieka*, C.H. Beck, Warszawa 2010, p. 332.

[20]René Cassin, *Speech on 7 July 1947*, as quoted in: A. Davidson, op. cit., p. 461.

[21]Which is particularly important for our analysis and for the very idea of rights whose "legal concept (. . .) is secondary to the philosophical concept." M. Jabłoński, S. Jarosz-Żukowska, op. cit., p. 20.

[22]As pointed out by H. Lauterpacht, thanks to the Convention the individual radically changed its status from being the object of the law of international empathy to being the subject of international law. (cf. M. Nowicki, op. cit., p. 19). Marek Nowicki adds that the Convention is "an original enterprise compared to the classical concepts of international law, mostly in view of the supranational control of the acts and activities of state authorities which may be exercised also on the initiative of the wronged parties themselves." Ibid.

"foundations" he understands solutions fundamental "in the sense that they are the substantiation for other—generally speaking—more detailed axiological and normative settlements," and include also "the problems of relationships between values and fundamental rights, and the ontological status of values and rights."[23] This way, an analysis of axiology and rights reveals the fundamental anthropological pre-assumptions of the normative system concerned.

10.1.1 Dignity: A Pillar of the Anthropology of Human Rights

Authors of the Universal Declaration of Human Rights, which provided the foundation for the European Convention, were aware that the basis for the proper understanding of rights was the adopted anthropology.[24] It is not a coincidence that the first Article of the Declaration says that "[a]ll human beings are born free and equal in dignity and rights. They are endowed with reason and conscience and should act towards one another in a spirit of brotherhood."[25]

The adoption of a solution which results in that Article 1 of the Declaration of Rights does not formulate any rights whatsoever is a rather peculiar measure. This paradox was explained by one of the authors of the Declaration, René Cassin, who pointed out that a reference to these values in the first Article was essential because the war had shown what happens if they are flouted.[26] These values were not presented as self-contained properties, but as properties anchored in the human being. In other words, authors of the Declaration found in necessary, in order to secure human rights against distortion, particularly considering the experiences of German Nazism which emphatically demonstrated the possible "iniquity of law," to guarantee respect for an explicitly worded pre-judgment about who man is. Thus, anthropology stands here directly and openly at the source of the order of values and human rights.

The declaration shows the human person as a social being endowed with dignity, reason and conscience, equal in dignity to other people and endowed with freedom. Before we discuss in more detail the "anthropological data" of the Declaration, we should note the general significance of this solution. It reflects the "recognition that being a man, i.e. a certain fact, is the basis of rights, irrespective of positive law or any other (...) normative structures. (...) The relation to the good of man as a whole is an integral element of any law and may not be disregarded when determining the

---

[23]M. Piechowiak, *Aksjologiczne podstawy...*, p. 6.

[24]J. Maritain suggested at UNESCO that human dignity may prove to be a foundation that is acceptable to every culture. Cf. W. Osiatyński, op. cit., p. 294.

[25]*Universal Declaration of Human Rights*, Article 1.

[26]M. Piechowiak, *Filozofia praw...*, pp. 77–78.

contents of any formulated postulates."[27] This perspective explains the essence of human rights discourse noted by Freeman "which distinguishes it from other moral discourses (. . .) [namely] that if you have a right to X, and you do not get X, then this is not only wrong, but it is also a wrong to you."[28] Consequently, human rights—defending basic human goods—must start with a pre-analytic belief about who man is. It is this belief that stands at the bottom of the entire, intricate structure of positive law guaranteeing human rights.

As a key anthropological category, the UDHR refers to the inherent dignity of man whose respect, along with respect for the rights it entails, is presented as "the foundation of freedom, justice, and peace in the world." This approach is paradigmatic. The International Covenants proclaimed nearly 20 years later explicitly say that human rights "derive from the inherent dignity of the human person."[29] Dignity as the fundamental legal principle—as noted by Józef Krukowski—would be referred to in most other essential acts of international law and in the constitutions of individual states.[30] Consequently, it is legitimate to assume that statements about the inherent dignity of man as the source of rights and their universal, inherent, inalienable and equal nature are the fundamental elements of the universally accepted concept of human rights.

It is worth considering why the category of dignity has been made central and what it in fact means. While it has no explicit legal definition,[31] its meaning seems self-evident. To perceive it, it is enough to consider the not infrequent objection that saying someone has certain rights because he is a man is "[n]ot a satisfactory formulation. It is not clear why one has any rights simply because one is a human being. It is particularly unclear why one has the rights listed in the Universal Declaration."[32] The category of dignity is a philosophical and legal construct which provides answers to such questions. It determines, to use Spaemann's language, the difference between a someone and a something, while at the same time warranting "that the normative system remains open to being complemented and is always in touch with the concrete good of individual people."[33]

The category of dignity shows that "human animality—as emphasized by Robert Spaemann—never was mere animality, but the medium of personal realization. The

---

[27]Ibid., p. 78. Consequently, the ultimate point of reference for a positive legal order protecting or respecting human rights are not the rights themselves, but the human person.

[28]Michael Freeman, *Human Rights: An Interdisciplinary Approach*, Polity 2011, p. 67. Naturally, the question still remains whether it is indeed a special type of moral discourse; it seems, actually, that this is what the very essence of this discourse consists in.

[29]Preamble to the *International Covenant on Civil and Political Rights*, https://www.ohchr.org/en/professionalinterest/pages/ccpr.aspx [22.05.2020].

[30]J. Krukowski, "Godność człowieka podstawą konstytucyjnego katalogu praw i wolności jednostki," in: L. Wiśniewski (ed.), *Podstawowe prawa jednostki i ich sądowa ochrona*, Wydawnictwo Sejmowe, Warszawa 1997, p. 44.

[31]M. Piechowiak, *Filozofia praw. . .*, p. 79.

[32]M. Freeman, op. cit., p. 67.

[33]M. Piechowiak, *Filozofia praw. . .*, p. 88.

nearer and more distant kinship relations in which human beings stand to one another are of personal, and so of ethical, importance." Consequently, "humanity, unlike animality, is more than an abstract concept that identifies a category; it is the name of a concrete community of persons to which one belongs not on the basis of certain precise properties objectively verified, but by a genealogical connection with the human family."[34]

In the above context, the definitional ambiguity of dignity proves to be an asset and a necessity. As pointed out by Piechowiak: "If a specifically existing reality cannot be captured adequately and with the use of unambiguous categories, as is the case with the cognitive understanding of the human being in the aspect of his good, then the postulate to build normative concepts and systems based solely on concepts which explicitly capture the contents of being that are relevant for the normative order must either result in a failure to include elements which are essential for ensuring the comprehensive development of a person, or—if an attempt is made at removing the ambiguity—in adopting as the basis of law a certain abstract 'model' of man, which in turn represents a major threat to a person's freedom."[35] At the same time, "in view of the troubles involved in formulating a positive definition, negative definitions are sometimes proposed, specifying what the violation of dignity consists in. It is asserted that such a violation is any situation in which man becomes solely the object of someone else's actions, and his role is reduced to a purely instrumental one."[36] This clearly shows that "the function of this category consists first of all not in referring to conceptual structures or theoretical constructs, but in pointing to a certain area of reality that determines the contents of postulates concerning both particular actions and positive law (. . .). In order to point to elements of that reality, it is not necessary to be able to offer a concept which encompasses all contents relevant for understanding the right; it is enough e.g. to say that the point is what decides about the difference between man and other beings, and what is the basis for the special treatment of man."[37] In this sense, the central meaning of dignity will ultimately ground the central relevance of anthropology to human rights, linking the law to a concrete human reality.

In light of these comments it comes as no surprise that the key characteristic of dignity is its inherency. It essentially describes the inseparability of man and personhood in international law, showing that personal dignity is an inseparable, "intrinsic property of man."[38] Consequently, dignity is also universal (in the sense of the unity of human nature), inalienable and non-acquirable (since it is inherent to

[34]R. Speamann, *Persons: The Difference Between 'Someone' and 'Something'*, Oxford University Press 2006, p. 240.

[35]M. Piechowiak, *Filozofia praw. . .*, p. 88.

[36]W. Janyga, *Przestępstwo obrazy uczuć religijnych w polskim prawie karnym w świetle współczesnego pojmowania wolności sumienia i wyznania*, Wydawnictwo Sejmowe, Warszawa 2010, p. 97.

[37]M. Piechowiak, *Filozofia praw. . .*, p. 87.

[38]Ibid., p. 80.

every man and to man alone), substantiating the inherency, inalienability and non-acquirability of rights.

Note that the fact dignity is inherent does not mean it is static. On the contrary, in international law dignity is dynamic: it is invoked both as the "direct standard of conduct" and as "the state towards which man's development is oriented," and which may be described as "the fullness of personal development."[39] In anthropological terms, this means that dignity is always inherent to man and must be respected, and that it is never fully realized and may be developed towards fulfillment. Reference to dignity thus reveals the concept of man as a dynamic being, whose essence encompasses ethical development, growth in humanity, and who is, at the same time, always endowed with dignity which is inviolable and which makes it imperative to ensure that he can exercise his fundamental rights.

10.1.1.1   The Right to Life as a (Fundamental) Dignity Right

Owing to the nature of dignity which encompasses the entire human being, and due to the dynamic nature of this category, it is relevant not only for the substance but also for the systematics or structure of human rights. As pointed out by Wiktor Osiatyński, "it is the relation to dignity that endows the classification of rights with a deeper meaning, so that each category of rights serves dignity in a different way,"[40] and that justifies the non-severability of "all human rights for this simple reason that the elimination of any of them endangers human dignity."[41] Thus, reference to dignity represents not only the *raison d'être* of human rights as a phenomenon related to the exceptional status of man compared to other beings, but also of their systematic perception.

Even though dignity lies at the source of every human right, it is also possible to distinguish those rights which are particularly strongly or directly related to the idea of dignity. In literature, they are sometimes called fundamental or basic rights,[42] "those that are necessary to other rights."[43] They become clearly visible when we try to understand the special status of the right to life, located "at the head of the

---

[39]Ibid., p.81.

[40]W. Osiatyński, op. cit., p. 295. He believes that "civil liberties protect individual autonomy and prohibit the state from interfering with the area of the individual's freedom. (...) Political rights give the individual an understanding of communal matters and enable him to participate in the process of decision-making. (...) Economic and social rights provide the individual with minimum economic security, (...) pave the way for dignity and more convenient conditions for individual development, made possible by civil liberties." Ibid., pp. 295–298.

[41]Ibid., p. 298.

[42]Cf. e.g. Roman Kuźniar, *Prawa człowieka. Prawo, instytucje, stosunki międzynarodowe*, Scholar, Warszawa 2004.

[43]M. Freeman, op. cit., p. 83. This idea is a proposal to solve a situation of conflict between human rights. It says that "to secure [basic rights] other rights may be violated if necessary, but basic rights may not be violated to secure non-basic rights." Ibid, p. 84.

catalogue of the rights of an individual—both in international legal acts and in many national constitutions."[44] If—as is emphasized in literature—the right to life is a special right,[45] this is not only for "pragmatic" reasons, namely because "its observance is the first and basic condition for the existence of any other rights and liberties,"[46] but also because it expresses one of the main values of democratic societies:[47] the belief that man has such a dignity, that his life is a special, irreplaceable and non-exchangeable value. Rejection of the logic of human dignity necessarily undermines the point of protecting the life of every human being.[48]

In the European context, only the paradigm of dignity makes it possible to understand why there is Article 2 ECHR at all which states that "everyone's right to life shall be protected by law," and why it translates into a very broad range of the state's duties. As noted by Marek Nowicki based on ECtHR case law which specifies the minimum scope of the protection of this right across Europe, this article formulates a great positive duty to "take appropriate steps to protect life."[49] This includes, without limitation the duty to protect individuals against acts of violence from other persons or themselves (in the case of suicide), to take preventive operational measures to protect the life of a person whose life is in danger, to ensure access to information about risks to life (e.g. in industrial occupations) or to carry out a court investigation in every case of death, etc.[50] Consequently, if a complaint is brought before the Court, "due to the fundamental character of the right protected in Article 2, it is sufficient to demonstrate—in the case of an objection that the authorities have failed to comply with the duty to protect the right to life—that they knew or should have known about an actual and direct risk and did not take action within their terms of reference such as could reasonably be expected."[51] The life of a human being as the only being in the world which is endowed with a special, inherent dignity, requires absolute and comprehensive protection.

Since the scope of protection afforded human life is currently the object of a fundamental dispute, it is worth adding how it should be viewed in light of the human rights law. Since at the time the Declaration was drafted, the issue of abortion was not yet a socially relevant topic, we do not find in it an explicit answer as to the moment from which life is protected. There can be no doubt, however, as to the negative answer, namely that in the Declaration "the caesura specifying the

---

[44]Adam Szymaniak, "Podstawowe prawa jednostki i mechanizmy ich ochrony," in: L. Koba, W. Wacławczyk, *Prawa człowieka...*, p. 172.

[45]Cf. e.g. M. Nowicki, op. cit., p. 155.

[46]Ibid.

[47]Ibid.

[48]Thus for example according to Peter Singer "to give preference to the life of a being simply because that being is a member of our species would put us in a position uncomfortably similar to that of racists who give preference to those who are members of their race." P. Singer, op. cit., p. 75.

[49]Note that it exceeds the minimum standard provided for in the UN system (Covenants), which essentially formulates negative obligations. Cf. Article Szymaniak, op. cit., pp. 172–173.

[50]M. Nowicki, op. cit., pp. 156–176.

[51]Ibid., p. 158.

beginning of human life is certainly not the fact of birth,"[52] and thus it does not rule out the protection of life in the prenatal phase. To apprehend the approach characteristic of the human rights tradition, we must therefore go beyond the strictly legal context and capture its spirit, as Zbigniew Stawrowski puts it.[53] Given the context in which the Declaration was drafted and considering its preamble which, formulated by René Cassin, was a combination of the 1789 declaration and the lesson of the Holocaust,[54] it is clear that its authors intended to safeguard man's dignity in all of its dimensions. It appears that in the early 1950s, the issue of human life in the prenatal phase was simply quite clear. Let us note that also the ECHR drafted in 1950 does not specifically refer to this issue, and the Declaration of the Rights of the Child of 1959 considers it obvious that the child "needs special safeguards and care, including appropriate legal protection, before as well as after birth."[55] This logic seems to be confirmed by the American Convention on Human Rights, also referring to the UDHR, but drafted later, in the early 1970s, which states explicitly that the right to life "shall be protected by law and, in general, from the moment of conception."[56] Also the context of the 1980s discussion on the execution of the death penalty at the UN General Assembly, where "the postulate that the death penalty not be executed on pregnant women, for an obvious reason—the good of the unborn child,"[57] and the Convention on the Rights of the Child adopted in the early 1990s, citing the above statement from the Declaration of the Rights of the Child, clearly show that "even though acts of international law do not explicitly identify man with every human being from the moment it comes into existence, still, given the fundamental solutions concerning dignity, hardly any other possibilities could be accepted without being inconsistent."[58]

Apart from the right to life, there are also other fundamental rights that have a special relation to dignity. Both in the Universal Declaration of Human Rights and the European Convention they are formulated in the Articles following the one concerning the right to life. They include first of all the prohibition of torture, inhuman or degrading treatment,[59] the right to liberty and security,[60] and the

---

[52]M. Piechowiak, *Filozofia praw…*, p. 84. See also the explanation on pp. 82–83.

[53]Cf. Z. Stawrowski, "Aksjologia i duch Konstytucji III Rzeczypospolitej," *Nowa Konfederacja* No 37/2014, http://www.nowakonfederacja.pl/stawrowski-aksjologia-i-duch-konstytucji-iii-rzeczypospolitej/ [12.09.2014].

[54]Cf. A. Davidson, op. cit., p. 458.

[55]*United Nations Convention on the Rights of the Child, Preamble*, 1989, https://www.ohchr.org/en/professionalinterest/pages/crc.aspx [02.06.2020].

[56]*American Convention on Human Rights*, Article 4 § 1, https://www.cidh.oas.org/basicos/english/basic3.american%20convention.htm [02.06.2020].

[57]A. Szymaniak, op. cit., p. 174.

[58]M. Piechowiak, *Filozofia praw…*, p. 84.

[59]Cf. Articles 4 and 5 UDHR, and Article 3 ECHR.

[60]Cf. Article 3 UDHR and Article 5 ECHR.

prohibition of slavery and forced labor.[61] In its rulings, as the key criterion in determining whether a case involves inhuman or degrading treatment, the European Court of Human Rights invokes the question whether an activity "undermines (...) human dignity."[62] It has stated that it is undermined by definition by a situation when "attributes of the right of ownership, or some of them, are applied"[63] to an individual, i.e. when a human being is treated as a thing. In a fundamental way this contradicts the intuition about dignity which says that, in accordance with the well-known Kantian formula, man must never be treated only as a means, but always as an end.

10.1.1.2 Dignity and Other Anthropological "Data"

Pursuant to Article 1 UDHR, dignity entails equality and freedom. It is not a coincidence that a major portion of rights provided for in the Declaration and subsequently guaranteed in the constitutional systems of particular countries or the European Convention are rights which warrant, on the one hand, various kinds and dimensions of freedom: from personal liberty[64] to freedom of thought, conscience, confession,[65] and opinion,[66] to freedom of assembly;[67] on the other hand they espouse the principles of equal treatment: from a general prohibition of discrimination,[68] to equality before law (as the right to legal personality,[69] the right to a fair trial,[70] the right to an effective remedy,[71] or the prohibition of punishment without law[72]), to civil, social, and cultural rights.[73]

What is the significance of their relation to dignity? In the context of equality, it should be noted that since "the purpose of protecting the rights is to enable the personal development of a concrete person who has his own goals etc., (...) it is

---

[61]The right to personal freedom is sometimes included in fundamental rights as well. Cf. Adam Szymaniak, *Podstawoweprawa...*, p. 172.

[62]Cf. Chember vs. Russia of 2 July 2008, Application No. 7188/03. In addition, the Court distinguished between degrading and inhuman treatment—more on this subject, cf. M. Nowicki, *WokółKonwencji*, pp. 175–204.

[63]Ibid., p. 205.

[64]Cf. Article 5 ECHR.

[65]Cf. Article 9 ECHR.

[66]Cf. Article 10 ECHR.

[67]Cf. Article 11 ECHR.

[68]Cf. Article 3 and 7 UDHR, Article 14 ECHR.

[69]Cf. Article 6 UDHR.

[70]Cf. Article 6 ECHR.

[71]Cf. Article 13 ECHR.

[72]Cf. Article 7 ECHR.

[73]Cf. Articles 21-26 UDHR.

clear that not for everyone the same thing will be a basic good."[74] Equality in light of the anthropology of human rights does not always mean identical treatment. The anthropology of human rights takes into account the diversity of man's choices and possibilities. It thus contends that man's dignity requires equal (identical) treatment only when the subjects have to the same degree a feature that is relevant in a given case. In other situations, i.e. when one of the subjects does not have a particular feature (or has it to a different degree), the requirement of dignity is satisfied by unequal (different) treatment. Consequently, discrimination is not differentiation itself, but an action taken in view of a particular feature which endangers the individual's dignity.[75]

Likewise, dignity is most relevant for the approach to freedom. The perspective of dignity does not permit the claim that freedom is a good for the sake of which other goods should be sacrificed. On the contrary, it is dignity that forms the basis of freedom. Consequently, the idea of human rights rooted in dignity limits an individual's freedom to act. The purpose of human rights, as pointed out by Marek Piechowiak, is not to maximize freedom, but to provide protection against the arbitrary actions of others.[76] In the anthropology expressed in the human rights law, "man is treated as a being whose decisions are referred to a reality that is independent from him, and whose recognition and understanding is a necessary condition for action that is consistent with who man is. When treating the protection of freedom as a protection against arbitrariness, the substance of freedom cannot be determined without a knowledge of reality, and thus without reason and conscience."[77]

In light of the above comments, it becomes self-evident that while freedom and equality are the formal criteria of just action which takes into account human dignity, reason, conscience and brotherhood refer to the substantive criteria. These elements "emphasize that man is not only a free, but also a rational and moral being. They recognize that the human person is not pure freedom, but has other features as well which are the basis of human rights."[78] The logic of human rights is thus founded on the recognition that human reason is capable of discovering the fundamental truth about man, and therefore that it is first and foremost a theoretical reason that transcends, as Wojciech Chudy puts it, social truth and moves towards the truth

---

[74]M. Piechowiak, *Filozofia praw...*, p. 90.

[75]Ibid., p. 91 The Universal Declaration says that "[e]veryone is entitled to all the rights and freedoms set forth in this Declaration, without distinction of any kind, such as race, colour, sex, language, religion, political or other opinion, national or social origin, property, birth or other status."

[76]M. Piechowiak, *Filozofia praw...*, p. 94.

[77]Ibid., p. 95.

[78]Ibid.

about society,[79] capable of discovering the normative boundaries of possible choices.[80]

Ultimately, the belief about the epistemic capabilities of man, also in terms of objective moral evaluation (by the conscience),[81] determines the possibility of codifying the rights and substantiates e.g. protection of the freedom of thought and opinion, as well as their possible limitations. It also demonstrates why human rights include ones other than those referring to quality or freedom. A special place among the latter belongs—in addition to the above-mentioned rights grounding the minimum requirements of dignity—to social rights related to the belief about the social nature of man, expressed in the idea of brotherhood.

As noted by Wiktor Osiatyński, the Universal Declaration of Human Rights (UDHR) reveals a "strong community trait."[82] It is expressed right in Article 1, in the call to action "in a spirit of brotherhood," the guaranteed rights applicable to groups and associations (as the right to assembly (Article 20) or the freedom of speech (Article 19)), as well the essential individual values, such as religious freedom (whose point is essentially related to community rights), or civil rights; finally, the assertion about duties to the community (Article 29). In accordance with the Universal Declaration, community is evidently "a necessary complement—i.e. a complementary formation—enabling personal development which in its chief meaning represents the common good"[83] and the goal of human rights.

10.1.2 Marriage in the Logic of Human Rights

If the UDHR understands man as a social being and not an individual, the foundation of this conviction is a moral pre-judgement about the significance of marriage and

---

[79]Cf. Wojciech Chudy, "Prawo naturalne albo zasada przemocy – alternatywa rozłączna metafizyki społecznej," *Civitas* No. 6, p. 35.

[80]Consequently, the logic of human rights, referring to the tradition of natural law, establishes on the one hand an objective criterion for the evaluation of the acts of public authorities, a check on its arbitrariness. On the other hand, it defines the possible conditions of international intervention in the event such basic rights are violated.

[81]Some interesting comments on how the conscience is understood in the UDHR can be found in M. Piechowiak, *Filozofia praw...*, pp. 96–98.

[82]W. Osiatyński, op. cit., p. 264. As pointed out by Joseph Raz, "[m]any rights were advocated and fought for in the name of individual freedom. But this was done against a social background which secured collective goods without which those individual rights would not have served their avowed purpose." Id., *The Morality of Freedom*, Clarendon Press, Oxford, 1988, p. 251. It may be added that it was the recognition of collective rights that was one of the sources of the support provided to the UDHR by non-European countries.

[83]M. A. Krąpiec, op. cit., pp. 57–58. As the author emphasizes in a poetics resembling that of Thomas Aquinas: "This does not mean, however, that the human person is only an embodied existential relationship. He is in itself an existing substance saturated with relations to other persons as a community which provides a 'niche' for man's personal development."

family for personal development. In the structure of the UDHR, its meaning is reflected in the fact that the series of Articles concerning social matters opens with Article 16 on marriage and family. It reads as follows:

1. Men and women of full age, without any limitation due to race, nationality or religion, have the right to marry and to found a family. They are entitled to equal rights as to marriage, during marriage and at its dissolution.
2. Marriage shall be entered into only with the free and full consent of the intending spouses.
3. The family is the natural and fundamental group unit of society and is entitled to protection by society and the State.[84]

In light of Article 16, reflected in the European Convention on Human Rights and many other documents of international law and constitutional acts, it is obvious that the entire concept of the person, directly expressed in Article 1 of the UDHR, as a social being (as well as the idea of community rights) is anchored in the recognition of the fundamental role of monogamous marriage and a family built on its basis as the primary community. It is only from the perspective of family that the meaning of brotherhood referred to in Article 1 becomes clear. It reflects the conviction that by his very nature man is not an island, to use Merton's famous phrase. The concept of brotherhood makes no sense outside the category of family, i.e. a community which one does not choose but of which one is naturally a member.

The issue of marriage and the family that is built on it, treated as a fundamental unit of society, is strictly related to the idea of human dignity. On the one hand, it is an essential precondition for personal development. Suffice it to say that contemporary sociology lists more than a dozen functions of the family: material and economic, caregiving and protective, procreative, sexual, legalizing and controlling, socializing, stratifying, cultural, religious, recreational and social, emotional and expressive.[85] Their number and nature point to the fundamental significance of marriage and family for the integral human development. On the other hand, it should be noted that in the light of human rights marriage and family are understood as a natural phase of man's life.[86] Being a natural and fundamental unit of society,

---

[84] A similar logic is found in the ECHR which confirms in Article 12 the inherent right to marriage by stipulating that "[m]en and women of marriageable age have the right to marry and to found a family, according to the national laws governing the exercise of this right," related to the guarantees of respect for family life in Article 8:

"Article 8. Right to respect for private and family life

1. Everyone has the right to respect for his private and family life, his home and his correspondence. 2. There shall be no interference by a public authority with the exercise of this right except such as is in accordance with the law and is necessary in a democratic society in the interests of national security, public safety or the economic well-being of the country, for the prevention of disorder or crime, for the protection of health or morals, or for the protection of the rights and freedoms of others."

[85] Cf. Zbigniew Tyszka, "Struktura i funkcja rodziny oraz świadomość rodzinna," in: id., Adam Wachowiak, *Podstawowe pojęcia i zagadnienia socjologii rodziny*, Poznań 1997.

[86] Cf. Janusz Balicki, "Rodzina," in: B. Szlachta, *Słownik społeczny*..., p. 1119.

family is not merely "an option," but a form of life that is intrinsic to human nature, fundamental, and therefore guaranteed by human rights. This applies both to the rights of children[87] and the right of adults who, having come "of age (. . .) have the right to marry."[88]

It is worth adding that it is not by accident that the Declaration presents monogamous marriage as the basis of family. Pursuant to the UDHR and the ECHR, the complementariness of the sexes represents an objective precondition for marriage. In the view of man that the two documents reflect, sex is not constructed, but inherent and anthropologically significant. Consequently, the natural sexual attraction to a person of the opposite sex (of man to woman and of woman to man) is not, in accordance with the Declaration, an act of preference or orientation, but a fact that has its moral (i.e. related to the objective good of man) and social significance which requires positive legal protection. Consequently, the good protected in the Universal Declaration of Human Rights and in the European Convention on Human Rights is not sexuality itself, or the possibility to express or realize it,[89] but the marriage between a man and a woman. The logic behind this solution is based on a conviction about the inseparability of the spiritual and the corporeal dimension of man, which clearly expresses an integral, or personalist, view of humanity.[90] Marriage, precisely as a spiritual and corporeal union, is seen here as a good that is necessary for the development in humanity of both the man and the woman, as well as their offspring (family). It is protected as an essential element guaranteeing living conditions corresponding to man's dignity. Society, as a natural community, appears only as "an extension" of marriage and family which is considered the fundamental unit of society. Consequently, the harmony of the sexes is seen here as the foundation of harmony in society.

10.1.3   Anthropology of Human Rights and Anthropological Models

The anthropological position reflected in human rights law clearly refers to constrained anthropology. Firstly, it is an approach based on defining boundaries which are not limitative, but constitutive in nature. Even the very concept of human nature invoked by the category of "inherent dignity and rights" is symptomatic. The

---

[87]Note that in Polish family law "divorce is not permitted if it would be detrimental to the welfare of the minor children of both spouses" (Article 56 of the Family and Guardianship Code).

[88]Article 16 UDHR.

[89]Hence prostitution, for example, is not a human right.

[90]As noted by Cardinal Karol Wojtyła, in this vision man "signifies not only his being ('an individual substance of a rational nature') but also his quality. In fact, only when considered as a quality can this being become a gift: it can objectively offer a gift and at the same time be accepted as a gift and be experienced as such." Id., *The Anthropology. . .*, p. 739.

entire edifice of human rights is based on the conviction that such a nature exists, and consequently that it is possible to know the good that is proper to this nature and that must be protected in order to guarantee the possibility of man's development. Consequently, understanding rights as an effect of the recognition of what belongs to the good of man is related to the need to define boundaries: the space of what is proper to man and his nature, and that which is not proper to his nature and offends his dignity. In its classical form, the logic of human rights thus defines Spaemann's normality: the space of freedom that must not be transgressed (even if possible) if humanity is not to be forsaken. It delineates the moral (related to good) boundaries of man's sovereignty, and consequently also of the sovereignty (arbitrariness) of government. As has been demonstrated, the particular boundaries of this sovereignty consist in respect for human life, and respect for marriage and family. The first boundary guarantees the possibility to exercise any rights, and thus becomes the basic precondition for and requirement of respect for human dignity; the second makes it possible for society to emerge, and thus becomes the basic requirement of respect for the social nature of man. This clearly reflects the *inclinationes naturales* identified by Thomas Aquinas, which naturally leads to a question about the status of the third of his "first principles." We will come back to this question later on.

Secondly, this anthropological standpoint avoids a reductive logic. By noting and acknowledging the significance of sex, and consequently of marriage and family for the identity of human being, the UDHR adopts a holistic logic. It views the human being in all of its complexity, embracing a personal perspective which goes beyond the logic of individualism. By placing the right to marriage and family at the foundation of social rights, it shows that it is through marriage, based on a covenant between the spouses and shaped by the relations which result from it as they give birth to or adopt children (establish a family), that man moves from looking at himself as an "I" towards an interpersonal relationship between "you" and "I,"[91] without forsaking his special, personal dignity. The reference to family as a natural and fundamental community is a guarantee protecting the logic of human rights from the logic of atomism, both as individualism and as collectivism. For even though it requires perceiving man as a being whose *telos* entails entering an interpersonal relationship, a person (endowed with inherent dignity) is always at the centre of its attention as an end rather than a means.[92]

---

[91]In other words, towards an "us" which does not, however, nullify the fundamental meaning of the "I."

[92]Pontifical Council for Justice and Peace, *Compendium. . .*, p. 145.

Thirdly, it should be noted that this anthropological standpoint is a strong one.[93] Its grounding of rights and values is sometimes called metaphysical.[94] In this perspective, considering "something to be right, just, good, etc. [is] generally independent from the will of the subjects, the contents of agreements, or the changing conditions (including cultural ones), but is a matter of knowledge, first of all knowledge of man and that which contributes to his development."[95] The issue of what constitutes a value is not a matter of opinion, but of recognizing the objective requirements of human dignity. This approach enables an integral view of values and rights. Such a stance is present, in fact, in today's human rights narration. The Vienna Declaration of 1991 emphasizes, for example, that "the international community must treat human rights globally in a fair and equal manner."[96] Moreover, its founding on the imperative of dignity understood as a strong anthropological position makes it possible, as noted by Zbigniew Stawrowski, "to develop a reasonable form of political order where individuals—even those who are not able or willing to act morally—are subject to external regulations that are morally just, which is to say: that respect their dignity."[97] It thus helps ensure, in the created institutions and legal regulations (including human rights law), conditions which are objectively conducive to personal development, thus curbing the potential arbitrariness of the government. Consequently, an adequate anthropology which expresses pre-analytic, certain convictions (pre-judgements, to use Burke's term), proves to be a foundation on which the axiological edifice of human rights is erected.

Fourthly, the logic of boundaries and strong anthropology result in man being understood as a being who has his own *telos*. Even the very identification of reason and conscience as the basic attributes of humanity, which then substantiate the protection of the freedom of conscience, opinion, or thought, shows that man is understood here as a being driven by the search for truth, including moral truth. A broader look may be taken, however: all human rights secure the area of goals/goods that are proper to man and that—if properly used—contribute to his growth in humanity. In other words, human rights turn out to be a normative reflection of the conviction that man is oriented towards values. And consequently also able to arrange them in a proper hierarchy. As pointed out by Roman Ingarden, "without directly and intuitively relating to values (...) man is profoundly miserable. He is happy when he can realize values and give in to their special appeal. And this is

---

[93] As noted by Bogdan Szlachta, such foundation of human rights "is very strong: it consists in the concept of a transcendental dimension of the human person who aims at fulfilling his existence and who enjoys the freedom to do so guaranteed by legally protected rights, rather than merely an obligation of other persons who enter into a social contract and grant mutual claims in the event the rights of the other party are violated." Bogdan Szlachta, *Wokół katolickiej myśli politycznej*, WAM, Kraków 2008, p. 209.

[94] Cf. Rev. P. Mazurkiewicz, *Wspólne wartości. . .*

[95] Marek Piechowiak, *Karta Praw Podstawowych UE a tradycyjne wartości*, in: M. Gierycz, J. Grosfeld [ed.], op. cit., p. 200.

[96] *Vienna Declaration*, p. I.5.

[97] Z. Stawrowski, *Wokół idei. . .*, p. 166.

not—at least not primarily—about relative values related to his strictly vital needs (e.g. food) or pleasures (e.g. good health or bliss), but about values which are absolute in their immanence (...) in short: moral values and aesthetic values."[98] Man's happiness, his sense of fulfillment is not the effect of unconstrained self-creation, but of choosing those goods which correspond to his inner structure, which are objectively good for him.

The most troublesome element in this, so far consistent, edifice of constrained logic seems to be the reference to Transcendence. Authors of the Universal Declaration of Human Rights aimed to avoid making any metaphysical statements. As argued by Jacques Maritain at the UNESCO, an agreement was possible "not on the basis of common speculative ideas, but on common practical ideas, not on the affirmation of one and the same conception of the world, of man, and of knowledge, but upon the affirmation of a single body of beliefs for guidance in action."[99] Consequently, the presented anthropological concept, particularly its foundation: the inherent dignity of man, is accepted as an axiom, a self-evident moral obviousness. As such, it represents a basic value protected in the international legal order, from which other rights are derived.[100] Such an approach may be called secular. It is also present in some constitutional traditions. The Spanish Constitution, for example, says in Article 10 that "[t]he dignity of the person, the inviolable rights which are inherent, the free development of the personality, the respect for the law and for the rights of others are the foundation of political order and social peace."[101]

In the constitutions of twentieth century Europe we also discover a different meta-axiology, however. The 1997 Constitution of the Republic of Poland is a modern example of this approach. A specific characteristic of its preamble is the conviction that political order is anchored in a community of values, based on universal values of truth, goodness and beauty which is entailed by belief in God, even though it is not shared by all citizens.[102] It also emphasizes the key significance of human dignity as the supreme principle of social and political order. A special meaning of man's inherent dignity is intrinsically related both to belief in God and to the placement of truth and good in the centre of the axiological landscape: truth about man's condition and protection of his good in order to create conditions for personal development as are worthy of man in the created institutions and legislation. In this way, truth, good, and human dignity rooted in God constitute the ethical foundations of state order, and thus the basic criteria of justice. In view of their grounding, both values and

---

[98]Ibid., p. 23.

[99]As quoted in W. Osiatyński, op. cit., p. 274.

[100]Ibid., p. 59.

[101]It is worth adding, however, that while the secular model of grounding values in the Constitutions of Spain or France may legitimately be seen as an expression of a worldview (anti-religious) manifesto, the solution adopted in the UN system results from the intention to present human rights as a supra-cultural experience.

[102]And—consequently—derive these values from other sources. Nevertheless, they are precisely those values which come with belief in God. Their content can therefore be objectively specified.

human rights, like in the German or Irish constitutions,[103] are rooted simultaneously in God and in man's inherent dignity. Consequently, as pointed out by Benedict XVI in his address to the Bundestag, the criteria of law are framed here both "in the awareness of man's responsibility before God and in the acknowledgment of the inviolable dignity of every single human person."[104]

The fact that reference to God does not cancel out reference to man's inherent dignity leads, in the first step, to the observation that the standpoint expressed in the UDHR, and consequently in the entire system of human rights protection under international law, is at least potentially open to theologization,[105] and so cannot be a position that is contrary to it. The case here seems to be more than just one of non-contradiction, however. As discussed in Part II, the logic of man's inherent personal dignity cannot be ultimately substantiated without referring to the conviction that man has been created by a personal God. In other words, in order to uphold the constrained, dignity-based anthropology, it is necessary to allow—at least hypothetically—for the existence of Transcendence, and thus for man as a created being. It is not a coincidence, as Wojciech Janyga points out in his monograph, that religious freedom is the first of all freedoms in the philosophy of human rights.[106] Consequently, the logic of inherent dignity appears to be one of the forms, so to say, of a pro-theistic agnosticism, which agrees to invert the Enlightenment postulate and organize the political sphere "as if God existed" (*velutisi Deus daretur*). This is also clearly understood by the opponents of the logic of dignity who publicly endorse fighting the idea of the sanctity of life, being a reflection of the idea of dignity, as an ethical relict of the Christian cultural formation.[107] Nevertheless, it is this secularized relict of a profoundly religious conviction about human dignity, *implicitly* referring to Transcendence, that is the foundation of the anthropology of human rights.[108]

---

[103]The Preamble to the Irish Constitution says: "In the Name of the Most Holy Trinity, from Whom is all authority and to Whom, as our final end, all actions both of men and States must be referred. We, the people of Éire; Humbly acknowledging all our obligations to our Divine Lord, Jesus Christ, Who sustained our fathers through centuries of trial; Gratefully remembering their heroic and unremitting struggle to regain the rightful independence of our Nation; And seeking to promote the common good, with due observance of Prudence, Justice and Charity, so that the dignity and freedom of the individual may be assured, true social order attained, the unity of our country restored, and concord established with other nations, Do hereby adopt, enact, and give to ourselves this Constitution." The religious sources of values are much more strongly present here than in the Constitution of Poland or Germany. Nevertheless, the basic values of political community are also here related to assuring the "dignity and freedom of the individual."

[104]Benedict XVI, "The Listening Heart". . . .

[105]Thus, "the ultimate explanation of moral norms and evaluations concerning social life in light of the truths of faith." Aniela Dylus, "Nauka solidarnego rozwoju," in: Paweł Kozacki OP, *Przewodnik po encyklikach*, W drodze, Poznań 2003, p. 137.

[106]Cf. W. Janyga, *Przestępstwo obrazy uczuć religijnych*. . ., pp. 86–92.

[107]Cf. P. Singer, op. cit., p. 94.

[108]A theological substantiation of human rights could easily be provided. On the grounds of Christianity, as the basic cultural substratum for the idea of human dignity, it would suffice to cite the idea of *imago Dei* and that of Incarnation and Redemption of man by Christ as probably the

10.2 Anthropology of Fundamental Rights in the European Union

From the perspective of European integration, the issue of values and human rights is a relatively recent one. While the Schuman Declaration, which marked the beginning of the integration process, extensively adapted in the Preamble to the Treaty establishing the first European community, i.e. the European Coal and Steel Community (ECSC), shows that moral values—such as solidarity/brotherhood, peace, or reconciliation—were presented as the fundamental reason for integration, in the second half of the 1950s such references were considerably toned down. This was related, first of all, to the failure of the two large-scale integration initiatives: the European Defence Community and the European Political Community. Their characteristic "axiological reserve" also had a positive source. Already in 1950, "the Council of Europe adopted the Convention for the Protection of Human Rights and Fundamental Freedoms which introduced an effective system of protecting and enforcing first generation rights."[109] It appeared that this issue did not need to be taken care of in the framework of the newly-created European economic structures.

---

most powerful substantiation of man's uniqueness compared to other beings imaginable. Philosophical substantiations could be sought as well—with slightly more ambivalent effects—for example in the philosophy of Kant and the theory of dignity developed on its basis. Indeed, both of these leads can be found in the Declaration. Nevertheless, the Declaration, as well as the entire tradition of international law, deliberately avoids pointing to any explicit religious or philosophical sources of the conviction about human dignity. Already in 1947, Jacques Maritain, "as a French delegate to the International UNESCO Conference in Mexico City, said that (...) it seemed impossible to reach a consensus on the substantiation of human rights. He suggested, however, that the dignity of the human person may prove to be a foundation of human rights that can be accepted by every culture." (W. Osiatyński, op. cit., p. 296, note 6). He made it clear, however, that "human dignity means nothing if it does not necessarily imply that a person naturally has the right to be respected, and, as a subject of the law, has rights" (ibid., p. 294). Thus, the point of reference here is an axiomatic conviction about human dignity, resulting from the natural recognition of this fact by human reason in all cultures of the world. Of course, as is effectively demonstrated by contemporary authors, this "neutral" substantiation is not (and cannot be) entirely neutral. It refers to a considerable degree (which comes as no surprise considering the intellectual interests of J. Maritain) to the Thomist concept of person and natural law. For St. Thomas, "the basis of being a person, and consequently also of that which is proper to a person, of what is rightly due to a person, is dignity—a specific mode of existence that is not reducible to any particular feature of the human being, while at the same time encompassing the entire human being (all of his properties and potentialities) which may for this reason be the basis for all rights." This assumption characterizes the contemporary understanding of dignity, situating—according to Marek Piechowiak—Thomas's philosophy as the most adequate substantiation of human rights. Whether or not this interpretation is fully accepted, it is certain that owing to the idea of inherent dignity, human rights on the anthropological plane are founded on the conviction about an exceptional existential status of man, his autotelicity, rationality, freedom and conscience, and the equal dignity of all men. Cf. M. Piechowiak, *Filozofia praw...*, pp. 265–342.

[109]Renata Mazur, "Karta Praw Podstawowych UE," in: A. Florczak [ed.], *Ochrona praw podstawowych...*, p. 41.

In the Treaties of Rome which provided the basis for the European Economic Community (EEC) on whose foundations the European Union was subsequently established, the space of proclaimed values was generally reduced to economic values, such as harmonious development of economies, improvement of living standards, economic and social progress, etc. In accordance with the functionalist logic which prevailed for many years to come, focusing on the satisfaction in the EEC of concrete, mostly economic, needs, the issue of human rights was generally not addressed.[110] Even though the axiological substantiation did not disappear, it was—to a large extent deliberately—pushed to the background. Foreground issues were dominated by relative values, mostly economic ones. As noted by Jacques Santer, commenting on the 1950s position of Konrad Adenauer, the Chancellor "was aware that the values he advocated would only be accepted by the Europeans if they live in prosperity and in a world of social justice."[111] It was effective, in a way. As long as the gains of the EEC's existence evidently outweighed the losses, and integration was limited so that the member states retained actual control (or at least had a reasonable sense of control) of the political process, the functionalist logic was essentially sufficient to continue the integration project. It allowed the EEC not only to effectively act within the jointly established frameworks and principles, but also to gradually expand them.

This does not mean, of course, that the issue of values and human rights was entirely absent in the communities. And yet it was not until 1969 that the Court of Justice first used the term fundamental right to refer to "constitutionally protected human rights,"[112] and in subsequent years (prior the adoption of the TEU) issued 20 rulings (i.e. on the average—one ruling a year) in which it referred to this term linking it to general principles of law. After nearly a decade, in 1977, "interest in fundamental rights was expressed by other community bodies: the European Parliament, the Council, and the Commission, who wrote in a common statement that the Communities would observe fundamental rights resulting from the constitutions of the member states and the European Convention on Human Rights and Fundamental Freedoms."[113] In primary law this term was first used in 1986 in the Preamble to the Single European Act which stated that one of the Communities' founding goals was to promote democracy on the basis of "the fundamental rights recognized in the constitutions and laws of the Member States, in the Convention for the Protection of Human Rights and Fundamental Freedoms, and the European Social Charter." Finally, in 1989 the European Parliament adopted the Declaration of Fundamental Rights and Freedoms which essentially anticipated the Charter of Fundamental Rights proclaimed at the threshold of the twenty-first century.[114] This clearly

---

[110]The only exception was the 1970 Declaration of European Identity.

[111]Jacques Santer, *Spór cywilizacyjny Europy*, in: *Cywilizacyjne zmagania Europy*, Wokół nas, Gliwice 2007, p. 23.

[112]J. Sozański, op cit., p. 39.

[113]R. Mazur, op. cit., p.42.

[114]Ibid.

shows that until the 1980s the issue of values and fundamental rights was on the margin of the integration process. In fact, until the end of the 1970s it remained entirely outside of the area of interest of the main institutions. It only gained in significance in the course of the integration process leading to establishing the Union.

Proclamation of the European Union, a political structure with clear federal ambitions,[115] renewed keen interest in values more profound than the economic ones, which was reflected in the new Treaties. In this context, the 1992 Maastricht Treaty on the European Union contains a reference to human rights. In its preamble, the treaty declared the Union's commitment "to the principles of liberty, democracy and respect for human rights and fundamental freedoms and of the rule of law," in fact formulating the catalogue of the Union's fundamental values. Furthermore, in the second paragraph of Article F it said that "the Union shall respect fundamental rights, as guaranteed by the European Convention for the Protection of Human Rights and Fundamental Freedoms signed in Rome on 4 November 1950 and as they result from the constitutional traditions common to the Member States, as general principles of Community law." Thus, human rights became, at least *de iure*, the leading principles of European integration.[116]

From then on, the axiological anchorage of the Union began to develop quite rapidly. The 1997 Amsterdam Treaty which modified the TEU not only upheld the solutions adopted in Maastricht but also, as though for the avoidance of doubt, introduced the principles which had so far existed only in the Preamble to the contents of Article 6 TEU (previously Article F). Furthermore in its new wording the TEU stated that membership of the EU was made conditional on respect for the above-mentioned principles, and that their violation could result in sanctions being applied to the Member States concerned. In this way, respect for human rights and democracy was made part of the treaty as a condition for accession to the Union and participation in its decision making process. Then, in 2000, the EU Charter of Fundamental Rights was proclaimed which, even though presented as a utilitarian text which consolidated human rights provisions dispersed across EU legislation, represented, as Joseph Weiler has aptly pointed out, the axiological and constitutional keystone of the developing European identity.[117]

The never fully realized project of a European Constitution referred directly to the concept of values rather than the concept of principles used in the TEU, even after the Amsterdam reform. It presented as values, for example, the principles of freedom, democracy, equality, rule of law, present already in the TEU, and complemented their catalogue with the dignity of the human person. It upheld the

---

[115]Cf. e.g. Hans Laufer, Tomas Fischer, *Föderalismus als Strukturprinzip für die Europäische Union*, Verlag Bertelsmann-Stiftung, Gütersloh 1996.

[116]As Marcin Dybowski points out, activities of the CJEU are characterized by "careful recourse to provisions of the Convention, despite its declared primacy among the sources of inspiration for rulings concerning fundamental rights." Cf. M. Dybowski, op. cit., p. 116.

[117]Cf. J.H.H. Weiler, *Un' Europa Cristiana. . . .*

principle of membership in the Union being conditional on respect for its values (Article I-59) and provided for sanctions, known since the Amsterdam, for their violation by Member States. The Treaty not only adopted and developed solutions found in the TEU, but also incorporated the Charter of Fundamental Rights which was thus to become an act of primary law.

Without going into the details of the axiological solutions of the Constitutional Treaty, substantially repeated in the Lisbon Treaty which will be analyzed further on in this chapter, it should be noted that from the Maastricht Treaty to the Lisbon Treaty (2009) the EU axiological potential was gradually strengthened. As its area of influence began to expand, the Union turned towards values and tried to find a meaningful basis for legitimizing its actions. To this end, it went beyond the area of economic values which clearly dominated in the Treaties of Rome, and moved towards fundamental values and rights, so values that provide the meaning, identification and direction to actions taken by social and political communities.

10.2.1   The Anthropological Bases of EU Axiology

The starting point for discovering the anthropological vision which stands today at the basis of EU axiology are the essential provisions of primary law referring to the issue of values. In accordance with our adopted methodology of looking for "foundations," the point is not to present all axiological references found in the Treaties and, or first of all, in the Charter of Fundamental Rights, which at the Summit in Nice was called the "declaration of European morality."[118] Rather, the goal is to discover and analyze those values which substantiate other axio-normative, or meta-axiological, solutions. As regards the international and national protection of human rights, as discussed above, the key category is dignity, ultimately referring to the constrained anthropological vision. The central question is whether the EU, when defining its catalogue of values at the dawn of the twenty-first century, when the tensions around fundamental values and therefore, as discussed in Part II, the vision of man were very advanced, embraced the classical standpoint or whether it tried to follow its own path.

One more methodological comment should be made at this point. It seems natural that a presentation of the foundations of EU axiology should follow chronological order. The timeline perspective reflects the dynamics of EU discussion about values which, at least in the beginning, was characterized by some ambivalence. It is revealed in the objective of the EU's first axiological manifesto, the Charter of Fundamental Rights. The third recital of its Preamble states that the reason for adopting the Charter is to strengthen "the protection of fundamental rights in the light of changes in society, social progress and scientific and technological

---

[118]M. Piechowiak, *Aksjologiczne podstawy...*, p. 6.

developments by making those rights more visible."[119] The matter does not seem to require any comment. On closer look, however, the declared goal of addressing the issue of values in EU law seems unclear, to say the least. On the one hand, the role of the Charter ultimately appears to be secondary: "making those rights more visible" is a formal task which does not contribute anything to the core of the integration project. On the other hand, however, this formal goal is represented as substantively fundamental, leading to strengthening "the protection of fundamental rights in the light of changes in society, social progress and scientific and technological developments." Indeed, this duality of viewing the role of the Charter was visible already at the opening of the Convention, as the Chairman, Roman Herzog, emphasized the declarative nature of the document, while his deputy, Ingo Mendez de Vigo, clearly stated that "a mere declaration is not enough (...). The Charter of Fundamental Rights must be binding and must be incorporated into the Treaty."[120] One saw in it a non-legally binding instrument of public debate, the other—the constitutive consolidation of the vision of federal Europe á la Monnet and Spinelli.[121]

Grainne de Burca points out that even the very decision about the composition,[122] operating principles and practices of the body which worked on the Charter showed that it was "a significant initiative and not simply another of many Sage reports or working groups proposals which have gathered dust on Community shelves over the years."[123] This awareness was enhanced by the name used by the body constituted by the decision of the Council in Tampere. The term "Convention" symbolically emphasized the significance of its works, which was momentous on its own, anyway.[124] Ultimately, their goal was to set out "in a single text, for the first time in the European Union's history, the whole range of civil, political, economic and social rights of European citizens and all persons resident in the EU."[125] Despite all declarations, keen observers of European integration clearly saw already in 2001 that the Charter would sooner or later become an object of judicial protection and would

---

[119]*Preamble*, in: *Charter of Fundamental Rights*, Official Journal of the European Union, 2010/C 83/02 of 30.3.2010.

[120]As quoted in: Grainne de Burca, "The Drafting of the European Union Charter of Fundamental Rights," *European Law Review*, April 26 (2001), p. 134.

[121]Ibid., p. 127.

[122]The Convention was composed of "high-level" politicians, beginning with the former President of the FRG Roman Herzog as its Chairman.

[123]G. de Burca, op. cit., p. 132.

[124]Also in the institutional sense. As Marek A. Cichocki points out, the fact that in 2000 the Convention adopted "the Charter of Fundamental Rights was considered an exceptionally promising experiment (...). For the first time, an important common document had been drafted in an open, democratic process at the European level, without the exclusive 'hard' participation of the Member States' government representatives. Based on this experience, it was considered that the Convention formula (...) could soften the seemingly fixed division of interests between the Member States." Marek A. Cichocki, *Porwanie Europy*, OMP, CSM, Warszawa-Kraków 2004, pp. 118–119.

[125]Amelia Conte, *A Europe of Rights: History of the EU Charter*, European Parliament, Luxembourg 2012, p. 34.

influence the Union's constitutional structure in functional terms.[126] And that is what ultimately happened after the Lisbon Treaty was adopted. In 2009, less than a decade after it was adopted, the Charter of Fundamental Rights became an integral part of the Union's primary law.

The Lisbon Treaty did not merely incorporate the Charter as the Union's axiological and human rights law manifesto; on the contrary, not only did it make corrections to comments to the CFR, but also introduced its own separate fundamental axiological and meta-axiological regulations in the Preamble and in the first Articles of the Treaty on the European Union, "being (chronologically) the last word of European politicians on the subject of European values."[127] This way, the chronological perspective also turns out to be the theoretical one. In other words, the Treaties seem to be the hermeneutic key to understanding of the Charter within the European Union. The Charter is the first text in the history of the Union that "plays a threefold role: it articulates the values, expresses their connection to practices (actions), and derives from these values the norms of action."[128] The European Treaties, which after Lisbon have acquired an axiological trait, are not just "footnotes to the Charter." On the contrary, they clarify, definitively for now, the direction of thinking about man followed by the Union in its presentation of values and rights. This means that when looking for the direction of the Union's anthropological thought, the Charter should be read in the context of the more general provisions of the Treaty.[129] The approach to be taken is not only chronological, therefore, but theoretical as well, so as to capture the anthropological significance of the evolution of EU values over a span of several years.

10.2.1.1 The Charter of Fundamental Rights

The fundamental values of the Union, in terms of constituting a basis upon which the European political structure is constructed, are expressly defined for the first time in recital 2 of the Preamble to the Charter of Fundamental Rights. It reads: "Conscious of its spiritual and moral heritage, the Union is founded on the indivisible, universal

---

[126]Christoph Engel, *The European Charter of Fundamental Rights A Changed Political Opportunity Structure and its Dogmatic Consequences*, Max-Planck-ProjektgruppeRecht der Gemeinschaftsgüter, Bonn 2001, p. 12. It is also worth noting in this context that the Charter included "rights which exceed the Community's competences: it referred to the right to social security (...), the right to healthcare (Article 35), and the right of access to services of general economic interest (Article 36), although the Union's institutions did not have the competence to act in these areas." Agnieszka Maria Nogal, *Ponad prawem narodowym. Konstytucyjne idee Europy*, ISP PAN, Warszawa 2009, p. 131.

[127]Piotr Mazurkiewicz, "Wokół Karty Praw Podstawowych," *Chrześcijaństwo-Świat-Polityka. Zeszyty myśli społecznej Kościoła*3(8)2008, p. 29.

[128]Marta Bucholc, "Karta Praw Podstawowych – jaki projekt społeczeństwa?," *Civitas* 12/2010, p. 13.

[129]Cf. P. Mazurkiewicz, "Wokół Karty...," pp. 29–32.

values of human dignity, freedom, equality and solidarity; it is based on the principles of democracy and the rule of law." The fundamental meaning of these values for the Union's axiological system is emphasized by the fact that the rights declared in the Charter are linked to each of these values in the very structure of the document.[130] This also shows an awareness of their anthropological anchorage.

As emphasized by Marek Piechowiak, "in this formula there are elements analogous to those found in Article 1 of the 1948 Universal Declaration of Human Rights, which is the undisputed cornerstone of the post-war concept of human rights."[131] Indeed, the categories of equality, freedom, and dignity are explicitly present in the Declaration and in the Charter, and the declaration of brotherhood is reflected in the category of solidarity.[132] The key categories of reason and conscience are more problematic as far as their content is concerned, however. Marek Piechowiak points out that recognition of the role of conscience can be inferred from the awareness of moral heritage.[133] The reference to morality would thus be another form of expressing the same content, as in the case of solidarity and brotherhood.

This view is open to criticism, however. As the author of *Filozofia Praw Człowieka* (*The Philosophy of Human Rights*) points out himself, the category of conscience may refer to different phenomena: the affective and subjective human sense as well as rational judgment associated with knowledge, referring actions to objective truth. In the text of the Declaration, the legal meaning of conscience may be discovered by analyzing the different language versions of the original.[134] This procedure does not work in the case of the Charter's "moral heritage," however. It may mean both the morality of Rousseau and that of St. Thomas, and it is impossible to know what the author actually had in mind. All the more so because Christian heritage—which may provide a key to identifying the core reservoir of values—has been mentioned in a very general way as religious heritage,[135] and in fact only in the German version of the Charter. Consequently, the German version is an exception compared to other language versions, even if during the negotiations between Roman Herzog and Jacques Chirac it was agreed that the French *spirituel* reflected the meaning of the German *geistig-religiös*. Nevertheless, it was clearly *spirituel* that became the reference category for most language versions of the Charter.[136] In this

---

[130]Subsequent chapters of the Charter are entitled: I—Dignity, II—Freedoms, III—Equality, IV—Solidarity, V—Citizens' Rights, and VI—Justice.

[131]M. Piechowiak, "Karta Praw Podstawowych UE a tradycyjne wartości," in: M. Gierycz, J. Grosfeld [ed.], *Zmagania początku* . . . p. 200.

[132]M. Piechowiak, *Aksjologiczne podstawy. . .*, p. 16.

[133]Ibid.

[134]Marek Piechowiak, *Filozofia praw. . .*, p. 98.

[135]In the Convention, the inspirer behind the appeal to God and Christian tradition was Ingo Friedrich, then the European People's Party (Christian Democracy) Vice President of the European Parliament. In the end, "the formulas proposed in the working group were abandoned in favor of the 'weaker' formula which referred to religious heritage." M. Piehowiak, *Aksjologiczne podstawy. . .*, p. 14.

[136]M. Piechowiak, *Aksjologiczne podstawy. . .*, p.14.

context, it seems that Stefan Hambura and Mariusz Muszyński are right that the different language versions provide different solutions to the same problem while entailing substantially different content.[137] This view seems to be especially legitimate considering the genesis of the solution adopted in the Charter. The starting point (the first proposal) was reference to God and Christian heritage. The direction of the evolution which led to the reference to "spiritual heritage" clearly shows the authors' intention to minimize the presence of the religious dimension in the Charter.[138] This objective was effectively achieved.

The question of how moral heritage is to be understood is at least unclear, and with a hint of irony it might be said that inferring the claim that the Union considers man to have a conscience (in its classical meaning) from the reference to this heritage is just as legitimate as inferring the meaning of righteous reason for the EU's anthropological concept from the word "conscious" in the expression "conscious of its spiritual and moral heritage." This is possible, but the analysis begins to look more like a torture device. It seems, therefore, that Marek Piechowiak's statement should be construed literally. If he says that in the Charter's formula "there are elements analogous to those found in Article 1 of the UDHR," that is exactly what we find: elements. More specifically: certain elements, for other elements are different. The vision of man in the Charter fully reflects the formal dimension of values in the UDHR, but does not reflect, at least not fully, its substantive dimension. We will need to come back the question of why this is so later on.

At this point, we should refer to the key anthropological category of dignity. Marek Piechowiak points out that thanks to the Charter the category of dignity, so explicitly absent from the ECHR, "reappears on the European scene 'in its full glory'."[139] Indeed, explanations on Article 1 of the Charter, which the authors designed as "a tool of interpretation intended to clarify the provisions of the Charter,"[140] say that "the dignity of the human person is not only a fundamental right in itself but constitutes the real basis of fundamental rights."[141] Consequently, the Explanations emphasize that "none of the rights laid down in this Charter may be used to harm the dignity of another person, and that the dignity of the human person is part of the substance of the rights laid down in this Charter. It must therefore be respected, even where a right is restricted."[142] Moreover, the first chapter, "entitled 'Human Dignity,' generally refers to rights in the narrower sense of the word, as different from freedoms. Both the taxonomy employed in the Charter and the taxonomy of values on which it is based indicate the primacy of rights over freedoms

---

[137]Stefan Hambura, Mariusz Muszyński, "W jakim języku o Bogu," *Rzeczpospolita* 5.04.2002.

[138]In fact, Marek Piechowiak points it out himself. Cf. *Aksjologiczne podstawy...*, p. 15.

[139]M. Piechowiak, "Karta Praw Podstawowych – wróg czy sprzymierzeniec tradycyjnych wartości?," *Chrześcijaństwo – Świat – Polityka* No. 3 (7) 2008, p. 23.

[140]*Explanations Relating to the Charter of Fundamental Rights*, OJEU 2007/C 303/02.

[141]Ibid., *Explanation on Article 1*.

[142]Ibid.

(. . .) [The Charter recognizes—M.G.] 'rights' in the broader sense as an overriding category covering rights in the narrower sense together with freedoms. This recognition of the primacy of rights over freedoms or freedom is very significant from the axiological point of view—it is dignity that is of primary importance, and its is dignity that determines rights, which do not depend in their existence on the decisions of individuals or societies, and which can be known."[143]

These findings are particularly important in that in the traditional system of values, which provides the basis for the contemporary international protection of human rights,[144] it is recognized that it is precisely man's inherent, inalienable dignity that forms their foundations. If, therefore, the category of dignity reappears in the Charter "in its full glory," it must be assumed that, despite the above-mentioned lack of anthropological clarity, the Charter reflects the anthropological model characteristic of the universal system of human rights.

Even the term dignity is problematic, however. In the Charter, "dignity is not defined as inherent, unlike in other instruments of international law and elsewhere."[145] In *Explanations Concerning the Charter*, inherency appears only in the UDHR quote. It is not clear from the *Explanations*, however, whether this view is shared by the Charter's authors. Rather, it is a reference to a historically momentous text: the first declaration of the primacy of human dignity, the dignity narrative which prevailed at the time. In the EU narrative, the inherent nature of dignity is no longer present. It is especially problematic that, as discussed above, it is inherency that substantiates the universality, non-acquirability, and inalienability of dignity.

This disappearance of inherency may be swept aside. Marek Piechowiak argues that "it may be assumed that recognition of the universality of dignity and, therefore, recognition that it is enjoyed by everyone, regardless of their characteristics or circumstances in life, expresses essentially the same truths as the recognition of inherency."[146] This thesis is far from obvious, however. Universality can express various contents. The meaning attributed to universality in international law stems precisely from the primacy of inherency.[147] If we evict it, we also remove the key to a conclusive interpretation of its meaning. As noted by Piotr Mazurkiewicz, universality may then be construed differently: "while the constitutions of European countries refer to absolute and indisputable values, this is but our European way of narrating. Human rights/the rights of a human person are therefore 'inviolable and inalienable', but only within our European 'valley'. In the neighbouring 'valley', on the other side of the hill, people have had a different history and entered into another ethical agreement, which is as good 'for them' as ours is 'for us'."[148] It is therefore "our" universality, historically and culturally established, but not universality in the

---

[143]M. Piechowiak, *Aksjologiczne podstawy. . .*, pp. 20–21.

[144]Ibid., p. 24.

[145]Ibid., p. 20.

[146]Ibid.

[147]In fact, Marek Piechowiak himself writes about this at length in *Filozofia praw. . .*, pp. 79–88.

[148]P. Mazurkiewicz, "Wokół Karty. . .," p. 29.

strong sense of the word. If this interpretation were to be adopted, it would seem reasonable to remove conscience and reason from the anthropological concept of the Charter. As mentioned above, these two elements provide for the possibility of a uniform reading and understanding of human rights around the globe. It is our shared nature, endowed with conscience and reason, that enables us to speak of universal rights, independent of the characteristics of a particular person or of the historical or cultural context; it allows us to perceive inherent dignity and to define its basic requirements. The Charter is not firm, to say the least, in recognizing this nature.

In view of the above observations, it seems reasonable to say that the axiological basis of the Charter leaves the reader in a state of anthropological confusion. Although it refers—and apparently in a strong way—to the anthropological categories found in the UDHR, it does so in a selective manner. Even though it might seem that the "majority stake," to use economic terminology, remains the same, the missing elements are crucial to upholding the anthropological position found in international and constitutional law. The one reflected in the Charter seems to be not so much identical but similar, even if at times very much so. It is not simply an "updated" version of the earlier model (in the sense that solidarity is an "updated" version of brotherhood), but a new approach, abandoning certain elements constitutive to the former one, to the axiological foundations of political community and human rights.

10.2.1.2   Treaty on European Union

There seems to be no doubt that the Treaty on European Union, in the wording of Lisbon, reinforces the Union's axiological anchoring present in the Charter. As the inspiration for creating the Union, it refers to Europe's heritage, related to universal and therefore fundamental values which constitute "inviolable and inalienable human rights," as well as freedom, democracy, equality, and the rule of law. These values, now as principles (except for equality), are cited almost entirely in the fourth recital of the Preamble as particularly relevant to the design of the EU, and democracy is cited once again in the fourth recital in relation to EU institutions. Thus, the Preamble to the TEU specifically emphasizes fundamental and democratic values. Furthermore, in the fifth and sixth recitals it refers to a number of social values (social rights, solidarity), followed by economic (economic cohesion, progress) and ecological ones (sustainable development) in the eighth recital. In addition, the principle of subsidiarity may be considered a reference to individual values.

A catalogue of EU values is then found in Article 2 of the TEU. It states that "the Union is founded on the values of respect for human dignity, freedom, democracy, equality, the rule of law and respect for human rights, including the rights of persons belonging to minorities. These values are common to the Member States in a society in which pluralism, non-discrimination, tolerance, justice, solidarity and equality between women and men prevail."[149] The values already mentioned in the Preamble are therefore complemented by the dignity of the human person, as well as pluralism, non-discrimination, tolerance, justice, solidarity, and equality between women and men.

Axiological problems are then elaborated in Article 3 of the TEU. It provides that the basis for EU activity in the area of economy is "sustainable development of Europe based on balanced economic growth and price stability, a highly competitive social market economy, aiming at full employment and social progress, and a high level of protection and improvement of the quality of the environment."[150] The Article also stipulates that the Union "shall combat social exclusion and discrimination, and shall promote social justice and protection, equality between women and men, solidarity between generations and protection of the rights of the child," and that "economic, social and territorial cohesion, and solidarity among Member States," ensure "that Europe's cultural heritage is safeguarded and enhanced", and contribute to "peace, security, the sustainable development of the Earth, solidarity and mutual respect among peoples, free and fair trade, eradication of poverty and the protection of human rights, in particular the rights of the child."[151]

The axiological landscape of the EU sketched out above shows that its legal solutions reflect a wide range of values—from fundamental to democratic, social, individual, environmental, and economic ones. There can be no doubt, therefore, that EU axiology is much more extensive today than in the previous versions of the Treaties. It seems to have been particularly enhanced in the area of fundamental values (dignity, equality, freedom) and democratic ones (pluralism, democracy, the rule of law). In this light, the EU is beginning to look almost like a human rights organization, which in fact it is not.[152]

While acknowledging the legitimacy of talking about an enhanced axiological anchorage of the Union, it should be noted that there hardly seems to be any internal logic to the collection of EU values. As a whole, the axiology reflected in the TEU appears to lack coherence. Indeed, it repeats the errors of the Constitutional Treaty in which the canon of European values—as noted by Helmut Juros—did not seem to aspire "either to adequacy or completeness."[153]

The noticeable lack of a logical arrangement of values appears to be the result of changes introduced into the axiological foundations of the Treaty much more decisively than in the Charter. The Charter of Fundamental Rights, as mentioned, refers to "human dignity" as the fundamental value, and erects the entire structure of

---

[149]*Treaty on European Union*, Article 2.

[150]Ibid, Article 3.

[151]Ibid.

[152]Marek Jeżewski, "Karta Praw Podstawowych w Traktacie Reformującym Unii Europejskiej," in: C. Mik, K. Gałka [ed.], *Prawa podstawowe w prawie i praktyce Unii Europejskiej*, Toruń 2009, pp. 22–23. The Union does not have the competence to protect these rights. They constitute (only) a specific boundary and the principle governing the activities of European institutions and EU Member States in the development and implementation of Community law.

[153]H. Juros, op. cit., p. 40.

values and rights on its basis. The positioning of human dignity at the heart of its axiological landscape means that, with all of the above-mentioned provisos, "relationship to the good of man as a whole is an integral part of any law,"[154] establishing a relatively clear hierarchy of values and their relation to human rights. We will not find it in the EU Treaty.

In this context, it appears characteristic that justice and solidarity have been excluded from the catalogue of values—listed in Article 2—on which the Union is based. It is particularly surprising in that both of these values are included in an analogous catalogue in the Charter of Fundamental Rights. Anne-Laure Chavier explains that the idea was that the values should be indisputable: "the editors could not include those values as fundamental which are controversial from the legal point of view (. . .). This explains why terms such as 'pluralism,' 'tolerance,' 'justice,' etc. were added to describe the model of European society, but were not explicitly classified as 'values'."[155] The logic of compromise, in which "the editors" decide about the catalogue of European values, is most poignant: both justice and solidarity may be excluded if they are found to be controversial. The fact that the exclusion of solidarity means breaking with the existing anthropological position is of little importance.

This approach seems to be deeply rooted in the TEU logic. It should be noted that the recognition of values on which the Union is built, found in Article 2 of the TEU, is not ontological. In light of this Article, the Union is based on these values not because they are intrinsic to human nature and therefore universal, but because they are shared by the Member States.[156] Its recognition of values is determined not so much by the knowledge of man, but by the current social and cultural situation. While the Charter could still be regarded as a document referring to the metaphysics of values, in the context of solutions found in the Treaty of Lisbon this tradition of understanding values has clearly been abandoned. Values are not derived from the knowledge of truth about being, but from the cultural and historical context and arrangements made between people. The metaphysics of values is therefore replaced, so to speak, by a sociology of values—the criterion for recognizing a particular value as the value of the European Union is not knowledge of man, but the social and cultural situation and the will of the Member States. In this logic, the editors of the Treaty—for the sake of compromise—do indeed have the right to abandon certain values as too controversial.

An even clearer declaration in this regard is found in the second recital to the TEU Preamble, added in Lisbon, which states: "Drawing inspiration from the cultural, religious and humanist inheritance of Europe, from which have developed the universal values of the inviolable and inalienable rights of the human person,

---

[154]M. Piechowiak, *Filozofia praw. . .*, p. 78.

[155]Anne – Laure Chavier, *Les valeurs de l'Union dans la Constitution europeenne*, Fondation Robert Schuman, Le suplement de la Lettre no 185, 25.10.2004, as quoted in: Rev. Piotr Mazurkiewicz, "Wspólne wartości . . .," p. 221.

[156]More on this subject, see: ibid.

freedom, democracy, equality and the rule of law."[157] As noted by Marek Piechowiak, "from the point of view of meta-axiological solutions, this recital clearly recognizes cultural relativism. In accordance with the adopted formula, values arise from the cultural, religious and humanist heritage of Europe. Since values are recognized in view of cultural developments, then the same applies to the recognition of their universality."[158] Piechowiak points out that "in this perspective, it makes sense to exclude dignity which is understood as an inherent source of rights that is essentially independent from culture."[159] Let us emphasize that the Preamble to the TEU does not mention dignity among its fundamental values—it does so only in Article 2, but precisely in the context of values recognized "by the Member States." It therefore appears that "the standpoint adopted in the Treaty may be referred to as one of consistent contextualism."[160]

* * *

If, in line with the arguments set out at the beginning of this section, we view solutions found in the Charter in the light of those adopted in the Lisbon Treaty, they seem to be a first step towards a de-ontologization of values, and thus also a move away from constrained anthropology related to the recognition of human nature and the objective, knowable requirements it entails. If we do not agree with this argumentation, we must conclude that there are two different meta-axiological standpoints in EU law. The first one, contained in the Charter, is potentially open to interpretations characteristic of the later regulations found in the Treaty.

It should be added that the meta-axiological position particularly characteristic of the TEU is often regarded as a special achievement of the EU reflection on values. As pointed out by one commentator, "agreement about values (. . .) does not imply agreement about their ontology. The incorporation of ontological justifications into axiology (. . .) is not necessary and even seems inadvisable in the pluralistic and differentiated European society."[161] The above analysis shows, however, that the lack of a strong anthropological anchoring of EU axiology translates into a free, if not arbitrary, prioritization or, more broadly, understanding of the relationship between values. The question is whether decisions concerning the axiological basis do not in fact affect the "agreement about values;" whether the way in which the specific values are understood is not affected by the de-ontologization of values? From the anthropological point of view, the question is whether the vision of man derived from the concept of fundamental rights, having lost its universality, does not also lose its essential content? Does it remain the same, yet referring to a specific social and cultural context; or does its content change as a result of abandoning the attribute of inherency? In view of the conclusions to Chap. 9, when answering this

---

[157] *Treaty on European Union, Preamble.*

[158] M. Piechowiak, *Karta Praw Podstawowych a tradycyjne wartości. . .*, p. 202.

[159] Ibid.

[160] P. Mazurkiewicz, "Wokół Karty. . .," p. 29.

[161] D. Bunikowski, *Podstawy aksjologiczne Konstytucji dla Europy*, http://www.racjonalista.pl/kk.php/s,4577 (31.03.2011).

question particular attention should be paid to the area of those rights which are of key importance for morality policy—for this is where the bitter cultural dispute has been held since the beginning of modernity.

10.2.2 Rights in the Logic of Compromise

When looking at the Charter of Fundamental Rights annexed to the EU Treaty, it is clear that the de-ontologization of values does not have to affect the contents of human rights. The proclaimed rights "for the most part do not raise doubts as to their embedding in the European tradition of thinking about human dignity and human rights (. . .) [introducing] however, some changes that result from a deeper understanding of human rights than in the past, elaboration of specific provisions, and the emergence of new challenges, such as the technical possibility of cloning human beings, which needed to be reconsidered from the point of view of these rights."[162] Nevertheless, commentators point out that at least in three cases "the reason for change is (. . .) different."[163]

The first problem concerns the structure of the right to life. Article 2 of the CFR says that "everyone has the right to life." It is based on Article 2 ECHR which says: "Everyone's right to life shall be protected by law. No one shall be deprived of his life intentionally save in the execution of a sentence of a court following his conviction of a crime for which this penalty is provided by law." Given that the dispute currently held in the context of the European civilization is not so much about the recognition of the right to life but about the "extent of mandatory protection by the state/European Union," the solution adopted in the CFR, avoiding the definition of the legal scope of the protection of the right to life, can be interpreted as the taking of a concrete standpoint in the dispute, namely the recognition that "the obligation of public authorities to protect the right to life does not cover situations related to abortion or euthanasia."[164] Even if this interpretation seems rather radical, there is no doubt that, in the case of this Article, the response of the Charter's editors to "changes in society (. . .) and scientific and technological developments" is not to strengthen the guarantee of protection of the right to life entailed by human dignity in situations resulting from these changes. On the contrary, the Charter's provisions "do not resolve Europe's most swollen problems concerning the protection of life."[165] In the context of biomedicine, "there are therefore two fundamental questions about the status of human life before birth, as

---

[162]P. Mazurkiewicz, "Wokół Karty. . .," p. 30.

[163]Ibid. Cf. also Andrzej Zoll, "Prawa człowieka: źródła i zakres w ujęciu chrześcijańskim i w Unii Europejskiej," in: Godność-wolność-prawa człowieka, Wokół nas, Gliwice 2016, pp. 42–52.

[164]P. Mazurkiewicz, "Wokół Karty. . .," p. 30.

[165]A. Zoll, op. cit., p.48.

well as the question of the admissibility of euthanasia."[166] Simply put, "the Charter of Fundamental Rights does not address the admissibility of abortion, embryo testing, or embryonic stem cell research. The wording of Article 2 (...) does not explicitly exclude the admissibility of euthanasia, including active euthanasia,"[167] so that it is possible in its context to actually consider "the existence of a 'right to death' which is not warranted either by the Biomedical Convention or the ECHR."[168]

If the construction of the right to life adopted in the CFR is, so to speak, as flexible as possible, then in the current cultural climate it supports narrowing interpretations of the right to life, without excluding "permissive interpretation of new phenomena resulting from scientific developments."[169] Consequently, as pointed out by Andrzej Zoll, former President of Polish Constitutional Tribunal, restraint in the protection of the right to life in fact "calls into question the existence of values sufficiently common to build the foundations of legal order. The issue of the protection of life is fundamental and very closely linked to the position of human dignity vis-à-vis other rights."[170] It appears that this is where the strong criticism of the Charter comes from St. John Paul II, who pointed out that the right to life is "threatened in many countries by policies that promote abortion, almost universally legalized, by an attitude that is increasingly permissive of euthanasia, by certain projects in the field of genetic technology" and "it is not enough to effuse about the dignity of the human being if it is right away grossly violated by the very norms of the European legal system."[171]

The anthropological logic behind Article 2 seems to be fully unveiled in the next Article of the CFR. It declares that everyone has the right to respect for his or her physical and mental integrity.[172] When clarifying this right in the context of biology and medicine, the CFR prohibits "reproductive cloning."[173] It refers at this point to the Convention on Human Rights and Biomedicine which expressly states that "any intervention seeking to create a human being genetically identical to another human being, whether living or dead, is prohibited." The Union prohibits only one form of cloning, however. This is due to the fact that "in some EU Member States, the cloning of human beings and even the creation of human-animal hybrids is, under certain conditions, permitted."[174] The desire to avoid a dispute within the Union has therefore led the authors, in the context of the protection of human dignity, to

---

[166]M. Grzymkowska, op. cit., p. 238.

[167]Ibid.

[168]Ibid., p. 239.

[169]Ibid.

[170]A. Zoll, op. cit., p. 48.

[171]As quoted in: Filip Jasiński, *Karta Praw Podstawowych Unii Europejskiej*, Dom Wydawniczy ABC, Warszawa 2003, p.199.

[172]*Charter...*, Article 3.

[173]Ibid.

[174]P. Mazurkiewicz, "Wokół karty...," p. 31.

"refrain from opposing what clearly infringes this dignity."[175] This is not changed by the fact that in their explanations to the Charter the authors stress that the solution they adopted "does not in any way prevent the legislature from prohibiting other forms of cloning."[176]

The above two Articles clearly show that the logic adopted by the authors, despite the declared supreme value of human dignity, looks like an attempt at "getting around" the consistent protection of that dignity precisely in those places where it is especially put to the test by civilizational progress. This is consistent with the meta-axiological orientation of EU axiology, rooted not so much in the objective knowledge of human nature as in cultural and social contextualism. Consequently, the declaratory logic of the metaphysics of values and inherency of rights is undermined in practice by the logic of the sociology of values.

Article 9 of the CFR, which concerns the guarantee of the right to marry and found a family, presents a similar problem. It reads: "The right to marry and the right to found a family shall be guaranteed in accordance with the national laws governing the exercise of these rights."[177] Since neither marriage nor family, i.e. the protected good, are defined here, it may be assumed that the good is so self-evident that it does not need defining. For example, the constitutions of the interwar period do not define the institution of marriage which is taken for granted. The other possibility, however, is that the Charter does indeed make the protected good subject to the decision of the national legislator. Since the first possibility must be considered anachronistic today, it must be concluded that the second one is the case. If this is so, however, from the perspective of the philosophy of human rights, the Article is quite a mystery. To put it bluntly: on the grounds of human rights, it makes no sense not to define a protected good, and make its content dependent on the legislator's decision instead. If it is inherent, it cannot depend on the legislator. If it depends on the legislator, it is no longer inherent. In an attempt to overcome this impasse, the lack of a legal definition of marriage in Article 9 is compensated for by the definition set out in the *Explanations* which, according to the authors of the Charter, are the key to its interpretation. Let us quote them at length:

> This Article is based on Article 12 of the ECHR, which reads as follows: 'Men and women of marriageable age have the right to marry and to found a family according to the national laws governing the exercising of this right.' The wording of the Article has been modernized to cover cases in which national legislation recognizes arrangements other than marriage for founding a family. This Article neither prohibits nor imposes the granting of the status of marriage to unions between people of the same sex. This right is thus similar to that afforded by the ECHR, but its scope may be wider when national legislation so provides.[178]

The concepts of "modernizing" and of a "similarity" of this Article to Article 12 ECHR is somewhat puzzling. If we perform an anthropological analysis of what

---

[175]Ibid.

[176]Explanations relating to the Charter of Fundamental Rights, OJ C 303, 14.12.2007.

[177]*The Charter...*, Article 9.

[178]*Explanations relating to the Charter...*

has been modernized, we will see that we are faced with a completely new philosophy of man and the institution of marriage and family.

As stated in the *Explanations*, Article 9 "neither prohibits nor imposes the granting of the status of marriage to unions between people of the same sex." In other words, it allows for a homosexual interpretation of marriage, in fact performing, in a way that is obvious not only to lawyers, a redefinition of marriage which has hitherto been necessarily linked to the logic of the complementarity of the sexes. As pointed out by Andrzej Zoll, "the constitutive function of marriage and family, although not exclusive, is, of course, procreation and the upbringing of a new generation. In the process of upbringing, each of the sexes plays an essential and irreplaceable role. Every child has the right to the closest contacts in the family with the mother and the father, with a man and a woman."[179] This right is not guaranteed by Article 9 of the Charter. What primary law considers to be a value protected by the EU, and therefore an element of common good, is different from its interpretation in international law and the approach characteristic of most constitutions of European states.[180]

It is worth noting, however, that it is clear from the *Explanations* that it was not so much a change in the concept of marriage, but a change in the concept of family that was the source of a new definition of the right protected by Article 9 of the CFR. The modification of the classic wording of the provision on marriage and family found in the European Convention on Human Rights in the EU Charter of Fundamental Rights was intended to "cover cases in which national legislation recognizes arrangements other than marriage for founding a family." In fact, the understanding of family in the Charter follows what the sociologist Jeffrey Weeks describes as a "family by choice." It is worth stressing that family is "defined not by ties of blood, marriage, or adoption, but by varieties of relationships and habitations among 'autonomous,' 'consensual' adults and their offspring."[181] The only condition for their recognition in light of the Charter is recognition by the positive law of a Member State. In this context the assurance found in Article 33 that "[t]he family shall enjoy legal, economic and social protection" is somewhat problematic, since it is not clear what entity the legislator actually has in mind.

This approach, whose sources should be sought in the logic of compromise, or better, of the "smallest common denominator," or the efforts to meet, or even anticipate, the changes taking place in European societies, considerably alters the understanding of man. If it is similar to the logic of international law, then it is so just as Averroes's comments to Aristotle's thoughts on the soul are similar to those of

---

[179] A. Zoll, op. cit., p. 50.

[180] It is worth noting that in one of its recent rulings, the European Court of Human Rights made it clear that European human rights legislation does not provide for the institution of "gay marriage." It also pointed out that "protection of the traditional institution of marriage is an important interest of the state. Since same-sex relationships and unions are not identical to the marriage between a man and a woman, they can be treated differently in legislation." http://www.hli.org.pl/drupal/pl/node/9563 [27.09.2014].

[181] G. Himmelfarb, op. cit., p. 51.

Thomas of Aquinas.[182] In other words, although the anthropology of the CFR is similar to the anthropology reflected in international and constitutional law, on this particular point the former ultimately proves to contradict the latter. And this is not a trivial point. As mentioned above, it was the family that founded the understanding of man as a social being in the UDHR, this way avoiding the logic of individualism and collectivism. In light of the CFR, a person may validly be understood as a consistent individual. Yes, he is a member of various groups, but they are instrumental, or else his membership results from natural (biological) necessity, with no moral or anthropological content being entailed.[183] This is clearly indicated by the fact that the right to marry and to found a family is placed under the heading of "Freedom." It seems to justify a construction in which marriage between a man and a woman, which is the basis of family, is no longer a natural (in the moral sense) and fundamental unit of society. On the contrary, it becomes "an option in life," no longer a form of life resulting from human nature. In other words, it becomes a freedom, not a right.

The above logic is confirmed and complemented by the principles of EU's non-discrimination law. This is particularly important as these principles are currently "not only part of the functioning of the internal market or European citizenship, but constitute the basis for the protection of the rights of individuals within the EU."[184] Article 21(1) of the Charter reads: "Any discrimination based on any ground such as sex, race, colour, ethnic or social origin, genetic features, language, religion or belief, political or any other opinion, membership of a national minority, property, birth, disability, age or sexual orientation shall be prohibited."[185] The *differentia specifica* of this regulation as seen against the background of international and constitutional non-discrimination regulations is that it includes sexual orientation as one of the characteristics protected against discrimination. The Agency for Fundamental Rights is right when it says: "Let us not forget that the EU Charter of Fundamental Rights is the first international human rights charter to explicitly include the term 'sexual orientation'."[186] This is indeed a significant modification. All the more so since this concept is not defined in the Charter.

---

[182]They both claimed that the soul was immortal, but Averroes believed that this applied only to the soul of mankind, as individual souls die with the body, while St. Thomas defended the immortality of the human soul.

[183]As a side remark, already in the 1980s Joan Aldous and Wilfrid Dumon highlighted the different dynamics of family policy in the US and in Europe. While in Europe it was targeted at individuals as involved in family roles, in the US it was aimed at the wellbeing of the entire group. Cf. Joan Aldous, Wilfrid Dumon, "European Union and United States perspectives on family policy: summing up," in: ids. [ed.], *The Politics and Programs of Family Policy: United States and European Perspectives*, Lueven University Press, Louvain 1980, pp. 253–289.

[184]Anna ŚledzińskaSimon, "Zasada równości i zasada niedyskryminacji w prawie Unii Europejskiej," *Studia BAS*, No. 2(26) 2011, pp. 41–42.

[185]*Charter...*, Article 21.

[186]European Union Agency for Fundamental Rights, *Homophobia and Discrimination on Grounds of Sexual Orientation in the EU Member States. Part I – Legal Analysis*, Vienna 2008, p. 10.

However, the category of "sexual orientation" as a basis for discrimination is not a *novum* of the Charter. It was introduced into Community law by the Treaty of Amsterdam which provided in Article 13 that, without prejudice to the provisions of the Treaty and within the limit of powers conferred on the Community (the Union), the Council, "acting unanimously on a proposal from the Commission and after consulting the European Parliament, may take the necessary measures to combat any discrimination on grounds of sex, racial or ethnic origin, religion or belief, disability, age or sexual orientation."[187] Consequently, "the first provisions protecting homosexual orientations were introduced by Directive 2000/78/EC of 27 November 2000 establishing a general framework for equal treatment in employment and occupation."[188]

It is worth noting that in the logic of constrained anthropology, it is not entirely clear what sexual orientation is actually supposed to be. If this concept means the natural sexual attraction to a person of the opposite sex (of a man to a woman and of a woman to a man), then the new grounds would be no different from the prohibition of discrimination on account of sex. Its meaning becomes intelligible only when we make unconstrained anthropology our point of departure. By referring to the concept of sexual orientation as a variable independent of the category of sex, a new division of the human species is performed. Being a man or a woman is no longer related to human sexuality. The latter is determined according to other criteria, distinguishing between hetero, homo, bi, trans, etc. -sexual persons.[189] This is an important observation, as it potentially sheds light on the deep-seated reasons of the Charter's treatment of marriage as merely one of man's freedoms. In line with the spirit of atomistic anthropology, all relationships are casual, dependent on the discretion and willingness of the individual. In this perspective, marriage, its permanence, form and content should also depend on the decision of the intending spouses.

In this context, one more observation may be added to the above reflections. Perhaps the replacement of brotherhood with solidarity, in view of the Charter's new anthropology, could mean more than a mere semantic modification. As mentioned above, the concept of brotherhood refers to the category of family and natural obligations to others. Solidarity, of course, can express the same content. Christian ethics of solidarity, developed by John Paul II and Rev. Joseph Tischner, considers this concept as synonymous with that of Christian brotherhood ("carry each other's burdens"). Nevertheless, the concept is double-faceted. It appears also in discourse in relation to the development of an individualistic mentality and the tendencies toward de-Christianization. Thanks to Pierre Leroux, who borrows this concept from Roman law, *la solidarité* is presented as the successor of Christian *caritas*.[190] In light

---

[187]Jacek Sobczak, "Orientacja seksualna jako prawo człowieka," *Studia Prawnicze* 1/2 2009, pp. 88–89.

[188]Ibid., p. 89.

[189]Cf. B. Francis, op. cit.

[190]Cf. M. Gierycz, *Chrześcijaństwo i Unia...*, pp. 74–79.

of the approach to marriage and family reflected in the Charter, it may be legitimate to ask which tradition is being referred to in the EU manifesto of fundamental rights.

10.2.3 The Anthropology of Fundamental Rights and Anthropological Models

The anthropological contours discovered in the EU's primary law cause some confusion. On the one hand, the standpoint they reflect refers to constrained anthropology. The reference to human dignity as the basis for fundamental rights suggests that the rights are protected by the good that is proper to human nature. On the other hand, the attempts at "getting around" the metaphysics of value mentioned above give rise to a model of thinking characteristic of the unconstrained perspective, in which man is his own creator. It seems characteristic that anthropological confusions come to the fore in areas related to the key problems of morality policies (the so-called primary morality policies), and it is in these areas that the Charter "is much more open to new interpretations of the established catalogue of human rights"[191] than other acts of international law. However, it is precisely the problems of primary morality policies, as mentioned in Chap. 9, that are the area of the most serious anthropological dispute today. In other words, while in the context of human dignity as understood in the Charter of Fundamental Rights we may refer to the law of nature theory and the philosophy of Thomism,[192] as regards marriage and human sexuality logically coherent ideological sources should be sought in the anthropology of J.J. Rousseau, the "founding father" of modernity.[193] This can also be seen in the inconsistent use of terms, where "sex" appears to be a category with no points in common with the category of "sexual orientation."

The key question seems to be whether two anthropological positions may "coexist" within a single constitutional order. The answer to this question is ambiguous. Even if we note that the anthropological standpoint of the Charter approximates the logic of reduction, and therefore that, by reducing the anthropological relevance of

---

[191]M. Grzymkowska, op. cit., p. 240.

[192]Which is most justified in the case of the human rights philosophy standing at the basis of international law regulations.

[193]As mentioned above, although family was depicted in *The Social Contract* as a natural community, this naturalness meant something radically different than in the natural law tradition. It was natural because it belonged to the forms of existence which resulted from "hunger and other appetites," which in fact boiled down, however, to satisfaction of sexual needs, upon whose gratification, according to Rousseau, "the two sexes knew each other no more and even the offspring was nothing to its mother, as soon as it could do without her". In this view of nature (in its primitive state) it is understood in physical rather than moral terms. The individual was king; it was only occasionally, and driven merely by natural instincts, that the opposite sexes turned to each other "as accident, opportunity or inclination brought them together," and parted "with the same indifference."

sex for the identity of human beings, it implicitly adopts an individualistic vision of man, it may be pointed out that the anthropological standpoint it represents is not an ontologically strong one. Its "weakness" seems to be highlighted by the Explanations to the CFR which seek not to settle the issue of human sexual orientation, or the meta-axiological solutions of the Lisbon Treaty, referring to the logic of contextualism. Consequently, it may be argued that the contents of the concept of man in the logic of constrained anthropology may be preserved, but in new framework conditions which are open to different views. Based on these assumptions, it actually seems justified to say that the EU model is much more effective in achieving the objective of the universality of rights. The EU's anthropological stance seems more inclusive than the UDHR's position: it allows for various anthropological narratives without demanding that any one of them be treated as exclusive.

This approach has one weak point, however, that is not immediately apparent. It does not take into account the fact that the above-mentioned change in framework conditions is also an anthropological one. As more extensively discussed in Part II, the ontologically "weak" anthropology is normatively just as strong as the ontologically "strong" one. Just as the former requires the recognition of objective limits of human nature, the latter requires recognition of their absence. If it allows for boundaries, it allows for them as relative boundaries, established by some as a form of their particular identity, not as something that is essential to man. Consequently, rights derived from respect for these boundaries, and therefore assertions which aspire to universality, must be regarded in the perspective of unconstrained anthropology as discrimination and disrespect for human freedom.

A good example seems to be the approach to marriage. The Charter of Fundamental Rights does not deny the possibility of recognizing a monogamous relationship as marriage. Nevertheless, in the light of Article 21 and the Explanations on Article 9, a situation in which same-sex unions do not have the same status can hardly be considered desirable, i.e. satisfying the requirements of human rights. Ultimately, this limits human freedom of which marriage is to be a manifestation; moreover, it borders on discrimination on the grounds of sexual orientation. It can be tolerated in view of the cultural and social circumstances with which the Treaty associates the configuration of human rights, but can hardly be regarded as an objective requirement of human dignity. Clearly, the coexistence of constrained and unconstrained anthropology ultimately seems to be impossible. The logic of unconstraint undermines the assumptions of constrained anthropology. Even if it may enable the absorption of a significant portion of anthropological beliefs, they are deprived of their objective anchoring in the human being, and therefore also of permanence and certainty.

Given the above findings concerning values and human rights in the EU, it may be concluded that the EU's primary law does not present a coherent anthropological model, but tries to reconcile two contradictory paradigms. Nevertheless, given the evolution of these solutions, it may be said that the anthropology adopted in the Treaty tends towards unconstrained anthropology, although it still upholds major categories and concepts characteristic of the hitherto prevailing view of man in international law. For even if it refers—as it does in most cases—to the classic human rights solutions, it changes their grounding, and changes or opens up to change the content of those rights which are today's most salient civilizational problems.

The provisions of EU primary law reveal that the dispute over the vision of man within it is primarily related to a dispute over morality policy: a dispute over the protection of the value of human life, which is a legal reflection of the anthropological dispute over whether man is an exchangeable value, and a dispute over marriage which, due to the intellectual climate of late modernity, today reflects the anthropological theory of androgyny. These two issues must therefore constitute a specific research area of functional analyses. The working hypothesis will be that the EU system contributes to the shaping of secondary legislation and policies in the Union—in the problem areas that are open to this—on the basis of an unconstrained anthropological approach. For ultimately, what—if not the Charter of Fundamental Rights and the Lisbon Treaty, developed consensually by Conventions[194] made up of representatives of all States and major EU institutions, and approved by the governments of Member States as part of the intergovernmental conference—reflect the foundations of the Union's institutional ethos? And as has been pointed out above, these documents tend towards unconstrained anthropology.

In the context of positioning the EU's vision of man against the models developed in Part II, one more comment ought to be added. As previously discussed, the unconstrained approach entails a horizontal vision of man. In this context, the fact that neither the Treaty nor the Charter refers to God or to Christianity should be regarded as consistent with the anthropological solution prevailing in the EU. While, as mentioned above, constrained anthropology is at least potentially open to theology, unconstrained anthropology structurally denies the possibility of recognizing "that which is Higher." It remains true to the Enlightenment postulate of organizing the public sphere *etsi Deus non daretur*, in which man is his only master. In its realm, "the sacred foundation for history and for the existence for the State was rejected; history was no longer gauged on the basis of an idea of a pre-existent God who shaped it; the State was henceforth considered in purely secular terms, founded on reason and on the will of the citizens."[195] While the idea of dignity that is inherent to man and independent of our will expresses the idea of "as if God existed," calling for a search—independent of human will or cultural conditions—for the requirements of human dignity, once it has been deprived of the attribute of inherency and became culturally and socially anchored, it is now a function of human freedom. Values no longer have the status of objectively known, ontological properties. They are not so much discovered as they are created, or—to use more modern categories—constructed by man.

---

[194]Obviously, the Lisbon Treaty was adopted by the intergovernmental conference. Nevertheless, the contents of its axiological (as well as most other) solutions were developed during the Convention drafting the Constitution for Europe.

[195]J. Ratzinger, *Europe: Today and...*, pp. 20–21.

Chapter 11
Anthropological Analysis of the Language and Contents of EU Documents

As mentioned in Chap. 9, the European Union, despite the limitations provided for in the Treaties, is clearly entering the area of primary morality policies. Consequently, in view of the close link between these policies and anthropology, and considering the "flexible" solutions provided in the Treaties and constituting the anthropological pillars of EU policy described in Chap. 10, a question arises about the anthropology adopted in the EU's political practice. The nature of morality policy makes it impossible, as indicated above, to "abstain from voting." Even if primary law does not clearly define the EU's position, its institutions must, at least implicitly, adopt an operational definition. In other words, they need to take a stance in the dispute over man. It should be added that, given the flexibility of the EU's axiological pillars[1] and the institutional and decision-making specificities of the Union, characterized by disparities in the organizational, political and cultural identities of its major institutions, it may be assumed that the anthropological perspective adopted by each institution may differ as well. At the same time, the socialization processes within the Brussels elites[2] and the consensual logic of the decision-making process, manifested not only in the fact that the EU Council rarely resorts to voting, but above all in the fact that decisions are taken in the course of interinstitutional agreements made outside of the official mechanisms provided for in the Treaty,[3] seem to suggest that these differences will not be fundamental. They may, therefore, be visible more in the scale of engagement than in the general orientation of its policies. The analysis carried out in this chapter, following the theoretical

---

[1]Cf. Michał Gierycz, "The European Union's axiological credo and morality policy tensions," *Studia Philosophiae Christianae* No. 3, 2015, pp. 159–193.

[2]Cf. J. Ruszkowski, "Europeizacja ad personam" in: Jacek Czaputowicz (ed.), *Zastosowanie konstruktywizmu...*

[3]The most spectacular manifestation of this decision-making formula seem to be the trialogues, which are currently used to adopt around 90% of EU legislation in the so-called ordinary legislative procedure. Cf. Adam Kirpsza, "Zastosowanie konstruktywizmu w wyjaśnianiu przebiegu i efektów procesu legislacyjnego UE," in: Jacek Czaputowicz (ed.), *Zastosowaniekonstruktywizmu...*

© Springer Nature Switzerland AG 2021
M. Gierycz, *European Dispute over the Concept of Man*, Contributions to Political Science, https://doi.org/10.1007/978-3-030-61520-8_11

assumptions made in Part I and the findings made in Chap. 9 on the role of language in morality policy, focuses on the language of EU institutions. For if "it is the institutions that are the carriers of culture, ideas, etc.,"[4] the basic communication channel of these ideas is always the language. Given that in the literature of the subject it is recognized that "one source of EU integration has been the development of a common discursive political vocabulary that constitutes a source of political legitimation,"[5] there can be no doubt about the importance of the use of terms for the orientation of European policy. The study has therefore been focused on the main institutional actors[6] of the European Union: the European Commission, the European Parliament, the Council of the European Union, and the Court of Justice of the European Union.

The analysis will be an inductive one. It will begin with collecting the most elementary data by identifying the notions that dominate the legal and political documents of the European Union. Given the importance of concepts for morality policy discourses, it seems reasonable to assume that the discovery of the linguistic code prevailing in the language of EU institutions may lead to identifying their dominant way of anthropological thinking. The statistical analysis performed as the first step should therefore allow for preliminary hypotheses to be made regarding the anthropological orientation of the Union's policy. Nevertheless, considering the above-mentioned disputes over concepts and their possible reinterpretation,[7] a statistical analysis can hardly be considered as sufficient evidence of the anthropological orientation of EU policy. What should be examined in the first place is the content attributed to the dominant concepts and the related political objectives articulated by the EU's institutional actors. Only then can a strong hypothesis be put forward about the anthropology prevailing in European institutions, which, in accordance with the principles of building a grounded theory, will be further verified—to the extent conclusions developed in this chapter will require additional saturation—in the course of analyses concerning the decision-making processes.

---

[4]Zbigniew Czachór, Adam Jaskulski, op. cit., p. 167.

[5]Sylvia Walby, "The European Union and Gender Equality: Emergent Varieties of Gender Regime," *Social Politics*, Spring 2004, Vol. 11, No. 1, p. 18.

[6]Cf. Z. Czachór, A. Jaskulski, op. cit., pp. 164–165. The authors argue for a much greater transparency of the term and its separation from the concept of institution.

[7]In reference to the findings made in Chap. 9, it may be concluded that the dispute between the two anthropological visions translates into different languages of morality policy discourses. At the same time, the analyses carried out there have shown that terms which belong to the language of one side of the dispute can be reinterpreted or at least made ambiguous, the crowning evidence being the case of the term "person."

11.1   Quantitative Perspective

The analyses performed in Chap. 9 revealed the different conceptual structures of constrained and unconstrained anthropology in disputes over primary morality policies. It is therefore worth taking a closer look at the language of European institutions and the concepts prevailing in their documents. The analyses will be focused on central concepts, i.e. those which constitute the basic expression of the anthropological contours characteristic of each of the two anthropologies and which, from the functional point of view, cannot easily be taken over by the other side of the discourse. Based on data available in the "Eur-Lex" search engine of EU documents, comparisons of all central concepts mentioned above have been made. For each of the discourses (concerning bioethics and sexuality), the first comparison presents the overall number of references to a given concept in EU documents by major institutions; the second shows the change in the number of references in subsequent years between 1 January 2000 and 31 December 2019.

If the contraposition of the terms "procreation" and "reproduction" is considered crucial to the dispute between bioethical discourses, it is striking to note that over the last 20 years the former term "procreation"[8] has been used 56 times, compared to more than 7500 references to the term "reproductive"[9] in EU documents. However, given that the latter concept is often used in EU documents in a context not related to man (e.g. zoological), procreation should be compared with reproductive rights and reproductive health instead, which categories are only used to describe human states and behaviours. Even in this comparison, however, procreation is referred to several

---

[8]The category of "procreation" was referred to in EU documents the total of 56 times, including in 7 documents of the European Parliament, 32 documents of the European Commission, 3 times in documents of the EU Council and 4 times in documents of the Court of Justice, https://eur-lex. europa.eu/search.html?textScope0=ti-te&qid=1588341011578&DTS_DOM=ALL& type=advanced&lang=en&andText0=%22procreation%22&SUBDOM_INIT=ALL_ALL& date0=ALL:01012000%7C31122019&DTS_SUBDOM=ALL_ALL [2.05.2020]. As a side remark, it may be added that the adjective "procreative" being the counterpart of the "reproductive" category appears in EU documents only three times, with the most recent document dating back to 1994. Cf. http://eurlex.europa.eu/search.html?textScope0=tite&qid=1467062832471&CASE_ LAW_SUMMARY=false&DTS_DOM=ALL&type=advanced&lang=en&andText0=%22pro creation%20health%22&SUBDOM_INIT=ALL_ALL&DTS_SUBDOM=ALL_ALL [27.06.2016].

[9]https://eur-lex.europa.eu/search.html?textScope0=tite&qid=1588341793503&DTS_ DOM=ALL&type=advan-ced&lang=en&andText0=reproductive&SUBDOM_INIT=ALL_ ALL&date0=ALL:01012000%7C31122019&DTS_SUBDOM=ALL_ALL [02.05.2020].

times less often than "reproductive rights"[10] and "sexual health,"[11] and nearly 12 times less often than reproductive health to which the EU referred to more than seven hundred times in the years 2000–2019.[12] Only the category of sexual rights was referred to less often than the concept of procreation.[13] All in all, references to sexual and reproductive health and rights (SRHR) over the last 20 years appeared more than 17 times more often in EU documents than the concept of procreation.[14] It might be added that the category of procreative health does not appear at all (Diagram 11.1).

From the institutional perspective, it is noteworthy that while the category of "procreation" is essentially alien to the language of the main European institutions, the terminology of the SRHR seems quite close especially to some of them, with the European Parliament and the European Commission taking the lead. The Parliament's leadership as regards the use of the categories of bioethical discourse associated with unconstrained anthropology is unrivalled, both in absolute and in relative terms. On the one hand, the Parliament's references to SHRH terminology represent more than half of all references to this terminology in EU documents. On the other hand, there are twice as many of such references in EP documents as in those of the European Commission, which also excels in the language of unconstrained anthropology. It should be emphasised that the Court of Justice of

---

[10]The category of "reproductive rights" was used in EU documents the total of 145 times, including 101 times in documents of the European Parliament, 18 times in documents of the European Commission, 6 times in documents of the EU Council, and once in documents of the Court of Justice, https://eur-lex.europa.eu/search.html?textScope0=tite&qid=1588341243485&DTS_DOM=ALL&type=advanced&lang=en&andText0=%22reproductive%20rights%22&SUBDOM_INIT=ALL_ALL&date0=ALL:01012000%7C31122019&DTS_SUBDOM=ALL_ALL [02.05.2020].

[11]The category of "sexual health" was referred to in EU documents the total of 169 times, including in 96 documents issued by the European Parliament, 45 documents of the European Commission, 17 documents of the EU Council, and one document of the Court of Justice, https://eur-lex.europa.eu/search.html?textScope0=tite&qid=1588341313745&DTS_DOM=ALL&type=advanced&lang=en&andText0=%22sexual%20health%22&SUBDOM_INIT=ALL_ALL&date0=ALL:01012000%7C31122019&DTS_SUBDOM=ALL_ALL [02.05.2020].

[12]The category of "reproductive health" was referred to in EU documents the total of 711 times, including 356 times in documents of the European Parliament, 222 times in documents of the European Commission, 36 times in documents of the EU Council, and three times in documents of the EU Court of Justice, https://eur-lex.europa.eu/search.html?textScope0=tite&qid=1588341313745&DTS_DOM=ALL&type=advanced&lang=en&andText0=%22sexual%20health%22&SUBDOM_INIT=ALL_ALL&date0=ALL:01012000%7C31122019&DTS_SUBDOM=ALL_ALL [02.05.2020].

[13]The category of' "sexual rights" was referred to in EU documents the total of 31 times, including in 22 documents of the European Parliament and 6 documents of the European Commission, https://eur-lex.europa.eu/search.html?textScope0=tite&qid=1588341726932&DTS_DOM=ALL&type=advanced&lang=en&andText0=%22sexual%20rights%22&SUBDOM_INIT=ALL_ALL&date0=ALL:01012000%7C31122019&DTS_SUBDOM=ALL_ALL [02.05.2020].

[14]http://eurlex.europa.eu/search.html?textScope0=tite&qid=1467062832471&CASE_LAW_SUMMARY=-false&DTS_DOM=ALL&type=advanced&lang=en&andText0=%22procreation%20health%22&SUBDOM_INIT=ALL_ALL&DTS_SUBDOM=ALL_ALL [27.06.2016].

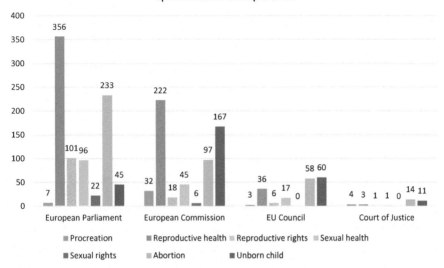

Diagram 11.1 Central concepts of bioethical discourses in the documents of main EU institutions between 2000 and 2019—a combined quantitative comparison

the European Union has been using the language of reproductive rights quite sporadically and only since recently,[15] and that the EU Council has referred to it with much restraint: almost ten times less often than the Parliament and five times less often than the Commission (Diagram 11.1).

It is interesting in this context that the concepts of "abortion" and "unborn child," linguistically representing the two opposite anthropological perspectives, appear in EU documents with a similar frequency: unborn child—402 times,[16] and abortion—

---

[15]It is referred to in rulings rendered after 2016. Cf. https://eur-lex.europa.eu/search.html? textScope0=ti-te&lang=en&SUBDOM_INIT=ALL_ALL&DTS_DOM=ALL& type=advanced&DTS_SUBDOM=ALL_ALL&qid=1588326641126&date0=ALL% 3A01012001%7C31122019&andText0=%22reproductive+rights%22&AU_CODED=GCEU [2.05.2020] or https://eur-lex.europa.eu/search.html?textScope0=ti-te&qid=1588342181013& DTS_DOM=ALL&AU_CODED=GCEU&type=advanced&lang=en&andText0=%22reproduc tive%20health%22&SUBDOM_INIT=ALL_ALL&date0=ALL:01012000%7C31122019& DTS_SUBDOM=ALL_ALL [2.05.2020].

[16]References to "unborn child" in EU documents were made 402 times, including 45 times in documents of the European Parliament, 167 times in documents of the European Commission, 45 times in documents of the EU Council, and 11 times in documents of the Court of Justicehttps:// eur-lex.europa.eu/search.html?textScope0=tite&qid=1588339974506&DTS_DOM=ALL& type=advanced&lang=en&andText0=%22homosexual%20inclination%22&SUBDOM_ INIT=ALL_ALL&date0=ALL:01012001%7C31122019&DTS_SUBDOM=ALL_ALL [02.05.2020].

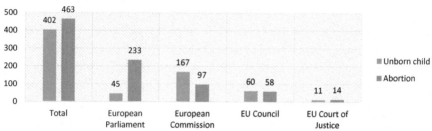

Diagram 11.2 The concepts of "unborn child" and "abortion" in EU documents between 2000 and 2019

463 times.[17] In the institutional perspective, the European Parliament stands out here again, accounting for more than half of the references to abortion in European Union documents during the analysed period. This also means that it was more than five times more likely to refer to the category of "abortion" in its documents than to that of the "unborn child." This is particularly interesting seeing that in other institutions there was either a balance in the use of the analysed terms (vide Council of the European Union or Court of Justice) or, as in the case of the European Commission, the opposite was true: for the Commission's 166 references to "unborn child" there were 95 references to "abortion" (Diagram 11.2).

The diagram showing the evolution of references to the above terms (Diagram 11.3) in the documents of European institutions does not come as a particular surprise. In the EU's bioethical discourse, the category of sexual and reproductive health and rights clearly has the upper hand. It permanently prevails over the concept of procreation. As regards the *nasciturus*, a decline in the general trend occurred in 2019. For the first time since 2000, the term "unborn child" was then referred to nearly as frequently in EU documents as abortion and sexual and reproductive rights/ health, and significantly more often than abortion. Considering the curve over the last 20 years, it appears to be more of a temporary aberration than a lasting change in trends. Nevertheless, a broader context needs to be taken into account, as will be done in the analyses further on.

With regard to human sexuality discourses, as indicated above, the basic dichotomy is that of sex v. gender. Those standpoints which refer to constrained anthropology clearly prefer the former category, while those which refer to unconstrained anthropology prefer the latter. A statistical analysis shows that the overwhelming

[17]References to "abortion" in EU documents were made 463 times, including 233 times in documents of the European Parliament, 97 times in documents of the European Commission, 58 times in documents of the EU Council, and 14 times in documents of the Court of Justice. https://eur-lex.europa.eu/search.html?textScope0=tite&qid=1588340582717&DTS_ DOM=ALL&type=advanced&lang=en&andText0=%22abortion%22&SUBDOM_INIT=ALL_ ALL&date0=ALL:01012000%7C31122019&DTS_SUBDOM=ALL_ALL [2.05.2020].

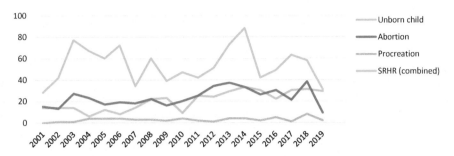

Quantitative change in references to central concepts
of bioethical discourses in EU documents between 2000-2019

Diagram 11.3 Quantitative change in references to central concepts of bioethical discourses in EU documents between 2000 and 2019

majority of references is to "gender"[18] (the total of 9424) over references to "sex"[19] (the total of 5359) in European Union documents. Diagram 11.4 shows that this proportion characteristic of all EU documents is particularly clearly reflected in Parliament and Commission documents, and (albeit somewhat less clearly) in thoseof the Council. It can be seen that the ratio of references to these categories over time (see Diagram 11.5) reflects an "opening scissors" effect. While in 2000 the number of references to "sex" and "gender" in EU documents was similar (with a slight predominance of references to "sex"), in the last 10 years the category of "gender" has always been used twice, and sometimes (vide year 2018) three times more often than the category of "sex". In this context, it is worth noting the category of "gender identity". This category, used only occasionally until 2010, appears to have become an important reference category in the last decade, which EU documents cite several dozen times a year. This observation seems important in the context of the qualitative analysis of the present understanding of the category of "gender" in the EU.

---

[18]During the analysed period, 9424 references were made in EU documents to the category of gender, including 2706 in documents of the European Parliament, 2958 in documents of the European Commission, 1797 in documents of the EU Council, and 149 in documents of the Court of Justice, https://eurlex.europa.eu/search.html?textScope0=tite&qid=1588579022341& DTS_DOM=ALL&type=advanced&lang=en&andText0=%22gender%22&SUBDOM_ INIT=ALL_ALL&date0=ALL:01012000%7C31122019&DTS_SUBDOM=ALL_ALL [04.05.2020].

[19]During the analysed period, 5359 references were made in EU documents to the category of "sex", including 1145 in documents of the European Parliament, 1613 in documents of the European Commission, 1064 in documents of the EU Council, and 650 in documents of the Court of Justice. https://eurlex.europa.eu/search.html?textScope0=tite&qid=1588578643850& DTS_DOM=ALL&type=advanced&lang=en&andText0=%22sex%22&SUBDOM_ INIT=ALL_ALL&date0=ALL:01012000%7C31122019&DTS_SUBDOM=ALL_ALL [04.05.2020].

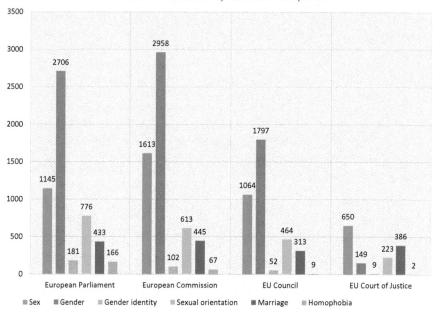

Diagram 11.4   Central concepts of human sexuality and sexual behavior discourses in the documents of main EU institutions between 2000 and 2019—a combined quantitative comparison

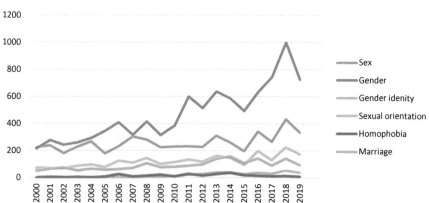

Diagram 11.5   Quantitative change in references to central concepts of human sexuality and sexual behavior discourses in EU documents between 2000 and 2019

The Court of Justice represents an exception among the main institutions as regards the use of linguistic categories. Globally, the semantics used in its rulings reflect the opposite trend than in other EU institutions: categories related to constrained anthropology (such as "sex" or "marriage") clearly prevail in the Court over categories related to unconstrained anthropology. This may suggest a gap between the legal and political discourse on the subject of human sexuality in the EU. It is worth noting that the general prevalence of the term "sexual orientation" is disturbed only in the case of the Court of Justice, which is the only major EU institution to have referred more often to the term "marriage". However, in view of the Court's nearly 150 references to the category of "gender", this issue requires a consideration more thorough than just the quantitative view. Particularly that chronologically speaking there has been a significant increase, as in the Union as a whole, in the Court's references to categories characteristic of unconstrained anthropology in recent years. While until 2005 the Court's rulings referred to the category of "sexual orientation" only occasionally, with more than a dozen judgments referring to the category of marriage every year, in 2017 the number of the Court's documents referring to these two categories became almost the same.[20] It is therefore also possible that the Court has adopted the same anthropological profile as the other European institutions, except that it has done so with a delay and at a slower pace.

It seems significant from the anthropological perspective that in the last 20 years "sexual orientation" has appeared more frequently in EU documents (and markedly more often in the case of the Parliament, the Commission, and the Council) than "marriage." Considering the fact that regulations concerning the rights of spouses have had a long tradition in the course of European integration, starting with the first regulations on the movement of workers, the prevalence of the term "sexual orientation" is especially puzzling.[21] This issue requires an in-depth qualitative analysis. It should be emphasised that, as in the case of bioethical discourses, the European Parliament has been the most reserved in its use of semantics associated with constrained anthropology. In the case of this institution, there is a particularly large disparity in the use of the category of gender compared to sex, as well as sexual orientation compared to marriage, in favour of the former two. The Parliament also excelled in references to homophobia. Out of the 263 mentions in EU

---

[20]The Court of Justice made 17 references to sexual orientation, and 18 references to marriage. Cf. https://eur-lex.europa.eu/search.html?textScope0=tite&qid=1588579854000&DTS_DOM=ALL&type=advanced&lang=en&andText0=%22marriage%22&SUBDOM_INIT=ALL_ALL&date0=ALL:01012000%7C31122019&DTS_SUBDOM=ALL_ALL&AU_CODED=CJ [04.05.2020] and https://eurlex.europa.eu/search.html?DB_AUTHOR=justice&textScope0=tite&qid=1588580974899&DTS_DOM=ALL&type=advanced&lang=en&andText0=%22sexual%20orientation%22&SUBDOM_INIT=ALL_ALL&date0=ALL:01012000%7C31122019&DTS_SUBDOM=ALL_ALL [04.05.2020].

[21]It may be added that in 2009, 2004 and 2003, references are found in the EP documents to "homosexual marriage." http://eurlex.europa.eu/search.html?textScope0=tite&qid=1467050794610&CASE_LAW_SUMMARY=false&DTS_DOM=ALL&type=advanced&lang=en&andText0=%22homosexual%20marriage%22&SUBDOM_INIT=ALL_ALL&date0=ALL:01062001%7C31052016&DTS_SUBDOM=ALL_ALL [27.06.2016].

documents, 166 came from those of the European Parliament.[22] It is worth noting that, as shown in Diagram 11.5, the concept of homophobia had practically not been used in EU documents until 2005. A sudden spike occurred in 2006, when the EU referred to it 25 times. The data presented in Diagram 11.5 also show that the prevalence of terms characteristic of unconstrained anthropology has been a lasting phenomenon for the last 20 years. This is confirmed by the results of one last comparison which does not require a graphic form. In the description of homosexualism in EU documents in the past 20 years, one document referred to the category of "homosexual inclination,"[23] linked to the approach of constrained anthropology. At the same time, EU documents referred 297 times to the LGBT category[24] and 171 times to the category of "homosexuals"[25]: both linked to the perspective of unconstraint.

Summing up the above findings, it may be concluded that the European Union refers to terms characteristic of both anthropological standpoints. Nevertheless, a quantitative analysis of the language of its documents supports the hypothesis that it is permanently dominated by concepts characteristic of unconstrained anthropology. In this regard, an incomparably greater number of references to the central categories of unconstrained anthropology and their clear prevalence over concepts reflecting the views of constrained anthropology has been observed in the discourse on sexuality. While, for example, in bioethical discourse the number of references to "unborn child" and "abortion" is similar, no such opposite concepts with a similar number of references can be found in EU documents relating to the dispute over human sexuality. In addition, it may be noted that the total number of references to sexual and reproductive health/rights is only half the number of references to sexual orientation, not to mention the concept of gender. It therefore seems that an initial hypothesis may be made about a more pronounced domination of unconstrained anthropology in the dispute over human sexuality compared to the bioethical dispute.

---

[22]https://eur-lex.europa.eu/search.html?textScope0=ti-te&qid=1588581462283&DTS_DOM=ALL&type=advanced&lang=en&andText0=%22homophobia%22&SUBDOM_INIT=ALL_ALL&date0=ALL:01012000%7C31122019&DTS_SUBDOM=ALL_ALL [04.05.2020]. As far as the other institutions are concerned, 67 references were made in documents of the European Commission, 9 in documents of the Council, and 2 in documents of the Court of Justice.

[23]https://eurlex.europa.eu/search.html?textScope0=tite&qid=1588578564449&DTS_DOM=ALL&type=advan-ced&lang=en&andText0=%22homosexual%20inclination%22&SUBDOM_INIT=ALL_ALL&date0=ALL:01012000%7C31122019&DTS_SUBDOM=ALL_ALL [04.05.2020].

[24]https://eurlex.europa.eu/search.html?textScope0=tite&qid=1588581579608&DTS_DOM=ALL&type=advan-ced&lang=en&andText0=%22LGBT%22&SUBDOM_INIT=ALL_ALL&date0=ALL:01012000%7C31122019&DTS_SUBDOM=ALL_ALL

[25]https://eur-lex.europa.eu/search.html?textScope0=tite&qid=1588581628987&DTS_DOM=ALL&type=advan-ced&lang=en&andText0=%22HOMOSEXUALS%22&SUBDOM_INIT=ALL_ALL&date0=ALL:01012000%7C31122019&DTS_SUBDOM=ALL_ALL [04.05.2020].

At the same time, differences should be noted between the languages used by European institutions. Concepts used in the bioethical discourse, such as the semantics of the discussion concerning sexuality, suggest that the European Parliament seems to be particularly committed to the logic of unconstraint. The Court of Justice appears to be at the opposite extreme, using language which usually referred proportionally to the categories associated with constrained anthropology. The EU Council and the Commission are somewhere in between these two extremes. In light of the illustrative statistical data, the EU Council seems to be the more restrained one of these two institutions in terms of references to the concepts related to unconstrained anthropology.

11.2   Qualitative Analysis: Bioethical Issues

As mentioned in the previous chapter, the concepts associated with unconstrained anthropology often remain semantically "open," allowing for a variety of interpretations. This also means that the legislator can potentially "close" them, thus taking away—at least to a large extent—their potential to support cultural change. In order to understand the importance of the prevalence of particular terms, it is necessary to examine what content is attributed to them in the documents of European institutions. And this is what this part of the study will be focused on. It should be added that an analysis of the contents of terms used in documents entails, provided that such contents are relatively unequivocal, an analysis of the goals of the institutions' activities in a given area. In this sense, qualitative research on the language of European politics, which touches upon the problem of the functioning of European institutions, may lead to forming initial conclusions about their anthropological position.

11.2.1   Sexual and Reproductive Health and Rights

In 2003, the European Union defined, and did so in a legally binding manner, its understanding of sexual and reproductive health. Regulation No. 1567/2003 of the European Parliament and of the Council of 15 July 2003 on aid for policies and actions on reproductive and sexual health and rights (SRHR) in developing countries states that "[t]he Community is deeply concerned by the reproductive and sexual health conditions of women and men, in particular those aged 15 to 49, in developing countries," and declares its intention to "make a full contribution towards achieving the Millennium Development Goals of reducing by three-quarters the rate of maternal mortality, achieving gender equality, and attaining access to sexual and reproductive health care and services worldwide."[26] Pursuant to the Regulation, "the Community shall support actions to improve reproductive and sexual health in developing countries and to secure respect for the rights relating thereto", and "shall provide financial assistance and appropriate expertise with a view to promoting a holistic approach to, and the recognition of, reproductive and sexual health and rights as defined in the ICPD Programme of Action, including safe motherhood and universal access to a comprehensive range of safe and reliable reproductive and sexual health care and services."[27] These declarations, rather vague due to the vagueness of the very concept of "reproductive health," may seem even more puzzling in the context of the Preamble which says that the Union, while recognizing "the right of individuals to decide freely on the number and spacing of their children," condemns "any violation of human rights in the form of compulsory abortion, compulsory sterilization, infanticide, or the rejection, abandonment or abuse of unwanted children as a means of curbing population growth."[28] Thus, the Union does not condemn abortion or sterilization as such. Rather, it is the inability to take an autonomous decision concerning them that is condemned.

Despite all the ambiguities contained in the text,[29] the Regulation explicitly states that no support is to be given under its provisions to "incentives to encourage sterilisation or abortion, or to the improper testing of contraception methods in developing countries. When cooperation measures are implemented, the decisions adopted at the ICPD [International Conference on Population and Development], in particular point 8.25 of the ICPD Programme of Action, according to which, inter alia, abortion should in no case be promoted as a method of family planning, must be rigorously observed. Post-abortion counselling, education and family planning services should be offered promptly, which will also help to avoid repeat abortions."[30]

This declaration is important for two reasons. On the anthropological level, it explicitly settles the way in which reproductive rights are understood in EU policies. The Regulation leaves no doubt that abortion is not part of the reproductive rights guaranteed by the Union. It is worth noting that in addition to negative obligations (prohibition of the promotion and financing of abortion), it includes a positive obligation to prevent further abortions. Consequently, despite the emphasis on the will of autonomous individuals with regard to the above-mentioned rights, the Union remains within the framework of the anthropology of constraint, recognizing the objectively existing moral limits to man's will.

---

[26]EU Council, EU Parliament, *Regulation (EC) No 1567/2003 of the European Parliament and of the Council of 15 July 2003 on aid for policies and actions on reproductive and sexual health and rights in developing countries*, Official Journal of the EU L 224, 11/v.48, *Preamble*, p. 9, p. 24.

[27]Ibid., Article 1.

[28]Ibid., *Preamble*, p. 5.

[29]Cf. also Natalia Brachowicz,"Prawa reprodukcyjne w polityce Unii Europejskiej. Parlament i Komisja Europejska wobec aborcji," *Pressje* 2009, p. 216.

[30]Ibid.

Politically, this declaration means that the Union has officially joined the US position. The passage which says that "in no case should abortion be promoted as a method of family planning" refers directly to the Helms amendment[31] adopted after Roe vs. Wade, prohibiting the United States from funding abortions as part of their foreign policy.[32] Its significance was enhanced in 1984 when the Reagan administration implemented a principle which "prohibited foreign nongovernmental organizations (NGOs) that receive U.S. family planning assistance from using non-U.S. funding to provide abortion services, information, counselling or referrals and from engaging in advocacy to promote abortion."[33] Consequently, to this day the US Agency for International Development (USAID) does not allow the financing of "abortion services," or equipping in or purchasing the means necessary to perform them,[34] or the practical "co-financing" of such activities. Given the financial importance of U.S. contribution to global health aid,[35] the American approach is crucial for the standards of developmental and humanitarian aid respected by all its providers. Since "most international humanitarian organizations rely in some part on U.S. funding, they are reluctant to take the risk"[36] related to the provision of abortion services. Consequently, abortion used to be, in principle, absent from the aid they provide.

The EU Regulation of 2003, like the U.S. solutions, reflected the recognition, characteristic of constrained anthropology, that due to the special dignity and "non-exchangeability" of man, human life must be protected from the very beginning. However, this document was repealed by the Commission's proposal for a financing instrument for development cooperation (DCI, Development Cooperation Instrument) in 2004.[37] The instrument, initially objected to by the European Parliament in

---

[31]Following the 1973 ruling in Roe vs. Wade which recognized the constitutionality of abortion in the United States, in an attempt to limit its practical consequences the Congress adopted an amendment that said: "No foreign assistance funds may be used to pay for the performance of abortion as a method of family planning or to motivate or coerce any person to practice abortions."

[32]Sneha Barrot, "Abortion Restrictions in U.S. Foreign Aid: The History and Harms of the Helms Amendment," *Guttmacher Policy Review* 3 (16) 2013, p. 9. More specifically, pro-abortion circles consider it scandalous that "while 'as a method of family planning' is not defined in the amendment, the federal status quo on abortion restrictions suggests that this excludes, at the very least, cases of rape, incest, and life endangerment," thus standing in contradiction to U.S. legislation.
Cf. http://www.genderhealth.org/the_issues/us_foreign_policy/helms/ [29.04.2016].

[33]S. Barrot, op. cit., p. 10.

[34]http://www.genderhealth.org/the_issues/us_foreign_policy/helms/ [29.04.2016].

[35]Cf. S. Barrot, op. cit., p. 13.

[36]Aryn Baker, *The Secret War Crime*, http://time.com/war-and-rape/?xid=homepage [02.05.2016]. Compared to other publications arguing for the funding of abortion for victims of war rape, this article stands out in that it documents conversations conducted with raped women in refugee camps. The author shows that due to the loss of their own families and loved ones during the war, the children conceived as a result of rape are often the only meaning of life for their mothers.

[37]It was originally intended as an instrument for financing development cooperation and economic cooperation, combining the development and economic policy with developed countries. Cf. European Commission, *Proposal for a Regulation of the European Parliament and of the Council*

view of a possible limitation of its competences,[38] was finally adopted by the Council and the Parliament through a conciliation procedure, entering into force on January 1, 2007 to replace more than a dozen earlier regulations on development policy.[39] Although apparently the main motivation for its adoption was to simplify EU legislation on development cooperation accumulated over the years, it reopened the question of how EU institutions understand reproductive rights.

The Instrument refers to the issue of reproductive health in three places. In the Preamble, the Union declares that "actions should be supported to improve reproductive and sexual health in developing countries and to secure respect for the rights relating thereto; financial assistance and appropriate expertise should be provided with a view to promoting a holistic approach to, and the recognition of, reproductive and sexual health and rights as defined in the Programme of Action of the International Conference on Population and Development (ICPD), including safe motherhood and universal access to a comprehensive range of safe and reliable reproductive and sexual health care and services. When cooperation measures are implemented, the decisions adopted at the ICPD must be rigorously observed, where relevant"[40]. Moreover, Article 5 explains that the purpose of the DCI is to increase "access to and provision of health services (...) with a central focus on the related MDGs [Millennium Development Goals], namely reducing child mortality, improving maternal and child health and sexual and reproductive health and rights as set out in the Cairo Agenda of the International Conference on Population and Development (ICPD),"[41] and Article 12, as part of the efforts aimed at eliminating diseases related to poverty, provides for supporting "actions to improve reproductive and sexual health in developing countries and to secure the right of women, men and adolescents to good reproductive and sexual health and provide financial assistance and appropriate expertise with a view to promoting a holistic approach to, and the recognition of, reproductive and sexual health and rights as defined in the ICPD Programme of Action, including safe motherhood and universal access to a comprehensive range of safe and reliable reproductive and sexual health care and services, supplies, education and information, including information on all kinds of family planning methods, including reducing maternal mortality and morbidity rates."[42]

---

establishing a financing instrument for development cooperation and economic cooperation, COM (2004) 629 final 2004/0220 (COD).

[38]Cf. Gay Mitchell, *I Report on the proposal for a regulation of the European Parliament and of the Council establishing a financing instrument for development cooperation and economic cooperation (COM(2004)0629—C6-0128/2004—2004/0220(COD))*, A6-0060/2005 and the extraordinarily consistent opinions it contains of other Committees of the Parliament.

[39]Cf. *Regulation (EC) No. 1905/2006 of the European Parliament and of the Council of 18 December 2006 establishing a financing instrument for development cooperation*, Official Journal of the European Union L 378, p. 41.

[40]Ibid., Preamble, p. 18.

[41]Ibid., Article 5.2.b) i.

[42]Ibid., Article 12.2.a) ii.

At least two changes can be identified, relevant from the anthropological perspective, compared to the previously adopted solutions. Firstly, there is a certain ambivalence in the approach to the arrangements made by the International Conference on Population and Development in Cairo (ICPD). Previously, ICPD decisions had been considered mandatory. This is particularly important considering that access to abortion is not part of the Cairo view of sexual and reproductive rights. Even though the Regulation states that its decisions "must be rigorously observed," it is nevertheless with the express proviso that this only applies "where relevant." Thus, there may be areas where provisions of the ICPD should be read differently, for example, as the 2014–2020 Instrument clarifies, in light of the "outcomes of their review conferences,"[43] or interpretations of UN agencies, whose opinions differ markedly. For example, the Committee for the Elimination of all Forms of Discrimination Against Women officially includes access to abortion in reproductive rights.[44]

Another, much more important, change in the Instrument is leaving out some essential content present in the 2003 Regulation. One may easily notice that all references which required the exclusion of abortion from the concept of reproductive rights have disappeared. Their deletion, in view of the political agenda for considering abortion as part of these rights described above,[45] makes the calls in the Regulation to promote "a holistic approach to, and the recognition of, reproductive and sexual health and rights" sound ambiguous, to say the least. Consequently, actions taken by the EU to provide information on "all kinds of family planning methods" may even be read as a foretoken of breaking the alliance with the Helms amendment, at least in the area of development policy. Furthermore, considering that Article 12 repeats the category of reproductive health four times in a single sentence, more blurring than clarifying the proper meaning of this concept, it appears that a wildcard category has been deliberately introduced here in place of an unambiguous one.

It is worth noting that none of these references to reproductive health were present in the Commission's original proposal. They are the outcome of the joint work of the Council and the Parliament in the conciliation procedure. Defending its legislative prerogatives, the Council was interested in adding specific development policy areas and topics.[46] While the content of these "thematic provisions," to use the Council's

---

[43] *Regulation (EU) No. 233/2014 of the European Parliament and of the Council of 11 March 2014 establishing a financing instrument for development cooperation for the period 2014-2020*, Official Journal of the European Union L 77/44.

[44] Cf. European Dignity Watch, *The Funding of Abortion through EU Development Aid. An Analysis of EU's Sexual And Reproductive Health Policy*, Brussels 2012, p. 6.

[45] Even if this is logically contradictory—cf. EDW, *The Funding...*, pp. 6–7.

[46] Cf. Council of the European Union, *Statement of the Council's Reasons [behind] the Common Position (EC) No. 28/2006 adopted by the Council on 23 October 2006 with a view to the adoption of a Regulation of the European Parliament and of the Council establishing a financing instrument for development cooperation*, Official Journal of the European Union C 301E/52. The Statement explains that "Article 3 of the initial Commission proposal merely stated that measures should be

nomenclature, was based on existing Regulations, the Council stressed that their content had been "adapted to changing needs and realities."[47] In the case of reproductive rights, the "changing realities" seem to have made it necessary to reject clear-cut concepts. This is reflected in the fact that in view of the radical differences between the States in their approach to abortion, the Council was unable to work out a consensus on the financing of abortion services as part of development aid[48] and adopted a formula "acceptable" to all representatives of the States that make it up. One might say that it reflected the anthropological strategy inherent in the Charter of Fundamental Rights.

Members of the European Parliament took note of the introduction of reproductive health passages into the text. Their reactions were radically different. Gay Mitchell, Member of the European Parliament who served as rapporteur, proposed an amendment to the draft calling for all three passages to be removed from the final text of the Regulation.[49] However, most MEPs reacted differently, and Mitchell's amendments were not approved by the Chamber. They voted against the rapporteur's position and in favor of upholding the text agreed upon with the Council. The Parliament's position came as no surprise, as it was consistent with its understanding of reproductive rights in other situations. Already in 2002, a report by the Socialist MP Anne E.M. van Lancker, approved by the Parliament, recommended that "in order to safeguard women's reproductive health and rights, abortion should be made legal, safe and accessible to all."[50] In a resolution adopted several years later on improving maternal health, proposed jointly by representatives of all political groups,[51] the European Parliament urged the EU "to remain in the vanguard of efforts to support sexual and reproductive health rights," pointing to the problem with their implementation reflected, among others, in the fact that in sub-Saharan Africa "30% of all maternal deaths (...) are caused by unsafe abortions."[52]

---

financed under geographical or thematic programmes, which would be drawn up by the Commission, that would equally specify their geographical scope. The Council, however, chose to take a different way in order to preserve its legislative powers. Rather than reducing the initial Commission proposal to a procedural instrument, requiring the Commission to make use of its right of initiative to present proposals for additional policy regulations, the Council felt that it would be more appropriate to introduce policy content in the provisions of the Regulation. Therefore, Articles 5 to 10 of the Common Position set the policy for geographical programmes, while Articles 11 to 16 provide for the content of thematic programmes." (p. 83).

[47]EU Council, *Statement . . .*, p. 7.

[48]Cf. European Dignity Watch, *The Funding of Abortion through EU Development Aid. . .*, p. 10.

[49]*Amendments 1, 2, 3 by Gay Mitchell and others* of 8.12.2006, A6-0448/1, A6-0448/2, A6-0448/3, Financing instrument for development cooperation.

[50]European Parliament, *European Parliament Resolution on Sexual and Reproductive Health and Rights (2001/2128 (INI))*, P5_TA(2002)0359, p. 12.

[51]394:182 with 34 abstentions http://www.europarl.europa.eu/oeil/popups/sda.do?id=16011& l=en [28.06.2016].

[52]European Parliament, *European Parliament resolution of 4 September 2008 on Maternal Mortality ahead of the UN High-level Event on the Millennium Development Goals to be held on 25 September 2008*, P6_TA(2008)0406, p. 13.

Consequently, the Resolution called for an increase in the level of EU funding for reproductive rights, since "if not, women will continue to die from pregnancy."[53] In the same Resolution, the Parliament "condemns the US's 'global gag rule' which prevents foreign NGOs that receive USAID (United States Agency for International Development) family planning funding from using their own, non-US funds to provide legal abortion services, medical counselling or abortion referrals."[54]

   The Parliament began to regularly speak on abortion as part of reproductive rights in a more explicit way during the 2009–2014 term. Already in the resolution on equality between women and men adopted in February 2010 by a majority of 381 to 253 votes,[55] the Parliament expressly stated that "women must have control over their sexual and reproductive rights, notably through easy access to contraception and abortion; (...) that women must have access free of charge to consultation on abortion," thus supporting "measures and actions to improve women's access to sexual and reproductive health services and to raise their awareness of their rights and of available services."[56] Similar passages can be found in subsequent resolutions devoted to this topic. In its 2011 resolution, the European Parliament "advocates access for women and men to adequate information and support on reproductive health, and stresses that women should have the same rights and opportunities as men to avail themselves of services in this area; stresses that women must have control over their sexual and reproductive rights, particularly through easy access to contraception and abortion; calls on the Member States and the Commission to adopt measures and actions raising awareness among men about their responsibilities in sexual and reproductive matters."[57] This trend continued in the next term of office. For example, in the 2015 resolution on progress on equality between women and men in the European Union, the European Parliament "maintains that women must have control over their sexual and reproductive health and rights, not least by having ready access to contraception and abortion; supports, accordingly, measures and actions to improve women's access to sexual and reproductive health services and inform them more fully about their rights and the services available."[58] The Resolution was adopted by a majority of 441:205 votes, with 52 abstentions.[59] Considering these and many other statements[60] by the European Parliament on reproductive

---

[53]Ibid., p. 14.

[54]Ibid., p. 22.

[55]http://www.europarl.europa.eu/oeil/popups/sda.do?id=17914&l=en [28.06.2016].

[56]European Parliament, *European Parliament resolution of 10 February 2010 on equality between women and men in the European Union—2009(2009/2101(INI))*, P7_TA(2010)0021.

[57]http://uniaeuropejska.org/kontrowersyjne-stanowisko-parlamentu-europejskiego-w-sprawie-aborcji/ [28.06.2016].

[58]European Parliament, *European Parliament resolution of 10 March 2015 on progress on equality between women and men in the European Union in 2013 (2014/2217(INI))*, P8_TA(2015) 0050, p. 47.

[59]http://www.europarl.europa.eu/oeil/popups/sda.do?id=25230&l=en [28.06.2016].

[60]Some of them are discussed by Natalia Brachowicz in "Prawa reprodukcyjne w polityce Unii Europejskiej...", pp. 208–218.

rights, as well as the absence of any resolutions over the last 20 years explicitly presenting an anthropologically different standpoint,[61] it may be concluded that the European Parliament permanently recognizes abortion as a reproductive right, clarifying any semantic ambiguities in anthropological terms.

While the Council's understanding of reproductive and sexual health and rights remains deliberately indeterminate, and the Parliament's position is consistently based on unconstrained anthropology, it is interesting, in the absence of a legal definition of reproductive rights in the EU, to see what is the Commission's official standpoint on the matter. The Commission has not presented its position *expressis verbis* in any document. The answer came from an unexpected source. In April 2014, the Socialist MEP from Malta Claudette Abela Baldacchino asked the Commission whether they could provide an analysis of the Member States' interpretation of the term SRHR in view of the diversity its interpretations in international and national law.[62] In reply, the Commissioner for Health Tonio Borg wrote on behalf of the Commission that they were aware of divergences in the understanding of reproductive and sexual health and rights by the Member States.[63] He then cited the WHO's definition of sexual health which states that "sexual health is a state of physical, emotional, mental and social well-being in relation to sexuality. Reproductive health addresses the reproductive processes functions and system at all stages of life."[64] He also stated that "Member States are responsible for the definition of their health services policy and for the organization and delivery of health services and medical care. As such, sexual and reproductive rights fall under the exclusive responsibility of Member States." The Commission themselves did not feel obligated, therefore, to define these rights in detail, or to implement them. Consequently, Commissioner

---

[61]Though following the European Parliament's resolutions closely, one may find a few passages suggesting the possibility for a different anthropological standpoint being expressed in the Parliament. For example, in the 2011 resolution on violence against women, the European Parliament "asks the Commission to focus more closely on violence against pregnant women in which the offender harms more than one party." European Parliament, *European Parliament resolution of 5 April 2011 on priorities and outline of a new EU policy framework to fight violence against women* (2010/2209(INI)), P7_TA(2011)0127, p. 22. This position suggests recognition of the personal dignity of life in the prenatal phase, implicitly contrasting the Parliament's pro-abortion position reiterated in many other Resolutions.

[62]Claudette Abela Baldacchino, *Question for written answer to the Commission on Rule 117. Subject: Definition of sexual and reproductive health rights*, P-004206-14. The question was: "The notion of sexual and reproductive health rights appears to be interpreted in varying ways in international treaties and national legislation. Can the Commission provide an analysis of how Member States interpret the notion of sexual and reproductive health rights?".

[63]Tonio Borg, *Answer given by Mr Borg on behalf of the Commission*, P-004206/2014.

[64]It is worth noting that the Commission has indeed funded EU studies relating to such a broad understanding of these rights without entering into anthropologically problematic areas. Cf. e.-g. *Project No. 2004314 under EU Health Programme 2008-2013 Improving the sexual and reproductive health of persons living with HIV in Europe (EUROSUPPORT V)* http://ec.europa.eu/chafea/projects/database.html?prjno=2004314 [28.06.2016].

Borg tried not to settle the anthropological dispute around the approach to abortion, keeping to the exceedingly general definition provided by the WHO.

While the Commission's response may be considered binding as regards internal politics,[65] it can hardly be considered other than evasive with regard to external politics. It operates on the basis of the Development Cooperation Instrument (DCI) described above, so it must have adopted some operational definition of reproductive rights, in particular in view of the divergent interpretations among the Member States. Since no answer to these questions can be found in the Commission's declarations concerning the notion of SRHR as regards abortion, they must be sought in functional analysis in next chapter. Summing up, it should be said that between 2003 and 2008 the European Union departed from an interpretation of reproductive and sexual health and rights which tried to link them to the logic of anthropological boundaries. The EU's indeterminate approach has been upheld in the DCI for the years 2014–2020, which embraced the vagueness characteristic of the 2007 Regulation. It states in two places that the Union's objective is to promote "the full and effective implementation of the Beijing Platform for Action and the Programme of Action of the International Conference on Population and Development and the outcomes of their review conferences and in this context sexual and reproductive health and rights."[66] Consequently, there is a discrepancy between the institutions in their understanding of the goals of the policy related to these rights, as well as an anthropological discrepancy. The European Parliament seems to stand unequivocally on the unconstrained position by including the right to abortion in the heart of reproductive rights. The Council is internally divided between States which conceive of these rights in a manner similar to the EP and (the smaller number of) States which reinterpret them in the spirit of constraint (such as Poland, Hungary or Malta). Consequently, it avoids presenting an explicit anthropological position. The Commission also tries to avoid defining the concept, although it is binding on it through secondary legislation. The EU Court of Justice has so far not addressed the subject of reproductive rights at all.

Despite the ambiguity of the standpoint adopted by the Commission and the Council, one should be careful about concluding that only the European Parliament follows unconstrained anthropology in its activities. Of course, its position is the most explicit in anthropological terms. However, looking at the evolution of the understanding of SRHR in the EU that has led to the increasing ambiguity of this concept, which in itself is a characteristic feature of the conceptual network associated with unconstrained anthropology, and the fact that in their documents after 2007 none of these institutions has challenged the legitimacy of treating abortion as an

---

[65]Tonio Borg, *Answer given by Mr Borg on behalf of the Commission*, P-004206/2014.

[66]*Annex I Areas of Cooperation Under Geographic Programmes, in: Regulation (EU) No. 233/2014 of the European Parliament and of the Council of 11 March 2014...*, Official Journal of the European Union L 77/59. This is repeated in one other place where the Union declares its support for "promoting the full and effective implementation of the Beijing Platform for Action and the Programme of Action of the International Conference on Population and Development and the outcomes of their review conferences and in this context sexual and reproductive health and rights."

element of reproductive rights, it is clear that even in the understanding of these rights the logic of unconstraint comes to the fore. It may be hypothesized that it will be more pronounced in the Commission than in the Council, which ultimately needs to achieve a consensus between the Member States for its decisions. Verification of this hypothesis will require further analyses, however, of the institutions' behavior in the course of the EU decision-making processes.

11.2.2   Abortion

Although, as already mentioned, the Court of Justice of the European Union has not taken a stance in the discussion concerning reproductive rights, it has participated in it indirectly, playing an important role in shaping the approach to abortion in the EU. The Court of Justice referred to this issue directly in the early 1990s in Case C-159/90 *The Society for the Protection of Unborn Children Ireland Ltd (SPUC) v. Grogan and others*. This issue has already been mentioned above, but at this point it is worth taking a look at the broader context of the case.

In 1989, SPUC called upon Stefan Grogan and others to desist from disseminating in Ireland information about English abortion clinics, and when they did not comply, petitioned "the District Court for an injunction prohibiting assistance in abortion."[67] Abortion, permitted in the UK, had always been a crime under "Irish law, first at common law, and since 1861 by statute as an offence against the person. In addition, in 1983 an amendment to the Irish Constitution was approved by referendum (Article 40, Section 3, third subsection), which says that 'The State acknowledges the right to life of the unborn and, with due regard to the equal right to life of the mother, guarantees in its laws to respect, and, as far as practicable, by its laws to defend and vindicate that right.' It is settled case-law that helping a pregnant woman to travel abroad [for the purpose of having an abortion—M.G.] (...) is a form of assisting in abortion and is contrary to Article 40, Section 3, third subsection of the Irish Constitution."[68]

In view of the provisions of the EEC Treaty, the Court referred three questions to the EU Court of Justice: "1. Does the organized activity or process of carrying out an abortion or the medical termination of pregnancy come within the definition of 'services' provided for in Article 60 of the Treaty establishing the European Economic Community? 2. In the absence of any measures providing for the approximation of the laws of Member States concerning the organized activity or process of carrying out an abortion or the medical termination of pregnancy, can a Member State prohibit the distribution of specific information about the identity, location and means of communication with a specified clinic or clinics in another Member State where abortions are performed? 3. Is there a right at Community law in a person in

---

[67]Leszek Bosek, "Aborcja a swoboda...," p. 128.
[68]Ibid., p. 128.

Member State A to distribute specific information about the identity, location and means of communication with a specified clinic or clinics in Member State B where abortions are performed, where the provision of abortion is prohibited under both the Constitution and the criminal law of Member State A but is lawful under certain conditions in Member State B?"[69].

In its reply to the first question, the Court of Justice ruled that "[w]hatever the merits of those arguments on the moral plane, (. . .) the answer (. . .) must be that medical termination of pregnancy, performed in accordance with the law of the State in which it is carried out, constitutes a service within the meaning of Article 60 of the Treaty."[70] As for the second and third questions, the Court in fact evaded them, stating that since "students associations distributing the information at issue in the main proceedings are not in cooperation with the clinics whose addresses they publish,"[71] then "the reply to the (. . .) second and third questions must (. . .) be that it is not contrary to Community law for a Member State in which medical termination of pregnancy is forbidden to prohibit students associations from distributing information about the identity and location of clinics in another Member State (. . .) where the clinics in question have no involvement in the distribution of the said information."[72] Thus, considering the earlier rulings of the CJEU, if the clinics had been involved, the judgment might have been different.

Commentators have pointed out that in this judgment "for no apparent reason, the Court prefers economic values over human values." It seems that the case is a little more nuanced. As Leszek Bosek rightly points out, the Court did not ignore the "axiological background" of its judgment. Nevertheless, it avoided resolving the ethical problem related to the status of abortion, consequently leaving the issue of universal human values to the discretion or "legislative autonomy" of the Member State concerned, in this case Ireland. Thus, although it did not negate its position, it did not support it either. This can be evaluated positively, as did the above-mentioned author, since such an approach makes it possible to "reconcile the Community's generally accepted goals with the principle of protecting the cultural diversity of the Member States declared in the Treaty of Lisbon (Article 3 TEU)."[73] It is worth considering, however, on the basis of what meta-axiological solution this

---

[69] *Judgment of the Court of 4 October 1991 in Case C-159/90, Reference to the Court under Article 177 of the EEC Treaty by the High Court of Ireland for a preliminary ruling in the action pending before that Court between The Society for the Protection of Unborn Children Ireland Ltd and Stephen Grogan and Others*, s. I-4736 – I-4737, http://curia.europa.eu/juris/showPdf.jsf; jsessionid=9ea7d2dc30d51acd24139990478ab79aad18e62e51c.
e34KaxiLc3qMb40Rch0SaxyKbhf0?
text=&docid=97366&pageIndex=0&doclang=EN&mode=lst&dir=&occ=first&part=1&cid-
=1090638 [15.09.2016].
[70] Ibid.
[71] Ibid.
[72] Ibid., p. 131.
[73] Ibid., p. 132.

is possible. Why does the Court "allow for balancing economic interests protected by freedoms provided for in the Treaty with guarantees of human rights"?[74]

The fact that in its judgment the Court does not engage in moral reflection on the substance of the matter at all and thus avoids the metaphysics of values is compensated for with its replacement by the "neutral" logic of the sociology of values. In evading a moral assessment of the merits of Ireland's arguments, the Court *ex definitione* did not regard those values which "are not based on principles or values currently recognized by the entire Community or by a majority of its Member States"[75] as a moral limit to the logic of economy, even if such values are enshrined in a constitution. However, as Maja Grzymkowska pointed out, "even considering abortion a service and making it subject to free market rules is irreconcilable with the Irish Constitution. The European Court of Justice applies the term service to behaviour which is a violation of fundamental constitutional law. Moreover, the CJEU protects the free provision of this service."[76] It is also worth noting that the CJEU did not attempt by way of derogation to cite Article 46 TEC which allows for imposing restrictions on the provision of services.

The Grogan case shows that the CJEU's adoption of the logic of the sociology of values, and thus an attempt at avoiding fundamental anthropological decisions and the adoption of the logic of the "lowest common denominator" ultimately means standing in opposition to constrained anthropology, at least in the sense of its weakening characteristic of the logic of late modernity. From the practical point of view, the application of this approach does not imply the freedom of the States to apply a "higher level of protection" to human life, "because the existence of the internal market makes it possible to 'circumvent' restrictions resulting from national law."[77] The costs of the CJEU's rejection of the maximalist approach based on metaphysics are therefore the higher "the greater the disparities in standards of protection between a particular State and other Member States." [78] In the analyzed case, it is therefore worth noting that the judgment rendered by the CJEU was "the direct reason for the Member States to supplement the Maastricht Treaty with Additional Protocol No. 17, which guarantees that 'no provision in the Treaty on European Union nor in the Treaties establishing the European Communities (...), the Treaties or the Acts supplementing or modifying those Treaties, shall affect the application by Ireland of Article 40 Section 3, third subsection of the Irish Constitution.'"[79]

The fact that the Court made no reference to the issue of abortion in its ruling seems to be a characteristic feature of the European institutions' approach to this issue. The European Commission, even when promoting reproductive rights, has

---

[74]Ibid.

[75]Ibid.

[76]M. Grzymkowska, op. cit., p. 247.

[77]Ibid., p. 252.

[78]Ibid.

[79]L. Bosak, *Aborcja a swoboda...*, p. 133.

consistently refused to initiate any regulations concerned with abortion, arguing that this is an area of the exclusive competence of the Member States. The European Parliament which in its political activities explicitly includes abortion in human rights stands out against this background. For example, in its resolution adopted in 2015 on the Annual Report on Human Rights,[80] the Parliament "finds it regrettable that women's and girls' bodies, specifically with respect to their sexual and reproductive health and rights, still remain an ideological battleground, and calls for the EU and its Member States to recognise the **inalienable rights** [emphasis—M.G.] of women and girls to (. . .) safe and legal abortion,"[81] finding the refusal of abortion to a woman to be a "gross violation of human rights." Examples of such declarations are many. It seems characteristic, however, that although the above issues can easily be found in the EP's Resolution on the Report, in the Report on Human Rights itself, published by the Council of the European Union, the issue of abortion is not mentioned among human rights at all.[82]

11.2.3   The Beginning of Human Life

As noted in Chap. 10, primary law does not define the moment after conception from which a human being is entitled to the protection of life. Nevertheless, this issue must *nolens volens* be settled by the EU's secondary legislation, adopted by the Parliament and the Council on a proposal from the Commission, for example as regards the use of human embryos in the course of scientific research. Moreover, as the significance of bioethical questions in EU politics keep increasing, the question of how the beginnings of human life are understood and protected has become a subject of decisions made by the CJEU.

The first reason for bringing this issue to the Court was the Biotechnological Directive adopted in 1998, which provided that although "the human body, at the various stages of its formation and development, and the simple discovery of one of its elements, including the sequence or partial sequence of a gene, cannot constitute patentable inventions,"[83] nevertheless "an element isolated from the human body or otherwise produced by means of a technical process, including the sequence or partial sequence of a gene, may constitute a patentable invention, even if the

---

[80]European Parliament, *European Parliament resolution of 12 March 2015 on the Annual Report on Human Rights and Democracy in the World 2013 and the European Union's policy on the matter(2014/2216(INI)), P8_TA(2015)0076.*

[81]Ibid., p. 136.

[82]Though in the 2014 Report there are references to other comments by the Parliament. Cf. Council of the European Union, *EU Annual Report on Human Rights and Democracy in the World in 2014*, 10152/15, pp. 67–72.

[83]*Directive 98/44/EC of the European Parliament and of the Council of 6 July 1998 on the legal protection of biotechnological inventions*, Article 5 Section 1.

structure of that element is identical to that of a natural element."[84] The Netherlands brought an appeal against the Tribunal the very same year pointing out that "elements of the human body are not patentable"[85] and argued that particularly in Article 5(2) "the Directive violates fundamental rights despite citing them in the 16th and 43rd recital of the Preamble;"[86] it also pointed out that the human body is a necessary instrument for the existence of human dignity. Consequently, "in view of this dignity an instrumental use of the human body is not permissible."[87]

The standpoint of the Kingdom of the Netherlands—stemming from premises characteristic of constrained anthropology and challenging the position of the Commission, the Parliament and the Council leaning towards unconstrained anthropology—was rejected by the Court. It resolved that in principle Article 5(1) of the Directive provides adequate safeguards for human dignity, and did not find any problems with the broad exception provided for in Articles 5(2) and 6 of the Directive. The Court stated that in the light of Article 5, neither elements of the human body in themselves nor their discovery can be the subject of protection: "Only inventions which combine a natural element with a technical process enabling it to be isolated or produced for an industrial application can be the subject of an application for a patent."[88] The possibility of an instrumentalization of the human body in this process was not of interest to the Court of Justice.[89]

An even clearer perspective for the instrumentalization of human life was approved in the Seventh Framework Programme for Research adopted in 2006, in which the EU institutions stipulated that "[r]esearch on the use of human stem cells, both adult and embryonic, may be financed, depending both on the contents of the scientific proposal and the legal framework of the Member state(s) involved."[90] Even though the said legislative resolution stated that "[a]ny such application for financing must include details of the licensing and control measures that will be taken by the competent authorities of the Member States", and that "[a]s regards the use of human embryonic stem cells, institutions, organisations and researchers must

---

[84]Ibid., Sect. 2.

[85]Agata Skorek, "Zdolność patentowa wynalazków biotechnologicznych a godność ludzka w regulacji Wspólnoty Europejskiej," *Studia Europejskie* 4/2008, p. 112.

[86]Ibid.

[87]Ibid., p. 112.

[88]Court of Justice, *Judgment of the Court 9 October 2001 in Case C-377/98, Netherlands v. Parliament and Council* http://curia.europa.eu/juris/showPdf.jsf; jsessionid=9ea7d2dc30d5e48086928a5443bd839f81d292779d18. e34KaxiLc3qMb40Rch0SaxuTa3r0?text=&docid=46255&pageIndex=0&doclang=EN& mode=lst&dir=&occ=first&part=1&cid=816316 [17.05.2016].

[89]Cf. Leszek Bosek, *Aksjologia Unii Europejskiej na przykładzie europejskiego prawa medycznego*, http://orka.sejm.gov.pl/WydBAS.nsf/0/210C10FB59F8520FC12578E300436679/ $file/AKSJOLOGIA%20UNII%20EUROPEJSKIEJ%20-%20L.Bosek.pdf [27.05.2016].

[90]European Parliament, *European Parliament legislative resolution on the proposal for a decision of the European Parliament and of the Council concerning the Seventh Framework Programme of the European Community for research, technological development and demonstration activities (2007 to 2013)*, P6_TA(2006)0265.

be subject to strict licensing and control in accordance with the legal framework of the Member State(s) involved,"[91] it explicitly allowed (on the condition it was permitted under the law of the Member State concerned) for an instrumental treatment of the human embryo. *Ergo*, it considered that life in the embryonic phase did not require the protection of human life under European law.

Although this solution was not challenged before the Court, it took up the issue of determining the dignity of human life in the prenatal phase in its 2011 judgment in Case C-34/10 Oliver Brüstle v Greenpeace eV.[92] Even though this judgment also reflects the tendency to evade "an unequivocal resolution of the philosophical status of the concept of dignity present in EU legal acts,"[93] it deviates from the logic of "getting around" the issue, but addresses a key ethical problem.

During the hearing, the Court considered the case of Dr. Olivier Brüstle, the holder of a German patent "which concerns isolated and purified neural precursor cells, processes for their production from embryonic stem cells and the use of neural precursor cells for the treatment of neural defects,"[94] which was ruled invalid by the Bundespatentgericht (Federal Patent Court) as it covered "precursor cells obtained from human embryonic stem cells and processes for the production of those precursor cells."[95] The defendant appealed against this ruling to the Bundesgerichtshof, which referred the following questions to the Court for a preliminary ruling:

> 1. What is meant by the term "human embryos" in Article 6(2)(c) of [the Directive]? (a) Does it include all stages of the development of human life, beginning with the fertilisation of the ovum, or must further requirements, such as the attainment of a certain stage of development, be satisfied? (b) Are the following organisms also included:—unfertilised human ova into which a cell nucleus from a mature human cell has been transplanted;—unfertilised human ova whose division and further development have been stimulated by parthenogenesis? (c) Are stem cells obtained from human embryos at the blastocyst stage also included? 2. What is meant by the expression 'uses of human embryos for industrial or commercial purposes'? Does it include any commercial exploitation within the meaning of Article 6 (1) of [the Directive], especially use for the purposes of scientific research? 3. Is technical teaching to be considered unpatentable pursuant to Article 6(2)(c) of the Directive even if the use of human embryos does not form part of the technical teaching claimed with the patent, but is a necessary precondition for the application of that teaching:—because the patent concerns a product whose production necessitates the prior destruction of human

---

[91] Ibid.

[92] Court of Justice of the European Union, *Judgment of the Court (Grand Chamber) of 18 October 2011 in Case C-34/10: reference for a preliminary ruling under Article 267 TFEU from the Bundesgerichtshof (Germany), made by decision of 17 December 2009, received at the Court on 21 January 2010, in the proceedings: Oliver Brüstle v Greenpeace eV, pp. I-9849 – I-9877*.

[93] Jędrzej Maśnicki, "Godność człowieka w świetle orzeczenia Oliver Brüstle przeciwko GreenpeaceV (C-34/10)," *Zeszyty Prawnicze* 13/4, pp. 206 and 208.

[94] Court of Justice of the European Union, *Judgment of the Court (Grand Chamber) of 18 October 2011 in Case C-34/10...*, p. 15, s. I-9864.

[95] Court of Justice of the European Union, *Judgment of the Court (Grand Chamber) of 18 October 2011 in Case C-34/10...*, p.19, s. I-9865. The judgment concerned the destruction of embryos.

embryos,—or because the patent concerns a process for which such a product is needed as base material?[96]

As pointed out by Jędrzej Maśnicki, "comments in the doctrine indicate that the questions referred for a preliminary ruling were formulated in such a way as to suggest a possible answer contrary to the previous decision of the Enlarged Board of Appeal of the European Patent Office in the WARF/Thomson case. In the decision of the European Patent Office, the controversial patent was refused because the principle of the protection of dignity was also extended to human embryos (. . .). However, the intention of the referring court in Brüstle v Greenpeace was to have the exemptions provided for in the Directive interpreted as narrowly as possible by the CJEU to allow for an interpretation that is favourable to the further development and use of inventions based on the use and destruction of embryos."[97]

The Court did not comply with the referring court's intention and pointed out that "[t]he context and aim of the Directive (. . .) show that the European Union legislature intended to exclude any possibility of patentability where respect for human dignity could thereby be affected."[98] Consequently, it ruled that "the concept of 'human embryo' within the meaning of Article 6(2)(c) of the Directive must be understood in a wide sense."[99] This judgment did not follow the logic of the sociology of values either,[100] even though it avoided metaphysical arguments.[101] In its detailed interpretation of this paragraph, the Court stated, without going into the decisions on this matter made by the Member States, that the human embryo is "any human ovum after fertilisation, any non-fertilised human ovum into which the cell nucleus from a mature human cell has been transplanted and any non-fertilised human ovum whose division and further development have been stimulated by parthenogenesis."[102] Consequently, it stated that "the exclusion from patentability concerning the use of human embryos for industrial or commercial purposes in Article 6(2)(c) of the Directive also covers use for purposes of scientific research, only use for therapeutic or diagnostic purposes which is applied to the human embryo and is useful to it being patentable,"[103] and that "Article 6(2)(c) of Directive 98/44 excludes an invention from patentability where the technical teaching which is

---

[96]Ibid., p. 23.

[97]J. Maśnicki, op.cit., pp. 196–197.

[98]Court of Justice of the European Union, *Judgment of the Court (Grand Chamber) of 18 October 2011 in Case C-34/10. . .*, p. 34, s. I- 9871.

[99]Ibid.

[100]As pointed out by Maśnicki: "the argument often raised against the merits of the decision in Brüstle v Greenpeace is the lack of consensus in the legislation of the Member States as regards identification of the issue of embryos and stem cell research. However, it does not appear that it is the consensus on the admissibility of research on human embryos that is the best measure of the rightness of the decision taken in this case." Op. cit., p. 204.

[101]Ibid.

[102]Court of Justice of the European Union, *Judgment of the Court (Grand Chamber) of 18 October 2011 in Case C-34/10. . .*, s. I- 9876.

[103]Ibid., s. I-9877.

the subject-matter of the patent application requires the prior destruction of human embryos or their use as base material, whatever the stage at which that takes place."[104]

This way, the Court defined and legally guaranteed that human dignity is vested in man also in the embryonic phase of life,[105] *de facto* referring to the way man and protection of human life is understood in European law.[106] Starting with teleological logic, it extended protection to all human organisms, even those which have not been fertilized in the strict sense of the word (e.g. in parthenogenesis), and which are capable of commencing the process of development of a human being just as an embryo created by the fertilization of an ovum.[107] In addition, it ruled out patenting inventions that require the previous killing of human life in the embryonic phase. This way, the CJEU has made man the subject of European law from the moment of conception. Despite all objections raised as to the explicitness of this judgment,[108] it should be emphasized that it departed from the earlier judicial tradition which avoided taking a stance on the ethical nature of the problem and "weighed" ethical and economic reasons, this time presenting a clear anthropological standpoint.

Three years after this ruling, in Case C-364/13 International Stem Cell Corporation v Comptroller General of Patents, Designs and Designs Trade Marks, the EU Court of Justice addressed the question of whether biotechnological inventions based on the use of parthenogenetically activated unfertilized human ova can be patented.[109] The British High Court of Justice "referred to the Court with the question whether the concept of 'human embryo' as it had been interpreted in the judgement in *Brüstle*, is limited to organisms which are capable of commencing the process of development of a human being. In this respect the British court

---

[104]Ibid.

[105]More on this subject, see J. Maśnicki, op. cit., pp. 200–201, where he reconstructs elements of the arguments proposed by the Advocate General.

[106]Even if the judgment only concerns the Biotechnological Directive.

[107]Court of Justice of the European Union, *Judgment of the Court (Grand Chamber) of 18 October 2011 in Case C-34/10...*, p. 36, s. I-9872.

[108]Opinions are divided here as well, however. For example, Marcin Naruszewicz and Piotr Muraszko point out that, despite such a clear definition, the CJEU, "did not manage to infer the simple conclusions it entails and (consistently—i.e. without leaving a margin of discretion in this regard to the Member States) to unequivocally rule on the question which it referred to the German court applying for a preliminary ruling—that is to say, to take a stand in favour of the view that the parent cell obtained from a human embryo at the stage of the blastocyst constitutes a human embryo under the Directive in question." Cf. Marcin Naruszewicz, Piotr Muraszko, "Pojęciei status embrionuludzkiego   w   świetlewyrokuTrybunałuSprawiedliwościUniiEuropejskiej—Oliver Brüestleprzeciwko Greenpeace eV," *Polski Rocznik Praw Człowieka i Prawa Humanitarnego* 3 (2012), pp. 164–165. The authors point out that this has implications for the meaning of the entire judgment, representing, in their view, a form of "moderated patent protection" which "entitles third parties to use that invention for industrial and commercial purposes," (ibid., p. 165) but not for scientific purposes, for example.

[109]Parthenogenesis consists in activating the division and development of an ovum without the participation of sperm, by means of chemical and electrical stimuli. A multicellular organism formed this way is called a "parthenote."

explained that in the light of current scientific knowledge organisms such as those being the subject of patent applications can never develop into a human being."[110]

In its ruling the Court stated that "an unfertilised human ovum whose division and further development have been stimulated by parthenogenesis does not constitute a 'human embryo', within the meaning of that provision, if, in the light of current scientific knowledge, it does not, in itself, have the inherent capacity of developing into a human being, this being a matter for the national court to determine."[111]

Such a definition allows for methods using unfertilized human ova to be patented and used for industrial or commercial purposes. While this opens up new pathways for the development of biotechnology in the EU, it raises new ethical problems. As noted by Bishop Ignacio Carrasco de Paula, President of the Pontifical Academy "Pro Vita," it is not simply that "we are not dealing with an embryo and therefore it can be made the subject of patents and trade (...). Think, for example, of donations of kidneys or other organs for transplantation: these are not embryos, and yet trade in these organs is absolutely prohibited in any serious ethics or medicine (...). This can become dangerous, because such an approach may be gradually extended to other areas, very sensitive ones particularly in our times (...). Especially striking is, for example, the possibility of (...) stimulating in a certain way the initiation of human existence."[112]

The example of these two patent judgments shows that the question of understanding the requirements of human dignity during the prenatal period and the scope of human life is linked by the Court, at least to a certain extent, to individual cases, and does not represent a fully coherent anthropological vision. Nevertheless, it should be noted that compared to the 1990s, the Court now places a much stronger emphasis on the importance of moral content, reorienting from positions akin to unconstrained anthropology towards constrained standpoints. It is particularly interesting in that both the understanding of reproductive rights and evolution of the approach to the protection of human life in its early stages in other EU institutions over the last 15 years has followed the opposite trend.

---

[110]http://www.lex.pl/czytaj/-/artykul/ets-definiuje-pojecie-embrionu-ludzkiego [27.05.2016].

[111]Court of Justice of the European Union, *Judgment of the Court (Grand Chamber) of 18 December 2014 in Case C-364/13 REQUEST for a preliminary ruling under Article 267 TFEU from the High Court of Justice (England & Wales), Chancery Division (Patents Court) (United Kingdom), made by decision of 17 April 2013, received at the Court on 28 June 2013, in International Stem Cell Corporation v Comptroller General of Patents, Designs and Trade Marks,* European Court Reports, ECLI:EU:C:2014:2451, p. 8.

[112]http://www.fronda.pl/a/watykanski-bioetyk-krytycznie-o-orzeczeniu-trybunalu-sprawiedliwosci-ue,45343.html [27.05.2016].

11.3   Qualitative Analysis: Sexuality and Sexual Behavior

In the discourse on human sexuality and sexual behavior in the European Union we have noted the quantitative prevalence in EU documents of references to a number of terms generally present in the so-called gender discourse associated with unconstrained anthropology. A special point of reference in this discourse is the concept of "gender." As indicated in Chap. 9, however, this concept is a double-faceted one: it was initially used in international documents interchangeably with the category of sex, and only over time, due to an extension of its meaning and the breaking of its link with the man/woman dichotomy, it became a category unequivocally related to the anthropology of unconstraint. The initial question to be asked is therefore whether the concept of "gender" in EU institutions is understood in a "broad" or "narrow" sense.

11.3.1   Gender

The concept of gender appears in the European Union in the context of gender equality. It is proposed that "[t]he three main manifestations of this principle are: equal treatment, which is based on the concept of equal rights and implemented through the law; equal opportunities, which is based on the concept of difference and incarnated politically through positive action or positive discrimination measures; and equal impact, which is based on the concept of gender and primarily operates through instruments such as gender mainstreaming."[113] In this view, gender does not appear to be at odds with the concept of sex, with emphasis on the cultural and social dimension of the latter category. It is no coincidence that its promotion has been linked to the influence of feminist circles in the European Commission. As noted by Sylvia Walby, the gender equality unit within the Commission, strongly influenced by feminist groups, "has been central to developing the many Directives to promote gender equality, establishing programmes of action on equalities issues, and building EU-wide networks of experts on gender equalities issues."[114] Consistently, some authors write about equality policy as an evolution of EU standards on equality of the sexes.[115] In this approach, the evolution of EU equality policy in terms of gender would consist in extending the narrowly conceived "equal treatment of women and men as workers in standard forms of employment,"[116] to "the regulation of working-time and (...) non-standard forms of employment, especially part-time and

---

[113]Sophie Jacquot, *Transformations in EU Gender Equality: From emergence to dismantling*, Palgrave Macmillan, 2015, p. 3.

[114]S. Walby, op. cit., p. 17.

[115]Theresa Wobbe, "From Protecting to Promoting: Evolving Sex Equality Norms in an Organisational Field," *European Law Journal* 9 (1), p. 88.

[116]S. Walby, op. cit., p. 25.

temporary work,"[117] so as to "address gender equality more generally."[118] In this perspective, the semantic replacement of "sex" with "gender" in EU documents does not seem to cause anthropological complications, its meaning functionally amounting to the same as man or woman.

From that perspective it is no surprise, that the European Institute for Gender Equality,[119] a EU's agenda tasked with developing, analyzing, evaluating and disseminating "methodological tools in order to support the integration of gender equality into all Community policies and the resulting national policies and to support gender mainstreaming in all Community institutions and bodies."[120] defines "gender mainstreaming," which "became central to the fight against gender inequalities at the beginning of the 1990s,"[121] based on the definition provided by the Council of Europe in 1998 and linked to the anthropology of constraint.[122] It explicitly states that in the Union gender mainstreaming is a "strategy for promoting equality between women and men."[123] This approach is common in the documents of major European institutions. For example, the European Pact for Gender Equality adopted by the Council of the European Union for the years 2011–2020 states that "equality between women and men is a fundamental value of the European Union and that gender equality policies are vital to economic growth, prosperity and competitiveness." Similarly, the European Parliament, in its resolution on commitment to the principle of gender mainstreaming in its own work, "commits itself to regularly adopting and implementing a policy plan for gender mainstreaming in Parliament with the overall objective of promoting equality between women and men through the genuine and effective incorporation of the gender perspective into all policies and activities, so that the different impact of measures on women and on men is assessed, existing initiatives are coordinated, and objectives and priorities, as well as the means of achieving them, are specified."[124] Also the European Commission's Strategy for Equality between Men and Women 2010–2015 and many other

---

[117]Ibid.

[118]Ibid.

[119]Polish translation of the name European Institute for Gender Equality is Europejski Instytut ds. Równości Kobiet i Mężczyzn, which translates as European Institute for the Equality of Men and Women.

[120]European Parliament, *European Parliament resolution of 17 November 2011 on gender mainstreaming in the work of the European Parliament (2011/2151(INI))*, Preamble, p. J.

[121]Sophie Jacquot, op. cit., p. 57.

[122]It says that "[g]ender mainstreaming is the (re)organisation, improvement, development and evaluation of policy processes, so that a gender equality perspective is incorporated into all policies at all levels and all stages."

[123]EIGE, *Mainstreaming gender into the policies and the programmes of the institutions of the European Union and EU Member States*,Publications Office of the European Union, Luxembourg 2013, p. 10.

[124]European Parliament, *European Parliament Resolution of 17 November 2011...*, p. 1.

EU policy positions[125] suggest a close link between sex and gender. It is worth stressing that they do so not only by explicitly referring gender to men and women, and thereby clearly linking "sex" and "gender," but also by the postulates made in these documents which are part of the classic set of postulates for non-discrimination on grounds of sex. For example, the Commission's strategy mentions "equal pay for equal work, equality in decision-making, no more gender-based violence, gender equality in international relations, etc.".

In the above postulates of European institutions there seem to be two layers which, according to Sophie Jacquot, may be viewed as a record of the developing understanding of gender equality. In different periods the term referred to "very different understandings of what might constitute a category of legitimate public action at the European level. In the first instance, the slogan 'Equal work for equal pay!' is a direct demand for equality of rights between men and women; they must be treated the same. To achieve this, existing inequalities must be corrected by trans- posing European dispositions into national legislation. In the second case, the reference to 'gender' calls for inequalities between men and women to be made visible; for an awareness of the differentiation that exists between the social and cultural classifications of male and female and the recognition that this hierarchy is the basis for the power relations and domination that women are victims of."[126] This approach does not lead only to affirmative actions or so-called positive discrimina- tion, however, as was the case in the first stage: "gender mainstreaming as a new strategy recognizes fundamental differences between men and women just like affirmative actions, but treats them in a very different way – the point is not simply to eliminate the consequences of existing differences, but to see in these differences benefits for both sexes and to take advantage of their potential. It turns towards diversity. The declared aim is therefore to change the systems and structures that cause discrimination – to introduce gender policy and equality thinking at all levels, in the private sector and in the public sector. Any political decision in any institution or company should be preceded by an analysis of its possible impact on gender relations. This, too, should be emphasized—gender mainstreaming is aimed not so much at combating the exclusion of women, but at ensuring that the potential of men and women can be fully taken advantage of."[127]

In the context of the above findings, the very concept of gender and its evolving meaning seem to remain most explicitly based on the understanding of sex that is characteristic of the anthropology of constraint. It is worth noting, however, the results of functional studies on the impact of EU policies on gender policy innova- tion in the Member States. Researchers point to three areas that fall under the

---

[125]Cf. eg. LodewijkAsscher, Helena Dalli, BronislavOndrus, *Trio Presidency Declaration*, 7.12.2015.

[126]Sophie Jacquot, op. cit., pp. 1–2.

[127]Patrycja Krysiak, "Jak mówić o gender-mainstreaming aby być zrozumianym/zrozumianą?" http://akademiagender.cba.pl/index.php/gender/87-jak-mowic-o-gender-mainstreaming-aby-byc-zrozumianym-zrozumiana [04.07.2016].

jurisdiction of the Member States where significant changes have resulted from the EU policy of gender mainstreaming.[128] The first are various policies concerning taxation and support provided by the welfare state; the second are "issues of fertility and sexuality, especially contraception, abortion, and sexual preference;" and the third concern "combating of violence against women."[129] While the first and third issues—even if they may be questioned in view of the EU acting outside its competence—are not cause for concern in the context of equal rights and the understanding of gender, the second dimension of political changes resulting from "gender mainstreaming" touches on the very heart of primary morality policies. It shows that in functional terms EU policy in this respect operates as an instrument of socio-cultural change in the area of reproductive rights and sexual orientation, thus clearly leaning, despite expressly made declarations, towards the anthropology of unconstraint.

This issue becomes even more ambiguous if we refer to the second key phrase where the concept of "gender" is used in the European Union, namely the category "gender identity." It appears in EU documents not so much in the context of equal rights for women, but accompanying the concept of "sexual orientation,"[130] and is an important point of reference for documents on guaranteeing equality rights for LGBTI groups. For example, when reporting on the issue of discrimination in 2014, Commissioner Věra Jourová, responsible, *inter alia*, for gender equality in the European Commission, treated sexual orientation and gender identity as cumulative grounds for discrimination.[131] She stressed that based on these combined grounds, the Commission will "continue to champion fundamental rights in its legislative and policy proposals whenever they cover aspects relevant for the rights of LGBTI persons under EU law."[132] The Commission considers policy areas that are relevant for LGBTI people to include non-discrimination, education, employment, health, free movement, asylum, hate speech/hate crime, enlargement and foreign policy.[133] Therefore, the Commission guarantees that "sexual orientation and gender identity

---

[128]The author points out that they go beyond the EU's competences provided for in the Treaties. S. Walby, op. cit., p. 20.

[129]Ibid.

[130]Cf. e.g. European Commission, *List of actions by the Commission to advance LGBTI equality*, Brussels 2015, where all references to gender identity are related to a reference to sexual orientation; European Parliament, *European Parliament Resolution of 4 February 2014 on the EU Roadmap against homophobia and discrimination on grounds of sexual orientation and gender identity (2013/2183(INI))*; Federica Mogherini, *Declaration by the High Representative, Federica Mogherini, on behalf of the European Union on the occasion of the International Day Against Homophobia, Transphobia and Biphobia*, 17 May 2015, http://www.consilium.europa.eu/pl/press/press-releases/2015/05/17-international-day-against-homophobia-transphobia/   [04.07.2016]; Agency for Fundamental Rights, *Homophobia, transphobia and discrimination on grounds of sexual orientation and gender identity*, Vienna 2010.

[131]Cf. Věra Jourová, *Foreword*, in: European Commission, *List of actions by the Commission to advance LGBTI...*, p. 3.

[132]European Commission, *List of actions...*, p. 5.

[133]Ibid.

will be mainstreamed in the daily work of the Commission."[134] This declaration seems particularly important in that it shows that gender mainstreaming as understood by the European Commission is given a much broader meaning here than would result from our findings so far. The category of gender is no longer a category relating exclusively to man and woman, but adopts a broad understanding of sex which includes so-called transgender and intersex persons, for instance.

The fact the Commission refers to gender identity as grounds for discrimination is particularly interesting in that, as pointed out by Anna Śledzińska-Simon, the Charter of Fundamental Rights "does not mention gender identity as prohibited grounds for different treatment of persons."[135] Moreover, as recently as 2002, when specifying the applicability of the anti-discrimination Directive 2000/78/EC, the European Commission claimed that it did not cover the issue of gender identity. And yet, the Commission already noted at that point that this ground for discrimination may be "inferred from CJEU case-law."[136] In 2014, it considered it to be its obligation and objective to monitor the Directive from the perspective of this case-law.[137]

The importance of the case-law of the EU Court of Justice for the broad understanding of the category of gender may be dated back to the P. v S. ruling of 1995 in which the Court addressed the problem of transsexualism for the first time. The case concerned a manager in the education sector who "informed his supervisor about (...) his planned gender reassignment surgery. He also began to dress like a woman."[138] After being dismissed from work, he brought a lawsuit against his former employer, in the course of which the English court ruled that "whilst there was a case for redundancy, the true reason for the dismissal was objection to P.'s undergoing a gender reassignment operation. It also noted that the situation 'fell outside' the circumstances regulated by the English Sex Discrimination Act,"[139] and asked the CJEU whether "in light of Directive 76/207/EC transsexuals are afforded special protection against discrimination on account of sex."[140]

In the course of the case before the CJEU, Advocate General Tesauro presented a broad understanding of gender identity. "He argued that it is necessary to go beyond the traditional man/woman dichotomy, which also has a sociological dimension. For there is a range of characteristics, behaviours and roles shared by men and women,

---

[134]Ibid., p. II 3, pp. 9–10.

[135]Anna Śledzińska—Simon, "Prawa osób transseksualnych w raportach Agencji Praw Podstawowych Unii Europejskiej," in: id. [ed.], Prawa osób transseksualnych..., p. 158, footnote 3.

[136]Patrycja Pogodzińska, "Tożsamość płciowa w prawie międzynarodowym. Wybrane zagadnienia," in: A. Śledzińska-Simon [ed.], Prawa osób transseksualnych..., p. 138.

[137]European Commission, List of actions..., p. II, pp. 9–10.

[138]Konrad Osajda, "Orzecznictwo Europejskiego Trybunału Sprawiedliwości dotyczące transseksualizmu," in: A. Śledzińska – Simon [ed.], Prawa osób transseksualnych..., p. 120.

[139]Ibid., pp. 120–121.

[140]Ibid., p. 121.

so that 'sex itself ought rather to be thought of as a continuum.'"[141] This claim, clearly linked to the logic of unconstrained anthropology, provided the intellectual basis for the Advocate General's thesis that "the prohibition of discrimination on grounds of sex [. . . is] *per se* under the protection of Community law even to a greater extent than would result from a linguistic and logical interpretation of the Directive."[142] The Advocate General's arguments for a linguistic and logical reinterpretation of the document was shared by the Court of Justice which agreed "with the Advocate General's conclusions (. . .) [and] stated that Directive 76/207/EC precludes the dismissal of a transsexual on account of a change of sex."[143] The new anthropology has thus established a new understanding of the notion of gender identity and non-discrimination.

This judgment became a point of reference for subsequent judgments rendered by the Court.[144] Of particular importance seems to be case C-117/01, which concerned K.B. living with R. who underwent a surgery to change her sex to male, but could not make a legal change of sex under UK law. As a result, K.B. and R. were not allowed to marry. Since K.B. was insured for life under a special pension fund, she "wanted to know whether, in the event of her death, R. could count on that benefit. The Fund informed her that, in the event of her death, R. would not be entitled (. . .) because R. was not her husband. K.B. therefore challenged the provisions governing the payment of the 'survivor's pension,' claiming that their operation in relation to a transsexual (. . .) was an example of discrimination on account of sex."[145] The UK court referred the question to the CJEU. In the course of the case pending before the CJEU, the British Government stressed that this was in no way a case of discrimination since no "cohabitation couples are entitled to the 'survivor's pension,' regardless of the reason why they are not married."[146]

In his opinion, the Advocate General argued referring to the 1995 case "that the prohibition of discrimination on grounds of sex should be understood broadly."[147] Consequently, he found that "there is no doubt that the United Kingdom legislation at hand is contrary to Community law. Fundamental rights which the Union is to protect (. . .) are an important element of Community law. The right of a transsexual to marry a representative of the sex to which he or she originally belonged is a fundamental right. Therefore prevention of the exercise of this right (. . .) infringes Community law."[148] He also said that "national legislators are required to regulate legal   issues   related   to   transsexualism   separately,   independently   and

---

[141]Patrycja Pogodzińska, op. cit., p.138.

[142]Konrad Osajda, op. cit., p. 122.

[143]Ibid., p. 123.

[144]See Cases *C-117/01, K.B. v National Health Pensions Agency,* and *C-423/04 Richards v Secretary of State for Work and Pensions.*

[145]Konrad Osajda, op. cit., p.124.

[146]Ibid., p. 124. Thus, this applied e.g. to homosexual couples who did not have the right to marry.

[147]Ibid., p. 126.

[148]Ibid., p. 125.

comprehensively. At the same time, until these normative changes are introduced, national courts are responsible for the protection of transsexuals, in particular by applying to them the principle of equal treatment of men and women."[149]

This argumentation is particularly noteworthy from the anthropological point of view. On the one hand, the Advocate General referred to a "broad interpretation of sex" based on P. v S., in which "sex is thought of as a continuum." This broad approach was the basis for the claim that there is a need for a "separate, independent and comprehensive" regulation of the status of transsexual persons; *ergo*, for their being treated in the legal order separately from the "traditional sexes." On the other hand, "pending" those regulations, he "expected the principle of equal treatment between men and women to be applied to them,"[150] actually finding the law of the United Kingdom to be a violation of fundamental rights as regards marriage. Thus, the category of sex was treated instrumentally here as a temporary solution until a proper approach to transgender gender identity was established.

As in the previous case, "the Court agreed with the Advocate General's theses."[151] It held that British law infringed the former Article 141 TEC which provided that each Member State was to ensure equal pay for equal work performed by men and women, but also the European Convention on Human Rights as regards the right to marry. On the latter point, let us add, it has openly gone beyond its jurisdiction. As pointed out by Konrad Osajda, "one can hardly view the Court's comments on the right of transsexuals to marry otherwise, since the regulation of family law, and therefore of marriage law, is the exclusive competence of the national legislators and their courts."[152] In the context of these rulings of the CJEU, it is easier to understand Sylvia Walby's comment on the EU's influence in the area of regulations concerning sexuality and sexual preferences. They also reveal the CJEU's leaning towards unconstrained anthropology in its understanding of gender.

It should be added that the broad understanding of gender presented by the CJEU and the EC is embraced by other European institutions. A broad understanding of gender is also advocated by the European Parliament which has "asked 10 times for a comprehensive European Union policy instrument for equality on grounds of sexual orientation and gender identity."[153] In its resolutions, it "strongly condemns any discrimination on the basis of sexual orientation and gender identity, and strongly regrets that the fundamental rights of lesbian, gay, bisexual, transgender and intersex (LGBTI) people are not yet always fully upheld in the European Union,"[154] and believes that "the Commission should continue working within the World Health

---

[149]Ibid., p. 126.

[150]Ibid., p. 126.

[151]Ibid., p. 126.

[152]Ibid., p. 127.

[153]European Parliament, *European Parliament Resolution of 4 February 2014 on the EU Roadmap against homophobia and discrimination on grounds of sexual orientation and gender identity (2013/2183(INI))* Preamble, p. I.

[154]Ibid., p.1.

Organisation to withdraw gender identity disorders from the list of mental and behavioural disorders and to ensure a non-pathologising reclassification,"[155] and further that "[r]elevant European Union agencies, including the European Union Agency for Fundamental Rights (FRA), the European Institute for Gender Equality (EIGE), the European Foundation for the Improvement of Living and Working Conditions (Eurofound), the European Police College (CEPOL), the European Union's Judicial Cooperation Unit (Eurojust), the European Judicial Network (EJN) and the European Asylum Support Office (EASO), should mainstream issues related to sexual orientation and gender identity in their work, and continue to provide the Commission and Member States with evidence-based advice on the fundamental rights of LGBTI people."[156]

The Council of the European Union takes a slightly more nuanced position. It says in its Guidelines[157] that "the promotion of human rights on grounds of sexual orientation and gender identity in many areas around the world, including within the EU, can lead to sensitive discussions." Nevertheless, "building on international standards and its own legislative framework," the EU stands together, to cite Federica Mogherini, "with LGBTI people all around the world in the struggle to end discrimination on the grounds of sexual orientation and gender identity."[158]

Although the category of "gender identity," unambiguously referring to the anthropology of unconstraint, occurs statistically much less often than other concepts related to "gender" in the sense referring to the anthropology of constraint, the very coexistence of their two understandings results in a reinterpretation of the concept of "gender." A good example of this situation is the European Parliament resolution on the application of Directive 2006/54/EC on the implementation of the principle of equal opportunities and equal treatment of men and women in matters of employment and occupation.[159] Although the title of the Resolution refers to men and women, suggesting a narrow understanding of "gender," in the text the concept is understood broadly. For example, the Parliament "calls on the Commission to closely monitor the effectiveness of national complaint bodies and procedures in the context of the implementation of the gender equality directives with regard to gender identity, gender expression and gender reassignment,"[160] "reiterates the importance of Member States clearly including in their national legislation the prohibition of any

---

[155]Ibid., p. 4 E i.

[156]Ibid., p. 4 A iii.

[157]Council of the European Union, *Guidelines to Promote and Protect the Enjoyment of All Human Rights by Lesbian, Gay, Bisexual, Transgender and Intersex (LGBTI) Persons*, Luxembourg, 24 June 2013.

[158]F. Mogherini, *Declaration...*

[159]European Parliament, *European Parliament Resolution of 8 October 2015 on the application of Directive 2006/54/EC of the European Parliament and of the Council of 5 July 2006 on the implementation of the principle of equal opportunities and equal treatment of men and women in matters of employment and occupation (2014/2160(INI))*.

[160]Ibid., p. 17.

discrimination based on sexual orientation or gender identity"[161] and "calls, in this connection, for the explicit inclusion in any future recast of a ban on discrimination on grounds of gender identity."[162]

Summing up the above findings, we must conclude that the category of gender in the language of European institutions is just as ambiguous as in other discourses on sexual behavior (as demonstrated in other studies). It clearly refers to the anthropology of unconstraint. A specific feature also seems to be the fundamental agreement of all European institutions on a broad view of gender identity which goes beyond the man-woman dichotomy. The Parliament's support of efforts taken by the Commission to "withdraw gender identity disorders from the list of mental disorders," or the CJEU's position acceding to the idea of sex "as a continuum" clearly show the unconstraint of their adopted anthropological perspective. Although the position of the Council of the European Union is less clear, it is also high on its agenda to promote and formulate human rights on the basis of gender identity.

11.3.2 Sexual Orientation

The concept of sexual orientation was added to the characteristics which may provide grounds for discrimination in the Treaty of Amsterdam which was adopted in 1997 and entered into force in 1999. It could not rely on any existing legal definition, as none of the primary acts of international law before the Amsterdam Treaty "explicitly provided for the right to the protection of sexual orientation."[163] Moreover, "at that time, not all the Member States condemned discrimination based on that criterion."[164] This concept was not clarified either in the Treaty of Amsterdam or in the Charter of Fundamental Rights, however. It would appear to have been considered as self-evident as sex or disability.

The first references to sexual orientation were made in documents of the European Parliament which explicitly referred to the category of sexual orientation in its resolutions as early as 1986, citing it as the cause for acts of intolerance.[165] The concept itself was explained in the 1994 report on discrimination against gays and lesbians in the European Union in which the term sexual orientation was understood as referring to "orientation towards the same or the opposite sex."[166] It was thus

---

[161] Ibid., p. 18.

[162] Ibid.

[163] Jacek Sobczak, op. cit., p. 74.

[164] Court of Justice of the European Union, *Opinion of Advocate General Niilo Jääskinen delivered on 15 July 2010, Case C147/08, Jürgen Römer v Freie und Hansestadt Hamburg*, ECLI:EU: C:2010:425, p. 127.

[165] European Commission, *Combating Sexual Orientation Discrimination in the European Union*, Directorate-General for Justice and Consumers, Directorate D – Equality, Brussels 2014, p. 21.

[166] Ibid., p. 21.

initially assumed that heterosexual and homosexual orientation existed as two variants of sexual orientation. Nevertheless, over the next 10 years the term was extended to all forms of non-heterosexual ways of experiencing sexuality. For example, in 2009 the Fundamental Rights Agency used the term discrimination based on sexual orientation and discrimination against LGBT people interchangeably in its report,[167] which suggests that the concept of orientation was *de facto* intended to protect non-heterosexual forms of sexuality. This interpretation seems to be confirmed by the fact that, in principle, all issues concerning the relationship between men and women, including those relating to discrimination, are regulated by reference to sex.

The answer as to which of the above approaches is the "official definition" of discrimination in the EU is not to be found in its secondary legislation; even Directive 2000/78/EC, which was to be implemented by December 2, 2003,[168] while establishing a general framework for equal treatment in matters of employment and occupation, does not define sexual orientation. At the same time, it was the first act of secondary law to prohibit direct and indirect discrimination on this basis in respect of: conditions of access to employment, occupation, promotion including conditions of dismissal and remuneration,[169] including with respect to persons from outside the Union.[170]

The case-law of the Court of Justice is perhaps the best illustration of the importance of introducing the category of "sexual orientation" into anti-discrimination law, and in particular into the above-mentioned Directive 2000/78. In Grant, a case settled even before 1999, which dealt with the issue of discount ticketing entitlements for persons in a homosexual relationship, the Court held that "in the present state of the law within the Community, stable relationships between two persons of the same sex are not regarded as equivalent to marriages or stable relationships outside marriage between persons of opposite sex."[171] Consequently, it found different treatment of same-sex unions as consistent with Community law. In Romer, a case held 10 years later, the Advocate General was already convinced that even though "the protection of marriage and the family provided for in German law by Paragraph 6(1) of the Basic Law may in itself constitute a legitimate aim," it nevertheless seemed to him "to go without saying that the aim of protecting marriage

---

[167]Cf. Fundamental Rights Agency, *Homophobia and Discrimination on Grounds of Sexual Orientation and Gender Identity in the EU Member States, Part II: The Social Situation,* Vienna 2009.

[168]J. Sobczak, op. cit., p. 89.

[169]C. Waaldijk, M.T. Bonini-Baraldi, op. cit., p. 32.

[170]J. Sobczak, op. cit., p. 89.

[171]Court of Justice of the European Union, *Judgment of the Court of 17 February 1998, Lisa Jacqueline Grant v South-West Trains Ltd., Reference for a preliminary ruling: Industrial Tribunal, Southampton—United Kingdom, Case C-249/96,* ECLI:EU:C:1998:63, p. I-648.

or the family cannot legitimize discrimination on grounds of sexual orientation,"[172] and postulated that prohibition of discrimination on grounds of sexual orientation "should be regarded as a general principle of Union law."[173] Over time, the Court generally upheld this interpretation, finding in 2015 that the prohibition of discrimination on grounds of sexual orientation "is a particular expression of the principle of equal treatment, which is a general principle of EU law."[174] Nevertheless, even though in Romer the Court stated that the provisions of "Directive 2000/78 preclude a provision (. . .) under which a pensioner who has entered into a registered life partnership receives a supplementary retirement pension lower than that granted to a married, not permanently separated, pensioner,"[175] it added two provisos. It made it clear that this is the case as long as "in the Member State concerned, marriage is reserved to persons of different gender and exists alongside a registered life partnership (. . .) which is reserved to persons of the same gender, and there is direct discrimination on the ground of sexual orientation because, under national law, that life partner is in a legal and factual situation comparable to that of a married person as regards that pension."[176] Thus, contrary to Case C-117/01 K.B. v NHSPA discussed above, the Court did not go as far as to evaluate the regulation of family law; it remained the limit for applying the principle of non-discrimination on grounds of sexual orientation which could *de facto* restrict its applicability in certain countries, despite its being regarded as a general principle of the European Union.

Although the Court has considered the issue of sexual orientation in its judgments on several occasions, in none of them has it provided its definition. However, it pointed to two of its essential characteristics. Firstly, it referred to the permanence of sexual orientation, the question being whether, as shown by recent studies, it may be temporal in nature, without creating, at least in some cases, a lasting preference,[177] or whether it is always permanent. The CJEU stated in one of its judgements that "it is common ground that a person's sexual orientation is a characteristic so fundamental

---

[172]Court of Justice of the European Union, Opinion of Advocate General NiiloJääskinen delivered on 15 July 2010, *Case C147/08, Jürgen Römer v Freie und Hansestadt Hamburg*, ECLI:EU: C:2010:425, pp. 174–175.

[173]Ibid., p. 131.

[174]Court of Justice of the European Union, *Judgment of the Court (Fourth Chamber) 29 April 2015, Case C528/13, Geoffrey Léger v Ministre des Affaires sociales, de la Santé et des Droits des femmes, Ministre des Affaires sociales, de la Santé et des Droits des femmes, Établissement français du sang*, ECLI:EU:C:2015:288, p. 48.

[175]Court of Justice of the European Union, *Judgment of the Court (Grand Chamber),Jürgen Römer v Freie und Hansestadt Hamburg*, ECLI:EU:C:2011:286, p. 67.

[176]Ibid.

[177]Steven E. Mock, Richard P. Eibach, "Stability and Change in Sexual Orientation Identity Over a 10-Year Period in Adulthood," *Archives of Sexual Behaviour*, June 2012, Vol. 41 (3), pp. 641–648. The authors observed that "heterosexuality was the most stable identity. For women, bisexuality and homosexuality were equally unstable and significantly less stable than heterosexuality, suggesting that sexual orientation identity fluidity is a pattern that applies more to sexual minority women than heterosexual women. For men, heterosexuality and homosexuality were both relatively stable compared to bisexuality, which stood out as a particularly unstable identity."

to his identity that he should not be forced to renounce it (...) [and—M.G.] according to the conditions prevailing in the country of origin, a specific social group may be a group whose members have sexual orientation as the shared characteristic."[178] Sexual orientation is thus treated in the EU as a permanent characteristic which is the basis of gender identity and which therefore opens up space for the emergence of the above discussed settlements as regards the latter category and undermining the understanding of the concept of gender heretofore present in international law.

At the same time, however, the Court of Justice has found sexual orientation to be a characteristic that is difficult to objectively verify. In the combined cases C-148-150/13 concerning the ability of a Member State to verify the claims of asylum seekers about their being persecuted on the basis of sexual orientation, the Court stated that, although statements of sexual orientation alone are not sufficient grounds for granting asylum, EU law does not allow "in the context of the assessment by the competent national authorities, acting under the supervision of the courts, of the facts and circumstances concerning the declared sexual orientation of an applicant for asylum, whose application is based on a fear of persecution on grounds of that sexual orientation" for "the statements of that applicant and the documentary and other evidence submitted in support of his application" to be "subject to an assessment by those authorities founded on questions based only on stereotyped notions concerning homosexuals,"[179] or for the competent national authorities to carry out "detailed questioning as to the sexual practices of an applicant for asylum in the context of that assessment."[180] Thus, in light of the Court's judgments sexual orientation ultimately remains both a permanent and a highly subjective characteristic which is difficult to verify objectively. In this sense, it is an exception to other characteristics protected by the EU anti-discrimination law.

The lack of a legal definition does not mean that there is no definition of sexual orientation in the EU, however. The Fundamental Rights Agency, whose first task commissioned by the European Parliament in 2007 was to prepare a report on discrimination on the basis of sexual orientation, adopted its own operational definition which says that sexual orientation is "each person's capacity for profound emotional, affectional and sexual attraction to, and intimate and sexual relations with, individuals of a different gender or the same gender or more than one

---

[178]Court of Justice of the European Union, *Summary: Judgment of the Court (Fourth Chamber) of 7 November 2013, Joined Cases C-199/12 to C-201/12, Minister voorImmigratieenAsiel v X and Y and Z v Minister voorImmigratieenAsiel*, http://curia.europa.eu/juris/document/document.jsf?text=orientacja%2Bseksualna&docid=159860&pageIndex=0&doclang=pl&mode=req&dir=&occ=first&part=1&cid=1724838#ctx1 [11.07.2016].

[179]Court of Justice of the European Union, *Judgment of the Court(Grand Chamber) of 2 December 2014 in Joined Cases C148/13 to C150/13, A (C148/13), B (C149/13), C (C150/13) v Staatssecretaris van VeiligheidenJustitie*ECLI:EU:C:2014:2406, p. 73.

[180]Ibid.

gender."[181] Thus, in its reports, it repeats almost verbatim the definition found in a footnote to so-called Yogyacarta Principles, adopted by a group of 29 "human rights experts from 25 countries at a meeting held at Gadjah Mada University in Yogyakarta, Indonesia, on November 6–9, 2006."[182] During the conference, the participants, who were not the official representatives of their respective countries, produced a non-legally and non-politically binding document aimed at "reconstructing international human rights standards with regard to sexual orientation and gender identity,"[183] identifying, with an exaggeration acknowledged even by its own authors,[184] more than one hundred commitments concerning "LGBT rights" in universal human rights.[185] In view of the authority of the persons proclaiming the Principles, as well as the publicity afforded to their work, this document has become an important reference point for movements promoting LGTB rights, which consider it a "highly important step"[186] towards ensuring human rights.

In accordance with the above-mentioned footnote to the Yogyakarta Principles, "sexual orientation is each person's capacity for profound emotional, affectional and sexual attraction to, and intimate and sexual relations with, individuals of a different gender or the same gender or more than one gender."[187] Despite the above-mentioned scientific studies which essentially undermine this claim, this capacity is regarded as permanent and unchanging as the basis of gender identity. It also

---

[181]Fundamental Rights Agency, *Homophobia and Discrimination on Grounds of Sexual Orientation and Gender Identity in the EU Member States, Part II: The Social Situation*, Vienna 2009, p. 28. https://fra.europa.eu/sites/default/files/fra-hdgso-report-part2_pl.pdf [11.07.2016].

[182]https://ms.gov.pl/pl/prawa-czlowieka/miekkie-prawo-miedzynarodowe/zasady-z-yogakarty/ [11.07.2016].

[183]Roman Wieruszewski, "Zasady Yogakarty – geneza i znaczenie," in: Katarzyna Remin [ed.], *Zasady Yogakarty. Zasady stosowania międzynarodowego prawa praw człowieka w stosunku do orientacji seksualnej oraz tożsamości płciowej*, Kampania Przeciw Homofobii, Warszawa 2009, p. 16.

[184]As noted by Roman Wieruszewski, one of the Principles' co-authors, "in drafting this document, attempts were made at reconstrucing the standards legally binding on the States (. . .). I am aware, however, that when reading some of the principles, doubts may arise as to whether they are indeed a reconstruction, or more of a construction, perhaps." Ibid., p. 18.

[185]Cf. Michał Gierycz, Piotr Mazurkiewicz, "Europejska antropologia i europejska polityka – obserwacja współczesności," in: Christian Bohr, Christian Schmitz [ed.], *Europa i jej antropologia polityczna. Człowiek jako droga historii – o filozofii Karola Wojtyły*, Konrad Adenauer Stiftung, Warszawa 2016, pp. 136–137.

[186]http://www.lgbtnet.dk/human-rights/yogakarta-principles [11.07.2016].

[187]Katarzyna Remin [ed.], op. cit., p. 22. As a side remark it may be added that the connection between the Yogacarta Principles and the Fundamental Rights Agency has now been strengthened by the election of a new Director of the Fundamental Rights Agency, Michael O'Flaherty, who was the rapporteur for the meeting in Indonesia and who "has made immense contributions to the drafting and revision of the Yogyakarta Principles". Participants in the meeting say that "his commitment and tireless efforts have been critical to the successful outcome of the process." Cf. Sonia Onufer Correa, Vitit Muntarbhorn, *Introduction to the Yogyakarta Principles*, https://yogyakartaprinciples.org/introduction/

seems to be in a loose relationship with sex. In fact, however, it undermines the logic of sex, which, from the theoretical point of view, should ultimately be replaced by the category of sexual orientation.[188]

Even though, in one of its recent recommendations, the European Commission pointed to the need for a binding definition to be legally adopted as part of the *aquis*,[189] it generally seems to be pleased with the absence of an official interpretation of sexual orientation. The Commission's report on discrimination on grounds of sexual orientation states that, although "it may be argued that providing an explicit legal definition of the meaning of 'sexual orientation' could have the potential to serve the LGB community in the EU with respect to the protection of their right to equal treatment, in particular in a situation where statistics show that discrimination based on sexual orientation remains a problem in many Member States, (. . .) it might be better for there to be no legal definition, as this approach enables a broad interpretation in practice."[190] Aware also of the risk that "the lack of a legal definition might lead to a limiting and strict construction of the concept by the national courts, leaving some groups with a specific sexual orientation (e.g. asexuality) without protection,"[191] the Commission ultimately recommends that "it is important for the authorities, courts and equality bodies to recall the broad definition of 'sexual orientation' under the Yogyakarta Principles."[192] Thus the Commissions takes the lack of a *de iure* definition to mean that sexual orientation should *de facto* be defined in accordance with Yogyakarta Principles, as is done by the Fundamental Rights Agency. In other words, the absence of a definition means a broad definition. An analogous strategy has been adopted by the European Parliament, which does not, in principle, define sexual orientation in its resolutions and reports. At the same time, however, it regularly cites conclusions from Fundamental Rights Agency reports which use the definition based on Yogyakarta Principles, and "calls on the Commission and Member States" to comply with FRA's "opinions contained therein to the greatest possible extent."[193]

Understanding sexual orientation as a permanent and unchanging disposition in the spirit of Yogyakarta Principles means that this concept may easily turn non-discrimination into promotion of LGBT postulates. As pointed out by John Finnis in reference to the discussion on sexual orientation in Europe, "laws or proposed laws outlawing 'discrimination based on sexual orientation' are always interpreted by 'gay rights' movements as going far beyond discrimination based

---

[188]This issue has been discussed at length in Sect. 9.3.2.1.

[189]European Commission, *Recommendation*, Plenary meeting of the "Structured Dialogue on Justice and Additional Rule of Law Matters between the European Union and Bosnia Herzegovina," Sarajevo, Bosnia and Herzegovina (13–14 May 2014), p.8.

[190]European Commission, *Combating Sexual Orientation Discrimination in the European Union. European Network of Legal Experts in the Non-discrimination Field*, Brussels 2014, p. 58.

[191]Ibid.

[192]Ibid.

[193]European Parliament, *European Parliament Resolution of 28 September 2011 on human rights, sexual orientation and gender identity at the United Nations, P7_TA(2011)0427*, p. 14.

merely on A's belief that B is sexually attracted to persons of the same sex. Instead (it is observed), 'gay rights' movements interpret the phrase as extending full legal protection to public activities intended specifically to promote, procure and facilitate homosexual conduct."[194] It seems that we are witnessing an analogous situation in some EU institutions.

Activities which European institutions consider discriminatory on grounds of sexual orientation include a very wide range of issues. An analysis of the outcomes of the annual good practice seminars on combating discrimination on the grounds of sexual orientation, initiated and co-chaired by the European Commission and attended by representatives of the Member States,[195] the Agency for Fundamental Rights, and the Network of Socio-Economic Experts, shows that they generally identify the problem of combating discrimination with the policy of advocating LGBT demands. Consequently, the 2011 report on discrimination based on sexual orientation states that there are various "barriers to policy making on LGBT issues. There are political barriers which range from political hostility, to policy making that responds to public opinion rather than LGBT needs, to lack of prioritisation of LGBT issues, and to invisibility for and inaction on LGBT issues. There are societal barriers that range from physical and verbal abuse of LGBT people to negative and judgmental attitudes in relation to LGBT people."[196] Clearly, any action other than advocacy of LGBT postulates, or any refusal to affirm them, is considered discriminatory. The authors also identify "cultural barriers in the value base of societies. These were evidenced in values held in relation to gender and gender roles and in relation to family, marriage and the raising of children. These cultural barriers—the Report states—can be exacerbated in times of hardship and situations of economic inequality."[197] Consequently, the prevailing cultural values of the Member States, including for example the concept of marriage, are considered discriminatory with regard to sexual orientation.

In this context, it is not surprising that in its most recent documents the European Commission talks not so much about discrimination on grounds of sexual orientation, but about efforts to improve LGBTI equality.[198] Citing Article 21 CFR on non-discrimination as the grounds of its activities, the Commission presents a kind of decalogue, a list of ten actions in the policy areas it considers to be "relevant for LGBTI people: non-discrimination, education, employment, health, free movement, asylum, hate speech/hate crime, enlargement and foreign policy. The Commission's

---

[194]John Finnis, *Law, Morality, and Sexual Orientation*, "Notre Dame Law Review" Vol. 69, Issue 5, 2014, p. 1054.

[195]Members of the Non-Discrimination Governmental Expert Group (GEG).

[196]Niall Crowley, *Final Seminar Report. Good practice exchange seminar: Discrimination on the ground of sexual orientation – how to overcome the barriers to public policy making*, Estonia, 29-30 September 2011, http://www.humanconsultancy.com/Publications/2011_II_EE_seminar%20report.pdf [11.07.2016], p. 5.

[197]Ibid.

[198]European Commission, *List of actions by the Commission to advance LGBTI equality*, Brussels 2015.

objectives are to support progress in all EU and accession countries in all these policy areas, improve the social acceptance of LGBTI people and enforce EU legislation."[199] In addition to monitoring the adopted anti-discrimination and hate crime Directives and preparing new projects (e.g. on LGBTI families), the Commission plans to "support LGBTI human rights defenders"[200] and other key actors, and to conduct "a broad and inclusive communications campaign (. . .), including specific actions aiming at: (a) improving the social acceptance of LGBTI persons and making societies more open and inclusive throughout Europe; (b) combatting the negative stereotypes that LGBTI persons endure (. . .); (c) raising awareness about the rights of LGBTI persons. Special focus areas will include homophobia in sports, young LGBTI, bullying at schools and transgender and intersex people."[201] Graphically, the Commission's involvement in these ten areas is presented in Fig. 11.1.

The Commission's list of activities refers to the list of actions for LGBTI people proposed by the European Parliament, included in the "EU Roadmap against homophobia and discrimination on grounds of sexual orientation and gender identity"[202] adopted a year earlier. In the document, the European Parliament "strongly condemns any discrimination on the basis of sexual orientation and gender identity, and strongly regrets that the fundamental rights of lesbian, gay, bisexual, transgender and intersex (LGBTI) people are not yet always fully upheld in the European Union,"[203] and "calls on the Commission to use its competences to the fullest extent"[204]. It also "calls on the Commission, Member States and relevant agencies to work jointly on a comprehensive multiannual policy to protect the fundamental rights of LGBTI people, i.e. a roadmap, a strategy or an action plan featuring the themes and objectives hereunder,"[205] providing a long list of desirable actions grouped into 12 categories.

As part of its horizontal actions, the Parliament advocates LGBTI mainstreaming, pointing out that "the Commission should work to secure existing rights throughout its work and across all domains in which it is competent by mainstreaming issues linked to the fundamental rights of LGBTI people in all relevant work—for instance when drafting future policies and proposals or monitoring the implementation of EU law."[206] Without going into all the details of this report, it should be noted that it calls for "the Yogyakarta Principles to be recognized as legal recommendations for

---

[199]Ibid., p. 5.

[200]Ibid., p. 16.

[201]Ibid., p. 10.

[202]European Parliament, *European Parliament resolution of 4 February 2014 on the EU Roadmap against homophobia and discrimination on grounds of sexual orientation and gender identity (2013/2183(INI))*, 14.02.2014,P7_TA(2014)0062.

[203]Ibid., p. 1.

[204]Ibid., p. 3.

[205]Ibid., p. 4.

[206]Ibid., p. A(i).

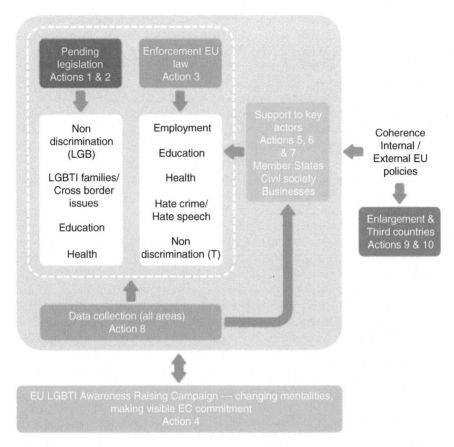

Fig. 11.1 Forms of the European Commission's commitment to LGBTI equality. Source: European Commission, List of actions by the Commission to advance LGBTI equality, Brussels 2015

the European Union ... [by adopting—M.G.] a radical reinterpretation of human rights in its provisions. Through its demands on the Commission and the Member States, it aims to ensure that no EU law adopted in the future fails to take into account the interests of the LGBT group."[207] For example, while the Roadmap says that "the Commission should promote equality and non-discrimination on grounds of sexual orientation and gender identity throughout its youth and education programmes,"[208] it makes no mention of the parents' rights to educate their own children, their protection against the promotion of ideas and actions incompatible with the religious and moral beliefs of the parents, or the right to conscientious objection; while guaranteeing freedom of expression to the LGBTI community, it stresses that "the

---

[207]Michał Gierycz, Piotr Mazurkiewicz, *Europejska antropologia...*, p. 137.

[208]European Parliament, *European Parliament resolution of 4 February 2014 ...*, p. 4 D(i).

freedom to express and display one's beliefs and opinions in keeping with the principle of pluralism of ideas, and provided that it does not incite to hatred, violence or discrimination, should be respected."[209]

Considering that, as has already been shown, traditional cultural values are considered discriminatory, the European Parliament thus seems to be "trying to impose double standards on Member States: unlimited freedom of expression for the LGBTI community and a limited freedom for their possible critics."[210] One other noteworthy postulate of the Parliament is that the EU should make the World Health Organization withdraw gender identity disorders from the list of mental and behavioral disorders entirely.[211] It shows that the category of sexual orientation ultimately leads to a legal recognition of behaviors which, in accordance with current medical knowledge, constitute some kind of disorder.

Although the Council of the European Union does not have as rich a dossier of documents on sexual orientation as the European Parliament or the Commission, it addressed this issue as well by adopting a Toolkit in 2010,[212] Guidelines to promote and protect the enjoyment of all human rights by lesbian, gay, bisexual, transgender and intersex (LGBTI) persons in 2013,[213] and the Conclusions on LGBTI equality in 2016.[214] These documents, like the analyzed documents of the Parliament and the Commission, link non-discrimination on grounds of sexual orientation closely to the implementation of LGBTI demands;[215] they also adopt a broad understanding of sexual orientation.[216] Nevertheless, they define the objectives of the Council's activities with some more precision. In light of the Guidelines, there are four main areas of the Union's commitment to LGBTI postulates. Firstly, they include decriminalization of sexual practices in third countries and combatting discriminatory laws,

---

[209]Ibid., p. 6.

[210]M. Gierycz, P. Mazurkiewicz, *Europejska antropologia . . .*, p. 137.

[211]Cf. Section E(II) where the Parliament "calls on the Commission and the World Health Organization to withdraw gender identity disorders from the list of mental and behavioural disorders, and to ensure a non-pathologising reclassification in the negotiations of the 11th version of the International Classification of Diseases (ICD-11)."

[212]Council of the European Union (Working Party on Human Rights), *Toolkit to Promote and Protect the Enjoyment of all Human Rights by Lesbian, Gay, Bisexual and Transgender (LGBT) People*, 11179/10, LIMITE, COHOM 162, PESC 80.

[213]Council of the European Union, *Guidelines to promote and protect the enjoyment of all human rights by lesbian, gay, bisexual, transgender and intersex (LGBTI) persons*, Foreign Affairs Council meeting, Luxembourg, 24 June 2013.

[214]Council of the European Union, *Council conclusions on LGBTI equality*, PRESS RELEASE 338/16 of 16.06.2016.

[215]Thus considering LGTBI activists to be a particularly valuable group of modern human rights defenders. Cf. Council of the European Union, *Guidelines. . .*, p. 29.

[216]Cf. e.g. Council of the European Union, *Guidelines. . .*, p.13, which say that "sexual orientation refers to each person's capacity for emotional, affective and sexual attraction to, and intimate and sexual relations with, individuals of a different or the same gender or more than one gender," i.e. repeating the definition found in the Yogyakarta Principles.

including, above all, the death penalty for homosexual relations.[217] Secondly, promoting equality and non-discrimination by encouraging states to promote equality and non-discrimination in the enjoyment of human rights by LGBTI people (particularly in the work place, health sector, and in education), raising social awareness, and support for government and non-government initiatives which provide "added value."[218] Thirdly, combating LGBTI-phobic violence, discussed below, and fourthly, support for LGBTI groups.[219] The document also lists dozens of different alternative ways to support LGBTI communities.

Despite the Council's declaration of strong commitment to promoting the rights of persons of different sexual orientations, one cannot fail to see that the list of its objectives is less extensive than the one proposed by the Commission, and that the first document on internal relations in the context of LGBTI appeared as late as 2016.[220] Moreover, the only anti-discrimination directive so far, whose adoption required the Council's unanimity, addresses only a limited portion of LGTBI postulates, without regulating such areas as education, access to goods and services, healthcare and social security. It is also noteworthy that while using a language similar to that of the Commission and the Parliament, documents of the EU Council seem to be much more careful in the choice of words. For example, when the Guidelines say that "the EU aims to promote and protect all human rights of LGBTI persons," this is immediately followed by the proviso: "on the basis of existing international legal standards in this area."[221] Similarly, in the 2016 Conclusions, when the Council "invites the European Commission to promote the measures outlined in its List of actions to advance LGBTI equality," it adds that this should be done "while fully respecting the Member States' national identities and constitutional traditions as well as the competence of the Member States in the field of family law,"[222] etc. Some of the observations contained in the document may even be taken as a criticism of the Fundamental Rights Agency.[223] It therefore appears that, despite

---

[217]Cf. Council of the European Union, *Guidelines...*, pp. 15–18.

[218]Ibid., p. 23.

[219]Ibid., pp. 24–30.

[220]Which was taken note of by the LGBT community. Cf. http://www.pinknews.co.uk/2016/06/20/all-28-eu-member-states-reach-consensus-on-lgbt-rights-for-first-time/ [11.07.2016].

[221]Council of the European Union, *Guidelines...*, p. 5.

[222]Council of the European Union, *Council Conclusions...*, p.8

[223]Ibid. In Sect. 11 the Council "calls on the European Union Agency for Fundamental Rights to further study the situation of LGBTI people by compiling high-quality statistics based on the most reliable methods", which would not be surprising if not for the fact that the recent wide-ranging studies performed by the FRA on gays and lesbians have been widely criticized as regards the methodology they employed. It was pointed out for example that "the studies were conducted through an online questionnaire which was open to the public. Respondents were able to recommend that others participate in the study. In addition, the questionnaire available on the website could be completed by anyone and any number of times. The description of the methodology indicates that it is not known how many persons started the survey again because they chose to use one of the many categories to qualify themselves as a member of the LGBTI movement, although they had previously indicated otherwise. Such a sampling of respondents makes the survey

its adoption of the same terms and definitions, the Council's position is not so unequivocally oriented toward satisfying the demands of the LGBTI community, and consequently that the category of discrimination on grounds of sexual orientation is conceived by the Council in a narrower sense than by the Commission or the Parliament, and similar to the way it is understood by the Court of Justice of the European Union.

11.3.3 Homophobia

As pointed out in the quantitative part of this study, the concept of homophobia appears explicitly in the language of EU institutions after 2006/2007. An important role in this process was played by the European Parliament which adopted two resolutions on this issue during that period: the resolution on homophobia of January 18, 2006, and the resolution on the increase in racist and homophobic violence in Europe of June 15, 2006. Less than a year later, on April 27, 2007, these resolutions were supplemented with yet another resolution on homophobia in Europe. In the same year, at the Parliament's request, the newly established EU Agency for Fundamental Rights launched a wide-ranging project concerning homophobia and discrimination on grounds of sexual orientation in Europe, which resulted in three reports by the year 2010. At the same time, the concept of "homophobia" entered the language of EU institutions which have since then celebrated the Day Against Homophobia on the 17th of May each year.[224]

When looking for the proper meaning of the concept of homophobia, it is therefore necessary to first explain how this concept is understood by the Parliament, which, by the way, "recalls the need for sound and clear definitions"[225] in one of the above resolutions. In fact, in its first resolution on homophobia the Parliament defined the phenomenon by saying that "homophobia can be defined as an irrational fear of and aversion to homosexuality and to lesbian, gay, bisexual and transgender (LGBT) people based on prejudice and similar to racism, xenophobia, anti-Semitism

---

non-representative. Furthermore, there was no control group for the study against which to compare the results of the respondents." Ordo Iuris, *Uwagi do dokumentu Agencji Praw Podstawowych Unii Europejskiej "Protection against discrimination on grounds of sexual orientation, gender identity and sex characteristics in the EU. Comparative legal analysis,"* http://www.ordoiuris.pl/uwagi-do-dokumentu-agencji-praw-podstawowych-unii-europejskiej%2D%2Dprotection-against-discrimina tion-on-grounds-of-sexual-orientation%2D%2Dgender-identity-and-sex-characteristics-in-the-eu %2D%2Dcomparative-legal-analysis-,3760,analiza-prawna.html, p. 2.

[224] http://www.lgbt-ep.eu/press-releases/eu-leaders-on-idaho-2011/ [07.06.2016].

[225] European Parliament, *European Parliamentre solution on the increase in racist and homophobic violence in Europe*, 15.06.2006, P6_TA(2006)0273, § 17.

and sexism."[226] It is worth noting three aspects of this definition: the objects of discrimination, the manifestations of homophobia and, finally, its psychological and political classification.

As regards the first issue, the Parliament's definition not only repeats the etymological mistake, characteristic of the discourse on sexual behavior in the context of unconstrained anthropology discussed more extensively in Chap. 9, by identifying homophobia as a phobia directed against homosexuals, but actually makes it worse. The prefix "homo" as understood by the Parliament refers not only to homosexuals, but also to bisexuals and transsexuals. This approach has also been adopted by other EU institutions.[227] The Fundamental Rights Agency highlighted the issue of transgender people who are victims of homophobia already in 2008.[228] Consequently, in a Statement issued on May 17 on behalf of the European Union, 10 years after the above-mentioned resolution, High Representative Federica Mogherini talks not of an International Day Against Homophobia, but an "International Day Against Homophobia, Transphobia and Biphobia," stressing that "the EU will continue working with all partners to advance the human rights of all people regardless of their sexual orientation and gender identity."[229] Consequently, these three groups do not constitute a closed catalogue, but one that is open to other gender identities. The hermeneutic importance of this fact consists in that everything that will be said below in the context of homosexuality may be just as adequately applied to bisexualism, transsexualism, and given the EU's efforts to remove the categories of sexual disorders from the list of diseases, in the future probably also to various other forms of sexual behavior.

It seems to be of key importance to establish what EU institutions understand as "an irrational fear of and aversion to" homo/trans/bisexualism, emotions which, as the European Commission makes clear, "are an unacceptable violation of human dignity (…) [that is] completely incompatible with the founding values of the EU."[230] To begin with, it is worth looking at the enumeration of behaviors considered to be homophobic in resolutions of the European Parliament. As noted by Rev. Piotr Mazurkiewicz, "among the manifestations of homophobia, authors enumerate both murders and acts of physical violence committed on this ground, as well as hateful speech, ridicule or verbal abuse; both prohibition of gay parades, and the fact that same-sex partners cannot enjoy all the rights and protections enjoyed by

---

[226]European Parliament, *European Parliamentre solution on homophobia in Europe*, 18.01.2006, P6_TA(2006)0018.

[227]Cf. Viviane Reding, *The Commission's actions are making LGBT rights a reality,* Speech at first International Day Against Homophobia and Transphobia (IDAHO) Forum, The Hague, 17 May 2013, http://europa.eu/rapid/press-release_SPEECH-13-424_en.htm?locale=en [06.07.2016].

[228]Agency for Fundamental Rights, *Homophobia and Discrimination on Grounds of Sexual Orientation in the EU Member States. Part I – Legal Analysis*, Vienna 2008, p. 4.

[229]Federica Mogherini, *Declaration by the High Representative, Federica Mogherini, on behalf of the EU on the occasion of the International Day Against Homophobia, Transphobia and Biphobia* (17 May 2019), Press release 249/16, 16.5.2016.

[230]*Fight against homophobia in Europe (debate)*, Viviane Reding, Strasbourg 22 May 2012.

heterosexual couples, including recognition of families with same-sex partners."[231] He concludes that "the term homophobia as used by the authors of these resolutions is extremely broad, and therefore ideological. It refers both to actual forms of discrimination and to situations where same-sex unions—legal in every European country in the sense of not being penalized—are not afforded the special legal protection and privileges which state legislation affords to heterosexual marriage."[232] This standpoint is reflected in the documents of the European Commission and the EU Council. Although in 1999, in the context of the then proposed anti-discrimination directive, the European Commission pointed out that a distinction should be made between "sexual orientation" protected by the directive and sexual behavior that it did not protect,[233] in 2013 it stressed its commitment to counteracting homophobia by "working to challenge stereotypes and change attitudes,"[234] considering so called equality parades (LGBT Pride) as "the litmus-tests for the openness of our societies."[235] A broad understanding of homophobia is also evidenced by the fact that the EU Fundamental Rights Agency, an independent advisory body providing "evidence-based assistance and expertise on fundamental rights"[236] to major EU institutions, classified a citizens' proposal submitted in Latvia postulating that schools educate children based on the constitutional principle of marriage being understood solely as a union between a man and a woman and prohibiting the participation of children in performances and events promoting homosexual behavior,[237] or the fact that "at retirement homes awareness of LGBT persons' needs can be non-existent,"[238] as a homophobia-related problems.

A similar perspective, though not identical to that embraced by the Commission and the Parliament, is adopted by the Council of the European Union. In its guidelines, it refers not so much to homophobia but to LGTBI-phobia,[239] in a way documenting the "broad" understanding of the "homo" prefix mentioned above. It

---

[231]Piotr Mazurkiewicz, *Między homo- a heterofobią*, Warszawa 2008 (author's archive).

[232]Ibid.

[233]C. Waaldijk, M.T. Bonini-Baraldi, op. cit., p. 32.

[234]Viviane Reding, op. cit.

[235]Ibid.

[236]*Introducing FRA*, http://fra.europa.eu/pl [11.07.2016].

[237]Fundamental Rights Agency, *Protection against discrimination on grounds of sexual orientation, gender identity and sex characteristics in the EU. Comparative legal analysis. Update 2015*, http://fra.europa.eu/sites/default/files/fra_uploads/protection_against_discrimination_legal_ update_2015, p. 51.

[238]Fundamental Rights Agency, *Homophobia and Discrimination on Grounds of Sexual Orientation and Gender Identity in the EU Member States, Part II: The Social Situation*, Vienna 2009, p. 4, https://fra.europa.eu/sites/default/files/fra-hdgso-report-part1_pl.pdf [11.07.2016]. The FRA report on homophobia says that "under these circumstances 'invisibility' becomes a survival strategy." (Ibid., p. 4).

[239]Council of the European Union, *Guidelines to promote and protect the enjoyment of all human rights by lesbian, gay, bisexual, transgender and intersex (LGBTI) persons*, Foreign Affairs Council meeting, Luxembourg, 24.06.2013, pp. 24–28.

considers LGBTI-phobic violence to include "murder, rape, beatings, torture, cruel, inhuman or degrading treatment or punishment, and physical attacks in public space."[240] It should be noted that while the Council stresses that "countries that continue to criminalize consenting same-sex and transgender adult relations, or that lack legislation explicitly protecting LGBTI persons from discrimination and violence, have notably higher rates of LGBTI-phobic violence,"[241] it does not describe these countries as LGBTI-phobic. The term LGBTI-phobic is used here in a narrow context, referring to violence. In other contexts, reference to discrimination is made instead. The noticeable difference in emphasis present in the Council's documents is less evident, however, in the speeches of its representatives, who, like President of the European Council in years 2009–2014 Herman van Rompouy consistently equate homophobia and discrimination on grounds of sexual orientation, amalgamating the two terms.[242]

This amalgamation is particularly significant in that homophobia, in the meaning attributed to this term in EU documents, is presented as something much worse than ordinary discrimination. To understand this difference, it is enough to look at other terms in whose company the notion of homophobia appears. While discrimination is referred to in the context of women, the disabled, national minorities, etc., homophobia appears in the context of anti-Semitism, racism and xenophobia. Thus, while discrimination, though undesirable and negatively evaluated, is regarded as a "blooper" which may happen in civilized societies, homophobia, just like racism and anti-Semitism, has no right to be present in public life. Considering the broad spectrum of content associated with the concept of homophobia, it may be concluded that putting this term on the same list with anti-Semitism and racism is intended to block the possibility of any discussion with the postulates of the LGTBI community. In other words, the idea is to make the conviction that homosexualism/bisexualism/transsexualism . . . is "a departure from the norm become an embarrassing relic for which there is no place not only in the mainstream of the public debate, but generally among the views acceptable among civilized people, just as was the case—and rightly so—with the other terms on the list."[243] In this sense, the concept of homophobia seems to be a tool of ultimate control exerted over the discourse about human sexuality and sexual behavior by the logic of anthropological unconstraint. This is particularly important in that the fight against homophobia is presented today as a determinant of the EU community of values. As President of the European Council Herman van Rompuy said on the occasion of the Day Against Homophobia: "The European Union can take some pride in being at the vanguard of combating homophobia and other forms of prejudice and discrimination (. . .). In this

---

[240]Ibid., p. 20.

[241]Ibid.

[242]Cf. Herman Van Rompuy, *Statement by President Herman Van Rompuy on the International Day Against Homophobia*, Brussels, 6.05.2010, PCE 88/10.

[243]P. Mazurkiewicz, *Między hetero. . .* Cf. Tomasz Wiścicki, "Kościół, homoseksualizm, człowiek i. . . kultura," *Więź* No. 3 (569) 2006, pp. 87–88.

respect, discrimination on the basis of gender and sexual orientation (. . .) is something that distinguishes Europe from many other parts of the world."[244] It should be added that this pride and distinctiveness of the EU is rooted in an anthropological concept underlying EU policy which is different from the one that is universally embraced.

11.4   Initial Conclusions on the Anthropological Orientation of the European Union

An inductively oriented analysis of the language and contents of EU documents from the perspective of political studies based on an analysis of concrete linguistic data shows that in terms of the categories used in EU policies, the content attributed to them, and the objectives furthered by EU institutions, the process of European integration as regards morality policy as a whole displays a significant leaning towards the anthropology of unconstraint. Looking globally and in statistical terms, EU documents are dominated by concepts typical of the anthropological discourse characteristic of the said anthropological perspective. Historically, their meaning used to be expressed so that they could be linked to the perspective of constrained anthropology. Classic examples include the understanding of reproductive rights or gender at the threshold of the twentieth century. Their definitions in EU law were then constructed, to use geopolitical categories, in line with the doctrine of containment: they did not allow an interpretation, already used in public discussion, that went beyond clear anthropological boundaries (for example, the definition of reproductive rights prevented abortion from being included in their framework). Nevertheless, in the context of the political process developing over the last 20 years, these legal definitions have either been deconstructed (*vide* reproductive and sexual health and rights) or supplemented by categories which deprive them of any anthropological clarity (*vide* gender equality and gender identity; or marriage and sexual orientation). Consequently, the objectives of EU politics as a whole as regards morality policy, both in the internal and the dimension, have also been to a large extent oriented in accordance with this logic. At the same time, studies have shown that the logic of containment has not been entirely eliminated, and at times helps restore the Union's anthropological boundaries in important places (*vide* CJEU judgment in Brüstle described in Sect. 11.2.3).

The process of containing unconstraint is possible because, as indicated above, European institutions do not form a monolith as regards their anthropological orientation. In light of the above analyses, the anthropological position they adopt is related both to the nature of the institution itself, and the type of moral problems it addresses. It seems that this division is irrelevant only in the case of the European Parliament. It stands unequivocally on the position of unconstrained anthropology,

---

[244]H. Rompuy, op. cit.

regardless of whether the issue concerns the protection of human life or the concept of human sexuality and sexual behavior, pushing in its resolutions such radical demands as the removal of sexual disorders from the list of mental diseases (and thus also pedophilia, for example), or the right to abortion. In the case of other institutions, the above-mentioned division is clearly visible. While, following the EU's non-discrimination law, the Court of Justice of the European Union supports recognition of the equivalence of marriage and same-sex unions, provided that there are grounds for doing so in national law, it stands on the antipodes of the Parliament's logic when it comes to protecting the right to life in that it considers all, even the earliest, phases of human development as requiring legal protection. Similarly, while clearly defining their position as regards LGTBI advocacy and the fight against homophobia, the Council of the European Union and the Commission do not explicitly define their understanding of reproductive and sexual health and rights. And yet, an analysis of their documents reveals that the Council is much more precise and cautious than the Commission in defining the key terms of the discourse of unconstraint (such as LGTBI-phobia or discrimination on grounds of sexual orientation), and, given the timing of their publication and the importance of documents published on this matter, less committed to pushing the political agenda in this area. An analysis of the documents also suggests, therefore, that the so-called transnational institutions (EC, EP) are more likely to adopt the logic of unconstraint than the international ones (CEU).

The studies carried out so far thus make it possible to lay foundations for a theory of the anthropology of the European Union in the area of morality policy. Its guiding thesis is the claim that despite trying "not to take a stance" in the anthropological dispute in its primary legislation, in the area of morality policy the European Union as a whole is moving away from constrained towards unconstrained anthropology. A particular role in this process is played by transnational institutional actors. Indeed, in view of the political objectives of the Parliament, the Commission and the Council, it may be concluded that the greater the independence from the states, the greater the commitment to anthropological unconstraint. A special case in this regard is the EU Court of Justice which appears to be following a different logic in its actions, largely autonomous from strictly political institutions, without presenting a uniform anthropological position. As stated above, in the area of bioethics it clearly refers to the logic of constraint, while in the area of sexuality and sexual behavior it has rendered a variety of judgments, some of which, like P. v S., represent the logic of unconstraint, while others reflect, to the extent possible under primary law, the logic of constraint.

While this theory seems saturated as regards the Court of Justice and the European Parliament, that is, the institutions whose actions involve mainly verbal decisions on the political objectives of the EU or the ways of understanding EU legislation, it requires saturation as regards the anthropological standpoint of the Commission and the Council, which not only make political and legal claims, but have an important practical role as well: by enacting them (the Parliament), initiating and implementing them (the Commission), or ultimately deciding on their applicability (the Council). The key question here is whether it is indeed possible to argue that the Commission represents the unconstrained anthropological position more emphatically than the Council. Another important, and related, question seems to be the role of the Member States, both in the process of containing unconstrained anthropology, and strengthening it in EU policy. Furthermore, the thesis on the specific role of supranational institutions in the EU's shift towards and the deepening of anthropological unconstraint needs to be verified.[245] After all, it is not without reason that the Parliament is repeatedly described in literature as the weakest of the main decision-making institutions, with no real driving force. An important question is therefore whether and how it is able to anthropologically channel the direction of European politics. In other words, can it be demonstrated that the deepening shift towards anthropological unconstraint is linked to the activity of the European Parliament. Another interesting question, which could perhaps be answered along the way, is how come the Parliament, being dominated by Christian Democrats, is involved in this kind of channelling European policy at all. All these questions lead directly to analyses of decision-making processes in the EU.

---

[245] As emphasized in Part II, unconstraint does not necessarily mean abandoning all boundaries, but merely a departure from limits which are not up to man to decide about.

Chapter 12
Anthropological Analysis of EU Decision-Making Processes

The analysis of the language and contents of EU documents from the perspective of political studies carried out in the previous chapter has shown that as regards the categories used in EU policies, their content, and their objectives, a marked leaning may be observed in the process of European integration towards unconstrained anthropology. At the same time, the study has shown that the degree of this leaning for a particular institution may vary both depending on the type of morality policy concerned (bioethics or sexuality/sexual behavior) and the nature of the institution itself. Generally speaking, supranational institutions (particularly the Parliament) seem to be more prone to unconstrained thinking than international ones (the Council). At the same time, decisions concerning the protection of human life were less susceptible to the logic of unconstraint than the issues of human sexuality, which were clearly dominated by this logic, at least on the verbal level.

The study has shown in particular the need to saturate claims concerning the Commission and the Council, including the role of Member States, and to examine the dynamics of deepening the anthropological unconstraint. It is also worth verifying the claims, which already seem to be well-grounded, concerning anthropological orientation of European Parliament as well as exploring its impact on anthropological orientation of other EU's institutions.

In line with the theoretical and methodological assumptions discussed in Part I, in order to saturate the inductively built claims, the case study method focused on a detailed analysis of specific decision-making processes has been employed in this chapter. The selection of cases presented below was aimed at maximizing the usefulness of information obtained from small samples and individual instances. Consequently, they generally represent two types: so-called critical cases, and paradigmatic cases.

Critical cases are those which help "to achieve information which permits logical deductions of the type, 'if this is (not) valid for this case, then it applies to all

© Springer Nature Switzerland AG 2021
M. Gierycz, *European Dispute over the Concept of Man*, Contributions to Political Science, https://doi.org/10.1007/978-3-030-61520-8_12

(no) cases."[1] They have been used to saturate the claim about the dominance of anthropological unconstraint in the Commission's policy in relation to its activity concerned with the protection of human life. Paradigmatic cases highlight the more general characteristics of the examined subjects, establishing "a school for the domain which the case concerns."[2] They refer to relevant situations in which the typical, here: consistent with what has been established so far, activity of institutional actors may be expected. The selected cases include: adoption of the seventh Framework Programme, the Horizontal Anti-Discrimination Directive, and resolutions concerned with the equality between women and men. The first touches on the core of bioethical problems; the second relates to sexual behavior and the understanding of human sexuality; the third concerns how to define reproductive and sexual rights and the attitude to abortion. Clearly, if the behavior of institutional actors in these cases deviated from the tendencies outlined in the previous chapter, their correctness would have to be verified.

While the classical case study method should help saturate the theoretical claims made in the previous chapter, it does not in itself explain the dynamics of the anthropological evolution of the EU moral policy over the last 15 years. The last part of this chapter will therefore employ process tracing within the case study method. It consists in an attempt to capture the causal mechanisms by which, in certain contexts or conditions, some entities transmit "energy, information or matter" to others, resulting in certain "characteristics, capabilities or tendencies" changing in a relatively permanent way[3]—at least until they are subjected to the operation of further mechanisms. The case analyzed here will be the evolution of the approach to the protection of human life in the prenatal phase as part of humanitarian policy.

12.1   Bioethical Aspects of the 7th Framework Programme[4]

In view of the open formula of guaranteeing the right to life in the Charter, the increasing significance of biotechnology for the progress of scientific research and, finally, divergences in the approach to the scope of lawful activity in this area in the legal orders of the Member States, the debate on the Union's funding of scientific research has been related to important ethical dilemmas practically since the end of the twentieth century. As noted by Maja Grzymkowska, already "in the decision establishing the 3rd Research Framework Programme (. . .) reference was made to

[1]Bent Flyvbjerg, "Five Misunderstandings About Case-Study Research," *Qualitative Inquiry*, Vol. 12, No. 2, April 2006, p. 34.

[2]Ibid.

[3]Cf. Kamil Ławniczak, "Process tracing. Śledzenie mechanizmów przyczynowych," in: id. [ed.], *Metody jakościowe i ilościowe w badaniu organizacji i działania Unii Europejskiej*, WDiNP UW, Warszawa 2013.

[4]In this paragraph, I have used fragments of my articles "Chrześcijańscy politycy w ponadnarodowych sporach. . .," and "Unijne spory o wartości podstawowe. . .".

'basic ethical standards' as a criterion in evaluating projects," and "in the next edition (...) a step further was made by specifying what kind of research would be excluded from funding."[5] Nevertheless, a look at EU regulations in this area does not reveal only a growing concern for the protection of life. As the said author observes, "the ethical requirements under the 6th Framework Programme were not as firm as those resulting from the earlier editions."[6] As pointed out by Wolfgang Wodarg (SPD) the Union's actions based on these requirements allowed, among other things, to fund "destruction of 'supernumerary' embryos in order to produce new 'European' stem cell lines."[7] Furthermore, based on the principle of respect for the pluralism of the Member States, the European Group on Ethics in Science and New Technologies established by the European Commission took the view that the possibility of Community funding of research on embryos should not be excluded *a priori*.[8] In addition, it agreed to "the patenting of human embryos and embryonic stem cells."[9]

12.1.1 European Commission Proposal

Due to the experience with the 6th Framework Programme, and to a significant increase in EU research funding and the development of biomedicine in the middle of the first decade of the twenty-first century, the bioethical problem was explicitly addressed in the EU on the occasion of drafting the 7th Framework Programme (FP7), whose solutions are largely continued under the current Horizon 2020 programme.[10] A particular area of controversy in the FP7 debate was the possibility of EU funding of embryonic stem cell research. Even though the funds allocated for such research accounted for 0.1% of the Programme's funding,[11] as emphasized by Jerzy Buzek, the Programme's rapporteur at the time, it was important "from the point of view of what world of values the European Union is based on."[12] Awareness of the ethical significance of this issue was shared by all institutions: consent to the financing of such activities from the EU budget would mean that a considerable number of the Member States would have to finance activities which were

---

[5]Ibid.

[6]Ibid.

[7]http://p-ntzp.com/dok/12Wodarg-p.pdf [30.07.2016].

[8]M. Grzymkowska, *Standardy...*, pp. 227–228.

[9]http://p-ntzp.com/dok/12Wodarg-p.pdf [30.07.2016].

[10]Cf. European Commission, *Declarations of the Commission (Framework Programme)*, (2013/C 373/02): "For the Horizon 2020 Framework Programme, the European Commission proposes to continue with the same ethical framework for deciding on the EU funding of human embryonic stem cell research as in the 7th Framework Programme," p. C 373/12.

[11]http://www.europarl.europa.eu/sides/getDoc.do?pubRef=-//EP//TEXT+IM-PRESS +20060615STO09076+0+DOC+XML+V0//PL [30.07.2016].

[12]Ibid.

manifestly contrary to their legal order. Moreover, the EP Committee on Legal Affairs issued a decision which explicitly opposed EU funding of such activities.

The direct subject-matter of the axiological dispute was, first of all, the wording of point 25 of the justification and Article 6 of the Framework Programme. Point 25 in the original version proposed by the European Commission read: "Research activities supported by this Framework Programme should respect fundamental ethical principles, including those reflected in the Charter of Fundamental Rights of the European Union. The opinions of the European Group on Ethics in Science and New Technologies are and will be taken into account."[13] Article 6 said, however: "All the research activities carried out under the seventh Framework Programme shall be carried out in compliance with fundamental ethical principles."[14] Clearly, the Commission proposed flexible wording that did not necessarily determine its final interpretation. Considering the experience with FP6, a heated discussion broke out in the European Parliament around the above articles, with a view to defining the applicability of the ethical principles they refer to.

12.1.2   Position of the European Parliament

Amendments were submitted to each of the above-mentioned passages. Amendment 47 made it clear that "research on the use of human stem cells may be financed under the seventh Framework Programme"[15] and was adopted by a majority of 286 votes, with 260 votes against and 28 abstentions.[16] Amendment 66 clarified the principles of conducting such research by modifying Article 6; it stated that "[r]esearch on the use of human stem cells, both adult and embryonic, may be financed, depending both on the contents of the scientific proposal and the legal framework of the Member state(s) involved. Any such application for financing must include details of the licensing and control measures that will be taken by the competent authorities of the Member States. As regards the use of human embryonic stem cells, Institutions, organisations and researchers must be subject to strict licensing and control in accordance with the legal framework of the Member State(s) involved."[17] This amendment was also adopted by a majority of 284 votes. This time, 249 Members

---

[13] *Report on the proposal for a decision of the European Parliament and of the Council concerning the seventh framework programme of the European Community for research, technological development and demonstration activities (2007 to 2013)*, COM(2005)0119 – C6-0099/2005 – 2005/0043(COD).

[14] Ibid.

[15] Cf. *European Parliament legislative resolution on the proposal for a decision of the European Parliament and of the Council concerning the seventh framework programme of the European Community for research, technological development and demonstration activities (2007 to 2013)*, COM(2005)0119 – C6-0099/2005 – 2005/0043(COD), § 51.

[16] http://www.votewatch.eu/cx_vote_details.php?id_act=1860&lang=pl (27.12.2010).

[17] Ibid., Article 6.

were against, and 32 abstained from voting.[18] In parallel to this vote, a similar majority rejected amendments attempting to ban the financing of research on embryos or embryonic stem cells from the EU budget, proposed, among others, by Anna Zaborska and Giuseppe Gargani (Amendments 352–357).[19] Not only amendments explicitly prohibiting the funding of such research from the EU budget were rejected,[20] but also those in which evaluation of the legitimacy of funding referred to documents of international law which presented a more clear-cut position concerning such research than the CFR, for example the Oviedo Convention,[21] or its Additional Protocol on the Prohibition of Cloning Human Beings.[22] The Parliament did not even pass an amendment which attempted not so much to prohibit embryo research but to limit it to embryos created before December 31, 2003—Amendment 319.[23] In this sense, the anthropology of constraint lost with the logic of unconstraint, while violating the principle of subsidiarity in the field of science.[24]

It is worth taking a closer look at the ratio of votes that led to this decision. In the vote on Amendment 47, as can clearly be seen from Table 12.1, the overwhelming majority of socialist (PES), liberal (ALDE) and radical left (GUE) groups voted in favor of an amendment which allowed for procedures not accepted in some Member States to be financed from the EU budget. In general, the right (EPP, UEN, IND) and, notably, the greens (Greens/EFA) were against. It can be easily calculated that, considering the support from the greens and the non-iscrits (NI), this vote should easily have been won by the Christian democratic party, which is the largest parliamentary grouping. In order to understand why this did not happen, it is worth noting the structure of votes in the two largest groups: PES and EPP. The socialists achieved a vote cohesion[25] of 92%, compared to 51% among Christian

---

[18]http://www.euro-fam.org/scripts/spop/articleINT.php?&XMLCODE=rollcallV2006_06_15_A&LG=PLeuro (4.03.2010).

[19]Amendments 356, 357 concerned point 4 of the justification, and 352 – point 21 of the justification. Amendments 354 and 355 concerned Article 6 of the Programme.

[20]Like Amendment 352, for instance: 294 votes against, 248 votes for, 34 abstentions.

[21]*The Convention for the Protection of Human Rights and Dignity of the Human Being with regard to the Application of Biology and Medicine,* Oviedo Convention 1997.

[22]Like Amendment 353, rejected by a majority of 249/280/8.

[23]*MEPs back €50bn programme for research and development,* http://www.europarl.europa.eu/sides/getDoc.do?language=EN&type=IM-PRESS&reference=   20060615STO09 076 (04.03.2010).

[24]For it may hardly be argued that it is consistent with the principle of subsidiarity for a higher level to finance activities from funds contributed by a lower level which are contrary to the latter's constitutional order.

[25]Vote cohesion of particular factions is provided citing votewatch.eu which employs a two-step method for calculating this parameter. In the first step, the so-called agreement index is calculated according to the Hix-Noury-Roland formula: $Ai = (max(Y,N,A)-(0.5((Y + N + A)-max(Y,N,A))))/(Y + N + A)$, where Y is the number of votes "For", N means the number of votes "Against", and A is the number of abstentions. Then, the cohesion rate of the group is determined by the arithmetical average of the scores of the Agreement Index. Cf. http://www.votewatch.eu/blog/guide-to-votewatcheu/#sthash.PDl1i7gi.dpuf

Table 12.1 Results of European Parliament vote on Amendment 47 to FP7 political group perspective

Group	For	Against	Abst.	Present	Absent	Members	Cohesion (%)
EPP	53	140	14	207	48	264	54.45
PES	147	5	3	155	39	201	92.26
ALDE	53	15	1	69	13	89	65.22
Greens/EFA	4	32	2	38	3	42	76.32
GUE-NGL	22	7	1	30	10	41	60.00
UEN	2	26	0	28	6	35	89.29
NI	3	15	6	24	5	33	43.75
IND/DEM	2	20	1	23	7	30	80.43
Total	286	260	28	574	131	735	

Source: www.votewatch.eu

democrats—which means that more than 25% (53 Members) voted against moral requirements which seem to be self-evident from the Christian perspective.[26] Given that the amendment was passed by a minimum majority, one may not fail to conclude that it was in fact carried by the votes of Christian democrats, without which it would not have stood a chance of being enacted.

Let us also note the vote on the amendment opposing research on embryos, proposed by Christian democrats. The data presented in Table 12.2 show that even in supporting its own proposals, the Christian democrats were the most divided. The EPP did not even reach a 50% vote cohesion. More than 30% of Christian democratic voters were against the amendment. Interestingly, the Gargani/Zaborska amendment was fairly well supported by the liberals (almost 30% of the voters were in favor) and, again, the greens. A consistently high support for solutions in line with the European ethical tradition was displayed by UEN and IND Members. Despite a high vote cohesion in smaller right-wing parties (the UEN reached a rate of 94%) and the greens, and the substantial support from the liberals, the amendment was rejected for the same reasons for which Amendment 47 was adopted: the ambiguity of Christian democrats and the clear-cut position of the European left. It is worth highlighting this phenomenon, as it shows the sources of the European Parliament's strong tilt towards unconstrained anthropology. The axiological unequivocalness of the left, which supports the logic of unconstraint, is not matched by an unequivocalness from the right, which is largely influenced by the logic of unconstraint. This issue be discussed further on in the context of the approach to sexuality and sexual behavior.

---

[26]For more on this subject, see my article "Christian politicians...", pp. 428–437.

Table 12.2 Results of European Parliament vote on Amendment 353 to FP7—a political group perspective

Group	For	Against	Abst.	Present	Absent	Members	Cohesion (%)
EPP	129	61	17	207	48	26	43.48
PES	9	140	5	154	39	201	86.36
ALDE	20	46	4	70	13	89	48.57
Greens/EFA	31	6	2	39	3	42	69.23
GUE-NGL	6	23	1	30	10	41	65.00
UEN	27	1	0	28	6	35	94.64
NI	18	1	6	26	5	33	53.58
IND/DEM	17	2	4	23	7	30	60.87
Total	257	281	39	577	131	735	

Source: www.votewatch.eu

It is worth looking at the results of votes from a national perspective. Table 12.3 clearly shows that alongside the Germans, Irish, Slovaks, Latvians, Lithuanians, Luxembourgers, Maltese and Hungarians, the Polish delegation was in a broad group of delegations strongly (more than half the Members from the national group concerned) opposed to the funding of research on embryos. Although the Polish delegation was not as unanimous on this issue as the Maltese or the Latvians, they showed the highest cohesion in voting among the large national groups opposed to the financing of this research from the EU budget.[27] Split votes (roughly 50/50) came from Austria, Italy, the Netherlands and the Czech Republic. In the remaining fifteen national groups, the majority of Members supported the funding of such research from the EU budget. The Polish delegation with its 40 votes was consequently a significant and visible group among opponents of the funding of this type of research, as a national group taking this standpoint second only to Germany in absolute numbers, but with a higher vote cohesion (70% to 53%). Among the opponents of such research, a voting cohesion greater than that of the Polish group was displayed by representatives of small countries: Latvia and Malta (100%), as well as Ireland (73%).[28] Consequently, it may be said that as regards the protection of human life in the embryonic phase, a position grounded in the anthropology of constraint was related to the citizenship of a particular country rather than the membership of a particular ideological faction.

---

[27] It may be added that a comparison of data presented by votewatch.eu on the participation of MPs from the largest national groups shows that only in the Polish and Spanish groups the absence/non-voting rate was about 10%. In the other groups it ranged between 20% and 30%.

[28] Source: votewatch.eu.

Table 12.3 Results of European Parliament vote on Amendments 47 and 252 to FP7—a national group perspective

Country	Amendment 47				Amendment 352			
	For	Against	Abst.	Voting	For	Against	Abst.	Voting
Austria	8	10	0	18	11	7	0	18
Belgium	16	3	0	19	3	15	1	19
Cyprus	2	1	0	3	2	1	0	3
Czech Republic	10	10	0	20	7	10	3	20
Denmark	11	1	0	12	2	10	0	12
Estonia	3	1	0	4	1	3	0	4
Finland	8	4	0	12	2	10	0	12
France	44	10	4	58	7	46	6	59
Germany	23	55	2	80	53	25	1	79
Greece	19	1	0	20	2	18	0	20
Hungary	3	8	4	15	7	3	6	16
Ireland	2	9	0	11	9	2	0	11
Italy	26	27	2	55	30	23	3	56
Latvia	0	7	0	7	7	0	0	7
Lithuania	1	3	1	5	3	2	0	5
Luxembourg	2	4	0	6	2	4	0	6
Malta	0	5	0	5	5	0	0	5
Netherlands	13	11	0	24	10	14	0	24
Poland	9	40	1	50	40	9	1	50
Portugal	13	4	0	17	4	13	0	17
Slovakia	3	7	2	12	7	4	1	12
Slovenia	2	2	1	5	2	3	0	5
Spain	28	17	3	48	17	29	2	48
Sweden	7	4	1	12	4	7	1	12
United Kingdom	33	16	7	56	11	36	9	56

Source: Own compilation based on votewatch.eu

12.1.3   Position of the Council of the European Union

In this context, it is not surprising that the dispute over the shape of the 7th Framework Programme finally moved to the level of the Council of the European Union. In its official position before the vote, Austria stated that although it generally supported FP7, it must "once again" emphasize its standpoint, "already expressed frequently, that activities which imply the use of human embryos must not be funded through the 7th Framework Programme for research."[29] Stressing that Austria "is strictly against this kind of research for fundamental ethical reasons," its representative said that it "regrets that Article 6 of the 7th Framework Programme Decision allows the financing of research on human embryonic stem cells," and stated that "[t] herefore, Austria cannot agree to the overall 7th Framework Programme of the EC."[30] Poland, Lithuania, Malta and Portugal, who also believed that the agreed wording of the FP7 was not morally acceptable, took a position similar to that of Austria. As observed by Malta, "the Seventh Framework Programme does not adequately address the ethical concerns regarding research with human embryos and human embryonic stem cells. In view of this, Malta cannot agree to the overall Seventh Framework Programme, and is therefore voting against the Council's common position."[31] Along the same lines, Poland appealed "to the Presidency and the European Commission to take this aspect from the currently discussed text of the proposal for the decision on the 7th Framework Programme for a separate consideration. Such a move would allow Poland to support the suitably amended proposal."[32] As this appeal was not considered, the decision on FP7 was adopted by a qualified majority vote, in which the above countries were outvoted.[33]

It should be emphasized that the loss by a group of states in the Council was linked to a change in the position of one previous member of the coalition blocking the Programme, namely Germany. In fact, the change in its position is documented by the existence of a statement made by Germany as one of the countries opposed to solutions proposed in the Regulation, as well as its internally inconsistent content. While stating that the "protection of human dignity and the right to life necessitate the comprehensive protection of human life from the moment of its creation," and despite finding "the provisions concerning research with human embryos and human embryonic stem cells to be still insufficient," it nevertheless "approves the Seventh Research Framework Programme because of its outstanding importance for European research and for social development in the European Union."[34]

---

[29]Statement by Austria in: *Council of the European Union, Proposal for a Decision of the European Parliament and of the Council concerning the 7th Framework Programme of the European Community for research, technological development and demonstration (2007–2013) [first reading]—Adoption (cp + s) (a) of the common position (b) of the statement of the Council's reasons—Statements,* Brussels, 19 September 2006 (19.09), 2005/0043 (COD), p. 2.

[30]Ibid.

[31]Statement by Malta in: Ibid., p. 5.

[32]Statement by Poland in: Ibid., pp. 3–4.

[33]Marcin Kawa, *Polskie Nie dla komórek macierzystych z ludzkich embrionów,* http://www. biotechnolog.pl/polskie-nie-dla-komorek-macierzystych-z-ludzkich-embrionow [30.07.2016].

[34]Statement by Germany in: *Council of the European Union, Proposal for a Decision of the European Parliament and of the Council concerning the 7th Framework Programme of the European Community for research, technological development and demonstration (2007–2013), [first reading]—Adoption (cp + s) (a) of the common position (b) of the statement of the Council's reasons—Statements,* Brussels, 19 September 2006 (19.09), 2005/0043 (COD), pp. 1–2.

The example of "outvoting" in the Council reveals three important issues. First, that it is an institution considerably divided as regards fundamental questions of morality policy. Secondly, and as a consequence, it is an institution capable, depending on the decision-making formula, of effectively containing the logic of unconstraint. Suffice it to say that if the decision in this case had required unanimity, it would not have been made. Thirdly, the case described above shows the impact of big players on the final decisions made by the Union. If Germany had upheld its opposition to embryo research, visible for example in its voting in the Parliament, the regulation would have been amended.

It is worth noting that the Commission also participated in the Council's discussion. Its position was not as flexible there as in the legislative proposal. In fact, the Commission clearly defended the solutions which had been agreed upon and were now being challenged by the above-mentioned countries. In its argumentation, it stressed that "the decision on the 7th Framework Programme explicitly excludes three fields of research from Community funding: research activities aimed at human cloning for reproductive purposes; research activities intended to modify the genetic heritage of human beings which could make such changes heritable; research activities intended to create human embryos solely for the purpose of research or for the purpose of stem cell procurement, including by means of somatic cell nuclear transfer,"[35] which, as is not difficult to see, did not address the problem of the potential instrumentalization of human embryos. Also, the assurance that "no activity will be funded that is forbidden in all Member States," and that "no activity will be funded in a Member State where such activity is forbidden" did not address the problems of Member States that did not so much refuse to fund such research in their own country (this was not subject to dispute), but did not want to fund it in other EU countries. Finally, the assurance that "in calling for proposals, the European Commission does not explicitly solicit the use of human embryonic stem cells," that "in practice, by far the largest part of Community funds for stem cell research is devoted to the use of adult stem cells," and that "there is no reason why this would substantially change in FP7,"[36] may hardly be considered an answer that dispels any ethical concerns.

Summing up the above findings, it may be concluded that the analyzed case confirms the assertion, resulting from what had previously been established, that the logic of unconstraint clearly prevails in the European Parliament, and that the Council distances itself from this logic due to the difference in views on related issues among the Member States. Consequently, at least in the area of bioethics, the Council is not consistent in its positions and does not always take full advantage of its containment potential. Nevertheless, it should be noted that the logic of unconstraint—not without connection with the Member States' positions—is still held back from being fully applied in the Union. While the EU allows embryo testing, it clearly limits its scope. The analyses also provide important data on the sources of

---

[35]Statement by the Commission, in: Ibid., p. 5.

[36]Ibid., p. 6.

the Parliament's ideological involvement, dominated by a unconstrained anthropological orientation, which is not only clearly dominating at the left side of European Parliament, but also shared by important group of it's right-wing members. Finally, they seem to support the thesis that the Commission's declared neutrality in the area of bioethics in practice implies a leaning towards the logic of unconstraint, although conclusive data would still need to be collected to confirm it.

12.2 European Commission's Policy on the Protection of Human Life in the Prenatal Phase

In looking for a conclusive answer as to the Commission's standpoint on the protection of human life in the prenatal phase, it is best to ask about its attitude to abortion and initiatives for the protection of life. In recent years, the Commission has often been confronted with these issues and, consequently, forced to present its position. This is particularly important seeing that the Commission has repeatedly declared that abortion remains outside its competence and that of the Union as such.[37] It is therefore worth confronting these claims with the Commission's activities where the subject matter of its decisions was the attitude to pro- or anti-abortion initiatives. Three cases have been selected for this purpose which may be considered critical: the Commission's position on financing pro-life campaigns in Hungary from European funds, the Commission's position on financing major abortion organizations from European funds, the Commission's position on an initiative to ban the financing of research involving the destruction of human embryos from the EU budget (the *One of Us* initiative).

12.2.1 European Commission and Pro-Life/Pro-Choice Funding

In 2011, a campaign was launched in Hungary, partly funded from the EU's PROGRESS programme, which included public transport posters showing a baby in the prenatal phase asking the mother: "Well, I understand that you are not ready to accept me, but think twice and give me over to adoption services. LET ME LIVE."

---

[37]Cf. e.g. questions asked by Vierling: Parliamentary questions, 27 September 2007, E-4666/07 WRITTEN QUESTION by Robert Kilroy-Silk (NI) to the Commission E-4666/2007, answer given by Mr. Frattini on behalf of the Commission: "However, this matter and regulations related thereto are under exclusive control of the Member States." WRITTEN QUESTION by Alexandros Alavanos (GUE/NGL) to the Commission, answer given by Mr. Verheugen on behalf of the Commission: "It should be recalled in any event that Member States remain competent to decide upon their national legislation on abortion and that abortion is subject to various restrictions in current Member States."

As reported by the media, the idea for such a large-scale campaign was related to the fact that in Hungary "several thousand lives are lost every year as a result of so-called abortions, while thousands of marriages wait very long for adoption."[38] In May 2011, fourteen MEPs approached the Commission about this matter, questioning the legitimacy of the Union's funding of this campaign, and in June, during a debate in the EP, the issue was raised by the French Socialist MEP Sylvie Guillaume, the then Vice-President of the European Parliament. In response to these interpellations, the Commissioner for Justice and Fundamental Rights, Viviane Reding, stated on behalf of the Commission that "this campaign goes against European values," and expressed a desire that "European funds (. . .) be returned as quickly as possible."[39] The Commissioner said that the Hungarian campaign "[did] not correspond to the project put forward by the Hungarian authorities, and therefore the Commission [called] on the Hungarian authorities to end part of this campaign and to withdraw the posters without delay."[40] As pointed out by pro-life commentators, "although Mrs. Reding expressed her disapproval for the campaign, she did not explain in her answer to the European Parliament the basis upon which she disapproved of the campaign. She did not cite any legal basis for her comments, nor did she say how it contradicted the European Social Agenda."[41] Although in the end the Commission failed to force Hungary to return the money, the Commission made a clear assessment of the legitimacy of funding pro-life campaigns. As Commissioner Reding subsequently argued, the lack of competence as regards abortion "means that the EU cannot promote or condemn abortion; that is why the Commission considers that the use of EU money for an anti-abortion campaign is not in line with EU competence."[42]

This explanation, although it does not justify declaring the Hungarian campaign to be contrary to European values, might be considered convincing. Note, however, that it was no longer considered applicable when it came to the Commission's funding of pro-abortion activities. After the high-profile International Planned Parenthood Federation (IPPF) case of 2015, when it was proven that the organization sold body parts of aborted children, the European Commission was confronted with the question of the legitimacy of financing IPPF from EU funds in view of its evident connection to abortion. In response to the MEPs' question: "Has the Commission ever funded the IPPF, and if so what is the total amount provided to date? What action does it intend to take now, given that trafficking in human organs is a crime in the EU and that the international scope of IPPF's activities would suggest that the

---

[38]https://prawy.pl/279-ue-wegry-oddajcie-te-pieniadze/ [30.07.2016].

[39]https://www.euractiv.com/section/justice-home-affairs/news/eu-funds-used-for-hungarian-anti-abortion-campaign/ [30.07.2016].

[40]https://prawy.pl/279-ue-wegry-oddajcie-te-pieniadze/ [30.07.2016].

[41]EU threatens Hungary for promoting adoption instead of abortion http://protectthepope.com/?p=3238

[42]Planned Parenthood Selling Aborted Baby Parts. Suspend EU Funding Now! http://www.europeandignitywatch.org/planned-parenthood-selling-aborted-baby-parts/

trafficking in organs from aborted foetuses might also be taking place within the EU?,"[43] the Commission confirmed that "[t]he International Planned Parenthood Federation is a recipient of EU development aid both through the general budget of the Union and through the European Development Fund (...) [and] received from the European Commission 20.4 million euros to implement 20 projects in various development cooperation partner countries and regions." In reply to concerns voiced by the MEPs, the Commission stated that it was "not aware of any cases of organ trafficking linked to International Planned Parenthood Federation's activities. Any information about such activities taking place in the EU should be reported to the appropriate national law enforcement and transplant agencies for further investigation, and, if necessary, for prosecution under the national legislative provisions."[44] It did not therefore see any reason for monitoring the funds transmitted to IPPF, finding their activities to be lawful and essentially non-problematic.[45]

This is particularly significant considering that a well-documented report published 2 years earlier by one of the lobbying institutes, European Dignity Watch, proved that since the mid-2010s the European Commission had funded the International Planned Parenthood Federation (IPPF) and Marie Stopes International (MSI), registered in the UK as non-profit charities. Both of these organizations are leading global providers of abortion services.[46] The European Commission has allocated funds "for projects in such countries as Cambodia, South Africa, Bangladesh or Papua New Guinea. It is worth noting that in the latter two countries abortion is only legal in the case of saving the life of the mother."[47] As demonstrated by European Dignity Watch, between 2005 and 2009 the European Commission transferred nearly £16 million to Marie Stopes International (MSI) and millions of pounds—the exact amount cannot be established due to the absence of financial reports—by the International Planned Parenthood Federation (IPPF).[48]

---

[43]Jadwiga Wiśniewska (ECR), Janusz Wojciechowski (ECR), Stanisław Ożóg (ECR), Zbigniew Kuźmiuk (ECR), *Question for written answer E-012709-15 to the Commission under Rule 130. Subject: Commission funding for the International Planned Parenthood Federation*, 10.09.2015, E-012709-15.

[44]*Answer given by Mr Mimica on behalf of the Commission*, 10.11.2015, E-012709/2015.

[45]Cf. *Joint answer given by Mr Mimica on behalf of the Commission, Written questions: P-012161/15, E-011611/15*.

[46]The Marie Stopes website explains: "We believe women everywhere, regardless of where they live, should have access to comprehensive sexual and reproductive health services—including a range of contraceptive methods and, where legal, access to safe abortion—so they can make informed choices about their reproductive health. Where the law allows, we offer women the choice of both surgical and medical abortion. In these settings, we work to empower women to make their own decisions and give training to existing healthcare providers on how to provide safe medical abortion. We also train these providers on how to counsel women through this process, and on how to provide post-abortion care."

[47]https://prawdaoaborcji.wordpress.com/tag/international-planned-parenthood-federation-ippf-i-marie-stopes-international-msi/ [30.07.2016].

[48]European Dignity Watch, *The Funding of Abortion through EU Development Aid: an analysis of EU's sexual and reproductive health policy*, pp. 9–10.

In their reports, both organizations openly informed the Commission about the fact they provided abortion training and treatments through EU-funded grants. For example, "MSI reported in an interim report from its Cambodia Project, a project that began in 2006, that MSI-run clinics in four provinces had succeeded in performing some 6807 abortions,"[49] and in a report from Bangladesh more than 12,000 such procedures were recorded.[50] In its report on a £1.7 m project funded by the Union, IPPF declared it had distributed more than 1102 "emergency contraception units" directly or through affiliated organisations in Peru, Bolivia and Guatemala.[51] Crucial to the significance of this declaration is the fact that these units, usually containing substances such as progestin, mifepristone or misoprostol and therefore having abortive effects, were distributed with Union money in states whose laws prohibit abortion. Similar examples are many. Suffice it to note that an analysis of the joint EU and UNFPA programme "Reproductive Health Initiative for Youth in Asia,"[52] conducted with the support of the global pro-abortion organization Marie-Stopes International, showed that abortion was funded by the EU in at least seven Asian countries: Pakistan, Bangladesh, Cambodia, Laos, Nepal, Sri Lanka and Vietnam.[53] Data officially reported to the Commission on abortion procedures performed in places where abortion was legal, or on "menstrual regulation" and pharmacological abortion where it was officially illegal,[54] was not considered by the Commission as a reason to withdraw funding.

12.2.2 European Commission and the Prohibition of Funding the Destruction of Embryos

In a particular way, the Commission's approach to the protection of human life in the prenatal phase was revealed in relation to the "One of Us" initiative. The European Citizens' Initiative "One of Us" in defense of human life was made possible by two events which preceded it. The first was the introduction into the Lisbon Treaty of a

---

[49]Ibid., p. 13.

[50]In view of the illegality of abortion in Bangladesh, called "menstrual regulation." Ibid.

[51]International Planned Parenthood Federation, *Improving the Sexual and Reproductive Health and Rights of Street Youth and Other Youth in Especially Difficult Circumstance in Bolivia, Guatemala, and Peru,* Final Project Report, Commission Contract, 100428, 2009, 11 (EC), as quoted in: European Dignity Watch, *The Funding of Abortion through EU Development Aid...*, p. 14.

[52]Reproductive Health Initiative for Youth in Asia—RHIYA http://www.asia-initiative.org

[53]C. Vierling, *Los derechos de la mujer y la regulación del aborto en el Parlamento Europeo,* http://www.prolifeworldcongress.org/zaragoza2009/index.php?option=com_content&task=view&id=192&Itemid=109 (31.03.2011).

[54]*Application to the General Court of the European Union in the case of European Citizen's Initiative ONE OF US and others versus the European Commission, the Council of the EU, and the European Parliament Strasbourg, on the 25th of July 2014,* http://eclj.org/pdf/Application-One-of-US-v-EC.pdf [02.08.2016], par. 109, p. 19.

new tool of so-called "participatory democracy:" one million European Union citizens from at least seven countries can petition the European Commission to propose legislation on a matter within the EU's competence. The other was the above-discussed judgment of the European Court of Justice in Brüstle vs. Greenpeace (Case C-34/10) which recognized the human embryo as the beginning of the development of a human being. Based "on the definition of the human embryo as the beginning of the development of the human being, which was given in a recent ECJ judgment (Brüstle vs. Greenpeace), "One of Us" asks the EU to end the financing of activities which presuppose the destruction of human embryos, in particular in the areas of research, development aid and public health. This will be done through a change of the financial regulation of the EU that determines the spending of the EU budget. A ban of such funding will greatly contribute to the consistency within the EU."[55]

Three legislative proposals were submitted as part of the initiative: introduction into the financial rules of the general budget (Regulation 1605/2002 of 25 June 2002) of an article stating that "[n]o budget allocation will be made for the funding of activities that destroy human embryos, or that presume their destruction;"[56] introduction into the Regulation on the "Horizon 2020" program of a section saying that "research activities that destroy human embryos, including those aimed at obtaining stem cells, and research involving the use of human embryonic stem cells in subsequent steps to obtain them are not to be financed from EU funds;"[57] and the addition of paragraph 5 in Article 2 of Regulation 1905/2006 of 18 December 2006 establishing a financial instrument for development cooperation discussed in the previous chapter, saying that: "The assistance of the Union, on the basis of this Regulation, shall not be used to fund abortion, directly or indirectly, through the funding of organizations that encourage or promote abortion. No reference is made in this Regulation to reproductive and sexual health, health care, rights, services, supplies, education and information at the International Conference on Population and on Development, its principles and Program of Action, the Cairo Agenda and the Millennium Development Goals, in particular MDG n. 5 about health and maternal mortality, can be interpreted as providing a legal basis for using EU funds to directly or indirectly finance abortion."[58]

The European Commission registered the "One of Us" initiative on May 11, 2012, and received from the organizers, as part of the application, proposals for legislative changes to which at the time it did not raise any objections.[59] The initiative has so far proved to be the most significant citizens' initiative in terms of popular engagement, with the support of "more than 1.7 million citizens with

---

[55]http://www.oneofus.eu/pl/initiative-explanation/ [02.08.2016].

[56]*Application to the General Court. . .*, par. 6, p. 3.

[57]Ibid.

[58]Ibid., pp. 3–4.

[59]Ibid., p. 3.

thresholds reached in 18 Member States."[60] Yet in May 2014, the Commission decided not to present the broadly supported citizens' proposal to the Parliament and the Council, as it did "not see a need to propose changes to the Financial Regulation."[61] On July 25, 2014, the European Citizens' Initiative "One of Us" lodged an appeal before the Court of Justice in Luxembourg against the European Commission, the Council of the European Union and the European Parliament, seeking annulment of the European Commission's decision not to refer the initiative to be proceeded by the European Parliament and the Council of the European Union.[62]

At this stage, without going into the disturbing questions about the point of establishing a citizens' initiative that—despite satisfying exacting requirements—may be dismissed by a single communication from the Commission and not even referred for consideration to legislative bodies,[63] it is worth looking at the Commission's explanatory memorandum which negates the legitimacy of the postulates made by the "One of Us" initiative. After all, as indicated in the above paragraphs, there is no doubt that the EU was involved in financing activities whose goal (as in the case of financing abortion in the Third World) or an element of which (as in the case of scientific research) was the destruction of human embryos. In this sense, the citizens' initiative was aimed at changing EU policy in the spirit of anthropological constraint.

What is intriguing in the Commission's response is that it does not provide any arguments in favor of the policy allowing, in certain situations, the destruction of human embryos. On the contrary, the Commission's ethical argumentation is based on the assertion that the EU's financial regulations already respect human dignity, the right to life, and the right to the integrity of the human person, and therefore do

---

[60]European Commission, *Communication from the Commission on the European Citizens' Initiative "One of us,"* 28.5.2014, COM(2014) 355 final, p. 2.

[61]Ibid., p. 17.

[62]Cf. "Europejska Inicjatywa Obywatelska 'Jeden z Nas' przed Sądem Unii Europejskiej," http://www.ordoiuris.pl/europejska-inicjatywa-obywatelska-jeden-z-nas-przed-sadem-unii-europejskiej,3440,i.html

[63]I have looked at this issue together with Fr. Piotr Mazurkiewicz in another article. Cf. M. Gierycz, P. Mazurkiewicz, *Europejskapolityka. . .* where we point out, among other things, that discussions accompanying the introduction of the European Citizens' Initiative into the Treaties were "a mixture of fear and hope. Hope for democratization, and fear of what ordinary citizens might demand from their elites. Hence the rather strict conditions: one million citizens and exceeding the minimum required number of signatures in at least seven countries. Even this did not disperse the bureaucrats' fears of confrontation with the will of the citizens, however. The initiative was deprived of the one element which gave it meaning: that of being a genuine legislative initiative of the citizens. It was reduced to the role of a petition to "our graciously planning" bureaucrats at Berlaymont Castle. The point of a citizens' initiative in a democracy is to equip citizens with the same right to take a specific legislative initiative as the president, the government or the parliament in European countries. In other words, citizens resorting to this instrument may sort of "rise up against" political elites without waiting for elections and try to correct their plans with regard to themselves. The Parliament, elected by the citizens, is obliged to consider its content whenever citizens wish to express their will directly and not only through the mouths of their representatives. Citizens are not a group of claquers. This is the meaning of the famous words: 'We, the people.'"

not need to be amended.[64] This thesis was supplemented by utilitarian and pragmatic argumentation.

In the case of funding research, the Commission argues that research on embryonic stem cells has unique scientific significance,[65] with promising results for the treatment of many diseases.[66] At the same time, it stresses that Horizon 2020 provisions on human stem cells are based on a "carefully calibrated" triple lock mechanism developed within the 7th Framework Programme, which protects the EU against financing unethical activities. This system, which the Commission referred to several times in its communication, includes respect for the law of the Member State, scientific and "rigorous" ethical review of planned research, and a ban on financing the creation of new stem cell lines and research which involves the destruction of embryos.[67] While it may be inferred from the Commission's reply that it has found a way to maximize the benefits of research while ensuring that the fundamental moral principles are upheld, it should be noted that the Commission does not specify in any way the principles according to which the ethical evaluation of proposed projects is to be carried out. In its second link, the "triple lock" reveals the lack of any substantive criteria for the evaluation of applications according to which they are to be "rigorously" reviewed. Furthermore, it should be noted that in its third element the "triple lock" does not refer at all to the fact that, despite the ethical restrictions mentioned (only) in this element, cell lines from previously killed embryos may be used for research purposes.[68] To put it bluntly: in its communication, the Commission did not at all address the problem, already clearly present in FP7, of financing research involving the destruction of human embryos, which were treated merely as the object of scientific research despite the existence of the "triple lock."

As regards abortion and the development policy, the Commission emphasizes the thesis on the compatibility of EU policy with human rights principles,[69] observing that "a funding ban would constrain the Union's ability to deliver on the objectives set out in the MDGs, particularly on maternal health."[70] This way, it considers abortion to be part of the Millennium Development Goals,[71] suggesting that access to abortion services is aimed at reducing abortion.[72] The Commission does not refer to the problem of the embryo's subjectivity, which is in line with the logic of unconstraint described above. In this context, it is also worth noting that, as the authors of the "One of Us" initiative pointed out in their application to the EU Court of Justice against the Commission's decision, the language used by the Commission

---

[64]European Commission, *Communication...*, p. 15.

[65]Ibid., p. 4.

[66]Ibid., p. 4.

[67]Ibid., p. 15.

[68]Cf. *Application...*, par. 86, p. 15.

[69]Ibid., p. 11.

[70]European Commission, *Communication...*, p. 19.

[71]Ibid., p. 17.

[72]Which was, in fact, criticized by the "One of Us" Federation. Cf. *Application...*, par. 107, p. 19.

in its communication employs a terminology dehumanizing the embryo,[73] that is to say, hiding the fact that it is "human beings that are being destroyed and used for research purposes."[74] The authors of the initiative point out that "one might also ask in this context whether it is appropriate to speak of 'donation' (which would imply that one human being can 'own' and 'donate' another human being), or of 'explicit, written, informed consent' (as if it were the embryo who had given explicit consent to its own destruction)."[75] Nevertheless, General Court of the European Union in its judgment from 2018 confirmed the decision of the Commission not to submit legislative proposal. Judgment states i.a. that "the Commission's communication is sufficiently reasoned" and "explained that current EU legislation already meets numerous requests of the authors of the initiative".[76]

* * *

The above discussed examples, which may be legitimately considered as critical cases in the context of the Commission's approach to the protection of human life, show that despite its declared "lack of competence" as regards abortion, the Commission conducts its policy concerning the protection of life in the prenatal phase in the spirit of anthropological unconstraint. Naturally, in relation to the Parliament's standpoint openly proclaiming the right to abortion, the Commission's position may appear to be much more nuanced. Nevertheless, it is much closer to that of the Parliament than of the Council, clearly divided in their opinions, with the standpoint of anthropological constraint still playing an important role. The Commission's position is not internally torn apart or self-contradictory. On the contrary, it is internally consistent in the reinterpretation of human rights and the concept of man itself. It therefore does not appear to be based on the recognition of the existence of objective limits to human actions, but on the logic of discretion, establishing and changing the limits of what is permissible depending on factors other than the recognition of anthropological limits. If this observation is correct, it should be possible to demonstrate its susceptibility to modification and, therefore, to further pushing the boundaries of political action. This issue will reappear in the last case analyzed in this chapter.

12.3 Horizontal Anti-discrimination Directive

Just as the discussion concerning the research framework program may be considered a paradigmatic case as regards the approach to the protection of human life, so the proposal for a Council directive on implementing the principle of equal treatment

---

[73]The terms included, for example: "spare blastocysts," "leftovers."

[74]Ibid., par. 72, p. 13.

[75]Ibid.

[76]General Court of European Union, *Press release No 52/18,* Luxembourg 23 April 2018, https://curia.europa.eu/jcms/upload/docs/application/pdf/2018-04/cp180052en.pdf

between persons irrespective of religion or belief, disability, age or sexual orientation, that is, the so-called Horizontal Anti-Discrimination Directive, may be considered a paradigmatic case for the approach to human sexuality and sexual behavior.[77]

12.3.1 European Commission Proposal

The Directive was initially drafted with a view to preventing discrimination against people with disabilities. Nevertheless, in 2008, "the European Commission also added provisions to the proposal referring to discrimination based on religion, belief, age and sexual orientation,"[78] with a view to implementing a uniform "framework for the prohibition of discrimination on these grounds" outside the labour market and introducing "a uniform minimum level of protection within the European Union for people who have suffered such discrimination."[79] An important role in extending the scope of the Directive in the months immediately preceding publication of the proposal was played by political circles related to sexual minority groups[80] which promoted a horizontal (covering all areas of discrimination) understanding of its scope[81] and were consulted in the course of its drafting.[82] In fact, text of the proposal reveals that as regards the scale of discrimination based on sexual orientation, in addition to Eurobarometer statistics the Commission relied mainly on data compiled by the European Evaluation Policy Consortium (EPEC) and the International Lesbian and Gay Association—Europe.[83]

---

[77]European Commission, *Proposal for a Council Directive on implementing the principle of equal treatment between persons irrespective of religion or belief, disability, age or sexual orientation*, COM/2008/0426, final version (hereinafter: "Proposal for an Anti-Discrimination Directive").

[78]*Dyrektywa antydyskryminacyjna ograniczy wolność gospodarczą w UE*, http://www.ordoiuris.pl/dyrektywa-antydyskryminacyjna-ograniczy-wolnosc-gospodarcza-w-ue,3521,i.html [02.08.2016].

[79]European Commission, *Proposal for a Council Directive on implementing the principle of equal treatment between persons irrespective of religion or belief, disability, age or sexual orientation*, p. 2

[80]https://agendaeurope.wordpress.com/general-anti-discrimination-directive/ [03.08.2016].

[81]Cf. ILGA-Europe, European Network Against Racism, *Why does the European Commission need to propose a Horizontal Directive on the principle of equal treatment? The Case for a Horizontal Anti-Discrimination Directive*. It is also worth noting that KathalijneBuitenweg, the rapporteur for this Directive in the European Parliament, gave particular thanks in her speech to Michael Cashman, leader of the LGBTI group in the Parliament, for his advice, all his lobbying activities, and inspiration. Cf. KathalijneBuitenweg, *Statement in debate*, 1.04.2009, PV 01/04/2009 – 14.

[82]Cf. ILGA – Europe, *Evidence of discrimination based on sexual orientation outside employment Submitted by ILGA – Europe following its written responses to the European Commission Consultation on New Anti-Discrimination Measures* (December 2007), http://www.ilga-europe.org/sites/default/files/Attachments/discrimination_based_on_sexual_orientation_-_additional_evidence_01dec07_www.pdf [02.08.2016].

[83]Cf. European Commission, *Commission Staff Working Document accompanying. . .*, p. 17. Data were also provided to the Commission by the EU Network of Independent Experts, but from the

The key goal of the Directive is to guarantee equal rights "to all persons, as regards both the public and private sectors, including public bodies, in relation to: (a) social protection, including social security and healthcare; (b) social advantages; (c) education; (d) access to and supply of goods and other services which are available to the public, including housing."[84] Its adoption would mean, for example, that it would be impossible to apply social privileges to marriages and families, to evaluate marriage and same-sex unions differently in education, or to refuse to provide services contrary to the service provider's convictions (e.g. to offer bed and breakfast accommodation to a same-sex couple in one's own home). Consequently, the Directive reflected a clear affiliation with anthropological unconstraint, raising concerns, for example, among churches[85] in view of the potential pressure on religious institutions as regards the way they recruit their employees in the area regulated by Community law,[86] entrepreneurs,[87] and the broadly understood right. For even though "the text makes it clear that matters related to marital and family status, which includes adoption, are outside the scope of the directive,"[88] as pointed out by Manfred Weber (EPP), the Directive results in "harmonisation [of family law] by the back door."[89] And sometimes even by the front door: for even though marriage or family issues (including adoption) remain outside the application area of the Directive, at the same time the Directive applies in cases where national law confers on civil partnerships rights comparable to marriage.[90]

The problematic nature of the Commission's proposal was not limited to issues of content. It also included important procedural issues. The Directive introduced an unconventional logic of proving guilt, or in fact innocence. The Commission explained that although "the general rule is that a person who alleges something must prove it, (...) in discrimination cases, it is often extremely difficult to obtain the evidence necessary to prove the case."[91] Consequently, the Commission suggested a "shift of the burden of proof" in all cases, except criminal actions, "alleging breach of the principle of equal treatment, including those involving associations and

---

document it turns out that they concerned mostly discrimination on the grounds of other protected characteristics.

[84]European Commission, *Proposal for an Anti-Discrimination Directive*, p. 20.

[85]Cf. M. Weber, *Equal treatment of persons irrespective of religion or belief, disability, age or sexual orientation (debate)*, 1.04.2009, PV 01/04/2009 – 14.

[86]Cf. *Amendment 52 and 95, European Parliament legislative resolution of 2 April 2009 on the proposal for a Council directive on implementing the principle of equal treatment between persons irrespective of religion or belief, disability, age or sexual orientation*, COM(2008)0426 – C6-0291/ 2008 – 2008/0140(CNS), P6_TA(2009)0211.

[87]Mostly for financial reasons. Cf. European Commission, *Proposal for an Anti-Discrimination Directive*, p. 10.

[88]European Commission, *Proposal for an Anti-Discrimination Directive*, p. 10.

[89]M. Weber, *Equal treatment. . . .*

[90]European Commission, *Proposal for an Anti-Discrimination Directive*, p. 10.

[91]Ibid., p. 11.

organisations under Article 7(2)."[92] Thus for example a person accused of discriminating against people of a different sexual orientation in education would have to demonstrate his or her innocence; the plaintiff would not have to prove guilt.

The directive proposal presented by the Commission was enthusiastically received by the LGTB community. The European Region of the International Lesbian and Gay Association (ILGA-Europe) not only "warmly welcomed" the proposal, but also considered it "an essential and much-needed step" towards equal protection against discrimination, and a "crucial" proposal which "provides for real protection where there is clear evidence of discrimination happening, including in housing, access to goods and services, access to health and education."[93] Comments made by ILGA-Europe were detailed in nature, aimed mainly at eliminating the few clauses in the text which potentially enabled Member States to evade fully implementing it with regard to gay and lesbian rights.[94] It was not concerned with the substance of the Commission's proposal, which clearly undertook to implement the postulates made by these communities.

12.3.2   Position of the European Parliament

As the Commission's legislative proposal had been submitted before the Lisbon Treaty entered into force, it was presented to the European Parliament for an opinion. The proposal sparked a debate within the EP, even though—apart from non-attached Members—critical remarks in the course of the parliamentary debate were only made by representatives of Christian democrats and conservatives. Their statements, particularly those made by the head of the Christian democratic faction, clearly reflected their sense of being "pilloried."[95] Indeed, the other factions: the socialists, liberals, communists and greens clearly supported the Commission's proposal, strongly criticizing any dissenting voices and pushing for amendments that further enhanced the "progressive" potential of the Commission's proposal.[96] By way of example, it is worth noting that amendments adopted by the Parliament included almost all of those proposed by ILGA-Europe in its memorandum. Some in the exact

---

[92]Ibid.

[93]*ILGA-Europe's position on the proposal for a Council Directive on the principle of equal treatment between persons irrespective of religion or belief, disability, age or sexual orientation. A Working Document*, October 2008, http://www.ilga-europe.org/sites/default/files/Attachments/ilga-europes_position_on_the_proposed_directive_october_2008_www.pdf [03.08.2016].

[94]Cf. *ILGA-Europe's position. . . .*

[95]For example, almost the entire statement by Manfred Weber, who was repeatedly referred to by other participants in the debate, was an appeal for an open discussion on the form of fighting against discrimination. *Equal treatment of persons irrespective of religion or belief, disability, age or sexual orientation (debate)*, 1.04.2009, PV 01/04/2009 – 14.

[96]Ibid.

Table 12.4 Results of European Parliament vote on the Proposal for a Horizontal Anti-Discrimination Directive—a political group perspective

Group	For	Against	Abst.	Present	Absent	Non Voters	Members	Cohesion (%)
EPP	35	154	59	248	29	11	288	43,15
PES	179	1	0	180	26	11	217	99,17
ALDE	78	5	2	85	9	6	100	87,65
Greens/EFA	4	33	0	37	5	2	44	83,78
GUE-NGL	37	1	0	38	4	1	43	96,05
UEN	29	0	1	30	9	2	41	95,00
NI	2	22	0	24	6	0	30	87,50
IND/DEM	3	10	0	13	6	3	22	65,38
Total	367	226	62	655	94	36	785	

Source: votewatch.eu

same wording as proposed by the International Lesbian and Gay Association,[97] others, in the absence of concrete proposals for solutions, simply responding to the concerns expressed in the ILGA position.[98] From the anthropological perspective, after having been processed in the Parliament, the logic of unconstraint already present in the proposal was significantly strengthened. The proposal was carried in the Parliament by 367 votes for to 226 votes against, with 62 abstentions.[99]

Table 12.4 documents the radical difference in the structure of votes cast on the right and on the left. While on the left more than 95%, including more than 87% of the "least cohesive" liberals, supported the Commission's initiative, the most cohesive group on the right were conservatives (their club at the time, the UEN, was made up mainly of Poles from the Law and Justice party, however) whose opposition was almost as cohesive as the support of the liberals. The key actor, the European People's Party, did not even achieve a 50% vote cohesion. Out of the 288 EPP Members, 154 voted against the Commission's proposal, the remaining 134 either

---

[97] See e.g. amendment to Article 2(8), or recital 16 of the Preamble. Cf. *ILGA- Europe's position. . .*, pp. 4 and 6; and European Parliament, *European Parliament legislative resolution of 2 April 2009 on the proposal for a Council directive on implementing the principle of equal treatment between persons irrespective of religion or belief, disability, age or sexual orientation* (COM(2008)0426 – C6-0291/2008 – 2008/0140(CNS)), P6_TA(2009)0211, Amendments 27 and 45.

[98] Cf. e.g. *ILGA- Europe's position. . .*, p. 7 and European Parliament, *European Parliament legislative resolution of 2 April 2009. . .*, Amendment 50.

[99] Cf. http://www.votewatch.eu/cx_vote_details.php?id_act=5750&lang=en

abstained (59), were in favor (35), or did not take part in the vote. In order to understand the political importance of the lack of cohesion in the Christian democratic vote, it is sufficient to note that if all EPP Members had voted in line with the party's prevailing position, the resolution would have been carried by as few as seven votes.

Some light on the divergences within the EPP is cast by the structure of votes in the national perspective. It shows that some national groups (such as Belgium, Ireland, Sweden and Denmark) supported the Commission's proposal practically as a whole, and some significant groups (including those significant within the EPP, such as France) as a great majority. At the same time, there was no country whose Members were mostly against that exceeded 60% of vote cohesion. The most cohesive, of those opposing the Commission's proposal, was the Polish national group, achieving a vote cohesion of 57% (Table 12.5).

To summarize, it may be said that the vote on the Horizontal Anti-Discrimination Directive proceeded in the Parliament in a manner similar to the vote on the 7th Framework Programme. One apparent difference was perhaps that the cohesion of votes cast by the greens significantly increased, which clearly strengthened the left's position. The People's Party, representing a position based on the logic of anthropological constraint in the debate, did not present their point in a cohesive manner when it came to their votes cast. Consequently, the proposal referred by the Parliament to the Council was marked by the logic of unconstraint even more than the Commission's initial proposal.

12.3.3 Position of the Council of the European Union

The proposal for the Directive, with the Parliament's amendments, was received at the Council of the European Union in the spring of 2009. Nevertheless, it had first been considered by the Council already in the autumn of 2008, during the French Presidency. As reported in a release on the Council's meeting of October 2, 2008, the Council then conducted "a policy debate, open to the public, on a proposal for a Directive on implementing the principle of equal treatment between persons irrespective of religion or belief, disability, age or sexual orientation,"[100] which revealed significant divergences between the Member States: "a large number of Ministers favoured a high level of ambition,"[101] while "some Ministers questioned the need to establish Community rules in this area, while supporting the principle of equal treatment."[102] Consequently, some delegations, not seeing the need for a horizontal approach, "would have preferred more ambitious provisions concerning

---

[100]Council of the European Union, Press release 2893rd Council meeting, *Employment, social policy, health and consumer affairs*, Luxembourg, 2 October 2008, C/08/271, 13405/08, p. 6.

[101]Ibid.

[102]Ibid.

Table 12.5 Results of European Parliament vote on the Proposal for a Horizontal Anti-Discrimination Directive—a national group perspective

Country	For	Against	Abst.	Present	Absent	Cohesion (%)
Austria	11	6	0	17	0	47.06
Belgium	19	3	0	22	1	79.55
Bulgaria	10	2	4	16	2	43.75
Cyprus	1	1	1	3	2	0.00
Czech Republic	8	11	1	20	3	32.50
Denmark	11	1	1	13	1	76.92
Estonia	3	1	0	4	2	62.50
Finland	9	3	0	12	2	62.50
France	40	7	13	60	13	50.00
Germany	37	46	0	83	12	33.13
Greece	8	5	6	19	3	13.16
Hungary	12	4	4	20	2	40.00
Ireland	10	0	1	11	2	86.36
Italy	33	27	1	61	12	31.15
Latvia	2	6	0	8	1	62.50
Lithuania	7	3	2	12	1	37.50
Luxembourg	3	1	1	5	0	40.00
Malta	2	0	1	3	2	50.00
Netherlands	15	8	1	24	2	43.75
Poland	14	35	0	49	5	57.14
Portugal	16	3	4	23	1	54.35
Romania	11	15	0	26	7	36.54
Slovakia	4	4	1	9	4	16.67
Slovenia	4	1	2	7	0	35.71
Spain	26	19	0	45	6	36.67
Sweden	17	1	0	18	0	91.67
United Kingdom	34	13	18	65	8	28.46
Total	367	226	62	655	94	

Source: votewatch.eu

measures to combat discrimination on grounds of disability."[103] Ultimately, "most delegations asked for certain parts of the proposal to be clarified in order to guarantee

---

[103]Ibid.

its legal certainty,"[104] and "a large number of delegations requested clarifications regarding the proposal's economic and financial impact."[105]

The debate on the Directive continued in the Council during the Czech Presidency which followed the French Presidency. The Presidency's progress report documents the Council's considerable concerns about the proposal, as well as their divided opinion as regards its merits, mainly concerning its horizontal dimension. The report says that even though "at the time, a large majority of delegations welcomed the proposal in principle, (. . .) some delegations would have preferred more ambitious provisions in regard to disability instead of the horizontal approach. While emphasising the importance of the fight against discrimination, certain delegations have put forward the view that more experience with the implementation of existing Community law is needed before further legislation is adopted at the Community level."[106] As a consequence, the Presidency's report documents a long list of unsettled and unaddressed concerns about the Commission's proposal,[107] concluding that although "tangible progress has been made (. . .) in the attempt to clarify the provisions on disability, there is a clear need for extensive further work on the proposal."[108]

The next two Presidencies, the Swedish and the Spanish one, in addition to taking into account the procedural changes resulting from the Lisbon Treaty's entry into force, did not achieve any particular results in their works on the directive. The report of November 2009 says that while "significant progress has been made under the Swedish Presidency in the attempt to clarify the scope, the division of competences, the disability provisions, and the implementation calendar, there is a clear need for extensive further work on the proposal."[109] An identical formula is found in the report of the Spanish Presidency.[110] It reiterates the conclusion found in the previous reports that "for the time being, all delegations have maintained general scrutiny reservations on the proposal. CZ, DK, FR, MT and UK have maintained parliamentary scrutiny reservations, CY and PL maintaining linguistic scrutiny reservations. The Commission has meanwhile affirmed its original proposal at this stage and has

---

[104]Ibid.

[105]Ibid.

[106]Council of the European Union, The Presidency, *Proposal for a Council Directive on implementing the principle of equal treatment between persons irrespective of religion or belief, disability, age or sexual orientation – Progress Report,* 2 June 2009, Brussels, SOC 349, JAI 312, MI 213, 2008/0140 (CNS), p. 2.

[107]Ibid., pp. 4–6.

[108]Ibid., p. 7.

[109]Council of the European Union, The Presidency, *Proposal for a Council Directive on implementing the principle of equal treatment between persons irrespective of religion or belief, disability, age or sexual orientation – Progress Report,* 17 November 2009, Brussels, 15575/09, p. 7.

[110]Ibid.

maintained a scrutiny reservation on any changes thereto,"[111] documenting the gap between the positions of the Council and of the Commission.

Given that the successive (Hungarian and Polish) Presidencies also failed to carry the Directive through with the Council, often focusing (as was the case, for instance, with the Polish Presidency) on a single detailed aspect,[112] and in subsequent years the topic in fact died down with the Council, it is worth asking about the primary sources of this institution's distancing itself from the Commission's proposal. Experts point out that "countries such as Germany and the Netherlands, as well as numerous NGOs and business associations, protested against its adoption,"[113] which was due to the fact that "the proposal for the Directive contained a number of solutions which significantly restricted the freedom of contract and freedom of economic activity."[114] Germany's strong resistance, in particular, was linked to the fear of "too much financial burden for entrepreneurs."[115] Nevertheless, there is no doubt that its "ethically sensitive" character also played an important role: "the greatest controversy is the special treatment of persons who engage in homosexual practices the proposal provides for."[116] This was actually confirmed by the Commission itself. Commissioner Viviane Reding, in her statement made in the European Parliament on the fight against homophobia, noted that while "the Commission is fully committed to combating this phenomenon with all the powers at our disposal, (...) unfortunately [emphasis added—M.G.], this text needs unanimity in the Council and that is the reason why it is blocked, but it is clear also that there is a vast majority of Member States who would back it."[117] Indeed, to date the Directive has not left the Council of the European Union, despite the fact that it was also a priority for the next President of the Commission, Jean Claude Juncker. Even though he announced in his inaugural address in 2014 that "[t]he Anti-Discrimination Directive [would] remain on the table and [he would] try to persuade the Council

---

[111]Ibid., p. 2.

[112]Cf. Council of the European Union, The Presidency, *Proposal for a Council Directive on implementing the principle of equal treatment between persons irrespective of religion or belief, disability, age or sexual orientation – Progress Report,* 15 November 2011, Brussels, 16525/11.

[113]Ordo Iuris, *Analiza Dokumentu Komisji Europejskiej "List of actions by the Commission to advance LGBTI equality" w kontekście jego zgodności z polskim porządkiem prawnym,* p. IV, http://www.ordoiuris.pl/analiza-dokumentu-komisji-europejskiej-list-of-actions-by-the-commis sion-to-advance-lgbti-equality%2D%2Dw-kontekscie-jego-zgodnosci-z-polskim-porzadkiem-prawnym,3786,analiza-prawna.html [03.08.2016].

[114]Ibid.

[115]Krzysztof Śmiszek, "Powolny proces dostosowywania polskiego systemu polityki antydyskryminacyjnej do standardów unijnych," *Problemy Polityki Społecznej* no. 15/2011, p. 57.

[116]*Dyrektywa antydyskryminacyjna ograniczy wolność gospodarczą w UE,* http://www.ordoiuris. pl/dyrektywa-antydyskryminacyjna-ograniczy-wolnosc-gospodarcza-w-ue,3521,i.html [02.08.2016].

[117]*Council and Commision statements: Fight against homophobia,* Bruksela, 4.06.2012.

to adopt at least the core proposals as soon as possible,"[118] he was unable to achieve this goal by the end of his term of office.

The case of the Anti-Discrimination Directive shows not only the difference in the positions of the Commission and the Council, despite their similar political rhetoric described in the previous chapter, as regards their approach to the so-called "LGTBI rights," but also confirms the significance, identified in the analysis of the FP7, of the CEU decision-making process for the anthropological orientation of EU decisions. Unanimity, which requires the positions of all Member States to be taken into account, by overriding the logic of transnationality,[119] in the anthropological context turns out to be the guardian of anthropological constraint. In addition, the case has confirmed the earlier claims about a particular dominance of the logic of unconstraint in the decisions of the European Parliament, deepening the logic of the Commission's unconstrained anthropological position.

12.4 Two Areas of Primary Morality Policies in Three Reports of the European Parliament

The analysis of the content and language of EU political documents, as well as the two previously examined cases, indicate a clear and unequivocal leaning of the European Parliament's anthropological orientation towards the logic of unconstraint. At the same time, an analysis of the votes shows that there is a significant, albeit minority, group of Members in this institution who are opposed to such an interpretation. The question is whether it is possible for their point of view to win a majority in the House, and whether it would mean that the Parliament is able to adopt a constrained anthropological perspective in the dispute over human life and sexuality. A good example based on which this issue may be examined is the history and implications of the report on reproductive and sexual health and rights prepared in the Committee on Women's Rights and Gender Equality by the Portuguese socialist Edite Estrela (S&D).

---

[118] Jean Claude Juncker, "Opening Statement in the European Parliament Plenary Session," in: Jean Claude Juncker (ed.), *A New Start for Europe: My Agenda for Jobs, Growth, Fairness and Democratic Change. Political Guidelines for the next European Commission. Opening Statement in the European Parliament Plenary Session*, Strasbourg, 15 July 2014, p. 20.

[119] Cf. Luuk van Middelaar, *The Passage to Europe: How a Continent Became a Union*, Yale University Press 2013.

12.4.1   Edite Estrela's Report

A report on reproductive and sexual health and rights[120] was presented to the Parliament in the autumn of 2013 and was intended as a kind of culmination of the EP's activity in this area in its 7th term. The aim was, first of all, to strengthen the EU's policy in this area at a time when, as stated in the explanatory memorandum "the anti-choice opposition is becoming stronger and more vocal" as clearly manifested "in countries such as Spain and Hungary, and in regional forums such as the Parliamentary Assembly of the Council of Europe, the European Committee on Social Rights, and even at the EP."[121] The specific context of the "opposition becoming stronger" in the EU was the "One of Us" Citizens' Initiative described above, which received far more signatures than required under EU law and was presented to the Commission.[122] It is interesting in the context of the Parliament's anthropological self-definition that the Members' reaction to the gradual change in the socio-political attitude towards abortion in Europe was to recognize that "it is more critical than ever that the EP stands up for sexual and reproductive rights as human rights and provides a useful summary of the current state of play of SRHR at the European level."[123] This was precisely the purpose of the proposed report.

In the context of this goal, it is not surprising that in the document containing the explanatory statement, the opinion and the text of the report on reproductive health itself, referring also to issues which do not give rise to any major doubts, such as, for example, support for the victims of HIV, or support for perinatal care, the term "abortion" is used 80 times.[124] No attempt was made here to conceal the fact that abortion is considered part of these rights. In accordance with the Estrela report, the Parliament "recommends that, as a human rights and public health concern, high-quality abortion services should be made legal, safe, and accessible to all within the public health systems of the Member States, including non-resident women, who often seek these services in other countries due to restrictive abortion laws in their country of origin;"[125] "[u]nderlines that even when legal, abortion is often prevented or delayed by obstacles to the access of appropriate services, such as the widespread use of conscientious objection (...) [and therefore] stresses that Member States should regulate and monitor the use of conscientious objection in the key

---

[120]Committee on Women's Rights and Gender Equality (FEMM), *Report on Sexual and Reproductive Health and Rights* (2013/2040(INI)), A7-0306/2013.

[121]Ibid.

[122]As an interviewee observed in one in-depth interview, the Estrela Report was "compiled in the context of the entire 'One of Us' European citizens' initiative and was also intended as a counterweight." *In-Depth Interview (IDI)—3*. UKSW Institute of Sociology, UKSW Institute of Political Science. Another interviewee said: "The Estrela report was an attempt to put all the most leftist and radical ideas together in a single text in order to anticipate the hearing of 'One of Us.'" *In-Depth Interview (IDI)– 6*. UKSW Institute of Sociology, UKSW Institute of Political Science.

[123]Explanatory Statement in: FEMM, *Report on Sexual and Reproductive Health and Rights*, p. 22.

[124]By way of comparison, the terms mother(s) and motherhood appears a total of 36 times.

[125]FEMM, *Report . . ., par.* 34

professions, so as to ensure that reproductive health care is guaranteed as an individual's right;"[126] "calls on all Member States to ensure that health care professionals who perform abortion and abortion related services are not prosecuted or penalised under any criminal law instruments, on the grounds of having provided these services;"[127] finally, "calls on the governments of the Member States and the candidate countries to refrain from prosecuting women who have undergone illegal abortions."[128] As regards the EU's international relations, the report called on the Commission to "to allow a specific line on SRHR under the thematic lines of the Development Cooperation Instrument, as well as sufficient funding for the broad SRHR agenda in all appropriate instruments."[129] Moreover, it urged "the EU to ensure that European development cooperation adopts a human rights-based approach and that it has a strong and explicit focus, and concrete targets on SRHR, paying particular attention to family planning services, maternal and infant mortality, safe abortion, contraceptives."[130]

However, abortion issues were not the only ones mentioned in the report. It also broadly addressed the second area of primary morality policies—the issue of human sexuality and sexual behavior. Second in length only to the general recommendations was the section entitled "As regards comprehensive sexuality education and youth-friendly services." Observing in it that "the sexual and reproductive health needs of adolescents differ from those of adults,"[131] the report called on the Member States "to ensure that adolescents have access to user-friendly services"[132] by employing "various methods in reaching out to young people, such as publicity campaigns, social marketing for condom use and other methods of contraception,"[133] "which are to be accessible without the consent of parents or guardians."[134] The draft report also recommended that "sex education classes [should be made] compulsory for all primary and secondary school children,"[135] and "must include non-discriminatory information and convey a positive view of LGBTI persons, in order to underpin and protect in an effective manner the rights of young LGBTI people,"[136] be held "in a safe, taboo-free, interactive atmosphere between students

---

[126]Ibid., par. 35.

[127]Ibid., par. 37.

[128]Ibid., par. 39.

[129]Ibid., par. 73.

[130]Ibid., par. 78.

[131]Ibid., par. 45.

[132]Ibid.

[133]Ibid., par. 42. In number 47, the Parliament "urges the Member States to take measures to remove all barriers hindering the access of adolescent girls and boys to safe, effective, affordable methods of contraception, including condoms, and to provide clear information on contraceptives."

[134]Ibid., par. 46.

[135]Ibid., par. 43.

[136]Ibid., par. 53.

and educators"[137] and "include the fight against stereotypes, prejudices, all forms of gender violence and violence against women and girls, shed light on and denounce discrimination on the grounds of gender and sexual orientation, and structural barriers to substantive equality."[138]

As is rarely the case, the Estrela report aroused widespread interest in Europe and significant public opposition. Mobilized by the circles associated with the "One of Us" European Citizens' Initiative, EU citizens *en masse* started sending letters to the Parliament to protest against the proposed measures.[139] As a result, the legislative process of this report took an unusual turn. On October 22, 2013, the Parliament decided to send the report back to the Commission by a majority of 351:319 votes, with 18 abstentions.[140] This decision was opposed almost unanimously by practically all left-wing parties.[141] Right-wing factions, in support of the report's referral to the Commission, presented an equally strong vote cohesion. Having more votes at their disposal, they settled the issue.[142]

Following minor changes made by the Commission, the report was presented to the MEPs again on December 3, 2013 in practically the very same wording. Two amendments were proposed, both as alternative resolutions. This means that instead of amending certain provisions of the proposed report, they called for it to be rejected in its entirety and for the text proposed in its place to be adopted.

The first alternative resolution, proposed by Bastiaan Belder, Tadeusz Cymański, Philippe de Villiers, Rolandas Paksas, Claudio Morganti and Lorenzo Fontan on behalf of the EFD Group,[143] was a negative, so to say, of Estrela's proposal. In accordance with this resolution, the Parliament was to invite "the Member States to include the promotion of (natural) family planning methods in their public health policy, and to ensure access to non-judgmental information about post-abortion trauma syndrome (PAS) as well as immediate and universal access to PAS treatments, provided in a safe and non-judgmental manner;" to recall "Section 8.25 of the Programme of Action of the International Conference on Population and

---

[137]Ibid., par. 44.

[138]Ibid., par. 52.

[139]The petition submitted by Matteo Cattaneo*No al rapporto Estrela* alone won the support of nearly 50,000 votes. http://www.citizengo.org/it/1224-no-al-rapporto-estrela Similar petitions were made in other languages.

[140]http://term7.votewatch.eu/en/sexual-and-reproductive-health-and-rights-motion-for-resolution-request-for-referral-back-to-committ.html#/##vote-tabs-list-2

[141]It may be observed, however, that as in previous cases, none of the Maltese voted against. Two supported the proposal (these were the only two votes "for" in the socialist faction), one abstained, two did not vote. Cf. http://term7.votewatch.eu/en/sexual-and-reproductive-health-and-rights-motion-for-resolution-request-for-referral-back-to-committ.html#/##vote-tabs-list-2

[142]http://term7.votewatch.eu/en/sexual-and-reproductive-health-and-rights-motion-for-resolution-request-for-referral-back-to-committ.html#/##vote-tabs-list-2

[143]Bastiaan Belder, Tadeusz Cymański, Philippe de Villiers, Rolandas Paksas, Claudio Morganti, Lorenzo Fontana on behalf of the EFD Group, *Motion for a resolution (Rule 157(4) of the Rules of Procedure) replacing non-legislative motion for a resolution A7-0426/2013 on sexual and reproductive health and rights*, 4 December 2010, A7-0426/1.

Table 12.6 Results of the vote on EFD's alternative resolution to the Estrela Report—a political group perspective

Group	For	Against	Abst.	Present	Absent	Non voters	Number of MEPs	Cohesion (%)
EPP	29	205	11	245	10	16	271	75.51
S&D	2	171	5	178	8	9	195	94.1
ALDE	0	71	5	76	5	3	84	90.13
Greens/EFA	0	55	0	55	3	0	58	100
ECR	33	4	12	49	4	4	57	51.02
GUE-NGL	0	30	0	30	2	3	35	100
EFD	16	1	13	30	2	0	32	30
NI	15	11	2	28	3	1	32	30.36

Source: http://term7.votewatch.eu/en/sexual-and-reproductive-health-and-rights-motion-for-resolu
tion-alternative-motion-for-a-resolution%2D%2D2.html#/##vote-tabs-list-2

Development stating: 'In no case should abortion be promoted as a method of family planning,'[144] and the fact that "abortion is not mentioned in any internationally binding UN human rights treaty and that no human right to abortion exists under international law;" and invite "the Commission and the European External Action Service (EEAS) to fully respect the reservations on sexual and reproductive health rights (SRHR) and abortion expressed by national governments in the relevant international treaties, conventions and programmes."[145] In addition, it reaffirmed the right to conscientious objection in the context of abortion,[146] and stressed the primacy of parents and the exclusive competence of the Member States to decide on the issue of sex education.[147]

The structure of the vote on this amendment is presented in Table 12.6. It is worth noting that the greatest support for this resolution came not from the party which proposed it (30% vote cohesion, 16 supporting Members), but from the European Conservatives and Reformists (ECR) (51.02% vote cohesion, 33 supporting Members), where it was supported by more Members than in the European People's Party as a whole. The EPP voted against the resolution, together with the socialists, communists and liberals. As a side remark, it is worth noting that this was perhaps the only "ethically sensitive" resolution during that term in which the votes of the EPP and S&D groups remained consistent with each other. Here, the factional

---

[144]Ibid., p. 4.

[145]Ibid., par. 7.

[146]Ibid., par. 8.

[147]Ibid., nn. 9–11.

strategy seems to have defeated the ethical strategy (especially since it was clear that there was no chance of adopting the EFD resolution).

This conclusion seems to be confirmed by the structure of votes in the national perspective. It reveals that only the Maltese Members voted by a majority (both from EPP and S&D) for the EFD resolution (except for Mr. Mizzi (S&D) who voted against). Aside from one more exception from Lithuania, where the number of votes "for" and "against" was equal, in all other national groups a majority of Members voted against the amendment. In terms of the scale of support, the Polish group *ex aequo* with the Italian group provided the most numerous support for the EFD resolution in the entire Parliament (Table 12.7).

The opposition of the EPP and the majority of national delegations[148] to the resolution proposed by the EFD was mainly due to the fact that its Members had proposed their own alternative resolution.[149] It was short in content and avoided entering into ethical disputes. Stressing the limited competence of the Union and bearing in mind that "the Cairo ICPD Programme of Action gives a definition of sexual and reproductive health and rights (SRHR),"[150] it provided that "the formulation and implementation of policies on SRHR and on sexual education in schools is a competence of the Member States,"[151] and "the EU can contribute to the promotion of best practices among Member States."[152] The House adopted this amendment by a majority of 334 to 327 votes, with 35 abstentions. The decision came as a shock not only to the left, causing the rapporteur to ask for her name to be removed from the resolution;[153] it was just as much of a shock to the right. Suffice it to note that one of the persons actively involved in the EU's axiological disputes had stated in an interview held in October 2014: "The Estrela report will be adopted on December 10. I think there is no other option, but at least it was not adopted right away. And 2 years ago, it probably would have been adopted right away."[154] From the right wing's perspective, it was therefore a success even to postpone the vote and send the report back to the Commission. The structure of votes in this landmark vote is presented in Tables 12.8 and 12.9.

It is glaringly obvious that the EPP amendment owed its success to a cohesive vote on the right side of the political scene: the Christian democrats and

---

[148]Given that S&D, ALDE, as well as green and communist groups were by definition against, the majority of Members belonged to political groups opposing the resolution.

[149]Together with one ECR Member. Cf. Doris Pack, Astrid Lulling, Angelika Niebler, Christa Klaß, Joanna Katarzyna Skrzydlewska, Regina Bastos, Nuno Teixeira, Paulo Rangel on behalf of the PPE Group Marina Yannakoudakis on behalf of the ECR Group, *Motion for a resolution (Rule 157(4) of the Rules of Procedure) replacing non-legislative motion for a resolution A7-0426/2013*.

[150]Ibid., rec. A.

[151]Ibid., par. 1.

[152]Ibid., par. 2.

[153]http://www.europarl.europa.eu/sides/getDoc.do?pubRef=-//EP//TEXT+PV+20131210+ITEM-009-04+DOC+XML+V0//PL

[154]*In-Depth Interview (IDI)* No. 5, UKSW Institute of Sociology, UKSW Institute of Political Science.

Table 12.7 Results of the vote on EPP's alternative resolution to the Estrela Report—a national group perspective

Country	For	Against	Abst.	Present	Absent	Non Voters	Number of MEPs	Vote cohesion (%)
Austria	9	10	0	19	0	0	19	28.95
Belgium	3	18	0	21	1	0	22	78.57
Bulgaria	1	15	1	17	1	0	18	82.35
Croatia	1	6	0	7	0	5	12	78.57
Cyprus	0	6	0	6	0	0	6	100.00
Czech Republic	4	11	2	17	1	4	22	47.06
Denmark	0	11	2	13	0	0	13	76.92
Estonia	1	5	0	6	0	0	6	75.00
Finland	1	9	2	12	1	0	13	62.50
France	4	65	0	69	4	1	74	91.30
Germany	5	86	3	94	3	2	99	87.23
Greece	0	17	2	19	2	1	22	84.21
Hungary	2	12	2	16	5	1	22	62.50
Ireland	2	5	5	12	0	0	12	12.50
Italy	16	36	6	58	9	6	73	43.10
Latvia	0	7	1	8	0	1	9	81.25
Lithuania	5	5	0	10	1	1	12	25.00
Luxembourg	0	6	0	6	0	0	6	100.00
Malta	4	1	0	5	1	0	6	70.00
Netherlands	2	21	0	23	0	3	26	86.96
Poland	16	31	1	48	1	0	49	46.88
Portugal	1	20	1	22	0	0	22	86.36
Romania	1	27	1	29	1	3	33	89.66
Slovakia	2	9	1	12	0	1	13	62.50
Slovenia	0	8	0	8	0	0	8	100.00
Spain	0	49	1	50	0	4	54	97.00
Sweden	0	18	0	18	2	0	20	100.00
United Kingdom	15	34	17	66	4	3	73	27.27

Source: http://term7.votewatch.eu/en/sexual-and-reproductive-health-and-rights-motion-for-resolu tion-alternative-motion-for-a-resolution%2D%2D2.html#/##vote-tabs-list-4

conservatives exceeded a 90% vote cohesion, plus the proposal received significant support from EFD. In the case of EFD, it was important that those who did not support it, abstained from vote instead of voting against it. In this situation, while remaining essentially cohesive in their standpoint, the left were not in a position to defeat the right-wing majority in the Parliament. Thus, the vote showed that the dominance of anthropological unconstraint in the EP is mainly due to the lack of

Table 12.8 Results of the vote on EPP's alternative resolution to the Estrela Report—a political group perspective

Political Group	For	Against	Abst.	Present	Absent	Non voters	Number of MEPs	Cohesion (%)
EPP	239	4	8	251	10	10	271	92.83
S&D	3	167	8	178	8	9	195	90.73
ALDE	7	64	3	74	5	5	84	79.73
Greens/ EFA	0	55	0	55	3	0	58	100.00
ECR	49	1	0	50	4	3	57	97.00
GUE- NGL	0	29	1	30	2	3	35	95.00
EFD	18	0	12	30	2	0	32	40.00
NI	18	7	3	28	3	1	32	46.43

Source: http://term7.votewatch.eu/en/sexual-and-reproductive-health-and-rights-motion-for-resolu tion-alternative-motion-for-a-resolution-.html#/##vote-tabs-list-2

anthropological cohesion of the right and the centre faced with the essentially cohesive unconstrained position of the left and the liberals.

A look at the results of the vote from the national perspective offers equally interesting insights. In addition to the Italians and the Germans, the Poles were the largest national group of pro-lifers in the abortion dispute (nearly twice as numerous as the Spanish group which has a similar number of MEPs). At the same time, however, in the German group there were more opponents than supporters of the alternative resolution which was ultimately adopted. Among the other large countries, the distribution of votes between its supporters and opponents was more or less equal (England), with a slight majority of opponents (France, Spain). Against this background, the fact that the overwhelming majority of the Polish group (both the EPP and the ECR) voted in favor of the EPP amendment and, ultimately, achieved the highest cohesion in this vote is interesting, not only because it suggests the importance of the Polish delegation in the EP's axiological disputes for defending the logic of anthropological constraint but also because, as observable from the previously analyzed cases, the Poles' vote cohesion was usually lower than that of Swedes, Belgians or Danes, who consistently supported a progressive axiological standpoint. In this vote, the roles were reversed.

In this context, it should be noted that the reversal of the trend in the Member States' vote cohesion was influenced precisely by the consistently high support of the right for the EPP amendment. It was only possible, however, through a "demoralization" of the issue at hand. Unlike the EFD amendment, the alternative resolution did not address the ethical qualification of abortion, but merely the issue of systemic competence, calling for respect for the subsidiarity and competence of the Member States. As pointed out by one of the initiators of this resolution, the idea

Table 12.9 Results of the vote on EPP's alternative resolution to the Estrela Report—a national group perspective

Country	For	Against	Abst.	Present	Absent	Non voters	Number of MEPs	Vote cohesion (%)
Austria	9	9	0	18	0	1	19	25.00
Belgium	7	14	0	21	1	0	22	50.00
Bulgaria	7	9	1	17	1	0	18	29.41
Croatia	6	6	0	12	0	0	12	25.00
Cyprus	0	4	1	5	0	1	6	70.00
Czech Republic	7	10	0	17	1	4	22	38.24
Denmark	2	10	1	13	0	0	13	65.38
Estonia	1	5	0	6	0	0	6	75.00
Finland	5	7	0	12	1	0	13	37.50
France	31	34	4	69	4	1	74	23.91
Germany	41	51	1	93	3	3	99	32.26
Greece	6	12	1	19	2	1	22	44.74
Hungary	13	4	0	17	5	0	22	64.71
Ireland	8	4	0	12	0	0	12	50.00
Italy	38	14	7	59	9	5	73	46.61
Latvia	4	4	0	8	0	1	9	25.00
Lithuania	5	4	2	11	1	0	12	18.18
Luxembourg	3	3	0	6	0	0	6	25.00
Malta	4	1	0	5	1	0	6	70.00
Netherlands	9	13	1	23	0	3	26	34.78
Poland	41	7	0	48	1	0	49	78.13
Portugal	10	12	0	22	0	0	22	31.82
Romania	14	11	3	28	1	4	33	25.00
Slovakia	6	4	1	11	0	2	13	31.82
Slovenia	4	4	0	8	0	0	8	25.00
Spain	23	28	0	51	0	3	54	32.35
Sweden	1	14	3	18	2	0	20	66.67
United Kingdom	29	29	9	67	4	2	73	14.93

Source: http://term7.votewatch.eu/en/sexual-and-reproductive-health-and-rights-motion-for-resolution-alternative-motion-for-a-resolution-.html#/##vote-tabs-list-4

was precisely for a majority of the Parliament to refer to "the principle of subsidiarity and not to the substance of the matter. That was our idea, not to attack them in the discussion about the beginning of life (. . .) but show that we should not be dealing with such issues."[155] It should be stressed, however, that the strategy of an ethically neutral framing of the issue of reproductive rights and the approach to human sexuality (including sex education) was not really aimed at winning the votes of the left and the liberals. In any case, it certainly did not succeed on this account. The left side of the EP, with a vote cohesion known from earlier votes, was not interested in "defusing" the ethical sensitivity of the two primary issues of morality policy. It seems, therefore, that this strategy was mainly addressed to the right side of the political scene, with the aim of ensuring cohesion in its political actions. Here, in any case, it actually had the expected effect. From the perspective of anthropological analyses this ultimately proves, however, that constrained anthropology, with an entirely marginal impact on the left side,[156] also has a limited impact on the right side of the EP's political scene. It is characteristic that the EFD resolution which referred to it did not have the slightest chance of being adopted, and that the EPP did not even attempt to follow such a line of argumentation in its proposal.

To provide a complete picture of the situation, it should be added that the mass mobilization of citizens also had a significant impact on the cohesion of the EPP and ECR's opposition to the Estrela report. All the more so because it took place a few months before the next EP elections. As observed by one of the politicians actively involved in those events, the point was that "the Catholic community have practically buried [the MEPs] with thousands of emails. (. . .) And this matters a lot, as the Members get angry because this is blocking their inboxes, but they know very well that it is no longer two crazy medieval Taliban who think whatever they think, but that this is an avalanche."[157] Considering that the right-wing MPs' fight against an "avalanche of electoral hyperactivity" right before the elections is not a particularly sensible strategy, it seems that an ethically neutral framework for the approach to reproductive rights was a convenient solution for both the EPP and the ECR. On the one hand, it helped meet the expectations of the right-wing electorate which right-wing politicians associated with the Church. On the other hand, it did not force a cohesive adoption of the perspective of constraint in the anthropological dispute, which, as shown by previous votes, would probably not have been feasible. Consequently, the thesis about the Parliament's marked leaning towards unconstrained anthropology seems to find its particular *a contrario* confirmation.

---

[155] *In-Depth Interview (IDI)* – 6. UKSW Institute of Sociology, UKSW Institute of Political Science.

[156] It is not entirely non-existent, though. An analysis of the above votes from the national perspective reveals that nationality is of essential importance. For example, in the votes examined above, S&D Members from Malta were usually unanimously against the position of their respective political groups. Cf. http://term7.votewatch.eu/en/equality-between-women-and-men-in-the-european-union-2011-motion-for-a-resolution-paragraph-47-2.html#/##vote-tabs-list-4 [10.10.2016].

[157] *In-Depth Interview (IDI)* – 2. Instytut Socjologii UKSW, Instytut Politologii UKSW.

12.4.2   Christina Zuber's Report

It is also worth noting the political consequences of the failure of the Estrela report, as some conclusions may also be drawn from them as regards the EU anthropological debate. Within a month of the above vote, the Parliament voted on two more "ethically sensitive" documents. The first was the 2013 report on equality between women and men prepared by Ines Christina Zuber of the Portuguese Communist Party, who sat in the Parliament in the colors of the Confederal Group of the United European Left/Nordic Green Left. It openly referred to the issue of abortion. In the proposal for this report, the Parliament "strongly urges the Member States to increase their investment in public services, education and health, particularly primary care health services relating to sexual and reproductive health; recommends to the Member States that they safeguard women's right to free, high-quality public gynaecological and obstetric healthcare services and to sexual and reproductive health in general, including the right to voluntary termination of pregnancy; stresses that Member States should ensure that all women share the same rights when it comes to contraception, maternity or sexuality,"[158] and "calls therefore on the Member States to collect data to establish knowledge of the situation faced by women regarding sexual and reproductive health and rights."[159]

The report was voted on January 31, 2014. 289 Members voted for, 298 voted against, and 87 abstained from voting. Consequently, the report was rejected. The structure of votes in factional terms is presented in Table 12.10.

It is worth noting that, contrary to previous reports on equality between women and men, almost the entire EPP, ECR and EFD groups opposed the report. Compared to previous years, vote cohesion in these groups was strikingly similar to that of the groups supporting the project. Nevertheless, it should also not be overlooked that the EPP's vote cohesion dropped by 10% compared to the Estrela vote, meaning that more than 30 fewer Members were against. In fact, if the liberal group and the left had maintained the vote cohesion of the Estrela report, the outcome of this vote could have been different. The Zuber report could be rejected due to the decreased vote cohesion among the liberals (down to 61% from nearly 90% in the previous vote) and the greens/EFA (23%) compared to the previous tendency of achieving a nearly 100% support. This was mainly due to the large number of Members who abstained from voting.

These results seem puzzling, especially in view of the fact that the previous pro-abortion legislation had been outvoted by a clear and consistent majority in the 2009–2014 term.[160] Only one new element can be seen in the text itself which could have led to possible protests. Christina Zuber's report clearly tried to go "a step further" than previous reports in defining reproductive rights. Until then, resolutions

---

[158]FEMM, *Report on equality between women and men in the European Union – 2012,* (2013/2156 (INI)), A7-0073/2014, par. 42.

[159]Ibid.

[160]The most apparent in a situation when the project originated from Christian democrats.

Table 12.10 Results of the vote on the Zuber Report—a political group perspective

Political group	For	Against	Abst.	Present	Absent	Non voters	Number of MEPs	Cohesion (%)
EPP	11	209	16	236	28	8	272	82.84
S&D	166	4	4	174	10	11	195	93.10
ALDE	55	0	19	74	7	3	84	61.49
Greens/ EFA	25	2	26	53	3	2	58	23.58
ECR	1	47	3	51	4	2	57	88.24
GUE- NGL	28	0	4	32	2	1	35	81.25
EFD	0	14	10	24	4	4	32	37.50
NI	3	22	5	30	0	2	32	60.00

Source: http://term7.votewatch.eu/en/equality-between-women-and-men-in-2012-motion-for-reso lution-vote-femm-committee-resolution-as-a-who.html#/##vote-tabs-list-2

had included the "possibility of abortion." Even this wording, let us add, was a significant change from the EP resolutions of 2004–2009 which avoided openly defining reproductive rights in resolutions on equal rights of men and women, settling only for their promotion.[161] However, Christina Zuber's report proposed a further change in language, calling for the "right to voluntary termination of pregnancy," thus including voluntary abortion no longer indirectly, but directly now into human rights. While this change should not be ignored, it can hardly be seen as a possible reason for the conservative group's opposition to the report (which had so far mostly supported abortion as part of reproductive rights) or, even more so, as a source of the decomposition of support from liberals and some of the left who sought to have abortion recognized as part of women's rights, after all.[162] It seems the failure of the Zuber report can only be understood in the context of the unexpected failure of the Estrela report a month earlier. Although it essentially reiterated the pro-abortion theses known from the 2009–2011 reports on equality between women

---

[161]Characteristic in this context is Article 8 of the resolution on equality between women and men adopted in 2008, i.e. the last one to be adopted in the 2004–2009 term. The Parliament "notes" in it "the importance to women's empowerment of their control over their sexual and reproductive rights; therefore supports measures and actions to improve women's access to sexual and reproductive health services and to raise their awareness of their rights and available services." European Parliament, *Report on Equality between women and men – 2008* (2008/2047(INI)), P6_TA(2008) 0399, art. 8. Cf. also European Parliament, *Report on Equality between women and men – 2007* (2007/2065(INI)), P6_TA(2007)0423, or European Parliament, *Report on Equality between women and men – 2004* (2004/2159(INI)), P6_TA(2006)0039.

[162]It may be noted, as a side remark, that the greens were involved in supporting the "black protests" in Poland in 2016 advocating liberalization of Polish abortion law. Cf. https://europeangreens.eu/ news/discussion-polish-greens-abortion-and-womens-rights [21.10.2016].

and men, the argument referring to subsidiarity and the social mobilization at that point provided the right-wing with a sufficient weapon for consolidating and defeating liberals and the left in the vote.

The structure of votes in the national perspective reveals a similar position of national groups in ethically sensitive votes as that observed in the case of the Estrela report. Among MEPs from large countries, votes "for" and "against" were divided almost equally (Italy, Spain, United Kingdom—mostly "against;" Germany, France—mostly "for"). Against this background, the Polish delegation stood out again, opposing the Zuber proposal by a vast majority (though smaller than in the case of the vote on the Estrela report), maintaining a high level of vote cohesion. Next to Malta and Hungary, it had the highest vote cohesion of all the countries opposing the project. Among the supporting national groups, the highest level of cohesion was achieved by Sweden, Denmark, and Cyprus (Table 12.11).

Despite the failure of the Zuber report, the "subsidiarity" argument proved to be easy to neutralize, though in more than just 1 month. This is demonstrated by the success of another report on equality between women and men, submitted by Marc Tarabella less than a year later, already in the European Parliament's new term of office.[163] While in point 46 the Parliament states that "the formulation and implementation of policies on sexual and reproductive health and rights and on sexual education is a competence of the Member States," it stresses that "the EU can contribute to the promotion of best practice among Member States."[164] Consequently, in point 47 it says that "women must have control over their sexual and reproductive health and rights, not least [emphasis added—M.G.] by having ready access to contraception and abortion."[165] Thus, the resolution reiterated the theses known from the 2009–2014 term. Nevertheless, this time it was adopted by a majority of nearly 2/3 votes. The resolution was supported by 443 Members and opposed by 205, with 52 abstentions. Such high support was possible owing to the almost even distribution of votes "for" and "against" within the EPP.[166] It may therefore be said that the failure of the Zuber report was "an exception confirming the rule" rather than evidence of a change in the Parliament's anthropological orientation.

---

[163] *European Parliament resolution of 10 March 2015 on progress on equality between women and men in the European Union in 2013* (2014/2217(INI)), P8_TA(2015)0050.

[164] Ibid., par. 46.

[165] Ibid., par. 47.

[166] http://www.votewatch.eu/en/term8-progress-on-equality-between-women-and-men-in-the-eu-in-2013-motion-for-resolution-vote-resolution.html#/##vote-tabs-list-2 [22.10.2016].

Table 12.11 Results of the vote on the Zuber Report—a national group perspective

Member state	For	Against	Abst.	Present	Absent	Non voters	Total MEPs	Cohesion (%)
Austria	7	9	2	18	0	1	19	25.00
Belgium	9	8	1	18	4	0	22	25.00
Bulgaria	7	6	2	15	1	2	18	20.00
Croatia	6	6	0	12	0	0	12	25.00
Cyprus	4	1	0	5	0	1	6	70.00
Czech Republic	12	7	1	20	2	0	22	40.00
Denmark	10	1	2	13	0	0	13	65.38
Estonia	4	1	1	6	0	0	6	50.00
Finland	7	3	2	12	1	0	13	37.50
France	27	26	11	64	9	1	74	13.28
Germany	39	40	11	90	4	4	98	16.67
Greece	8	1	6	15	5	2	22	30.00
Hungary	4	14	3	21	1	0	22	50.00
Ireland	3	3	5	11	0	1	12	18.18
Italy	25	28	6	59	13	1	73	21.19
Latvia	4	3	1	8	0	1	9	25.00
Lithuania	4	2	2	8	3	1	12	25.00
Luxembourg	2	3	1	6	0	0	6	25.00
Malta	0	5	0	5	1	0	6	100.00
Netherlands	6	10	9	25	1	0	26	10.00
Poland	7	35	2	44	4	3	51	69.32
Portugal	10	10	0	20	0	2	22	25.00
Romania	14	13	1	28	4	1	33	25.00
Slovakia	4	7	2	13	0	0	13	30.77
Slovenia	3	3	1	7	1	0	8	14.29
Spain	23	21	3	47	2	5	54	23.40
Sweden	16	1	2	19	0	1	20	76.32
United Kingdom	24	31	10	65	2	6	73	21.54

Source: http://term7.votewatch.eu/en/equality-between-women-and-men-in-2012-motion-for-reso
lution-vote-femm-committee-resolution-as-a-who.html#/##vote-tabs-list-4

12.4.3   Urlike Lunacek's Report

The other document was a report on an EU plan to fight against homophobia and discrimination on grounds of sexual orientation and gender identity, prepared by Urlike Lunacek, an Austrian Member of the Green Alternative (Die Gruenne Alternative), which in the EP is part of the Greens/EFA group. In the report, the Parliament "strongly condemns any discrimination on the basis of sexual orientation and gender identity, and strongly regrets that the fundamental rights of lesbian, gay, bisexual, transgender and intersex (LGBTI) people are not yet always fully upheld in the European Union,"[167] calling on the Commission "to use its competences to the fullest extent" in order to prepare "a roadmap, a strategy or an action plan" for LGBTI advocacy.[168]

The actions it recommended included "LGBTI mainstreaming," that is the postulate to mainstream "issues linked to the fundamental rights of LGBTI people in all relevant work—for instance when drafting future policies and proposals or monitoring the implementation of EU law,"[169] and include the specific issues concerning "transgender and intersex people throughout the relevant EU policies, mirroring the approach adopted in the Gender Equality Strategy;"[170] it called for the Commission to "promote equality and anti-discrimination on grounds of sexual orientation and gender identity throughout its youth and education programmes,"[171] and take action "within the World Health Organisation to withdraw gender identity disorders from the list of mental and behavioural disorders and to ensure a non-pathologising reclassification in the negotiations on the 11th version of the International Classification of Diseases (ICD-11);"[172] it demanded that Member States ensure that "rights to freedom of expression and assembly are guaranteed, particularly with regard to pride marches and similar events, by ensuring these events take place lawfully and by guaranteeing the effective protection of participants,"[173] and to "refrain from adopting laws and reconsider existing laws which restrict freedom of expression in relation to sexual orientation and gender identity,"[174] while taking care, however, to "register and investigate hate crimes against LGBTI people, and adopt criminal legislation prohibiting incitement to hatred on grounds of sexual orientation and gender identity."[175] Among the particularly important demands, it is worth noting the postulate of automatic mutual recognition of civil status documents and their legal consequences. Its implementation "may, indirectly, contribute to forcing Member States to legally recognise unions of same-sex persons."[176]

In brief, the Lunacek report *de facto* sought recognition of the "Yogyakarta Principles," discussed in the previous chapter, as political and legal guidelines for

---

[167] Ibid., p. 1.

[168] Ibid., par. 3.

[169] Ibid., par. 4. A (i).

[170] Ibid., par. 4G (ii).

[171] Ibid., par. 4 D (i).

[172] Ibid., par. 4 E (ii).

[173] Ibid., par. 4 I (i).

[174] Ibid., par. 4 I (ii).

[175] Ibid., par. 4 J (v).

[176] M. Gierycz, P. Mazurkiewicz, *Europejska polityka i europejska antropologia...*, p. 137. In practice, this would mean that countries where same-sex unions are not legally recognized would be obliged by EU law to recognize such unions concluded in other countries, together with all their legal consequences (adoption of children, equal access to methods of artificial procreation, etc.).

Table 12.12 Results of the vote on the Lunacek Report—a political group perspective

Group	For	Against	Abst.	Present	Absent	Non voters	Number of MEPs	Cohesion (%)
EPP	69	129	25	223	22	28	273	36.77
S&D	159	0	0	159	15	21	195	100
ALDE	73	0	1	74	6	4	84	97.9
Greens/ EFA	52	0	0	52	3	3	58	100
ECR	2	15	30	47	5	5	57	45.74
GUE-NGL	30	0	2	32	3	0	35	90.63
EFD	4	17	8	29	2	1	32	37.93
NI	5	15	6	26	4	2	32	36.54

Source: http://term7.votewatch.eu/en/homophobia-and-discrimination-on-grounds-of-sexual-orien
tation-and-gender-identity-motion-for-resolu-2.html#/##vote-tabs-list-2 [24.10.2016]

the European Union, in an attempt to impose on Member States a double standard: unlimited freedom of expression for the LGBTI community and the limited freedom of their possible critics. While promoting LGBTI-friendly education, the report made no mention of the parents' rights to educate their own children, protect them from the promotion of ideas and actions incompatible with the parents' religious and moral beliefs, or the right to conscientious objection. In this regard, the EU's call for the WHO to remove gender identity disorders from the list of mental and behavioral disorders entirely seems particularly significant. It shows that the category of sexual orientation linked to the new anthropology ultimately leads to the legal recognition of behaviors which, according to contemporary medical knowledge, require treatment.

The vote on the report took place on the February 4, 2014, less than a week after the vote on the Zuber report. It was passed by a majority of 394:176, with 72 abstentions. More precisely, the second amendment to the report was adopted, submitted by its author and representatives of four other groups, including Christian democrats and communists.[177] This amendment, an alternative resolution in fact, repeated in its entirety the text of the original report, adding one paragraph on restrictions on freedom of expression. The submission and voting on this kind of amendment excluded the possibility of voting on individual passages of the report in the roll-call vote system. The results of the vote in factional terms are presented in Table 12.12.

---

[177]Cf. Roberta Metsola on behalf of the PPE Group, Michael Cashman on behalf of the S&D Group, Sophia in 't Veld on behalf of the ALDE Group, Ulrike Lunacek on behalf of the Verts/ALE Group, Cornelis de Jong on behalf of the GUE/NGL Group, *Amendment 2*, A7-0009/2.

Given the EPP's commitment to the Lunacek project even before it was voted on (the fact it participated in drafting the alternative resolution), it is not surprising that the proposal received significant support (69 Members) and that a large number of Members avoided taking a stance on the issue (75 Members in total abstaining and not voting/absent). All in all, they outnumbered the EPP Members who opposed the report (144:129). A similar phenomenon can be observed in the ECR, where a majority of the group abstained from voting.[178] The liberals, greens, socialists and communists were present at the meeting and voted consistently for the report. As a result, it received more than 100 more votes than was required for its adoption, confirming the unconstrained anthropological orientation of the European Parliament and recalling the case of the Anti-Discrimination Directive which also received high support in the Parliament (367:226).

The structure of votes in the national perspective is presented in Table 12.13. It is worth noting that the national groups of only seven Member States (Hungary, Latvia, Austria, Italy, Slovakia, Croatia, France) did not exceed 40% of vote cohesion, so there was no clear majority in their votes "for" and "against," unlike in the other 21 countries; in five of them the majority was complete. Groups of MEPs from Cyprus, Finland, Luxembourg, Sweden and Malta achieved a 100% vote cohesion. It is characteristic, however, that the representatives of all these countries voted "for" the report. Indeed, the high cohesion of the national groups in this vote essentially meant cohesion in support of the Lunacek proposal. Only in the case of Members from Italy, Lithuania, Poland, Romania and Slovenia did more Members vote "against" than "for." In this group, only Poland achieved a high (65%) vote cohesion, meaning that 30 out of the 39 voting Members opposed the report. Next to the Germans (31 against, 57 for), Poles (30 against, 9 for) were the second largest group of the "coalition" opposed to the Lunacek report. It also seems interesting that a group of MEPs from Malta, unequivocally opposed to the pro-abortion proposals of Estrela's and Zuber's reports, equally unequivocally supported Lunacek's proposals. This indicates not only a general prevalence of the unconstrained anthropological position with regard to human sexuality among national groups in the EP, but also the fact that it may gain support among MEPs representing a constrained anthropological position in disputes over human life.

The case of the Lunacek report, as well as the earlier case of the Anti-Discrimination Directive, also shows that the change concerning the definition of marriage in the Charter of Fundamental Rights has a functional relevance. The scope of protection of human life, not specified in the Charter, opens up a space of dispute the outcome of which—even in the Parliament, as can be seen from the case of the Estrela and Zuber reports—in certain circumstances may not be obvious and may weaken the support for the logic of unconstraint. However, the position expressed in the CFR regarding marriage and family, undermining the anthropology adopted in

---

[178]In the group voting against, 11 out of the 15 Members were from Poland: http://term7.votewatch. eu/en/homophobia-and-discrimination-on-grounds-of-sexual-orientation-and-gender-identity-motion-for-resolu-2.html#/##vote-tabs-list-2 [24.10.2016].

Table 12.13 Results of the vote on the Lunacek Report—a national group perspective

Member State	For	Against	Abst.	Present	Absent	Non voters	Total MEPs	Cohesion (%)
Austria	9	9	1	19	0	0	19	21.05
Belgium	19	3	0	22	0	0	22	79.55
Bulgaria	10	1	4	15	1	2	18	50.00
Croatia	5	4	0	9	2	1	12	33.33
Cyprus	5	0	0	5	1	0	6	100.00
Czech Republic	11	3	4	18	1	3	22	41.67
Denmark	10	0	2	12	0	1	13	75.00
Estonia	4	1	0	5	0	1	6	70.00
Finland	10	0	0	10	1	2	13	100.00
France	41	27	1	69	3	2	74	39.13
Germany	57	31	5	93	4	2	99	41.94
Greece	13	0	4	17	5	0	22	64.71
Hungary	6	3	6	15	5	2	22	10.00
Ireland	11	0	1	12	0	0	12	87.50
Italy	26	27	3	56	13	4	73	22.32
Latvia	3	3	1	7	1	1	9	14.29
Lithuania	3	5	0	8	2	2	12	43.75
Luxembourg	6	0	0	6	0	0	6	100.00
Malta	5	0	0	5	1	0	6	100.00
Netherlands	18	2	3	23	1	2	26	67.39
Poland	9	30	0	39	2	10	51	65.38
Portugal	14	3	0	17	3	2	22	73.53
Romania	7	11	1	19	2	12	33	36.84
Slovakia	4	5	1	10	1	2	13	25.00
Slovenia	4	1	0	5	3	0	8	70.00
Spain	37	4	2	43	2	9	54	79.07
Sweden	19	0	0	19	1	0	20	100.00
United Kingdom	28	3	33	64	5	4	73	27.34

Source: http://term7.votewatch.eu/en/homophobia-and-discrimination-on-grounds-of-sexual-orien
tation-and-gender-identity-motion-for-resolu-2.html#/##vote-tabs-list-4 [25.10.2016]

international law, although constructed as a mediational position, in political action
becomes a strong, non-mediational one. In view of the above-mentioned standpoints
of the national groups, it opens the way for the Parliament to push for new
anthropological solutions, unequivocally depriving monogamous marriage and the
family based on it of the status of a specially protected value. In this case, the logic of
unconstraint seems impregnable.

12.5   Abortion in Humanitarian Policy: A Process-Tracing Analysis

The case studies performed so far have contributed to satiating theoretical claims concerning the anthropological orientation of the main European institutions, as well as the role of Member States in blocking the deepening of anthropological unconstraint in the Council. Nevertheless, they do not provide much data on the mechanisms of cross influence among supranational institutions, or the role of Member States in strengthening unconstraint. Of course, the fact that the Parliament enhances the logic of unconstraint as observed in the previous cases suggests the significance of the role it plays, which does not seem limited merely to correcting the Commission's proposals in the legislative process. It is much more likely that it also affects the shape of these proposals. The question, therefore, is whether it may be demonstrated that the Parliament's political standpoints with a significant anthropological potential affect the shape of laws proposed by the Commission; that there is a mutual feedback in the operation of these two supranational institutions which has significant anthropological consequences. If so, what does it look like? And what role can Member States and their policy play in this process?

In answering these questions, it may be helpful to perform a process-tracing analysis of the humanitarian policy. There has been a marked change in the attitude to abortion in recent years: from its exclusion from to inclusion into humanitarian policy. Tracing this transformation may provide some important insights, as the issue of abortion is a particular gauge of the anthropological orientation of the political process. Humanitarian policy is, by definition, a policy specifically oriented towards human life, and for the Union itself it is the essence of the axiological involvement of its policies. It should therefore be especially protected from attempts at thinking about man in terms of an "exchangeable value." The emergence of a different way of thinking in itself indicates a significant role of the logic of anthropological unconstraint.

In light of the findings made so far, and according to the principles of process-tracing analysis,[179] it is necessary to formulate the hypotheses subject to verification. Firstly, it may be assumed that the European Union will, whenever legally possible, be involved in the financing of abortion as part of its humanitarian policy. Secondly, that an important role in the EU's pro-abortion orientation will be played by the ambiguity of the Commission's standpoint, the political involvement of the European Parliament supported by active lobbying groups, as well as the support of "big players," i.e. important Member States.

One more remark needs to be made content-wise. For those unversed in the problems related to humanitarian aid, it may be puzzling how the problem of abortion could appear in it at all. It should therefore be noted that humanitarian aid is directed not only to the victims of natural disasters, but above all to victims of

---

[179]Cf. Kamil Ławniczak, op. cit.

armed conflicts. An important aspect of much of these conflicts is the sexual exploitation of women. The European Union, which has been politically and financially involved in humanitarian aid over the last 11 years in connection with armed conflicts in the world, mainly Africa and the Middle East, has always expressed strong opposition to such practices. At the same time, in relation to its developing reproductive health agenda, the question of the right to life of children conceived by rape as opposed to women's reproductive rights has increasingly become more and more politically relevant. Especially that EU secondary legislation, as indicated in the previous chapter, no longer rules out abortion as an SRHR instrument.

12.5.1   Starting Point: EU Position on the Congo Homicide

A particularly dramatic moment for the EU to address the problem of war rape and its consequences were the events in the Democratic Republic of Congo in the years 2006–2007. During that time, "over a period of 12 months, more than 400,000 women and girls were raped in the east of the country,"[180] a crime on an unprecedented scale. This was due to the fact that in Congo a "large-scale rape strategy" was "used by both sides of the conflict as a tool to punish and intimidate civilians suspected of aiding the opposing military and political formations."[181]

In its resolution of January 17, 2008, the European Parliament made a very clear reference to the events which shook the world opinion at the time.[182] Recalling "the Rome Statute of the International Criminal Court, adopted in 1998, and particularly Articles 7 and 8 thereof, which define rape, sexual slavery, enforced prostitution, forced pregnancy and forced sterilisation or any form of sexual violence as crimes against humanity and war crimes and equate them with a form of torture and a serious war crime,"[183] it strongly condemned "rape as a weapon of war," recalling the jurisdiction of the International Criminal Court and calling on the government of Congo and the international community to "investigate those acts and prosecute those responsible," and on the fighting forces "to cease all attacks on women and other civilians."

It is worth taking a closer look at the Parliament's strategy of support for the victims of violence in Congo, as it says a lot about the political consensus at the time in understanding reproductive rights within the framework of humanitarian policy. Firstly, it includes legal and criminal postulates aimed at more effectively punishing the perpetrators of such crimes. In this context, the European Parliament called on

---

[180]Damian Żuchowski, *Gwałty w Demokratycznej Republice Konga*, https://estuariumsumienia. wordpress.com/2014/04/20/gwalty-w-demokratycznej-republice-konga/ [27.04.2016].

[181]Ibid.

[182]European Parliament, *European Parliament resolution of 17 January 2008 on the situation in the Democratic Republic of Congo and rape as a war crime*, P6_TA(2008)0022.

[183]Ibid.

the UN and the Union "to recognise rape, forced impregnation, sexual slavery and any other forms of sexual violence as crimes against humanity, serious war crimes and a form of torture, whether or not they are carried out in a systematic manner."[184] Secondly, the resolution suggests mechanism for the control and prosecution of crimes, calling upon "all UN member states that send personnel on the MONUC peacekeeping mission to follow up all claims of sexual abuse and exploitation, particularly those which concern minors, and to bring individuals who have committed sexual abuse to court as quickly as possible;"[185] upon "the UN, the African Union, the EU and the other partners of the DRC to do everything possible to put in place an effective mechanism for the monitoring and documenting of sexual violence in the DRC and to provide efficient and adequate aid and protection for women;"[186] finally, upon participants of the Conference on Peace, Security and Development in Goma (in North Kivu) "to address the issue of sexual violence against women and girls and to commit themselves to bringing the perpetrators to justice."[187] The third, key dimension of the resolution consists in direct assistance to the affected women. In this regard, the Parliament calls for "efficient and adequate aid and protection for women, particularly in the east of the country,"[188] allowing "humanitarian agencies to come to the assistance of victims,"[189] and "calls on the EU to allocate substantial funds to providing medical, legal and social support for victims of sexual abuse and empowering women and girls as a way of preventing further sexual abuse,"[190] as well as financial and any other support for the peace process.[191]

In summary, in the face of the unprecedented series of rapes during the wars in Congo, the Parliament's position was aimed at explicit legal sanctioning of rape as a war crime, prosecution of the perpetrators and, above all, providing humanitarian aid to victims of rape. This last point was understood as supporting women in their tragic situation by ensuring safety, medical aid, but also social assistance. In this context, the resolution refers to the category of "empowerment," bearing in mind it is not uncommon that "women and girls who are victims of rape suffer widespread social discrimination and rejection by their families and communities."[192] As pointed out by Jurgen Schroeder, the then President of the Parliament's Delegation to Congo: "on the one hand women and girls, even small children down to 3 years are rejected in general by their husbands, by their families, by their villages, because according to the standard of morality or ethics the reputation of the family is affected. On the other

---

[184]Ibid., par. 6.

[185]Ibid., par. 8.

[186]Ibid., par. 9.

[187]Ibid., par. 11.

[188]Ibid., par. 9.

[189]Ibid., par. 6.

[190]Ibid., par. 5.

[191]Ibid., par. 12.

[192]Ibid., par. H.

hand they suffer physical pain. The perpetrators know that they do not affect only the dignity of the woman but that they also destroy the structure of the society."[193] Consequently, it was the Parliament's goal to "help women of that country, not only to be free from those human rights violations but to be able to play the leading role of the society."[194]

These objectives, let us add, were not only those of the Parliament, but in fact reflected the objectives of the Union as a whole. As Luiza Wojnicz points out, "interest in Africa's security problems was more explicitly reflected only after the implementation of Operation ARTEMIS, i.e. in 2004, when the Council of the European Union adopted its Common Position on Africa of January 26."[195] The document stated that the goal of the European Union is to "contribute to the prevention, management and resolution of violent conflicts in Africa by strengthening African capacity and means of action in this field," and expressed the EU's commitment to "develop long-term conflict prevention and peace-building initiatives,"[196] which became the basis for the 2006 EUFOR DR Congo military mission and the civilian missions in Congo[197] aimed at reorganizing the army and the police.[198] Furthermore, as stressed by the then Commissioner Meglena Kuneva, the European Commission dealt in particular with the problem of sexual violence and crime through a "project in the eastern part of the Democratic Republic of Congo, focusing *inter alia* on building the capacity of judicial actors and reinforcing the provision of legal assistance to the victims of sexual violence,"[199] and by providing "significant humanitarian assistance—roughly 40 million euros per year—to the Democratic Republic of Congo, especially to Uturi and the Kivus."[200] All in all, between 2003 and 2012 the Union invested more than 1.9 billion euros in the reconstruction of the Democratic Republic of the Congo.

---

[193]*MEPs see devastating effect of rape in DR Congo,* 2 April 2008, https://www.europarl.europa. eu/sides/getDoc.do?pubRef=-//EP//TEXT+IM-PRESS+20080331STO25211+0+DOC+XML +V0//EN

[194]Ibid.

[195]Luiza Wojnicz, "Wpływ procesów europeizacyjnych w Afryce na przykładzie cywilnych misji Unii Europejskiej w Demokratycznej Republice Konga," *Rocznik Integracji Europejskiej* 8/2014, p. 273.

[196]Ibid., p. 274.

[197]EUPOL Kinshasa in 2005 (completed) and EUSEC Congo of 2005 and EUPOL Kongo of 2007 which continued until 2014.

[198]EUSEC – EU mission to advise and assist in the reform of the security sector of the Democratic Republic of Congo. It aims to help the Congolese to reform their army. EUPOL: EU police mission to the Democratic Republic of Congo. It may thus be said that EUPOL is the EUSEC equivalent in the security forces. http://www.euractiv.pl/wersja-do-druku/artykul/europa-zostanie-w-kongu-005044 [27.04.2016].

[199]*Situation in the Democratic Republic of Congo and rape as a war crime (debate): Meglena Kuneva,* Strasbourg 17.01.2008, CRE 17/01/2008 – 11.2.

[200]Ibid.

It is worth stressing that, across the spectrum of the EU's political, legal and financial influence, with explicit condemnation of crimes and as strong[201] a support to women and humanitarian engagement as the EU was able to provide, it seems that the Union's actions were not accompanied by undermining the right to life of children conceived by rape. The lives of the victims of rape and of the children conceived as a result were not subject to any "weighing" procedure. In the above-discussed proposals for a resolution of the European Parliament, only the political group of the European United Left/Nordic Green Left (GUE/NGL) postulated that it should include a reference to "the importance of access to reproductive health services in conflict situations and refugee camps," and to guarantee access "for all women and girls who have been victims of rape to post-coital contraception."[202] No reference to this issue was made in the joint proposal for a resolution, however, not even in the euphemistic form of reproductive rights. Moreover, none of the political forces raised the abortion issue in the debate.[203] Likewise, in the context of political documents relating to analogous problems within the Union, this issue was absent.[204] It will therefore not be an exaggeration to say that as recently as 2008 the postulate of abortion as a form of European humanitarian aid to women raped during the war was articulated only by the most ideologically radical left-wing groups. No other political group considered it appropriate to raise the idea of abortion clinics in refugee camps or promote this solution as an EU approach.

12.5.2 Reorientation of the Debate: the Role of UK and Ambiguity of the EU Commission

The next term of EP's office came during a period when the situation in Congo relatively calmed down. Although there were no crimes against women in any country between 2009 and 2013 comparable to those of the years 2005–2008, the problem of war rape remained a major issue due to the number of ongoing wars and

---

[201] As rightly pointed out by MEP Marcin Libicki in the debate around this resolution, "[u]ntil the European Union creates a police force that would not, of course, intervene in every civil war but could at least supervise the camps, the so-called refugee camps where the very worst crimes are being committed in the Democratic Republic of Congo, all we will be able to do is continue debating the matter. People will continue to suffer and die whilst we debate endlessly." Ibid.

[202] *Motion for resolution with request for inclusion in the agenda for the debate on cases of breaches of human rights, democracy and the rule of law pursuant to Rule 115 of the Rules of Procedure by Eva-Britt Svensson, Luisa Morgantini on behalf of the GUE/NGL Group on Democratic Republic of Congo and mass rape as war crime and crime against humanity*, B60030/2008.

[203] Cf. European Parliament, *Situation in the Democratic Republic of Congo and rape as a war crime (debate)*, Strasbourg 17.01.2008, CRE 17/01/2008 – 11.2.

[204] Cf. e.g. *European Parliament resolution of 26 November 2009 on the elimination of violence against women*, P7_TA(2009)0098.

conflicts, "of which rape was an integral part."[205] At the same time, these problems lost some of their political relevance and did not represent a particularly important current in the European human rights policy until 2012.

Nevertheless, in 2012 the UK launched its Preventing Sexual Violence Initiative (PSVI), aimed not only at better detecting and documenting sexual offenses, but also at implementing gender equality reforms in the area of security and justice.[206] The initiative was conducted at the highest political level and led to the adoption of a G8 declaration devoted to this issue already in 2013, as well as, in the same year, the UN Security Council's Resolution no. 2016.[207] In this context, it is easier to understand why in 2012 the postulate of abortion as part of humanitarian aid appeared in the Parliament's resolution on equality between women and men. The resolution, generally dealing with intra-European matters, on a few points also referred, *en passant* so to say, to the Union's external relations. Not only did the European Parliament condemn in it "the fact that rape is still used in certain regions of the world as a weapon,"[208] but also called for "the provision of EU humanitarian aid to be made effectively independent from the restrictions on humanitarian aid imposed by the USA, in particular by ensuring access to abortion for women and girls who are victims of rape in armed conflicts."[209]

The above postulate was made in the proposal put forward by the liberal (ALDE) MEP Sophia in 't Velt, and no amendment to it was submitted by any of the political factions. It was therefore adopted together with the document as a whole. The only sign of internal division in the Parliament was the fact that in 't Velt's report was carried by a relatively small (albeit already clear) majority of 361:268 votes, with 70 abstentions.[210] At the same time, MEPs participating in the working group on HIV/AIDS and development, co-led by Sophia in 't Velt,[211] sent a letter to President Barack Obama urging him to "immediately issue an executive order lifting U.S. abortion restrictions on humanitarian aid for girls and women raped in armed conflict."[212]

---

[205]Inga Hajdarowicz, *Bezdomne we własnym ciele – sytuacja kobiet w czasie wojny na Bałkanach*, http://krytyka.org/bezdomne-we-wlasnym-ciele-sytuacja-kobiet-w-czasie-wojny-na-balkanach/ [29.04.2016].

[206]Paul Kirby, "Ending Sexual Violence in Conflict: Preventing Sexual Violence Initiative (PSVI) and its Critique," *International Affairs* 91:32015, p. 457.

[207]Ibid.

[208]European Parliament, *European Parliament resolution of 13 March 2012 on equality between women and men in the European Union – 2011* (2011/2244(INI)), art. 55.

[209]Ibid., art. 61.

[210]http://www.europarl.europa.eu/oeil/popups/printsda.pdf?id=21255&l=en [29.04.2016].

[211]http://www.epwg.org/members.aspx [13.05.2016].

[212]*Letter from Working Group, Reproductive Health, HIV/AIDS and Development in the European Parliament, International AIDS Society, to President Barack Obama, President of the United States*, 6.03.2013, as quoted in: Susan Yoshihara, "Abortion and the Laws of War: Subverting Humanitarianism by Executive Edict," *University of St. Thomas Journal of Law & Public Policy*, Vol. IX, 2015, p. 12.

The Commission did not respond to its being "reminded" of the need to "become independent" from the US.[213] It was forced to react, however, by a question asked by the author of the above amendment, along with other MEPs,[214] seeking to have the Commission recognize that the US were blocking EU humanitarian aid as regards abortion. Krystalina Georgieva, the then Commissioner for development and humanitarian aid, replied that "[t]he Commission provides (. . .) needs-based humanitarian aid and it is not subject to any restrictions unilaterally imposed by other donors."[215] It also pointed out that part of this aid, based on the Minimum Initial Service Package standard,[216] was the so-called "emergency contraception," granted as part of what she called "post-exposure prophylaxis" [PEP]. As it must be applied up to 72 h after the incident, she concluded that the main problem to be addressed by EU humanitarian aid was not so much non-funding of abortion or US pressures, but "quick access to medical care."

It is worth noting that the Commission's reply indicated that, contrary to what might be concluded from its position in 2008, the European Union was structurally involved in early, pharmacological abortion. This response clearly closed the issue of funding abortion, however, setting out the limits of EU commitment. This position, although it may be considered as anthropologically inconsistent, seems to reflect the inconsistency of solutions adopted in the EU's primary law.

Commissioner Georgieva's response not only did not close the subject, but triggered another letter, this time from a non-governmental organization. Jane Benshoof, head of the Global Justice Center which focuses on "progressive interpretation and enforcement of international law" as "a powerful catalyst for social and structural change" and promoting "the right to abortion,"[217] sent a letter to the Commission upholding in 't Velt's comments and accusing the Commission of breaching the Geneva Convention. A lengthy correspondence ensued, in which it is worth noting the letter from Claus Sorensen, Director General for Humanitarian Aid and Civil Protection. In its discussion with the Global Justice Center, he stressed on behalf of the Commission that "neither international humanitarian law nor international human rights law explicitly refer to abortion rights and therefore the legal primacy of international frameworks on this issue is not clear. Even if international humanitarian law were to give unequivocal rights in this field (which does not currently appear to be the case), in many countries this law is only enforceable if

---

[213]Cf. European Commission, *Follow up to the European Parliament resolution on equality between women and men in the European Union – 2011, adopted by the Commission on 6 June 2012*, SP(2012)387.

[214]Sophia in 't Velt (ALDE), AntonyiaParvanova (ALDE), Renate Weber (ALDE), Baroness Sarah Ludford (ALDE), Jean Lambert (Verts/ALE), Véronique Mathieu (PPE), SirpaPietikäinen (PPE), Norbert Neuser (S&D), Françoise Castex (S&D) and Charles Goerens (ALDE), *Question for written answer to the Commission*, 30.05.2012, E-005386/12 (hereinafter: S. in'tVelt, *Question. . .*).

[215]*Answer given by Ms Georgieva on behalf of the Commission*, 17.07.2012, Question for written answer E-005386/12.

[216]http://www.unhcr.org/4e8d6b3b14.html [02.05.2016].

[217]https://www.globaljusticecenter.net/about-us/mission [02.05.2016].

integrated into domestic law. Generally speaking, our humanitarian partners advise their staff operating in country to abide by the laws of the land. Violating domestic law would carry the risk of prosecution, which would put humanitarian aid at risk."[218] The Commission's standpoint was therefore quite explicit and, in view of the clarity of international law, did not provide for the financing of abortion as humanitarian aid.

12.5.3 The Parliament's Pro-Abortion Stance

A political discussion was thus opened, however, and in a resolution proposed a year later the European Parliament *de facto* made it clear that it did not accept the Commission's explanations. In the 2013 resolution on the framework for achieving the Millennium Development Goals post 2015, the EP demands that the EU's provision of humanitarian aid which contributes to the achievement of the Millennium Development Goals "should effectively be excluded from the restrictions on humanitarian aid imposed by the USA or other donors, in particular by ensuring access to abortion for women and girls who are victims of rape in armed conflicts."[219] This postulate, although non-existent in the original proposal for a resolution prepared by Filip Kaczmarek (EPP),[220] but added to the draft at an early stage by MEP Anne Delvaux[221] as part of the demands of the Committee on Women's Rights and Gender Equality, was carried in the European Parliament together with the entire resolution by a significant majority of 335:172 votes, with 26 abstentions.[222] It is worth noting that at the stage of voting in the Committee on Women's Rights where the passage was added, support for the report was almost unanimous (25:0, with 1 abstention). It may therefore be concluded that a form of consensus within the Parliament had begun to take shape, allowing for abortion as part of humanitarian aid. Like in 2012, the Commission did not address this postulate in its

---

[218]*Letter from Claus Sorensen, Director General, European Commission, to Janet Benshoof, President, Global Justice Center*, 10.10.2012, as quoted in: Susan Yoshihara, "Abortion and the Laws ...," pp. 14–15.

[219]European Parliament, *European Parliament resolution of 13 June 2013 on the Millennium Development Goals – defining the post-2015 framework* (2012/2289(INI)), P7_TA(2013)0283, art. 33.

[220]Cf. European Parliament's Development Committee, *Motion for a European Parliament Resolution on the Millennium Development Goals – defining the post-2015 framework* (2012/2289 (INI)), PE504.341.

[221]Cf. *Opinion of the Committee on Women's Rights and Gender Equality for the Committee on Development on the Millennium Development Goals – defining the post-2015 framework (2012/ 2289(INI)*, PE504.148.

[222]http://www.europarl.europa.eu/oeil/popups/sda.do?id=22911&l=en [29.04.2016].

information on the prospects for implementing the ideas contained in the report.[223] The Union's ideological position did not, therefore, translate as yet into specific practices within the framework of its policies.

Nevertheless, in 2014 there was an increase in the activity of ISIS in Syria and the related Islamist groups in Africa, which, like Boko Haram, adopted a war strategy against women similar to that employed in Congo.[224] This opened up opportunities for re-addressing the issue of abortion for victims of rape. On March 31, 2014, Sophie in 't Velt asked Commissioner Georgieva again a question requiring a written answer.[225] Noting that the media, focusing on the use of chemical weapons in Syria, often ignored the use of rape as a form of violence, she pointed out that women were denied safe abortions, and consequently attempted unsafe abortion or even committed suicide. In this context, recalling its questions and answers from the Commission in 2012, she reiterated the question of whether the Commission was aware of the importance of US restrictions on the provision of abortion in Syria, and pointed out that life-saving abortion was not part of the PEP. Finally, she demanded detailed information on new measures taken to increase the "gender sensitivity" of humanitarian aid.[226]

Like in 2012, at the same time as the MEP, the Global Justice Center sent its letter as well, beginning an exchange of correspondence with the Commission which continued until December.[227] In essence, the goals of the GJC and in 't Velt were similar, they both lobbied for the Commission to recognize the right to abortion as a humanitarian right, and tried to highlight the negative role of the US in this regard. A particular context of this correspondence was the fact that as part of its PSIV initiative, the United Kingdom presented its position on abortion in the framework of humanitarian aid in the first half of 2014[228] referring to the arguments put forward by the GJC, which, interestingly, then referred to the UK standpoint in its activities.[229]

---

[223]Cf. European Commission, *Follow up to the European Parliament resolution on Millennium Development Goals – defining the post 2015 framework, adopted by the Commission on 8 October 2013*, SP(2013)626.

[224]Cf. Piotr Kowalski, *ONZ potępia dżihadżystów*, http://www.kowalski.pch24.pl/niewolnictwo-seksualne%2D%2Dgwalty-oraz-przymusowe-malzenstwa%2D%2Donz-potepila-dzihadystow,35161,i.html [27.04.2016].

[225]Sophia in 't Veld (ALDE), MarietjeSchaake (ALDE), *Question for written answer to the Commission Rule 117. Subject:Rape as a weapon of war in Syria*, 31.03.2014, E-003947-14.

[226]Ibid.

[227]The correspondence of 25.04.2014 (to EC), 30.06.2014 (answer), 7.07.2014 (to EC), 8.09.2014 (answer), 10.10.2014 (open letter to EC) is available at: http://www.globaljusticecenter.net/publications/letters [02.05.2016].

[228]Department for International Development, *Safe and unsafe abortion. The UK's policy position on safe and unsafe abortion in developing countries*, December 2013, London.

[229]The mutual interpretive interrelations are also evident in the subsequent British document on sexual violence. Cf. http://globaljusticecenter.net/blog/288-victory-uk-house-of-lords-report-on-sexual-violence-in-conflict-cites-to-gjc [02.05.2016].

Without going into the details of the entire correspondence,[230] which Commissioner Georgieva carried on simultaneously with the Global Justice Center and with Ms. in 't Velt, it is worthwhile noting one of the Commissioner's last answers before the end of her term of office. In response to repeated enquiries about ensuring abortion to victims of rape, she wrote: "as already mentioned in our previous letter, it is the European Commission's understanding that under neither international humanitarian law nor international human rights law is there at present an explicit 'right to abortion' or a universal obligation to provide abortions to rape victims. This interpretation (...) is also in agreement with the UK's interpretation that 'it is the UK's view that in situations of armed conflict or occupation where denial of abortion threatens the woman's or girl's life or causes unbearable suffering, international humanitarian law principles may justify offering a safe abortion rather than perpetuating what amounts to inhumane treatment in the form of an act of cruel treatment or torture. Clearly this will depend on the woman's choice, her condition and the safety and security of the humanitarian staff, as well as other contextual factors. The illegality of abortion under national law may represent one of such contextual factors."[231]

The Commissioner's answer is interesting. On the one hand, it upholds the Commission's unequivocal normative position of 2012. At the same time, however, it is worth noting a slightly different distribution of emphasis. While Director Sorensen stressed the incompatibility of abortion with the principles of humanitarian law, the Commissioner's letter of 2014 already mentions the "Commission's interpretation of international law," which is different from the UK interpretation. The illegality of abortion is no longer an expression of a universal principle, but merely a "contextual factor." From the theoretical point of view, it may be said that as a result of political debate and changes in the approach of its members, the Commission, while upholding the same normative position, moved from a realistic to a constructivist standpoint.

12.5.4   Political Pressures on the European Commission

Meanwhile, the European Parliament, already in its new composition elected in 2014, had been monitoring the situation in the Middle East[232] and Africa and responded to the dramatic events with resolutions concerning Syria or Nigeria. With regard to the issue of abortion, both of these resolutions contain postulates

---

[230]Cf. *Answer given by Ms Georgieva on behalf of the Commission*, 27.05.2014, E-003947/2014, Sophia in 't Veld, *Re.: Your answer on Written Question E-003947/2014*, Bruksela, 8.07.2014.

[231]Kristalina Georgieva, *Letter to Ms. Benshoof*, 08.09.2014, Ares(2014)2934591.

[232]For example, representatives of the UNHCR and other organizations presented the situation in Syria at a meeting of the Subcommittee on Human Rights (16.3.2015), http://www.europarl.europa.eu/news/pl/news-room/20141013IPR73812/Syria-and-Iraq-debate-on-the-human-rights-situation-of-refugees [29.04.2016].

referring to proposals from the previous parliamentary term, in a way reopening the debate. Especially that the European Commission's term of office expired in 2014 as well and the Commissioner responsible for humanitarian aid changed.

In order to illustrate the dynamics of the discourse on abortion in the EU after 2014, let us take a look at the Nigerian resolution. All political groups in the Parliament submitted their proposals for resolutions to the President. The proposal submitted by Verts/ALE proposed that the Parliament urge "that girls and women who are victims of rape in the context of armed conflict be offered the full range of sexual and reproductive health services, including abortion, in EU-funded humanitarian facilities, in accordance with the Geneva Conventions' common Article 3 guaranteeing all necessary medical care required by the condition of the wounded and sick, and without adverse distinction."[233] Similarly, GUE/NGL demanded in their proposal that the Parliament urge "the Commission to acknowledge that international humanitarian law mandates that women and girl victims of war rape be provided with all the necessary medical care required by their condition, including abortions." In the same paragraph, they proposed that the Parliament call on the Commission "to update its humanitarian aid policy to affirm that in situations of armed conflict the Geneva Conventions apply, and therefore require humanitarian actors to provide necessary medical care required by victims' conditions and the full range of sexual and reproductive health services, including abortions; [stress] that the denial of abortion to women and girls impregnated by war rape breaches the prohibition of torture and cruel treatment under the Geneva Conventions' common Article 3."[234] None of the other political groups—and therefore also neither of the two dominant parliamentary factions—included similar content in their proposals. Nevertheless, in the joint motion for a resolution, which was subsequently sent to a plenary session, there is a passage in which the European Parliament "urges that wounded soldiers receive the appropriate treatment, and that girls and women who are victims of rape in the context of armed conflict be offered the full range of sexual and reproductive health services, in EU-funded humanitarian facilities, in accordance with common Article 3 of the Geneva Conventions, which guarantees all necessary medical care required by the condition of the wounded and sick, without making adverse distinctions."[235]

---

[233]Jean Lambert, Maria Heubuch, Heidi Hautala, Judith Sargentini, Michèle Rivasi, Ernest Urtasun, Barbara Lochbihler, TamásMeszerics, Jordi Sebastià, Davor Škrlec, *Motion for resolution with request for inclusion in the agenda for a debate on cases of breaches of human rights, democracy and the rule of law pursuant to Rule 135 of the Rules of Procedure* (2015/2520(RSP)), art. 7.

[234]Lola Sánchez Caldentey, Marisa Matias, Malin Björk, Rina Ronja Kari, Merja Kyllönen, Patrick Le Hyaric, Miloslav Ransdorf, Marie-Christine Vergiat, Younous Omarjee on behalf of the GUE/NGL Group, *Motion for a resolution to wind up the debate on the statement by the Vice-President of the Commission / High Representative of the Union for Foreign Affairs and Security Policy pursuant to Rule 123(2) of the Rules of Procedure on the situation in Nigeria* (2015/2520 (RSP)), B8-0371/2015, art. 13.

[235]Santiago Fisas Ayxelà, Davor Ivo Stier, Cristian Dan Preda, Francesc Gambús, Joachim Zeller, Michael Gahler, Maurice Ponga, Fernando Ruas, Tokia Saïfi, Bogdan Brunon Wenta, Daniel Caspary, Elisabetta Gardini, Dubravka Šuica, Claude Rolin, Philippe Juvin, József Nagy, Arnaud

This point was adopted by the Parliament, and appears in exactly the same wording as in the joint motion for a resolution in the text of the Parliament's resolution of 30 April 2015.[236] It is worth noting that the EP resolution was adopted by an overwhelming majority (516:11, with 26 abstentions).[237] This contrasts sharply with the Parliament's position in 2008, when postulates that abortion be treated as part of humanitarian law remained on the margins of the ideological discourse. While it is clear that the Parliament's mass support for the resolution on Nigeria was not primarily linked to the guarantee of reproductive rights, but to the desire to protest against violence and to support the local population, the European Parliament—this time almost unanimously—agreed to accept abortion as an element of humanitarian aid.

This ideological declaration by the Parliament was quickly used by the supporters of including abortion in humanitarian aid to translate their ideas into EU's political practice. Although the Commission was not obliged to comment on the above-mentioned resolution and did not address it, less than a month after its adoption a group of 39 left-wing Members of the European Parliament (S&D, GUE/NGL, ALDE and one ECR Member) sent a letter to Federica Mogherini, the newly appointed Vice-President of the European Commission and EU High Representative for Foreign Affairs and Security Policy, and Christos Stylianides, Commissioner for Foreign Affairs and Security Policy, the successor of Kristelina Georgieva in this position.[238] Although the letter was signed by only 39 Members, the rank of the signatories, including Elena Valenciano, Chair of the Subcommittee on Human

---

Danjean on behalf of the PPE Group, Eric Andrieu, Hugues Bayet, Nicola Caputo, Ana Gomes, Alessia Maria Mosca, Momchil Nekov, Demetris Papadakis, Vincent Peillon, Arne Lietz, Maria Arena, Linda McAvan, Victor Boştinaru, KashetuKyenge, Doru-Claudian Frunzulică, Carlos Zorrinho, Elena Valenciano, Michela Giuffrida, Seb Dance, Afzal Khan, Nicola Danti on behalf of the S&D Group, Charles Tannock, Angel Dzhambazki, Beatrix von Storch on behalf of the ECR Group, Javier Nart, PetrasAuštrevičius, Dita Charanzová, Gérard Deprez, Filiz Hyusmenova, Beatriz Becerra Basterrechea, Izaskun Bilbao Barandica, Marielle de Sarnez, José InácioFaria, Alexander Graf Lambsdorff, Juan Carlos Girauta Vidal, Antanas Guoga, Ivan Jakovčić, Petr Ježek, Ilhan Kyuchyuk, Fernando Maura Barandiarán, Louis Michel, UrmasPaet, Maite Pagazaurtundúa Ruiz, Jozo Radoš, Robert Rochefort, MarietjeSchaake, Pavel Telička, Yana Toom, Ramon TremosaiBalcells, FrédériqueRies, Ivo Vajgl, Johannes Cornelis van Baalen, Hilde Vautmans on behalf of the ALDE Group, Lola Sánchez Caldentey, Marie-Christine Vergiat on behalf of the GUE/NGL Group, Jean Lambert on behalf of the Verts/ALE Group, Fabio Massimo Castaldo, Ignazio Corrao, Piernicola Pedicini on behalf of the EFDD Group, *Joint motion for a resolution pursuant to Rule 123(2) and (4) of the Rules of Procedure replacing the motions by the following groups: S&D (B8-0370/2015), GUE/NGL (B8-0371/2015), PPE (B8-0374/2015), Verts/ALE (B8-0394/2015), ECR (B8-0396/2015), EFDD (B8-0398/2015), ALDE (B8-0400/2015) on the situation in Nigeria (2015/2520(RSP))*, RC-B8-0370/2015, art. 15.

[236]European Parliament, *European Parliament resolution of 30 April 2015 on the situation in Nigeria* (2015/2520(RSP)), P8_TA(2015)0185, art. 15.

[237]http://www.votewatch.eu/en/term8-situation-in-nigeria-joint-motion-for-resolution-vote-resolution.html#/##vote-tabs-list-2 [30.04.2016]. Interestingly, it was only opposed by the MEPs from Greece and Holland.

[238]Who was appointed Commissioner for Budget.

Rights of the European Parliament, Iratxe García-Perez, Chair of the Committee on Women's Rights and Gender Equality, as well as Gianni Pittella, Chair of the Progressive Alliance of Socialists and Democrats (S&D), and Guy Verhofstadt, Chair of the Alliance of Liberals and Democrats for Europe (ALDE), gave it particular weight.

Referring inter alia to the recently adopted EP resolution on Nigeria, the authors of the letter call on the Commission to respect international law by guaranteeing access to abortion. In doing so, they reveal their logic of understanding human rights, implicitly presented in the resolution. They claim, in line with the content of the resolution, that since under international law all those "wounded and sick" during the war must receive the necessary medical assistance, then "medical care for girls and women impregnated by war rape must include abortion."[239] In fact, they point out that "failing to provide an abortion to a victim of war rape, thereby forcing her to continue her unwanted pregnancy, can constitute an act of torture and inhuman treatment in violation of common Article 3 of the Geneva Conventions."[240] To put it bluntly: not guaranteeing abortion is presented here as a violation of international humanitarian law. They further reinforce this argumentation by referring to UN Security Council resolutions nos. 2016 and 2212 adopted in 2013, and a report by the UN Secretary-General.[241]

Both substantive arguments presented by the authors are open to criticism. The content of Article 3, common to all the Geneva Conventions,[242] or even the Additional Protocol II stating that the "all the wounded, sick and shipwrecked, to whichever Party they belong, shall be respected and protected" and "in all circumstances they shall be treated humanely and shall receive, to the fullest extent practicable and with the least possible delay, the medical care and attention required

---

[239]Elena Valenciano, Iratxe García-Perez, Gianni Pittella, Guy Verhofstadt, Sophie in 't Veld, et at., *EU humanitarian aid fails female victims of war rape*, Letter to Federica Mogherini and Christos Stylianides,29 May 2015, Brussels.

[240]Ibid.

[241]Ibid.: "Provisions in Security Council adopted resolutions 2106 and 2122 respond to the UN Secretary-General's recommendations that all humanitarian actors (inter alia EU-funded organisations operating in conflict areas) ensure women impregnated by war rape are provided all necessary medical services, including 'safe termination of pregnancies resulting from rape,' 'without discrimination,' and 'in accordance with international humanitarian law.'"

[242]It says: "Persons taking no active part in the hostilities, including members of armed forces who have laid down their arms and those placed 'hors de combat' by sickness, wounds, detention, or any other cause, shall in all circumstances be treated humanely, without any adverse distinction founded on race, colour, religion or faith, sex, birth or wealth, or any other similar criteria. To this end, the following acts are and shall remain prohibited at any time and in any place whatsoever with respect to the above-mentioned persons. (a) violence to life and person, in particular murder of all kinds, mutilation, cruel treatment and torture; (b) taking of hostages; (c) outrages upon personal dignity, in particular humiliating and degrading treatment; (d) the passing of sentences and the carrying out of executions without previous judgment pronounced by a regularly constituted court, affording all the judicial guarantees which are recognized as indispensable by civilized peoples. (2) The wounded and sick shall be collected and cared for. . ." *Convention (III) relative to the Treatment of Prisoners of War,* Geneva, 12 August 1949.

by their condition,"[243] do not refer to the issue of reproductive rights or abortion. A pregnant woman can hardly be considered sick, wounded or shipwrecked. This remark is not ironic. The Convention does not ignore the problem of rape, but deliberately does not approach its consequences in the way suggested by the parliamentarians. The above-mentioned Protocol to the Convention states *expressis verbis* that "the following acts are and shall remain prohibited at any time and in any place whatsoever: (a) violence to the life, health (. . .) (e) outrages upon personal dignity, in particular humiliating and degrading treatment, rape, enforced prostitution and any form of indecent assault."[244] Nevertheless, not once does it call, even as a suggestion, for abortion to be used as a measure of humanitarian aid. This is profoundly justified. Humanitarian aid is intended to serve human life and its protection. Abortion, being a form of destroying human life, could not be regarded in the Convention as part of such aid. Consequently, it must be stated that both the Parliament's resolution and the parliamentarians in their letter used the Geneva Convention in an instrumental manner. Its authority was used to support a right to abortion on humanitarian grounds which is nowhere to be found in its provisions.

Similar doubts arise in the context of the second "legal" argument of the letter's signatories. The reference to the Security Council's resolution, and thus to a document of international law, seems to suggest an objective contradiction between the EU policy and the requirements of that law as regards abortion. The matter thus becomes serious. The problem is that if we look at these resolutions, the Security Council's strongest call turns out to be to ensure the provision of "medical, legal, psychosocial and livelihood services to women affected by armed conflict and post-conflict situations," and to note in the Preamble "the need for access to the full range of sexual and reproductive health services, including regarding pregnancies resulting from rape, without discrimination."[245] These statements are vague and therefore open to various interpretations. Particularly considering the fact that "the term 'sexual and reproductive health' has only been defined once by member states, in the 1994 Cairo conference (. . .) where a right to abortion was rejected."[246] Moreover, the remark made in the Preamble does not have a normative value. Therefore, one can hardly argue that it substantiates the obviousness of there being an obligation under international law to ensure abortion as part of humanitarian aid.

More explicit in this regard is the UN Secretary-General's Report, which is the main reference point for the letter. It calls on Member States and aid donors to "step up their efforts to reduce maternal mortality and expand access to sexual and reproductive health services," commending UNFPA for "emergency reproductive

---

[243]*Protocol Additional to the Geneva Conventions of 12 August 1949, and Relating to the Protection of Victims of Non-International Armed Conflicts (Protocol II)* adopted on 8 June 1977 by the Diplomatic Conference on the Reaffirmation and Development of International Humanitarian Law applicable in Armed Conflicts, art. 7.

[244]Ibid., art. 4.

[245]United Nations Security Council, *Resolution 2122 (2013) Adopted by the Security Council at its 7044th meeting, on 18 October 2013*, S/RES/2122 (2013).

[246]Susan Yoshihara, "Abortion and the Laws. . .," p. 7.

health kits, which include essential medical supplies for post-rape care and can be delivered anywhere in the world within hours of a request."[247] However, the UN Secretary-General—in line with the Committee on the Status of Women—notes that ensuring "safe abortion" is only possible where this practice is "permitted by national law"[248] —without attempting to make it a standard of international law. Consequently, the call of the signatories of the letter to the Commission, who, referring to the above documents, claim that "the EU must do more to meet its international obligations"[249] as regards guaranteeing the right to abortion as part of humanitarian aid, must be seen as a form of political manipulation.[250]

12.5.5   A Change in the EU Position

Even more interesting than the letter, however, is the European Commission's response. Federica Mogherini and Christos Stylianides are clearly aware of the interpretative ploys employed by the Members in their letter. This is demonstrated, for example, by the fact that, unlike the Members, they do not claim that abortion is a requirement of international law, but rather than in certain situations "international humanitarian law and/or international human rights law may justify offering a safe abortion."[251] Nevertheless, both the design of the letter and its arguments are aimed not so much at correcting the Members' way of thinking, but at its strengthening and justification.

The third and fourth paragraphs which open the Commission's substantive reply are not so much an answer to the signatories' question but a presentation of arguments supplementing those included the letter, showing the importance of the question referred to the Commission and its empathy with the view it expresses. The Commissioners say that they are "highly concerned with the fate of women and girl survivors of rape, including those who do not have access to safe abortions or are

---

[247] United Nations Security Council, *Report of the Secretary-General on women and peace and security*, S/2013/525, art. 53.

[248] Ibid., art. 11.

[249] Elena Valenciano, Iratxe García-Perez, Gianni Pittella, Guy Verhofstadt, Sophie in 't Veld, et at., *EU humanitarian aid fails female victims of war rape*, Letter to Federica Mogherini and Christos Stylianides, 29 May 2015, Brussels, p. 3.

[250] Cf. Mirosław Karwat, *Sztuka manipulacji politycznej*, Adam Marszałek, Toruń 1998. The author notes that an important aspect of manipulation is inducing "desirable states of affairs and events by one's own actions," "creating something" (p. 12), which includes "disinformation and disorientation in the scope of manipulation activities in politics" (ibid.). Among the various manipulation techniques, Karwat distinguishes the so-called "paragraph attack" in which "the criticism of our adversary is transferred—really or apparently—to the sphere of legal criteria, reinforcing the suggestion with legal or pseudo-legal terminology, which is to make our accusations as objectified as they are indisputable, and turn ourselves into the judge of the dispute" (pp. 148–149).

[251] Federica Mogherini, Christos Stylianides, *Letter addressed to Ms. Elena Valenciano et al.*, 11.09.2015, Ares (2015)3757306.

forced to carry to term unwanted pregnancies." They point out that "some rape survivors expose themselves to risky illegal abortions in unsafe conditions—and may die as a consequence—others attempt to self-abort and some even commit suicide." These claims, let us add, are taken as self-evident and general knowledge. The Commissioners do not provide any specific data in the context of the consequences of Boko Haram's actions they refer to.

Moving from comments on the situation in Nigeria to a more general level, the Commission notes that "unsafe abortion is listed by the World Health Organization as one of the three leading causes of maternal mortality," and women "in all these situations face heightened health risks (both physical and psychological) and exacerbated social suffering."[252] The Commissioners—which is particularly interesting in the context of justifying abortion—look not only at the fate of women, but also of the children conceived as a result of rape. They point out that "children born from rape and their mothers are often rejected by their families and communities, including in conflict situations, where they may be associated with the enemy. This exacerbates the already high vulnerability of women and girl survivors of sexual assault and their children, who are often excluded from their social system and condemned to live in dire conditions."[253] In line with this reasoning, abortion would therefore be a humane solution to the potential problems of unborn children.

In the next paragraph, the Union presents its approach as survivor-centered,[254] which leads it to the following conclusion on the merits of the question it was asked: "in cases where the pregnancy threatens a woman's or a girl's life or causes unbearable suffering, international humanitarian law and/or international human rights law may justify offering a safe abortion rather than perpetuating what amounts to inhumane treatment. Women and girls who are pregnant as a result of rape should first receive appropriate and comprehensive information and be provided access to the full range of sexual and reproductive health services. Naturally, these will depend on the woman's wishes, on her condition, on the security of the humanitarian workers, as well as on other context-related factors."[255] It is not difficult to see that the Commission's position quotes almost verbatim the United Kingdom's position of 2014. While a year earlier the Commission, if it did not argue with that position, at least sought to justify the possibility of reconciling its different standpoint with the UK approach, a year later it embraced it wholly as its own. Moreover, it presented the EU as a party supporting UN resolutions previously referred to by the GJC and in 't Velt in their questions to the Commission[256] about the right to abortion for rape victims, and as an active party in developing the G8 position in 2013 and 2015.[257]

---

[252]Ibid.

[253]Ibid.

[254]Ibid.

[255]Ibid.

[256]Ibid.

[257]Ibid.

This position of the Commission was enthusiastically received by the co-chairs of the European Parliament's working group on reproductive and sexual health and rights: Sophie in 't Veld and Heidi Hautala. They interpreted the Commission's answer as a recognition that "war rape victims have the right, under international humanitarian law, to receive all the medical care required by their condition, including abortion, irrespective of local laws in war zones." While "until now the Commission has tacitly agreed on a total ban on abortion under the pressure of the United States, (. . .) with the new position, the Commission finally acknowledges the rights of female war rape victims (. . .) to safe abortion."[258]

The Commission's new position was reflected in the European Parliament's resolution on preparations for the World Humanitarian Summit adopted later that year. Endorsing the proposal of the rapporteur Enrique Guerrero Salom,[259] the Parliament insists in it that "the provision of humanitarian aid follows international humanitarian law, and that EU humanitarian aid [should] not be subject to restrictions imposed by other partner donors," and "calls for a global commitment (. . .) ensuring that women and girls have access to the full range of sexual and reproductive health services, including safe abortions, in humanitarian crises, rather than perpetuating what amounts to inhumane treatment, as required by international humanitarian law and as foreseen in the Geneva Conventions and their Additional Protocols."[260] The Parliament's position was adopted by a majority of 395 votes, with 63 votes against and 244 abstentions,[261] which revealed a significant discrepancy in the document's evaluation by the two main parliamentary groups.

As the change in the Commission's approach occurred in the process of adopting the 2016 budget, the Parliament's postulates also left their mark on the 2016 budget. The abortion discourse spread to the financial debate, which included the principles of financing humanitarian aid. In its budget proposal, the Commission suggested a provision to the effect that "the aid is granted to victims without discrimination on the grounds of race, ethnic origin, religion, disability, sex, age, nationality or political affiliation. That assistance is provided as long as it is necessary to meet

---

[258]*EU recognizes the right to abortion for war rape victims*, http://www.sophieintveld.eu/eu-recognises-the-right-to-abortion-for-war-rape-victims/ [02.05.2016]. Sophie in 't Veld said: "Finally the EU speaks out on behalf of all those women and girls raped and impregnated by their rapists in war zones. At last the EU recognises that these women and girls should have access to safe abortion. These victims are often under-aged girls, sometimes even 12 years old, like the girls abducted by Boko Haram. It would be both physically and mentally devastating for these traumatised female victims to be forced to carry an unwanted pregnancy to term. These women finally get the help they are entitled to."

[259]Cf. Enrique Guerrero Salom, *Report on preparing for the World Humanitarian Summit: Challenges and opportunities for humanitarian assistance* (2015/2051(INI)), 18.11.2015, A8-0332/2015, art. 21.

[260]European Parliament, *European Parliament resolution of 16 December 2015 on preparing for the World Humanitarian Summit: Challenges and opportunities for humanitarian assistance* (2015/2051(INI)), P8_TA(2015)0459, art. 21.

[261]http://www.votewatch.eu/en/term8-preparing-for-the-world-humanitarian-summit-challenges-and-opportunities-for-humanitarian-assistance-3.html#sthash.pCnDuHVZ.dpuf [02.05.2016].

the humanitarian needs to which such situations give rise."[262] The Council of the European Union did not comment on this part of the budget,[263] and no proposals for amendments to this section were submitted by the Parliamentary Committees in the autumn of 2015. Nevertheless, in view of the Commission's new standpoint and the strong position of the Parliament, the language of that section was amended during the works on the budget,[264] with the result that in its final form the EU budget for 2016 states that: "the aid is granted to victims without discrimination or adverse distinction on the grounds of race, ethnic origin, religion, disability, sex, age, nationality or political affiliation. That assistance is provided in accordance with international humanitarian law and **should not be subject to restrictions imposed by other partner donors** (emphasis added—M.G.), as long as it is necessary to meet the humanitarian needs to which such situations give rise."[265] Considering that the budget is a document representative of all EU institutions, it does not seem unfair to say that the European Union has thus distanced itself from the Helms amendment as regards the objectives of its humanitarian aid. In fact, it has therefore accepted that abortion is its legitimate element.

* * *

The above analysis of the paradigmatic shift in the humanitarian policy makes it possible to distinguish several key elements of this process, confirming the hypotheses. Firstly, attention should be paid to the political significance of the role of the European Parliament. Its non-legally binding resolutions have ultimately provided a fulcrum for the change in European policy. The above example shows that the Parliament's prevalent anthropological position may translate directly into EU policy in just a few years. A key role in this process is played by "creative minorities" which create ways of interpreting terms then taken over by entire interpretive communities, and engage in lobbying and other political action for paradigmatic change. In this case, it was a collaboration between Sophi in 't Velt and the Global Justice Center, not only "assailing" the Commission with their questions, but also consistently promoting a politically manipulative reinterpretation of humanitarian law in a pro-abortion spirit and gaining political support for this position. In this respect, the above analysis may also help understand the importance

---

[262]European Commission, *Draft General budget of the European Union for the financial year 2016, Volume 3, Section III: Commission,* COM(2015) 300 – EN, 24.06.2015, 230201, p. 1082.

[263]The only amendment concerned item 23 01 06 01, i.e. reducing the appropriations for the Education, Audiovisual and Culture Executive Agency – Contribution from EU Aid Volunteers initiative. Cf. Council of the European union, *Explanatory Memorandum. Subject: Draft general budget of the European Union for the financial year 2016: Council position of 4 September 2015,* 04.09.2015, (OR.en) 11706/15, p. 67.

[264]This achievement is attributed to Sophie in 't Velt, yet the author has not been able to find independent sources to confirm this. Cf. *EU finalizes divorce from US abortion ban,* http://globaljusticecenter.net/press-center/press-releases/241-eu-finalizes-divorce-from-us-abortion-ban [02.05.2016].

[265]*Budgets. Definitive Adoption (EU, Euratom) 2016/150 of the European Union's general budget for the financial year 2016,* 24.2.2016, p. 1435.

of lobbying in other cases, such as the Anti-Discrimination Directive discussed above.

It has also confirmed the importance of the Member States' position and the Commission's lack of a clear-cut standpoint. There is no doubt that in this respect the fact the UK government joined the progressive interpretive community gave new impetus to political actions supported by NGOs and Members from minority political groups. In the context of the Commission's role, it seems striking that its departure from the logic of anthropological constraint (consent to pharmacological abortion) ultimately deprives it of weapons to defend itself against the deepening logic of unconstraint, making decisions in this regard dependent on the prevailing political climate. The divergence of Georgieva and Mogherini's positions shows that in the absence of clear legal regulations or a clear political declaration as regards the recognition of reproductive rights, the decision on the Union's approach to abortion is an arbitrary, clerical one. It is worth noting that, within a few years, the initially very divergent positions of the Commission and the Parliament merged into one. Looking at this process more generally, it should be noted that the dynamics of political processes in the EU and the tendency of its transnational institutions to think in terms of anthropological unconstraint makes it possible for the Union to move very quickly from moderate to radical unconstrained positions. In the case discussed above, within 7 years the ideological position of the marginal communist-socialist group GUE/NGL became the official position of the European Union on abortion in humanitarian policy.

Chapter 13
Conclusion

If there is a thesis of Jean-Claude Juncker's which seems to be still valid after ending of his cadency, it is the assertion that within EU "the crisis is of course not finished."[1] The recent years of the European Union have been marked by "spectacular" crises: economic, migration, epidemic and political ones, the most obvious manifestation of which is the United Kingdom's decision to leave the EU. Nevertheless, Europe has long been suffering from a cultural crisis that attracts less attention from European officials, but which is no less serious for it.[2] It may be seen as the essential source of all other crises. As noted by Cardinal Joseph Ratzinger, "although, on the one hand, Christianity found its most influential form in Europe, we must also say, on the other hand, that Europe has developed a culture that most radically contradicts, not only Christianity, but the religious and moral traditions of humanity as well. This helps us understand that Europe is going through a 'stress test;' it also helps us understand the radical nature of the tensions that our continent has to face."[3]

If culture "embodies answers to fundamental questions about good and evil,"[4] then its core is the anthropological question. It is precisely "that which is human," as emphasized by Remi Brague, "that is currently experiencing a frontal attack on legitimacy and is under threat as a whole. This is happening either in Europeanised parts of the world or as a result of events that began on the Old Continent."[5] In this

---

[1]European Parliament News, *Refugee crisis must be first priority, says Juncker in 2015 State of the Union debate*, 09.09.2015: https://www.europarl.europa.eu/news/en/headlines/eu-affairs/20150909STO92301/refugee-crisis-must-be-first-priority-says-juncker-in-2015-state-of-eu-debate

[2]Cf. Krzysztof Wielecki, *Alpinizm bez asekuracji, czyli Unia wobec zmiany cywilizacyjnej*, "Chrześcijaństwo-Świat-Polityka" No 17/182014/2015, pp. 51–60.

[3]J. Ratzinger, *Europe's crisis of culture*, p. 348.

[4]Remi Brague, *Europe, Christianity and the Modern Age*, lecture (in German) delivered during the International Conference "John Paul II and the Spiritual Foundations of European Unity" organized by the Konrad Adenauer Foundation and the Centre for the Thought of John Paul II on June 11–12, 2014.

[5]Ibid.

© Springer Nature Switzerland AG 2021

M. Gierycz, *European Dispute over the Concept of Man*, Contributions to Political Science, https://doi.org/10.1007/978-3-030-61520-8_13

work, I have therefore tried to look at the concept of man behind the European Union's policy. An analysis of the EU's role in the cultural dispute is, in a sense, justified *ex natura rei* as regards the political form of united Europe. Nevertheless, it seems particularly important seeing that, in parallel with the intensification of the cultural dispute, the Union has grown in competences and strengthened its axiological anchorage, describing itself, in the Treaty of Lisbon, as a community of values. In an age of disputes about fundamental matters, this meant deliberately entering into the heart of a discussion which the Communities and then the Union, as an economy-centered organization, had almost been able to avoid for many years. As promised in the Introduction, this work has undertaken to reconstruct the sources and specificities of EU thinking about man, as well as its political consequences.

As regards the sources of EU anthropology, studies have shown that today's disputes over the first principles, held in the Union and elsewhere, can be seen as a continuation, or indeed the fulfillment, of the dispute about man initiated by the Enlightenment. The horizontal concept created at the time of man as a plastic being, with unlimited possibilities and aspirations, being the source and creator of all values, was opposed to the idea of man, established by Christianity and dating back to the ancient reflection on the *nous* and the law of nature, as a subject who has his own ontology or, to use a different language, identity,[6] and his inherent borders. This concept of man, challenging the human ability to perceive the proper measures of being itself, is defined here as unconstrained anthropology by reference to the typology of Thomas Sowell. In history, it manifested itself *inter alia* in the claims of utilitarian liberalism and Marxism, yet particularly favorable conditions for its development appeared in the age of late modernity. Its characteristic assertion that "nothing can be known for certain,"[7] leading to Vattimo's accomplished nihilism, ultimately undermines even those elements of anthropology which had so far been considered permanent also by the advocates of unconstrained thought. These include, first of all, the pre-judgements associated with the first two *inclinationes naturales*, i.e. the conviction about the non-exchangeability of human life (linked to a particular human dignity), and the recognition of sexuality (being a man or a woman) as a constitutive element of the human condition.

The contemporary negation of these first principles has swung the door wide open to morality policy. As an area of disputes about fundamental values, it is particularly relevant in the study of anthropological disputes. As results from the above analyses, two types of morality policies may be distinguished: primary and secondary. While the latter accept the traditional axiological system by demanding some room in the area of law for human weakness (e.g. through the legalization of gambling), primary policies involve an attempt to redefine values and win public affirmation for actions

---

[6] As pointed out by Rev. Jacek Grzybowski, in accordance with its Greek etymology and semantics, "the term *identity, identical* refers to (...) to the property of being—to being 'the same,' to the unchanging and inviolable essence of being, without which being would no longer be the same, would not be itself." Id, *Byt, Tożsamość, Naród. Próba wyjaśnienia formuły 'tożsamość narodowa' w perspektywie metafizyki*, Wyd. Marek Derewiecki, Kęty 2012, p. 6.

[7] Ibid.

hitherto considered to contradict human dignity. In their case, the dispute is primarily about yes/no questions.[8] Primary morality policies are therefore linked to the dispute over the first principles, placing themselves at the core of the anthropological dispute. Secondary policies are more concerned with the dispute over the political and legal implementation of these principles. As the study has demonstrated, the European Union is now exerting its influence in the area of primary morality policies.

The second research problem was concerned with the place and role of the European Union in the anthropological dispute. As demonstrated in the analysis of primary law concerning fundamental values and rights, the Union avoids referring to the holistic concept of man in areas where this would entail settling axiological disputes between the Member States. As a consequence, European Union law reflects the coexistence of contradictory anthropological concepts, referring both to the logic of constraint and that of unconstraint. Their coexistence presents a much more considerable challenge to constrained than to unconstrained anthropology. While the former entails the conviction that there exists an objective "measure of being" and therefore, by definition, does not allow for the coexistence of "multiple truths," the latter asserts that "all talk about the world, in the sense of attributing to it a relationship to the objective truth about things, is constructed by man and imposed on others by violence in order to subjugate them."[9] Consequently, it is not hindered by the coexistence of contradictory standpoints, unless they claim to be judgements about truth. For in the logic of late modernity, it is precisely truth as such that is considered synonymous with violence which should not be succumbed to.

The thesis about the EU's leaning towards unconstrained anthropology has been confirmed by functional studies. An analysis of the language and content of documents issued by the EU's institutional actors (including their formulation of political objectives) reveals the prevalence of the anthropological discourse characteristic of unconstrained anthropology. Although it is not uncommon for the meaning attributed to these concepts in EU to have been initially linked to the perspective of constrained anthropology (e.g. at the beginning of the twentieth century, reproductive rights did not include abortion), in recent years these restrictions have mostly been deconstructed or supplemented by categories that deprive them of anthropological clarity. Consequently, the objectives of EU politics as a whole with regard to morality policy, both internally and externally, have also become to a large extent oriented along the lines of unconstrained anthropology. Nevertheless, the studies have shown that the capacity for containing the unconstraint has not become completely eliminated, and it helps at times to restore the Union's anthropological boundaries in important places.

The process of containing the unconstraint is possible because, as indicated in the analysis of the decision-making process, European institutions are not monolithic in terms of their anthropological orientation. An important factor in favor of

---

[8]"Is X the case?"—"Is X not the case?".

[9]P. Mazurkiewicz, *Ideologia gender...*

unconstrained logic is transnationality: given the activity of the Parliament, the Commission and the Council, it is clear that dependence on the national sovereign promotes anthropological constraint. Among the institutions involved in the legislative process, a strong promoter of unconstrained anthropology is the European Parliament, whose actions are usually hampered at the level of the Council of the European Union, which generally takes the position closest to constrained anthropology (and often addresses morality policy issues much later than the Commission or the Parliament) owing to the lack of unanimity between the Member States in this area. The European Commission is positioned between these two standpoints, but in recent years it has clearly seconded the European Parliament's position. A *sui generis* situation is presented by the Court of Justice of the EU, which appears to be subject to a different logic in its actions, largely autonomous from the strictly political institutions, without presenting a homogeneous anthropological standpoint.

It is worth pointing out that analyses of the positions of political groups in the European Union show that the model of constrained vs. unconstrained anthropology in the EU does not simply entail a division into right-wing and left-wing parties. The analyses have revealed that the logic of unconstraint is clearly present in the political standpoints of liberals, socialists, as well as communist and green groups in disputes over the first principles. Nevertheless, they have also shown that it is significantly represented in the European circles of the Christian democrats and the conservatives. As has been pointed out, one of the greatest political success of the advocates of the logic of constraint in the European Parliament was made possible by the right effectively avoiding substantive discussions and, therefore, abandoning the moral and anthropological issue in the dispute over the first principles. It was only in this way that the initiators could win the support of the right side of the political scene for their proposal.

On the other hand, the analysis of votes carried out from the perspective of national states shows that a position on ethically sensitive matters is often linked more to nationality than to factional affiliation. The example of Members from Malta or Sweden who voted on morality policy issues regardless of belonging to a particular political group, often achieving 100% vote cohesion within their respective national groups, shows that anthropological visions rooted in the Member States' cultural traditions are sometimes clearly reflected in the activity of their politicians. In this context, the role of Polish politicians should be noted. As the case studies have shown, the Polish delegation in the European Parliament, irrespective of the term of office under consideration, was a pillar of the "coalition" of Members seeking to found EU decisions on constrained anthropology. Also in the Council of the European Union, the Polish delegation played a similar role. Given that in the context of Poland's integration into the European Union it has been repeatedly stressed that "Polish culture in the united Europe may become an impetus for combining the modern and the traditional,"[10] we may actually be witnessing this

---

[10]Sławomir Sowiński, "Papież, Polska i europejskość," *Tygodnik Powszechny* no. 17 (2807), 23.04.2003.

process in the political dimension.[11] Of course, this issue would require separate studies.

If the analyses carried out in this study have generally confirmed the legitimacy of claims evoked in the public space about the EU's role in promoting new standards in the area of primary morality policies, one surprising finding seems to be the pace of changes in the Union's approach to these issues. An analysis of the approach to abortion as part of humanitarian policy shows that radical unconstrained positions, rejected by most EU political forces, may become part of mainstream European politics in just a few years. This confirms the adequacy of the thesis, formulated in the context of the history of ideas in the long term perspective, on the self-deepening of unconstraint also as regards the political process, that is, in the short term perspective.

The comment on the relationship of long-term and short-term duration also leads to noting the validity of the methodological orientation used in this study, called in-depth system analysis. Its employment makes it possible to reveal the significance of the relationship between the political system and its cultural environment. In the perspective of the specific research goal of political science, it allows to integrate the research techniques characteristic of philosophical and theological anthropology, with particular regard to the hermeneutic method, and techniques developed in the framework of cultural anthropology.[12] This study clearly shows that political anthropology may be considered as a subdiscipline of political science. Just as cultural anthropology is based on an analysis of the products of culture, and philosophical anthropology on intellectual reflection, so political anthropology is based on an analysis of political thought, laws and political documents, in order to unveil the concepts of man behind them adopted within the political system.

One more comment should be made about the consequences of EU's leaning towards anthropological unconstraint in the context of the cultural crisis. If "the fundamental intuition about the moral character of Being itself and about the necessary harmony between the human being and the message of nature is common to all the great cultures, and therefore the great moral imperatives are likewise held in common,"[13] this leaning entails a gradual shift away from this supra-cultural intuition. This study confirms, therefore, the validity of theoretical conclusions on the uniqueness of primary morality policies as an area marked by an attempt at "reversing values," thus becoming the focus of the contemporary cultural dispute. While this ethical positioning of the EU is inconsistent due to the heterogeneity of the positions of its institutional actors, the law and political objectives within these

---

[11]This also seems to be an important contribution to the discussion about modernization. Cf. Dariusz Karłowicz, "Modernizacji nie da się skserować," *Teologia polityczna* no. 52009/2010, pp. 73–77.

[12]Discussed at length in Chap. 3.

[13]J. Ratzinger, *A Turning Point...*, p. 36.

policies are based in the EU not "on the discernible reality of right and wrong, but on the authority of the person with the power to enact it."[14]

The study has shown, therefore, that the problem of the Union's "democracy deficit" often mentioned in literature is probably deeper than is generally believed.[15] The structural inadequacy of the procedural ideal of democracy and the EU's political system based on an elitist logic is now additionally compounded by incongruity of content. It is also worth noting that both the idea of elite leadership[16] and the idea, evoked by leading EU politicians, of deepening the integration towards an ultimately undefined objective is characteristic of an unconstrained vision of politics. Deepening integration as a remedy for its crisis[17] seems therefore to be yet another variation on Condorcet's spirit of progress which will lead human affairs to their fulfillment. In reference to the distinctions, made in the Introduction, between authentic and apparent democracy, the study shows the need for caution in assessing the current state of the Union, which may right now be at a time of breakthrough, redefining the meaning of the democratic ideal. This issue would require further studies, however.

The Union's leaning towards unconstrained anthropology also sheds some light on the reason for treating integration as a "secular project." The logic of secularism, as mentioned above, is inherent in the anthropological assumptions of unconstraint in which man has no authority other than himself. The debate on the Constitutional Treaty, and then on the Treaty of Lisbon, rejection of the *invocatio Dei* or even any mention of Europe's Christian sources, or the earlier disputes over the reference to religious heritage in the Charter of Fundamental Rights are just some of the manifestations of the conviction of European elites that there is no place for Christianity in the Union[18] other than in some fenced-in, reserved areas.[19]

---

[14]Ibid., p. 56.

[15]More on this topic, see Tomasz Grzegorz Grosse, *Europa na rozdrożu*, ISP, Warszawa 2008, pp. 99–144; or Jacek Czaputowicz, "Demokracja a suwerenność w Unii Europejskiej," in: Konstanty Adam Wojtaszczyk, Małgorzata Mizerska-Wrotkowska, *Polska w procesie integracji europejskiej. Dekadadoświadczeń (2004–2014)*, WDiNP UW, Warszawa 2014, pp. 147–166.

[16]It is emblematic in this context that "the ideas for improving the efficiency of the functioning of the European Union indicate the need to strengthen technocratic institutions. (...) [In line with these ideas] the influence of majority-based institutions and democratically elected politicians should be limited. Such separation is aimed at eliminating *ad hoc* decisions, related to the electoral cycle. It is also intended to provide a strategic direction in decision making." T.G. Grosse, *Europa na rozdrożu...*, p. 122.

[17]Cf. e.g. Jean-Claude Juncker, *State of the Union 2015: Time for Honesty, Unity and Solidarity*, Strasburg, 9 September 2015, SPEECH/15/5614.

[18]Questioning the need to make any reference to God in the Constitutional Treaty, Valery Giscard d'Estaing explained that "Europeans live in secular political systems." D'Estaing's point of view was based on the assumption present in the European political elites that religion, as a category belonging to the private space at the very most, has essentially no relevance for the political sphere.

[19]Interesting comments on such a treatment of religion in liberalism can be found in Jürgen Habermas, "Religion in the Public Sphere," *European Journal of Philosophy*, Vol. 14 issue 1, April 2006, pp. 1–25.

Secularism seems to be synonymous with a kind of impermeability of European politics: it is separated from religion by a high and deep-seated wall,[20] even if the *Ode to Joy*, the EU's informal anthem, proclaims in the words of Schiller: "Brüder—überm Sternenzelt Muss ein lieber Vater wohnen" (Brothers, beyond the starry vault of the sky there must be a Father who loves us).

Rocco Buttiglione points out, however, that the secular idea ultimately poses a huge challenge to integration. He asks: "Why should a German be willing to make sacrifices for the Greeks or why should an Englishman or an Italian be ready to die for Gdansk? Schiller gives a very simple and straightforward answer: because we are brothers. But: do we want to be brothers? And can we be brothers if we have no common roots, if we do not have a father who loves us and makes us brothers? The question of the Christian roots is not so abstract and far from the concrete problems of the political everyday life as some imagine."[21]Buttiglione's comments not only show the legitimacy of the conviction that the cultural crisis is of fundamental significance for other European crises, but also suggest that one final look should be taken at the ongoing anthropological dispute in the EU also from the perspective of political and social utility.

There is no doubt that strengthening the EU's axiology in the Lisbon Treaty was linked to the hope of overcoming the Union's major legitimation deficit and building a European identity. The reference to values at least potentially has an irreplaceable integrating quality. It helps clearly define for every citizen the deepest motives for which the Union should be created and developed. As a community of values, in the long term it may become an object of attachment for more than just financial reasons. Not only the problem of the deficit of solidarity emphasized by Buttiglione, but also the associated neo-imperial evolution of the Union diagnosed by some political scientists[22] show that these hopes have come true to a very limited extent. Indeed,

---

[20]The European Parliament has defined secularism as "strict separation between non-confessional political authorities and religious authorities." This approach calls into question some traditional ways of regulating state-church relations in Europe (e.g. Germany). It also seems to be implicitly related to a distrust of Christianity. In the same resolution, the Parliament "calls on the Member States to protect (. . .) freedom of those without a religion not to suffer discrimination as a result of excessive exemptions for religions from laws on equality and Anti-Discrimination," and to depenalize blasphemy (offense against religious feelings) since "they are often applied to persecute, mistreat, or intimidate persons belonging to religious or other minorities, [and] can have a serious inhibiting effect on freedom of expression". *European Parliament resolution of 27 February 2014 on the situation of fundamental rights in the European Union (2012)* (2013/2078(INI)), P7_TA (2014)0173, articles 34–35.

[21]R. Buttiglione, "Can Europe be saved? "*Chrześcijaństwo-Świat-Polityka* No. 17/182014/ 2015, p. 15.

[22]As noted by Jacek Czaputowicz, the empire is "a hierarchical system in which [...] sovereignty of states is not upheld. It is defined as 'relations of political control of effective sovereignty, imposed by some political communities on other political communities" (Jacek Czaputowicz, *Suwerenność*, PISM, Warszawa 2013, p. 252). Further on the author refers to the theses of Urlich Beck, Edgar Lagrande, and Jan Zielonka, who demonstrate, in a different way, the legitimacy of the claim of the Union's imperial nature. Ibid., pp. 364–365. Cf. also Marek A. Cichocki, *Political Problem of European Unity*, PISM, Warszawa 2012, pp. 49–92.

the anthropological position of the EU has, from the very beginning, generated axiological disputes within the Union. Suffice it to note Poland's objections to the adoption of the CFR,[23] or the EU vs Hungary clashes.[24] The lasting consequences of these tensions can be seen in the difference between the EC/EP's and the CEU's position in resolving "ethically sensitive" issues. Moreover, the social shift towards parties which emphasize national ideas and Euroscepticism witnessed in recent years, at least in some countries, seems to suggest a growing distance of some European societies from the horizontal and unconstrained logic prevailing in the EU.

Important problems can also be seen from the perspective of social utility. Given that in the next 30 years Europe will be facing a 30% decline in its population,[25] one can hardly fail to see that the Union's anthropological standpoint does little to address this frightful challenge.[26] On the other hand, considering the migration crisis, including the fact that cultural minorities, especially Muslims, do not usually share the interpretation of values prevailing in European institutions, the question is how these interpretations influence the process, never easy, of integrating these numerous minorities with European societies.[27] Finally, a question arises in this context whether the undermining of the anthropology established in Europe by Christianity does not further undermine the cultural cohesion of the Union, which is already facing a major challenge due to the migration crisis. Such questions are many. They show that the outcome of the dispute over the concept of man will be fundamental not only to the survival of the European Union as a Community of Equals,[28] but also to the future of Europe as a continent of culture.

---

[23]As pointed out by Jerzy Jaskiernia, Poland joined the UK Protocol primarily because of its concern that the Charter (in fact, its application by the European Court of Justice) may impose moral standards, in particular the prohibition of discrimination on grounds of sexual orientation and, subsequently, standards relating to family law, abortion and euthanasia. Jerzy Jaskiernia, Współczesny system wartości społeczno-kulturowych a aksjologia Karty Praw Podstawowych Unii Europejskiej, http://www.jaskiernia.eu/index.php?view=article&catid=14%3Adorobek-naukowy&id=40% 3Awspoczesny-system-wartoci-spoeczno-kulturowych-a-aksjologia-karty-praw-podstawowych-unii-europejskiej&option=com_content&Itemid=52 [07.08.2009].

[24]The head of the liberal faction in the EP accused Victor Orban, whose party changed the Constitution by introducing, *inter alia*, protection of human life from conception and the definition of marriage as a union between a man and a woman, of departing from European principles and values. Cf. http://www.tvn24.pl/wiadomosci-ze-swiata,2/wegry-w-ogniu-europejskiej-krytyki-czy-to-jeszcze-panstwo-prawa,311506.html [24.10.2016].

[25]Andrzej Kurasiewicz, "Zadania i wyzwania polityki rodzinnej w UE," in: Z. Biegański, J. Jackowicz [ed.], *Unia Europejska społeczne i gospodarcze aspekty integracji*, TWP, Warszawa 2008, p. 62.

[26]I have alaborated on this subject in "Unii Europejskiej (re)definicja małżeństwa i rodziny. Antropologiczne i polityczne znaczenie w kontekście starzenia się Europy," *Annales. Universitatis Mariae Curie-Skłodowska. Sctrio K. Politologia* Vol. XXII, 2, 2015, pp. 69–83.

[27]Cf. Mariusz Sulkowski, Cezary Żołędowski, "Europejskie kłopoty z wielokulturowością," in: W. Anioł, M. Duszczyk, P. W. Zawadzki, *Europa socjalna. Iluzja czy rzeczywistość?*, IPS UW, Warszawa 2011, pp. 57–78.

[28]Cf. Robert Schuman, *For Europe*.

Bibliography

Political Documents and Legal Acts

American Convention on Human Rights, https://www.cidh.oas.org/basicos/english/basic3.american%20convention.htm

"Annex I: Areas of cooperation under geographic programmes," in: *Regulation (EU) No 233/2014 of the European Parliament and of the Council of 11 March 2014 establishing a financing instrument for development cooperation for the period 2014-2020,* Official Journal of the European Union, L 77/44.

Application to the General Court of the European Union in the case of European Citizen's Initiative "One of Us" and others versus the European Commission, the Council of the EU, and the European Parliament, Strasbourg, 25.7.2014, https://7676076fde29cb34e26d759f611b127203e9f2a0021aa1b7da05.ssl.cf2.rackcdn.com/eclj/Application-One-of-US-v-EC.pdf.

Asscher Lodewijk, Dalli Helena, Ondrus Bronislav, *Trio Presidency Declaration,* 7.12.2015, http://www.lm.gov.lv/upload/eng/trio_presidency_declaration_signed.pdf

Ayxelà Santiago Fisas, Stier Davor Ivo, Preda Cristian et al., *Joint Motion for a Resolution pursuant to Rule 123(2) and (4) of the Rules of Procedure replacing the motions by the following groups: S&D (B8-0370/2015), GUE/NGL (B8-0371/2015), PPE (B8-0374/2015), Verts/ALE (B8-0394/2015), ECR (B8-0396/2015), EFDD (B8-0398/2015), ALDE (B8-0400/2015) on the situation in Nigeria (2015/2520(RSP)),* RC-B8-0370/2015.

Baldacchino Claudette Abela, *Question for written answer to the Commission on Rule 117. Subject: Definition of sexual and reproductive health rights,* P-004206-14.

Belder Bastiaan, Cymański Tadeusz, Villiers Philippe de, Paksas Rolandas, Morganti Claudio, Fontana Lorenzo on behalf of the EFD Group, *Motion for a resolution (Rule 157(4) of the Rules of Procedure) replacing non-legislative*

© Springer Nature Switzerland AG 2021   457
M. Gierycz, *European Dispute over the Concept of Man*, Contributions to Political Science, https://doi.org/10.1007/978-3-030-61520-8

motion for a resolution A7-0426/2013 on sexual and reproductive health and rights, A7-0426/1, 4.12.2010.

Budgets. Definitive Adoption (EU, Euratom) 2016/150 of the European Union's general budget for the financial year 2016, OJ L48, 24.2.2016.

Buitenweg Kathalijne, *Statement made during Equal treatment of persons irrespective of religion or belief, disability, age or sexual orientation debate*, PV 01/04/2009-14, 1.4.2009.

Caldentey Lola Sánchez, Matias Marisa, Björk Malin et al., *Motion for a Resolution to wind up the debate on the statement by the Vice-President of the Commission/ High Representative of the Union for Foreign Affairs and Security Policy pursuant to Rule 123(2) of the Rules of Procedure on the situation in Nigeria (2015/2520(RSP)) on behalf of the GUE/NGL Group*, B8-0371/2015.

Charter of Fundamental Rights of the European Union, Official Journal of the European Union, 2010/C 83/02, 30.3.2010.

Committee on Women's Rights and Gender Equality, *Report on Sexual and Reproductive Health and Rights (2013/2040(INI))*, A7-0306/2013

Consolidated Version of the Treaty on European Union, OJ C115/13, 9.5.2008.

Convention on the Elimination of All Forms of Discrimination against Women adopted and opened for signature, ratification and accession by General Assembly, resolution 34/180, 18.12.1979, *https://www.ohchr.org/documents/ professionalinterest/cedaw.pdf.*

Convention on the Rights of the Child Proclaimed by the General Assembly, resolution *1386 (XIV)*, A/RES/14/1386, 20.11.1959.

Council and Commission statements: Fight against homophobia, Brussels, 4.6.2012.

Council of the European Union, *Common Position (EC) No 28/2006 adopted by the Council on 23 October 2006 with a view to the adoption of Regulation of the European Parliament and of the Council of establishing a financing instrument for development cooperation*, 2006/C 301 E/02.

Council of the European Union, *Council conclusions on LGBTI equality*, Press Release 338/16, 16.6.2016.

Council of the European Union, Council of the European Union, Press release 2893rd Council meeting, *Employment, social policy, health and consumer affairs*, C/08/271, 13405/08, Luxembourg, 2.10.2008.

Council of the European Union, *Council Regulation (EU) No 1259/2010 of 20 December 2010 implementing enhanced cooperation in the area of separation the law applicable to divorce and legal*, L 343/10.

Council of the European Union, *EU Annual Report on Human Rights and Democracy in the World in 2014*, 10152/15.

Council of the European Union, Explanatory Memorandum. *Subject: Draft general budget of the European Union for the financial year 2016: Council position of 4 September 2015*, 11706/15, 4.9.2015.

Council of the European Union, *Guidelines to promote and protect the enjoyment of all human rights by lesbian, gay, bisexual, transgender and intersex (LGBTI) persons*, Foreign Affairs Council meeting, Luxembourg, 24.6.2013.

Council of the European Union, *Human Rights and Democracy: EU Strategic Framework and EU Action Plan*, 11855/12.

Council of the European Union, The Presidency, *Proposal for a Council Directive on implementing the principle of equal treatment between persons irrespective of religion or belief, disability, age or sexual orientation - Progress Report*, SOC 349, JAI 312, MI 213, 2008/0140 (CNS), 2.6.2009.

Council of the European Union, The Presidency, *Proposal for a Council Directive on implementing the principle of equal treatment between persons irrespective of religion or belief, disability, age or sexual orientation - Progress Report*, 15575/09, 17.11.2009.

Council of the European Union, The Presidency, *Proposal for a Council Directive on implementing the principle of equal treatment between persons irrespective of religion or belief, disability, age or sexual orientation - Progress Report*, 9535/10, Brussels, 17.5.2010.

Council of the European Union, The Presidency, *Proposal for a Council Directive on implementing the principle of equal treatment between persons irrespective of religion or belief, disability, age or sexual orientation - Progress Report*, 16525/11,Brussels, 15.11.2011.

Court of Justice of the European Union, Judgement of the Court (Fourth Chamber), *Case C-528/13, Geoffrey Léger v Ministre des Affaires sociales, de la Santé et des Droits des femmes, Ministre des Affaires sociales, de la Santé et des Droits des femmes, Établissement français du sang*, ECLI:EU:C:2015:288, 29.4.2015.

Court of Justice of the European Union, Judgement of the Court (Grand Chamber), *Jürgen Römer v Freie und Hansestadt Hamburg*, ECLI:EU:C:2011:286.

Court of Justice of the European Union, Judgement of the Court (Grand Chamber) of 2 December 2014 in Joined Cases C-148/13 to C-150/13, *A (C148/13), B (C149/13), C (C150/13) v Staatssecretaris van VeiligheidenJustitie*ECLI:EU:C:2014:2406.

Court of Justice of the European Union, Judgment of the Court (Fourth Chamber) of 7 November 2013, Joined Cases C-199/12 to C-201/12, *Minister voor Immigratie en Asiel v X and Y and Z v Minister voor Immigratie en Asiel*, Summary, http://curia.europa.eu/juris/document/document.jsf?text=orientacja%25252Bseksualna&docid=159860&pageIndex=0&doclang=EN&mode=req&dir=&occ=first&part=1&cid=1724838%23ctx1.

Court of Justice of the European Union, *Judgment of the Court (Grand Chamber) of 18 October 2011*, Oliver Brüstle v Greenpeace eV., Reference for a preliminary ruling: Bundesgerichtshof - Germany, Case C-34/10, European Court Reports 2011 I-09821, ECLI:EU:C:2011:669.

Court of Justice of the European Union, *Judgment of the Court (Grand Chamber), 18 December 2014, International Stem Cell Corporation v Comptroller General of Patents, Designs and Trade Marks, Request for a preliminary ruling from the High Court of Justice (England & Wales), Chancery Division (Patents Court), Reference for a preliminary ruling — Directive 98/44/EC — Article 6(2), Case C-364/13*, ECLI:EU:C:2014:2451.

Court of Justice of the European Union, *Judgment of the Court 9 October 2001 in Case C-377/98, Netherlands v. Parliament and Council,* http://curia.europa.eu/ j u r i s / s h o w P d f . j s f ; jsessionid=9ea7d2dc30d5e48086928a5443bd839f81d292779d18. e34KaxiLc3qMb40Rch0SaxuTa3r0?text=&docid=46255&pageIndex=0& doclang=EN&mode=lst&dir=&occ=first&part=1&cid=816316.

Court of Justice of the European Union, *Press release No 112/11*, Luxembourg, 18.10.2011.

Declaration by United Nations, Washington, 1.1.1942, https://avalon.law.yale.edu/ 20th_century/decade03.asp.

Declaration of the 21st Session of the ACP Parliamentary Assembly on the peaceful co-existence of religions and the importance given to the phenomenon of homosexuality in the ACP-EU Partnership, 2/3/15, vol.1, no. 10, Brussels, 28.9.2010.

EIGE, *Mainstreaming gender into the policies and the programmes of the institutions of the European Union and EU Member States*, Publications Office of the European Union, ISBN: 978-92-9218-164-2, Luxembourg, 2013.

Enrique Guerrero Salom, *Report on preparing for the World Humanitarian Summit: Challenges and opportunities for humanitarian assistance* (2015/2051(INI)), A8-0332/2015, 18.11.2015.

EU recognizes the right to abortion for war rape victims, http://www.sophieintveld. eu/eu-recognises-the-right-to-abortion-for-war-rape-victims/ [02.05.2016].

European Citizens' Initiative, *One of Us* against the judgment of the General Court, http://www.ordoiuris.pl/europejska-inicjatywa-obywatelska-jeden-z-nas-przed-sadem-unii-europejskiej,3440,i.html

European Commission, *Proposal for a Council Directive on implementing the principle of equal treatment between persons irrespective of religion or belief, disability, age or sexual orientation,* COM/2008/0426 final.

European Commission, *Answer given by Mr Mimica on behalf of the Commission,* E-012709/2015, 10.11.2015.

European Commission, *Answer given by Mr Borg on behalf of the Commission,* P-004206/2014.

European Commission, *Answer given by Ms Georgieva on behalf of the Commission,* E-005386/12, 17.07.2012.

European Commission, *Answer given by Ms Georgieva on behalf of the Commission,* E-003947/2014, 27.05.2014.

European Commission, *Combating Sexual Orientation Discrimination in the European Union, Directorate-General for Justice and Consumers, Directorate D — Equality,* JUST/D1,B-1049, Brussels, 2014.

European Commission, *Combating Sexual Orientation Discrimination in the European Union. European Network of Legal Experts in the Non-discrimination Field,* Brussels, 2014, https://op.europa.eu/en/publication-detail/-/publication/c01db252-847d-474b-b397-d0f41eccecd1.

European Commission, *Communication from the Commission on the European Citizens' Initiative "One of us",* COM(2014) 355 final, 28.5.2014.

European Commission, *Declaration of the Commission (Framework Programme)*, 2013/C 373/02, 20.12.2013.

European Commission, *Draft General budget of the European Union for the financial year 2016, Volume 3, Section III: Commission*, COM(2015) 300 — EN, 230201, 24.6.2015.

European Commission, *Follow up to the European Parliament resolution on equality between women and men in the European Union – 2011*, SP(2012)387, 6.6.2012.

European Commission, *Follow up to the European Parliament resolution on Millennium Development Goals – defining the post 2015 framework*, SP(2013)626, 8.10.2013.

European Commission, *Joint answer given by Mr Mimica on behalf of the Commission. Written questions: P-012161/15, E-011611/15*, https://www.europarl.europa.eu/doceo/document/E-8-2015-011611-ASW_EN.html.

European Commission, *List of actions by the Commission to advance LGBTI equality*, Brussels, 2015, https://ec.europa.eu/info/sites/info/files/lgbti-actionlist-dg-just_en.pdf.

European Commission, *Proposal for a Council Directive on implementing the principle of equal treatment between persons irrespective of religion or belief, disability, age or sexual orientation*, COM(2008) 426 final, 2008/0140 (CNS), Brussels, 2.7.2008.

European Commission, *Proposal for a Regulation of the European Parliament and of the Council establishing a financing instrument for development cooperation and economic cooperation*, COM(2004) 629 final 2004/0220 (COD).

European Commission, *Recommendation*, Plenary meeting of the "Structured Dialogue on Justice and Additional Rule of Law Matters between the European Union and Bosnia Herzegovina", Sarajevo, Bosnia and Herzegovina, 13-14.5.2014.

European Court of Human Rights, *European Convention on Human Rights (Convention for the Protection of Human Rights and Fundamental Freedoms) as amended by Protocols Nos. 11 and 14, supplemented by Protocols Nos. 1, 4, 6, 7, 12, 13 and 16*, Strasbourg, n.d.

European Dignity Watch, *The Funding of Abortion through EU Development Aid. An analysis of EU's sexual and reproductive health policy*, EDW, Brussels, 2012, https://agendaeurope.files.wordpress.com/2014/11/funding_of_abortion_through_eu_development_aid_full_version.pdf.

European Parliament Committee on Civil Liberties, Justice and Home Affairs, *Report on the EU Roadmap against homophobia and discrimination on grounds of sexual orientation and gender identity (2013/2183(INI))*, A7-0009/2014.

European Parliament Committee on Development, *Draft Report on the Millennium Development Goals – defining the post-2015 framework (2012/2289(INI))*, PE504.341.

European Parliament, Gay Mitchell et al., *Amendment 1, 2, 3* to the *Financing instrument for development cooperation*, A6-0448/1, A6-0448/2, A6-0448/3, 8.12.2006.

European Parliament, *Amendment 52 and 95, European Parliament legislative resolution of 2 April 2009 on the proposal for a Council directive on implementing the principle of equal treatment between persons irrespective of religion or belief, disability, age or sexual orientation,* COM(2008)0426 – C6-0291/2008 – 2008/0140(CNS), P6_TA(2009)0211.

European Parliament, *Equal treatment of persons irrespective of religion or belief, disability, age or sexual orientation (debate),* PV 01/04/2009 – 14, 1.4.2009.

European Parliament, *European Parliament legislative resolution of 2 April 2009 on the proposal for a Council directive on implementing the principle of equal treatment between persons irrespective of religion or belief, disability, age or sexual orientation* (COM(2008)0426 – C6-0291/2008 – 2008/0140(CNS)), P6_TA(2009)0211, 2.4.2009.

European Parliament, *European Parliament legislative resolution on the proposal for a decision of the European Parliament and of the Council concerning the seventh framework programme of the European Community for research, technological development and demonstration activities (2007 to 2013),* COM(2005) 0119 – C6-0099/2005 – 2005/0043(COD).

European Parliament, *European Parliament resolution of 10 February 2010 on equality between women and men in the European Union – 2009 (2009/2101 (INI)),* P7_TA(2010)0021, 10.2.2010.

European Parliament, *European Parliament resolution of 10 March 2015 on progress on equality between women and men in the European Union in 2013* (2014/2217(INI)), P8_TA(2015)0050, 10.3.2015.

European Parliament, *European Parliament resolution of 12 March 2015 on the Annual Report on Human Rights and Democracy in the World 2013 and the European Union's policy on the matter (2014/2216(INI)),* P8_TA(2015)0076, 12.3.2015.

European Parliament, *European Parliament resolution of 13 June 2013 on the Millennium Development Goals – defining the post-2015 framework(2012/2289 (INI)),* P7_TA(2013)0283.

European Parliament, *European Parliament resolution of 13 March 2012 on equality between women and men in the European Union - 2011(2011/2244(INI)).*

European Parliament, *European Parliament resolution of 16 December 2015 on preparing for the World Humanitarian Summit: Challenges and opportunities for humanitarian assistance (2015/2051(INI)),* P8_TA(2015)0459, 16.12.2015.

European Parliament, *European Parliament resolution of 17 January 2008 on the situation in the Democratic Republic of Congo and rape as a war crime,* P6_TA (2008)0022, 17.1.2008.

European Parliament, *European Parliament resolution of 2 April 2009 on the application of Directive 2004/38/EC on the right of citizens of the Union and their family members to move and reside freely within the territory of the Member States (2008/2184(INI),* 2.4.2009.

European Parliament, *European Parliament resolution of 26 November 2009 on the elimination of violence against women,* P7_TA(2009)0098, 26.11.2009.

European Parliament, *European Parliament resolution of 27 February 2014 on the situation of fundamental rights in the European Union (2012)*, 2013/2078(INI), P7_TA(2014)0173, 27.2.2014.

European Parliament, *European Parliament resolution of 28 September 2011 on human rights, sexual orientation and gender identity at the United Nations*, P7_TA(2011)0427, 28.9.2011.

European Parliament, *European Parliament resolution of 30 April 2015 on the situation in Nigeria* (2015/2520(RSP)), P8_TA(2015)0185, 30.4.2015.

European Parliament, *European Parliament resolution of 4 February 2014 on the EU Roadmap against homophobia and discrimination on grounds of sexual orientation and gender identity (2013/2183(INI))*, 4.2.2014.

European Parliament, *European Parliament resolution of 4 September 2008 on Maternal Mortality ahead of the UN High-level Event on the Millennium Development Goals to be held on 25 September 2008*, P6_TA(2008)0406, 4.9.2008.

European Parliament, *European Parliament resolution of 5 April 2011 on priorities and outline of a new EU policy framework to fight violence against women (2010/2209(INI))*, P7_TA(2011)0127, 5.4.2011.

European Parliament, *European Parliament resolution of 8 March 2011 on equality between women and men in the European Union – 2010 (2010/2138(INI))*, P7_TA(2011)0085, 8.3.2011.

European Parliament, *European Parliament resolution on homophobia in Europe*, P6_TA(2006)0018, 18.1.2006.

European Parliament, *European Parliament resolution on sexual and reproductive health and rights (2001/2128 (INI))*, P5_TA(2002)0359.

European Parliament, *European Parliament resolution on the increase in racist and homophobic violence in Europe*, P6_TA(2006)0273, 15.6.2006.

European Parliament, European Parliament, *Report on Equality between women and men - 2007* (2007/2065(INI)), P6_TA(2007)0423.

European Parliament, *Gender mainstreaming in the work of the European Parliament European Parliament resolution of 17 November 2011 on gender mainstreaming in the work of the European Parliament (2011/2151(INI))*, 17.11.2011.

European Parliament, *MEPs back €50bn programme for research and development*, http://www.europarl.europa.eu/sides/getDoc.do?language=EN&type=IM-PRESS&reference=20060615STO09 076 [04.03.2010].

European Parliament, *MEPs see devastating effect of rape in DR Congo*, 2.4.2008, https://www.europarl.europa.eu/sides/getDoc.do?pubRef=-//EP//TEXT+IM-PRESS+20080331STO25211+0+DOC+XML+V0//EN

European Parliament, *Motion for resolution with request for inclusion in the agenda for the debate on cases of breaches of human rights, democracy and the rule of law pursuant to Rule 115 of the Rules of Procedure by Eva-Britt Svensson, Luisa Morgantini on behalf of the GUE/NGL Group on Democratic Republic of Congo and mass rape as war crime and crime against humanity*, B60030/2008.

European Parliament, *Opinion of the Committee on Women's Rights and Gender Equality for the Committee on Development on the Millennium Development Goals – defining the post-2015 framework (2012/2289(INI)*, PE504.148.

European Parliament, *Report on Equality between women and men - 2004 (2004/2159(INI))*, P6_TA(2006)0039.

European Parliament, *Report on Equality between women and men - 2008 (2008/2047(INI))*, P6_TA(2008)0399.

European Parliament, *Resolution of 8 October 2015 on the application of Directive 2006/54/EC of the European Parliament and of the Council of 5 July 2006 on the implementation of the principle of equal opportunities and equal treatment of men and women in matters of employment and occupation (2014/2160(INI))*, 8.10.2015.

European Parliament, *Situation in the Democratic Republic of Congo and rape as a war crime (debate): Meglena Kuneva*, Strasbourg, CRE 17/01/2008 - 11.2, 17.01.2008.

European Parliament, Wiśniewska Jadwiga (ECR), Wojciechowski Janusz (ECR), Ożóg Stanisław (ECR), Kuźmiuk Zbigniew (ECR), *Question for written answer E-012709-15 to the Commission, Rule 130, Subject: Commission funding for the International Planned Parenthood Federation*, E-012709-15, 10.9.2015.

European Union Agency for Fundamental Rights, *Homophobia and Discrimination on Grounds of Sexual Orientation in the EU Member States. Part I – Legal Analysis*, Vienna, 2008.

European Union Agency for Fundamental Rights, *Homophobia and Discrimination on Grounds of Sexual Orientation and Gender Identity in the EU Member States, Part II: The Social Situation*, Vienna, 2009.

European Union Agency for Fundamental Rights, *Homophobia, transphobia and discrimination on grounds of sexual orientation and gender identity*, ISBN 978-92-9192-695-4, Vienna, 2010.

European Union Agency for Fundamental Rights, *Protection against discrimination on grounds of sexual orientation, gender identity and sex characteristics in the EU. Comparative legal analysis. Update 2015*, ISBN 978-92-9239-892-7, 10.2811/556190, TK-02-15-554-EN-C.

Explanations relating to the Charter of Fundamental Rights, OJ C 303, 14.12.2007.

Federika Mogherini, *Declaration by the High Representative, Federica Mogherini, on behalf of the EU on the occasion of the International Day Against Homophobia, Transphobia and Biphobia*, Press release 249/16, 17.5.2019, https://www.consilium.europa.eu/en/press/press-releases/2015/05/17/international-day-against-homophobia-transphobia/

General Secretariat of the Council and European Parliament, *Directive 2004/23/EC of The European Parliament and of The Council of 31 March 2004 on setting standards of quality and safety for the donation, procurement, testing, processing, preservation, storage and distribution of human tissues and cells*, L 102/48, 7.4.2004.

General Secretariat of the Council and European Parliament, *Directive 2004/38/EC of the European Parliament and of the Council of 29 April 2004 on the right of citizens of the Union and their family members to move and reside freely within the territory of the Member States amending Regulation (EEC) No 1612/68 and repealing Directives 64/221/EEC, 68/360/EEC, 72/194/EEC, 73/148/EEC, 75/34/EEC, 75/35/EEC, 90/364/EEC, 90/365/EEC and 93/96/EEC.*

General Secretariat of the Council and European Parliament, *Directive 98/44/EC of The European Parliament and of The Council of 6 July 1998 on the legal protection of biotechnological inventions,* L 213/13.

General Secretariat of the Council and European Parliament, *Regulation (EC) No 1567/2003 of the European Parliament and of the Council of 15 July 2003 on aid for policies and actions on reproductive and sexual health and rights in developing countries,* OJ L 224, 6.9.2003.

General Secretariat of the Council and European Parliament, *Regulation of The European Parliament and of The Council on advanced therapy medicinal products and amending Directive 2001/83/EC and Regulation (EC) No 726/2004,* OJ L 324, 10.12.2007.

General Secretariat of the Council and European Parliament, *Regulation (EC) No 1905/2006 of the European Parliament and of the Council of 18 December 2006 establishing a financing instrument for development cooperation,* OJ L 378, 27.12.2006.

General Secretariat of the Council and European Parliament, *Regulation (EU) No 233/2014 of the European Parliament and of the Council of 11 March 2014 establishing a financing instrument for development cooperation for the period 2014-2020,* OJ L 77, 15.3.2014.

General Secretariat of the Council, Working Party on Human Rights, *Toolkit to Promote and Protect the Enjoyment of all Human Rights by Lesbian, Gay, Bisexual and Transgender (LGBT) People,* 11179/10, LIMITE, COHOM 162, PESC 80.

Georgieva Kristalina, *Letter to Ms. Benshoof,* Ares(2014)2934591, 8.9.2014.

Global Justice Centre, *EU finalizes divorce from US abortion ban,* 24.2.2016, http://globaljusticecenter.net/press-center/press-releases/241-eu-finalizes-divorce-from-us-abortion-ban [02.05.2016].

Havel Vaclav, *Speechin European Parliament,* Brussels, 11.11.2009.

ILGA – Europe, *Evidence of discrimination based on sexual orientation outside employment Submitted by ILGA - Europe following its written responses to the European Commission Consultation on New Anti-Discrimination Measures,* December 2007, https://www.ilga-europe.org/sites/default/files/Attachments/discrimination_based_on_sexual_orientation_-_additional_evidence_01dec07_www.pdf.

ILGA-Europe, European Network Against Racism, *Why does the European Commission need to propose a Horizontal Directive on the principle of equal treatment? The Case for a Horizontal Anti-Discrimination Directive,* n.d., https://www.ilga-europe.org/sites/default/files/Attachments/the_case_for_a_horizontal_anti-discrimination_directive_ilga-europe_enar_www.pdf.

ILGA-Europe, *ILGA-Europe's position on the proposal for a Council Directive on the principle of equal treatment between persons irrespective of religion or belief,*

disability, age or sexual orientation. A Working Document, October 2008, https://
www.ilga-europe.org/sites/default/files/Attachments/ilga-europes_position_on_
the_proposed_directive_october_2008_www.pdf.

Juncker Jean-Claude, *Opening Statement in the European Parliament Plenary Session*, in: id., *A New Start for Europe: My Agenda for Jobs, Growth, Fairness and Democratic Change. Political Guidelines for the next European Commission. Opening Statement in the European Parliament Plenary Session*, Strasbourg, 15.7.2014.

Juncker Jean-Claude, *State of the Union 2015: Time for Honesty, Unity and Solidarity*, SPEECH/15/5614, Strasburg, 9.9.2015.

Juorova Vera, *Foreword*, in: European Commission, *List of actions by the Commission to advance LGBTI equality*, Brussels, 2015.

"Komunitariańska Platforma Programowa. Społeczeństwo Responsywne: Prawa i Obowiązki," in: P. Śpiewak [ed.], *Komunitarianie. Wybórtekstów*, Aletheia, Warszawa, 2004.

Metsola Robertaon behalf of the PPE Group, Cashman Michael on behalf of the S&D Group, in 't Veld Sophia on behalf of the ALDE Group, Lunacek Ulrike on behalf of the Verts/ALE Group, Jong Cornelis de on behalf of the GUE/NGL Group, *Motion for a resolution (Rule 157(4) of the Rules of Procedure) replacing non-legislative motion for a resolution, Amendment 2*, A7-0009/2014.

Mitchell Gay, *I Report on the proposal for a regulation of the European Parliament and of the Council establishing a financing instrument for development cooperation and economic cooperation (COM(2004)0629 – C6-0128/2004 – 2004/0220 (COD))*, A6-0060/2005.

Mogherini Federica, *Declaration by the High Representative, Federica Mogherini, on behalf of the EU on the occasion of the International Day Against Homophobia, Transphobia and Biphobia*, Press release 249/16, 17.5.2016.

Mogherini Federica, Stylianides Christos, *Letter adressed to Ms. Elena Valenciano et al.*, Ares (2015)3757306, 11.9.2015.

Protocol Additional to the Geneva Conventions of 12 August 1949 and Relating to the Protection of Victims of Non-International Armed Conflicts (Protocol II), Diplomatic Conference on the Reaffirmation and Development of International Humanitarian Law applicable in Armed Conflicts, 8.6.1977, https://www.ohchr. org/EN/ProfessionalInterest/Pages/ProtocolII.aspx

Report of the International Conference on Population and Development, Cairo, 1994, https://www.un.org/en/development/desa/population/events/pdf/expert/27/SupportingDocuments/A_CONF.171_13_Rev.1.pdf.

Report on the proposal for a decision of the European Parliament and of the Council concerning the seventh framework programme of the European Community for research, technological development and demonstration activities (2007 to 2013), COM(2005)0119 – C6-0099/2005 – 2005/0043(COD), https://www. europarl.europa.eu/sides/getDoc.do?pubRef=-//EP//TEXT+REPORT+A6-2006-0202+0+DOC+XML+V0//EN.

Secretariat of Commission of Bishops' Conferences of the European Union, *An Overview Report on Bioethics in the European Union*, COMECE, Brussels, 2009.

"Statement by Austria," in: *Council of the European Union, Proposal for a Decision of the European Parliament and of the Council concerning the 7th Framework Programme of the European Community for research, technological development and demonstration (2007-2013) [first reading]. - Adoption (cp + s) (a) of the common position (b) of the statement of the Council's reasons - Statements*, 2005/0043 (COD), Brussels, 15.9.2006 (19.09).

"Statement by Commission," in: Council of the European Union, *Proposal for a Decision of the European Parliament and of the Council concerning the 7th Framework Programme of the European Community for research, technological development and demonstration (2007-2013) [first reading]. - Adoption (cp + s) (a) of the common position (b) of the statement of the Council's reasons - Statements*, 2005/0043 (COD), Brussels, 15.9.2006 (19.09).

"Statement by Germany," in: Council of the European Union, *Proposal for a Decision of the European Parliament and of the Council concerning the 7th Framework Programme of the European Community for research, technological development and demonstration (2007-2013) [first reading]. - Adoption (cp + s) (a) of the common position (b) of the statement of the Council's reasons - Statements*, 2005/0043 (COD), Brussels, 15.9.2006 (19.09).

"Statement by Malta," in: Council of the European Union, *Proposal for a Decision of the European Parliament and of the Council concerning the 7th Framework Programme of the European Community for research, technological development and demonstration (2007-2013) [first reading]. - Adoption (cp + s) (a) of the common position (b) of the statement of the Council's reasons - Statements*, 2005/0043 (COD), Brussels, 15.9.2006 (19.09).

"Statement by Poland," in: Council of the European Union, *Proposal for a Decision of the European Parliament and of the Council concerning the 7th Framework Programme of the European Community for research, technological development and demonstration (2007-2013) [first reading]. - Adoption (cp + s) (a) of the common position (b) of the statement of the Council's reasons – Statements*, 2005/0043 (COD), Brussels, 15.9.2006 (19.09).

The Constitution of The Republic of Poland, POL-1997-C-48187, 2.4.1997, http://www.ilo.org/dyn/natlex/docs/ELECTRONIC/48187/73135/F401971080/POL48187%20English.pdf.

UN General Assembly, *Vienna Declaration*, The World Conference on Human Rights, A/CONF.157/23, 12.6.1993, https://rm.coe.int/0900001680536c83.

Veld Sophia in 't (ALDE), Parvanova Antonyia (ALDE), Weber Renate (ALDE) i in., *Question for written answer to the Commission*, E-005386/12, 30.5.2012.

Veld Sophia in 't (ALDE), Schaake Marietje (ALDE), *Question for written answer to the Commission Rule 117. Subject: Rape as a weapon of war in Syria*, E-003947-14, 31.3.2014.

Veld Sophia in 't, *Re.: Your answer on Written Question E-003947/2014*, Brussels, 8.7.2014.

Vierling Catherine, *Los derechos de la mujer y la regulación del aborto en el Parlamento Europeo*, http://www.prolifeworldcongress.org/zaragoza2009/index.php?option=com_content&task=view&id=192&Itemid=109 [31.03.2011].

Weber Manfred, *Equal treatment of persons irrespective of religion or belief, disability, age or sexual orientation debate*, PV 01/04/2009 - 14, 1.4.2009.

Sources of Voting and Statistical Data

https://eur-lex.europa.eu/search.html?textScope0=ti-te&qid=1588341011578&DTS_DOM=ALL&type=advanced&lang=en&andText0=%22procreation%22&SUBDOM_INIT=ALL_ALL&date0=ALL:01012000%7C31122019&DTS_SUBDOM=ALL_ALL [2.05.2020].

http://eurlex.europa.eu/search.html?textScope0=tite&qid=1467062832471&CASE_LAW_SUMMARY=false&DTS_DOM=ALL&type=advanced&lang=en&andText0=%22procreation%20health%22&SUBDOM_INIT=ALL_ALL&DTS_SUBDOM=ALL_ALL [27.06.2016].

https://eur-lex.europa.eu/search.html?textScope0=tite&qid=1588341793503&DTS_DOM=ALL&type=advan-ced&lang=en&andText0=reproductive&SUBDOM_INIT=ALL_ALL&date0=ALL:01012000%7C31122019&DTS_SUBDOM=ALL_ALL [02.05.2020].

https://eur-lex.europa.eu/search.html?textScope0=tite&qid=1588341243485&DTS_DOM=ALL&type=advanced&lang=en&andText0=%22reproductive%20rights%22&SUBDOM_INIT=ALL_ALL&date0=ALL:01012000%7C31122019&DTS_SUBDOM=ALL_ALL [02.05.2020].

https://eur-lex.europa.eu/search.html?textScope0=tite&qid=1588341313745&DTS_DOM=ALL&type=advanced&l ang=en&andText0=%22sexual%20health%22&SUBDOM_INIT=ALL_ALL&date0=ALL:01012000%7C31122019&DTS_SUBDOM=ALL_ALL [02.05.2020].

https://eur-lex.europa.eu/search.html?textScope0=tite&qid=1588341313745&DTS_DOM=ALL&type=advanced&lang=en&andText0=%22sexual%20health%22&SUBDOM_INIT=ALL_ALL&date0=ALL:01012000%7C31122019&DTS_SUBDOM=ALL_ALL [02.05.2020].

https://eur-lex.europa.eu/search.html?textScope0=tite&qid=1588341726932&DTS_DOM=ALL&type=advanced&lang=en&andText0=%22sexual%20rights%22&SUBDOM_INIT=ALL_ALL&date0=ALL:01012000%7C31122019&DTS_SUBDOM=ALL_ALL [02.05.2020].

http://eurlex.europa.eu/search.html?textScope0=tite&qid=1467062832471&CASE_LAW_SUMMARY=-false&DTS_DOM=ALL&type=advanced&lang=en&andText0=%22procreation%20health%22&SUBDOM_INIT=ALL_ALL&DTS_SUBDOM=ALL_ALL [27.06.2016].

https://eur-lex.europa.eu/search.html?t ex tScope0=t i - te&lang=en&SUBDOM_INIT=ALL_ALL&DTS_DOM=ALL&type=advanced&DTS_

SUBDOM=ALL_ALL&qid=1588326641126&date0=ALL%3A01012001%
7C31122019&andText0=%22reproductive+rights%22&AU_CODED=GCEU
[2.05.2020]

https://eur-lex.europa.eu/search.html?textScope0=ti-te&qid=1588342181013&
DTS_DOM=ALL&AU_CODED=GCEU&type=advanced&lang=en&
andText0=%22reproductive%20health%22&SUBDOM_INIT=ALL_ALL&
date0=ALL:01012000%7C31122019&DTS_SUBDOM=ALL_ALL
[2.05.2020]

https://eur-lex.europa.eu/search.html?textScope0=tite&qid=1588339974506&
DTS_DOM=ALL&type=advanced&lang=en&andText0=%22homosexual%
20inclination%22&SUBDOM_INIT=ALL_ALL&date0=ALL:01012001%
7C31122019&DTS_SUBDOM=ALL_ALL [02.05.2020]

https://eur-lex.europa.eu/search.html?textScope0=tite&qid=1588340582717&
DTS_DOM=ALL&type=advanced&lang=en&andText0=%22abortion%22&
SUBDOM_INIT=ALL_ALL&date0=ALL:01012000%7C31122019&DTS_
SUBDOM=ALL_ALL [2.05.2020]

https://eurlex.europa.eu/search.html?textScope0=tite&qid=1588579022341&
DTS_DOM=ALL&type=advanced&lang=en&andText0=%22gender%22&
SUBDOM_INIT=ALL_ALL&date0=ALL:01012000%7C31122019&DTS_
SUBDOM=ALL_ALL [04.05.2020]

https://eurlex.europa.eu/search.html?textScope0=tite&qid=1588578643850&
DTS_DOM=ALL&type=advanced&lang=en&andText0=%22sex%22&
SUBDOM_INIT=ALL_ALL&date0=ALL:01012000%7C31122019&DTS_
SUBDOM=ALL_ALL [04.05.2020]

https://eur-lex.europa.eu/search.html?textScope0=tite&qid=1588579854000&
DTS_DOM=ALL&type=advanced&lang=en&andText0=%22marriage%22&
SUBDOM_INIT=ALL_ALL&date0=ALL:01012000%7C31122019&DTS_
SUBDOM=ALL_ALL&AU_CODED=CJ [04.05.2020]

https://eurlex.europa.eu/search.html?DB_AUTHOR=justice&textScope0=tite&
qid=1588580974899&DTS_DOM=ALL&type=advanced&lang=en&
andText0=%22sexual%20orientation%22&SUBDOM_INIT=ALL_ALL&
date0=ALL:01012000%7C31122019&DTS_SUBDOM=ALL_ALL
[04.05.2020].

http://eurlex.europa.eu/search.html?textScope0=t ite&qid=1467050794610&
CASE_LAW_SUMMARY=false&DTS_DOM=ALL&type=advanced&
lang=en&andText0=%22homosexual%20marriage%22&SUBDOM_
INIT=ALL_ALL&date0=ALL:01062001%7C31052016&DTS_
SUBDOM=ALL_ALL [27.06.2016].

https://eur-lex.europa.eu/search.html?textScope0=ti-te&qid=1588581462283&
DTS_DOM=ALL&type=advanced&lang=en&andText0=%22homophobia%
22&SUBDOM_INIT=ALL_ALL&date0=ALL:01012000%7C31122019&
DTS_SUBDOM=ALL_ALL [04.05.2020]

https://eurlex.europa.eu/search.html?textScope0=tite&qid=1588578564449&
DTS_DOM=ALL&type=advan-ced&lang=en&andText0=%22homosexual%

20inclination%22&SUBDOM_INIT=ALL_ALL&date0=ALL:01012000%
7C31122019&DTS_SUBDOM=ALL_ALL [04.05.2020]

https://eurlex.europa.eu/search.html?textScope0=tite&qid=1588581579608&
DTS_DOM=ALL&type=advan-ced&lang=en&andText0=%22LGBT%22&
SUBDOM_INIT=ALL_ALL&date0=ALL:01012000%7C31122019&DTS_
SUBDOM=ALL_ALL [04.05.2020]

https://eur-lex.europa.eu/search.html?textScope0=tite&qid=1588581628987&
DTS_DOM=ALL&type=advan-ced&lang=en&andText0=%22HOMOSEX
UALS%22&SUBDOM_INIT=ALL_ALL&date0=ALL:01012000%
7C31122019&DTS_SUBDOM=ALL_ALL [04.05.2020]

http://term7.votewatch.eu/en/equality-between-women-and-men-in-the-european-
union-2009-motion-for-a-resolution-paragraph-38-1.html#/##vote-tabs-list-2
[22.10.2016].

http://term7.votewatch.eu/en/equality-between-women-and-men-in-the-european-
union-2011-motion-for-a-resolution-vote-resolution-te.html [22.10.2016].

http://term7.votewatch.eu/en/equality-between-women-and-men-in-the-european-
union-2011-motion-for-a-resolution-paragraph-47-2.html#/##vote-tabs-list-4
[10.10.2016].

http://term7.votewatch.eu/en/equality-between-women-and-men-in-the-european-
union-2011-motion-for-resolution-paragraph-47-2.html#/##vote-tabs-list-4
[10.10.2016].

http://term7.votewatch.eu/en/homophobia-and-discrimination-on-grounds-of-sex
ual-orientation-and-gender-identity-motion-for-resolu-2.html#/##vote-tabs-list-2
[24.10.2016].

http://term7.votewatch.eu/en/homophobia-and-discrimination-on-grounds-of-sex
ual-orientation-and-gender-identity-motion-for-resolu-2.html#/##vote-tabs-list-4
[25.10.2016].

http://term7.votewatch.eu/en/sexual-and-reproductive-health-and-rights-motion-
for-resolution-request-for-referral-back-to-committ.html#/##vote-tabs-list-2
[22.10.2016].

http://term7.votewatch.eu/en/sexual-and-reproductive-health-and-rights-motion-
for-resolution-request-for-referral-back-to-committ.html#/##vote-tabs-list-2
[10.10.2016].

http://www.europarl.europa.eu/sides/getDoc.do?pubRef=-//EP//TEXT+PV
+20131210+ITEM-009-04+DOC+XML+V0//PL [10.10.2016].

http://www.votewatch.eu/cx_vote_details.php?id_act=1860&lang=pl
[27.12.2010].

http://www.votewatch.eu/cx_vote_details.php?id_act=5750&lang=en
[27.12.2010].

http://www.votewatch.eu/en/term8-preparing-for-the-world-humanitarian-summit-
challenges-and-opportunities-for-humanitarian-assistance-3.html#sthash.
pCnDuHVZ.dpuf [02.05.2016].

http://www.votewatch.eu/en/term8-progress-on-equality-between-women-and-
men-in-the-eu-in-2013-motion-for-resolution-vote-resolution.html#/##vote-tabs-
list-2 [22.10.2016].

http://www.votewatch.eu/en/term8-progress-on-equality-between-women-and-men-in-the-eu-in-2013-motion-for-resolution-paragraph-45-1.html#/##vote-tabs-list-2 [22.10.2016].

http://www.votewatch.eu/en/term8-situation-in-nigeria-joint-motion-for-resolution-vote-resolution.html#/##vote-tabs-list-2 [30.04.2016].

Other Sources and Research Papers

Abeles Marc, "Virtual Europe," in: I. Bellier, T.M. Wilson [ed.], *The Anthropology of European Union. Building, Imagining and Experiencing the new Europe*, Routledge, Berg, Oxford, New York, 2000.

Acton John Emerich Edward Dalberg Lord, "The History of Freedom in Antiquity," in: *The History of Freedom, and Other Essays,* New York, 1967.

Aldous Joan, Dumon Wilfrid., "European Union and United States perspectives on family policy: summing up," in: id. [ed.], *The politics and programs of family policy: United States and European perspectives*, Leuven University Press, 1980.

Allison Lincoln, "Politics," in: McLean Iain, Mcmillan Alistair [ed.], *The Concise Oxford Dictionary of Politics*, Oxford University Press, 2003.

Amitai Etzioni [ed.], *The Essential Communitarian Reader*, Rowman & Littlfield Publishers, 978-0-8476-8827-2, 1998.

Anatrella Tony, *Definition of therms in the neo-language of the philosophy of constructivism and gender*, Pontificum Consilium Pro Familia, Vatican City, 2008.

Anonymous, *The Cloud of Unknowing,* trans. J. Walsh, Paulist Press, 1981.

Antoszewski Andrzej, "Politologia," in: id., R. Herbut [ed.], *Leksykonpolitologii*, atla 2, Wroclaw, 2004.

Antoszewski Andrzej, Herbut Ryszard [ed.], *Leksykon politologii*, atla2, Wroclaw, 2003.

Apthorpe Raymond, "Writing development policy and policy anaysis plain or clear. On language, genre and power," in: C. Shore, S. Wright [ed.], *Anthropology of Policy. Critical perspectives on governance and power*, Routledge, London & New York, 2005.

Aquinas Thomas, *De Regno: On Kingship,* Divine Providence Press, 2014.

Aquinas Thomas, *Summa Theologiae,* 2nd rev. ed., trans. Fathers of the English Dominican Province, New Advent, 2008.

Arendt Hannah, *Between Past and Future: Eight Exercises in Political Thought*, The Viking Press, 1968.

Arendt Hannah, *The Human Condition,* University of Chicago Press, 2018.

Aristotle, "Magna Moralia" in: *Aristotle's Ethics: Writings from the Complete Works*, Princeton University Press, 2014.

Aristotle, *The Nicomachean Ethics*, Harvard University Press, 1934.

Aristotle, *Politics*, Penguin Classics, Harmondsworth, 1981.

Babbie Earl, *The practice of social research*, Cengage Learning, 2007.

Bäcker Roman, *Czym jest teoria w politologii? O znaczeniu kategorii typu idealnego*, "Czym jest teoria w politologii?" Conference paper, Poznan, 12.5.2010, wnpid.amu.edu.pl/attachments/787_Prof.%20Backer%20-%20referat.pdf [10.09.2013].

Baker Aryn, *The Secret War Crime, http://time.com/war-and-rape/?xid=homepage* [02.05.2016].

Balandier Georges, *Political Anthropology*, Random House, New York, 1970.

Balicki Janusz Rev., *Rodzina*, in: B. Szlachta, *Słownik społeczny*, WAM, Krakow, 2004.

Bandow Doug, "Roe v. Wade: Four Decades of Tragedy," in: N. Merino [ed.], *Abortion*, Greenhaven Press, Farmongton Hills, 2014.

Barcz Jan, *Unia Europejska na rozstajach. Traktat z Lizbony. Dynamika i główne kierunki reformy ustrojowej*, 2nd ed., EuroPrawo, Warszawa, 2010.

Bardel Michał, Gadacz Tadeusz, "Osoba," in: B. Szlachta [ed.], *Słownik społeczny*, WAM, Krakow, 2006.

Barnard Alan, *History and Theory in Anthropology*, Cambridge University Press, 2000.

Barrot Sneha, "Abortion Restrictions in U.S. Foreign Aid: The History and Harms of the Helms Amendment," *Guttmacher Policy Review*, vol. 3, no. 16, 2013.

Bartky Sandra Lee, "Foucault, Femininity and the Modernization of Patriarchal Power," in: K. Conboy, N. Medina, S. Stanbury [ed.], *Writing on the Body: Female Embodiment and Feminist Theory*, Columbia University Press, New York, 1997.

Baszkiewicz Jan, Ryszka Franciszek, *Historia doktryn politycznych i prawnych*, PWN, Warszawa, 1973.

Bauman Zygmunt, Postmodernity and its discontents, Polity, 1997.

Beijing Declaration and Platform for Action, The Fourth World Conference on Women, Beijing, 1995, https://www.un.org/en/events/pastevents/pdfs/Beijing_Declaration_and_Platform_for_Action.pdf.

Bellier Irene, Wilson Thomas [ed.], *An anthropology of European Union. Building, Imagining and Experiencing the New Europe*, Berg, Oxford, New York, 2000.

Bellier Irene, Wilson Thomas M., "Building, Imagining and Experiencing Europe: Institutions and Identities in the European Union," in: id. [ed.], *The Anthropology of European Union. Building, Imagining and Experiencing the new Europe*, Berg, Oxford, New York, 2000.

Benedict XVI, "Interview of Benedict XVI with the journalists during the flight to Lebanon," *L'Osservatore Romano*, 9-10(346), 14.9.2012.

Benedict XVI, *Encyclical Letter Spe Salvi to the Bishops, Priests and Deacons, Men and Women Religious, and All the Lay Faithful on Christian Hope*, http://www.vatican.va/content/benedict-xvi/en/encyclicals/documents/hf_ben-xvi_enc_20071130_spe-salvi.html

Benedict XVI, *The Listening Heart. Reflections on the Foundations of Law*, Visit to the Bundestag, Reichstag Building, Berlin, 2011, *https://insidethevatican.com/news/the-listening-heart-reflections-on-the-foundations-of-law/*

Benedict XVI, *To the participants in the International Congress on natural moral law*, Clementine Hall, 12.2.2007.

Berg-Schlosser Dirk, Stammen Theo, *Einführung in die Politikwissenschaft*, 7.te Auflage, Verlag C.H. Beck, München, 2003.

Berlin Isaiah, "Political Ideas in the Twentieth Century," in: id., H. Hardy [ed.], *Liberty*, Oxford University Press, 2002.

Berman Paul, *A Tale of Two Utopias: The Political Journey of the Generation of 1968*, W. W. Norton & Company, 1997.

Bernacki Włodzimierz, *Marksizm*, in: B. Szlachta [ed.], *Słownik społeczny*, WAM, Krakow, 2004.

Bertky Sandra Lee, "Foucault, Femininity and the Modernization of Patriarchal Power," in: K. Conboy, N. Medina, S. Stanbury, *Writing on the Body: Female Embodiment and Feminist Theory*, Columbia University Press, 1997.

Bertolis Ottavio De, "Elementi di antropologia giuridica," *Edizioni Scientifiche Italiane*, 2010.

Bielik-Robson Agata, *Kryptoteologie późnej nowoczesności*, Universitas, Krakow, 2008.

Bierstedt Robert, *The Social Order*, McGraw Hill, 1957.

Boas Franz, "The Aims of Anthropological Research," in: *Race, Language and Culture*, University of Chicago Press, 1982.

Boas Franz, *Race and Democratic Society*, Biblo and Tannen Publishers, 1969.

Bobko Aleksander, "Wstęp: Człowiek w filozofii Immanuela Kanta," in: I. Kant, *Antropologia w ujęciu pragmatycznym*, trans. E. Drzazgowska, P. Sosnowska, IFiS PAN, Warszawa, 2005.

Bodnar Adam, *Wprowadzenie*, in: A. Śledzińska-Simon [ed.], *Prawa osób transseksualnych. Rozwiązania modelowe a sytuacja w Polsce*, Wolters Kluwer business, Warszawa, 2010.

Boeckenfoerde Ernst-Wolfgang, "Teoria polityki a teologia polityczna. Uwagi na temat ich wzajemnego stosunku," in: id. *Teologia polityczna*, 3/2005-2006.

Bosek Leszek, "Aborcja a swoboda przepływu usług," in: M. Safjan [ed.], *Prawo wobec medycyny i biotechnologii: Zbiór orzeczeń z komentarzami*, Wolters Kluwer bussines, Warszawa, 2011.

Bosek Leszek, *Aksjologia Unii Europejskiej na przykładzie europejskiego prawa medycznego*, *http://orka.sejm.gov.pl/WydBAS.nsf/0/210C10FB59F8520FC12578E300436679/$file/AKSJOLOGIA%20UNII%20EUROPEJSKIEJ%20-%20L.Bosek.pdf* [27.05.2016].

Bostrom Nick, *Transhumanist Values*, *https://www.nickbostrom.com/ethics/values.html*.

Böttcher Winfrid, Krawczynski Johanna, *Europas Zukunft: Subsidiaritaet*, Shaker Verlag, Aachen, 2000.

Brachowicz Natalia, "Prawa reprodukcyjne w polityce Unii Europejskiej. ParlamentiKomisjaEuropejskawobecaborcji," *Pressje*, 2009.

Brague Remi, *Europe, Christianity and the Modern Age*, lecture (in German) delivered during the International Conference "John Paul II and the Spiritual

Foundations of European Unity" organized by the Konrad Adenauer Foundation and The Centre for the Thought of John Paul II, 11-12.6.2014.

Brague Remi, *The Legitimacy of the Human,* trans. P. Seaton, St. Augustine's Press, Chicago, 2017.

Braudel Fernand, *A History of Civilizations,* Penguin Books, 1995.

Brożek Bartosz, "Pojęcie osoby w dyskursie bioetycznym," in: Z. Liana [ed.], *Prace Komisji Polskiej Akademii Umiejętności 'Fides et Ratio',* PAU, Krakow, 2011.

Bucholc Marta, "Karta Praw Podstawowych – jaki projekt społeczeństwa?," *Civitas,* 12/2010.

Bunikowski Dawid., *Podstawy aksjologiczne Konstytucji dla Europy,* http://www. racjonalista.pl/kk.php/s,4577 [31.03.2011].

Burca Grainne de, "The drafting of the European Union Charter of Fundamental Rights," *European Law Review,* 26.4.2001.

Burgoński Piotr Rev., "Judaizm," in: P. Burgoński, M. Gierycz [ed.], *Polityka i religia. Perspektywa politologiczna,* Elipsa, Warszawa, 2014.

Burgoński Piotr Rev., "Europeizacja polskiej polityki równościowej i antydyskryminacyjnej," *Przegląd Europejski,* vol. 2, 2012.

Burgoński Piotr Rev., Gierycz Michał, "Politologia i religia," in: P. Burgoński, M. Gierycz [ed.], *Polityka i religia. Zarysproblematyki,* Elipsa, Warszawa, 2014.

Butler David i Ranney Austey [ed.], *Referendums around the world: the growing use of direct democracy,* American Enterprise Institute for Public Policy Research, Washington, DC, 1994.

Butler Judith, *Gender Trouble. Feminism and the Subversion of Identity,* Routledge, 1990.

Buttiglione Rocco, "Can Europe be saved?," *Chrześcijaństwo-Świat-Polityka,* no. 17/18, 2014/2015.

Catechism of the Catholic Church, 2nd ed., Libreria Editrice Vaticana, 2012.

Charles Taylor, *The Ethics of Authenticity,* Harvard University Press, 1992.

Chlipała Paweł, *Podejście etnograficzne w gromadzeniu wiedzy o konsumentach,* Zeszyty naukowe Uniwersytetu Szczecińskiego, no. 660.

Chmaj Marek, Marszałek-Kawa Joanna, Sokół Wojciech [ed.], *Encyklopedia Wiedzy Politycznej,* Wyd. Adam Marszałek, Torun, 2006.

Chodubski Andrzej, *Analiza polityczna,* in: W. Sokół, M. Żmigrodzki [ed.], *Encyklopedia politologii,* book I: *Teorie polityki,* Zakamycze, Krakow, 1999.

Chudy Wojciech, "Miejsce prawdy w systemie wartości. Postawa klasyczna a postawa liberalistyczna i ich konsekwencje aksjologiczne," in: *Liberalizm i katolicyzm dzisiaj,* Wydawnictwo DiG, Warszawa, 1994.

Chudy Wojciech, "Prawo naturalne albo zasada przemocy – alternatywa rozłączna metafizyki społecznej," *Civitas,* vol. 6.

Chyrowicz Barbara SSpS, "Eutanazja i spór na argumenty," in: id. [ed.], *Eutanazja. Prawo do życia. Prawo do wolności,* TN KUL, Lublin, 2005.

Cicero, *On the Republic,* trans. C.W. Keyes, Harvard University Press, 1928.

Cichocki Marek A., *Polityczny problem jedności Europy,* PISM, Warszawa, 2012.

Cichocki Marek A., *Porwanie Europy,* OMP, CSM, Warszawa-Krakow, 2004.

Citowicz Rafał, *Prawnokarne aspekty ochrony życia człowieka a prawo do godnej śmierci*, Kodeks, Warszawa, 2006.

Clifford James, *Routes: Travel and Translation in the Late Twentieth Century*, Harvard University Press, Cambridge, MA, 1997.

Clifford Scott, Jerrit Jennifer, "How Words Do the Work of Politics: Moral Foundations Theory and the Debate over Stem Cell Research," *The Journal of Politics*, no. 75, 2013.

Condorcet Antonie Nicolas, *Sketch for a Historical Picture of the Progress of the Human Mind*, J. Johnson, 1795.

Constant Benjamin, *Réflexions sur les constitutions, la distribution des pouvoirs et les garanties dans une monarchie constitutionnelle*, Forgotten Books, 2018.

Conte Amelia, *A Europe od Rights: history of the EU Charter*, European Parliament, Luxembourg, 2012.

Correa Sonia Onufer, Muntarbhorn Vitit, "The Yogyakarta Principles," in: K. Remin [ed.], *The Yogyakarta Principles on the Application of International Human Rights Law in relation to Sexual Orientation and Gender Identity*, Campaign Against Homophobia, Warszawa, 2009.

Cribb Alan, *Values and Comparative Politics. An introduction to the philosophy of political science*, Avebury, Adershot, 1991.

Crowley Niall, *Final Seminar Report. Good Practice Exchange seminar Discrimination on the ground of sexual orientation – how to overcome the barriers to public policy making*, Estonia, 29-30.9.2011, *http://www.humanconsultancy. com/Publications/2011_II_EE_seminar%20report.pdf* [11.07.2016].

Culp-Ressler Tara, *A New Google Extension Will Change Every Mention Of 'Pro-Life' To 'Anti-Choice'*, *http://thinkprogress.org/health/2016/02/20/3751397/ extension-anti-choice/* [13.06.2016].

Czachór Zbigniew, Jaskulski Adam, "Instytucje i instytucjonalizm w analizie integracji i Unii Europejskiej," in: J. Czaputowicz [ed.], *Studia europejskie. Wyzwania interdyscyplinarności*, WDiNP UW, Warszawa, 2014.

Czaputowicz Jacek, "Demokracja a suwerenność w Unii Europejskiej," in: K.A. Wojtaszczyk, M. Mizerska-Wrotkowska, *Polska w procesie integracji europejskiej. Dekada doświadczeń (2004-2014)*, WDiNP UW, Warszawa, 2014.

Czaputowicz Jacek, *Suwerenność*, PISM, Warszawa, 2013.

Czernikiewicz Wiesław, *Czy homoseksualizm można wyleczyć?*, http://www. medonet.pl/zdrowie/zdrowie-dla-kazdego,czy-homoseksualizm-mozna-wyleczyc-,artykul,1643684.html [23.06.2016].

d'Onorio Joël-Benoit, *Le Vatican et la politique européenne*, Paris, 1994.

Davidson Alstair, *The Immutable Law sof Mankind. The Struggle for Universal Human Rights*, Springer, Heidelberg, New York, London, 2012.

Davis Creston, Milbank John, Ziżek Slavoj [ed.], *Theology and the political. The new debate*, Duke University Press, 2005.

Department for International Development, *Safe and unsafe abortion. The UK's policy position on safe and unsafe abortion in developing countries*, London, 2013.

Dijk T.A. van, *The Study of Discourse – an Introduction*, in: id. [ed.], *Discourse Studies*, vol.1, Sage, London, 2007.

Dilthey Wilhelm, *Hermeneutics and the Study of History*, Princeton University Press, 2018.

Dohnal Wojciech, *Antropologia polityczna*, in: M. Drozd-Piasecka, A. Posern-Zieliński [ed.], *Antropologia polityki i polityka w antropologii*, Komitet Nauk Etnologicznych PAN, Warszawa, 2010.

Dohnal Wojciech, Posern-Zieliński Aleksander, "Introduction," in: id. [ed.], *Antropologia i polityka. Szkice z badań nad kulturowymi wymiarami władzy*, KNE PAN, Warszawa, 2011.

Doris Pack, Astrid Lulling, Angelika Niebler, Christa Klaß, Joanna Katarzyna Skrzydlewska, Regina Bastos, Nuno Teixeira, Paulo Rangel on behalf of the PPE Group Marina Yannakoudakis on behalf of the ECR Group, *Motion for a resolution (Rule 157(4) of the Rules of Procedure) replacing non-legislative motion for a resolution*, A7-0426/2013.

Drozdowski Zbigniew, "Antropologia a nauki stosowane. Antropologia polska nadchodzących lat,", *Przegląd Antropologiczny*, vol. 52, no. 1-2, 1986.

Drozd-Piasecka Mirosława, Posern-Zieliński Aleksander [ed.], *Antropologia polityki i polityka w antropologii*, KNE PAN, Warszawa, 2010.

Dubrzyńska Hanna, *Elementy teorii polityki*, University of Gdansk, 1998.

Duchliński Piotr, "Uwagi o stylu klasycznej antropologii filozoficznej," in: P.S. Mazur [ed.], *Spór o osobę w świetle klasycznej koncepcji człowieka. Studia i rozprawy*, Ignatianum, WAM, Krakow, 2012.

Duchliński Piotr, Hołub Grzegorz [ed.], *Oblicza natury ludzkiej. Studia i rozprawy*, Ignatianum, WAM, Krakow, 2010.

Dybowski Maciej, *Prawa fundamentalne w orzecznictwie ETS*, Beck, Warszawa, 2007.

Dylus Aniela, "Chrześcijaństwo," in: P. Burgoński, M. Gierycz [ed.], *Religia i polityka. Zarys problematyki*, Elipsa, Warszawa, 2014.

Dylus Aniela, "Nauka solidarnego rozwoju," in: Paweł Kozacki OP, *Przewodnik po encyklikach*, W drodze, Poznan, 2003.

Dylus Aniela, *Polityka w perspektywie etycznej i religijnej*, UKSW, Warszawa, 2016.

Dynarski Wiktor, "Glosariusz," in: Śledzińska-Simon Anna[ed.], *Prawa osób transseksualnych. Rozwiązania modelowe a sytuacja w Polsce*, Wolters Kluwer buisness, Warszawa, 2009.

Easton David., "An Approach to the Analysis of Political Systems," in: *World Politics*, vol. 9, no. 3, 1957.

Easton David., *The Political System. An Inquiry Into A State Of The Political Science*, H. Wolff, New York, 1959.

Ebeling Gerhard, "Przyczynek do definicji człowieka," in: *Człowiek w nauce współczesnej. Rozmowy w Castel Gandolfo*, Znak, Krakow, 2006.

Eckstein Harry, "Case Study and Theory in Political Science," in: *Regarding Politics. Essays on Political Theory, Stability, and Change*, University of

California Press, 1991, *https://publishing.cdlib.org/ucpressebooks/view? docId=ft0k40037v;brand=ucpress*

Edmund Burke, *Reflections on the Revolution in France*, Seeley, Jackson and Halliday, 1872.

Elo Satu, Kyngas Helvi, *The qualitative content analysis process*, "Journal of Advanced Nursing," vol. 62, no. 1, 2007.

"Embryo," in: *Encyclopaedia Britannica: Micropaedia* vol. 4, Encyclopaedia Britannica, Inc. 1993.

Enelow James, Hinch Melvin, *The Spatial Theory of Voting: An Introduction*, Cambridge University Press, 1984.

Engel Christoph, *The European Charter of Fundamental Rights A Changed Political Opportunity Structure and its Dogmatic Consequences*, Max-Planck-Projektgruppe Recht der Gemeinschaftsgüter, Bonn, 2001.

Engeli Isabelle, Greek-Pedersen Christogger, Larsen Lars Thorup, *Theoretical Perspectives on Morality Issues*, in: id. [ed.], *Morality Politics in Western Europe. Parties, Agendas and Policy Choices*, Palgrave Macmillan, New York, 2012.

Engels Friedrich, *The Origin of the Family, Private Property and the State,* Penguin Classics, 2010.

Engels Friedrich, *The Origin of the Family, Private Property and the State,* https://www.marxists.org/archive/marx/works/1884/origin-family/ch02d.htm.

Esposito Roberto, *Terms of the Political: Community, Immunity, Biopolitics (Commonalities)*,Fordham University Press, 2013.

Fabricio Paul J., *Evolving into Morality Politics: U.S. Catholic Bishops' Statements on U.S. Politics from 1792 to the Present*, in: Christopher Z. Mooney [ed.], *The Public Clash of Private Values. The Politics of Morality Policy*, Chatman House Publishers, New York-London, 2001.

Felmlee Diane, Sweet Elizabeth, Sinclair H. Colleen, "Gender Rules: Same- and Cross-Gender Friendships Norms", *Sex Roles*, April 2012.

"Fetus," in: *Encyclopaedia Britannica: Micropaedia* vol. 4, Encyclopaedia Britannica, Inc. 1993.

Filipowicz Stanisław*, Historia myśli polityczno-prawnej*, Arche, Gdansk, 2001.

Finkielkraut Alain, *L'Humanité perdue*, Seuil, 1996.

Finnis John, "Law, Morality, and Sexual Orientation," *Notre Dame Law Review*, vol. 69, no. 5, 2014.

Florczak Agnieszka, "Ewolucja ochrony praw człowieka w systemie prawa wspólnotowego," in: id. [ed.], *Ochrona Praw Podstawowych w Unii Europejskiej. Wybranezagadnienia*, WAiP, Warszawa, 2009.

Flyvbjerg Bent, "Five Misunderstandings About Case-Study Research," Qualitative Inquiry, vol. 12, no. 2, 2006.

Francis Babete, *Gender bending: let me count the ways, https://mercatornet.com/ gender_bending_let_me_count_the_ways/11552/*

Fredric Jameson, *Postmodernism, or, the Cultural Logic of Late Capitalism*, Duke University Press, 2013.

Friedman Samuel G., "Push Within Faith for Same-Sex Marriage Gets Little Attention", *The New York Times National*, 25.7.2015.

Fromm Erich, *Marx's concept of man*, Marino Publishing, Mansfield Centre, 2011.

Gadacz Tadeusz, *Historia filozofii XX wieku. Nurty*, book 1&2, Znak, Krakow, 2009.

Gawkowska Aneta, *Skandal i ekstaza. Nowy Feminizm na tle koncepcji pojednania Jana Pawła II*, WUW, Warszawa, 2015.

Geertz Clifford, "Thick Description: Toward an Interpretive Theory of Culture," in: M. Kempny, E. Nowicka [ed.], *The Interpretation of Cultures: Selected Essays*, Basic Books, New York, 1973.

Giddens Anthony, *The Consequences of Modernity*, John Wiley & Sons, 2013.

Gielarowski Andrzej, "Natura, jako to, co upragnione. Analiza koncepcji natury ludzkiej u J.J. Rousseau," in: G. Holub, P. Duchliński, *Oblicza natury ludzkiej*, WAM, Krakow, 2010.

Gierycz Michał, "Chrześcijańscy politycy w ponadnarodowych sporach o wartości. Perspektywa europejska," in: A. Solarz, H. Schroeiber [ed.], *Religia w stosunkach międzynarodowych*, WUW, Warszawa, 2012.

Gierycz Michał, "EU's Axiological Credo and Morality Policy tensions," *Studia Philosophiae Christianae,* vol. 3, 2015.

Gierycz Michał, "Kościół, teoria i kryzys polityki," in: J. Grosfeld [ed.], *50 lat później. Posoborowe dylematy współczesnego Kościoła*, IP UKSW, Centrum Myśli Jana Pawła II, Warszawa, 2014.

Gierycz Michał, "O pojmowaniu antropologii politycznej na gruncie politologii," *Roczniki Nauk Społecznych*, vol. 6, no. 42, 2014.

Gierycz Michał, "Religion: A Source of Fundamentalism or A Safeguard Against It?" *Religions* 11, 104, 2020, https://doi.org/10.3390/rel11030104

Gierycz Michał, "Unii Europejskiej (re)definicja małżeństwa i rodziny. Antropologiczne i polityczne znaczenie w kontekście starzenia się Europy," *Annales. Universitatis Mariae Curie-Skłodowska. Sctrio K. Politologia*, vol. 22, no. 2, 2015.

Gierycz Michał, "Unijne spory o wartości podstawowe. Źródła, kluczowe problemy i 'polski głos' w Parlamencie Europejskim," in: P. Burgoński, S. Sowiński [ed.], *Od akcesji do prezydencji. Kościół Katolicki w Polsce i Unia Europejska*, Wyd. Adam Marszałek, Torun, 2011.

Gierycz Michał, "The European Union's axiological credo and morality policy tensions", *Studia Philosophiae Christianae*, No.3, 2015

Gierycz Michał, *Axiology of European Union and the challenges of integration process*, in: W. Gizicki [ed.], *European Union. Present and Future*, KUL, Lublin, 2009.

Gierycz Michał, *Chrześcijaństwo i Unia Europejska. Rola religii w procesie integracji europejskiej*, WAM – IP UKSW, Krakow – Warszawa, 2008.

Gierycz Michał, Mazurkiewicz Piotr Rev., "Europejska antropologia i europejska polityka – obserwacja współczesności," in: Ch. Bohr, Ch. Schmitz [ed.], *Europa i jej antropologia polityczna. Człowiek jako droga historii – o filozofii Karola Wojtyły*, KAS, Warszawa, 2016.

Gierycz Michał, *Rola polskich posłów do Parlamentu Europejskiego VI kadencji w kształtowaniu jego polityki w obszarze aksjologii praw człowieka*, WDiNP UW, Warszawa, 2010.

Gill Seidel, Laurent Vidal, "The implications of 'medical', 'gender in development' and 'culturalist' discourses for HIV/AIDS policy in Africa," in: C. Shore, S. Wright, *Anthropology of Policy. Critical perspectives on governance and power*, Routledge, London-New York, 2005.

Gingrich Andrew, "Alliances and Avoidance: British Interactions with German-speaking anthropologists 1933-1953," in: D. James, E. Plaice, Ch. Toren [ed.], *Culture Wars. Context, Models and Anthropologists' Account*, Berghahn Books, New York-Oxford, 2012.

Giovanni Reale, *A History of Ancient Philosophy I: From the Origins to Socrates*, SUNY Press, 1987.

Giovanni Reale, *Karol Wojtyla un pellegrino dell'assoluto*, Bompiani, 2005.

Gładkowski Krzysztof, "Idealizacja, ideologizacja, indoktrynacja: mit 'ludu' w naukach o polityce, w etnologii oraz masowych ruchach XIX i XX wieku," in: W. Dochnal, A. Posern-Zieliński [ed.], *Antropologia i polityka. Szkice z badań nad kulturowymi wymiarami władzy*, KNE PAN, Warszawa, 2011.

Grabowski Marian [ed.], *O antropologii Jana Pawła II*, WUMK, Torun, 2004.

Graff Agnieszka, *Świat bez kobiet. Płeć w polskim życiu publicznym*, W.A.B., Warszawa, 2008.

Grat Ireneusz Stanisław, *Stanowisko prawnonaturalne Czesława Strzeszewskiego na tle poglądów polskich tomistów*, Temida 2, Bialystok, 2009.

Gray John, *Liberalism*, University of Minnesota Press, 1995.

Gray John, *Liberalisms: Essays in Political Philosophy*, Routlege, 2009.

Gray John, *Postliberalism: Studies in Political Thought*, Routledge, 1993.

Grosfeld Jan, "Żydowski wymiar chrześcijaństwa," in: M. Gierycz, J. Grosfeld [ed.], *Zmagania początku tysiąclecia*, Łośgraf, Warszawa, 2012.

Grosfeld Jan, *Mężczyzna i kobieta*, in: M. Gierycz, J. Grosfeld [ed.], *Zmagania początku tysiąclecia*, Łośgraf, Warszawa, 2012.

Grosse Tomasz Grzegorz, "Trzy oblicza konstruktywizmu w Europie. Rozważania o kryzysie metody integracyjnej," *Chrześcijaństwo-Świat-Polityka*, no. 17/18, 2014/2015.

Grosse Tomasz Grzegorz, *Europa na rozdrożu*, ISP, Warszawa, 2008.

Grzybowski Jacek, *Byt, Tożsamość, Naród. Próba wyjaśnienia formuły 'tożsamość narodowa' w perspektywie metafizyki*, Wyd. Marek Derewiecki, Kety, 2012.

Grzymkowska Maja, *Standardy bioetyczne w prawie europejskim*, Wolter Kluwers, Warszawa, 2009.

Habermas Jürgen, "Religion in the Public Sphere," *European Journal of Philosophy*, vol. 14, no. 1, 2006.

Habermas Jürgen, *The Future of Human Nature*, Polity Press, 2003.

Haeffner Gerd, *The Human Situation: A Philosophical Anthropology*, University of Notre Dame Press, 1989.

Haider-Markel Donald P., "Morality in Congress? Legislative Voting on Gay Issues," in: Ch. Z. Money [ed.], *The Public Clash of Private Values. The Politics of Morality Policy*, Chatman House Publishers, New York-London, 2001.

Hall Peter A., "Policy paradigms, social learning, and the state: the case of economic policymaking in Britain," *Comparative Politics,* vol. 25, no. 3, 1993.

Hallowell John, *The Moral Foundation of Democracy,* Liberty Fund, 2007.

Hambura Stefan, Muszyński Mariusz, "W jakim języku o Bogu", *Rzeczpospolita,* 5.4.2002.

Harrison Beverly Wildung, *Our Right to Choose. Toward a New Ethic of Abortion,* Beacon Press, Boston, 1983.

Hayek Friedrich von, *The Constitution of Liberty,* University of Chicago Press, 2011.

Heichel Stephan, Knill Christoph, Schmitt Sophie, "Public policy meets morality: conceptual and theoretical challenges in the analysis of morality policy change," *Journal of European Public Policy,* vol. 20, no.3, 2013.

Hervada Javier, *Historia de la Ciencia del Derecho Natural,* EUNSA, Pamplona, 1987.

Himmelfarb Gertrude, *One Nation, Two Cultures: A Searching Examination of American Society in the Aftermath of Our Cultural Revolution,* Vintage, 2001.

Hobbes Thomas, *Leviathan, or The Matter, Form and Power of a Commonwealth Ecclesiastical and Civil,* Hackett Publishing Company, 1994.

Höffe Otfried, "Subsidiaritaet als europapolitisches Prinzip," in: Rudolf Hrbek [Hg.], *Die Anwendung des Subsidiaritätsprinzips in der Europäischen Union – Erfahrungen und Perspektiven,* Nomos Verlagsgesselschaft, Baden-Baden, 1995.

Hoffman John, *A Glossary of Political Theory,* Edinburgh University Press, 2008.

Horkheimer Max, Adorno Theodor W., *Dialectic of Enlightenment,* Verso, 1997.

Immanuel Kant, *Lectures on Logic,* Cambridge University Press, 2004.

International Theological Commission, *In Search of a Universal Ethic: A New Look at the Natural Law,* 2009

Jabłoński Mariusz, Jarosz-Żukowska Sylwia, *Prawa człowieka i systemy ich ochrony. Zaryswykładu,* WUWr, Wroclaw, 2010.

Jack David Eller, *Cultural Anthropology: Global Forces, Local Lives,* Routlege, 2016.

Jacquot Sophie, *Transformations in EU Gender Equality. From Emergence to Dismantling,* Palgrave Macmillian, 2015.

Jakubowski Wojciech, *Społeczna natura człowieka,* Elipsa, Warszawa, 1999.

Jakubowski Wojciech, Załęski Piotr, Zamęcki Łukasz, "Aspekty współczesnych badań politologicznych," in: id., *Nauka o polityce. Zarys koncepcji dyscypliny,* Akademia Humanistyczna im. A. Gieysztora in Pułtusk, 2013.

Janicki Mirosław, Władyka Wiesław, "Gabinet grozy," *Polityka,* vol. 20, no. 2858, 16.5.2012.

JánosKis, *Politics as a Moral Problem,* Central European University Press, 2008.

Janssen-Jurreit Marielouise, "Die Zukunft der Reproduktion – Niederlage oder Befreiung der Frau?," in: id. [ed.], *Frauen und Sexualmoral,* Fischer Taschenbuch Verlag, Frankfurt am Main, 1986.

Janyga Wojciech, *Przestępstwo obrazy uczuć religijnych w polskim prawie karnym w świetle współczesnego pojmowania wolności sumienia i wyznania*, Wydawnictwo Sejmowe, Warszawa, 2010.

Janyga Wojciech, "Wolność religijna," in: P. Burgoński, M. Gierycz [ed.], *Religia i polityka. Zarys problematyki*, Elipsa, Warszawa, 2014.

Janyga Wojciech, "Wolność sumienia," in: P. Burgoński, M. Gierycz [ed.], *Polityka i religia*, Elipsa, Warszawa, 2014.

Jasiński Filip, *Karta Praw Podstawowych Unii Europejskiej*, Dom Wydawniczy ABC, Warszawa, 2003.

Jaskiernia Jerzy, *Współczesny system wartości społeczno-kulturowych a aksjologia Karty Praw Podstawowych Unii Europejskiej*, http://www.jaskiernia.eu/index. php?view=article&catid=14%3Adorobek-naukowy&id=40% 3Awspoczesny-system-wartoci-spoeczno-kulturowych-a-aksjologia-karty-praw-podstawowych-unii-europejskiej&option=com_content&Itemid=52 [07.08.2009].

Jeziński Marek, "Polityka," in: M. Chmaj, J. Marszałek-Kawa, W. Sokół [ed.], *Encyklopedia Wiedzy Politycznej*, Wyd. Adam Marszałek, Torun, 2006.

Johann Gottlieb Fichte, *Addresses to the German Nation*, Cambridge University Press, 2009.

John Paul II, *Apostolic Exhortation (Familiaris Consortio) of His Holiness Pope John Paul II to the Episcopate to the Clergy and to the Faithful of the Whole Catholic Church Regarding the Role of the Christian Family in the Modern World*, http://www.vatican.va/content/john-paul-ii/en/apost_exhortations/docu ments/hf_jp-ii_exh_19811122_familiaris-consortio.html

John Paul II, *Encyclical Letter Fides et Ratio of John Paul II to the Bishops of the Catholic Church on the Relationship Between Faith and Reason*, http://www. vatican.va/content/john-paul-ii/en/encyclicals/documents/hf_jp-ii_enc_ 14091998_fides-et-ratio.html

John Paul II, *Evangelium Vitae Encyclical to the Bishops, Priests and Deacons, Men and Women religious, lay Faithful and all People of Good Will on the Value and Inviolability of Human Life*, http://www.vatican.va/content/john-paul-ii/en/ encyclicals/documents/hf_jp-ii_enc_25031995_evangelium-vitae.html

John Paul II, *On the Hundredth Anniversary of Rerum Novarum: Encyclical Letter Centesimus Annus of the Supreme Pontiff*, no. 44, St. Paul Books & Media, 1991-93.

John Paul II, *The Encyclical Letter Redemptor Hominis to His Venerable Brothers in the Episcopate, the Priests, the Religious Families, the Sons and Daughters of the Church and to All Men and Women of Good Will at the Beginning of His Papal Ministry*, http://www.vatican.va/content/john-paul-ii/en/encyclicals/documents/ hf_jp-ii_enc_04031979_redemptor-hominis.html

John Paul II, *The Redemption of the Body and Sacramentality of Marriage*, Libreria Editrice Vaticana, 2005.

John Paul II, *Veritatis splendor*, http://www.vatican.va/content/john-paul-ii/en/ encyclicals/documents/hf_jp-ii_enc_06081993_veritatis-splendor.html

Johnson Janet Buttolph, Reynolds Henry T., Mycoff Jason D., *Political Science Research Methods*, CQ Press, 2015.

Joseph Cardinal Ratzinger, "Europe in the Crisis of Cultures," *Communio: International Catholic Review,* vol. 32, 2005.

Jouvenel Bertrand de, *On Power. The natural History of Its Growth,* Liberty Fund, Indianapolis, 1993.

Juros Helmut Rev., "Problem wartości w preambule Traktatu Konstytucyjnego Unii Europejskiej", in: K. Karbowska, A. Wnukowska, *Ustrojowo-polityczny wymiar Traktatu Konstytucyjnego Unii Europejskiej,* WSH, Pultusk, 2004.

Kaczorowski Paweł, *My i oni. Państwo jako jedność polityczna,* SGH, Warszawa, 1998.

Kamiński Stanisław, *Antropologia filozoficzna a inne działy poznania,* in: id. [ed.], *O Bogu i człowieku,* vol. 1, Warszawa, 1968.

Kamprowski Rafał, *Miejsce i rola kobiety w rodzinie na przestrzeni wieków. Od Antyku po I wojnę światową. Zarys problematyki,* https://repozytorium.amu.edu. pl/bitstream/10593/3835/1/kamprowski.pdf [07.09.2016].

Kant Immanuel, *Anthropology from a Pragmatic Point of View,* trans. R. B. Louden [ed.], Cambridge University Press, 2006.

Kantyka Zbigniew, "Nauki polityczne," in: W. Sokół, M. Żmigrodzki [ed.], *Encyklopedia politologii,* vol.1: *Teorie polityki,* Zakamycze, Krakow, 1999.

Karłowicz Dariusz, "Modernizacji nie da się skserować," *Teologia polityczna,* vol. 5, 2009/2010.

Karłowicz Dariusz, *Arcyparadoks śmierci,* Znak, Krakow, 2000.

Karwat Mirosław, *Sztuka manipulacji politycznej,* Wyd. Adam Marszałek, Torun, 1998.

Kaszewski Michał Rev., *Raj upragnionym przez Boga losem człowieka, http://www. teologia.pl/m_k/zag03-09.htm#5,* 25.3.2014.

Katha Pollitt, *Pro: Reclaiming Abortion Rights,* Picador, 2014.

Kelly J. M., *A Short History of Western Legal Theory,* Clarendon Press, 1992.

Kiereś Henryk, "Kultura klasyczna wobec postmodernizmu," *Człowiek w kulturze,* vol. 11, 1998.

Kirby Paul, "Ending Sexual Violence in Conflict: Preventing Sexual Violence Initiatve (PSVI) and its Critique," *International Affairs,* vol. 91, no. 3, 2015.

Kirpsza Adam, "Zastosowanie konstruktywizmu w wyjaśnianiu przebiegu i efektów procesu legislacyjnego UE," in: J. Czaputowicz [ed.], *Zastosowanie konstruktywizmu w studiach europejskich,* WUW, Warszawa, 2016.

Kłodkowski Piotr, *O pęknięciu wewnątrz cywilizacji. Ideologiczny spór między modernistami a fundamentalistami w islamie i hinduizmie w XX i na początku XXI wieku,* Dialog, Warszawa, 2005.

Knill Christoph, "The study of morality policy: analytical implications from a public policy perspective," *Journal of European Public Policy,* vol. 20, no.3, 2013.

Koba Laura, Zydel Robert, "Dzieje, charakter i treść praw człowieka," in: L. Koba, W. Wacławczyk, *Prawa człowieka. Wybrane zagadnienia i problemy,* Oficyna Wolters Kluwers, Warszawa, 2009.

Kołakowski Leszek, "O duchu rewolucyjnym," in: id., *Czy diabeł może być zbawiony i 27 innych kazań,* Znak, Krakow, 2006.

Kołakowski Leszek, "Samozatrucie otwartego społeczeństwa," in: id., *Cywilizacja na ławie oskarżonych*, Res publica, Warszawa, 1990.

Kołakowski Leszek, *Główne nurty marksizmu. vol. 1, Powstanie*, Zysk i ska, Poznań, n.d.

Kołakowski Leszek, *Kant i zagrożenie cywilizacji*, in: id., *Czy diabeł może być zbawiony i 27 innych kazań*, Znak, Krakow, 2006.

Kołakowski Leszek, Kapłan i błazen. "Rozważania o teologicznym dziedzictwie współczesnego myślenia," in: id., *Nasza wesoła apokalipsa. Wybór najważniejszych esejów*, Znak, Krakow, 2010.

Kołodziej Jacek K., *Wartości polityczne. Rozpoznanie, rozumienie, komunikowanie*, Księgarnia Akademicka, Krakow, 2011.

Kondratiewa-Bryzik Jelena, *Początek prawnej ochrony życia ludzkiego w świetle standardów międzynarodowych*, Wolters Kluwer, Warszawa, 2009.

Konecki Krzysztof, *Studia z metodologii badań jakościowych. Teoria ugruntowana*, PWN, Warszawa, 2000.

Kopczyńska Ewa, *Metoda i pasja. Antropologia kulturowa Franza Boasa z wyborem pism*, Nomos, Krakow, 2012.

Kostyło Hanna, "Rekonstrukcjonizm społeczny: wzajemność oddziaływań kultury i edukacji," *Forum Oświatowe*, vol. 2, no. 47, 2012.

Kováts Eszter, Põim Maari [ed.], *Gender as symbolic glue. The position and role of conservative and far right parties in the anti-gender mobilizations in Europe*, Foundation for European Progressive Studies, Friedrich Ebert Stiftung, Budapest, 2015.

Kowalczyk Stanisław Rev., *Zarys filozofii człowieka*, Wydawnictwo Diecezjalne, Sandomierz, 2002.

Kowalski Krzysztof, *Europa: mity, modele, symbole*, Międzynarodowe Centrum Kultury, Krakow, 2002.

Krąpiec Mieczysław Albert OP, *Człowiek i polityka*, The Society of Saint Thomas Acquinas, Lublin, 2007.

Krauz-Mozer Barbara, *Teorie polityki*, PWN, Warszawa, 2005.

Krawczyk Anna, *Hobbes i Locke. Dwoiste oblicze liberalizmu*, WDiNP UW, Warszawa, 2011.

Kroeber Alfred L., *The Nature of Culture*, University of Chicago Press, 1952.

Król Marcin, *Słownik demokracji*, Res Publica, Warszawa, 1991.

Kropiwnicki Jerzy, "Rodzina i ochrona życia poczętego na sesjach nadzwyczajnych ONZ (Kair plus pięć, Pekin plus pięć, Stambuł plus pięć)," *Annales. Etyka w życiu gospodarczym*, vol. 11, no. 2, 2008.

Krukowski Józef Rev., "Godność człowieka podstawą konstytucyjnego katalogu praw i wolności jednostki," in: *Podstawowe prawa jednostki i ich sądowa ochrona*, L. Wiśniewski [ed.], Wydawnictwo Sejmowe, Warszawa, 1997.

Kuder Taduesz, *Antropologia w zarysie*, WUJK, Kielce, 2011.

Kula Marcin, *Najpierw trzeba się narodzić*, WUW, Warszawa, 2011.

Kuneva Meglena, *Statement made during Situation in the Democratic Republic of Congo and rape as a war crime debate*, Strasbourg 17.01.2008, CRE 17/01/2008 - 11.2.

Kurasiewicz Andrzej, "Zadania i wyzwania polityki rodzinnej w UE," in: Z. Biegański, J. Jackowicz [ed.], *Unia Europejska społeczne i gospodarcze aspekty integracji*, TWP, Warszawa, 2008.

Kuźniar Roman, *Prawa człowieka. Prawo, instytucje, stosunki międzynarodowe*, Scholar, Warszawa, 2004.

Kuźniarz Bartosz, *GoodbyeMr Postmodernizm. Teorie społeczne myślicieli późnej lewicy*, FNP, Torun, 2011.

Kymlicka Will, *Contemporary Political Philosophy*, Oxford University Press, 2002.

Ladaria Louis,, *Introducción a la antropología teológica,* Editorial Verbo Divino, 2010.

Lakoff George, *Moral Politics. How Liberals and Conservatives Think*, University of Chicago Press, 2001.

Lambert Jean, Heubuch Maria, Hautala Heidi et al., *Motion for a Resolution to wind up the debate on the statement by the Vice-President of the Commission/High Representative of the Union for Foreign Affairs and Security Policy pursuant to Rule 123(2) of the Rules of Procedure on the situation in Nigeria (2015/2520 (RSP)) on behalf of the Verts/ALE Group*, B8-0394/2015.

Lasswell H. D., *Psychopathology and Politics*, University of Chicago Press, 1986.

Laufer Hans, Fischer Tomas, *Föderalismus als Strukturprinzip für die Europäische Union*, Gütersloh, 1996.

Ławniczak Kamil, "Processtracing. Śledzenie mechanizmów przyczynowych", in: id. [ed.], *Metody jakościowe i ilościowe w badaniu organizacji i działania Unii Europejskiej*, WDiNP UW, Warszawa, 2013.

Legutko Ryszard, *Sokrates*, Zysk i ska, Poznan, 2013.

Levi-Strauss Claude, *A World on the Wane,* Criteron Books, New York, 1961.

Levi-Strauss Claude, *Structural anthropology*, Basic Books, 1974.

Lewellen Ted C., Political Anthropology: An Introduction, Praeger, 2003.

Lewis Clive Staples, *Mere Christianity*, HarperOne, 2015.

Lewis Clive Staples, *The World's Last Night and Other Essays*, Harcourt Brace Jovanovich, 1973.

Lobkowicz Nicholas, *Das Erbe Europas*, Frankfurt a.M., 1989.

Locke John, The Second Treatise of Government and A Letter Concerning Toleration, Courier Corporation, Mineola, New York, 2012.

Locke John, Two Treatises of Government, Whitmore and Fenn, 1821.

Lockwood David., "Some Remarks on 'The Social System," *The British Journal of Sociology*, vol. 7, no.2, 1956.

Longchamps de Berier Franciszek Rev., "Rechtsautonomie und Moral," *Christentum-Welt-Politik*, no. 3, 2008.

Losinger Anton, "Einfluss auf das Menschen- und Gesellschaftsbild der Katholischen Soziallehre," in: W. J. Mückl [Hg.], *Subsidiarität. Gestaltungsprinzip fuer eine freiheitliche Ordnung in Staat, Wirtschaft und Gesellschaft*, Verlag Ferninand Schöningh, Paderborn-München-Wien-Zürich, 1999.

Louis Dumont, Homo hierarchicus. The Caste System and Its Implications, University of Chicago Press, 1981.

Lowi Theodore J., "New Dimensions in Policy and Politics," in: Moral Controversies in American Politics Cases in Social Regulatory Policy, R. Tatalovich [ed.], B. Daynes, M.E. Sharpe, Armonk, N.Y., 1998.

Luzbetak Louis J., The Church and Cultures, Orbis Books, 1989.

Lyotard Jean-Francois, "Answering the Question: What Is Postmodernism?" in: The Postmodern Condition: A Report on Knowledge, trans. R. Durand', Manchester University Press, 1984.

Machiavelli, *The Prince*, trans. W. K. Marriott, Dutton & Company, 1908.

Machinek Marian MSF Rev., "Embrion ludzki," in: *Wielka Encyklopedia Nauczania Jana Pawła II*, Polskie Wydawnictwo Encyklopedyczne, Radom, 2014.

Madison James, "The Federalist Papers," *Independent Journal,* no. 51, 6.2.1788.

Madison James, "Dalej na ten sam temat z tego samego punktu widzenia oraz wnioski", in: F. Quinn [ed.], *Eseje polityczne Federalistów*, Krakow - Warszawa, 1999.

Majewski Erazm, "Rasa a naród," *Światowid.,* no. 6, 1905, http://www.archeo.uw. edu.pl/swarch/Swiatowit-r1905-t6-s162-168.pdf [4.11.2015].

Malczewski Jacek, "Eutanazja – z dziejów pojęcia", *Diametros*, no. 1, 2004.

Małek Monika, *Liberalizm etyczny Johna Stuarta Milla. Współczesne ujęcia u Johna Graya i Petera Singera*, FNP, Wroclaw, 2010.

Malinowski Andrzej, "Introduction," in: id. [ed.], *Antropologia fizyczna*, PWN, Warszawa – Poznan, 1980.

Maliński Mieczysław Rev., *Katechizm dla niewierzących*, WAM, Krakow, http:// www.opoka.org.pl/biblioteka/K/kat_dla_nie3.html

Maliszewska-Nienartowicz Justyna, "Geneza i rozwój prawa antydyskryminacyjnego Unii Europejskiej," in: A. Zawidzka-Łojek, A. Szczerba-Zawada, *Prawo antydyskryminacyjne Unii Europejskiej*, Instytut Wydawniczy EuroPrawo, Warszawa, 2015.

Manent Pierre, An intellectual history of Liberalism, trans. R. Balinski, Princeton University Press, 1994.

Manners Ian, "Normative Power Europe: A Contradiction In Terms?," Journal of Common Market Studies, vol. 2, no. 40, 2002

Manninen Bertha Alvarez, Pro-life, pro-choice. Shared values in the abortion debate, Vanderbilt University Press, Nashville, 2014.

Marczewska-Rytko Maria, *Religia i polityka w globalizującym się świecie*, UMCS, Lublin, 2010.

Maritain Jacques, Man and the State, CUA Press, 1998.

Markiewicz Barbara A., "Nowożytne prawa obywatela – albo co można było kupić za 50 franków złotem, czyli 'markę srebra' (marc d'argent)", *Civitas*, vol. 6, 2002.

Marsh David., Furlong Paul, "A Skin Not a Sweater: Ontology and Epistemology in Political Science," in: D. Marsh, G. Stoker [ed.], Theory and Methods in Political Science, Pallgrave McMillan, 2002.

Marx Karl, Engels Friedrich, The Communist Manifesto, Wiley-Blackwell, 1995.

Marx Karl, *Theses on Feuerbach,* trans. C. Smith, Marxists Internet Archive, 2002.

Maśnicki Jędrzej, "Godnośćczłowieka w świetleorzeczenia Oliver Brüstleprzeciwko Greenpeace eV (C-34/10)", *Zeszyty Prawnicze*, no. 13/4.

Matteo Cattaneo, *No al rapporto Estrela zdobyłablisko 50 000 poparcia*.http://www.citizengo.org/it/1224-no-al-rapporto-estrela

Max Scheler, The Human Place in the Cosmos, Northwestern University Press, 2009.

Mazur Piotr Stanisław, "Spór o substancjalną koncepcję osoby," in: id. [ed.], *Spór o osobę w świetle klasycznej koncepcji człowieka. Studia i rozprawy*, Ignatianum, WAM, Krakow, 2012.

Mazur Renata, "Karta Praw Podstawowych UE," in: A. Florczak [ed.], *Ochrona Praw Podstawowych w Unii Europejskiej*, WAiP, Warszawa, 2009.

Mazurkiewicz Piotr Rev., "Chrześcijańskie korzenie Europy," in: M. Koźmiński [ed.], *Cywilizacja europejska. Wykłady i eseje*, Scholar, Collegium Civitas Press, Warszawa, 2004.

Mazurkiewicz Piotr Rev., "Grzech," in: B. Szlachta [ed.], *Słownik społeczny*, WAM, Krakow, 2004.

Mazurkiewicz Piotr Rev., "Odpowiedzialność uczonego w ponowoczesnym świecie," in: P. Mazurkiewicz, K. Wielecki [ed.], *Inny człowiek w innym społeczeństwie? Europejskie dyskursy*, Centrum Europejskie, Warszawa, 2008.

Mazurkiewicz Piotr Rev., "Polityka jako roztropna troska o dobro wspólne: koncepcja polityki w katolickiej nauce społecznej," in: W. Wesołowski [ed.], *Koncepcje polityki*, Scholar, Warszawa, 2009.

Mazurkiewicz Piotr Rev., "Wokół Karty Praw Podstawowych UE," in: M. Gierycz, J. Grosfeld [ed.], *Zmagania początku tysiąclecia*, Losgraf, Warszawa, 2012.

Mazurkiewicz Piotr Rev., "Wspólne wartości w Traktacie ustanawiających Konstytucję dla Europy," in: P. Mazurkiewicz, S. Sowiński [ed.], *Religia-Tożsamość-Europa*, Ossolineum, Wroclaw, 2005.

Mazurkiewicz Piotr Rev., *Europeizacja Europy. Tożsamość kulturowe Europy w kontekście procesów integracji*, IP UKSW, Warszawa, 2001.

Mazurkiewicz Piotr Rev., *Ideologia gender jako wyzwanie dla chrześcijańskiej antropologii*, http://tydzienwychowania.pl/wp-content/uploads/2015/08/TW-ks-Mazurkiewicz-gender.pdf [27.06.2016].

Mazurkiewicz Piotr Rev., *Między homo- a heterofobią*, author's archive, Warszawa, 2008.

Mazurkiewicz Piotr Rev., "Niepolityczna polityczność Kościoła," *Chrześcijaństwo-Świat-Polityka*, vol. 13, no. 1, 2012.

McLean Iain, McMillan Alistair [ed.], *The Concise Oxford Dictionary of Politics*, Oxford University Press, 2003.

Meier Kenneth J., "Drug, Sex and Rock and Roll The theory of Morality Politics," Policy Studies Journal, vol. 27, no. 4,1999. Reprinted, in: Ch. Z. Mooney, The Public Clash of Private Values. The Politics of Morality Policy, Chatman House Publishers, New York-London, 2001.

Michael Freeman, *Human Rights: An Interdisciplinary Approach,* Polity, 2011.

Michel Haar, "Nietzsche and Metaphysical Language," in: D. Allison [ed.], *The New Nietzsche: Contemporary Styles of Interpretation*, Delta, New York 1997, as quoted in: J. Butler, *Gender Trouble*...

Middelaar Luuk van, *The Passage to Europe: How a Continent Became a Union*, Yale University Press, 2013.

Mik Cezary, *Europejskie Prawo Wspólnotowe. Zagadnienia teorii i praktyki*, vol.1., Warszawa, 2000.

Mik Cezary, Gałka Katarzyna, *Prawa podstawowe w prawie praktyce Unii Europejskiej*, Dom Organizatora, Torun, 2009.

Milczarek Dariusz, "Rola międzynarodowa Unii Europejskiej jako „mocarstwa niewojskowego," *Studia Europejskie*, vol. 1, 2003.

Mill John Stuart, *On Liberty*, Fields, Osgood & Company, 1869.

Mill John Stuart, Utilitarianism, Batoche Books, Kitchener, 2001.

Millon-Delsol Chantal, *Éloge de la singularité, essai sur la modernité tardive*, La Table Ronde, 2007.

Millon-Delsol Chantal, *Qu'est-ce que l'homme? Cours familier d'anthropologie*, CERF edition, 2008.

Minogue Kenneth, The liberal mind, Liberty Fund, Indianapolis, 2003.

Mock Steven E.,. Eibach Richard P, "Stability and Change in Sexual Orientation Identity Over a 10-Year Period in Adulthood," Archives of Sexual Behaviour,, vol. 41, no. 3, 2012.

Money Christopher Z., "The Public Clash of Private Values," in: id. [ed.]. The Public Clash of Private Values. The Politics of Morality Policy, Chatman House Publishers, New York-London, 2001.

Morawski Lech, *Co może dać nauce prawa postmodernizm?*, Dom Organizatora, Torun, 2001.

Mozgoł Ryszard, *Kobieta, małżeństwo i rodzina w starożytnym Rzymie*, http://www. rodzinakatolicka.pl/index.php/kompendium/37-kompendium/40970-kobieta-maestwo-i-rodzina-w-staroytnym-rzymie [2016.09.07].

Mucciarioni Gary, "Are Debates about 'Morality Policy' Really about Morality? Framing Opposition to Gay and Lesbian Rights," The Policy Studies Journal, vol. 39, no. 2, 2011.

Muciek Elżbieta, "Antropologia polityczna – między etnologią a politologią," *Roczniki Nauk Społecznych*, vol. 6, no. 42, 2014.

Naruszewicz Marcin, Muraszko Piotr, "Pojęcie i status embrionu ludzkiego w świetle wyroku Trybunału Sprawiedliwości Unii Europejskiej - Oliver Brulstle przeciwko GreenpeaceeV," *Polski Rocznik Praw Człowieka i Prawa Humanitarnego*, vol. 3, 2012.

Nietzsche Friedrich, *Joyful Wisdom,* Macmillan, 1911.

Nietzsche Friedrich, On the Genealogy of Morality, Independently published, 2017.

Nogal Agnieszka Maria, *Ponad prawem narodowym. Konstytucyjne idee Europy*, ISP PAN, Warszawa, 2009.

Nowicka Ewa, *Świat człowieka – świat kultury,* New edition, PWN, Warszawa, 2006.

Nowicka Wanda, Solik Aleksandra, *Międzynarodowe standardy zdrowia i praw reprodukcyjnych oraz seksualnych a ich realizacja w Polsce*, Sekretariat Pełnomocnika Rządu ds. Równego Statusu Kobiet i Mężczyzn, Warszawa, 2003.

Nowicki Marek, *Wokół Konwencji Europejskiej. Komentarz do Europejskiej Konwencji Praw Człowieka*, vol. 4. updated, Wolters Kluwer business, Warszawa, 2009.

Nugent Neill, The Government and Politics of the European Union, Palgrave, London, 2017.

Oaksechott Michael, *Rationalism in Politics and Other Essays,* Basic Books, 1962.

Ordo Iuris, *Analiza Dokumentu Komisji Europejskiej "List of actions by the Commission to advance LGBTI equality" w kontekście jego zgodności z polskim porządkiem prawnym,* bookIV, http://www.ordoiuris.pl/analiza-dokumentu-komisji-europejskiej-list-of-actions-by-the-commission-to-advance-lgbti-equality%2D%2Dw-kontekscie-jego-zgodnosci-z-polskim-porzadkiem-prawnym,3786,analiza-prawna.html [03.08.2016].

Ordo Iuris, Uwagi do dokumentu Agencji Praw Podstawowych Unii Europejskiej "Protection against discrimination on grounds of sexual orientation, gender identity and sex characteristics in the EU. Comparative legal analysis," *http://www.ordoiuris.pl/uwagi-do-dokumentu-agencji-praw-podstawowych-unii-europejskiej--protection-against-discrimination-on-grounds-of-sexual-orientation--gender-identity-and-sex-characteristics-in-the-eu--comparative-legal-analysis-,3760,analiza-prawna.html* [03.08.2016].

Osajda Konrad, "Orzecznictwo Europejskiego Trybunału Sprawiedliwości dotyczące transseksualizmu," in: A. Śledzińska – Simon [ed.], *Prawa osób transseksualnych. Rozwiązania modelowe a sytuacja w Polsce*, Wolters Kluwer business, Warszawa, 2010.

Osiatyński Wiktor, *Prawa człowieka i ich granice,* Znak, Krakow, 2011.

Paczkowska – Łagowska Elżbieta, *O historyczności człowieka*, Słowo/obraz terytoria, Gdansk, 2008.

Paczkowska-Łagowska Elżbieta, "Wstęp: Natura ludzka, historia, polityka w antropologii HelmuthaPlessnera," in: H. Plessner, *Władza a natura ludzka. Esej o antropologii światopoglądu historycznego*, trans. E. Paczkowska-Łagowska, PWN, Warszawa, 1994.

Paczkowska-Łagowska Elżbieta, *Logos życia. Filozofia hermeneutyczna w kręgu Wilhelma Diltheya*, Słowo/obraz Terytoria, Gdansk, 2000.

Paine Thomas, Rights of Man, *http://www.let.rug.nl/usa/documents/1786-1800/thomas-paine-the-rights-of-man/text.php* [15.09.2016].

Pańkow Irena, Pańkow Julian, "Polityka jako sztuka skutecznego rządzenia: Niccolo Machiavelli," in: W. Wesołowski [ed.], *Koncepcje polityki*, Scholar, Warszawa, 2009.

Peeters Marguerite A., *The Globalization of the Western Cultural Revolution: key concepts, operational mechanisms,* Institute for Intercultural Dialogue Dynamics, 2012.

Pera Marcello, "Introduction: A proposal That Should Be Accepted," in: J. Ratzinger, *Europe in the Crisis of Cultures,* Ignatius Press, San Francisco, 2006.

Picker Eduard, *Menschenwürde und Menschenleben. Das Auseinanderdriften zweier fundamentaler Werte als Ausdruck der wachsenden Relativierung des Menschen,* Klett-Cotta, 2002.

Piechowiak Marek, "Aksjologiczne podstawy Karty Praw Podstawowych," *Studia Prawnicze,* vol. 1, no. 155, 2003.

Piechowiak Marek, "Karta Praw Podstawowych – wróg czy sprzymierzeniec tradycyjnych wartości?," *Chrześcijaństwo – Świat – Polityka,* vol. 3, no. 7, 2008.

Piechowiak Marek, "Karta Praw Podstawowych UE a tradycyjne wartości," in: M. Gierycz, J. Grosfeld [ed.], *Zmagania początku tysiąclecia,* Losgraf, Warszawa, 2012.

Piechowiak Marek, "Klasyczna koncepcja osoby jako podstawa pojmowania praw człowieka. Wokół św. Tomasza z Akwinu i Immanuela Kanta propozycji ugruntowania godności osoby," in: P. Dardziński, F. Longchamp de Berier, K. Szczucki [ed.], *Prawo naturalne – natura prawa,* C.H. Beck, Warszawa, 2011.

Piechowiak Marek, *Filozofia praw człowieka,* KUL, Lublin, 1999.

Pietila Hilkka, Vickers Jeanne, "Making Women Matter. The Role of the United Nations," Zed Books, London 1990, in: E. R. Amy, Sexual Politics and European Union: The New Feminist Challenge, New York, 1996.

Piluś Henryk, *Antropologia filozoficzna neotomizmu,* Wizja, Warszawa, 2010.

Plato, The Laws, trans. B. Jowett, Pantianos Classics, 2016.

Plato, *The Republic,* trans. B. Jowett, Neeland Media, 2016.

Plato, The Statesman, trans. E. Brann, P. Kalkavage, E. Salem, Focus, 2012.

Plessner Helmuth Political Anthropology, trans. N. F. Schott, Northwestern University Press, Evanston, Illinois, 2018.

Plessner Helmuth, "Zadanie antropologii filozoficznej," trans. E. Paczkowska – Łagowska, in: S. Czerniak, J. Rolewski [ed.], *Studia z filozofii niemieckiej, Antropologia filozoficzna,* vol.4, UMK, Torun, 2004.

Pogodzińska Patrycja, "Tożsamość płciowa w prawie międzynarodowym. Wybrane zagadnienia," in: A. Śledzińska-Simon [ed.], *Prawa osób transseksualnych.* Rozwiązaniamodelowe a sytuacja w Polsce, Wolters Kluwer Polska, 2010.

Pontifical Council for Justice and Peace, Compendium of the Social Doctrine of the Church, http://www.vatican.va/roman_curia/pontifical_councils/justpeace/docu ments/rc_pc_justpeace_doc_20060526_compendio-dott-soc_en.html

Popławska Anna, "Podejście antropologiczne a metody historyczne i socjologiczne na terenie nauk politycznych," in: B. Szklarski [ed.], *Mity, symbole i rytuały we współczesnej polityce,* Scholar, Warszawa, 2008.

Przebinda Grzegorz, *Od Czaadajewa do Bierdiajewa. Spór o Boga i człowieka w myśli rosyjskiej (1832-1922),* Znak, Krakow, 1998.

Przybylski Henryk, *Politologia. Zarys problematyki,* 2[nd]ext. ed., Wydawnictwo Naukowe Slask, Katowice-Warszawa, 2004.

Pudło Anna, "Niedyskryminacja osób transseksualnych w świetle prawa europejskiego," *Roczniki Administracji i Prawa*, year XIV.

Puppnick Gregor, "Abortion and the European Convention on Human Rights," Irish Journal of Legal Studies, vol. 3, no. 2, 2012.

Putnam Tong Rosmarie, *Feminist Thought: A Comprehensive Introduction,* Routledge, 1989.

Rapley Tim, *Analiza konwersacji, dyskursu i dokumentów*, trans. A. Gąsior-Niemiec, PWN, Warszawa, 2010.

Rapoport Anatol, "Some System Approaches to Political Theory," in: David Easton [ed.], Varieties of Political Theory, Prentice-Hall, Englewood Cliffs, 1966.

Ratzinger Joseph, Cardinal, A Turning Point for Europe?: The Church in the Modern World: Assessment and Forecast, Ignatius Press, 1994.

Ratzinger Joseph, Cardinal, Christianity and the Crisis of Cultures, Ignatius Press, 2006.

Ratzinger Joseph, Cardinal, Europe Today and Tomorrow: Addressing the Fundamental Issues, Ignatius Press, 2007.

Rau Zbigniew, "Wstęp," in: J. Locke, *Dwa traktaty o rządzie*, trans. Z. Rau, PWN, Warszawa, 1992.

Rau Zbigniew, *Liberalizm. Zarys myśli politycznej XIX i XX wieku*, Aletheia, Warszawa, 2000.

Rawl John, *A Theory of Justice*, Belknap Press, Harvard University Press, 2005.

Raz Joseph, The Morality of Freedom, Clarendon Press, Oxford, 1988.

Reding Viviane, The Commission's actions are making LGBT rights a reality, Speech at 1st International Day Against Homophobia and Transphobia (IDAHO) Forum, The Hague, 17.5.2013.

Regan Richard J., "Preface," in: Aquinas, Commentary on Aristotle's Politics, trans. R. J. Regan, Hackett Publishing Company, Indianapolis, Cambridge, 2007.

Reilly Robert R., Making Gay Okay. How Rationalizing Homosexual Behavior is Changing Everything, Ignatius Press, San Francisco, 2014.

Rembierz Marek, "Tropy transcendencji… Współczesne myślenie religijne wobec pluralizmu światopoglądowego i relacji międzykulturowych," *Świat i Słowo,* vol. 2, no. 23, 2014.

Remin Katarzyna [ed.], The Yogyakarta Principles on the Application of International Human Rights Law in relation to Sexual Orientation and Gender Identity, Campaign Against Homophobia, Warszawa, 2009.

Richard Dawkins, *The God Delusion,* Mariner Books, 2008.

Richard Rorty, Objectivity, Relativism, and Truth, Cambridge University Press, 1991.

Rompuy Herman Van, Statement by President Herman Van Rompuy on the International Day Against Homophobia, Brussels, 6.5.2010, PCE 88/10.

Romuald Piekarski, *Makiawelizm, patologia ducha, sacrum i polityka. Eseje z filozofii politycznej*, Spoldzielczy Instytut Naukowy, Sopot, 2016.

Rousseau Jean-Jacques, *Discourse on Inequality*, Penguin Classics, 1985.

Rousseau Jean-Jacques, *Emile: or On Education,* NuVision Publications, 2007.

Rousseau Jean-Jacques, The Social Contract, CreateSpace Independent Publishing Platform, 2014.

Roztworowski Piotr OSB Fr.,W szkolemodlitwy, 5th ed., Wydawnictwo Benedyktynów, Tyniec, 2011.

Ruszkowski Janusz, "Europeizacja *ad personam*," in: J. Czaputowicz [ed.], *Zastosowanie konstruktywizmu w studiach europejskich*, WUW, Warszawa, 2016.

Ruszkowski Janusz, *Wstęp do studiów europejskich*, PWN, Warszawa, 2007.

Ruth Benedict, Patterns of Culture, Houghton Mifflin Company, 2005.

Ryszka Franciszek, *Nauka o polityce. Rozważania metodologiczne*, PWN, Warszawa, 1984.

Safjan Marek [ed.], *Prawo wobec medycyny i biotechnologii: Zbiór orzeczeń z komentarzami*, Wolters Kluwer bussines, Warszawa, 2011.

Safjan Marek, "Prawo, wartości i demokracja," in: M. Gierycz, J. Grosfeld [ed.], *Zmagania początku tysiąclecia*, Losgraf, Warszawa, 2012.

Safjan Marek, "Recht, Werte, Demokratie", *Christentum-Welt-Politik*, vol. 3, 2008.

Salij Jacek OP, *Eseje tomistyczne*, W Drodze, Poznan, 1995.

Santer Jacques, "Spór cywilizacyjny Europy," in: *Cywilizacyjne zmagania Europy*, Wokol nas, Gliwice, 2007.

Sapir Edward, "The Status of Linguistics as a Science," in: Selected Writings of Edward Sapir, D.G. Mandelbaum [ed.], University of California Press, 1949.

Schafft Gretchen Engle, From Racism to Genocide: Anthropology in the Third Reich, University of Illinois Press, 2007.

Schafft Gretchen Engle, Zeidler G., "Antropologia Trzeciej Rzeszy," *Alma Mater. Miesięcznik Uniwersytetu Jagiellońskiego,* vol. 47, 2003. *http://www3.uj.edu.pl/ alma/alma/47/01/05.html* [13.09.2011].

Schecter David L., "Legislating morality outside of the legislature: Direct democracy, voter participation, and morality politics," The Social Science Journal, vol. 46, 2009.

Schmitt Carl, *Political Theology*, University of Chicago Press, 2006.

Schmitt Carl, *The Concept of the Political*, trans. G. Schwabb, Expanded edition, The University of Chicago Press, 2007.

Schoen Johanna, Abortion after Roe: Abortion after Legalization, University of North Carolina Press, North Carolina, 2015.

Schuman Robert, *For Europe,* Les Éditions Nagel, Geneva, 2010.

Schwaabe Christian, *Politische Theorie 1. Von Platon bis Locke*, 2., durchgesehende Auflage, Wilhelm Fink, Paderborn, 2010.

Scruton Roger, Fools, Frauds and Firebrands: Thinkers of the New Left, Longman Group, 1985.

Shore Cris, Wright Susan, "Policy. A new field of anthropology," in: Anthropology of Policy. Critical perspectives on governance and power, Routledge, London-New York, 2005.

Siewierska-Chmaj Anna, *Język polskiej polityki. Politologiczno-semantyczna analiza expose premierów Polski w latach 1919-2004*, Wyższa Szkoła Informatyki i Zarządzania, Rzeszow, 2005.

Silverman David., Interpreting Qualitative Research, SAGE Publications, 2019.

Silverman David., Qualitative Research, Sage Publications Ltd, 2016.

Singer Peter, Ethics, Oxford University Press, 1994.

Singer Peter, *Practical Ethics*, Cambridge University Press, New York, 2011.

Skarżyński Ryszard, *Od chaosu do ładu. Carl Schmitt i problem tego, co polityczne*, ISP PAN, Warszawa, 1992.

Skolimowska Anna [ed.], *Normatywna potęga Unii Europejskiej w obliczu umiędzynarodowionych konfliktów wewnętrznych*, Elipsa, Warszawa, 2015.

Skorek Agata, "Zdolność patentowa wynalazków biotechnologicznych a godność ludzka w regulacji Wspólnoty Europejskiej," *Studia Europejskie*, vol. 4, 2008.

Skorowski Henryk SDB, "Sumienie," in: B. Szlachta [ed.], *Słownik społeczny*, WAM, Krakow, 2006.

Skrzek Karolina, *Objawy homofobii*, http://www.psychiczne.objawy.net/Objawy +Homofobii [23.06.2016].

Skurowski Piotr, "Wprowadzenie," in: G. Himmelfarb, *Jeden naród, dwie kultury*, WAiP, Warszawa, 2007.

Ślebzak Krzysztof, "Antydyskryminacyjne prawo Unii Europejskiej w dziedzinie zatrudnienia w orzecznictwie TSUE — zakres i podstawowe pojęcia," *Praca i Zabezpieczenie Społeczne*, vol. 9, 2013.

Śledzińska-Simon Anna, "Prawa osób transseksualnych w raportach Agencji Praw Podstawowych Unii Europejskiej," in: id. [ed.], *Prawa osób transseksualnych. Rozwiązania modelowe a sytuacja w Polsce*, Wolters Kluwer business, Warszawa, 2010.

Śledzińska-Simon Anna, "Zasada równości i zasada niedyskryminacji w prawie Unii Europejskiej," *Studia BAS*, vol. 2, no. 26, 2011.

Śmiszek Krzysztof, "Powolny proces dostosowywania polskiego systemu polityki antydyskryminacyjnej do standardów unijnych," *Problemy Polityki Społecznej*, vol. 15, 2011.

Sobczak Jacek, "Orientacja seksualna jako prawo człowieka", *Studia Prawnicze*, 2009.

Sobkowiak Leszek, "Polityka," in: A. Antoszewski, R. Herbut, *Leksykon politologii*, Atla2, Wroclaw, 1998.

Sobolewski Marek, "Historyczne ujęcie zjawisk politycznych," in: K. Opałek [ed.], *Metodologiczne i teoretyczne problemy nauk politycznych*, PWN, Warszawa, 1975.

Sowell Thomas, *A Conflict of Visions. Ideological Origins of Political Struggles*, rev. edition, Basic Books, 2007.

Sowiński Sławomir, "Liberalizm. Przed kryzysem, po kryzysie," in: K. Wielecki, S. Sowiński [ed.], *Co po postindustralizmie?*, Centrum Europejskie UW, Warszawa, 2013.

Sowiński Sławomir, "Religia i polityka w tradycji liberalnej," *Studia Bobolanum*, vol. 1, 2013.

Sozański Jarosław, *Prawa człowieka w systemach prawnych Wspólnot i Unii Europejskiej*, PWP, Warszawa-Poznan, 2008.

Spaeamann Robert, *Grenzen. Zur ethischen Dimension des Handelns,* Klett-Cotta, 2001.

Spaemann Robert, *Rousseau – człowiek czy obywatel. Dylemat nowożytności,* Oficyna Naukowa, Warszawa, 2011.

Śpiewak Paweł, "Voegelina poszukiwanie Boga," in: E. Voegelin, *Od Oświecenia do Rewolucji,* WUW, Warszawa, 2011.

Staniszkis Jadwiga, *O władzy i bezsilności,* Wydawnictwo Literackie, Krakow, 2006.

Stawrowski Zbigniew, "Aksjologia i duch Konstytucji III Rzeczypospolitej," *Nowa Konfederacja,* vol. 37, 2014, http://www.nowakonfederacja.pl/stawrowski-aksjologia-i-duch-konstytucji-iii-rzeczypospolitej/ [12.09.2014].

Stawrowski Zbigniew, *Prawo naturalne a ład polityczny,* Instytut Myśli Józefa Tischnera, ISP PAN, Krakow-Warszawa, 2006.

Stawrowski Zbigniew, *Wokół idei wspólnoty,* OMP, Krakow, 2012.

Steiner Juerg, *Conscience in Politics: An Empirical Investigation of Swiss Decision Cases,* Routledge, 1996.

Stoch Magdalena, "Reprodukcja i reprezentacja – analiza związków w obrębie dyskursu feministycznego," *Annales Universitatis Paedagogicae Cracoviensis. Studia de Cultura,* vol. 7, 2015.

Stocking George W., *The Shaping of American Anthropology, 1883-1911: A Franz Boas Reader,* University of Chicago Press, New York, 1989.

Strauss Leo, Natural Right and History, University of Chicago Press, 1965.

Studlar Donley T., "What Constitutes Morality Policy? Cross-National Analysis," in: Ch. Z. Mooney [ed.], *The Public Clash of Private Values. The Politics of Morality Policy,* Chatman House Publishers, New York-London, 2001.

Studlar Donley T., Cagossi Alessandro, Duval Robert D., "Is morality policy different? Institutional explanations for postwar Western Europe," Journal of European Public Policy, vol. 20, no. 3.

Sulkowski Mariusz, Żołędowski Cezary, "Europejskie kłopoty z wielokulturowością," in: W. Anioł, M. Duszczyk, P. W. Zawadzki, *Europa socjalna. Iluzjaczyrzeczywistość?,* IPS UW, Warszawa, 2011.

Sussman Robert Wald, *The Myth of Race: The Troubling Persistence of an Unscientific Idea,* Harvard University Press, Cambridge, Massachusetts, London, 2014.

Świeżawski Stefan, *Święty Tomasz na nowo odczytany,* W drodze, Poznan, 2002.

Sykuna Sebastian, "Powszechna Deklaracja Praw Człowieka," in: M. Balcerzak, S. Sykuna [ed.], *Leksykon ochrony praw człowieka,* C.H. Beck, Warszawa, 2010.

Synowiec Aleksandra, "W stronę analizy tekstu – wprowadzenie do teorii dyskursu," *Zeszyty Naukowe Politechniki Śląskiej,* vol. 65, 2013.

Sytnik-Czetwertyński Janusz, "Pojęcie monady w koncepcjach Gottfrieda Wilhelma Leibniza i Immanuela Kanta," *Diametros,* vol. 15, 2008.

Szacki Jerzy, *Historia myśli socjologicznej.,* newedition, PWN, Warszawa, 2002.

Szahaj Andrzej, "Postmodernizm," in: B. Szlachta [ed.], *Słownik społeczny,* WAM, Krakow, 2006.

Szczeniowski Jerzy, *Metaantropologia filozoficzna. Zarys antropologii krytycznej,* Oficyna Wydawnicza Politechniki Warszawskiej, Warszawa, 1997.

Szczuka Kazimiera, *Milczenie owieczek*, WAB, Warszawa, 2004.

Szkołut Tadeusz, "Słowo wstępne: Spór o naturę ludzką i jego konsekwencje aksjologiczne," in: id. [ed.], *Antropologia filozoficzna i aksjologiczne problemy współczesności*, UMCS, Lublin, 1997.

Szlachta Bogdan, "Individualism" in: id., [ed.], *Słownik społeczny*, WAM, Krakow, 2006.

Szlachta Bogdan, "Katolicyzm – liberalizm: obszary konfliktu i dialogu," in: id., *Liberalizm i katolicyzm dzisiaj*, Wydawnictwo DiG, Warszawa, 1994.

Szlachta Bogdan, *Wokół katolickiej myśli politycznej*, WAM, Krakow, 2008.

Szpotański Janusz, *Towarzysz Szmaciak czyli wszystko dobre, co się dobrze kończy*, literat.ug.edu.pl/szpot/szmaciak.htm

Sztaba Mariusz Rev., *Przykładowe metody użyteczne w pisaniu pracy teoretycznej*, http://pracownik.kul.pl/files/12843/public/Metody_uzyteczne_w_pisaniu_prac_teoretycznych_z_pedagogiki.doc. [31.03.2016].

Sztompka Piotr, "Analiza systemowa w naukach politycznych. Próba rekonstrukcji," in: K. Opałek [ed.], *Metodologiczne i teoretyczne problemy nauk politycznych*, PWN, Warszawa, 1975.

Sztompka Piotr, *Socjologia. Analiza społeczeństwa*, Znak, Krakow, 2002.

Szyjewski Andrzej, "Miara, liczba i waga – Andrzeja Wiercińskiego droga do poznania," in: A. Wierciński, *Magia i religia. Szkice z antropologii religii*, Nomos, Krakow, 2010.

Szymaniak Adam, "Podstawowe prawa jednostki i mechanizmy ich ochrony," in: L. Koba, W. Wacławczyk, *Prawa człowieka. Wybrane zagadnienia i problemy*, Wolters Kluwer business, Warszawa, 2009.

Szymański Adam, "Systemowe podejście w badaniach europejskich," in: W. Jakubowski, K. A. Wojtaszczyk, *Studia europejskie. Zagadnienia metodologiczne*, WAiP, Warszawa, 2010.

Talmon Jacob L., *The Origins of Totalitarian Democracy*, Butler & Tanner Ltd., London, 1919.

Taylor Charles, "Cross-purposes: The Liberal-Communitarian Debate," in: Philosophical Arguments, Harvard University Press, 1995.

Taylor Edward B., *Primitive culture: researches into the development of mythology, philosophy, religion, language, art and custom*, John Murray, London, 1920.

Thomas Carlyle, *The Selected Works of Thomas Carlyle*, F. Randolph Ludovico [ed.], The Bibliotheca Cakravarti Foundation, 2014.

Timmermans Arco and Breeman Gerard, "Morality Issues in the Netherlands: Coalition Politics dunder Pressure," in: I. Engeli, Ch. Greek-Pedersen, *Morality Politics in Western Europe. Parties, Agendas and Policy Choices*, Palgrave Macmillan, New York, 2012.

Tischner Józef Rev., "Etyka wartości i nadziei. Wobec wartości," in: J. Tischner, J.A. Kłoczowski OP, *Wobec wartości,* W drodze, Poznan, 2001.

Tokarczuk Olga, "Kobieta nie istnieje," in: J. Butler, *Uwikłani w płeć. Feminizm i polityka tożsamości*, trans. K. Krasucka, Krytyki politycznej, Warszawa, 2008.

Tokarczyk Roman, *Filozofia prawa*, UMCS, Lublin, 2005.

Tokarska-Bakir Joanna [ed.], *Cóż po antropologii?*, Collegium Civitas, Warszawa, 2006.

Tönnies Ferdinand, *Community and Civil Society*, Cambridge University Press, 2001.

Turek Justyna, "Dobro wspólne w myśli politycznej Johna Locke'a," *Annales. Etyka w życiu gospodarczym*, vol. 1, no. 8, 2005.

Tyszka Zbigniew, "Struktura i funkcja rodziny oraz świadomość rodzinna," in: id., A. Wachowiak, *Podstawowe pojęcia i zagadnienia socjologii rodziny*, Poznan, 1997.

Vanberg Victor, "Conflict of Visions. Thomas Sowell," Cato Journal, vol.7, no.2, 1987.

Vance Carole S., "Social Construction Theory: Problems in the History of Sexuality," in: D. Altman [ed.], *Homosexuality, which Homosexuality?: International Conference on Gay and Lesbian Studies*, An Dekker/Schorer, 1989.

Vatican II, Pastoral Constitution on the Church in the Modern World *Gaudium et spes*, Pauline Books & Media, *1966*.

Vattimo Gianni, "Dialectics, Difference, Weak Thought," in: G. Vattimo, P. A. Rovatti [ed.], trans. P. Carravetta, Weak Thought, State University of New York Press, 2012.

Vattimo Gianni, "Kościół popełnia samobójstwo," *Europa. Tygodnik Idei*, 14-15.03.2009.

Vattimo Gianni, *The End of Modernity: Nihilism and Hermeneutics in Post-modern Culture*, The Johns Hopkins University Press 1991.

Voegelin Eric, *From Enlightenment to Oppression*, Duke University Press, Durham, 1975.

Voegelin Eric, *From Enlightenment to Revolution*, Duke University Press Books, 1982.

Voltaire Francois Marie Arouet, *Letters on England*, trans. L. Tancock, Penguin, London, 2005.

Voltaire Francois Marie Arouet, *The Ignorant Philosopher*, Haldeman-Julius Co., 1922.

Waaldijk Kees, Bonini-Baraldi M.T., Sexual Orientation Discrimination in the European Union: National Laws and the Employment Equality Directive, T.M.C. Asser Press, 2006.

Walby Sylvia, "The European Union and Gender Equality: Emergent Varieties of Gender Regime," *Social Politics*, vol.11, no. 1, 2004.

Wald Berthold, "Bycie człowiekiem jest byciem osobą. Kontekst chrześcijański i podstawy filozoficzne," in: P. S. Mazur [ed.], *Spór o osobę w świetle klasycznej definicji człowieka*. Studia irozprawy, Ignatianum, WAM, Krakow, 2012.

Weaver Richard M., Ideas Have Consequences, University of Chicago Press, 2013.

Weber Max, *The Vocation Lectures*, Hackett Publishing, 2004.

Węgrzecki Adam, "Od filozofii człowieka do antropologii filozoficznej. Maxa Schelera koncepcja człowieka," in: L. Kusak [ed.], *Filozofia człowieka. Wybrane koncepcje epoki nowożytnej*, Wydawnictwo Uniwersytetu Ekonomicznego w Krakowie, 2015.

Węgrzecki Janusz Rev., "Wartości podstawowe w polityce. Debata w latach 2005-2008," in: P. Burgoński, S. Sowiński [ed.], *Ile Kościoła w polityce, ile polityki w Kościele?*, Księgarnia św. Jacka, Katowice, 2009.

Weigel George, The Cube and the Cathedral. Europe, America and Politics Without God, Basic Books, 2006.

Weigel George, *The Final Revolution: The Resistance Church and the Collapse of Communism*, Oxford University Press, 2003.

Weil Simone, "Let Us Not Start Another Trojan War," *The Power of Words*, SWA,1936.

Weil Simone, "The Power of Words," in: id., S. Miles [ed.], *An Anthology*, Weidenfeld & Nicolson, New York, 1986.

Weiler Joseph H.H., *Un' Europa Cristiana: Un saggio esplorativo*, BUR Saggi, 2003.

Wejbert-Wąsewicz Ewelina, *Aborcja w dyskursie publicznym. Monografia zjawiska*, Wydawnictwo Uniwersytetu Łódzkiego, 2012.

White Kevin, Sexual Liberation or Sexual License? The American Revolt Against Victorianism, I. R. Dee Publ., Chicago, 2000.

Wielecki Krzysztof, "Alpinizm bez asekuracji, czyli Unia wobec zmiany cywilizacyjnej," *Chrześcijaństwo-Świat-Polityka*, vol. 17/18, 2014/2015.

Wieruszewski Roman, "ZasadyYogakarty – genezaiznaczenie", in: K. Remin[ed.], The Yogyakarta Principles on the Application of International Human Rights Law in relation to Sexual Orientation and Gender Identity, Campaign Against Homophobia, Warszawa, 2009.

Williams Andrew, The Ethos of Europe. Values, Law and Justice in the EU, Cambridge University Press, 2010.

Williams Mary Elisabeth, "The Choice to Abort Is Up to Women," in: N. Merino [ed.], Abortion, Greenhaven Press, Farmongton Hills, 2014.

Wiścicki Tomasz, "Kościół, homoseksualizm, człowiek i... kultura," *Więź*, vol.3, no. 569, 2006.

Wobbe Theresa, "From Protecting to Promoting: Evolving Sex Equality Norms in an Organisational Field," European Law Journal, vol. 9, no. 1, 2003.

Wojnicz Luiza, "Wpływ procesów europeizacyjnych w Afryce na przykładzie cywilnych misji Unii Europejskiej w Demokratycznej Republice Konga," *Rocznik Integracji Europejskiej*, vol. 8, 2014.

Wojtyla Karol Card., "The Anthropological Vision of Humanae Vitae," trans. William May, *Nova et Vetera* (English edition), vol. 7, no. 3, 2009, *https://stpaulcenter.com/13-nv-7-3-karol-wojtyla/*.

Wojtyla Karol Card., *Love and Responsibility*, Ignatius Press, 1993.

Wojtyla Karol Card., *The Acting Person*, Springer, 1979.

Woleński Jan, "Spór o status metodologiczny nauk o polityce," in: K. Opałek [ed.], *Metodologiczne i teoretyczne problemy nauk politycznych*, PWN, Warszawa, 1975.

Wright D.S., "The Book review: Conflict of visions," Progressive Friends of the Library Newsletter, https://www.dailykos.com/stories/2012/02/21/1052864/-Book-Review-A-Conflict-Of-Visions-Part-1 [12.09.2013].

Wróblewski Michał, "Zatarg Jeana - FrancoisaLyotarda czyli o postmodernizmie raz jeszcze," *Diametros*, vol. 24, 2010.

Yanow Dvora, Conducting Interpretive Policy Analysis, Sage Publications, Thousand Oaks, London, New Delhi, 1999.

Yoshihara Susan, "Abortion and the Laws of War: Subverting Humanitarianism by Executive Edict," University of St. Thomas Journal of Law & Public Policy, vol. 9, 2015.

Yoshihara Susan, "Lost in translation: the failure of the international reproductive rights norm," Ave Maria Law Review, vol. 11, no. 2, 2013.

Zając Kazimierz, "Św. Tomasz z Akwinu – Jego zapatrywania socjalne i ekonomiczne," *Annales. Etyka w życiu gospodarczym*, vol. 1, no. 8, 2005.

Zajadło Jerzy, *Godność jednostki w aktach międzynarodowej ochrony praw człowieka*, RPEiS, vol. 51, 1989.

Załęski Piotr, "Subdyscypliny empiryczne nauk o polityce," in: W. Jakubowski, P. Załęski, Ł. Zamęcki, *Nauki o polityce. Zarys koncepcji dyscypliny*, Typografia Pułtusk, 2013.

Zawadzki Andrzej, "Koniec nowoczesności: nihilizm, hermeneutyka, sztuka," in: G. Vattimo, *Koniec nowoczesności,* Universitas, Krakow, 2006.

Zawadzki Andrzej, "Pojęcie nihilizmu u Nietzschego, Heideggera i Vattimo," *Słupskie Prace Filologiczne*, Seria Filologia Polska, vol. 3, 2004.

Zawadzki Andrzej, *Literatura a myśl słaba*, Universitas, Krakow, 2009.

Żebrowski Waldemar, *Badanie polityki. Ogniwa procesu badawczego na studiach politologicznych*, INP UWM, Olsztyn, 2012.

Zenderowski Radosław, "Czym jest kultura? Kultura a cywilizacja. Spór o definicje podstawowych pojęć," in: R. Zenderowski, K. Cebul, M. Krycki, *Międzynarodowe stosunki kulturalne*, PWN, Warszawa, 2010.

Zenderowski Radosław, *Religia a tożsamość narodowa i nacjonalizm w Europie Środkowo-Wschodniej. Między etnicyzacją religii a sakralizacją etosu*, FNP, Wroclaw, 2011.

Zięba Maciej OP,. "Kościół wobec liberalnej demokracji," in: M. Novak, A. Rauscher SJ, M. Zięba OP, *Chrześcijaństwo. Demokracja. Kapitalizm*, Wydawnictwo Polskiej Prowincji Dominikanów W drodze, Poznan, 1993.

Zięba Ryszard, *UE jako aktor stosunków międzynarodowych*, Scholar, Warszawa, 2003.

Zielonka Jan, *Europa jako imperium*, PISM, Warszawa, 2010.

Ziółkowski Janusz, "Antropologia kulturowa i społeczna," *Przegląd Antropologiczny*, vol. 52, 1986.

Zoll Andrzej, "Prawa człowieka: źródła i zakres w ujęciu chrześcijańskim i w Unii Europejskiej," in: *Godność-wolność-prawa człowieka*, Wokół nas, Gliwice, 2016.

Życiński Józef abp, *Bóg postmodernistów*, RW KUL, Lublin, 2001.

Journal Publications, Information Materials and Press Releases

Babete Francis, *Gender bending: let me count the ways,* http://www.mercatornet. com/articles/view/gender_bending_let_me_count_the_ways [24.10.2016].

Baker Aryn, *The Secret War Crime,* http://time.com/war-and-rape/?xid=homepage [02.05.2016].

Charamsa Krzysztof Rev., *Manifest księdza Charamsy do Kościoła katolickiego. Po 1. Wyzbycie się homofobii...,* https://wiadomosci.gazeta.pl/wiadomosci/ 1,114871,18960940,manifest-ksiedza-charamsy-do-kosciola-katolickiego-po-1-wyzbycie.html [02.05.2016]

http://wiadomosci.gazeta.pl/wiadomosci/1,114871,18960940,manifest-ksiedza-charamsy-do-kosciola-katolickiego-po-1-wyzbycie.html[23.06.2016].

Dyrektywa antydyskryminacyjna ograniczy wolność gospodarczą w UE, http:// www.ordoiuris.pl/dyrektywa-antydyskryminacyjna-ograniczy-wolnosc-gospodarcza-w-ue,3521,i.html [02.08.2016].

Dziadzio Andrzej, *Skąd się wzięły rozwody? Historia prawa małżeńskiego,* https:// www.gloria.tv/article/Re9J8fh6WS1c2Q5uaHpKgALSo [23.06.2016].

Dziedzina Jacek, *Sól utracona, http://gosc.pl/doc/1121852.Sol-utracona* [20.08.2015].

Dziewicki Marek Rev., *Homofobia istnieje naprawdę!,* http://www.opoka.org.pl/ biblioteka/P/PS/md_homofofo.html [23.06.2016].

EU recognizes the right to abortion for war rape victims, http://www.sophieintveld. eu/eu-recognises-the-right-to-abortion-for-war-rape-victims/ [02.05.2016].

Europejska Inicjatywa Obywatelska "Jeden z nas" przed Sądem Unii Europejskiej, http://www.ordoiuris.pl/europejska-inicjatywa-obywatelska-jeden-z-nas-przed-sadem-unii-europejskiej,3440,i.html [15.09.2016]

Hajdarowicz Inga, *Bezdomne we własnym ciele – sytuacja kobiet w czasie wojny na Bałkanach,* http://krytyka.org/bezdomne-we-wlasnym-ciele-sytuacja-kobiet-w-czasie-wojny-na-balkanach [29.04.2016].

Kawa Marcin, *Polskie Nie dla komórek macierzystych z ludzkich embrionów,* http:// www.biotechnolog.pl/polskie-nie-dla-komorek-macierzystych-z-ludzkich-embrionow [30.07.2016].

Kowalski Piotr, *ONZ potępia dżihadżystów,* http://www.kowalski.pch24.pl/ niewolnictwo-seksualne%2D%2Dgwalty-oraz-przymusowe-malzenstwa%2D% 2Donz-potepila-dzihadystow,35161,i.html [27.04.2016].

Krysiak Patrycja, *Jak mówić o gender-mainstreaming aby być zrozumianym/ zrozumianą?,* http://akademiagender.cba.pl/index.php/gender/87-jak-mowic-o-gender-mainstreaming-aby-byc-zrozumianym-zrozumiana [04.07.2016].

Margasiński Andrzej, "Homofobia. Co to znaczy?", *Uważam Rze,* http://www. uwazamrze.pl/artykul/935705/homofobia-co-to-znaczy [23.06.2016].

FRA - Promoting and protecting your fundamental rights across the EU, https://fra. europa.eu/en

Sowiński Sławomir, "Papież, Polska i europejskość," *Tygodnik Powszechny,* vol. 17, no. 2807, 23.4.2003.

Żuchowski Damian, *Gwałty w Demokratycznej Republice Konga,* https://estuariumsumienia.wordpress.com/2014/04/20/gwalty-w-demokratycznej-republice-konga [27.04.2016].

http://ec.europa.eu/chafea/projects/database.html?prjno=2004314 [28.06.2016].

http://ec.europa.eu/european_group_ethics/platform/index_en.htm [2.11.2010].

http://ec.europa.eu/justice/fundamental-rights/homophobia/index_en.htm [6.07.2016].

http://europeandignitywatch.org/pl/codzienny/detail/article/planned-parenthood-selling-aborted-baby-parts-suspend-eu-funding-now.html [30.07.2016].

http://fakty.interia.pl/tylko-u-nas/news-in-vitro-przeciwnicy-kontra-zwolennicy-trwa-zbieranie-podpis,nId.,1853169 [24.07.2015].

http://globaljusticecenter.net/blog/288-victory-uk-house-of-lords-report-on-sexual-violence-in-conflict-cites-to-gjc [02.05.2016].

http://info.wiara.pl/doc/566000.Andrea-Bocelli-moja-matka-nie-dokonala-aborcji [15.09.2016].

http://leplus.nouvelobs.com/contribution/845347-je-suis-homo-contre-le-mariage-gay-m-hollande-arretez-la-democratie-a-deja-perdu.html [20.08.2015].

http://portalwiedzy.onet.pl/122853,,,,komorki_macierzyste,haslo.html [14.06.2016].

http://webcache.googleusercontent.com/search?q=cache:U85ykNPT79oJ:ec.europa.eu/polska/news/140127_grecja_pl.htm+&cd=2&hl=pl&ct=clnk&gl=pl&client=firefox-b [05.08.2016].

http://www.asia-initiative.org [27.06.2016]

http://www.euractiv.pl/wersja-do-druku/artykul/europa-zostanie-w-kongu-005044 [27.04.2016].

http://www.euro-fam.org/scripts/spop/articleINT.php?&XMLCODE=rollcallV2006_06_15_A&LG=PLeuro [4.03.2010].

http://www.europarl.europa.eu/elections2014-results/pl/turnout.html [30.03.2016].

http://www.europarl.europa.eu/elections2014-results/pl/turnout.html [30.03.2013].

http://www.europarl.europa.eu/news/pl/news-room/20141013IPR73812/Syria-and-Iraq-debate-on-the-human-rights-situation-of-refugees [29.04.2016].

http://www.europarl.europa.eu/news/pl/news-room/20150909STO92301/juncker-w-or%C4%99dziu-o-stanie-ue-migracja-kluczowym-priorytetem [2016.09.14].

http://www.europarl.europa.eu/oeil/popups/printsda.pdf?id=21255&l=en [29.04.2016].

http://www.europarl.europa.eu/oeil/popups/sda.do?id=16011&l=en [28.06.2016].

http://www.europarl.europa.eu/oeil/popups/sda.do?id=17914&l=en [02.10.2016].

http://www.europarl.europa.eu/oeil/popups/sda.do?id=22911&l=en [29.04.2016].

http://www.europarl.europa.eu/oeil/popups/sda.do?id=25230&l=en [28.06.2016].

https://www.europarl.europa.eu/sides/getDoc.do?pubRef=-//EP//TEXT+IM-PRESS+20060615STO09076+0+DOC+XML+V0//EN

https://www.europarl.europa.eu/sides/getDoc.do?pubRef=-//EP//TEXT+PV
+20131210+ITEM-009-04+DOC+XML+V0//EN

https://www.europarl.europa.eu/sides/getDoc.do?pubRef=-//EP//TEXT+CRE
+20110308+ITEM-009-11+DOC+XML+V0//EN

http://www.europeandignitywatch.org/day-to-day/detail/article/hungary-eu-funded-pro-life-poster-banned-by-the-commission.html?utm_source=Mailman&utm_medium=Email&utm_c [30.07.2016].

http://www.fronda.pl/a/watykanski-bioetyk-krytycznie-o-orzeczeniu-trybunalu-sprawiedliwosci-ue,45343.html [27.05.2016].

http://www.genderhealth.org/the_issues/us_foreign_policy/helms [29.04.2016].

http://www.lex.pl/czytaj/-/artykul/ets-definiuje-pojecie-embrionu-ludzkiego
[27.05.2016].

http://www.lgbt-ep.eu/press-releases/eu-leaders-on-idaho-2011 [07.06.2016].

http://www.oaza.pl/cdz/index.php/pl/2011/612-warszawa-marsz.html [15.09.2016].

http://www.prawaczlowieka.edu.pl/index.php?orzeczenie=ef9cb1abfdb1d45bb08bd2742f179591c8266187-b0 [15.09.2016].

http://www.tvn24.pl/wiadomosci-ze-swiata,2/wegry-w-ogniu-europejskiej-krytyki-czy-to-jeszcze-panstwo-prawa,311506.html [24.10.2016].

http://www.tvn24.pl/wiadomosci-ze-swiata,2/trzy-plcie-w-paszporcie-w-australii,184317.html [25.04.2016].

https://agendaeurope.wordpress.com/general-anti-discrimination-directive
[03.08.2016].

https://agendaeurope.wordpress.com/sexual-and-reproductive-health [14.06.2016]

https://europeangreens.eu/news/discussion-polish-greens-abortion-and-womens-rights [21.10.2016].

https://ms.gov.pl/pl/prawa-czlowieka/miekkie-prawo-miedzynarodowe/zasady-z-yogyakarty [11.07.2016].

https://prawdaoaborcji.wordpress.com/tag/international-planned-parenthood-federation-ippf-i-marie-stopes-international-msi [30.07.2016].

https://www.euractiv.com/section/justice-home-affairs/news/eu-funds-used-for-hungarian-anti-abortion-campaign [30.07.2016].

https://www.lifesitenews.com/pulse/abortionist-quits-when-he-holds-a-living-baby-in-his-hands-after-an-abortion [28.06.2016].

https://wydawnictwo.krytykapolityczna.pl/pro-odzyskajmy-prawo-aborcji-katha-pollitt-94#.V9rIgK1XrgY [15.09.2016].

http://eur-lex.europa.eu/search.html?textScope0=ti-te&qid=1467039715570&CASE_LAW_SUMMARY=false&DTS_DOM=ALL&type=advanced&lang=en&SUBDOM_INIT=ALL_ALL&date0=ALL:01062001%7C31052016&DTS_SUBDOM=ALL_ALL&andText0=%22reproductive%22
[27.06.2016].

http://eur-lex.europa.eu/search.html?textScope0=ti-te&qid=1467050794610&CASE_LAW_SUMMARY=false&DTS_DOM=ALL&type=advanced&lang=en&andText0=%22homosexual%20marriage%22&SUBDOM_INIT=ALL_ALL&date0=ALL:01062001%7C31052016&DTS_SUBDOM=ALL_ALL [27.06.2016].

http://eur-lex.europa.eu/search.html?textScope0=ti-te&qid=1467062832471&
    CASE_LAW_SUMMARY=false&DTS_DOM=ALL&type=advanced&
    lang=en&andText0=%22procreation%20health%22&SUBDOM_INIT=ALL_
    ALL&DTS_SUBDOM=ALL_ALL [27.06.2016].
http://eur-lex.europa.eu/search.html?textScope0=ti-te&qid=1467062832471&
    CASE_LAW_SUMMARY=false&DTS_DOM=ALL&type=advanced&
    lang=en&andText0=%22procreation%20health%22&SUBDOM_INIT=ALL_
    ALL&DTS_SUBDOM=ALL_ALL [27.06.2016].
http://www.lgbtnet.dk/human-rights/yogyakarta-principles [11.07.2016].
http://ec.europa.eu/european_group_ethics/index_en.htm [2.11.2010].
http://ec.europa.eu/budget/fts/ [1.12.2011].
http://www.lemonde.fr/societe/article/2013/04/21/pro-et-anti-mariage-homosexuel-
    manifestent-dimanche-a-paris_3163619_3224.html [26.07.2015].
http://www.hli.org.pl/drupal/pl/node/9563 [27.09.2014].
http://www.europedirect-bydgoszcz.byd.pl/index.php?id=244 [30.03.2016].
http://libr.sejm.gov.pl/tek01/txt/inne/1949-3-t1.html [30.04.2016].
http://www.globaljusticecenter.net/about-us/mission [02.05.2016].
http://www.unhcr.org/4e8d6b3b14.html [02.05.2016].
http://www.epwg.org/members.aspx [13.05.2016].
http://www.pinknews.co.uk/2016/06/20/all-28-eu-member-states-reach-consensus-
    on-lgbt-rights-for-first-time [11.07.2016].
http://sjp.pl/reprodukcja [22.06.2016].
http://dayagainsthomophobia.org/what-is-may-17th [23.06.2016].
http://kph.org.pl/o-kph/misja-i-wizja-dokumenty [23.06.2016].
http://sjp.pwn.pl/sjp/prokreacja;2572612.html [27.06.2016].
https://en.wikipedia.org/wiki/Gender_identity [27.06.2016].
http://p-ntzp.com/dok/12Wodarg-p.pdf [30.07.2016].
https://prawy.pl/279-ue-wegry-oddajcie-te-pieniadze [30.07.2016].
http://www.oneofus.eu/pl/initiative-explanation [02.08.2016].
http://www.biogimnazjum.w.interiowo.pl/start2/k1/k1t1.htm [15.09.2016].
http://jedenznas.pl [15.09.2016].
http://www.federa.org.pl [15.09.2016].
http://www.pro-life.pl [15.09.2016].
https://prawy.pl/28420-tak-dla-zycia [15.09.2016].
https://www.youtube.com/watch?v=10nryBtML_Q [15.09.2016].
http://www.globaljusticecenter.net/publications/letters [02.05.2016].

Information on the Methodology and Interlocutors of In-Depth Interviews [IDI]

The interviews were conducted between October 2013 and June 2014 in line with IDI principles. The interview scenario was only treated as a kind of guidance, direction for performing the interview, suggesting the issues around which to structure the IDI. In accordance with the methodology of social sciences, the IDI as a qualitative study of exploratory nature (as opposed to questionnaire interviews) has its own individual dynamics, and its course depends to a large extent on the answers given by the person being interviewed. Consequently, some issues may be emphasized and others treated more superficially on a case by case basis—depending on the knowledge of the interviewer and his or her willingness to share their thoughts. The scenario was developed by Rafał Wiśniewski, Ph.D. and Marcin Zarzecki, Ph.D. of UKSW Institute of Sociology.

Interlocutors

- Robert Biedroń, Member of the Polish Sejm, representative of the Parliamentary Assembly of the Council of Europe, co-founder and president of the Campaign Against Homophobia Association, rapporteur of the Parliamentary Assembly of the Council of Europe on LGTB
- Maria Hildingsson, Secretary General of the European Federation of Catholic Family Associations (FAFCE)
- Roger Kiska, lawyer, counsel in the European branch of Alliance Defending Freedom
- Paweł Kowal, Member of the European Parliament (2009–2013), European Conservatives and Reformists
- Agnieszka Kozłowska-Rajewicz, Government Representative of the Republic of Poland for Equal Treatment, Member of the European Parliament (2014–2019), European People's Party

© Springer Nature Switzerland AG 2021
M. Gierycz, *European Dispute over the Concept of Man*, Contributions to Political Science, https://doi.org/10.1007/978-3-030-61520-8

- Gudrun Kugler, Head of the Observatory on Intolerance and Discrimination Against Christians in Europe
- Jan Olbrycht, Member of the European Parliament, European People's Party
- Prof. Aleksander Stępkowski, lawyer, Director of the Ordo Iuris Foundation which monitors axiological disputes in the EU, University of Warsaw, Secretary of State at the Ministry of Foreign Affairs
- Prof. Magdalena Środa, philosopher, member of the Scientific Council of the European Institute for Gender Equality (EIGE), co-organizer of the Congress of Women, University of Warsaw

Printed by Printforce, the Netherlands